The Foundations of the Welfare State
Volume II

The Foundations of the Welfare State
Volume II

Edited by

Robert E. Goodin

Professor of Social and Political Theory, and Philosophy,
Research School of Social Sciences
Australian National University, Australia

and

Deborah Mitchell

Fellow in Economics, Research School of Social Sciences
Australian National University, Australia

An Elgar Reference Collection
Cheltenham, UK • Northampton, MA, USA

Published by
Edward Elgar Publishing Limited
Glensanda House
Montpellier Parade
Cheltenham
Glos GL50 1UA
UK

Edward Elgar Publishing, Inc.
136 West Street
Suite 202
Northampton
MA 01060
USA

A catalogue record for this book is available from the British Library.

Library of Congress Cataloguing in Publication Data

The foundations of the welfare state / edited by Robert E. Goodin and Deborah Mitchell.
    (Elgar mini series) (An Elgar reference collection)
    Includes bibliographical references and index.
        1. Public welfare. 2. Welfare state. 3. Social policy. I. Goodin, Robert E. II. Mitchell,
Deborah, Dr. III. Series. IV. Series.
HV31.F63   2000
361.6'5—dc21   99–089369

ISBN   1 85898 796 2 (3 volume set)

Printed and bound in Great Britain by MPG Books Ltd, Bodmin, Cornwall

Contents

Acknowledgements

The editors and publishers wish to thank the authors and the following publishers who have kindly given permission for the use of copyright material.

American Economic Association for article: János Kornai (1992), 'The Postsocialist Transition and the State: Reflections in the Light of Hungarian Fiscal Problems', *American Economic Review (Papers and Proceedings)*, **82** (2), May, 1–21.

Blackwell Publishers Ltd for article and excerpt: R.H. Tawney (1943), 'The Problem of the Public Schools', *Political Quarterly*, **XIV** (2), April–June, 117–49; Jonathan Swift (1729/1955), 'A Modest Proposal for Preventing the Children of Poor People in Ireland, from being a Burden to their Parents or Country; and for making them beneficial to the Publick', in Herbert Davis (ed.), *Irish Tracts 1728–1733*, 109–18.

Canadian Sociology and Anthropology Association for article: Gøsta Esping-Andersen (1989), 'The Three Political Economies of the Welfare State', *Canadian Review of Sociology and Anthropology*, **26** (1), 10–36.

Government and Opposition for article: Catherine Jones (1990), 'Hong Kong, Singapore, South Korea and Taiwan: Oikonomic Welfare States', *Government and Opposition*, **25** (4), Autumn, 446–62.

HarperCollins Publishers, Inc. for article and excerpt: Alexis de Tocqueville (1835/1983), 'Memoir on Pauperism', *Public Interest*, **70**, Winter, 102–20; Alva Myrdal (1945), 'Official Programs and Legislative Acts', in *Nation and Family: The Swedish Experiment in Democratic Family and Population Policy*, Chapter X, 157–74 and references.

Walter Korpi for his own article: (1990), *The Development of the Swedish Welfare State in a Comparative Perspective*, Reprint No. 309, 3–12.

Macmillan Press Ltd for excerpts: B. Seebohm Rowntree (1902), 'Summary and Conclusion', in *Poverty: A Study of Town Life*, Second Edition, Chapter IX, 295–305; John Maynard Keynes (1943/1980), 'Proposed Speech on Beveridge Report', in Donald Moggridge (ed.), *John Maynard Keynes, Volume XXVII: Activities 1940–1946 Shaping the Post-War World: Employment and Commodities*, 256–61.

Oxford University Press for excerpt and article: Jean Drèze and Amartya Sen (1991), 'Public Action for Social Security: Foundations and Strategy', in Ehtisham Ahmad, Jean Drèze, John Hills and Amartya Sen (eds), *Social Security in Developing Countries*, Chapter 1, 3–40; Chiara Saraceno (1994), 'The Ambivalent Familism of the Italian Welfare State', *Social Politics*, **1** (1), Spring, 60–82.

Oxford University Press, Inc. and the Frances Goldin Literary Agency, Inc. for excerpt: Claus Offe (1991), 'Smooth Consolidation in the West German Welfare State: Structural Change, Fiscal Policies, and Populist Politics', in Frances Fox Piven (ed.), *Labor Parties in Postindustrial Societies*, Chapter 6, 124–46.

Princeton University Press for excerpt: Margaret Weir, Ann Shola Orloff and Theda Skocpol (1988), 'Understanding American Social Politics', in Margaret Weir, Ann Shola Orloff and Theda Skocpol (eds), *The Politics of Social Policy in the United States*, 3–27.

Sage Publications, Inc. for article: Nancy Fraser (1994), 'After the Family Wage: Gender Equity and the Welfare State', *Political Theory*, **22** (4), November, 591–618.

Sage Publications Ltd for article and excerpt: Jane Lewis (1992), 'Gender and the Development of Welfare Regimes', *Journal of European Social Policy*, **2** (3), 159–73; Francis G. Castles (1996), 'Needs-Based Strategies of Social Protection in Australia and New Zealand', in Gøsta Esping-Andersen (ed.), *Welfare States in Transition: National Adaptations in Global Economies*, Chapter 4, 88–115.

Walter de Gruyter GMBH & Co. for excerpt: Jens Alber (1986), 'Germany: Historical Synopsis', in Peter Flora (ed.), *Growth to Limits: The Western European Welfare States Since World War II, Volume 2: Germany, United Kingdom, Ireland, Italy*, 4–15 and notes.

Every effort has been made to trace all the copyright holders but if any have been inadvertently overlooked the publishers will be pleased to make the necessary arrangement at the first opportunity.

In addition the publishers wish to thank the Library of the London School of Economics and Political Science, the Marshall Library of Economics, Cambridge University and B & N Microfilm, London for their assistance in obtaining these articles.

Part I
The Growth of an Idea: The British Welfare State

[1]

An Act for the Relief of the Poor.

BE it enacted by the Authority of this present Parliament, that the Churchwardens of every Parish, and four, three or two substantial Housholders there, as shall be thought meet, having respect to the Proportion and Greatness of the same Parish and Parishes, to be nominated yearly in *Easter* Week, or within one Month after *Easter*, under the Hand and Seal of two or more Justices of the Peace in the same County, whereof one to be of the *Quorum*, dwelling in or near the same Parish or Division where the same Parish doth lie, shall be called Overseers of the Poor of the same Parish: And they, or the greater Part of them, shall take order from Time to Time, by, and with the Consent of two or more such Justices of Peace as is aforesaid, for setting to work the Children of all such whose Parents shall not by the said Churchwardens and Overseers, or the greater Part of them, be thought able to keep and maintain their Children: And also for setting to work all such Persons, married or unmarried, having no Means to maintain them, and use no ordinary and daily Trade of Life to get their Living by: And also to raise weekly or otherwise (by Taxation of every Inhabitant, Parson, Vicar and other, and of every Occupier of Lands, Houses, Tithes impropriate, Propriations of Tithes, Coal-Mines, or saleable Underwoods in the said Parish, in such competent Sum and Sums of Money as they shall think fit) a convenient Stock of Flax, Hemp, Wooll, Thread, Iron, and other necessary Ware and Stuff, to set the Poor on Work: And also competent Sums of Money for and towards the necessary Relief of the Lame, Impotent, Old, Blind, and such other among them, being Poor, and not able to work, and also for the putting out of such Children to be Apprentices, to be gathered out of the same Parish, according to the Ability of the same Parish, and to do and execute all other Things as well for the disposing of the said Stock, as otherwise concerning the Premisses, as to them shall seem convenient:

II. Which said Churchwardens and Overseers so to be nominated, or such of them as shall not be let by Sickness or other just Excuse, to be allowed by two such Justices of Peace or more as is aforesaid, shall meet together at the least once every Month in the Church of the said Parish, upon the *Sunday* in the Afternoon, after Divine Service, there to consider of some good Course to be taken, and of some meet Order to be set down in the Premisses; (2) and shall within four Days after the End of their Year, and after other Overseers nominated as aforesaid, make and yield up to such two Justices as is aforesaid, a true and perfect Account of all Sums of Money by them received, or rated and sessed, and not received, and also of such Stock as shall be in their Hands, or in the Hands of any of the Poor to work, and of all other Things concerning their said Office, (3) and such Sum or Sums of Money as shall be in their Hands, shall pay and deliver over to the said Churchwardens and Overseers, newly nominated and appointed as aforesaid; (4) upon Pain that every one of them absenting themselves without lawful Cause as aforesaid, from such Monthly Meeting for the Purpose aforesaid, or being negligent in their Office, or in the Execution of the Orders aforesaid, being made by and with the Assent of the said Justices of Peace, or any two of them before-mentioned, to forfeit for every such Default of Absence or Negligence twenty Shillings.

III. And be it also enacted, That if the said Justices of Peace do perceive, that the Inhabitants of any Parish are not able to levy among themselves sufficient Sums of Money for the Purposes aforesaid; That then the said two Justices shall and may tax, rate and assess, as aforesaid, any other of other Parishes, or out of any Parish, within the Hundred where the said Parish is, to pay such Sum and Sums of Money to the Churchwardens and Overseers of the said poor Parish, for the said Purposes, as the said Justices shall think fit, according to the Intent of this Law: (2) And if the said Hundred shall not be thought to the

said

A. D. 1601.   Anno quadragefimo tertio Reginæ ELIZABETHÆ.   C. 2.   703

said Juftices able and fit to relieve the faid feveral Parifhes not able to provide for themfelves as aforefaid ; *Churchwardens, &c. may make a Rate to relieve burfe themfelves, &c.* then the Juftices of Peace, at their General Quarter-Seffions, or the greater Number of them, fhall rate, and affefs as aforefaid, any other of other Parifhes, or out of any Parifh within the faid County, for the Purpofes aforefaid, as in their Difcretion fhall feem fit.

IV. And that it fhall be lawful, as well for the prefent as fubfequent Churchwardens and Overfeers, or *13 & 14 Car. 2. c. 12. §. 18.* any of them, by Warrant from any two fuch Juftices of Peace as is aforefaid, to levy as well the faid Sums of Money and all Arrearages, of every one that fhall refufe to contribute according as they fhall *A Remedy for the levying of the Money affeffed.* be affeffed, by Diftrefs and Sale of the Offenders Goods, as the Sums of Money or Stock which fhall be behind upon any Account to be made as aforefaid, rendring to the Parties the Overplus, (2) and in De-fect of fuch Diftrefs, it fhall be lawful for any fuch two Juftices of the Peace, to commit him or them to *Imprifonment in Default of Diftrefs.* the common Gaol of the County, there to remain without Bail or Mainprife, until Payment of the faid Sum, Arrearages and Stock: (3) And the faid Juftices of Peace or any one of them, to fend to the *Imprifonment of thofe that will not work.* Houfe of Correction or common Gaol, fuch as fhall not employ themfelves to Work, being appointed thereunto as aforefaid: (4) And alfo any fuch two Juftices of Peace to commit to the faid Prifon every *Refufers to account, imprifoned.* one of the faid Churchwardens and Overfeers, which fhall refufe to account, there to remain without Bail or Mainprize, until he have made a true Account, and fatisfied and paid fo much as upon the faid Account fhall be remaining in his Hands.

V. And be it further enacted, That it fhall be lawful for the faid Churchwardens and Overfeers, or *17 Geo. 2. c. 38.* the greater Part of them, by the Affent of any two Juftices of the Peace aforefaid, to bind any fuch Chil- *Binding of Children Apprentices.* dren, as aforefaid to be Apprentices, where they fhall fee convenient, till fuch Man-Child fhall come to the Age of four and twenty Years, and fuch Woman-Child to the Age of one and twenty Years, or the *1 Jac. 1. c. 25.* Time of her Marriage ; the fame to be as effectual to all Purpofes as if fuch Child were of full Age, and *3 Car. 1. c. 4.* by Indenture of Covenant bound him or her felf. (2) And to the Intent that neceffary Places of Habita- *Farther Provifions relating hereto,* tion may more conveniently be provided for fuch poor impotent People ; (3) Be it enacted by the Au-thority aforefaid, that it fhall and may be lawful for the faid Churchwardens and Overfeers, or the *8 & 9 W. 3. c. 30. §. 5.* greater Part of them, by the Leave of the Lord or Lords of the Manor, whereof any Wafte or Common *Parifh Apprentices may be turned over to the Sea-Service,* within their Parifh is or fhall be Parcel, and upon Agreement before with him or them made in Writing, under the Hands and Seals of the faid Lord or Lords, or otherwife, according to any Order to be fet down by the Juftices of Peace of the faid County at their General Quarter Seffions, or the greater Part *by 2 & 3 Annæ, c. 6. §. 6.* of them, by like Leave and Agreement of the faid Lord or Lords in Writing under his or their Hands and *Building of Houfes on the Wafte for the Poor to inhabit.* Seals, to erect, build, and fet up in fit and convenient Places of Habitation, in fuch Wafte or Common, at the general Charges of the Parifh, or otherwife of the Hundred or County, as aforefaid, to be taxed, rated and gathered in Manner before expreffed, convenient Houfes of Dwelling for the faid impotent Poor ; (4) and alfo to Place Inmates, or more Families than one in one Cottage or Houfe ; one Act made *8 Geo. 1. c. 7.* in the one and thirtieth Year of her Majefty's Reign, intituled, *An Act againft the erecting and maintaining of* *31 Eliz. c. 7.* *Cottages,* or any Thing herein contained, to the contrary notwithftanding : (5) Which Cottages and Places for Inmates fhall not at any Time after be ufed or employed to or for any other Habitation, but only for Impotent and Poor of the fame Parifh, that fhall be there placed from Time to Time by the Churchwar-dens and Overfeers of the Poor of the fame Parifh, or the moft Part of them, upon the Pains and Forfei-tures contained in the faid former Act made in the faid one and thirtieth Year of her Majefty's Reign.

VI. Provided always, That if any Perfon or Perfons fhall find themfelves grieved with any Sefs or Tax, *A Remedy for them who find themfelves grieved with any Tax.* or other Act done by the faid Churchwardens, and other Perfons, or by the faid Juftices of Peace ; that then it fhall be lawful for the Juftices of Peace at their General Quarter Seffions, or the greater Number of them, to take fuch Order therein as to them fhall be thought convenient ; and the fame to conclude and bind all the faid Parties.

VII. And be it further enacted, That the Father and Grandfather, and the Mother and Grandmother, *Poor Perfons relieved by their Parents or Children.* and the Children of every poor, old, blind, lame, and impotent Perfon or other poor Perfon not able to work, being of fufficient Ability, fhall, at their own Charges, relieve and maintain every fuch poor *5 Geo. 1. c. 8.* Perfon in that Manner, and according to that Rate, as by the Juftices of Peace of that County where *2 Bulftr. 344.* fuch fufficient Perfons dwell, or the greater Number of them, at their General Quarter Seffions fhall be affeffed ; (2) upon Pain that every one of them fhall forfeit twenty Shillings for every Month, which they fhall fail therein.

VIII. And be it further hereby enacted, That the Mayors, Bailiffs, or other Head Officers of every *Officers of Corporate Towns have the Authority of Juftices of Peace.* Town and Place Corporate and City within this Realm, being Juftice or Juftices of Peace, fhall have the fame Authority by Virtue of this Act, within the Limits and Precincts of their Jurifdictions, as well out of Seffions, as at their Seffions, if they hold any, as is herein limited, prefcribed and appointed to Juftices of the Peace of the County, or any two or more of them, or to the Juftices of aPeace in their Quarter-Seffions, to do and execute for all the Ufes and Purpofes in this Act prefcribed, and no other Juftice or *Aldermen of London.* Juftices of Peace to enter or meddle there : (2) And that every Alderman of the City of *London* within his Ward, fhall and may do and execute in every Refpect fo much as is appointed and allowed by this Act to be done and executed by one or two Juftices of Peace of any County within this Realm.

IX. And be it alfo enacted, That if it fhall happen any Parifh to extend itfelf into more Counties *A Parifh extend-ing into two Counties, or into two Liberties.* than one, or Part to lie within the Liberties of any City, Town, or Place Corporate, and Part without, that then, as well the Juftices of Peace of every County, as alfo the Head Officers of fuch City, Town *2 Bulftr. 351.* or Place Corporate, fhall deal and intermeddle only in fo much of the faid Parifh as lieth within their Li-berties, and not any further : (2) And every of them refpectively within their feveral Limits, Wards and Jurifdictions, to execute the Ordinances before mentioned concerning the Nomination of Overfeers, the Confent to binding Apprentices, the giving Warrant to levy Taxations unpaid, the taking Account of

Church-

704   **C. 2.**   Anno xliii Reginæ ELIZABETHÆ.   **A. D. 1601.**

Churchwardens and Overseers, and the committing to Prison such as refuse to account, or deny to pay the Arrearages due upon their Accounts; (3) and yet nevertheless, the said Churchwardens and Overseers, or the most Part of them, of the said Parishes that do extend into such several Limits and Jurisdictions, shall, without dividing themselves, duly execute their Office in all Places within the said Parish, in all Things to them belonging, and shall duly exhibit and make one Account before the said Head Officer of the Town or Place Corporate, and one other before the said Justices of Peace, or any such two of them, as is aforesaid.

The Justices Forfeiture for not naming of Overseers.
X. And further be it enacted by the Authority aforesaid, That if in any Place within this Realm there happen to be hereafter no such Nomination of Overseers yearly, as is before appointed, That then every Justice of Peace of the County, dwelling within the Division where such Default of Nomination shall happen, and every Mayor, Alderman and Head Officer of City, Town or Place Corporate where such Default shall happen, shall lose and forfeit for every such Default five Pounds, to be imployed towards the Relief of the Poor of the said Parish or Place Corporate, and to be levied, as aforesaid, of their Goods, by Warrant from the General Sessions of the Peace of the said County, or of the same City, Town or Place Corporate, if they keep Sessions.

How the Forfeiture shall be levied and imployed.
XI. And be it also enacted by the Authority aforesaid, That all Penalties and Forfeitures before-mentioned in this Act to be forfeited by any Person or Persons, shall go and be employed to the Use of the Poor of the same Parish, and towards a Stock and Habitation for them, and other necessary Uses and Relief, as before in this Act are mentioned and expressed; (2) and shall be levied by the said Churchwardens and Overseers, or one of them, by Warrant from any two such Justices of Peace, or Mayor, Alderman, or Head Officer of City, Town or Place Corporate respectively within their several Limits, by Distress and Sale thereof, as aforesaid; (3) or in Defect thereof, it shall be lawful for any two such Justices of Peace, and the said Aldermen and Head Officers within their several Limits, to commit the Offender to the said Prison, there to remain without Bail or Mainprise till the said Forfeitures shall be satisfied and paid.

The Justices shall rate every Parish to a weekly Sum. 2 Bulstr. 353.
XII. And be it further enacted by the Authority aforesaid, That the Justices of Peace of every County or Place Corporate, or the more Part of them, in their General Sessions to be holden next after the Feast of *Easter* next, and so yearly as often as they shall think meet, shall rate every Parish to such a weekly Sum of Money as they shall think convenient; (2) so as no Parish be rated above the Sum of Six-pence, nor under the Sum of a Halfpenny, weekly to be paid, and so as the total Sum of such Taxation of the Parishes in every County amount not above the Rate of Two-pence for every Parish within the said County (3) Which Sums so taxed shall be yearly assessed by the Agreement of the Parishioners within themselves, or in Default thereof, by the Churchwardens and Petty Constables of the same Parish, or the more Part of them : Or in Default of their Agreement, by the Order of such Justice or Justices of Peace as shall dwell in the same Parish, or (if none be there dwelling) in the Parts next adjoining.

The Penalty for refusing to pay Money taxed.
XIII. And if any Person shall refuse or neglect to pay any such Portion of Money so taxed, it shall be lawful for the said Churchwardens and Constables, or any of them, or in their Default, for any Justice of Peace of the said Limit, to levy the same by Distress and Sale of the Goods of the Party so refusing or neglecting, rendring to the Party the Overplus : (2) And in Default of such Distress, it shall be lawful to any Justice of that Limit to commit such Person to the said Prison, there to abide without Bail or Mainprize till he have paid the same.

Relief for the Prisoners of the King's Bench, Marshalsea, Hospitals. Farther Provisions relating hereto. 19 Car. 2. c. 4.
XIV. And be it also enacted, That the said Justices of Peace at their General Quarter-Sessions to be holden at the Time of such Taxation, shall set down what competent Sums of Money shall be sent quarterly out of every County or Place Corporate, for the Relief of the Poor Prisoners of the King's Bench and Marshalsea, and also of such Hospitals and Alms-houses as shall be in the said County, and what Sums of Money shall be sent to every one of the said Hospitals and Alms-houses, so as there be sent out of every County yearly twenty Shillings at the least, to each of the said Prisons of the King's Bench and Marshalsea; (2) which Sums ratably to be assessed upon every Parish, the Churchwardens of every Parish shall truly collect and pay over to the High Constable, in whose Division such Parish shall be situate, from Time to Time, quarterly, ten Days before the End of every Quarter; (3) and every such Constable at every such Quarter-Sessions in such County, shall pay over the same to two such Treasurers, or to one of them, as shall by the more Part of the Justices of Peace of the County be elected to be the
Treasurers.
said Treasurers, to be chosen by the Justices of Peace of the said County, City or Town, or Place Corporate, or of others which were sessed and taxed at five Pounds Lands, or ten Pounds Goods at the least, at the Tax or Subsidy next before the Time of the said Election to be made; (4) and the said Treasurers so elected to continue for the Space of one whole Year in their Office, and then to give up their Charge, with a due Account of their Receipts and Disbursements, at the Quarter-Sessions to be holden next after the Feast of *Easter* in every Year, to such others as shall from Year to Year, in Form aforesaid, successively be elected Treasurers for the said County, City, Town or Place Corporate; (5) which said Trea-
Lord Chief Justice of England, Knight Marshal.
surers, or one of them, shall pay over the same to the Lord Chief Justice of *England*, and Knight Marshal for the Time being, equally to be divided to the Use aforesaid, taking their Acquittance for the same, or in Default of the said Chief Justice, to the next antientest Justice of the King's Bench, as aforesaid : (6) And if any Churchwarden or High Constable, or his Executors or Administrators, shall fail to make Payment in Form above specified, then every Churchwarden, his Executors or Administrators, so offending,
The Forfeiture of the Churchwardens or High Constables offending.
shall forfeit for every Time the Sum of ten Shillings; (7) and every High Constable, his Executors or Administrators, shall forfeit for every Time the Sum of twenty Shillings: (8) the same Forfeitures, together with the Sums behind, to be levied by the said Treasurer and Treasurers by Way of Distress and Sale of the Goods, as aforesaid, in Form aforesaid, and by them to be employed towards the charitable Uses comprised in this Act.   XV. And

XV. And be it further enacted, That all the Surplufage of Money which fhall be remaining in the faid Stock of any County, fhall by Difcretion of the more Part of the Juftices of Peace in their Quarter-Seffions, be ordered, diftributed and beftowed for the Relief of the poor Hofpitals of that County, and of thofe that fhall fuftain Loffes by Fire, Water, the Sea, or other Cafualties, and to fuch other charitable Purpofes, for the Relief of the Poor, as to the more Part of the faid Juftices of Peace fhall feem convenient. *How the Surplufage fhall be beftowed. 2 Salk. 605.*

XVI. And be it further enacted, That if any Treafurer elected fhall wilfully refufe to take upon him the faid Office of Treafurerfhip, or refufe to diftribute and give Relief or to account, according to fuch Form as fhall be appointed by the more Part of the faid Juftices of Peace, that then it fhall be lawful for the Juftices of Peace in their Quarter-Seffions, or in their Default, for the Juftices of Affize, at their Affizes to be holden in the fame County, to fine the fame Treafurer by their Difcretion; (2) The fame Fine not to be under three Pounds, and to be levied by Sale of his Goods, and to be profecuted by any two of the faid Juftices of Peace whom they fhall authorife. (3) Provided always, That this Act fhall not take Effect until the Feaft of *Eafter* next. *The Penalty for refuling to be Treafurer, to give Relief, or Account. This Act to take Effect at Eafter.*

XVII. And be it enacted, That the Statute made in the nine and thirtieth Year of her Majefty's Reign, intituled, ' An Act for the Relief of the Poor, fhall continue and ftand in Force until the Feaft of *Eafter* next; (2) and that all Taxations heretofore impofed and not paid, nor that fhall be paid before the faid Feaft of *Eafter* next, and that all Taxes hereafter before the faid Feaft to be taxed by Virtue of the faid former Act, which fhall not be paid before the faid Feaft of *Eafter*, fhall and may after the faid Feaft of *Eafter* be levied by the Overfeers and other Perfons in this Act refpectively appointed to levy Taxations, by Diftrefs, and by fuch Warrant in every Refpect, as if they had been taxed and impofed by Virtue of this Act, and were not paid. *For what Time, and to what Purpofe the Stat. of 39 Eliz. c. 3. fhall be put in Execution.*

XVIII. Provided always, That whereas the Ifland of *Fowlnefs* in the County of *Effex*, being environed with the Sea, and having a Chapel of Eafe for the Inhabitants thereof, and yet the faid Ifland is no Parifh, but the Lands in the fame are fituated within divers Parifhes far diftant from the faid Ifland; (2) Be it therefore enacted by the Authority aforefaid, That the faid Juftices of Peace fhall nominate and appoint Inhabitants within the faid Ifland, to be Overfeers for the poor People dwelling within the faid Ifland, and that both they the faid Juftices and the faid Overfeers fhall have the fame Power and Authority to all Intents, Confiderations and Purpofes for the Execution of the Parts and Articles of this Act, and fhall be fubject to the fame Pains and Forfeitures, and likewife that the Inhabitants and Occupiers of Lands there fhall be liable and chargeable to the fame Payments, Charges, Expences and Orders, in fuch Manner and Form as if the fame Ifland were a Parifh; (3) In Confideration whereof, neither the faid Inhabitants or Occupiers of Land within the faid Ifland, fhall not be compelled to contribute towards the Relief of the Poor of thofe Parifhes wherein their Houfes or Lands which they occupy within the faid Ifland are fituated, for or by reafon of their faid Habitations or Occupyings, other than for the Relief of the poor People within the faid Ifland, neither yet fhall the other Inhabitants of the Parifhes wherein fuch Houfes or Lands are fituated, be compelled, by reafon of their Refiancy or Dwelling, to contribute to the Relief of the poor Inhabitants within the faid Ifland. *The Ifland of Fowlnefs in Effex.*

XIX. And be it further enacted, That if any Action of Trefpafs or other Suit fhall happen to be attempted and brought againft any Perfon or Perfons, for taking of any Diftrefs, making of any Sale, or any other Thing doing, by Authority of this prefent Act, the Defendant or Defendants in any fuch Action or Suit fhall and may either plead Not guilty, or otherwife make Avowry, Cognifance or Juftification for the Taking of the faid Diftreffes, making of Sale, or other Thing doing by Virtue of this Act, alledging in fuch Avowry, Cognifance or Juftification, That the faid Diftrefs, Sale, Trefpafs or other Thing, whereof the Plaintiff or Plaintiffs complained, was done by Authority of this Act, and according to the Tenor, Purport and Effect of this Act, without any Expreffing or Rehearfal of any other Matter or Circumftance contained in this prefent Act: (2) To which Avowry, Cognifance or Juftification, the Plaintiff fhall be admitted to reply, That the Defendant did take the faid Diftrefs, made the faid Sale, or did any other Act or Trefpafs fuppofed in his Declaration, of his own Wrong, without any fuch Caufe alledged by the faid Defendant; (3) whereupon the Iffue in every fuch Action fhall be joined, to be tried by Verdict of twelve Men, and not otherwife, as is accuftomed in other Perfonal Actions: (4) And upon the Trial of that Iffue the whole Matter to be given on both Parties in Evidence, according to the very Truth of the fame; (5) and after fuch Iffue tried for the Defendant, or Nonfuit of the Plaintiff after Appearance, the fame Defendant to recover treble Damages, by reafon of his wrongful Vexation in that Behalf, with his Cofts alfo in that Part fuftained, and that to be affeffed by the fame Jury, or Writ to enquire of the Damages, as the fame fhall require. *The Defendant's Plea in a Suit commenced againft him againft this Statute. Treble Damages for the Defendant, and his Cofts.*

XX. Provided always, That this Act fhall endure no longer than to the End of the next Seffion of Parliament. [3 Car. 1. c. 4. continued until the End of the firft Seffion of the next Parliament, and further continued by 16 Car. 1. c. 4.] *Farther Provifions concerning Poor, 13 & 14 Car. 2. c. 12.*

22 & 23 Car. 2. c. 18. 1 Jac. 2. c. 17. 3 & 4 W. & M. c. 11. 8 & 9 W. 3. c. 30. 9 & 10 W. 3. c. 11. 12 Ann. Stat. 1. c. 18. 5 Geo. 1. c. 8. 9 Geo. 1. c. 7. 2 Geo. 2. c. 28. 3 Geo. 2. c. 29. 17 Geo. 2. c. 3, 37 & 38. and 31 Geo. 2. c. 11.

[2]

A MODEST

PROPOSAL

FOR

Preventing the Children of poor People in Ireland, *from being a Burden to their Parents or Country; and for making them beneficial to the Publick.*

Written in the Year 1729

IT is a melancholly Object to those, who walk through this great Town, or travel in the Country; when they see the *Streets*, the *Roads*, and *Cabbin-doors* crowded with *Beggars* of the Female Sex, followed by three, four, or six Children, *all in Rags*, and importuning every Passenger for an Alms. These *Mothers*, instead of being able to work for their honest Livelyhood, are forced to employ all their Time in stroling to beg Sustenance for their *helpless Infants*; who, as they grow up, either turn *Thieves* for want of Work; or leave their *dear Native Country, to fight for the Pretender in* Spain, or sell themselves to the *Barbadoes*.

I THINK it is agreed by all Parties, that this prodigious Number of Children in the Arms, or on the Backs, or at the *Heels* of their *Mothers*, and frequently of their *Fathers*, is *in the present deplorable State of the Kingdom*, a very great additional Grievance; and therefore, whoever could find out a fair, cheap, and easy Method of making these Children sound and useful Members of the Commonwealth, would deserve so well of the Publick, as to have his Statue set up for a Preserver of the Nation.

BUT my Intention is very far from being confined to provide only for the Children of *professed Beggars*: It is of a much greater

Extent, and shall take in the whole Number of Infants at a certain Age, who are born of Parents, in effect as little able to support them, as those who demand our Charity in the Streets.

As to my own Part, having turned my Thoughts for many Years, upon this important Subject, and maturely weighed the several *Schemes of other Projectors*, I have always found them grosly mistaken in their Computation. It is true a Child, *just dropt from its Dam*, may be supported by her Milk, for a Solar Year with little other Nourishment; at most not above the Value of two Shillings; which the Mother may certainly get, or the Value in *Scraps*, by her lawful Occupation of *Begging*: And, it is exactly at one Year old, that I propose to provide for them in such a Manner, as, instead of being a Charge upon their *Parents*, or the *Parish*, or *wanting Food and Raiment* for the rest of their Lives; they shall, on the contrary, contribute to the Feeding, and partly to the Cloathing, of many Thousands.

THERE is likewise another great Advantage in my *Scheme*, that it will prevent those *voluntary Abortions*, and that horrid Practice of *Women murdering their Bastard Children*; alas! too frequent among us; sacrificing the *poor innocent Babes*, I doubt, more to avoid the Expence than the Shame; which would move Tears and Pity in the most Savage and inhuman Breast

THE Number of Souls in *Ireland* being usually reckoned one Million and a half; of these I calculate there may be about Two hundred Thousand Couple whose Wives are Breeders; from which Number I subtract thirty thousand Couples, who are able to maintain their own Children; although I apprehend there cannot be so many, under *the present Distresses of the Kingdom*; but this being granted, there will remain an Hundred and Seventy Thousand Breeders. I again subtract Fifty Thousand, for those Women who miscarry, or whose Children die by Accident, or Disease, within the Year. There only remain an Hundred and Twenty Thousand Children of poor Parents, annually born: The Question therefore is, How this Number shall be reared, and provided for? Which, as I have already said, under the present Situation of Affairs, is utterly impossible, by all the Methods hitherto proposed: For we can *neither employ them in Handicraft* or *Agriculture*; we neither build Houses, (I mean in the Country) nor cultivate Land: They can very seldom pick up a Livelyhood *by Stealing* until they arrive at six Years old; except where they are of towardly Parts; although, I confess, they learn the Rudiments much earlier; during which Time, they can, however, be properly looked upon only as *Probationers*; as I have been informed by a principal Gentleman in the County of *Cavan*, who protested to me, that he never knew above one or two Instances under the Age of six, even in a Part of the Kingdom *so renowned for the quickest Proficiency in that Art.*

I AM assured by our Merchants, that a Boy or a Girl before twelve Years old, is no saleable Commodity; and even when they come to this Age, they will not yield above Three Pounds, or Three Pounds and half a Crown at most, on the Exchange; which cannot turn to Account either to the Parents or the Kingdom; the Charge of Nutriment and Rags, having been at least four Times that Value.

I SHALL now therefore humbly propose my own Thoughts; which I hope will not be liable to the least Objection.

I HAVE been assured by a very knowing *American* of my Acquaintance in *London*; that a young healthy Child, well nursed, is, at a Year old, a most delicious, nourishing, and wholesome Food; whether *Stewed, Roasted, Baked,* or *Boiled*; and, I make no doubt, that it will equally serve in a *Fricasie,* or *Ragoust.*

I DO therefore humbly offer it to *publick Consideration*, that of the Hundred and Twenty Thousand Children, already computed, Twenty thousand may be reserved for Breed; whereof only one Fourth Part to be Males; which is more than we allow to *Sheep, black Cattle,* or *Swine*; and my Reason is, that these Children are seldom the Fruits of Marriage, *a Circumstance not much regarded by our Savages*; therefore, *one Male* will be sufficient to serve *four Females.* That the remaining Hundred thousand, may, at a Year old, be offered in Sale to the *Persons of Quality* and *Fortune*, through the Kingdom; always advising the Mother to let them suck plentifully in the last Month, so as to render them plump, and fat for a good

Table. A Child will make two Dishes at an Entertainment for Friends; and when the Family dines alone, the fore or hind Quarter will make a reasonable Dish; and seasoned with a little Pepper or Salt, will be very good Boiled on the fourth Day, especially in *Winter*.

I HAVE reckoned upon a Medium, that a Child just born will weigh Twelve Pounds; and in a solar Year, if tolerably nursed, encreaseth to twenty eight Pounds.

I GRANT this Food will be somewhat dear, and therefore very *proper for Landlords*; who, as they have already devoured most of the Parents, seem to have the best Title to the Children.

INFANTS Flesh will be in Season throughout the Year; but more plentiful in *March*, and a little before and after: For we are told by a grave * Author, an eminent *French* Physician, that *Fish being a prolifick Dyet*, there are more Children born in *Roman Catholick Countries* about Nine Months after *Lent*, than at any other Season: Therefore reckoning a Year after *Lent*, the Markets will be more glutted than usual; because the Number of *Popish Infants*, is, at least, three to one in this Kingdom; and therefore it will have one other Collateral Advantage, by lessening the Number of *Papists* among us.

I HAVE already computed the Charge of nursing a Beggar's Child (in which List I reckon all *Cottagers*, *Labourers*, and Four fifths of the *Farmers*) to be about two Shillings *per Annum*, Rags included; and I believe, no Gentleman would repine to give Ten Shillings for the *Carcase of a good fat Child*; which, as I have said, will make four Dishes of excellent nutritive Meat, when he hath only some particular Friend, or his own Family, to dine with him. Thus the Squire will learn to be a good Landlord, and grow popular among his Tenants; the Mother will have Eight Shillings net Profit, and be fit for Work until she produceth another Child.

THOSE who are more thrifty (*as I must confess the Times require*) may flay the Carcase; the Skin of which, artificially dressed, will make admirable *Gloves for Ladies*, and *Summer Boots for fine Gentlemen*.

As to our City of *Dublin*; Shambles may be appointed for

* Rabelais.

this Purpose, in the most convénient Parts of it; and Butchers we may be assured will not be wanting; although I rather recommend buying the Children alive, and dressing them hot from the Knife, as we do *roasting Pigs*.

A VERY worthy Person, *a true Lover of his Country*, and whose Virtues I highly esteem, was lately pleased, in discoursing on this Matter, to offer a Refinement upon my Scheme. He said, that many Gentlemen of this Kingdom, having of late destroyed their Deer; he conceived, that the Want of Venison might be well supplied by the Bodies of young Lads and Maidens, not exceeding fourteen Years of Age, nor under twelve; so great a Number of both Sexes in every County being now ready to starve, for Want of Work and Service: And these to be disposed of by their Parents, if alive, or otherwise by their nearest Relations. But with due Deference to so excellent a Friend, and so deserving a Patriot, I cannot be altogether in his Sentiments. For as to the Males, my *American* Acquaintance assured me from frequent Experience, that their Flesh was generally tough and lean, like that of our School-boys, by continual Exercise, and their Taste disagreeable; and to fatten them would not answer the Charge. Then, as to the Females, it would, I think, with humble Submission, *be a Loss to the Publick*, because they soon would become Breeders themselves: And besides it is not improbable, that some scrupulous People might be apt to censure such a Practice (although indeed very unjustly) as a little bordering upon Cruelty; which, I confess, hath always been with me the strongest Objection against any Project, how well soever intended.

BUT in order to justify my Friend; he confessed, that this Expedient was put into his Head by the famous *Salmanaazor*, a Native of the Island *Formosa*, who came from thence to *London*, above twenty Years ago, and in Conversation told my Friend, that in his Country, when any young Person happened to be put to Death, the Executioner sold the Carcase to *Persons of Quality*, as a prime Dainty; and that, in his Time, the Body of a plump Girl of fifteen, who was crucified for an Attempt to poison the Emperor, was sold to his Imperial

Majesty's prime Minister of State, and other great *Mandarins* of the Court, *in Joints from the Gibbet*, at Four hundred Crowns. Neither indeed can I deny, that if the same Use were made of several plump young girls in this Town, who, without one single Groat to their Fortunes, cannot stir Abroad without a Chair, and appear at the *Play-house*, and *Assemblies* in foreign Fineries, which they never will pay for; the Kingdom would not be the worse.

SOME Persons of a desponding Spirit are in great Concern about that vast Number of poor People, who are Aged, Diseased, or Maimed; and I have been desired to employ my Thoughts what Course may be taken, to ease the Nation of so grievous an Incumbrance. But I am not in the least Pain upon that Matter; because it is very well known, that they are every Day *dying*, and *rotting*, by *Cold* and *Famine*, and *Filth*, and *Vermin*, as fast as can be reasonably expected. And as to the younger Labourers, they are now in almost as hopeful a Condition: They cannot get Work, and consequently pine away for Want of Nourishment, to a Degree, that if at any Time they are accidentally hired to common Labour, they have not Strength to perform it; and thus the Country, and themselves, are in a fair Way of being soon delivered from the Evils to come.

I HAVE too long digressed; and therefore shall return to my Subject. I think the Advantages by the Proposal which I have made, are obvious, and many, as well as of the highest Importance.

FOR, *First*, as I have already observed, it would greatly lessen the *Number of Papists*, with whom we are yearly over-run; being the principal Breeders of the Nation, as well as our most dangerous Enemies; and who stay at home on Purpose, with a Design to *deliver the Kingdom to the Pretender*; hoping to take their Advantage by the Absence *of so many good Protestants*, who have chosen rather to leave their Country, than stay at home, and pay Tithes against their Conscience, to an idola-trous *Episcopal Curate*.

SECONDLY, The poorer Tenants will have something valuable of their own, which, by Law, may be made liable to

A MODEST PROPOSAL   115

Distress, and help to pay their Landlord's Rent; their Corn and Cattle being already seized, and *Money a Thing unknown.*

THIRDLY, Whereas the Maintenance of an Hundred Thousand Children, from two Years old, and upwards, cannot be computed at less than ten Shillings a Piece *per Annum*, the Nation's Stock will be thereby encreased Fifty Thousand Pounds *per Annum*; besides the Profit of a new Dish, introduced to the Tables of all *Gentlemen of Fortune* in the Kingdom, who have any Refinement in Taste; and the Money will circulate among ourselves, the Goods being entirely of our own Growth and Manufacture.

FOURTHLY, The constant Breeders, besides the Gain of Eight Shillings *Sterling per Annum*, by the Sale of their Children, will be rid of the Charge of maintaining them after the first Year.

FIFTHLY, This Food would likewise bring great *Custom to Taverns*, where the Vintners will certainly be so prudent, as to procure the best Receipts for dressing it to Perfection; and consequently, have their Houses frequented by all the *fine Gentlemen*, who justly value themselves upon their Knowledge in good Eating; and a skilful Cook, who understands how to oblige his Guests, will contrive to make it as expensive as they please.

SIXTHLY, This would be a great Inducement to Marriage, which all wise Nations have either encouraged by Rewards, or enforced by Laws and Penalties. It would encrease the Care and Tenderness of Mothers towards their Children, when they were sure of a Settlement for Life, to the poor Babes, provided in some Sort by the Publick, to their annual Profit instead of Expence. We should soon see an honest Emulation among the married Women, *which of them could bring the fattest Child to the Market.* Men would become as *fond* of their Wives, during the Time of their Pregnancy, as they are now of their *Mares* in Foal, their *Cows* in Calf, or *Sows* when they are ready to farrow; nor offer to beat or kick them, (as it is too *frequent* a Practice) for fear of a Miscarriage.

MANY other Advantages might be enumerated. For instance, the Addition of some Thousand Carcasses in our

Exportation of barrelled Beef: The Propagation of *Swines Flesh*, and Improvement in the Art of making good *Bacon*; so much wanted among us by the great Destruction of *Pigs*, too frequent at our Tables, and are no way comparable in Taste, or Magnificence, to a well-grown fat yearling Child; which, roasted whole, will make a considerable Figure at a *Lord Mayor's Feast*, or any other publick Entertainment. But this, and many others, I omit; being studious of Brevity.

SUPPOSING that one Thousand Families in this City, would be constant Customers for Infants Flesh; besides others who might have it at *merry Meetings*, particularly *Weddings* and *Christenings*; I compute that *Dublin* would take off, annually, about Twenty Thousand Carcasses; and the rest of the Kingdom (where probably they will be sold somewhat cheaper) the remaining Eighty Thousand.

I CAN think of no one Objection, that will possibly be raised against this Proposal; unless it should be urged, that the Number of People will be thereby much lessened in the Kingdom. This I freely own; and it was indeed one principal Design in offering it to the World. I desire the Reader will observe, that I calculate my Remedy *for this one individual Kingdom of* IRELAND, *and for no other that ever was, is, or I think ever can be upon Earth.* Therefore, let no man talk to me of other Expedients: *Of taxing our Absentees at five Shillings a Pound: Of using neither Cloaths, nor Houshold Furniture except what is of our own Growth and Manufacture: Of utterly rejecting the Materials and Instruments that promote foreign Luxury: Of curing the Expensiveness of Pride, Vanity, Idleness, and Gaming in our Women: Of introducing a Vein of Parsimony, Prudence and Temperance: Of learning to love our Country, wherein we differ even from* LAPLANDERS, *and the Inhabitants of* TOPINAMBOO: *Of quitting our Animosities, and Factions; nor act any longer like the* Jews, *who were murdering one another at the very Moment their City was taken: Of being a little cautious not to sell our Country and Consciences for nothing: Of teaching Landlords to have, at least, one Degree of Mercy towards their Tenants. Lastly, Of putting a Spirit of Honesty, Industry, and Skill into our Shop-keepers; who, if a Resolution could now be taken to buy only our native Goods, would immediately unite to cheat and exact upon us in the Price, the Measure, and the Goodness; nor could ever yet be brought to make one fair Proposal of just Dealing, though often and earnestly invited to it.*

THEREFORE I repeat, let no Man talk to me of these and the like Expedients; till he hath, at least, a Glimpse of Hope, that there will ever be some hearty and sincere Attempt to put *them in Practice.*

BUT, as to my self; having been wearied out for many Years with offering vain, idle, visionary Thoughts; and at length utterly despairing of Success, I fortunately fell upon this Proposal; which, as it is wholly new, so it hath something *solid* and *real*, of no Expence, and little Trouble, full in our own Power; and whereby we can incur no Danger in *disobliging* ENGLAND: For, this Kind of Commodity will not bear Exportation; the Flesh being of too tender a Consistence, to admit a long Continuance in Salt; *although, perhaps, I could name a Country, which would be glad to eat up our whole Nation without it.*

AFTER all, I am not so violently bent upon my own Opinion, as to reject any Offer proposed by wise Men, which shall be found equally innocent, cheap, easy, and effectual. But before something of that Kind shall be advanced, in Contradiction to my Scheme, and offering a better; I desire the Author, or Authors, will be pleased maturely to consider two Points. *First*, As Things now stand, how they will be able to find Food and Raiment, for a Hundred Thousand useless Mouths and Backs? And *secondly*, There being a round Million of Creatures in human Figure, throughout this Kingdom; whose whole Subsistence, put into a common Stock, would leave them in Debt two Millions of Pounds *Sterling*; adding those, who are Beggars by Profession, to the Bulk of Farmers, Cottagers, and Labourers, with their Wives and Children, who are Beggars in Effect; I desire those Politicians, who dislike my Overture, and may perhaps be so bold to attempt an Answer, that they will first ask the Parents of these Mortals, Whether they would not, at this Day, think it a great Happiness to have been sold for Food at a Year old, in the Manner I prescribe; and thereby have avoided such a perpetual Scene of Misfortunes, as they have since gone through; by the *Oppres-*

sion of Landlords; the Impossibility of paying Rent, without Money or Trade; the Want of common Sustenance, with neither House nor Cloaths, to cover them from the Inclemencies of Weather; and the most inevitable Prospect of intailing the like, or greater Miseries upon their Breed for ever.

I PROFESS, in the Sincerity of my Heart, that I have not the least personal Interest, in endeavouring to promote this necessary Work; having no other Motive than the *publick Good of my Country, by advancing our Trade, providing for Infants, relieving the Poor, and giving some Pleasure to the Rich.* I have no Children, by which I can propose to get a single Penny; the youngest being nine Years old, and my Wife past Child-bearing.

[3]

Memoir
on
pauperism

ALEXIS DE TOCQUEVILLE

The "Memoir on Pauperism," de-
livered to the Royal Academic Society of Cherbourg in 1835 and
printed in the proceedings of the Academy, was not included in
the collected edition of Tocqueville's works published soon after
his death. Reprinted in a French academic journal in 1911, it was
little known until its translation into English by the American
scholar Seymour Drescher.[1]

The "Memoir" is a critique of the system of poor relief which
earned England the distinction of being, as Tocqueville said, "the
only country in Europe which has systematized and applied the
theories of public charity on a grand scale." That system had its
origins in the sixteenth century when rising prices and land en-
closures (the conversion of arable land to pasturage) created much
distress and unemployment, a situation aggravated by the dissolution of the monasteries which had traditionally played a large part
in the distribution of charity. After several attempts to control va-
grancy and provide some measure of relief, an act passed in 1601
consolidated earlier legislation and became the basis of the system
of relief that prevailed (with much modification and variation) until

---

[1] Reprinted here with Mr. Drescher's permission from *Tocqueville and Beau-
mont on Social Reform*, Seymour Drescher, ed. and trans., (New York: Harper
& Row, Harper Torchbooks, 1968), pp. 1-27.

it was superseded by the welfare state in 1945. These Elizabethan poor laws provided for relief for the aged and infirm, apprenticeship for the children of the poor, employment of the "able-bodied" poor, and punishment or confinement in "houses of correction" for the "sturdy beggars" who persisted in seeking alms. Although the parish was the unit of administration, the system was national and compulsory; each parish was required by law to levy taxes on property (the "poor rates," as they were known) to be used for the sole purpose of discharging its obligations to the poor who had a "settlement" (a legal residence) within its boundaries.

In the course of the following two centuries, the poor laws were repeatedly modified, sometimes made more harsh and restrictive (an act of 1662, for example, permitting the parish to evict any newcomer who might become a charge on the parish), sometimes more generous and expansive, but always within the framework of the original laws. The most dramatic expansion of relief came with the "Speenhamland policy" in 1795, which pegged relief to the price of bread and the size of the family, thus supporting those who were employed but whose earnings fell below a minimum standard. This policy, coming in the wake of a series of bad harvests, the French Revolutionary wars, the rapid increase of population, and the dislocations caused by the agricultural and industrial "revolutions," had the effect of vastly increasing the number of people dependent, entirely or partially, on relief (not, it is now thought, the one-sixth of the population cited by Tocqueville, although at times it almost reached that point). By the same token it also considerably increased the poor rates, which at one point amounted to one-fifth of the total national expenditure. Malthus's Essay on Population, published in 1799, was not the first but it was the most influential critique of the poor laws. In subsequent decades criticism mounted as relief was held responsible for a vicious cycle of evils: the decrease of wages (because wages could be supplemented out of the poor rates), the decline of productivity (pauper labor being less efficient than independent labor), and the increased dependency and demoralization of the poor (the "pauperization of the poor," as it was called).

In 1832 a Royal Commission was set up to inquire into the problem, and two years later the Poor Law Amendment Act was passed. The "New Poor Law," as it was commonly called, made no essential change in relief for the aged and sick who would continue to receive relief in money or kind while living in their own homes ("outdoor relief"). The real change came in the relief for the able-

bodied, who were to be assisted only in the workhouse and only under the principle of "less-eligibility"—under conditions that were less "eligible," less desirable, than those of the laboring poor. By these means the reformers hoped to prevent the laborer from being tempted to join the ranks of the pauper. And by these means they thought it possible to reform the poor laws rather than, as Malthus would have liked, to abolish them, thus retaining relief for the needy while making it so onerous for those capable of working as to discourage them from applying for relief.

It was against this background that Tocqueville wrote his "Memoir." What is interesting is his resistance to the prevailing sentiment in England, where both the critics and the defenders of the New Poor Law—with the notable exception of Malthus—thought that it had brought about a radical change in the system of relief. Tocqueville, focussing on the principle rather than the mechanism, saw the new law as prone to all the evils of the old because it was still committed to the idea of a legal right to public relief. That principle, like the principle of democracy (Tocqueville had just completed his Democracy in America), had its own imperatives and its internal logic, which no such "reform" could alter.

—Gertrude Himmelfarb

Part I

THE PROGRESSIVE DEVELOPMENT OF PAUPERISM
AMONG CONTEMPORARIES AND THE
METHODS USED TO COMBAT IT

WHEN one crosses the various countries of Europe, one is struck by a very extraordinary and apparently inexplicable sight.

The countries appearing to be most impoverished are those which in reality account for the fewest indigents, and among the peoples most admired for their opulence, one part of the population is obliged to rely on the gifts of the other in order to live.

Cross the English countryside and you will think yourself transported into the Eden of modern civilization—magnificently maintained roads, clean new houses, well-fed cattle roaming rich meadows, strong and healthy farmers, more dazzling wealth than in any country of the world, the most refined and gracious standard of the basic amenities of life to be found anywhere. There is a pervasive concern for well-being and leisure, an impression of universal prosperity which seems part of the very air you breathe. At

every step in England there is something to make the tourist's
heart leap.

Now look more closely at the villages; examine the parish registers, and you will discover with indescribable astonishment that
one-sixth of the inhabitants of this flourishing kingdom live at the
expense of public charity. Now, if you turn to Spain or even more
to Portugal, you will be struck by a very different sight. You will
see at every step an ignorant and coarse population; ill-fed, ill-
clothed, living in the midst of a half-uncultivated countryside and
in miserable dwellings. In Portugal, however, the number of indigents is insignificant. M. de Villeneuve estimates that this kingdom contains one pauper for every 25 inhabitants. Previously, the
celebrated geographer Balbi gave the figure as one indigent to
every ninety-eight inhabitants.

Instead of comparing foreign countries among themselves, contrast the different parts of the same realm with each other, and
you will arrive at an analogous result; you will see on the one hand
the number of those living in comfort, and, on the other, the number of those who need public funds in order to live, growing proportionately....

I think that it is not impossible to give a reasonable explanation
for this phenomenon. The effect that I have just pointed out is due
to several general causes which it would take too long to examine
thoroughly, but they can at least be indicated....

AT this point, I want to examine only a corner of that immense
tableau of the feudal centuries. In the twelfth century, what
has since been called the "third estate" did not yet exist. The population was divided into only two categories. On the one hand were
those who cultivated the soil without possessing it; on the other,
those who possessed the soil without cultivating it.

As for the first group of the population, I imagine that in certain regards its fate was less deserving of pity than that of the
common people of our era. These men were in a situation like that
of our colonial slaves, although they played their role with more
liberty, dignity, and morality. Their means of subsistence was almost always assured; the interest of the master coincided with their
own on this point. Limited in their desires as well as in their power, without anxiety about a present or a future which was not theirs
to choose, they enjoyed a kind of vegetative happiness. It is as
difficult for the very civilized man to understand its charm as it is
to deny its existence.

The other class presented the opposite picture. Among these
men hereditary leisure was combined with continuous and assured
abundance. I am far from believing, however, that even within this
privileged class the pursuit of pleasure was as preponderant as is
generally supposed. Luxury without comfort can easily exist in a
still half-barbarous nation. Comfort presupposes a numerous class
all of whose members work together to render life milder and

easier. But, in the period under discussion, the number of those not totally absorbed in self-preservation was extremely small. Their life was brilliant, ostentatious, but not comfortable. One ate with one's fingers on silver or engraved steel plates, clothes were lined with ermine and gold, and linen was unknown; the walls of their dwellings dripped with moisture, and they sat in richly sculptured wooden chairs before immense hearths where entire trees were consumed without diffusing sufficient heat around them. I am convinced that there is not a provincial town today whose more fortunate inhabitants do not have more true comforts of life in their homes and do not find it easier to satisfy the thousand needs created by civilization than the proudest medieval baron. If we look carefully at the feudal centuries, we will discover in fact that the great majority of the population lived almost without needs and that the remainder felt only a small number of them. The land was enough for all needs. Subsistence was universal; comfort unheard of.

It was necessary to establish this point of departure in order to make clear what follows.

As time passes, the population which cultivates the soil acquires new tastes. The satisfaction of the basic necessities is no longer sufficient. The peasant, without leaving his fields, wants to be better housed and clothed. He has seen life's comforts and he wants them. On the other hand, the class which lived off the land without cultivating the soil extends the range of its pleasures; these become less ostentatious, but more complex, more varied. Thousands of needs unknown to the medieval nobles stimulate their descendants. A great number of men who lived on the land and from the land leave their fields and find their livelihood by working to satisfy these newly discovered needs. Agriculture which was everyone's occupation is now only that of the majority. Alongside those who live in leisure from the productivity of the soil arises a numerous class who live by working at a trade but without cultivating the soil.

Each century, as it emerges from the hand of the Creator, extends the range of thought, increases the desires and the power of man. The poor and the rich, each in his sphere, conceive of new enjoyments which were unknown to their ancestors. In order to satisfy these new needs, which the cultivation of the soil cannot meet, a portion of the population leaves agricultural labor each year for industry.

If one carefully considers what has happened in Europe over several centuries, it is certain that proportionately as civilization progressed, a large population displacement occurred. Men left the plow for the shuttle and the hammer; they moved from the thatched cottage to the factory. In doing so, they were obeying the immutable laws which govern the growth of organized societies. One can no more assign an end to this movement than impose limits on human perfectibility. The limits of both are known only by God.

What has been, what is the consequence of this gradual and irresistible movement that we have just described? An immense number of new commodities have been introduced into the world; the class which had remained in agriculture found at its disposal a multitude of luxuries previously unknown. The life of the farmer became more pleasant and comfortable; the life of the great proprietor more varied and more ornate; comfort was available to the majority. But these happy results have not been obtained without a necessary cost.

I HAVE stated that in the Middle Ages comfort could be found nowhere, but life everywhere. This sentence sums up what follows. When almost the entire population lived off the soil great poverty and rude manners could exist, but man's most pressing needs were satisfied. It is only rarely that the earth cannot provide enough to appease the pangs of hunger for anyone who will sweat for it. The population was therefore impoverished but it lived. Today the majority is happier but it would always be on the verge of dying of hunger if public support were lacking.

Such a result is easy to understand. The farmer produces basic necessities. The market may be better or worse, but it is almost guaranteed; and if an accidental cause prevents the disposal of agricultural produce, this produce at least gives its harvester something to live on and permits him to wait for better times.

The worker, on the contrary, speculates on secondary needs which a thousand causes can restrict and important events completely eliminate. However bad the times or the market, each man must have a certain minimum of nourishment or he languishes and dies, and he is always ready to make extraordinary sacrifices in order to obtain this. But unfortunate circumstances can lead the population to deny itself certain pleasures to which it would ordinarily be attracted. It is the taste and demand for these pleasures which the worker counts on for a living. If they are lacking, no other resource remains to him. His own harvest is consumed, his fields are barren; should such a condition continue, his prospect is only misery and death.

I have spoken only of the case where the population restricts its needs. Many other causes can lead to the same effect: domestic overproduction, foreign competition, etc.

The industrial class which gives so much impetus to the well-being of others is thus much more exposed to sudden and irremediable evils. In the total fabric of human societies, I consider the industrial class as having received from God the special and dangerous mission of securing the material well-being of all others by its risks and dangers. The natural and irresistible movement of civilization continuously tends to increase the comparative size of this class. Each year needs multiply and diversify, and with them grows the number of individuals who hope to achieve greater comfort by working to satisfy those new needs rather than by remaining occupied in agriculture. Contemporary statesmen would do well to consider this fact.

To this must be attributed what is happening within wealthy societies where comfort and indigence are more closely connected than elsewhere. The industrial class, which provides for the pleasures of the greatest number, is itself exposed to miseries that would be almost unknown if this class did not exist.

HOWEVER, still other causes contribute to the gradual development of pauperism. Man is born with needs, and he creates needs for himself. The first class belongs to his physical constitution, the second to habit and education. I have shown that at the outset men had scarcely anything but natural needs, seeking only to live; but in proportion as life's pleasures have become more numerous, they have become habits. These in turn have finally become almost as necessary as life itself. . . . The more prosperous a society is, the more diversified and more durable become the enjoyments of the greatest number, the more they simulate true necessity through habit and imitation. Civilized man is therefore infinitely more exposed to the vicissitudes of destiny than savage man. What happens to the second only from time to time and in particular circumstances, occurs regularly to the first. Along with the range of his pleasures he has expanded the range of his needs and leaves himself more open to the hazard of fortune. Thus the English poor appear almost rich to the French poor; and the latter are so regarded by the Spanish poor. What the Englishman lacks has never been possessed by the Frenchman. And so it goes as one descends the social scale. Among very civilized peoples, the lack of a multitude of things causes poverty; in the savage state, poverty consists only in not finding something to eat.

The progress of civilization not only exposes men to many new misfortunes; it even brings society to alleviate miseries which are not even thought about in less civilized societies. In a country where the majority is ill-clothed, ill-housed, ill-fed, who thinks of giving clean clothes, healthy food, comfortable quarters to the poor? The majority of the English, having all these things, regard their absence as a frightful misfortune; society believes itself bound to come to the aid of those who lack them, and cures evils which are not even recognized elsewhere. In England, the average standard of living a man can hope for in the course of his life is higher than in any other country of the world. This greatly facilitates the extension of pauperism in that kingdom.

If all these reflections are correct it is easy to see that the richer a nation is, the more the number of those who appeal to public charity must multiply, since two very powerful causes tend to that result. On the one hand, among these nations, the most insecure class continuously grows. On the other hand, needs infinitely ex-

pand and diversify, and the chance of being exposed to some of
them becomes more frequent each day.

We should not delude ourselves. Let us look calmly and quietly
on the future of modern societies. We must not be intoxicated by
the spectacle of its greatness; let us not be discouraged by the
sight of its miseries. As long as the present movement of civilization
continues, the standard of living of the greatest number will rise;
society will become more perfected, better informed; existence will
be easier, milder, more embellished, and longer. But at the same
time we must look forward to an increase of those who will need
to resort to the support of all their fellow men to obtain a small
part of these benefits. It will be possible to moderate this double
movement; special national circumstances will precipitate or sus-
pend its course; but no one can stop it. We must discover the means
of attenuating those inevitable evils which are already apparent.

Part II

THERE are two kinds of welfare. One leads each individual, according to his means, to alleviate the evils he sees around him.
This type is as old as the world; it began with human misfortune.
Christianity made a divine virtue of it, and called it charity. The
other, less instinctive, more reasoned, less emotional, and often
more powerful, leads society to concern itself with the misfortunes
of its members and is ready systematically to alleviate their sufferings. This type is born of Protestantism and has developed only
in modern societies. The first type is a private virtue; it escapes social action; the second on the contrary is produced and regulated
by society. It is therefore with the second that we must be especially concerned.

At first glance there is no idea which seems more beautiful and
grander than that of public charity. Society is continually examining itself, probing its wounds, and undertaking to cure them. At
the same time that it assures the rich the enjoyment of their wealth,
society guarantees the poor against excessive misery. It asks some
to give of their surplus in order to allow others the basic necessities. This is certainly a moving and elevating sight.

How does it happen that experience destroys some of these beautiful illusions? The only country in Europe which has systematized
and applied the theories of public charity on a grand scale is England. At the time of the religious revolution under Henry VIII,
which changed the face of England, almost all the charitable foundations of the kingdom were suppressed; and since their wealth
became the possession of the nobles and was not at all distributed
among the common people, the poor remained as numerous as before while the means of providing for them were partly destroyed.

The numbers of the poor therefore grew beyond measure, and Elizabeth, Henry's daughter, struck by the appalling miseries of the people, wished to substitute an annual levy furnished by the local governments for the sharply reduced alms-giving caused by the suppression of the convents.

A law promulgated in the forty-third year of that ruler's reign declared that in each parish, overseers of the poor would be chosen, and that these overseers would have the right to tax the inhabitants in order to feed disabled indigents, and to furnish work for the others.

As time passed, England was increasingly led to adopt the principle of legal charity. Pauperism grew more rapidly in Great Britain than anywhere else. Some general and some special causes produced this unfortunate result. The English have surpassed the other nations of Europe in civilized living. All the observations that I made before are applicable to them; but there are others which relate to that country alone.

THE English industrial class not only provides for the necessities and pleasures of the English people, but of a large part of humanity. Its prosperity or its miseries therefore depend not only on what happens in Great Britain but in a way on every event under the sun. When an inhabitant of the Indies reduces his expenditure or cuts back on his consumption, it is an English manufacturer who suffers. England is therefore the country in the world where the agricultural laborer is most forcefully attracted towards industrial labor and finds himself most exposed to the vicissitudes of fortune. In the past century an event has occurred which, looking at the rest of the world's development, can be viewed as phenomenal. For a hundred years landed property has been breaking up throughout the known world; in England it continues to concentrate. Medium-sized holdings disappear into vast domains. Large-scale agriculture succeeds small-scale cultivation. One could offer some interesting observations on this subject, but it would divert me from my chosen topic: the fact must suffice—it is a constant. The result is that while the agricultural worker is moved by his interest to abandon the plow and to move into industry, he is in a way thrust in the same direction in spite of himself by the agglomeration of landed property. Comparatively speaking, infinitely fewer workers are required to work a large estate than a small field. The land fails him and industry beckons in this double movement. Of the 25 million people of Great Britain, no more than 9 million are involved in agriculture. Fourteen million, or close to two-thirds, make their perilous way in commerce and industry. Thus pauperism was bound to grow more quickly in England than in countries whose civilization might have been equal to that of the English. Once having admitted the principle of legal charity, England has not been able to dispense with it. For two hundred years English legislation for the poor has revealed itself as nothing more than an extended

development of the Elizabethan laws. Almost two and a half centuries have passed since the principle of legal charity was fully
embraced by our neighbors, and one may now judge the fatal consequences which flowed from the adoption of this principle. Let
us examine them successively.

Since the poor have an absolute right to the help of society, and
have a public administration organized to provide it everywhere,
one can observe in a Protestant country the immediate rebirth and
generalization of all the abuses with which its reformers rightly
reproached some Catholic countries. Man, like all socially organized beings, has a natural passion for idleness. There are, however, two incentives to work: the need to live and the desire to
improve the conditions of life. Experience has proven that the majority of men can be sufficiently motivated to work only by the first
of these incentives. The second is only effective with a small minority. Well, a charitable institution indiscriminately open to all
those in need, or a law which gives all the poor a right to public
aid, whatever the origin of their poverty, weakens or destroys the
first stimulant and leaves only the second intact. The English peasant, like the Spanish peasant, if he does not feel the deep desire
to better the position into which he has been born, and to raise
himself out of his misery (a feeble desire which is easily crushed
in the majority of men)—the peasant of both countries, I maintain,
has no interest in working, or, if he works, has no interest in saving. He therefore remains idle or thoughtlessly squanders the fruits
of his labors. Both these countries, by different causal patterns,
arrive at the same result: the most generous, the most active, the
most industrious part of the nation, which devotes its resources to
furnishing the means of existence for those who do nothing or who
make bad use of their labor.

W E are certainly far from that beautiful and seductive theory
     that I expounded above. Is it possible to escape the fatal con-
sequences of a good principle? For myself I consider them inevitable.
Here I might be interrupted by a rejoinder: You assume that, whatever its cause misery will be alleviated; you add that public assistance will relieve the poor of the obligation to work. This states as
a fact something questionable. What is to prevent society from in-
quiring into the causes of the need before giving assistance? Why
could work not be imposed as a condition on the able-bodied indigent who asks for public pity? I reply that some English laws have
used the idea of these palliatives; but they have failed, and understandably so.

Nothing is so difficult to distinguish as the nuances which separate unmerited misfortune from an adversity produced by vice.
How many miseries are simultaneously the result of both these
causes! What profound knowledge must be presumed about the
character of each man and of the circumstances in which he has
lived, what knowledge, what sharp discernment, what cold and in-

exorable reason! Where will you find the magistrate who will have the conscience, the time, the talent, the means of devoting himself to such an examination? Who would dare to let a poor man die of hunger because it's his own fault that he is dying? Who will hear his cries and reason about his vices? Even personal interest is restrained when confronted by the sight of other men's misery. Would the interest of the public treasury really prove to be more successful? And if the overseer's heart were unconcerned with such emotions, which are appealing even when misguided, would he remain indifferent to fear? Who, being judge of the joy or suffering, life or death, of a large segment of his fellow men, of its most dissolute, its most turbulent, its crudest segment, who would not shrink before the exercise of such terrible power? And if any of these intrepid beings can be found, how many will there be? In any event such functions can only be exercised with a restricted territory. A large number must be delegated to do so. The English have been obliged to put overseers in every parish. What inevitably follows from all this? Poverty is verified, the causes of poverty remain uncertain: the first is a patent fact, the second is proved by an always debatable process of reasoning. Since public aid is only indirectly harmful to society, while the refusal of aid instantly hurts the poor and the overseer himself, the overseer's choice cannot be in doubt. The laws may declare that only innocent poverty will be relieved; practice will alleviate all poverty. I will present plausible arguments for the second point, equally based on experience.

We would like work to be the price of relief. But, first, is there always public work to be done? Is it equally spread over the whole country in such a way that you never see a good deal of work to be done with few people to do it in one district and in another many indigents to be helped but little work to be undertaken? If this difficulty is present at all times, doesn't it become insurmountable when, as a consequence of the progressive development of civilization, of population growth, of the effect of the Poor Law itself, the proportion of indigents, as in England, reaches a sixth, some say a quarter, of the total population?

But even supposing that there would always be work to do, who will take responsibility for determining its urgency, supervising its execution, setting the price? That man, the overseer, aside from the qualities of a great magistrate, will therefore also possess the talents, the energy, the special knowledge of a good industrial entrepreneur. He will find in the feeling of duty alone what self-interest itself would be powerless to create—the courage to force the most inactive and vicious part of the population into sustained and productive effort. Would it be wise to delude ourselves? Pressured by the needs of the poor, the overseer will impose make-work, or even —as is almost always the case in England—pay wages without demanding labor. Laws must be made for men and not in terms of a perfect world which cannot be sustained by human nature, nor of models which it offers only very occasionally.

A NY measure which establishes legal charity on a permanent basis and gives it an administrative form thereby creates an idle and lazy class, living at the expense of the industrial and working class. This, at least, is its inevitable consequence, if not the immediate result. It reproduces all the vices of the monastic system, minus the high ideals of morality and religion which often went along with it. Such a law is a bad seed planted in the legal structure. Circumstances, as in America, can prevent the seed from developing rapidly, but they cannot destroy it, and if the present generation escapes its influence, it will devour the well-being of generations to come.

If you closely observe the condition of populations among whom such legislation has long been in force you will easily discover that the effects are not less unfortunate for morality than for public prosperity, and that it depraves men even more than it impoverishes them.

There is nothing which, generally speaking, elevates and sustains the human spirit more than the idea of rights. There is something great and virile in the idea of right which removes from any request its suppliant character, and places the one who claims it on the same level as the one who grants it. But the right of the poor to obtain society's help is unique in that instead of elevating the heart of the man who exercises it, it lowers him. In countries where legislation does not allow for such an opportunity, the poor man, while turning to individual charity, recognizes, it is true, his condition of inferiority in relation to the rest of his fellow men; but he recognizes it secretly and temporarily. From the moment that an indigent is inscribed on the poor list of his parish, he can certainly demand relief, but what is the achievement of this right if not a notarized manifestation of misery, of weakness, of misconduct on the part of its recipient? Ordinary rights are conferred on men by reason of some personal advantage acquired by them over their fellow men. This other kind is accorded by reason of a recognized inferiority. The first is a clear statement of superiority; the second publicizes inferiority and legalizes it. The more extensive and the more secure ordinary rights are, the more honor they confer; the more permanent and extended the right to relief is, the more it degrades.

The poor man who demands alms in the name of the law is, therefore, in a still more humiliating position than the indigent who asks pity of his fellow men in the name of He who regards all men from the same point of view and who subjects rich and poor to equal laws.

But this is still not all: individual alms-giving established valuable ties between the rich and the poor. The deed itself involves the giver in the fate of the one whose poverty he has undertaken to alleviate. The latter, supported by aid which he had no right to demand and which he may have had no hope of getting, feels inspired by gratitude. A moral tie is established between those two

classes whose interests and passions so often conspire to separate
them from each other, and although divided by circumstance they
are willingly reconciled. This is not the case with legal charity. The
latter allows the alms to persist, but removes its morality. The law
strips the man of wealth of a part of his surplus without consulting him and he sees the poor man only as a greedy stranger invited by the legislator to share his wealth. The poor man, on the
other hand, feels no gratitude for a benefit which no one can refuse
him and which could not satisfy him in any case. Public alms guarantee life, but do not make it happier or more comfortable than
individual alms-giving; legal charity does not thereby eliminate
wealth or poverty in society. One class still views the world with
fear and loathing while the other regards its misfortune with de-
spair and envy. Far from uniting these two rival nations, who have
existed since the beginning of the world and who are called the
rich and the poor, into a single people, it breaks the only link
which could be established between them. It ranges each one under a banner, tallies them, and, bringing them face to face, pre-
pares them for combat.

I HAVE said that the inevitable result of public charity was to perpetuate idleness among the majority of the poor and to provide
for their leisure at the expense of those who work.

If the idleness of the rich, an hereditary idleness, merited by
work or by services, an idleness immersed in public consideration,
supported by psychological complacency, inspired by intellectual
pleasures, moralized by mental exercise—if this idleness, I say, has
produced so many vices, what will come of a degraded idleness
obtained by baseness, merited by misconduct, enjoyed in ignominy?
It becomes tolerable only in proportion to the extent that the soul
subjects itself to all this corrupting and degrading.

What can be expected from a man whose position cannot improve, since he has lost the respect of his fellow men which is the
precondition of all progress, whose lot could not become worse,
since, being reduced to the satisfaction of his most pressing needs,
he is assured that they will always be satisfied? What course of
action is left to the conscience or to human activity in a being so
limited, who lives without hope and without fear? He looks at the
future as an animal does. Absorbed in the present and the ignoble
and transient pleasures it affords, his brutalized nature is unaware
of the determinants of its destiny.

Read all the books on pauperism written in England, study the
inquiries ordered by the British Parliament, look at the discussions
which have taken place in the Lords and Commons on this difficult question. They boil down to a single deafening cry—the degraded condition into which the lower classes have fallen! The
number of illegitimate children and criminals grows rapidly and
continuously, the indigent population is limitless, the spirit of foresight and of saving becomes more and more alien to the poor. While

throughout the rest of the nation education spreads, morals improve, tastes become more refined, manners more polished—the indigent remains motionless, or rather he goes backwards. He could be described as reverting to barbarism. Amidst the marvels of civilization, he seems to emulate savage man in his ideas and his inclinations.

Legal charity affects the pauper's freedom as much as his morality. This is easily proved. When local governments are rigorously obligated to aid the indigent, they necessarily owe relief only to the poor who reside in their jurisdiction. This is the only fair way of equalizing the public burden which results from the law, and of proportioning it to the means of those who must bear it. Since individual charity is almost unknown in a country of organized public charity, anyone whose misfortunes or vices have made him incapable of earning a living is condemned, under pain of death, to remain in the place of his birth. If he leaves, he moves through enemy country. The private interest within the parish, infinitely more active and powerful than the best organized national police could be, notes his arrival, dogs his every step, and, if he wants to establish a new residence, informs the public authority who takes him to the boundary line. Through their Poor Laws, the English have immobilized a sixth of their population. They have bound it to the earth like the medieval peasantry. Then, man was forced against his will to stay on the land where he was born. Legal charity keeps him from even wishing to move. That is the only difference between the systems. The English have gone further. They have reaped even more disastrous consequences from the principle of public welfare. The English parishes are so dominated by the fear that an indigent person might be placed on their rolls and acquire residency, that when a stranger whose clothes do not clearly indicate wealth temporarily settles among them, or when an unexpected misfortune suddenly strikes him, the municipal authorities immediately ask him to post bond against possible indigence, and if the stranger cannot furnish this security, he must leave.

Thus legal charity has not only taken freedom of movement from the English poor, but also from those who are threatened by poverty.

I KNOW of no better way to complete this sad picture than by reproducing the following fragment from my notes on England. I traveled through Great Britain in 1833. Others were struck by the imposing prosperity of the country. I myself pondered the secret unrest which was visibly at work among all its inhabitants. I thought that great misery must be hidden beneath that brilliant mask of prosperity which Europe admires. This idea led me to pay particular attention to pauperism, that hideous and enormous sore which is attached to a healthy and vigorous body.

I was staying at the house of a great proprietor in the south of

England at the time when the justices of the peace assemble to pass judgment on the suits brought to court by the poor against the parish, or by the parishes against the poor. My host was a justice of the peace, and I regularly accompanied him to court. I find in my travel notes this portrait of the first sitting that I attended. It gives a short concise summary and clarifies everything said before. I am reproducing it with scrupulous exactness in order to render a true picture.

The first individual who comes before the justices of the peace is an old man. His face is honest and ruddy, he wears a wig and is dressed in excellent black clothes. He seems like a man of property. However, he approaches the bar and passionately protests against the parish administration's injustice. This man is a pauper, and his share of public charity has just been unjustly diminished. The case is adjourned in order to hear the parish administrators.

After this hale and petulant old man comes a pregnant young woman whose clothes bear witness to recent poverty and who bears the marks of suffering on her withered features. She explains that some time ago her husband set out on a sea voyage, that since then she has received neither assistance nor news from him. She claims public charity but the overseer of the poor hesitates to give it to her. This woman's father-in-law is a well-to-do merchant. He lives in the very city where the court is sitting, and it is hoped too, that in the absence of his son, he will certainly want to take responsibility for the maintenance of his daughter-in-law. The justices of the peace summon this man; but he refuses to fulfill the duties imposed on him by nature and not by law. The judges insist. They try to create remorse or compassion in this man's egoistic soul. Their efforts fail, and the parish is sentenced to pay the requested relief.

After this poor abandoned woman come five or six big and vigorous men. They are in the bloom of youth, their bearing is resolute and almost insulting. They lodge a complaint against their village administrators who refuse to give them work, or, for lack of work, relief.

The administrators reply that at the moment the parish is not carrying out any public work; and gratuitous relief is not required, they say, because the plaintiffs could easily find jobs with private individuals if they wanted to.

Lord X [Radnor], with whom I had come, tells me, "you have just seen in microcosm part of the numerous abuses which the Poor Law produces. That old man who came first quite probably has the means to live, but he thinks that he has the right to demand that he be supported in comfort, and he does not blush to claim public charity, which has lost all of its afflicting and humiliating character in the people's eyes. That young woman, who seems honest and unfortunate, would certainly be helped by her father-in-law if the Poor Law did not exist; but interest silences the cry of shame within him and he unloads a debt on the public that he alone ought to discharge. As for those young people who appeared last, I know them, they live

in my village. They are very dangerous citizens and indeed bad subjects. They quickly squander the money they earn in taverns because
they know they will be given relief. As you see, they appeal to us at
the first difficulty caused by their own shortcomings."

The sitting continues. A young woman comes before the bar, followed by the overseer of the poor of her parish. She approaches without showing the slightest sign of hesitation, her gaze not at all lowered
by a sense of shame. The overseer accuses her of having had the baby
she is carrying through unlawful intercourse.

She freely admits this. As she is indigent and if the father remained
unknown the illegitimate child would become a public charge along
with its mother, the overseer calls on her to name the father; the court
puts her under oath. She names a neighborhood peasant. The latter,
who is present among the audience, very obligingly admits the accuracy of the fact, and the justices of the peace sentence him to support the child. The father and the mother retire and the incident does
not excite the least emotion in an audience accustomed to such scenes.

After this young woman comes another. She comes willingly. She
approaches the judges with the same shameless indifference shown by
the first. She declares herself pregnant and names the father of the
unborn child. This man is absent. The court adjourns the case in order
to have him summoned.

Lord X tells me: "Here again are the harmful effects produced by
the same laws. The most direct consequence of the Poor Laws is to
make the public responsible for the support of the deserted children
who are the neediest of all indigents. Out of this comes the parish's
desire to free themselves of the duty to support illegitimate children
whose parents would be in a position to nurture them. Out of this also
comes the paternity suits instigated by the parishes, proof of which is
left to the woman. For what other kind of proof can one delude one-
self into expecting in such a case? By obliging the parishes to become
responsible for illegitimate children and permitting the paternity suits
in order to ease this crushing weight, we have facilitated the misconduct of lower-class women as much as we could. Illegitimate pregnancy must almost always improve their material condition. If the father of the child is rich, they can unload the responsibility of raising
the fruit of their common blunder on him; if he is poor, they entrust
this responsibility to society. The relief granted to them in either way
exceeds the expenses caused by the infant. So they thrive from their
very vices, and it often happens that a woman who has become a
mother several times over concludes a more advantageous marriage
than the young virgin who has only her virtues to offer. They have a
dowry of infamy."

I repeat that I wanted to change nothing from this passage in
my diary. I have reproduced it exactly, because it seemed to me
that it rendered the impressions that I would have the reader share
with truth and simplicity.

SINCE the time of my English journey the Poor Law has been modified. Many Englishmen flatter themselves that these changes will exercise great influence on the indigents' future, on their morality, and on their number. I would like to be able to share these hopes, but I cannot do so. In the new law the present-day English have again reaffirmed the principle introduced two hundred years ago by Elizabeth. Like that ruler, they have imposed on society the obligation of feeding the poor. That is quite enough. All the abuses that I have tried to describe are contained in it, just as the biggest oak is contained in the acorn that a child can hide in its hand. It needs only time to develop and grow. To want to create a law which regularly, permanently, and uniformly relieves indigency without also increasing the indigent population, without increasing their laziness along with their needs, and their idleness with their vices, is to plant an acorn and to be stunned when a stem appears, followed by leaves, flowers, and fruits, which in turn will one day produce a whole forest from the bowels of the earth.

I am certainly far from wanting to put the most natural, the most beautiful, and the most holy of virtues on trial. But I think that there is no principle, however good, whose every consequence can be regarded as good. I think that beneficence must be a manly and reasoned virtue, not a weak and unreflecting inclination. It is necessary to do what is most useful to the receiver, not what pleases the giver, to do what best serves the welfare of the majority, not what rescues the few. I can conceive of beneficence only in this way. Any other way it is still a sublime instinct, but it no longer seems to me worthy of the name of virtue.

I recognize that individual charity almost always produces useful results. It devotes itself to the greatest miseries, it seeks out misfortune without publicity, and it silently and spontaneously repairs the damage. It can be observed wherever there are unfortunates to be helped. It grows with suffering. And yet, it cannot be unthinkingly relied on, because a thousand accidents can delay or halt its operation. One cannot be sure of finding it, and it is not aroused by every cry of pain.

I admit that by regulating relief, charitable persons in association could infuse individual philanthropy with more activity and power. I recognize not only the utility but the necessity of public charity applied to inevitable evils such as the helplessness of infancy, the decrepitude of old age, sickness, insanity. I even admit its temporary usefulness in times of public calamities which God sometimes allows to slip from his hand, proclaiming his anger to the nations. State alms are then as spontaneous as unforeseen, as temporary as the evil itself.

I even understand that public charity which opens free schools for the children of the poor and gives intelligence the means of acquiring the basic physical necessities through labor.

But I am deeply convinced that any permanent, regular, administrative system whose aim will be to provide for the needs of the poor, will breed more miseries than it can cure, will deprave the population that it wants to help and comfort, will in time reduce the rich to being no more than the tenant-farmers of the poor, will dry up the sources of savings, will stop the accumulation of capital, will retard the development of trade, will benumb human industry and activity, and will culminate by bringing about a violent revolution in the state, when the number of those who receive alms will have become as large as those who give it, and the indigent, no longer being able to take from the impoverished rich the means of providing for his needs, will find it easier to plunder them of all their property at one stroke than to ask for their help.

L ET us summarize in a few words. The progressive movement of modern civilization will gradually and in a roughly increasing proportion raise the number of those who are forced to turn to charity. What remedy can be applied to such evils? Legal alms comes to mind first—legal alms in all forms—sometimes unconditional, sometimes hidden in the disguise of a wage. Sometimes it is accidental and temporary, at other times regular and permanent. But intensive investigation quickly demonstrates that this remedy, which seems both so natural and so effective is a very dangerous expedient. It affords only a false and momentary stop to individual suffering, and however used it inflames society's sores. We are left with individual charity. It can produce only useful results. Its very weakness is a guarantee against dangerous consequences. It alleviates many miseries and breeds none. But individual charity seems quite weak when faced with the progressive development of the industrial classes and all the evils which civilization joins to the inestimable goods it produces. It was sufficient for the Middle Ages, when religious enthusiasm gave it enormous energy, and when its task was less difficult; could it be sufficient today when the burden is heavy and when its forces are so weakened? Individual charity is a powerful agency that must not be despised, but it would be imprudent to rely on it. It is but a single means and cannot be the only one. Then what is to be done? In what direction can we look? How can we mitigate what we can foresee, but not cure?

Up to this point I have examined the financial approach to poverty. But is this the only approach? After having considered alleviating evils, wouldn't it be useful to try to forestall them? Is there a way to prevent the rapid displacement of population, so that men do not leave the land and move into industry before the latter can easily respond to their needs? Can the total national wealth continue to increase without a part of those who produce this wealth having to curse the prosperity that they produce? Is it impossible to establish a more constant and exact relation between the production and consumption of manufactured goods? Can the working classes be helped to accumulate savings which would allow them to await a reversal of fortune in times of industrial calamity, without dying?

At this point my horizon widens on all sides. My subject grows. I see a path opening up, which I cannot follow at this moment. The present *Memoir*, too short for my subject, already exceeds the limits that I had thought it necessary to set for myself. The measures by which pauperism may be combatted preventively will be the object of a second work which I hope respectfully to submit next year to the Academic Society of Cherbourg.[2]

---

[2] The promised sequel to the *Memoir* never appeared and was apparently never written. It seems to have suffered the same fate as the continuation of his essay on the "Political and Social Condition of France," written for the *London and Westminster Review* in 1836. Both projects were pushed aside in deference to the task of writing the second part of *Democracy in America*, which took years longer than originally anticipated.

[4]

ENUMERATION *and* CLASSIFICATION *of* PAUPERS, *and* STATE PENSIONS *for the* AGED. *By* CHARLES BOOTH, ESQ.

CONTENTS :

PART I.

Pauperism at Stepney.

As a study of the class provided for under the Poor Law may be of use in considering what changes, if any, are desirable in this law or its administration, I have made an inquiry into two London unions, the results of which I now lay before the Royal Statistical Society.

The two London unions chosen for this purpose are Stepney and St. Pancras.

Stepney is one of those unions which have practically abolished out relief. At the beginning of April, 1870, there were 1,022 in-door and 3,126 out-door poor, and the yearly expenditure was about 12,600*l.* in-door and 12,300*l.* out-door. In April, 1888, there were 946 in-door and only 26 out-door, and the annual expense was about 10,500*l.* in-door and 500*l.* out-door.

The record of relief from 1876 to 1889 is preserved in books kept by the relieving officers, and to these books I have kindly been allowed access. The system employed is so admirable that it might with advantage be adopted elsewhere. The name and request of every applicant for relief is entered in the relieving officer's journal, and if relief is granted, and sometimes when it is not granted, the particulars of the case are entered in the "record "books." These particulars include the results of inquiries made, and what relief, if any, is given, and the books are so arranged and indexed that all entries referring to the same case are to be found together, and a reference is made to "allied" cases; that is, when other members of the same family have received assistance, "family" being here understood in its larger sense. It will readily be perceived how invaluable a picture of the pauper class is to be found in the pages of these records.

1891.] Booth—*Enumeration and Classification of Paupers, &c.* 601

The population of Stepney Union in 1881 was 58,543, and in 1891, 57,599. It is full of waterside poverty, and contains very few inhabitants above the working class level in means.

The institutions belonging to the union in which paupers live are as follow :—

    A. Poplar Workhouse (shared by Stepney), for the able bodied.
    B. Bromley Workhouse, for the infirm, including aged and any children not at school.
    C. Sick Asylum at Bromley (shared by Poplar).
    D. District schools (at Sutton in Surrey).

Roman Catholic children are sent to various schools belonging to that community, and the lunatics to various asylums.

There are also a very limited number of out pensioners, and there is some medical out relief.

The numbers receiving relief on 30th April, 1889, were as follow :—

Able bodied (Poplar Workhouse)	53	
Infirm, aged, &c. (Bromley Workhouse)	504	
Sick	155	In-door.... 1,163
School children	213	
Lunatics	238	
Pensioners	17	
Medical relief	137	Out-door 162[1]
Other „	8	
Total..		1,325

For most of these I have the materials of a short history. But before taking up this part of my subject I will complete the enumeration by going back twelve months. There is no absolute reason for choosing this period. A bottle of medicine or the drawing of a tooth in January might not be thought to pauperise for the whole year, while on the other hand to have been brought up in pauper schools may leave a stigma for life, but a year, bringing each season in its turn, is on the whole a convenient basis for estimating the total pauperism, and has been usually accepted.

The following table gives the numbers of fresh admissions to each institution separately, and shows the extent to which these overlap (the same person recurring in various institutions) so as finally to yield the total number of those who at one time or other, or in one way or other, did receive relief in the twelve months from 1st May, 1888, to 30th April, 1889. I show also how many of these poor people died during the year, so as to give finally the actual number of persons living on 30th April, 1889, who had received relief, in-door or out-door, during the preceding twelve months.

    [1] Number on 1st January, 1889.

Stepney.—*Number of In-door Poor Relieved during Twelve Months ending 30th April, 1889.*

Institution and Class of Pauper.	Number of Inmates 30th April, 1889.	Number to be added. Gross.	Number to be added. Net.	Total Number counted for Twelve Months.	
Poplar Workhouse, for the able bodied....	53	328	251	304	247 relieved Poplar Workhouse only 134 there and elsewhere also
Bromley Workhouse, for the infirm	504	538	254	758	562 relieved Bromley Workhouse only 480 there and elsewhere also
The sick asylum....	155	711	497	652	509 relieved sick asylum only 357 there and elsewhere also
The district and other schools	213	101	90	303	179 relieved in schools only 135 there and elsewhere also
Lunatic asylums...	238	42	40	278	252 relieved lunatic asylums only 28 there and elsewhere also
	1,163	1,720	1,132	2,295	

In order to arrive at the net number to add, those items of duplicate relief have been omitted which seemed least important, and especially such as are formal only—as the entry of children in the Bromley workhouse on their way to or from school. The difference between the gross and the net figures (588) is rather more than half the cases in which relief was given " elsewhere " also," because in some cases relief was obtained by the same person in three different institutions.

Of the 1,132 who had relief during the year but were not in receipt of relief at the end of it, we know that 130 had died, namely, 5 persons in Poplar, 10 in Bromley, 97 in the sick asylum, and 18 in lunatic asylums. The deduction of these dead from the roll of paupers gives us the final numbers of those who are to be counted in connection with each institution, thus :—

	Number of Inmates on 30th April, 1889.	Net Number to add (less Deaths).	Per Cent. to be added for Twelve Months.	Total.
Poplar (able bodied)	53	246	464 %	299
Bromley (infirm)................	504	244	48 „	748
Sick asylum	155	400	258 „	555
District and other schools	213	90	42 „	303
Lunatic asylums	238	22	9 „	260
	1,163	1,002	86 %	2,165

It should be borne in mind that the apportionment between institution and institution is, owing to overlapping, somewhat arbitrary, but the ratios given above may be taken as approximately true on the whole, and show that here 86 per cent. must be added to the paupers of one day to give the total for the year for in-door cases.

STEPNEY.—*Number of Out-door Poor Relieved during Twelve Months ending Lady-day,* 1889.

Form of Relief.	Number of Persons Relieved on 1st January, 1889.	Number to be added for Year ending Lady-day, 1889. Gross.	Number to be added. Net.	Net Total of Out-door Poor.
Pensions	17	3	—	17
Other out relief	8	103	84	92
Medical aid....................	137	1,491	996	1,133
	162	1,597	1,080	1,242

The "other out relief" includes 76 funerals, which must be deducted, and taking an estimated number of deaths from those in receipt of medical relief (as to whom I have no information) we get the following percentage table :—

	Number Relieved 1st January, 1889.	Net Number to add.	Addition per Cent.	Total.
Pensioners	17	—	—	17
Other out relief	8	8	100%	16
Medical aid	137	900	657 „	1,037
	162	908	560%	1,070

Percentages of increase are apt to be misleading when the initial number is small. What may be safely said is that apart from medical orders, out relief does not apply to double the number of one day, whereas medical orders apply to seven times as many as one day's list shows.

Those who were in receipt of relief at the end of the year have many of them been in receipt of relief for a length of time, but, except for these, they, like the others, are a floating population, coming and going, and moving about from institution to institution, and much care has to be taken not to count them more than once   It is indeed possible that with all the care taken some few may appear twice, but on the whole the company of the unfortunate or the unworthy who were in receipt of relief from the Stepney Union on the 30th April, 1889, or had been during the twelve months preceding, and were still living, may be summed up again as follows :—

In-door—

Able bodied	299
Infirm	748
Sick	555
Children	303
Insane	260
	2,165

Out-door—

Permanent list (pensioners)	17
Relief in kind	8
Medical aid	900
	925
	3,090

What manner of people these are will be shown sufficiently by an analysis of the stories of those (1,163 in all) who were actually in receipt of relief on the 30th April, 1889. In making this analysis I have found that the following are the principal causes of pauperism. To each cause I have affixed a letter for use in tabulation, thus :—

If Principal Cause.	Contributory.	Father or Husband.	Mother or Wife.	Both.
Crime ... C	c	c^1	c^2	c^3
Vice ... V	v	v^1	v^2	v^3
Drink ... D	d	d^1	d^2	d^3
Laziness ... L	l	l^1	l^2	l^3
Pauper association ... P	p	p^1	p^2	p^3
Heredity ... H	h	h^1	h^2	h^3
Mental disease ... M	m	m^1	m^2	m^3
Temper (queer) ... Q	q	q^1	q^2	q^3
Incapacity ... I	i	i^1	i^2	i^3
Early marriage (girl) ... G	g	g^1	g^2	g^3
Large family ... F	f	—	—	—
Extravagance ... E	e	e^1	e^2	e^3
Lack of work (unemployed) ... U	u	u^1	u^2	u^3
Trade misfortune ... T	t	t^1	t^2	t^3
Restlessness, roving, tramp ... R	r	r^1	r^2	r^3
No relations ... N	n	—	—	—
Death of husband ... W	w	—	—	—
Desertion (abandoned) ... A	a	—	—	—
Death of father or mother (orphan) } ... O	o	o^1	o^2	o^3
Sickness ... S	s	s^1	s^2	s^3
Accident ... X	x	x^1	x^2	x^3
Ill luck ... Y	y	—	—	—
Old age ... Z	z	z^1	z^2	z^3

Repetition of letters may be used for recurrence, as Ss recurrent sickness, or Vv habitual immorality.

As a further indication of character when the opposite of a fault is intended, the letter can be circled thus Ⓘ for industry, Ⓓ for known sobriety or teetotaler.

Any one who may follow me in this attempt to state pauper

circumstances in tabular form will find this system very useful. There are few stories that cannot be very forcibly expressed by married condition, age, and three letters, as the following examples will show :—

Martin Rooney	M.	86	I z d	Incapable old man, who drinks.
Patrick Rooney	S.	36	C h d	{ A criminal, hereditary pauper, and drunkard.
Sarah Truelove	M.	66	D z p	{ Drunken old woman of pauper associations.
John Curtis	S.	72	X z n	{ Single old man, without any relations, who has had an accident.
Eliza Green	Ch.	4	O¹ d²	{ Child whose father is dead and mother drinks.
Mary Carter	W.	59	(dl) S n z	{ Elderly widow of good character for sobriety and industry, with no relations, and ill.
Eliza Knight	M.	60	(dl) M¹ S	{ Husband insane. This woman, who is sick, has a good character for sobriety and industry.

The analysis of these Stepney stories is embodied in the following tables, which show the length of time those in each institution had been chargeable there, and separately the ages and civil condition, with the principal and contributory causes of pauperism.

TABLE I.—STEPNEY. *Table showing the Length of Time during which Persons Receiving In-door Relief on 30th April, 1889, had been in Receipt of Relief at the Institution in which they then were.*

Institution.	Less than 1 Year.		1—2 Years.		2—3 Years.		3—5 Years.		5—10 Years.		10—15 Years.		15—20 Years.		20 and over.		Total.		
	M.	F.	M.	F.	M.	F.	M.	F.	M.	F.	M.	F.	M.	F.	M.	F.	M.	F.	Together
Poplar Work-house	21	25	1	—	—	1	3	2	—	—	—	—	—	—	—	—	25	28	53
Bromley Workhouse	155	94	23	18	48	25	46	31	21	15	8	12	4	1	2	1	307	197	504
Sick asylum	71	60	2	2	5	3	3	3	2	1	—	2	—	1	—	—	83	72	155
Schools	37	20	13	6	19	14	33	17	24	27	1	2	—	—	—	—	127	86	213
Lunatic and Imbecile Asylums	15	19	8	1	4	7	9	8	16	22	22	38	13	37	5	14	92	146	238
	299	218	47	27	76	50	94	61	63	65	31	54	17	39	7	15	634	529	1,163
	517		74		126		446												

It will be seen that the moving stream is less in volume than the pool in and out of which it runs, leaving its deposit of those who become fixed. It is remarkable that in every institution those who have been in from two to three years exceed in numbers those who have been in for one to two years. I have no explanation at hand for this peculiar fact. It may be that it is only after two years that the habit of going out for a while ceases to operate with even the most regular.

TABLE II.—POPLAR. *(Able Bodied.)* Condition and Age.

	Children.		20—30.		30—40.		40—50.		50—60.		60—70.		Total.		
	M.	F.	M.	F.	M.	F.	M.	F.	M.	F.	M.	F.	M.	F.	Together
Single	1	1	6	1	2	2	1	1	3	2	—	—	13	7	20
Married	—	—	—	—	1	1	—	1	5	2	1	—	7	4	11
Widowed*	—	—	—	1	—	1	—	4	3	9	2	2	5	17	21
	1	1	6	2	3	4	1	6	11	13	3	2	25	28	53

24   29

* Including one deserted wife.

It will be seen that of the able bodied more than half, 29 out of 53, are over 50. Of these 29 we find 8 as to whom drink is given as the principal, and 4 as to whom it is given as a contributory cause; want of work accounts for 4, and incapacity for 3. Mental disease for 2, other illness for 6, and the death of the husband for 3 cases, as well as contributing in 5 more. Of the 24 younger people drink accounts for 2 in the first place, contributing in 7 more; immorality or crime for 7, and laziness for 3.

TABLE III.—BROMLEY. *Infirm.*

	Children.		20—50.		50—60.		60—70.		70—80.		80—		Total.		
	M.	F.	M.	F.	M.	F.	M.	F.	M.	F.	M.	F.	M.	F.	Together
Single	15*	8	15	11	8	4	15	5	11	4	1	—	65	32	97
Married	—	—	4	1	8	4	49	15	32	7	5	—	98	27	125
Widowed†	—	—	3	2	12	6	43	39	55	49	12	20	124	117	241
	15	8	21	15	28	14	107	59	98	60	18	20	287	176	463
Cases of over 13 years' standing.‡	—	—	3	2	3	1	5	6	6	4	3	8	20	21	41
	15	8	24	17	31	15	112	65	104	64	21	28	307	197	504

110   394

* Two of these are young people, 15—20.   † Including two deserted wives.
‡ Of which we have no record as to condition.

It will be seen that there are 394 above 60 out of a total of 504; of these 373 are returned as over 65.

Amongst the 362 of these old people of whom we have records, 35 are mentioned as owing their pauperism to drink as the principal cause, with 48 more cases in which drink is mentioned as contributing. Illness, including accidents, accounts for 66. Incapacity or temper for 8, and lack of work for 13. Old age is given as the principal cause for 187, and as contributing in 91

1891.]   *of Paupers, and State Pensions for the Aged.*   607.

more. As a principal cause it is combined with drink, sickness, want of work, and lack of those who might support them. It stands without qualification in 27 cases.

TABLE IV. —*Sick Asylum.*

	Children		20—50.		50—60.		60—70.		70—80.		80—		Total.		
	M.	F.	M	F.	M.	F.	M.	F.	M.	F.	M.	F.	M.	F.	Together.
Single	9	7	29	5	7	2	—	2	—	2	—	—	45	18	63
Married	—	—	9	10	8	3	5	6	3	1	1	—	26	20	46
Widowed*	—	—	4	3	3	5	3	10	1	10	1	6	12	34	46
	9	7	42	18	18	10	8	18	4	13	2	6	83	72	155
	16		60				79								

* Including one deserted wife.

Out of these 155 cases, drink is given as the principal cause of pauperism in 19, and as contributing in 15 more.

TABLE V.—*Children at School, divided for Sex and Age.*

Under 5.		5—10.		10—15.		15 and Over.		Total.		
M.	F.	M.	F.	M.	F.	M.	F.	M.	F.	Together.
4	2	34	34	80	45	9	5	127	86	213

The causes of their pauperism are given below :—

	Number.	Per Cent.	
Death of father	105	49·3	{ Combined with drink in 39 cases, immorality and laziness in 2 cases
„ mother	8	3·8	Combined with insanity in 4 cases
„ father and mother....	19	8·9	{ The only cause in 14 cases ; combined with immorality in 3 cases
Desertion of mother	16	7·5	{ Combined with drink in 8 cases, immorality in 5 cases
Insanity or imbecility of father	6	2·8	
Illness of father (accident)	22	10·3	{ Combined with drink in 2 cases, and trade misfortune in 4 cases
„ mother	2	0·9	
Incapacity .... Lack of work .... } of father Trade misfortune Old age	12	5·6	
Immorality .... ⎫ of father Laziness .... } or Pauper association ⎭ mother	7	3·3	Combined with drink in 5 cases
Drink, father	8	3·8	Combined with laziness in 3 cases
„ mother	1	0·5	
„ father and mother........	7	3·3	{ Combined with laziness and immorality in 3 cases, and with mental disease in 2 cases
	213	100·0	

TABLE VI.—STEPNEY.   *In-door Cases.   General Statement of Ages, &c.*
(Omitting Lunatics).

Condition.	Children.		15—20.		20—40.		40—50.		50—60.		60—70.		70—80.		80—		Total.		
	M.	F.	M.	F.	M.	F.	M.	F.	M.	F.	M.	F.	M.	F.	M.	F.	M.	F.	Together
Single	140	95	11	7	38	10	16	10	18	8	15	7	1	6	11	—	250	143	393
Married	—	—	—	—	6	8	8	5	21	9	55	21	35	8	6	—	131	51	182
Widowed*	—	—	—	—	3	4	3	8	18	20	48	51	56	59	13	26	141	168	309
Old cases†	—	—	—	—	1	—	2	2	3	1	5	6	6	4	3	8	20	21	41
Total	140	95	11	7	48	22	29	25	60	38	123	85	108	77	23	34	542	383	925
	235				240						450								

* Including four deserted wives.

† These date back beyond our recorded information, age and sex only being known.

The large proportion of old people is very noticeable. It may be interesting to note in connection with this table the relation which four of the principal causes of pauperism, viz., drink, sickness, accident, and lack of work, bear to age, sex, and civil condition.

Table showing connection between certain Causes of Pauperism and Age, Sex, and Civil Condition.

Cause.	Males.								Total Males	Females.								Total Females	Grand Total.
	Under 60.				Over 60.					Under 60.				Over 60.					
	S.	M.	W.	Total.	S.	M.	W.	Total.		S.	M.	W.	Total.	S.	M.	W.	Total.		
Drink	8	10	2	20	2	21	10	33	53	1	6	8	15	2	5	5	12	27	80
Sickness........	38	15	12	65	2	16	15	33	98	10	12	10	32	5	3	31	39	71	169
Accident	4	2	4	10	3	4	8	15	25	—	—	1	1	—	1	3	4	5	30
Lack of work	1	2	3	6	1	8	11	20	26	—	—	—	—	—	1	1	2	2	28
	51	29	21	101	8	49	44	101	202	11	18	19	48	7	10	40	57	105	307

It will be seen from this table that an extraordinary proportion of those who suffer because of drinking habits are or have been married. It is not to be supposed that the married drink much more than the single, but it may be taken that it is in connection with the responsibilities of married life that the consequences of drink are fatal. Single people, if they indulge, may do so with comparative impunity. On the other hand, a large proportion of the sick are single or widowed, having, I suppose, no home care. Accidents apply principally to men, but are fairly distributed between young and old, married and not. Lack of work applies chiefly to elderly men, married or widowers.

Principal Causes of Pauperism at Stepney (by Institutions).

Principal or Obvious Causes.	Poplar, Able Bodied.		Bromley, Infirm.		Sick Asylum.		Summary.				Contributory Causes.			
	Number.	Per Cent.	Number.	Per Cent.	Number.	Per Cent.	Males.	Females.	Total.	Per Cent.	Drink. (d.)	Pauper Association and Heredity. (p.)(h.)	Sickness. (a.)(x.)(m.)	Old Age. (z.)
Drink .... D	10	19·6	50	11·3	20	14·2	53	27	80	12·6	8	23	11	11
Immorality V	7	13·7	5	1·1	4	2·9	6	10	16	2·5	8	3	8	1
Laziness L	3	5·8	6	1·4	3	2·1	10	2	12	1·9	6	5	1	3
Pauper association and heredity. P&H	1	2·0	4	0·9	2	1·4	6	1	7	1·1	1	—	2	2
Incapacity, temper, &c. I&Q	5	9·8	19	4·3	—	—	17	7	24	3·8	4	5	2	6
Extravagance .... E	—	—	8	1·8	—	—	7	1	8	1·3	4	2	—	3
Lack of work, or trade misfortune } U	5	9·8	23	5·2	—	—	26	2	28	4·4	4	—	5	13
Accident X	—	—	25	5·7	5	3·5	25	5	30	4·7	4	2	1	14
Death of husband ... W	4	7·9	20	4·5	2	1·4	—	26	26	4·1	8	2	10	8
Desertion .... A	1	2·0	2	0·5	—	—	—	3	3	0·5	3	—	1	1
Mental derangement. M	3	5·8	7	1·6	1	0·7	8	3	11	1·7	1	2	—	2
Sickness .... S	8	15·7	76	17·2	85	60·3	98	71	169	26·7	24	38	5	41
Old age .... Z	—	—	192	43·4	16	11·4	113	95	208	32·8	22	18	44	—
Other causes	4	7·9	5	1·1	3	2·1	9	3	12	1·9	6	6	2	2
	51	100·0	442	100·0	141	100·0	373	261	634	100·0	85	106	87	107
Children	2	—	21	—	13	—	22	14	36	—	—	—	—	—
Old cases, no record	—	—	41	—	1	—	20	22	42	—	—	—	—	—
	53	—	504	—	155	—	415	297	712	—	—	—	—	—

The foregoing table will bear study as containing much in small compass. It will be seen that drink with a capital D stands for only 80 out of 634 cases, or 12·6 per cent., whilst as contributory it appears in 85 more, chiefly in connection with sickness and old age as principal cause. Altogether 25 per cent. are returned as affected by drink. This proportion is less than might have been expected, and it is possible that closer research into the circumstances and history of these people, if it could be made, might disclose a greater connection than here appears between pauperism and the public house. It is however noteworthy that the results shown agree on the whole with those of the two inquiries I have myself made previously into apparent causes of poverty. The first, regarding 4,000 cases of poverty known by certain of the school board visitors, gave 13 and 14 per cent. as due to drink, the higher percentage being for the greater degree of poverty. The second, regarding about 5,000 people living poor and irregular lives, showed 10 and 11 per cent., dropping to only 5 per cent. for about another 3,000 who, though poor, were more regularly employed; the information in this case coming from district visitors connected with religious organisations. The relieving officers, school board and district visitors, are all of them in daily contact with the people, and their various reports, in so far as they agree, make a strong force of evidence. That from 10 to 14 per cent. of poverty and pauperism should be directly connected with drink, and that perhaps as much more may be indirectly connected with it, is serious enough, although it is much less than has been asserted by the advocates of prohibition. I should say here that the analysis of poverty at St. Pancras, shortly to be given, shows a higher percentage, and should be taken into account.[2]

It will be seen that pauper association and heredity, while only accounting as principal cause for 7 cases, appear as contributory in no less than 106 cases. Incapacity and lack of work together account for 52 cases, or 8 per cent. of the whole. Accidents for 30 cases more. The large proportion of accidents, as well as the numerous out of work cases, are probably connected with risks and uncertainties of water side employment. Sickness accounts as principal cause for 169 cases, and old age for 208, whilst the latter contributes in 107 other cases. Sickness and old age are causes so overwhelming and obvious, as to draw a curtain over what has gone before; behind that curtain we doubtless might find some whose previous life offered another explanation of their condition.

In weighing the value of the evidence on which the foregoing tables are based, it is to be remembered that it was none of it

---

[2] Mr. McDougall, as the result of a searching inquiry into 254 cases at Manchester, gives 52 per cent. as the proportion of drink cases.

taken *ad hoc*, but was collected and noted down as a matter of business by those who had to report on each case for the guidance of the guardians in the administration of the law. I, however, do not wish to lay too much stress on the results shown, as the basis is insufficiently wide for safe generalisation, and I give these tables, and those which follow concerning St. Pancras, rather as types to show the use that might be made of such information if obtained on a larger scale, than as themselves of much conclusive value. On the whole the results obtained at St. Pancras support those shown at Stepney.

PART II.

Pauperism at St. Pancras.

In St. Pancras Union there is no systematic record of cases such as has been kept at Stepney, but from the personal knowledge possessed by the relieving officers of those in receipt of relief, and by obtaining an accurate account of the movements from institution to institution, and in and out, from the registers, I have been able to work out a parallel statement, which, though somewhat less complete, is yet of considerable value.

The time of investigation was December, 1889, and the numbers in receipt of relief were as follow, as recorded in the official returns for week ending 21st December :—[3]

	Work-house.	St. Anne's Home, Streatham.	Infir-mary.	Imbe-cile Asylum.	Lunatic Asylum.	Other Places.	Leaves-den Schools.	Other Schools.	Boarded Out.	Total.*
In-door	1,814	340	504	772	477	69	602	178	152	4,908
Out-door	{ 916 families, consisting of 1,713 individuals, and 92 wayfarers were relieved. (This does not include cases which had medical orders only.)									

* Seventy-five hospital (fever) cases omitted.

At Stepney, to find the actual number of persons relieved in twelve months, I worked back, including with those in receipt of relief on 30th April, 1889, all others who had been relieved during the preceding twelve months. At St. Pancras it was more convenient to work forward, and so to those in receipt of relief on 1st January, 1890, the names have been added of all others who received relief during any part of 1890.

The plan adopted was the somewhat laborious one of noting down in alphabetical order the name and age of every person to

[3] Population 1881, 236,208.   1891, 234,437.

whom relief was granted in each institution, and then striking off all except the first entry of any individual. Several persons appear and re-appear more than thirty times, and in one case the record extends to forty-eight entries; in all there are 4,000 readmissions. This multiplication of apparent numbers, though partly due to the system by which any transfer from one institution to another involves a fresh entry, reflects to a large extent the restless habits of many of the paupers, who obtain a species of liberty by claiming discharge and readmission as often or nearly as often as the law permits. The method of inquiry adopted will thus be found to throw some light upon the character as well as true volume of existing pauperism. The numbers that must be added to the total at the end of December, 1890, to cover the pauperism of a whole year are shown in the following table. Each institution is taken separately and the overlapping allowed for:—

ST. PANCRAS.—*Number of In-door Poor Relieved during Twelve Months ending 31st December, 1890.*

Institution and Class of Pauper.	On 1st January, 1890.	Gross Number to add.	Net Number to add.	Total for Twelve Months.
Workhouse (able bodied) .... St. Anne's Home (able bodied)........	} 2,164	4,425	2,431	4,595
Infirmary	579	2,029	1,197	1,776
District schools	602	355	355	957
Asylums (imbecile)	768	185	185	953
Other asylums (insane)	473	160	160	633
Hospitals, &c.	68	56	56	124
Certified schools	179	64	64	243
Children boarded out	155	9	9	164
Non-resident paupers	69	33	33	102
	5,057	7,316	4,490	9,547

The division of the net number to add amongst the various overlapping institutions is somewhat arbitrary—the total is correct, or nearly so.

The deaths which occurred amongst these people during the twelve months reduce their numbers by 841 in all, viz., 358 in the workhouse, 309 in the infirmary, and 174 in asylums. So that the total number of persons living on 31st December who had obtained relief during the twelve months was 8,706, or 3,649 more than were counted on 1st January, being an addition of 70 per cent. on all classes of in-door paupers together.

The particulars obtained at the outset were not confined to those in the workhouse on 1st January, but included all relieved there during December, or 2,188 persons. Of these 101 were discharged and re-entered during December.

631 were admitted before 1st January, 1888.
520   „   between 1st January, 1888, and 1st June, 1889 (seventeen
    months).
529 were admitted between 1st June, 1889, and 1st December, 1889 (six months).
609 were admitted during December.
—
2,289
101 [4] duplicates who were discharged and re-admitted in December.
—
2,188 actual number of persons relieved during December.

Some further analysis is necessary. Of the 631, who may be
called " old stagers," having been admitted two years before, I can
say nothing more; the cause of their poverty had passed out of
recollection. Of the rest we learn something from the manner and
date of their admission, as is shown in the subjoined table :—

Manner of Admission.	Date of Admission.		Total.
	1st January, 1888, to 31st May, 1889.	1st June, 1889, to 31st December, 1889.	
By order of master	165	203	368
„ relieving officer......................	336	642	978
At the gate, from police courts, &c.	14	44	58
Born in workhouse	5	28	33
Children with parents or from school........	—	120	120
	520	1,037	1,557

The 368 admitted by order of master, being usually transferred
from the infirmary or other institution, may most of them be
added to the 631 of " old stagers," making 999 in all of those
whose story dates back beyond our ken—nor had we any information about those who were admitted at the gate, nor of those
families whose children are here counted separately. The children
from school are most of them entered and discharged the same
day, their parents being outside. As to those unlucky enough to
be born in the workhouse, nothing more need be said; they do not
usually stay in, for we see that while 28 remain of those born in
seven months, ending on the 31st December, only 5 remain of
those born in seventeen months before.

It is, finally, to those admitted by the relieving officer that our
detailed particulars appertain. They are divided as above into
two parts by the summer of 1889. The line drawn is not so
arbitrary as may at first sight appear. In June, July, and August,
there is a very marked exodus of otherwise permanent paupers, who
leave the workhouse for the fruit, pea, and hop-picking season, or
take advantage of warmer weather to seek work or pleasure, or, at
any rate, variety outside. All who can, get out for a while, and

[4] These should be deducted mostly from the 609 December cases, but a few
would be re-entries from the 529 cases of six months previous.

those who do not do so, may be counted for practical purposes as permanent paupers. Of such we have 336 to describe. The remaining 642, being those relieved in December who were admitted after 1st June, are really composed of four different classes. (1.) Those (comparatively few) whom the lapse of another year will prove to be permanent.[5] (2.) Those (a considerable number) who divide their lives pretty regularly between the workhouse and the world outside, coming in for the winter or when work fails. (3.) The regular "ins and outs," to whom we have already referred, and of whom we shall have more to say, and finally (4.) Cases whose relief is genuinely of a temporary character.

The figures given so far are all taken from the St. Pancras "creed" register, verified by reference to the admission and discharge book. The table of causes of pauperism which now follows is based on the answers given by the relieving officers to questions put as to the previous history of the inmates admitted by their order between 1st June, 1888, and 31st December, 1889. In some cases they were, as might well be supposed, unable to give any information whatever as to inmates admitted long before. In the case of persons who, when they applied, had been but a short time in the district, they had sometimes not been able to ascertain even the facts needed, with a view to discovering relatives who might be liable for their support. Again, the information is often very meagre with regard to those who are admitted at once on account of illness, as the relieving officer will naturally dispense with the searching questions asked of those who seek admittance on the ground of destitution. It must be said, on the whole, that our knowledge does not go much beyond proximate causes, and that the original causes in the case of the aged and sick are frequently not given. Subject to this necessary proviso, the table attempts to show the part played by drink, immorality, laziness, mental derangement, desertion, illness, and old age, in producing this mass of pauperism.

[5] Of the 1,037 relieved in December who were admitted between 1st June and the end of the year (1,138, less 101 duplicates), we know that 249 were re-discharged in December, leaving 788 in the house on 1st January, and these took their discharges as follow :—

In January	257		Brought forward....	578
„ February	67		In September	3
„ March	95		„ October	7
„ April	54		„ November	13
„ May	44		„ December	3
„ June	30			—
„ July	9			604
„ August	22		Left in the house	184
	—			—
Carried forward....	578			788

From which it seems that of 1,037 current cases only about one-sixth remain continually, and are still in the house after twelve months.

Causes of Pauperism—St. Pancras Workhouse.

Principal or Obvious Causes.	Permanent Paupers.		Current Cases.		Ins and Outs.		Total.				Number of Cases in which the undernoted are contributory.			
	Number.	Per Cent.	Number.	Per Cent.	Number	Per Cent.	Male.	Female.	Total.	Per Cent.	Drink. (d.)	Pauper Association. (p. and h.)	Sickness. (s.)(x.)(m.)	Old Age. (z.)
D Drink	40	17.2	93	21.2	28	43.0	88	73	161	21.9	—	11	26	5
V Immorality	8	3.5	36	8.2	7	10.8	1	50	51	6.9	10	5	2	1
L Laziness	13	5.6	40	9.1	25	38.5	58	20	78	10.6	22	19	8	—
P&H Pauper association and heredity	4	1.7	7	1.6	2	3.1	6	7	13	1.8	1	—	2	—
I&Q Incapacity, temper, &c.	5	2.2	11	2.5	2	3.1	6	12	18	2.4	—	3	1	2
E Extravagance	3	1.3	—	—	—	—	2	1	3	0.4	—	—	1	1
U Lack of work or trade misfortune	1	0.4	15	3.4	—	—	7	9	16	2.2	1	—	1	1
X Accident	9	3.9	10	2.3	—	—	13	6	19	2.6	4	—	—	2
W Death of husband	1	0.4	2	0.5	—	—	—	3	3	0.4	—	—	—	2
A Desertion	7	3.0	11	2.5	1	1.5	1	17	18	2.4	—	—	4	—
M Mental derangement	7	3.0	24	5.5	—	—	11	21	32	4.3	1	3	1	7
S Sickness	44	19.0	108	24.6	—	—	90	62	152	20.7	8	3	7	25
Z Old age	90	38.8	82	18.6	—	—	46	126	172	23.4	4	—	9	—
Addition	232	100.0	439	100.0	65	100.0	329	407	736	100.0	45	44	57	46
Old cases	9	—	22	—	—	—	—	—	31	—	—	—	—	—
New comers, tramps, &c.	46	—	23	—	—	—	—	—	69	—	—	—	—	—
Children	5	—	52	—	—	—	—	—	57	—	—	—	—	—
No information	44	—	41	—	—	—	—	—	85	—	—	—	—	—
Total	336	—	577	—	65	—	—	—	978	—	—	—	—	—

Note.—Of the sick 29, and of the old 58, are marked as of known good character for industry, sobriety, or thrift.

The plan of marking each case with a capital letter to denote principal, and small letters to denote secondary causes of pauperism, has been adopted with these as with Stepney cases. But in making any comparison with the Stepney figures, it must be remembered that while our information at Stepney covers the infirm and sick as well as the able bodied, and all except quite a few old cases, the St. Pancras particulars are only for the workhouse itself, and omit 1,000 of the older cases there as being "old stagers," about whom we could gather no information.

It will be seen that drink, sickness, and old age stand about on an equality both as principal and subsidiary causes, differing from the Stepney figures, in which drink is much less prominent. The part which drink plays amongst the more permanent paupers is less than amongst the current cases, and very much less than with the "ins and outs," of whom over 40 per cent. are marked with big D, and if we had particulars of the 1,000 old cases, and of the 600 inmates of the infirmary, it is certain that the proportion of those with whom drink is the principal cause of pauperism would be less than 20 per cent., very possibly not more than 15 per cent.

That the current cases should be more drunken and immoral than the permanent ones is so probable as to require little proof, and amongst them the "ins and outs" are naturally the worst. One-sixth of the number (see note p. 614) may become permanent, others, after receiving help, do not recur, but the majority are regular customers seeking shelter at least once a year.

Mental disease accounts for more amongst current cases than amongst the permanent, simply because such cases after a while pass into the imbecile or lunatic asylums; similarly, sickness bears a greater proportion as a cause of current than of permanent pauperism, because those who are ill pass on into the infirmary. Miscellaneous causes affect the permanent as much as the current cases, and old age adjusts the balance, accounting as it seems for 38 per cent. in the permanent as against 18 per cent. in the current cases, and passing out of count altogether in the "ins and outs."

The "Ins and Outs."—This class consists of those who, while spending most of their time in the workhouse, are in the habit of constantly re-visiting their acquaintances outside. It does not include those who, under stress of want, are in the habit of occasionally revisiting the workhouse.

The inmates of any poor house are usually allowed a day out from time to time. This is at the pleasure of the guardians, and those who receive permission may be seen in the streets in their workhouse dress. It is not this privilege, nor yet any abuse of it, that is enjoyed by the "ins and outs." They leave the workhouse simply because they have a right to do so when they please, and re-enter (very often on the same day) because the law allows it. Relief in the house is a right, and the house is no prison. There is however some check on this; a man cannot quite use the workhouse as a free shelter. He may discharge himself at any time on giving notice of his intention, but in accordance with the Act of 1871 the guardians may direct that the discharge shall not be till twenty-four hours after notice has been given, and this period may be extended to forty-eight hours if the pauper has already discharged himself in the same calendar month, and to seventy-two hours if he has done so more than twice in the last two months. Of these curtailed privileges very extended use is made.

I have noted particularly the in and out movements in May and in December, and of the 65 members of this class who had relief some time in December, we find 30 who took their discharge at least twice in one or other month. Here they are :—

Laura P.	Age 27.	Admitted and discharged three times in each month.
Lucy C.	„ 39.	Not relieved in May; in and out five times in December.
Charles K.	„ 38.	Not relieved in May; in and out three times in December.
Elizabeth I........	„ 30.	Once in May and twice in December.
Maria P.	„ 72.	Five times in May and once in December.
Margaret S.	„ 40.	Four times in May; admitted three times and discharged twice in December.
Ann B.	„ 52.	Not relieved in May; three times in December.
Edward B.	„ 21.	Not relieved in May; admitted three times and discharged twice in December.
Frederick B.	„ 18.	Not relieved in May; four times in and out in December.

(These three are one family, Ann being the mother; the boys have been chargeable in and out since they were 4 or 5 years old. The relatives are all a bad lot.)

Emily C.	Age 31.	Three times in May; once in December.
Arthur F.	„ 45.	Not in May; four times in December.
John G.	„ 19.	Not in May; three times in December.
George G.	„ 36.	Not in May; three times in and twice out in December.
Edward H.........	„ 49.	Not in May; three times in and twice out in December.
Emily H.	„ 38.	Six times in May and six times in December.

(This woman's restlessness of habit was the precursor of insanity; she is now in the asylum for lunatics.)

Jane H.	Age 49.	Three times in and out in May; four times in and three out in December.
James H.	„ 52.	Not in May; three times in and out in December.
Hannah I.	„ 41.	Not in May; three times in and twice out in December.

Joanna M.	Age 34.	Not in May; twice in and out in December.
Frederick P.	„ 21.	Not in May; three times in and out in December.
Edward R.	„ 51.	Not in May; three times in and twice out in December.
Caroline R.........	„ 64.	Once in and out in May; twice in and out in December.
William S.	„ 47.	Not in May; four times in and three times out in December.
Isabella T.	„ 34.	Not in May; five times in and four times out in December.
George T.	„ 29.	Not in May; four times in and four times out in December.
William W........	„ 47.	Not in May; four times in and three times out in December.
Robert W.	„ 53.	Not in May; five times in and four times out in December.
Ellen C.	„ 36.	Twice in and out in May; three times in and twice out in December.
Ellen K.	„ 23.	Not in May; four times in and three times out in December.
John K.	„ 40.	Not in May; three times in and three times out in December.

It is hardly necessary to dwell in detail on the characters of these people. We have seen that drink, immorality, laziness and pauper associations, or heredity, are the evident causes of their condition; of the whole 65, no less than 42 are marked with big or little D. for drink, 20 with big or little V. for immorality, 31 with big or little L. for laziness, while 14 bear H. or P. for heredity or pauper associations.

Out Relief.—At St. Pancras I have so far considered in-door relief only, except that the number of out cases has been given for the week ending 21st December, 1889, viz., 916 families (or cases), consisting of 1,713 individuals.

For Ward VI, the poorest in the parish, and indeed in North London, I have the following particulars :—Relief here was given in December to 143 permanent and 66 temporary cases, and the whole number relieved for the year ending October, 1890, was 165 permanent and 456 temporary cases. It will be seen that the increase of numbers for the year is only 15 per cent. in the permanent cases, but is sevenfold in the temporary ones.[6]

The cost of the permanent relief for six months ending March, 1890, was 523*l*., or (assuming a similar amount for the second half year) 7*l*. 6*s*. 4*d*. per case on the average. The cost of temporary relief for the whole year was 201*l*., or an average of 8*s*. 10*d*. a head.

[6] I do not know to what extent these cases overlap those in which in-door relief was given.

Of the 143 permanent cases in December, there were :—

Widows.	Widowers.	Single Women.	Single Men.	Married.	
112	6	6	6	13	= 143

and their ages are given :—

65 and upwards.	60—65.	55—60.	Under 55.	
122	8	2	11	= 143

The average age of those over 65 was 75·2.

All those permanently assisted were of good character. Of the 11 under 55, 9 were blind, crippled, deformed, or epileptic, one had a husband in the lunatic asylum, and one was a widow with children.

Of the 66 temporary cases relieved in December, 1889, there were :—

Married.	Widows.	Widower.	Single.	
50	13	1	2	= 66

representing 95 adults and 263 children, or 358 persons in all. Of these 66 cases half were reported on favourably. Sickness[7] (including accidents) accounted for 18, old age for 8, and want of employment for 3 ; while crime on part of the husband, illness of children, mental derangement, widowhood and illness in a large family account for 1 each. As to the remainder, want of work is the ostensible ground for relief in nearly every case, but drink is reported as the principal cause in 21 cases, or one-third of the whole. Laziness proved by shamming paralysis was given as the sole cause in one case. Early marriage sufficiently explained the difficulties of a carpenter aged 19, whose wife aged 18 had just been confined. One woman, living apart from her husband and ill, received an allowance, and the rest were cases of sickness of which, as they were new comers, the relieving officer knew little, except one, the circumstances of which were to some extent an instance of depauperisation. The man, aged 48, was brought up in the workhouse, and five years ago married a woman who was also reared in the institution, and who had two illegitimate children, both now grown up. One of these, a son, is still in and out of the workhouse, and the other, a daughter,

---

[7] Sickness includes frequently the illness of children. The influenza may have had some effect in December, 1889.

has been lost sight of. For some time now this pair of married paupers have been getting along outside, and doing as well as could be expected with a little assistance.

[The foregoing particulars were collected at Stepney by Mr. George E. Arkell, and at St. Pancras by Miss C. E. Collet, to whose patient work, and the kind co-operation of the relieving officers, is due the success of the investigation]

PART III.

Statistics of Pauperism.

While bringing the results of these investigations before this Society, I wish to urge the desirability of such changes being made in the methods of official tabulation as shall cause the returns to show, more accurately than they now do, the whole volume of pauperism and something of its character.

In former times a return was made to the Local Government Board from each union, giving the total number of persons relieved from Lady Day to Michaelmas, and Michaelmas to Lady Day, in connection with the numbers actually receiving relief on 1st January and 1st July. For some years past these returns have not been demanded, and for many years earlier no use was made of them. There is a great possibility of error in such returns, as the strictest care is necessary to avoid a duplication of entries, which will have the effect of making the volume of pauperism appear much larger than it actually is; and we may assume that no use was made of these figures because of the probability of error in them. In basing their returns solely on the number of those in receipt of relief at any one time, it must be admitted that the Local Government Board stands on firm ground. To go further than this without running into error involves many difficulties; but I venture to think that these difficulties can be overcome, and it is the more necessary that they should be faced, because for lack of reliable official data very misleading estimates have been made as to the total amount of pauperism indicated by the published figures.

It has been usual to say that the pauperism of the day must be multiplied three or three-and-a-half times to give the pauperism of the year. Mr. Mulhall, in his "Dictionary of Statistics," comparing English with continental pauperism, says that the actual number on one day may be taken as one-third of the whole. He gives no authority, but may perhaps lean upon some figures published by Mr. Pashley when writing on pauperism and poor law. Mr. Pashley relied upon information not of a very complete or convincing character, privately obtained from certain unions in 1851. Then again Mr. Dudley Baxter, writing on " The " National Income," gives the ratio of $3\frac{1}{2}$, and says he obtained the figures from which this ratio is deduced from Mr. Purdy, of the Statistical Department of the Local Government Board, the return applying to 1857, and being, Mr. Baxter says, the only one of the kind ever made.

On Mr. Baxter's authority, a multiplier of $3\frac{1}{2}$ has been generally accepted, and has been used with confidence by Canon Blackley, Mr. Sydney Webb, and others, when discussing schemes of poor law reform or State pensions.

The full figures given by Mr. Baxter are as follows :—

Paupers, in-door and out-door, relieved during the half year ending Michaelmas, 1856	1,845,782
Paupers, in-door and out-door, relieved only on 1st July	796,102
" ending Lady Day, 1857 " during the half	1,934,286
Paupers, in-door and out-door, relieved only on 1st January	800,000

Mr. Baxter adds together the two half year's totals, and from the result (3,780,068) deducts a number (800,000) to represent those in receipt of relief on Michaelmas Day, 1856, who may be supposed to be carried forward and so repeated in the second half year's total. The total number then appears as 2,980,000, or fully three-and-a-half times 800,000.

This calculation would doubtless be true if the first half year's total included no duplicate entries of the same pauper, and further if no paupers received relief in the second half year who had been relieved in the previous six months, but who were not amongst those actually in receipt of relief on Michaelmas Day. Neither supposition is tenable. No record of Mr. Purdy's inquiry exists at the Local Government Board, and Mr. Purdy himself is dead. We have only the frank admission on the part of Mr. Baxter that Mr. Purdy considered that a greater reduction ought to be made; but Mr. Baxter says, " I am unable to see how this can be," and merely notes the fact. It may be that Mr. Purdy doubted the perfect accuracy of the half year's total, and he was probably aware that many of those relieved and discharged in the first six months, might again receive relief in the second six months.

The figures, if they were in themselves correct, would show that the paupers counted for six months were, thirty-five years ago, rather less than two-and-a-half times the number on one day. It is probable that this was then and would be now an exaggeration. They do not in any way indicate to what extent this ratio should be increased to give the pauperism of a year.

I do not know how it may be with other unions, but at bot Stepney and St. Pancras the officials have never discontinue

making up half-yearly returns in the old way, and by the kindness
of the guardians I have had access to the books in which these
returns are preserved.

At St. Pancras I understand no attempt has been made to
strike off duplicates due to those who pass from institution to
institution, and the figures are an example of the kind of error
which may be expected to creep in with large unions of complicated
administration. The six months' total given officially we find
amounts to nearly as large a number as can be counted correctly
in the whole year.

At Stepney the workhouse system is more simple, and
exceptional care appears to have been taken to avoid duplication;
the figures may therefore be fairly accepted as correct, and,
compared with the true twelve months' totals, show that with the
in-door poor the numbers for the half year must be increased by
17 per cent., for the ordinary out-door by 24 per cent., and for the
medical cases by 75 per cent., or on the average an increase of
31 per cent., whereas Mr. Baxter's assumption involves an increase
of over 61 per cent.

The following table shows the various ratios in detail, comparing the figures at Stepney in 1889, for one day, for six months,
and for twelve months :—

	Official Figures.			Special Inquiry.			Ratios.	
	Mean Day.	Six Months.	Per Cent. of Addition.	On 30th April.	Twelve Months.	Per Cent. of Addition.	Actual Increase from Six to Twelve Months.	Increase of Ratio.
In-door	1,147	1,958	71%	1,163	2,295	97%	17%	37% (on 71)
Out-door............	24	88	267%	25	109	336%	24% } 69%	26% (,, 267) } 55%
Medical orders..	124	648	423%	137	1,133	733%	75%	74% (,, 423)
	1,295	2,694	108%	1,325	3,537	167%	31%	55% (on 108)

The increase of ratio comparing six months with twelve months,
may, for any apparent reason to the contrary, be the same or
approximately the same elsewhere as at Stepney.[8] But with
regard to the actual additions it is not so, for the practical abolition
of all the more permanent forms of out relief exaggerates
abnormally the percentage which the new names bear to those
on the list at any one time. To get over this difficulty I have
gone back twenty years, as will be shown in the following table.
The figures given for each year are themselves the mean of two
half-yearly statements :—

---

[8] For this the whole of out-door relief must be taken together.

In-door.*

	One Day.				Six Months.				Ratio of Addition.			
	M.	W.	Ch.	Total.	M.	W.	Ch.	Total.	M.	W.	Ch.	Total.
									P. ct.	P. ct.	P. ct.	P. ct.
1870...............	345	421	392	1,158	575	621	579	1,775	67	47	48	54
'71...............	319	379	426	1,124	541	597	573	1,711	69	57	35	52
'72...............	327	374	336	1,037	681	612	548	1,841	108	63	63	78
'73.........	312	389	312	1,013	639	626	554	1,819	104	61	78	80
'74...............	317	422	313	1,052	607	659	624	1,890	91	56	99	80
Mean of 5 years ....}	324	397	356	1,077	609	623	575	1,807	88	56	62	68
1884...............	420	440	305	1,165	782	679	566	2,027	86	54	86	74
'85...............	440	444	309	1,193	876	803	628	2,307	99	81	103	93
'86	456	452	268	1,176	843	701	545	2,089	85	55	103	78
'87...............	456	436	278	1,170	788	669	549	2,006	73	53	97	71
'88...............	470	429	253	1,152	832	644	519	1,995	77	50	105	73
Mean of 5 years ....}	448	440	283	1,171	824	699	562	2,085	84	59	99	78
Mean of 10 years ....}	386	419	319	1,124	717	661	568	1,946	86	57	78	73
1889...............	472	426	249	1,147	831	623	528	1,937	76	46	112	69

* The lunatics in asylums, who for official purposes are counted as " out-door poor," are added to the " in-door poor " in this table.

It will be seen that the ratios vary a good deal, from 67 to 108 per cent. with men, from 46 to 81 per cent. with women, and from 35 to 112 per cent. with children. Also that while for adults the ratios show a slightly decreasing tendency, the increase in the case of children is very marked. The greater movement among the children is probably connected with the change in policy as to out relief, some of the children of widows being taken into the schools while the mother manages to maintain herself and the others outside. As this policy is exceptional, I take 70 per cent. as a fair ratio of increase for six months' pauperism among the in-door poor over that as counted on one day.

Out-door.

	One Day.				Six Months.				Ratio of Addition.			
	M.	W.	Ch.	Total.	M.	W.	Ch.	Total.	M.	W.	Ch.	Total.
									P. ct.	P. ct.	P. ct.	P. ct.
1870	263	1,033	1,087	2,383	1,035	1,928	2,993	5,956	294	87	175	150
'71	230	902	843	1,975	658	1,411	1,872	3,941	186	56	122	99
'72	107	491	306	904	293	815	861	1,969	174	66	181	118
'73	66	341	155	562	175	548	524	1,247	211	61	238	127
'74	51	273	104	428	121	361	274	756	137	32	163	77
Mean of 5 years }	143	608	499	1,250	456	1,012	1,305	2,774	206	66	161	122

In this case, owing to the subsequent extinction of out relief, I have to rely on these five earlier years only. They do not give a very satisfactory average, and I think it probable that the rate should be not less than 130.

' The greater amount of movement among the men as compared to the women is very noticeable throughout.

Medical.

	One Day.	Six Months.	Ratio of Addition.
			Per cnt.
1870	606	1,444	138
'71	479	1,419	196
'72	380	952	151
'73	165	491	197
'74	65	318	390
Mean of 5 years	339	925	173

Here too the effects of a changed policy are very noticeable, and in connection with 70 per cent. for in-door, and 130 per cent. for ordinary out-door, we may perhaps put the normal ratio for medical relief at 160 per cent.

Taking the numbers in receipt of medical relief on any day as one-fourth the number in receipt of other forms of out relief, as was the case at Stepney during these years, we obtain a ratio for all forms of out relief together of $\frac{520 + 160}{5} = 136$ per cent.

These ratios (70 per cent. in-door and 136 per cent. out-door) being for six months, we have still to allow for the difference between six months and twelve months, and we have to deduct for deaths occurring during the year among those who have had relief.

If we may adopt the increase of ratio from six months to twelve months shown at Stepney in 1889, the 70 per cent. for in-door (adding 37 per cent.) becomes 96 per cent.; the 130 per cent. for out-door (adding 26 per cent.) becomes 164 per cent.; the 160 per cent. for medical orders (adding 74 per cent.) becomes 278 per cent.; and finally, the combined out-door ratio of 136 per cent. becomes 187 per cent.

As to deaths, we know that 130 occurred at Stepney among the in-door poor in the year ending 30th April, 1889, and if we allow for these, our ratio is reduced from 96 per cent. to 85 per cent.[9] If it may be supposed that an equal proportion of deaths occurs amongst the out-door cases, the ratios would be reduced from

[9] At St. Pancras the ratio of addition for twelve months over one day, allowing for deaths, is 70 per cent.; without deaths, 88 per cent.

164 and 278, to 148 and 256 per cent. respectively, or taken together, 187 per cent. becomes 169 per cent. The ratios finally obtained are thus :—

	Per cent.	
In-door pauperism	85	
Out-door ordinary	148	} combined 169
Medical orders	256	

or say 85 per cent. in-door, and 170 per cent. out-door.

Combining the two we get 134 per cent., or in other words we find that we have to multiply by 2·34 in place of 3·5 as assumed by Mr. Dudley Baxter. It is noteworthy that the revised rate for twelve months is practically the same as that shown by Mr. Purdy's return for six months, and that this rule, as we have already said, nearly held good with regard to the tested figures for St. Pancras, indicating that the exaggeration due to error in the six months' figures is on the whole about enough to make good the further addition needed for the twelve months' enumeration.

It must be noted here that the proportion of "medical relief "only" cases at Stepney seems to be exceptional. I have obtained information on this subject from twenty other parishes selected to represent London and the great provincial towns, and manufacturing, mining, and agricultural districts, and find in few of them any such proportion as one-fourth, the average being only about one-seventeenth of other forms of out relief on the 1st January, 1891.

If we could assume that the reduction in "medical orders "only" meant a general reduction in the minor forms of relief, the result would be to reduce the total ratio for out-door cases from 170 to 154 per cent. But we have no right to assume this. Out relief consists of permanent or continuing assistance and occasional aid. This, and not that adopted officially between "medical only" and other relief, is the division needed for our purpose. The doctor's visit and his medicine are not counted as pauperising more than the sick person. If any form of food be added, though it be intended strictly for the invalid, the addition is held to pauperise the whole family when the patient is the head of the house; in other cases only the sick person and the responsible head of the family are returned as paupers.

The policy pursued in the matter of giving food as well as medicine, affects the proportion of "medical order only" cases to the rest, but there is no reason to suppose that the proportion of slight to serious cases is affected. It may therefore be assumed that any reduction of rates due to a small proportion of "medical "order only" cases would be counterbalanced by an increased

ratio on other forms of out relief. The figures we have from
Ward VI at St. Pancras confirm this, showing as they do for all
slight forms of relief a sevenfold ratio for the twelve months (see
p. 618), which is higher than any ratio made use of in the foregoing calculations. We know, moreover, that the proportion of
"medical order only" cases at St. Pancras to other forms of out-
door relief is as 1 to 12.

In reconsidering these ratios (85 per cent. in-door, 170 per
cent. out-door, and 134 per cent. mean) before making any use
of them, we must remember that much uncertainty attaches to
them, because they are compounded of varying factors which may
and probably do play a very different part in different unions.
Perhaps no two unions would be alike, and accurate details from
twenty unions, if we had them, might not represent the rest
correctly.

The percentage to be added to the six months' total of in-door
poor, which we have assumed to be 85 per cent., is itself, as we
have seen in the case of both Stepney and St. Pancras, compounded
of various ratios from 10 per cent. to 500 per cent., according to
the character of relief given, and further, wide differences apply
as between men and women, and as between those who are over or
under 60 years of age. With the out-door it is the same; there
are those in receipt of regular weekly allowances, whose numbers
are almost constant, and others receiving temporary assistance,
medical or otherwise, who may perhaps be increased tenfold before
the year is out. Moreover, for the out-door cases my own figures
are much less complete than for the in-door.

It is with great unwillingness that I lay such doubtful figures
before this Society, and my only excuse is that the matter is
important, and has become pressing, and no better can be obtained.
This being so, I trust I may not be thought presumptuous if I make
a suggestion as to the manner in which the Local Government
Board's periodical returns might be made to give the required
information. My proposal in brief is, that the statistics should
take the form of a running account from month to month, showing
the number in receipt of each kind of relief on the first of each
month, with the particulars of those who applied for and obtained
relief during the month, these being divided into (a) those who
had, and (b) those who had not been in receipt of any form of
relief during the twelve months preceding their present application. This form will show the magnitude, and to some extent the
character of the stream of pauperism, but would need to be supplemented by a half-yearly return, which should show in a similar
manner the movement for the half year, and the total number of
paupers who had at any time within twelve months sought and

obtained relief. In order to make myself quite clear, I subjoin examples of returns in the form I would suggest.

TABLE I.—*Monthly Return of Pauperism.*

Institution or Class.	Number in Receipt of Relief on 1st January.			Number of Persons who apply for and are granted Relief between 1st January and 1st February.						Number in Receipt of Relief on 1st February.		
				Those who have received Relief within Twelve Months of Present Application.			Those who have not received Relief within Twelve Months of Present Application.					
	M.	W.	Ch.	M.	W.	Ch.	M.	W.	Ch.	M.	W.	Ch.
In-door— Able bodied .... Not able bodied Insane												
Out-door— Able bodied ... Not able bodied Insane					(a)			(b)				
Medical only— Able bodied .... Not able bodied												

Note.—It is intended that those who are relieved twice or oftener in the month, should on the first occasion be counted in the *b* column, and on subsequent occasions in the *a* column. Transfers from one institution to another would be counted in the *a* column.

Memorandum as to TABLE II.

To find the total pauperism for any twelve months :—

On 30th June (1892) take numbers from column w + a + b + d + e + h.

„ 31st December (1892)   „   x + e + f + h + i + l.

From the number thus indicated must be deducted the deaths which have occurred amongst them, to give the actual total required.

TABLE II.—Return for Half Year ending 31st December, 1891.

Return for Half Year ending 31st December, 1891.

Institution or Class of Pauper.	Number in Receipt of Relief on 1st July, 1891.			Number of Applications Granted between 1st July, 1891, and 1st January, 1892.												Number in Receipt of Relief on 1st January, 1892.			Total Number of those who have been Relieved during Six Months ending 31st December, 1891.		
				Previously Relieved during									Having previously Received no Relief, or none since 1st July, 1890.								
				Second Half of 1890.			First Half of 1891.			Second Half of 1891.											
	M.	W.	Ch.	M.	W.	Ch.	M.	W.	Ch.	M.	W.	Ch.	M.	W.	Ch.	M.	W.	Ch.	M.	W.	Ch.
In-door— Able bodied Not able bodied Insane		(w)	(x)		(a)			(b)			(c)			(d)			(x)				
Out-door— Able bodied Not able bodied Insane																					
Medical only— Able bodied Not able bodied																					

Return for Half Year ending 30th June, 1892.

Institution or Class of Pauper.	Number in Receipt of Relief on 1st January, 1892.			Number of Applications Granted between 1st January, 1892, and 1st July, 1892.												Number in Receipt of Relief on 1st July, 1892.			Total Number of those who have been Relieved during Six Months ending 30th June, 1892.		
				Previously Relieved during									Having previously Received no Relief, or none since 1st January, 1891.								
				First Half of 1891.			Second Half of 1891.			First Half of 1892.											
	M.	W.	Ch.	M.	W.	Ch.	M.	W.	Ch.	M.	W.	Ch.	M.	W.	Ch.	M.	W.	Ch.	M.	W.	Ch.
(As above)		(w)	(x)		(e)			(f)			(g)			(h)			(y)				

Return for Half Year ending 31st December, 1892.

Institution or Class of Pauper.	Number in Receipt of Relief on 1st July, 1892.			Number of Applications Granted between 1st July, 1892, and 1st January, 1893.												Number in Receipt of Relief on 1st January, 1893.			Total Number of those who have been Relieved during Six Months ending 31st December, 1892.		
				Previously Relieved during									Having previously Receivd no Relief, or none since 1st July, 1891.								
				Second Half of 1891.			First Half of 1892.			Second Half of 1892.											
	M.	W.	Ch.	M.	W.	Ch.	M.	W.	Ch.	M.	W.	Ch.	M.	W.	Ch.	M.	W.	Ch.	M.	W.	Ch.
(As above)		(y)	(z)		(i)			(j)			(k)			(l)			(z)				

The returns at present are made every week, and if this is necessary it could be done exactly in the same way. I, however, do not myself see any advantage to be gained by returns more often than once a month.

The guardians ought to, and probably in nearly all cases do, know whether an applicant has had relief before within twelve months, and any systematic record of persons relieved would serve as the basis for such a return as the foregoing. This record, whether it took the shape of a journal with successive entries, or what might be better, of numbered "case papers," could be so indexed as to avoid any duplicate enumeration. The general adoption of such a system would in many ways lead to valuable results. We should learn the true annual amount of pauperism, and, in addition, all that "periodicity" showed of its character. A better and more uniform system might lead to better and more uniform administration; and, finally, the information accumulated in these records would form a reliable basis for that classification of paupers which must, I think, be the basis of any reform of the law.

More uniform and better administration of the present law must be our first object. It has been proved beyond possibility of dispute that that form of poverty which we call pauperism can be very largely decreased without to the same extent (or it would even seem to any extent) increasing the volume of poverty which is not pauperism. It cannot be done all at once, but it is certain that the gradual withdrawal of public charity in the form of out relief stimulates, or may be made to stimulate, every form of private effort. Greater exertions are made by those in distress to stand up against "a sea of trouble;" those who are bound by family or other ties will do more to help; and, finally, private charity flows more freely. Each of these is to be preferred to any form of public charity.

Part IV.

Old Age Pensions.

It is, however, a question whether by some system of deferred annuity, old age might not be eliminated entirely as a cause of pauperism, and as this question has been raised, and is now under public discussion, I will, without attempting a final judgment, state the case for and against as it appears to me.

First, as to the amount of old age pauperism. For this we mainly rely on Mr. Burt's return, which gives the number of aged people in receipt of relief on 1st August, 1890, in-door and out-door, male and female, able bodied and not able bodied, and by ages, as given below:—

Ages.	In-door.			Out-door.			Combined Total.		
	M.	F.	Total.	M.	F.	Total.	M.	F.	Total.
80—	4,949	4,803	9,752	12,456	22,652	35,108	17,405	27,455	44,860
75—80............	7,086	5,298	12,384	16,474	32,021	48,495	23,560	37,319	60,879
70—75............	9,953	6,856	16,809	17,633	43,266	60,899	27,586	50,122	77,708
65—70............	9,468	6,339	15,807	10,567	35,866	46,433	20,035	42,205	62,240
Total over 65	31,456	23,296	54,752	57,130	133,805	190,935	88,586	157,101	245,687
60—65............	8,018	5,354	13,372	5,959	21,849	27,808	13,977	27,203	41,180
Total over 60	39,474	28,650	68,124	63,089	155,654	218,743	102,563	184,304	286,867

It is to be noted that the women are very much more numerous than the men, being on the whole as 176 to 100 over 65, and 195 to 100 from 60 to 65. But it is among the out-door only that the excess occurs, as in-door the men predominate. The disproportion out-door is as 234 to 100 men over 65, and as 367 to 100 men from 60 to 65. The greater proportion of women below 65 seems to indicate that it is not till considerably later in life than with women that old age renders it necessary for men to obtain parish relief.

These are the numbers as returned on one day, and include those receiving "medical aid only." Some possible doubt exists as to the correctness of this return because of the tendency to exaggerate age, especially as improved conditions of pauper life are meted out to those over 60. On this point we can only say that the return has undoubtedly been made in good faith, and that those who may claim more than their true age must at least be apparently "aged" or their claim would be questioned. It also appears that it is not at 60 but later, at and after 65, that the numbers look so large. The possibility of some error should, however, be borne in mind. On the other hand, there is some addition to be made to these numbers if we are to count all as paupers who have had any form of relief during the twelve months. What this addition should be can only be the subject of a very rough estimate. If the addition to paupers of *all ages* be fairly put at 85 per cent. on the average in-door, and 170 per cent. on the average out-door (see *ante*), the ratios for the *old* will be something less, and in what follows, failing more accurate figures, I put the addition at 60 per cent. in-door and 120 per cent. out-door for the old, leaving the ratios for those under 60 and the insane (who are not included in Mr. Burt's return) at 102 per cent. in-door and 201 per cent. out-door respectively. On this assumption we can make the following table :—

Total Pauperism, distinguishing the Ages.

	In-door.				Out-door.			
	Under 60 and all the Insane.	60—65.	65—	Total.	Under 60 and all the Insane.	60—65.	65—	Total.
Total of paupers relieved on 1st July, 1890, divided by ages according to Mr. Burt's return for 1st August	99,983	13,372	54,752	168,107	346,788	27,808	190,935	565,531
Numbers to add to give total pauperism on twelve months' basis	*(102%)	(60%)	(60%)	(85%)	†(201%)	(120%)	(120%)	(170%)
	102,017	8,023	32,851	142,891	698,911	33,370	229,122	961,403
	202,000	21,395	87,603	310,998	1,045,699	61,178	420,057	1,526,934

* Insane.	Children.	Remainder.	† Insane.	Remainder.
9%	42%	226%	9%	224%
		102%		201%

On the same assumption, the following table gives the proportion of paupers to population under and over 60 and 65 years of age (estimated, pending full returns for 1891):—

Paupers under 60	1,247,699	Population under 60	26,866,294	Ratio	4·6%
,, 60—65	82,573	,, 60—65...	812,028	,,	10·2%
,, over 65....	507,660	,, over 65	1,322,696	,,	38·4%
Total	1,837,932		29,001,018		6·3%

To make this table tell a complete story, we should need to state the percentage of pauperism at every age, but failing this information it may be said roughly that the increase in ratio from 4·6 to 38·4 per cent. is the measure of the effect of old age *directly* or *indirectly* on pauperism. It is not possible to distinguish between the direct and the indirect influence of old age, all the causes of pauperism being aggravated by years; but premising this, it may be said that more than half of the pauperism from 60 to 65, and nearly eight-ninths of that from 65 upwards, must be accounted "old age pauperism," and of the remaining one-ninth not less than half will have fallen into pauperism earlier in life through such causes of misfortune as sickness or incapacity.

As the rate rises with age, it follows that the proportion of pauper deaths will be higher still. Of all who die over 65 it would seem that not less than 40 per cent., and probably more, have had public relief in one shape or other during the last years of their life, and out of these not more than one-ninth will have been chargeable before they were 60.

It is remarkable that Canon Blackley, by an entirely different method, arrives at exactly the same conclusion, the figures given by actual investigation in twenty-six parishes being 42·7 per cent.

Such a state of things is both startling and deplorable, and leaves a considerable margin for possible over statement in the figures I have used.[10]

It is true that "pauperism" means many things, and that of those counted as receiving out-door, and especially medical relief, there are many who are practically self supporting or supported by their friends to the very last. It is true also that it is such as these (obtaining a little assistance occasionally) who swell the list of names and make so great an addition necessary to the paupers of any.one day to indicate the total numbers relieved. But no considerations of this kind affect the broad fact that so large a proportion of our old people do, as things now are, seek State aid.

All pauperism no doubt might be said to argue some fault on the part of the pauper. He might have gone less often to the public house; have been more industrious or less lazy; with sufficient care he might have saved; he might have made friends and kept them; if his children had been well brought up they would have taken care of his old age, and so forth. If we all had equal opportunities in every respect this view might be completely true, but things being as they are, it is not tenable. The popular sentiment, which accounts as misfortune the lapse into pauperism of any who up to old age have kept clear of relief, is perhaps more just. Of these, as we have just seen, eight-ninths of aged pauperism consists. Similarly and with even more justice it is felt that those who suffer under long continued ill health, and so ultimately become paupers, are the victims of fate. Such of these invalids as survive must therefore be counted in old age with those who then

---

[10] For instance, if the ratio of addition for the in-door old be taken at 50 per cent., and for the out-door at 100 per cent., which would be a low estimate, we should obtain the following figures :—

In-door.			Out-door.		
	Per cnt.			Per cnt.	
Paupers over 60	50	} P. ct.	Paupers over 60	100	} P. ct.
Insane	9	} 85	Insane	9	} 170
Children	42		Remainder	240	
Remainder	245				

				Ratio.	
Paupers under 60 to population under 60........				4·8 per cent.	} 6·3 per cent.
„ 60—65	„	60—65	....	9·3 „	
„ over 65	„	over 65	....	35·1 „	

for the first time ask relief, claiming sympathy and gentle treatment as paupers by misfortune.

This common and popular view is reflected in our present law, and in its administration. Out relief is granted to a certain extent to respectable but destitute aged people, and exceptional indulgence within the workhouse is dealt out to the infirm; but neither plan is altogether satisfactory. A workhouse is at best a dreary residence. Decent old people who find refuge there cannot but be associated with very questionable companions. Whilst even if actual tyranny is avoided, it is difficult to prevent harsh callous treatment. By contrast out relief has many advantages. It offers for those who, without being able to earn a living, are still able to clean and cook for themselves, a far more desired and desirable existence. They can still remain members of the society to which they are accustomed, can still confer as well as receive neighbourly favours, mind a baby, sit up with the sick, chop firewood, or weed the garden. They are not cut off from the sympathies of daily existence, and their presence is often a valuable ingredient in the surrounding life. When the end comes, the presence of well known faces, the sound of well known voices, soothe and succour the last hours. The fact of the pauperism does not often intrude; it is never alluded to.

These advantages, combined with its apparent cheapness as compared to cost of workhouse maintenance, have given the system a strong hold on public opinion. With all classes the giving of out relief to the old is popular. But it has not the one saving virtue of in-door relief. If desirable, it is not deterrent, and it is only on the side of deterrence that our poor law encourages economic virtue. Here we have the weak place, and hence the demand for some pension system which, for most of the aged poor, shall take the place of either in-door or out-door relief, and which, if it does not positively encourage thrift, shall at least not discourage it, by making the exhaustion of all savings a first qualification for aid, as is the case under the present law.

It is held too that those who have worked for a lifetime have a claim to something more than social charity, and however this argument may be regarded as to men, it has a certain force with respect to women, who have often spent lives of the most active and invaluable citizenship without ever having the smallest opportunity for saving. Their husbands give them from their wages the sum they think necessary for current expenses of the household, and expect a very full *quid pro quo* in solid comfort. Men sometimes die leaving an elderly widow entirely destitute, or with little more than enough coming from some friendly society to defray her husband's funeral expenses, and there may or may not be children able or willing to give their mother a home.

There are a variety of pension schemes at present before the public, representing various economic schools, and various political tendencies, but all are based upon the considerations above mentioned. Few of them have been worked out in such detail as would make exact criticism possible. It seems however unlikely that any ingenuity can evade the difficulties which, being based on broad principles, affect them all. Particulars of two proposals are given in the Appendix.

Some would amend or extend the poor law by providing good character pensions on a large scale. The evident objection to this is that such pensioners would be still paupers, whatever they might be called, and that the granting of aid in this form would be no less dangerous in its results than any other description of out relief,

Others would ask the Government to assist voluntary effort by putting a premium on thrift. The objection to this proposal is, that it would be insufficient. Cheapening thrift will not necessarily make people thrifty, and all who were not so would still come upon the rates. Moreover, against this suggestion, as well as the preceding one, may be urged the great difficulty of carrying it into effect without seriously interfering with existing thrift agencies.

Another group would combine compulsion with State aid, and, either on the German system, or by demanding from every young person a payment (on Canon Blackley's original plan), obtain enough to provide, with the help of contributions from employers or from the State, a small pension in old age. Both payment and pension apply, as I understand it, only to those of the poorer class, whose future would be thus to a certain extent secured, and who to this State provision would add their private savings. This proposal is free from the objections which apply to the first two. No direct pauperisation is involved, and it is not necessary to abandon other forms of saving in order to qualify, whilst there is no reason to suppose that the business of thrift agencies would be adversely affected. But there are, I think, fatal objections in the complicated nature of these schemes, and in the practical impossibility of exercising any compulsion of this character on our people.

Finally, there are those who boldly propose universal pensions for the old, and wildly extravagant as it may seem, there is much to be said for this suggestion. It is at least complete, and is not open to the objections which affect the proposals already considered, though it may be itself objected to on other grounds.

In England and Wales there are at present about 733,000 women and 590,000 men over 65 years of age, or in all about 1,323,000 (estimated, pending full returns for 1891). At 13*l.* per annum each, a universal pension list would reach 17,000,000*l.* In taking 65 as the age, and 13*l.* (or 5*s.* per week) as the amount, I accept the bases on which this question is now usually discussed.[11]

Putting the total national income (England and Wales) at one thousand millions per annum, and assuming that taxation falls, or tends to fall, or can be arranged to fall, in true proportion to income, it seems that to maintain such a pension scheme every one would have to pay 1·7 per cent. of their income. What would they get in return? Manifestly they would benefit unequally. The rich as a class would pay much more in proportion to what they would receive than would the poor, but lying between the two there would be a middle class which would pay and receive about equally. Roughly speaking, this middle line of equality would consist of those who have a family income of about 150*l.* a year, shared by four or five persons, young and old. The quite poor, whose incomes for the same number of people is only one-fourth of this sum, would as a class pay in taxes only one-fourth the value of the annuities which would fall to their share, and the extra payments of the better to do and rich would balance the account.[12]

I have spoken of the people by classes, because for individuals other inequalities are involved. Considering a whole generation, those who die before 65 pay but receive nothing. Considering the facts of a single year, the young in every class pay for the old.

No measure involving so heavy a taxation could pass unless it were in itself exceedingly popular, and on this account these questions of incidence are very important, beyond the merits (yet to be considered) which the proposal may have as a matter of public policy.

The people for this purpose may be taken as belonging to five classes: (1) the quite poor—family income, 50*l.* or less; (2) fair working class position, income 60*l.* to 100*l.* and over; (3) lower middle class, 150*l.* to 200*l.*; (4) middle class, 300*l.* to 1,000*l.*; (5) more or less wealthy class, with income of 1,000*l.* and upwards.

The two classes whose incomes are below 100*l.* pay no income tax, and practically no succession duty, nor would they pay much, though they would pay something, if a tax were placed on all

[11] Scotland on the same calculation would figure for about 2,500,000*l.*, and Ireland with her excessive proportion of old people for over 4,000,000*l.* more.

[12] It may be noted that the working classes would pay through taxation (assuming taxation to fall in proportion to income) about the same contribution towards the cost of these deferred annuities as they do under the German plan, where employer, workman, and State contribute each about a third.

property. Taxation reaches them indirectly, firstly by way of customs and excise duties, which can be recognised in the prices of the things they buy, and secondly, by a gradual levelling process acting through their earnings, which makes it, I think, certain that the burthen of every tax, however levied, is gradually spread, and ultimately borne by them in common with the whole industrial community. In neither case is the pressure very obvious, whilst on the other hand it is probable they would be very much alive to the advantages accruing from the pension scheme in assuring provision at once for the aged, who are a pressing charge to them to-day, as well as in assisting to provide for their own old age. With the poorest class, most of whose old people are in the workhouse or are receiving some parochial assistance outside, the proposal would certainly be popular. These classes count up to more than half the population.

Of the lower middle class, who in numbers stand next, I am not so sure. They are keenly alive to questions of money, would know precisely what they paid, and deliberately weigh this against what they got for it. It is doubtful if they would readily sacrifice themselves for another class, nor would the annuities paid to their own old people appeal very much to them, as in this class the young look to the old rather than the old to the young for assistance. But there is the demonstrable fact that, in exchange for the increase of taxation involved, they would obtain a cheap and perfectly secure deferred annuity, which would tend to satisfy many of them. The class just above this would some of them share the simple view of "what do I get," but others would rather consider the question from the point of view of public policy.

Finally, the upper-middle and wealthy classes would certainly dread a proposal involving the principle of taxation of the rich for the benefit of the poor, and would therefore need to be very fully satisfied that the money would be well spent, and that the scheme has elements of finality, and is not to be regarded as an attack on private property.

Such being the probable attitude of each class, we may pass to more general considerations.

It must be remembered, in considering the cost of such a scheme, that the large sum involved would not be spent in the sense that it would be if used to employ labour, as for instance in armaments. Looked at nationally, it would be merely transferred from one pocket to another. It may also be said that the young in any case support the old; providing for their own old age, or for that of those who have failed to do so themselves. The scheme would be only a new adjustment of this common rule.

As a matter of public burthen the present cost of maintaining aged paupers would be saved. For those *in* the house the guardians would draw the pension (gradually it may be hoped that all except the very helpless or very reckless would manage to find homes outside); and out relief for the aged would naturally come to an end. We spend 8,500,000*l.* on poor relief; the aged poor are a third of the number, and must represent more than one third of the cost. Ultimately then 3 millions might be saved, but the establishments could not be at once cut down. This is the only public saving to be anticipated, and unless specially adjusted in some way would go to the ratepayers, and hence chiefly to the middle and lower middle classes. Nothing can be counted on from the pensions already paid to soldiers, policemen, postmen, and public servants great or small. It is evident that these people all pay their proportion of taxes, and would thus pay for their 5*s.* a week as much, and in the same way as others, by enhanced cost of living due to increased taxation. So that if the special pension of their calling was reduced (as it might be) there would be room for a proportionate rise in their daily pay. We must also disregard the idea that any old man would be above drawing his pension, as it is of the essence of the proposal that the pensions should be for all, and absolutely free from any poverty qualification whatever.

In addition to the poor who are relieved by the State, there are many other old people who are helped by private charity. Some of this charity might be withdrawn, and in so far those who now give it would save, and some would be transferred to other charitable claims. There would at any rate be a relieving of funds in many directions which might be taken advantage of in one way or the other.

We have seen that, on the plan proposed, year by year the young and middle aged lose to the advantage of the old, and the rich to the advantage of the poor, and it is the same with regard to men and women. Throughout it is those who are weakest who profit. As between young and old, time would balance the account if all had equal chances of prolonged life; as it is, there is here a turn in favour of the well to do, whose chances of life are on the whole better.

As between the sexes equality of the kind is hardly expected. It is usually only a question of what man is responsible for the provision for each elderly woman.

As between rich and poor life is a lottery, and comparatively few can say that they are beyond all chances of destitution in old age. It is not only those who were born poor who are found in the workhouse to-day. If the chances of poverty were equal, none could say that they lost while another gained by paying unfairly

for a general scheme of pensions. They are not equal. "One of
" the few lessons" (says Mr. Leslie Stephen) "which I have
" learnt from life, and not found already in copy books, is the
" enormous difficulty which a man of the upper classes finds in
" completely ruining himself even by vice, extravagance, and folly;
" whereas there are plenty of honest people who in spite of
" economy and prudence can scarcely keep outside of the
" workhouse."

So far as it goes (and it is not very far) this proposal would
tend to equalise our lots. It is not, however, this levelling
character which is the most alarming feature of any attempt to
amend the working of our socialistic poor law. Other considerations are more important. Any State action would be fatal if it
in any way disturbed the bases of work and wages, discouraged
thrift, or undermined in the slightest degree self respect or the
forces of individuality, upon which morality as well as industry
depends. If the scheme fails in these points it stands condemned,
but if it can be fairly held that universal pensions would have no
evil effect in these directions, and if it can be shown also that
besides reducing the existing mass of pauperism and lightening
much poverty outside, the whole problem of pauperism and poverty
would be simplified—then it would be worth while to consider
whether the financial difficulties could be faced.

Work, wages, thrift, self respect, and energy are the points in
question, and may be taken in the order given. First as to work:
the total amount done would be but little affected by the receipt of
a pension of 5s. a-week after 65. What old men do now they would
hardly cease to do, except in so far as a small fixed income would
encourage them earlier to turn to such duties as those of watchmen and caretakers. Old women do little beyond helping with
their grandchildren, or keeping house for those who are actively at
work. They would do this rather more than less as home life came
to be substituted for that in the workhouse. Then as to wages:
those required by caretakers and watchmen might be less (here
indirectly the rich would gain something), but otherwise there
seems little reason to fear any lowering effect.

Next as to thrift. Will the assurance of 5s. a week after 65 on
the whole make those who can lay by at all, less anxious to do
so? This sum may be enough to keep an old man or woman out
of the workhouse. Except when illness rendered them helpless,
or love of drink made them reckless, I believe it would have this
effect. But, so much secured, every shilling would tell on comfort.
" He who has wants more," is but a worldly version of " To him
" that hath shall be given," and I am not sure whether the greater
certainty of the enjoyment of saving (now by no means certain)

would not make thrift more attractive. Moreover the objects of saving are not exhausted when old age after 65 is provided for. The years of elderly existence and doubtful earnings before the age of 65 has been reached have still to be provided for. Here is a benefit within easy range of the imagination. To live to 60 is likely enough, the certainty of at any rate a pittance would lie beyond, and a bridge would have to be made, the building of which would be a very definite object. Insurance companies, friendly societies, and the government tables would doubtless cater for the demand which might be expected to arise in this direction. Then again there is death to provide for; and the certainty of being able to avoid the workhouse in old age would, one may reasonably suppose, increase the desire already so strong to avoid a pauper funeral. I am therefore inclined to think that such a provision as we are considering, underlying the whole social structure, would have no adverse effect on the business of thrift agencies, but might rather be expected, by raising the whole standard of life, to increase the demand for their services.

Self respect is a question as to which it is difficult to predicate with any certainty, a question of sentiment, beyond proof, and almost beyond argument. I do not see why this honourable feeling should be hurt by the receipt of a pension which all old people alike would draw.[13]

Finally, if the foregoing be true, if work, wages, and thrift and self respect, are not adversely affected, will it not follow that industrial energy and all the forces of individuality will be stimulated rather than checked by security afforded to old age?

This proposal of State pensions is, however, surrounded by dangers on every side, and it is these dangers which put indefeasible limits on what can be done, even stronger than would be found in the difficulties of finance, if the already enormous sum of 17 millions yearly were to be doubled or more.

To take a lower age than 65, or a larger amount than 5s. a week, would be dangerous, and increasingly dangerous for every year deducted or every shilling added. At 65 the working days of men are practically over; at 60 they are not. An allowance of 5s. a week is about balanced by the cost of maintenance by the guardians in the house, to which the law now gives every one a right. It represents the minimum cost of life, and as the pension would revert to the State (through the guardians) if at any time the

[13] I assume that the poor law officials would have nothing to do with the payment of the pensions, they would merely receive the amounts due to them for such old people as still came under their charge. Identification and registration might rest with the registrar-general's department, and payment be made through the banking department of the post office or other savings banks. Familiarity with the doors of a bank would perhaps help the cause of thrift.

pensioner failed to maintain himself outside, it could not be fore-stalled; there would be no security on which money could be borrowed. But if the pension exceeded 5s. a week, any one might, and many would, even if the transaction were made illegal, sell the surplus cost of maintenance for cash down to whomsoever would agree, in exchange for the pension, to board and lodge the pensioner under less galling restrictions than life in the workhouse involves. Further, an annuity from the State if raised from 5s. to (say) 10s. a week, might fairly be accounted an attack on the business of thrift agencies.

Sixty-five years of age and 5s. a week are as far as it would be safe to go, and may even involve some, though I think not serious, risks. On the other hand, to begin later, or to give less, would be of little use for the object in view. Within such close limits is this project confined.

Such is the case for a general pension scheme put as fairly as I am able to do. On the other hand, besides the great (perhaps insuperable) financial difficulties involved, it must be said that the highest authorities on poor law administration shrink from one and all of these pension schemes.

They point to the results in certain unions where out-door pauperism has been gradually abolished concurrently with no increase of any other form of pauperism, and with a very marked effect in the reduction of old age pauperism, and claim that the figures on which the need for a pension system rests are swollen by the careless giving of relief. They have confidence in the sufficiency of their methods. "We are," they say, "on the right "road, why be tempted to leave it, following false lights? All "now admit the principles of the great reform of 1834, in "adherence to which lies the promise of a sound and steady "improvement. We have survived the first outburst of unpopu-"larity and abuse. The people are now used to our methods. "There is no outcry on their part for change. The outcry is from "above, and of a theoretic, unpractical character."

To such authority and such experience all deference is due, but it would seem that it is only by the unremitting efforts of excep-tional men, such as Mr. Bland Garland, who for twenty years has influenced the administration of Bradfield Union, or Mr. John Jones, who for more than twenty years acted as relieving officer at Stepney, that these results can be attained. To attempt the enforcing of such a policy by law would be considered very harsh, and might not succeed, so that, besides being at best very slow in action, it is for the whole country in effect impracticable.

On the other hand it may be urged that the cause they have at heart, the constant improvement of the administration of the poor

law, the more thorough application of the principles of 1834, would
be aided, and their task lightened, by the practical withdrawal of
all the aged except those who are so ill as to be in need of hospital
care, or those who have no rag of respectability left. There would
still be difficulties enough; the question of widows would remain,
and in itself demand the utmost exercise of discrimination, judgment and firmness. The young, the sick, the feeble, and the
incapable, to say nothing of the idle, the vicious, and the drunken,
all demand wise, and to some extent distinctive treatment, but the
principles involved would be more clear when disentangled from
old age, and their application might be made more uniform and
more strict.

APPENDIX.

NATIONAL OLD AGE PENSIONS.

Although many proposals are " in the air " for the establishment
of a system of old age pensions, the two schemes appended seem
to be the only ones which have yet been published in a definite
detailed form :—

NATIONAL PROVIDENCE LEAGUE.

In a "Statement of Views" issued by this League, dated
August last, they say :—

"New proposals are now made for the establishment of a
" voluntary State aided old age pension scheme.

"These proposals the National Providence League cordially
" welcomes as tending in the direction of its own objects, namely,
" the extinction of old age pauperism, and will lend its best efforts
" to the advocacy of any scheme resolved upon by the newly
" formed 'Voluntary Parliamentary Committee on Old Age
" ' Pensions,' which does not contravene the following principles:—

"I.—*That contractors for an old age pension State benefit be*
" *required to make a contribution from their own resources.*

"II.—*That the contract made by contributors for their own share*
" *of the pension assured, be only recognised as entitled to State*
" *augmentation if effected through some financially sound organisa-*
" *tion ; whether a friendly society, an annuity office, a pensions' trust*
" *fund established by parliament, or the post office.*

"Subject to these main principles, the National Providence
" League ventures to recommend :—

" 1. That the pension secured by a contributor from his or her
     " own resources shall not be less than 6*l*. 10*s*. a year,
     " payable at 65 years of age.

" 2. That the amount of pension guaranteed by the State to
     " meet such sum should be another annual sum of
     " 6*l*. 10*s*.; so that each contributor be entitled at 65
     " years of age to a pension of 13*l*.[14] a year.

" 3. That the post office organisation be made use of for the
     " collection of funds if desired, and in all cases for the
     " payment of State pensions when due.

" 4. That every person on completion of his or her own pay-
     " ments shall receive a parchment certificate, stating
     " the name, age, and address of the insurer, the date of
     " the completion of the insurance, and also the name
     " and address of the friendly society, annuity office,
     " trust fund, or post office savings bank in which the
     " insurance was effected, and such certificate, after
     " being countersigned by a magistrate on proof of
     " identity, shall be presented by the person insured
     " when the State pension is demanded at any post office.

" 5. That the production, at any time, of such a certificate shall
     " entitle an applicant to receive any poor law relief
     " which may be necessary during any period of life, in
     " the form of out-door relief, if so desired.

" 6. That on the death of a certificate holder before drawing
     " pension, a sum, not exceeding 5*l*., be paid by the State
     " to his or her nominee.

" 7. That no pensioner shall have the right to assign or alienate
     " any portion of his or her pension of 13*l*. a year.

" 8. That as the great object of the National Providence
     " League is to prevent *pauperism*, it is most desirable
     " that no part of the State pension subventions should
     " be chargeable on the *poor rates;* but the League
     " recommend that the State contribution be divided
     " between *imperial* and *local* taxation."

Poor Law Reform Association.

The Committee of this Association has issued the following
suggestions upon a practical pension scheme :—

" I.—That considering the very large number of persons who,
" reaching old age, are driven to seek the assistance of the poor
" law, some system of pension is extremely desirable, as such
" pensions would enable them to dispense with poor law relief.

[14] 13*l*. a year is equivalent to 5*s*. a week.

" II.—That, in view of the fact that every person has neces-
" sarily contributed, directly or indirectly, to the public funds
" during his life, and has, under the present law, if destitute, a
" right to poor law relief, a *minimum* pension be receivable by
" everyone attaining the age of 65.[15]

" III.—That in order to disconnect all idea of pauperism from
" the State pension, to which every aged person should have a
" right, such pension should be payable through the post office or
" some agency other than that of the poor law system.

" IV.—That any person who shall not be in a position to main-
" tain himself by the aid of the State pension, shall be referred
" to the existing poor law authorities, and if poor law relief be
" afforded to him, the guardians shall have power to impound the
" State pension.

" V.—That with a view of affording every possible facility to
" persons to supplement by their own efforts of thrift the minimum
" State pension, the existing system of post office insurance should
" be so modified as to permit of a pension not exceeding 10*l.* a
" year for old age being secured by payment either of a lump sum
" or in weekly or other instalments, such modifications being :—

" 1. A subsidy from public funds, not exceeding 20 per cent. of
   " the pension above named.[16]

" 2. Special arrangements by the post office to facilitate the
   " collection of the insurance premiums from or through
   " employers of labour, for persons in their employment,
   " and exceptional facilities in those cases in which (as is
   " often the practice) the employers themselves make the
   " whole or part of the contributions, as in the German
   " system."

[15] Sixty-five being the age at which friendly society sick pay ceases.

[16] Thus, of a pension of 10*l.*, the pensioner's contribution would provide 8*l.*
and the State would provide 2*l.*

The Discussion on Mr. Booth's Paper will be printed in the
Journal for March, 1892 (vol. lv, part 1).

[5]

SUMMARY AND CONCLUSION

In this chapter it is proposed to briefly summarise the facts set forth in the preceding pages, and to consider what conclusions regarding the problem of poverty may be drawn from them.

Method and Scope of Inquiry.—As stated in the second chapter, the information regarding the numbers, occupation, and housing of the working classes was gained by direct inquiry, which practically covered every working-class family in York. In some cases direct information was also obtained regarding earnings, but in the majority of cases these were estimated, the information at the disposal of the writer enabling him to do this with considerable accuracy.

The Poverty Line.—Having thus made an estimate, based upon carefully ascertained facts, of the earnings of practically every working-class family in York, the next step was to show the proportion of the total population living in poverty. Families regarded as living in poverty were grouped under two heads :—

(*a*) Families whose total earnings were insufficient to obtain the minimum necessaries for the maintenance of merely physical efficiency. Poverty falling under this head was described as " primary " poverty.

(*b*) Families whose total earnings would have been sufficient for the maintenance of merely physical efficiency were it not that some portion of it was absorbed by other expenditure, either useful or wasteful. Poverty falling under this head was described as " secondary " poverty.

To ascertain the total number living in " primary " poverty it was necessary to ascertain the minimum cost upon which families of various sizes could be maintained in a state of physical efficiency. This question was discussed under three heads, viz. the necessary expenditure for (1) food; (2) rent; and (3) all else.

In Chapter IV. it was shown that for a family of father, mother, and three children, the minimum weekly expenditure upon which physical efficiency can be maintained in York is 21s. 8d., made up as follows :

	s.	d.
Food .	12	9
Rent (say) .	4	0
Clothing, light, fuel, etc.	4	11
	21	8

The necessary expenditure for families larger or smaller than the above will be correspondingly greater or less. This estimate was based upon the assumptions that the diet is selected with a careful regard to the nutritive values of various food stuffs, and that these are all purchased at the lowest current prices. It only allows for a diet less generous as regards variety than that supplied to able-bodied paupers in workhouses. It further assumes that no clothing is purchased which is not absolutely necessary for health, and assumes too that it is of the plainest and most economical description.

No expenditure of any kind is allowed for beyond that which is absolutely necessary for the maintenance of *merely physical efficiency.*

The number of persons whose earnings are so low that they cannot meet the expenditure necessary for the above standard of living, stringent to severity though it is, and bare of all creature comforts, was shown to be no less than 7230, or almost exactly 10 per cent of the total population of the city. These persons, then, represent those who are in "primary" poverty.

The number of those in "secondary" poverty was arrived at by ascertaining the *total* number living in poverty, and subtracting those living in "primary" poverty. The investigators, in the course of their house-to-house visitation, noted those families who were obviously living in a state of poverty, *i.e.* in obvious want and squalor. Sometimes they obtained definite information that the bulk of the earnings was spent in drink or otherwise squandered, some-

times the external evidence of poverty in the home
was so clear as to make verbal evidence superfluous.

In this way 20,302 persons, or 27·84 per cent of
the total population, were returned as living in poverty.
Subtracting those whose poverty is "primary," we
arrive at the number living in "secondary" poverty,
viz. 13,072, or 17·93 per cent of the total population.
The figures will be clearer if shown in tabular form :—

		Proportion of total Population of York.
Persons in " primary " poverty . . .	7,230	9·91 per cent
Persons in " secondary " poverty . .	13,072	17·93 ,,
Total number of persons living in poverty .	20,302	27·84 ,,

One naturally asks, on reading these figures, how
far they represent the proportion of poverty in other
towns.   The only statistics which enable us to form
an opinion upon this point are those collected in
London by Mr. Charles Booth, and set forth in his
Life and Labour of the People in London.   The
objects of Mr. Booth's inquiry, as explained by himself, were "to show the numerical relation which
poverty, misery, and depravity bear to regular earnings, and to describe the general conditions under
which each class lives." [1]

In East London Mr. Booth obtained information
from the School Board visitors regarding every family
scheduled by the Board in which there were children
of school age.   These families represented about one-

---

[1] *Life and Labour of the People in London,* by Charles Booth, vol. i. p. 6.

half of the working-class population, and Mr. Booth assumed that the condition of the whole population was similar to that of the part tested.

In the other districts of London Mr. Booth, in order to complete his inquiry in a reasonable time, was obliged to adopt a rougher classification.

From the information thus obtained, which he checked and supplemented in various ways, Mr. Booth estimated that 30·7 per cent of the total population of London were living in poverty.[1] *Supposing, then, that the same standard of poverty had been adopted in the two inquiries,* a comparison between the poverty in York and that of London would be possible. From the commencement of my inquiry I have had opportunities of consulting with Mr. Booth, and comparing the methods of investigation and the standards of poverty adopted. As a result I feel no hesitation in regarding my estimate of the total poverty in York as comparable with Mr. Booth's estimate of the total poverty in London, and in this Mr. Booth agrees.

The proportions arrived at for the total population living in poverty in London and York respectively were as under :—

London . . . 30·7 per cent
York . . . 27·84 „

the proportion of the population living in poverty in York may be regarded as practically the same as in London, especially when we remember that

[1] In estimating the poverty in London Mr. Booth made no attempt to differentiate between "primary" and "secondary" poverty.

Mr. Booth's information was gathered in 1887-1892, a period of only *average* trade prosperity, whilst the York figures were collected in 1899, when trade was unusually prosperous.

This agreement in result is so striking that it is perhaps best to say that I did not set out upon my inquiry with the object of proving any preconceived theory, but to ascertain actual facts, and that I was myself much surprised to obtain the above result.[1]

We have been accustomed to look upon the poverty in London as exceptional, but when the result of

[1] On this subject the present writer has received the subjoined letter from Mr. Booth :—

"9 ADELPHI TERRACE, STRAND, W.C.,
"*July* 25, 1901.

"DEAR MR. ROWNTREE—You know with what interest I have watched your investigation into the conditions of life at York, and in response to your question I certainly think that the slight difference in our methods ought in no way to prevent the possibility of a comparison being made between your results and mine.

"The methods adopted by you are more complete than those I found available for the large area of London. I made an estimate of the total proportion of the people visibly living in poverty, and from amongst these separated the cases in which the poverty appeared to be extreme and amounted to destitution, but I did not enter into the questions of economical or wasteful expenditure. You too have enumerated the cases of visible poverty, applying similar tests, and so far our estimates are fairly comparable ; but you enumerate separately those whose income is such that they cannot by any means afford the expenditure which your argument sets forth as an absolutely necessary minimum. It is very possible that few of those classed by you or me as poor would pass muster as sufficiently nourished, clothed, and housed, according to this standard; but your classification separates those who conceivably might be so, from those who certainly could not.

"It is in this respect that my classification falls short of yours ; but our totals may be correctly compared, and the comparison, as you have shown, is very close. At this I am not surprised. I have, indeed, long thought that other cities, if similarly tested, would show a percentage of poverty not differing greatly from that existing in London. Your most valuable inquiry confirms me in this opinion.—Yours faithfully,   CHARLES BOOTH."

careful investigation shows that the proportion of poverty in London is practically equalled in what may be regarded as a typical provincial town, we are faced by the startling probability that from 25 to 30 per cent of the town populations of the United Kingdom are living in poverty. If this be the fact, its grave significance may be realised when it is remembered that, in 1901, 77 per cent of the population of the United Kingdom is returned as " urban " and only 23 per cent as " rural." [1]

The Results of Poverty.—The facts regarding the *proportion* of poverty are perhaps the most important which have been dealt with in this volume, but the conditions under which the poor live, and the effects of those conditions, especially upon their physical stamina, will have also claimed the serious attention of the reader.

Housing.—It has been shown that in York 4705 persons, or 6·4 per cent of the total population, are living more than two persons to a room, whilst the actual number who are living, and especially sleeping,

---

[1] According to the official distinction of "urban" and "rural" adopted by the Registrar-General, the population of England and Wales in 1901, as given in the Preliminary Report of the Census, is as follows :—

Urban	25,054,268	77 per cent
Rural	7,471,242	23 ,,

If, however, the distinction between urban and rural be drawn at towns of 10,000 population, the figures are as follows :—

Urban	21,946,346	67 per cent
Rural	10,579,164	33 ,,

And if drawn at towns of 20,000 population they are :—

Urban	18,940,056	58 per cent
Rural	13,585,444	42 ,,

in rooms which provide inadequate air-space for the maintenance of health is undoubtedly very much greater. Moreover, the impossibility of maintaining the decencies of life in these overcrowded houses is a factor which cannot fail to affect the morals of their inhabitants.

The close relation which exists between over-crowding and poverty is indicated by the fact that 94 per cent of the overcrowded families are in poverty either " primary " or " secondary."

Rent.—Although rents in York are much lower than in many towns, still the proportion of total earnings spent in rent by the working classes in York is high, varying from 9 per cent in the few favoured cases where the total earnings reach or exceed 60s., to 29 per cent for those whose total family earnings fall below 18s. weekly. The average proportion of total family earnings spent in rent by all sections of the working classes in York is over 14 per cent. Although York is not a large city, and freehold land within three miles of the centre of the city may be bought for £60 to £80 an acre, it never-theless contains slums as degradingly filthy as any to be found in London.

Relation of Poverty to Health.—Turning now to the relation of poverty to health, it has been shown in the preceding pages how low is the standard of health amongst the very poor. This was tested not only by the general and infant mortality of the city, but by an examination of the physique of a large

number of school children.   The inferences drawn
from this latter examination are corroborated by the
general statistics which refer to the health standard
of those who seek enlistment in the army.   These
indicate that a low standard of health prevails among
the working classes.   It therefore becomes obvious
that the widespread existence of poverty in an
industrial country like our own must seriously
retard its development.

Workmen's Household Budgets.—In the last
chapter concrete evidence is advanced as to the inadequate nutrition of the poorer sections of the
labouring classes.   An inquiry into the diet of various
sections of the community revealed the facts (1) that
the diet of the middle classes is generally more than
adequate ; (2) that of the well-to-do artisan is on the
whole *adequate;* but (3) that of the labouring class
is seriously *inadequate.*   Indeed, the labouring class
receive upon the average 25 per cent less food than
has been proved by scientific experts to be necessary for the maintenance of physical efficiency.   This
statement is not intended to imply that labourers
and their families are chronically hungry, but that
the food which they eat (although on account of its
bulk it satisfies the cravings of hunger) does not
contain the nutrients necessary for normal physical
efficiency.   A homely illustration will make the point
clear.   A horse fed upon hay does not feel hungry,
and may indeed grow fat, but it cannot perform hard
and continuous work without a proper supply of corn.

Just so the labourer, though perhaps not hungry, is unable to do the work which he could easily accomplish upon a more nutritious diet.

As the investigation into the conditions of life in this typical provincial town has proceeded, the writer has been increasingly impressed with the gravity of the facts which have unfolded themselves.

That in this land of abounding wealth, during a time of perhaps unexampled prosperity, probably more than one-fourth of the population are living in poverty, is a fact which may well cause great searchings of heart. There is surely need for a greater concentration of thought by the nation upon the well-being of its own people, for no civilisation can be sound or stable which has at its base this mass of stunted human life. The suffering may be all but voiceless, and we may long remain ignorant of its extent and severity, but when once we realise it we see that social questions of profound importance await solution. What, for instance, are the primary causes of this poverty? How far is it the result of false social and economic conditions? If it be due in part to faults in the national character, what influences can be exerted to impart to that character greater strength and thoughtfulness?

The object of the writer, however, has been to state facts rather than to suggest remedies. He desires, nevertheless, to express his belief that however difficult the path of social progress may be, a

IX   SUMMARY AND CONCLUSION   305

way of advance will open out before patient and
penetrating thought if inspired by a true human
sympathy.

The dark shadow of the Malthusian philosophy
has passed away, and no view of the ultimate scheme
of things would now be accepted under which multi-
tudes of men and women are doomed by inevitable
law to a struggle for existence so severe as necessarily
to cripple or destroy the higher parts of their nature.

[6]

OLD-AGE PENSIONS BILL.
Order for Second Reading read.

*THE CHANCELLOR OF THE EX-CHEQUER (Mr. LLOYD-GEORGE, Carnarvon Boroughs): I do not propose to enter into an explanation of the provisions of this Bill. The Bill has been before the House for some time, it has been thoroughly criticised, both in the Press and on the platform, and hon. Members have been able to form an opinion one way or the other with regard to its general character. I propose rather this afternoon to take *seriatim* the main criticisms which have been levelled at the provisions of the measure. But before I come to consider these criticisms in detail I should like to make one or two preliminary observations. The first is this, that the scheme is necessarily an incomplete one. We have never professed that it was complete and dealt with the whole problem; we wished it to be treated as an incomplete one, and to be considered as such. It is purely the first step, and I may even say it is necessarily an experiment. The second observation I should like to make is this, that those who have criticised most severely the disqualifications which we have introduced into the Bill are those who are opposed to the principle of the payment of old-age pensions at the expense of the State at all. Therefore I should invite hon. Members to consider very cautiously those criticisms when they recollect the quarter from which in the main they have come. The first general criticism is that this is a non-contributory scheme. I am not sure that that is not the effect of the Amendments of the noble Lord the Member for Marylebone and my hon. friend the Member for Preston—these two anarchist leaders. I demur altogether to the division of the schemes into contributory and non-contributory. So long as you have taxes imposed upon commodities which are consumed practically by every family in the country there is no such thing as a non-contributory scheme. You tax tea and coffee, sugar, beer and tobacco, and you get a contribution from practically every family in the land one way or another. So, therefore, when a scheme is financed out of public funds it is as much a contributory scheme as a scheme which is financed directly by means of contributions arranged on the German or any other basis. A workman who has contributed health and strength, vigour and skill, to the creation of the wealth by which taxation is borne has made his contribution already to the fund which is to give him a pension when he is no longer fit to create that wealth. Therefore, I object altogether to the general division of these schemes

into contributory and non-contributory schemes. There is, however, a class of scheme which is known as a contributory one. There is the German scheme, in which the workmen pay into a fund. It is rather a remarkable fact that most social reformers who have taken up this question have at first favoured contributory schemes, but a closer examination has almost invariably led them to abandon them on the ground that they are unequal in their treatment of the working classes, cumbersome, and very expensive, and in a country like ours hopelessly impracticable. I would refer to the experience of the statesman who on the whole has done more to popularise the question of old-age pensions in this country than anyone else—I mean the right hon. Gentleman the Member for West Birmingham. He took up this question a good many years ago, and advocated it on public platforms. No doubt he urged it upon his party, for he got Committees appointed to examine the subject. His first idea was a contributory scheme, but he afterwards abandoned it, having come to the conclusion that it was quite impracticable. He got a Committee appointed, I think by the 1892 Government, for the examination of his plans, and he first of all summoned about sixty or seventy Members of this House to consider and formulate a plan of a contributory character. Gradually he gave up that position and in the course of the debates in this House he formally abandoned his adhesion to a contributory scheme. I do not think it is any secret that the scheme adopted by the Committee presided over by the right hon. Gentleman opposite, of which I had the privilege of being a member, was in substance the scheme which was pressed upon the Members by the right hon. Gentleman the Member for West Birmingham. By that time he had given up finally, I think, any notion of a contributory scheme. He had come to the conclusion that it was quite impracticable for a variety of reasons in this country. We sifted all the schemes which were brought before us, and I do not believe there was a scheme not submitted to us. We examined witnesses who gave evidence with regard to plans which had been adopted in other countries, and witnesses with regard to small schemes of old-age pensions which had been established in England more especially, and after examining all these schemes very carefully we came with practical unanimity to the conclusion that we could not recommend a contributory scheme, and in its main outlines the scheme recommended by the right hon. Gentleman's Committee is the one which the Government has followed on the present occasion. I should like to point out another circumstance. There has been a change in the character of the schemes submitted by Members or by groups of Members of this House and since 1899 there has become noticeable a tendency to substitute for contributory schemes schemes of a non-contributory character. There is the hon. Member for Worcestershire, who had a scheme which was purely non-contributory, and he, I believe, had the support of the vast majority of Members on his own side of the House when that Bill came before us on two or three occasions in the last Parliament. Therefore, practically all parties in this House, with two or three exceptions, have abandoned almost finally the contributory idea and have decided that the only plan which could be carried out successfully in this country is a non-contributory one. That is a very important consideration, and must be borne in mind by those who criticise the Government because we have not put forward a contributory plan. A good deal is made in the Press of this, and there seems to be a revival of the contributory idea. It follows practically the same course that it followed in this House. Those who approach the question of old-age pensions for the first time are rather taken with the contributory idea, and, although I will not say the Press approach the question for the first time, yet they have now seriously approached it as a practical proposal for the first time, and they are affected by the contributory plan exactly in the same way as this House was. It appeals to all at first. But the more they consider the matter the more will they realise the difficulties and the unfairness of such a scheme, and ultimately they will come to the same conclusion that all parties in this House seem to have come to for the last fifteen or twenty years. Let me give now two or three considerations why, in my judgment, a contributory scheme is impossible in this country. In the first place, it would practically exclude women from its benefits. Out of the millions of members

of friendly societies there is but a small proportion, comparatively, of women. Another consideration is that the vast majority are not earning anything and cannot pay their contributions. The second reason is that the majority of working men are unable to deflect from their weekly earnings a sufficient sum of money to make adequate provision for old age in addition to that which they are now making for sickness, infirmity, and unemployment. I do not know what the average weekly wage in this country is; we have not had a wages census since 1886. I hope the Board of Trade will soon be able to publish the result of the wages census initiated some months ago, but I do not suppose we shall have the Returns in time for our debates on this Bill. The average weekly wage in 1886 was 24s. 9d., and 57 per cent. of the working classes in this country were then earning 25s. or less. It is quite clear, therefore, that out of such wages they cannot make provision for sickness, for all the accidents and expenses of life, and also set aside a sufficient sum to provide a competence for old age as well. Take the agricultural labourer, with his 15s. or 16s. a week. How can he set aside 4d. a week for a period of forty years, in addition to what he has to set aside already for the purpose of sickness or infirmity? He must pay his subscriptions to the friendly societies steadily and regularly. I find that some of the friendly societies which have superannuation benefits demand that if you fail in your subscriptions you either make it up afterwards, sometimes with interest, or you forfeit your benefit altogether. Now it is obviously impossible that that could be done with the great majority of workmen. The friendly societies of this country have a membership of about 12,000,000. So far from the number being over 12,000,000 it would very likely be under, because a good many members of trade unions are also members of benefit societies. It is very gratifying that such a large number of workmen should have the prudence, foresight, and restraint to enable them to set aside out of earnings money which they might have spent on necessaries or the comforts of the moment. I point that out for this reason, that the House may depend upon it that, if it were within the compass of the means of the working classes to make provision for old age, the fact that they

Mr. Lloyd-George.

had provided for sickness, that a good many have provided against unemployment and accidents of that kind, would in itself be a proof that they would have provided superannuation for old age if they could have done it. And I would point out the fact that most of the great friendly societies in this country have discovered that a superannuation scheme is practically a failure—that they cannot get a sufficient number of subscribers to make it a substantial part of their great scheme. The noble lord the Member for Marylebone, I see, rather challenges that statement; but I wonder whether he has seen the remarkable letter in the *Spectator* from a past grand master of a lodge of Oddfellows? He points out that they have failed to make provision of from 1s. 4d. to 3s. 4d. a week for aged persons, and I think he says the working classes could not afford to sustain a contribution of this kind through life in addition to the other drain on their resources. Besides that, I do not think the State has a right to invite the workman earning from 15s. to 20s. or 25s. a week to make the sacrifice which is necessary—the sacrifice, really, of some of the absolute necessaries of life as far as he and his children are concerned, in order to make provision for old age, but that the State itself ought to make it. So much with regard to the non-contributory question. I am dealing first with criticisms which, even if they were substantiated, would not have the effect of increasing the cost of the scheme. The second criticism of that character is that which has been directed against the fixed income limit. It has been suggested that it would be far more equitable to have a sliding scale. The Prime Minister, when he gave an outline of the scheme in his Budget statement, made it perfectly clear that the Government had no very emphatic view on this question; that it was purely a balance of considerations, and that the balance, in his mind, very slightly tended in the direction of a fixed income limit. There is a good deal to be said on both sides, and I am quite prepared to give due weight to the consideration in favour of a sliding scale. It does seem to be rather unfair that a man who is earning 7s. should be better treated by the State than the man who is earning 12s. The man who earns 7s. gets a pension; the man who earns 12s. gets nothing. On the face of it, that

appears to be inequitable. If a sliding scale were established, there is one consideration which ought to weigh with the Chancellor of the Exchequer, whoever he may be, and that is that I do not think there will be the same inducement to reduce the income in order to claim the benefits of the scheme. I am not suggesting fraud, but I think that can be done in many ways without fraud. I can quite imagine a case where a liberal employer is giving a pension of 11s. or 12s. a week to one of his old workmen. If he gave him only 10s. the workman would be better off by 3s., and, therefore, it would be an inducement to the employer, not to save his own pocket, but to benefit his workman, to reduce the pension he was giving him. These are considerations which I should like the House to weigh very carefully, but the Government have an open mind on this question. Personally, I think there is a good deal to be said for a sliding scale. It is working very well in New Zealand. I have never heard any criticism against its operation there, and, if the House is of that opinion, they will find the Government will not resist that very strenuously. But I have got one word of warning to my hon. friends below the gangway. I do not mind a sliding scale so long as it does not increase substantially the charges upon the Exchequer, and I think it would be possible to suggest a sliding scale which will neither diminish nor increase the charges but which would be fair to all parties. But if the sliding scale takes as a minimum what we have adopted as a maximum, the result would be that we would be committing ourselves to an absolutely indefinite figure. There have been estimates based on an income of 10s.; there have been no estimates based on 15s.; and, therefore, it would be a great leap in the dark if the range were to extend from 10s. to 15s. That is all I have got to say about the sliding scale. I come to the criticisms and objections which, if they are maintained, will have the effect of increasing the charges on the Exchequer, and very substantially increasing them. But before I consider them in detail, I should like to make a few general observations as to the cost of the scheme. Hon. Members will find all the material for calculating its cost in the Budget statement of the Prime Minister. The number of persons over seventy is 1,262,632, and, obviously, the cost of the scheme will depend upon the deductions and whether those deductions will work out up to the estimate formed beforehand. Those deductions are in respect of crime and aliens who are not naturalised. Then there is the thrift and industry test, which will not effect a very substantial diminution in the cost. The two tests that will make a very considerable inroad upon the number of persons over seventy who can claim 10s. are, first, the persons with a 10s. limit of income, and, secondly, the pauper test. Making all necessary deductions in respect of all these tests, the Prime Minister has already told the House that the net pensionables—the number of people who can pass all these tests and claim a pension—aggregate 572,000. If 572,000 is multiplied by 13, it will be found to work out, in round figures, at £7,500,000. There is a deduction in respect of married couples, but the saving on that heading would practically be neutralised by the cost of administration, which would probably be £250,000, while the saving on couples would not be more than £300,000. That is the estimate, but it is purely an estimate. The cost of the scheme will, eventually, if these figures work out, be £7,500,000. We may be asked why did we say the cost was £6,000,000 ? My right hon. friend said the charge at first would be £6,000,000, but that, eventually, it would develop and extend. The reason why we came to the conclusion that at first the charge would not be more than £6,000,000 was this. Everything is in the realm of conjecture when you are dealing with human elements of this kind, but we find that in New Zealand and in Denmark even those who were entitled to claim a pension were at first a little shy and reserved about it—so much so that in New Zealand there were only 7,000 claimants the first year. The second year they ran up to 11,000, an increase practically of about 60 per cent. in the second, or, to be more accurate, in the third year. A number of persons who can claim a pension will be anxious to see how it works, what the effect of it will be, what the *status* of the pensioner is, how the drawing of a pension is regarded by the public opinion of the class they belong to. I think that must have a very great effect upon the applications for the first year. I have no doubt that in the course of two or three years, it may be in less,

Mr. Lloyd-George.

these pensions will become very popular. They will be regarded as an honourable recognition of services rendered to the State, and in course of time, perhaps a very short time, practically all the persons who can claim pensions will put in their claims and press them. They pressed them so hard in New Zealand that they had in the course of two years rather to limit than to extend the operation of their Acts. The second consideration which I think will affect the numbers for the first year or two is the pauper disqualification test. The full effect of that will be felt in the first year, but gradually it will disappear. It is a vanishing disqualification, and I want the House to remember that. It disqualifies those who from the 1st January onward are in receipt of relief. But the moment this pension is established, what will happen ? There are three or four persons, at any rate, whose business it will be to see that the class of persons who now get Poor Law relief will in future stand out for a State pension. In the case of every man about seventy years of age who applies for Poor Law relief, they will induce him to wait if he is not seventy, and after seventy they will refer him to the Excise officer, and it will be their business in the interest of the rates to bring all the pressure in their power, and it is very considerable, rather to push the applicants for Poor Law relief into the category of pensioners. There is the applicant himself, who will naturally prefer 5s. a week as a State pensioner to 3s. a week as a pauper. Then there are the relatives, and it will be to their interest to get 5s., because £13 a year given in consideration of maintaining an aged person is a gigantic addition to the annual income of a labourer. Therefore, you have the guardians, the aged persons themselves, their relatives, and all those people who are engaged in charitable work, clergymen, and others, in a conspiracy to reduce the number of possible paupers and to increase the number of possible State pensioners. That is why we have come to the conclusion that although at first the scheme may not cost more than £6,000,000, it may in the course of a year or two cost considerably more, and the figure I have given is by no means an under-estimate. I am not so sure that the 10s. limit is incapable of modification, but I shall not dwell upon that. I can quite understand that after the Bill comes into operation there are many old persons who are now earning 11s. by hard work who will, I will not say at once, throw up their jobs and draw their pension, but it may limit the sphere of their toil and cause them to give it up a little earlier than they otherwise would. An hon. friend has told me of a superannuation scheme in Wales where a good many men prefer drawing from 5s. a week of superannuation to earning their 10s., 12s. or 14s. by hard work in the quarry. I can quite understand it; they are not working merely for the sake of the 12s., but because they are obliged to do so in order to earn their daily bread, and if a pension is provided even to the limited extent of 5s., many of them will think the time has come when they have earned rest from their labour. That is why I should like to warn the House that these figures are elastic. Well, that is the experience of every country. Take New Zealand, and Denmark more especially; I am not quite sure about Germany. I do not know what the German estimate was, but I know that with regard to almost every country which has embarked on this experiment in no case has it gone beyond the resources of the State. I want the House to realise that at the present moment, even if the Bill passes without a single alteration, what the commitment of the Treasury is. It is a possible commitment of seven and a half millions, and the consideration that I wish to put to the House is that, at any rate, we should wait until we see how the thing works before we enlarge and widen the sphere of operation of so liberal a scheme. Another thing I should like to say is that it is much the most liberal scheme which has ever been suggested by any responsible authority in this House. It is true that the right hon. Gentleman the Member for Wimbledon's Committee proposed an age-limit of sixty-five, and that half the expense was to come out of the rates, and the sum of money to come out of the Exchequer was considerably less than the sum we are undertaking to provide now under this scheme. Take the pauper limit. This disqualification affects a smaller number of men than has ever been suggested to the House. Other schemes, that of the Member for Wimbledon, the scheme of the Member for Worcester and his colleagues, invariably provided that every person in receipt of Poor Law relief for twenty years before the application should be excluded. Our estimate of the number of those excluded by our disqualification is something between 278,000 to 280,000 persons. The estimate of the Hamilton Committee of the number of persons to be excluded under the pauper test of the right hon. Gentleman the Member for Wimbledon, and of hon. Members sitting behind him, was over 400,000, so that this is far and away the most liberal scheme that has ever been submitted to this House in that respect. It is a much more liberal scheme than any that has been submitted by any old country. The Colonies, it is true, have much more liberal schemes, but I think I am entitled to point this out in regard to the Colonies, that they are not in the same position as we are; they have not a great naval and military expenditure; the Navy that defends their shores is maintained by us, and therefore they can afford it. If we could have saved our naval and military expenditure, or even one-half of it—[An HON. MEMBER: "Why not?"]—then I can assure the House that this is not the scheme which we would have submitted, and that is equally true of any old-established country. They have enormous expenditure for naval and military purposes, and therefore they cannot afford what a new country like Australia or New Zealand can undertake. Another thing is that their local finance is totally different. They have great land grants to provide sites, which we buy with an enormous amount of money; and not only that, but the land grant subsidises local rates instead of being a burden on them. They are in a much better position financially to embark on liberal schemes, which we could not look at for the time being. But if you take countries like Germany, Belgium, Denmark and France, and examine the best of the schemes submitted in any or every one of these countries, this is infinitely more liberal than anything that has been brought before the legislature of any land. Germany has a prosperous scheme for old-age, for infirmity, for sickness, and for unemployment. It costs £2,500,000 in the aggregate to the State, and the State subscription to the old-age pension over seventy is 1s. a week. In this country we are embarking in a scheme which begins at £6,000,000, which climbs up in the direction of £7,000,000. I want the House of Commons or any Member of the House, who begins to scrutinise our plan and to object to the disqualifications that limit the expenditure, to remember that no great country has ever embarked on a bolder experiment than we are submitting to the House at the present moment. I now come to examine in detail some disqualifications and the objections raised to them. The first is the age limit. Hon. Members have suggested that we ought to reduce the limit from seventy to sixty-five. Of course, if we followed the plan which was adopted not merely by the right hon. Member for Wimbledon and several other Members on the other side, and had put half the charge on the local rates, we could have done it, but that is not quite consistent with the attitude taken up on this side of the House, and on the other side of the House also, that the charges for the local rates are much too high at the present time. I was a party to that scheme, but I do not think the right hon. Gentleman himself would now get up and suggest that a part of the cost should fall upon the local rates. That shows that we are not in a position to consider the only scheme which up to the present has been considered feasible with the view of reducing the age limit to sixty-five. The expenditure would be too great to begin with, and in my own judgment I do not think that is the best way of dealing with the period between sixty-five and seventy. I am not sure that the German method is not better there. It deals with infirmity rather than with age. That is the test under seventy. I can well understand a man of seventy saying, "I am willing to retire, I have earned my pension." There are many men of sixty-five, sixty-six, and sixty-seven who are much more effective and vigorous, and capable of doing good work, than many men of fifty-seven. I think when we come to deal, as I hope we will in the near future, with the problem of infirmity that will be the time to consider the question of the broken down old man of sixty-seven and sixty-eight who is left to charity. But we are now simply providing old-age pensions, and I think they ought to begin at seventy—the old-age pension as such—that is my answer to the proposal to reduce the limit from seventy to sixty-five. It is because of the fact that it costs more, that is my answer for the moment. I would rather not at the moment contemplate

Mr. Lloyd-George.

any expenditure beyond the £7,500,000. I come now to the second disqualification, or rather to the second proposal in the Bill, which has been criticised very severely. I refer to the treatment accorded to married couples, or to those living together, married or unmarried, such as brothers and sisters. We have been very severely attacked for this proposal. One would really imagine that such a proposal had never been put forward before. I have been through most of the schemes submitted to the House by hon. Members on either side, and I find that almost every plan proposes to deal with couples on this basis. The right hon. Member for Wimbledon's Committee had this proposal before them —namely, that you should have a fixed figure for the aged person, but that there should be an abatement in respect of couples.

MR. GOULDING (Worcester): In the case of two sisters living together?

*MR. LLOYD-GEORGE: We do not want to punish marriage, and this might conceivably be the effect if you confined it only to married couples. Does the hon. Member mean to suggest that you should give 7s. 6d. to a married couple and 10s. to an unmarried couple?

MR. GOULDING: Provide a sliding scale.

*MR. LLOYD-GEORGE: Provide a sliding scale of what? I do not want to discuss that. The reason that has prompted, not merely the Government, but every Committee that has considered this question, and every group of Members who have ever formulated a scheme, is the suggestion made that they would have nothing to do with the question of married or single. It is purely a question of household economy. You have this scheme in Denmark, and in Australia; and it has been proposed practically by every scheme which has been submitted to the House, with, perhaps, the exception of my hon. friend behind me. Every plan submitted in the form of a Bill or proposed by a Committee has involved an abatement in respect of couples living together. I repudiate, therefore, the kind of language that has been used about this and two or three other disqualifications. One might imagine that we were engaged as a Government in a nefarious attempt by crafty, harsh, and even immoral means to rob hundreds of thousands of old people of the honourable provision made for them by Tory Administrations in the past, and that this was the sole object of the Government Bill. No stranger coming to this country and following the controversy could imagine that we were trying for the first time to realise a scheme which men of all parties had been trying for the last twelve years to initiate. Although hon. Members opposite had been ten years in power, with an opportunity of dealing with the question, it is only now that we are attempting for the first time, in our third year of office, to provide about £7,000,000 of money. [Several OPPOSITION MEMBERS: You are not providing £7,000,000.] That is purely a quibble and hon. Members opposite will find that out. When a Government undertakes a task of this kind is it really supposed that we do not know absolutely what provision we have to make. Surely hon. Members must have a poor opinion of the present Government—and I know they have —but at the same time they cannot imagine any sane body of Britishers undertaking a task of this kind without knowing, and knowing pretty clearly, where they are going. I assure the House that we do know. Very well, we are making this provision, I repeat, for the first time ; and, therefore, I must protest against the language which has been addressed to us and the criticisms which have been levelled against us in respect of these disqualifications. At any rate, in spite of these disqualifications, we are finding for the first time a provision for very nearly 680,000 aged persons who have nothing but pauperism in front of them. I ask the House to remember this when we come to consider questions like the abatement on income and married couples. I have pointed out that every proposal practically up to the present time contained this particular abatement, and that it is in practical operation in one or two of the Australian Colonies and in Denmark. The reason is, of course, that we want our dole to go as far as it possibly will, not merely in order to save the taxpayer, but really because it is purely a beginning. Every penny that we spend which is not necessary for the establishment of the scheme, and for conferring on aged people its full benefit, is money which is *pro tanto* taken away from the development of the scheme in future. Therefore, we have to consider every penny from that point of view. It would cost £300,000 now, a very considerable sum ; but the cumulative effect would be also very considerable and would have a curtailing effect on any future plan to be presented to the country. I come now to the industry test. It is very difficult to find out what the full operation of this test will be. There has been a good deal of misapprehension as to its purpose, and I think it is largely due to the use of one or two words which were a little unfortunate in the drafting of the Bill. It is supposed from the use of the word " misbehaviour " that this implied a character test. It does not ; it is an industry test, which is a very different thing. The right hon. Gentleman opposite proposed a very stringent thrift test, and I find that the Hamilton Commission went into the figures very closely and came to the conclusion that this test excluded 43,000 persons altogether. I think that this was a very high estimate. But the test in the Bill is not so severe a test as that proposed by the right hon. Gentleman. That was to a certain extent a character test, and it was certainly a thrift test. In respect to a very considerable number of workmen, the ordinary application of the word " thrift " is impossible. You cannot ask a man earning 15s. or 20s. a week, with gaps, to save money in the sense of a workman earning £3 a week. If, therefore, the thrift test were strictly enforced, it would be unfair and unjust ; and therefore we dismiss the thrift test. But this is a test of a different kind. It is a test to exclude the loafer and the wastrel. I do not attach any importance to the mere wording of the clause, and if any hon. Member can suggest a better form of words, or if he thinks that the net is a little too wide, and that a good many men who it is not desired to catch, would possibly be caught by these words, we are perfectly willing to consider any form of alternative words. But I do attach very great importance to the principle that men of this category shall not be treated on the same basis as men who have given the best of their lives in honest service to the State. This is a class of man known very well in the small town and village. He shirks through life; he has never done his duty; he has managed somehow to get along without doing many days honest work in his life, and yet has escaped from applying for relief to the Poor Law. This man, I think, ought to be excluded for two reasons. One reason is applicable to the pensioners themselves. I think it is highly important that the receiver of the pension should be regarded as quite honourable, that there should be nothing in the nature of pauperisation, that the pension should be regarded as the recognition of faithful services to the State; and if every man, without distinction of conduct—if men who have never done an honest day's work in their lives, receive this pension in common with men who have really worked hard, I think that the receiver of the pension will be regarded in the same light as he who is actually known to be of that stamp which we wish ruthlessly to exclude, as they ought to be. In order, therefore, to raise the character of the gift, or, rather, the recognition of faithful service to the State, we eliminate the loafer and the wastrel from among the recipients of the bounty of the State. My second reason is this. I am thinking rather of the effect it will have on men whose sole interest in the scheme is to contribute by means of taxation to the finance of it. If men who are paying heavily for the right, see men of that kind receiving at their expense an honourable pension of £13 a year, depend upon it, although not numerous, they will be multiplied a hundredfold in the imagination of every man who has paid his taxes. He would naturally say: "I pay so much in income-tax and in a number of ways to the fund, and this is what the money goes for." I am certain the result would be that you would poison their minds against the whole proposal. It is very important that all classes of the community, not merely those who receive a pension, but also those who contribute towards it, should feel that it is fair, just, and equitable in all its essentials, and for that reason I adhere very strongly

Mr. Lloyd-George.

to the principle of this disqualification, that you should rule out rigidly men who would come within one or other of these two categories. This is not the last word which I have to say upon that matter. I apologise to the House for so long a speech, but before I conclude I shall have to say one other word on this. I can well understand the fear there is in the mind of hon. Members on both sides of the House that a test of this kind might in its application be oppressively used, that men whom no one could describe as loafers or wastrels, but who are obnoxious to the authorities for some reason or another, might be kept out by the operation of this test; but I do not think there is quite the same danger of that when you have officials who represent the Imperial rather than the local authority dispensing the grants. They are much more independent than local officials. Still, I think it is very desirable that the test should be as automatic as possible, and I would go to this extent. I will propose an Amendment which will exclude from the operation of this subsection all persons who have been members of benefit societies, friendly societies, trade unions, and societies of that kind for ten years before they attain the age of sixty. I can well understand that after the age of sixty they might not be able to keep up their payments to the society, and it would be unfair to take it beyond sixty. That at once excludes from the possibility of their ever being subjected to inquisitorial examination as to their past industrial record something like 12,000,000 of the workmen of this country. The rest, therefore, would only apply to those who had never been subscribers to a friendly society, and never been members of a trade union or other society of that kind, which would prove that a man had been steadily employed and had done something for himself. I think that will remove at any rate any danger of the test being converted into an inquisitorial machine.

AN HON. MEMBER: What about women?

MR. LLOYD-GEORGE: That is a difficulty, but a rapidly diminishing difficulty, because women are being organised very largely into trade unions.

[Cries of " Oh."] Well, they are being organised gradually. Apart from that, I do not think there is the same danger in regard to women. The real danger arises in the case of the man who has taken a prominent part in some agitation in a village or town, and so rendered himself obnoxious to the authorities. There is an apprehension that they may take advantage of a clause of this kind in order to punish him for his past record in that respect. That could not possibly apply to women. I come now to the last, and perhaps the most important, criticism, and that is the one which relates to the disqualification of paupers. I want the House to remember, first of all, what I have already pointed out, that in every scheme which has been submitted to this House the pauper disqualification is a much severer one than the one which we contemplate, and not only so, but our disqualification is a dwindling one in its effect. I do not deny for a moment that it may operate partially and perhaps inequitably in some cases. It does seem hard that a man who happens to be seventy years of age, and is in receipt of poor relief when the Bill comes into operation, and who, if this Bill had been in operation, would have passed every test and received 5s. a week, should, because he was born a year or two too soon, only receive 3s. a week, from the Poor Law, and that another man who was only a few years younger should get his 5s. The sufferings of the second man would not be greater but perhaps less, and if those two cases are put side by side it does seem, on the face of them, rather hard, but the House must remember that if it had not been for this Bill the other man would have been a pauper too. You cannot in the course of a single scheme at once deal with every hard case. Social reformers, I think, make a great mistake if, when Government takes a single step in their direction, they insist upon their either not taking it at all or leaping up the whole flight at once. That is not the way to get on ; it is the way to get a fall. This is a beginning, and a real beginning. It is obviously impossible to include paupers in the scheme until you have first of all dealt with the problem of the Poor Law. There is a Royal Commission sitting at

this moment on that question. If we had been really anxious to shirk facing the problem of old-age pensions we might easily have said : " We will deal with old-age pensions after the Commission on the Poor Law has reported." Instead of that we say we will not wait for the Report of the Commission. In order to have a logical and complete scheme you ought to have a scheme which deals with the pauper, but as we cannot have that we would rather begin with an incomplete scheme and do something for the 572,000 persons outside the Poor Law. We say therefore we will not let them wait until the Commission Reports. They are seventy years of age and cannot wait. We will make a real start and then, when we get the Report of the Commission, we will include all those who under its recommendations might be treated as pensioners rather than as paupers. Moreover, it is obviously impossible to include the paupers, because that would involve an addition of from £3,500,000 to £4,000,000 to the cost of the scheme. · I know that it has been suggested that we might go to the local authorities and ask them to refund us £2,000,000 which would be saved, but I should like to ask any hon. Member whether he would take the responsibility of saying that once this money is given away they are prepared to support a plan by which the local authorities shall refund the money to the Exchequer to that extent. It is obviously impossible that we should get the whole of this money back to the Exchequer. What makes it all the more difficult to deal with this problem is that we have to face two difficulties. In dealing with pauperism we shall have to discriminate and distinguish between deserving and undeserving paupers, and that will be much better done after we have received the Report of the Commission. Besides this difficulty of discrimination, we shall also have to deal with the further problem of the relations of local and imperial finance. These are two things which the Chancellor of the Exchequer must have in his mind and must deal with at the earliest possible moment. It may be said that we are postponing indefinitely the inclusion of the pauper. But if the House will only look very closely at the disqualifying clause, they will find it is

VOL. CXC. [FOURTH SERIES.]

to the interest of the Government to deal with this at the earliest possible moment, because otherwise by the action of boards of guardians pretty well all the pauper class over seventy years of age will be gradually put on to the pension list. Therefore, it will be to the interest of the Exchequer, in its own defence, to deal with this problem effectively, with a view both to discrimination, and also to adjusting the relations between the local and Imperial Exchequers in order to get a satisfactory, if not a logical, basis of operations with regard to these cases. The pauper disqualification is not merely on the face of it provisional, it is really provisional, until Parliament otherwise orders. Parliament will have to make its order at a very early opportunity, otherwise the Exchequer would suffer very severely, because a scheme for £10,000,000 would be converted into a scheme for something like £11,500,000, unless something be done in the course of the next three or four years to deal with this problem. I want the House to remember that. I think I have dealt with most of the disqualifications in this scheme. I must say, in summing up all these disqualifications, that we have to look at the finance at our disposal. Remember what a wealthy man does when he considers the charity which he is going to dispense in the course of a year. He does not look merely at the needs of the the locality ; he looks at his own means, and having made up his mind what his means are for the current year, he decides to dispense his charity within those means, picking out those objects which are most deserving of the funds at his disposal. That is exactly what we have done. We say that in the course of next year we shall be able to find a sum of money which will at any rate finance the scheme on these lines. Later on we shall be able to find more. Unless I am mistaken, I see that a tariff reformer opposite is already making a mental note of the effect of this admission. But there is one thing common to both schools of finance—that no financial proposals you can ever submit will mature at once. It is much more true of protectionist finance, but it is quite true also of free trade finance, that the taxes you put on do not mature at once ; they do not fructify in the course of a year.

Mr. Lloyd-George.

It is only in the course of two, three, or four years that you get the full benefit of any financial proposals submitted to the country. We have come to the conclusion that in the course of next year at any rate we cannot see our way to propose anything which will cost more than the figure which I have already indicated to the House. I would warn those who are sincerely friendly to old-age pensions, that if they will take the trouble to peruse the criticism directed against not this scheme merely, but every scheme of old-age pensions, by honest and sincere opponents, they will find that use is made of these disqualifications, not in order to widen or liberalise the scheme, but in order to destroy it. I wonder whether hon. Members read carefully a very able article whch appeared in the *Spectator* last Saturday week criticising the scheme of the Government. They have taken a very consistent course ; they are the official organ of the new anarchist party which has appeared in this House. They oppose the scheme, they have always been against it, they are against all schemes of this character. They are frankly and ruthlessly individualist. What is the line they take ? First of all they opposed old-age pensions at the expense of the State in any shape or form. Then they proceeded to analyse and condemn our disqualifications with regard to pauperism, in respect of thrift, and of merit, taking them one by one and condemning them all ; and then they said it might be objected that these two positions were inconsistent, that first of all they objected to any burden being placed on the community, and then they condemned disqualifications which had the effect of lessening that burden ; but they added that they were entitled to take their own way of opposing old-age pensions. I ask the House to bear that in mind. They put it quite frankly, and even said brutally—

"We know perfectly well that if you eliminate these disqualifications you will add so much to the burden of the State that the Government will have to abandon the scheme."

That may be true, and that is their way of killing old-age pensions. I invite the supporters of old-age pensions who are just as sincere in that support as opponents are sincere in their opposition, not to fall into the trap, and I ask them to support the Government not merely on the general principle of the Bill, establishing at the expense of the State provision for old age, but also in the disqualifications which on the face of them may appear harsh and unjust for the moment, and all for the same reason. This is purely an experiment. Every scheme of this kind must be. It is true that you have systems in operation in New Zealand and Australia, but that is a very different thing; you are dealing there with a much simpler civilisation. You have never had a scheme of this kind tried in a great country like ours, with its thronging millions, with its rooted complexities; and everyone who has been engaged in any kind of reform knows how difficult it is to make way through the inextricable tangle of an old society like ours. This is, therefore, a great experiment. It is made in an old country for the first time. We put it forward as an incomplete one; we say it is a beginning and only a beginning, but a real beginning. We do not say that it deals with all the problem of unmerited destitution in this country. We do not even contend that it deals with the worst part of that problem. It might be held that many an old man dependent on the charity of the parish was better off than many a young man, broken down in health, or who cannot find a market for his labour. The provision which is made for the sick and unemployment is grossly inadequate in this country, and yet the working classes have done their best during fifty years to make provision without the aid of the State. But it is insufficient. The old man has to bear his own burden, while in the case of a young man who is broken down and who has a wife and family to maintain, the suffering is increased and multiplied to that extent. These problems of the sick, of the infirm, of the men who cannot find means of earning a livelihood, though they seek it as if they were seeking for alms, who are out of work through no fault of their own, and who cannot even guess the reason why, are problems with which it is the business of the State to deal; they are problems which the State has neglected too long. In asking the House to give a Second Reading to this Bill, we ask them to sanction not merely its principle, but also its finance, having regard to the fact that we are anxious to utilise the resources of the State to make provision for undeserved poverty and destitution in all its branches.

Speech on National Insurance Bill

I desire this evening to address myself to the unemployment branch of our proposals, and the observations which I shall make upon that branch will deal with one or two general points. I should like the House to consider the true position and functions of the State subsidy. Voluntary schemes of unemployed insurance, schemes to which the individual may resort or not as he chooses, have always failed because those men likely to be unemployed resorted to them, and, consequently, there was a preponderance of bad risks against the office which must be fatal to the success of the scheme. There is much more to be said for the subsidising by the State of voluntary associations which pay unemployed benefits, if they are organised on a trade basis. We are adopting those general provisions which every voluntary insurance scheme has in association with the compulsory provision. I should like to say in regard to that that any such extension of the Ghent scheme will not produce any really substantial result in increasing the number of insured persons. The new persons who become insured will have so greatly increased the subsidy of the State that, considering that a large portion of your subsidy goes to persons who have already been able to make provision, you get a very small return from the new insured persons on the money invested. As a supplement to a compulsory scheme, as a precursor to an extension of a compulsory scheme voluntary insurance provisions are defensible, and even desirable, But to put them forward as a means of dealing with the evil of unemployment by insurance at the present time would not be grappling with any real needs or handling the subject with a serious or earnest mind. So much for voluntary schemes the result of which in regard to unemployment insurance must be insignificant.   [495]

On the other hand, compulsory schemes are exposed to this danger, that they inflict injustice on the superior workman by forcing him to bear the extra risks of the inferior workman, and it is for that reason that we come to the State subsidy. Herein lies the true function of the State subsidy. The Leader of the Opposition will appreciate the comparison I am making when I say its object is to bridge the gap between the two classes of workmen in the same way as we bridged the gap between Irish landowners and tenants under the Irish Land Purchase scheme. It is intended by State payment to make it just worth while for the superior workman to pool his luck with his comrades. It is not a payment to bribe or induce the workman to join the insurance society as it would be under a voluntary scheme. It is intended to do justice between man and man in a class of persons already compelled to insure. The State subsidy is actually fixed at a point where it makes the system good for all. I do not say it will be equally good for all, but possibly it will be good for everyone who is comprised within it. In other words, the State subsidy, in the region of unemployment insurance, enables the insured persons to share the advantages and not to share the risks, to divide the benefits but not to divide the risks. That is the function of a State subsidy, and that is why it is vital to any scheme of compulsory unemployment insurance.

It is only in the direction of compulsory unemployment insurance that any real advance is practicable. We have been told that our scheme is incomplete. We have been asked why our compulsory system, if it is good, is to be only partial in its application. We are asked why certain trades are to be picked out. The House will realise the answer that readily occurs to a Minister. "You must begin somewhere." The oldest habit in the world for resisting change is to complain that unless the remedy to the disease can be universally applied it should not be applied at all. But you must begin somewhere. You must begin on a definite basis. The materials for the actuarial calculation on the subject of unemployment insurance are admittedly incomplete. We are prepared because of the conservative estimates we have formed to be responsible with regard to unemployment insurance upon this basis. We are not prepared to be responsible for a universal scheme of compulsory insurance, nor could the   [496] actuaries aid us in this matter. They have declined to do so. We shall never be prepared to deal with a universal scheme—the actuaries will never be able to assist us in this respect—unless we begin with a limited scheme. The data for further progress will be obtained only when we make the first march. It is no use waiting doing nothing; it is no use hoping that the materials will accumulate, that theoretical inquiry will result in further knowledge, or that a Royal Commission or other methods of investigation will produce the facts that are now lacking. The facts will never come to hand in that way. But when the first stage of the journey has been completed the course of the second stage will become visible. It is the first stage that will give access to the second. It would be foolhardy to launch out now with a universal scheme of compulsory insurance, but it is sensible and prudent to make a well-considered experiment with a definite group of trades which will admit of steady and practical observation. Those therefore who demand in the country or in the newspapers or in this House an immediate universal system of compulsory unemployment insurance are in fact as much the enemies of compulsory insurance as those who are opposed to it *in toto.* To be in favour of compulsory insurance of unemployment at the present time is to be in favour of partial unemployment insurance, because no other scheme than one of partial insurance could be advaanced with any hope of success.

I come to the next question that has been greatly discussed, and that is why are these trades in the schedule selected? The reasons for that have already been indicated to the House, and I only propose to summarise them in their collective form. My right hon. Friend the Chancellor of the Exchequer has pointed out that these are in the main the trades concerned with producing the instruments of production, and of course the House will see that the trades concerned in producing the great instruments of production are subject to an almost total cessation of orders in a period of depression, and they cannot go on if they are short of orders. When these trades are confronted with a sudden stoppage of orders there is a sharp and sudden arrest, of course, of their industry. But whatever may be the explanation those trades are subject to special phenomena and characteristics, and they are the trades in which unemployment is very severe, and in which the fluctuations are most violent. They are the trades in which you can discern with unvarying regularity, or rather with an unvarying regular irregularity, seasonal or cyclical depressions. They are the trades which manifest themselves not in a short time or in other shifts of that sort, but in the total discharge of a certain number of workmen. Those are the trades whose unemployment when it occurs is exactly that kind of unemployment which can and should be remedied by a system of insurance. I mean they are not decaying trades, they are not overstocked trades. they are not congested with a surplus or an insufficient supply of labour, but they are trades whose unemployment is due not to a permanent contraction but to a temporary oscillation in their range of business, and that is the class of business in which unemployment insurance is marked out as the scientific remedy for unemployment.

It is not true, moreover, to say that these are well-paid trades. My right hon. Friend the President of the Board of Trade has shown that half of the men in these trades earn less than 25s. a week and half less than 30s. a week, so that they cannot be said to be exceptionally well-paid trades. They are, moreover, the trades about which we have good figures. We have in some of them trade unemployment statistics going back for a period of over fifty years, and we have them in regard to over 300,000 persons. We have statistics which go back for twenty years with reference to unemployed insurance at work in those trades. Here, if anywhere, is the foundation upon which you may start and begin to build. But it is said, why should you go to the aid of those who have already insured themselves? Why not begin with those who have been up to the present unable to effect that provision for insurance against unemployment? In reply to that question I will ask the House to consider this: Why is it that those trades in which unemployment is manifested in the way that I have described have exhibited the peculiar phenomenon of provision for unemployment insurance already? They are not the best organised trades in the country. On the contrary, the proportion of trade unionists in them is only one in five, whereas throughout the country it is one in four. They are therefore not the best organised trades. The textile and the coalminers are much better organised. And yet these much less organised trades protect themselves on lines of which a

[Mr. Churchill.]

permanent feature is unemployment insurance. Why is that? It is not because they need it less, it is not because they feel the pinch less acutely, though it does not come upon them in the same form when depression strikes these trades. It is because the fluctuations are greater than can be met by wage-spreading devices such as short time, which modify the effect of trade deprivation upon the individual worker in other trades, but when the pinch comes in the insured trades it is so sharp that it means that thirty or even forty men are turned off, and no employer can keep any but a nucleus of his hands in a period of almost total inactivity.

The provision which has been made in these trades I will not say is measured by their needs, but is due largely to their sense of the evil under which they suffer, just as we see in the natural world creatures in different stages of development putting forth defences against the particular dangers to which they are subjected. We have here in the insured trades in the unemployment provision an indication that it is in that direction that the need of the measure is most felt. When we talk of the scope of the compulsory scheme—I am only dealing with the compulsory part of it for the moment—being limited, let us do justice to it. Even if it be limited it nevertheless covers a very large area, and covers no less than 2,500,000 of those engaged in adult labour, and in that figure there are no less than 2,000,000 who are not insured and who are outside all provision. Of that 2,000,000 again there is 1,000,000 who receive less than 30s. a week; 2,500,000 adult men is one-third of the total number of adult males engaged in distinctively industrial operations, excluding professional and commercial workers, domestic service, agriculture, fishing, Government officials, and others of that character. Of the remaining two-thirds, nearly one-half are employed on the railway or in the mercantile marine or in textile, mining, or other employments, which are able to meet a period of unemployment by wage-spreading devices. It is, therefore, true to say, broadly speaking, that the compulsory provisions of this Bill are large and substantial, covering very nearly half of the whole field of unemployment; certainly more than half the field of what seems to be properly called insurable unemployment. I think these are very important facts, and I should like to point out to the

House that we are not only under these sections of the Bill, dealing with the evil of unemployment in this great body of workers in our midst, but we are giving them aid which is not merely important aid, but adequate aid, in the great majority of cases.

Already the benefits cover the greater part of the periods of unemployment which we expect to be incurred by the individual in these trades, and it covers the whole of the period with a great majority of the persons who become unemployed in those trades in a bad year. Not more than 5 to 10 per cent. of the persons in those trades are out of work for more than three weeks, and consequently not one-third of the number would run through their benefits, and the rest would be covered by the benefits provided by the scheme. Possibly, I say, we are not only affording protection to this great body of persons in regard to unemployment, but we are providing in the great majority of cases an adequate amount of protection. There are one or two points which were raised by the hon. Member for Liverpool which are points of detail, but which I should like to deal with. The hon. Member commented upon the different rates of benefit which we paid to certain trades, and he thought the benefits were illusory. Of course, if your money is small you cannot expect on any actuarial bases to receive the same benefits for your contribution, but we thought it better to start with the building trade on a little lower scale of benefit because the wages are less than in other trades. But there is power in the Bill to raise the benefits, and if there is money in the Fund the benefits will certainly be raised. The hon. Member asked me what would happen to a trade unionist if he refused to take a job below the trade union rate. We propose not to deprive any man of his unemployed benefit for refusing to take a job which is below his own customary rate in his own district. That is the position which, after a very great deal of thought, we take up, and we are satisfied that that will be a good solution of what is undoubtedly a very difficult point. Then the hon. Member raised the point in regard to the employer, and the encouragement given him to give long term engagements. As the House knows, the contribution of an employer in respect of a particular workman for a year can be franked at a lower rate by annual stamp than by a succession of short-time stamps

Mr. WILKIE: Would the workman have the same opportunity of compounding as the employer?

Mr. CHURCHILL: I would like to come to the case of the superior workman in its proper place, but I will deal with the point. The question has arisen whether the effect of the employer paying for some of his workmen a composition, and paying what others do weekly on a composition yearly basis would not be to erect a division between the different classes of workmen and put pressure unfairly upon the less prosperous class of them. It may be possible to meet that in another way.

Mr. AUSTEN CHAMBERLAIN: Must the composition be in respect of a named workman—of a particular man—or may it be a composition for a number?

Mr. CHURCHILL: The composition must be in regard to a particular workman. There is no point in the other case. Everybody keeps a sufficient number of workmen, but what we want to do is to encourage long-term engagements, and not to encourage casual employment. But there is this danger, and my right hon. Friend tells me he has carefully considered if we cannot get our point in another way. It may be possible to calculate at the end of the year individual workmen whom the employer has employed for the whole year, and then give a rebate backwards. Those are the special points of detail raised by the hon. Member. I should like to say this about criticisms which are generally addressed to the principle of unemployment insurance. They have been like the criticisms which my hon. Friend addressed to the larger subject of invalidity, they are in a very large degree mutually destructive criticisms. For instance, we are told there are no complete statistics, and then we are told we have dealt only or mainly with the organised trades. Only organised trades have statistics, and we only get statistics on this subject in so far as we are dealing with trades which are organised and so far as those trades are organised. Then we are told that the risk is indefinite, and in the same breath we are told the scheme is partial. It is the partiality and limited character of the scheme which is the certain restriction of our risks. Then we are told that only those who are able to make provision are helped, and in the same breath we are told this will impose a burden on the best workers. Then it is said only certain trades are to be favoured, and

in the same breath that only those certain trades are to be burdened by the restrictions which we impose. We are told that the system of unemployed insurance will injure trade unions. We have also been told it will arm their fighting funds. All these criticisms have a tendency to answer one another. But there is one criticism which to some extent was referred to in the very able and careful speech of the hon. Member (Mr. Worthington-Evans) which requires reference. He suggested, speaking not only of this, but also of invalidity, that the system of insurance might possibly cause more unemployment. It has been suggested to us when we have been preparing our unemployment insurance scheme that when an employer knows a man is insured he will not trouble to keep him in his works during his period of difficulty, but he will let him go into unemployment and draw his benefit. The answer to that is that our statistics are based on trade union workers who are insured against unemployment and in the insured trades they already receive a higher benefit than that which we are providing, and, therefore, every motive which has been operative on the employer to discharge men who are insured, because after all they are provided for, has already been operative in regard to the trade union insured with results which have been ascertained, and our figures are based on those ascertained results.

Then there was a danger that workmen would prefer to be idle and draw unemployed benefit, we are told, instead of remaining at work, but no workman in his senses would ever exchange the regular reward of wage payment for what are, after all, the very narrowly cut grants which alone will be payable under this scheme. I should like to say that there can really be no danger of malingering in the field of unemployment insurance, because a workman who will malinger in unemployment insurance—a workman who will not work when he has the chance and prefers to draw these very exiguous benefits—is only drawing his benefit out at a period when he does not want it instead of keeping it for a period when he will be really unemployed. If he malingers he malingers against himself. I hope I have convinced the House that the danger is not a very serious one.

Let me now look at it from the point of view of the employer. The responsibility of the employer is undoubted, and his co-operation in any attempt to deal with unemployment is indispensable. There is

[Mr. Churchill.]

already a great recognition by employers in this country of their duties towards their workmen, and legislation is not required to inculcate a new doctrine, but only to give scientific expression to a powerful impulse of just and humane endeavour. A system of compulsory unemployment insurance associates directly for the first time the interest of the employer and of the unemployed workmen. Both contribute to a common fund, and both are concerned in its maintenance and in its thrifty administration. I cannot but feel that the inauguration of this system must promote the gradual adoption of those methods of the collective regulation of labour hours and labour activity which give full and comforting security to the lives of the collier and the cotton operative, and that they will promote short time arrangements and wage - spreading arrangements wherever they are possible. I think the admission of apprentices and the engagement of new workmen will tend to be scanned and scrutinised with some greater regard to the permanent average needs of the industry, and we trust that in the arrangement of business contracts more attention will be paid in the future to the possibility of sudden ups and downs involving sudden wholesale discharges of workmen from the fact that such sharp changes will have the effect of draining the fund and possibly increasing the levy.

I admit that the scale on which these tendencies will be operative will not be a very great one, but so far as the common interest of the employer and the employed are associated in these funds to which they both are liable to contribute the tendency undoubtedly will be to lead to a more statesmanlike view of business undertakings and a less purely commercial view than hitherto has prevailed. We therefore say to the employer in advocacy of the system: "You hold the keys of enterprise, and you are responsible for its wise direction; your own humanity has already prompted you to make such provision—such provision has been made by the employers in many parts of the country—in regard to the prevention of distress through unemployment. We shall complete your provision and organise it effectively." We say, thirdly: "If your business is subjected to special regulations it will also receive substantial and special benefit," and, lastly, we say to the employer: "Nothing is more important to you than discipline and efficient workmen and the organisation of insurance will un-

questionably enable you to command superior efficiency from the insured workmen."

In regard to the less capable workmen, as there is a more or less in this—I am speaking of good normal workmen, and not mere inefficients, men of declining years, and so on—the benefits of the scheme are so obvious that I shall not enlarge upon them. It is clear they get greatly improved prospects from the association with their stronger comrades. Let us consider the case of the superior workman. What can we say to him to reconcile him to the discipline and machinery of this scheme? First, we say, no man can be certain that he may not lose his class. He may be a good workman to-day, but in a few years illness, accident, the bankruptcy of an employer, the invention of a new machine may cause a man to fall from his class to a lower class. Consequently we say to him: "You have an interest in the fortunes of your comrades," and the better the workmen in this country the more they have responded to the idea of the solidarity of labour interests, not only within the trade, but in all the broad areas of trade, and not only in this country, but this conception of solidarity has stretched out far over the surface of the civilised world. We say, in the third place: "Whatever sentiments you may hold upon that subject, at least you can keep the inferior workman from undercutting your standard rate of wages," and, as a matter of fact, trade union unemployed benefit has been largely dictated by a desire to prevent rates being pulled down by large numbers of men being thrown on the market in hard times.

We say, fourthly, to him: "Your risks are limited to sharing your comrades' burdens. You are not called upon to take mere inefficients on your back. They soon drop out of the scheme under the conditions, and you have only to share your risks with your normal comrades." We say to him, in the fifth place: "The State subsidy makes it worth your while to pool your luck within these limits, and. in fact, we say, sixthly: "We give you at least 150 per cent. increased value in addition to any that you can obtain anywhere else from your own investment." Lastly, we say to him: "If you need them you can draw the benefits of the scheme as you require them, but if you do not need them," or if you do need them all, then at sixty, if you survive, having all these years been safeguarded within the benefits of the scheme, having all these years helped to safeguard others within the benefits of the scheme, you can have every penny that you have contributed back at compound interest, and take it away with you so that if it is not drawn out in unemployment insurance it may repose as if in a bank, at compound interest at 2½ per cent."

I can quite see the House feels that that must be very difficult to manage, because, when one looks at it for the first time, one cannot see how it can possibly square with the solvency of the Fund. But the explanation is so simple that I am afraid the House will think it almost a conjuring trick. Let me explain the reason, and it will be seen that there is not so much in it as there seems. Every workman who subscribes to our Insurance Fund brings not only his own contribution but the contribution of the employer and the contribution of the State, so that he is only putting a little more than a third in, compared with the other two-thirds which go to enrich the Fund. It will be possible for every workman in the Fund to draw out every year benefits to the extent of his own contribution, plus the employer, plus the State, without destroying the solvency of the Fund. Therefore in the case of a workman who has subscribed all these years and reaches sixty without having even drawn out his own contribution, it is possible for us, especially as every one does not live to sixty, to give him back all his own contributions— not the State's or the employer's—without throwing any burden upon the Fund in spite of the compound interest. That is our apology and our reward to the best class of man who goes through this business to the end, and yet appears at the time to derive no benefit from it.

I think the Board of Trade comes before the House with good credentials in regard to unemployment insurance. This is the counterpart and the complement of that system of Labour Exchanges which was set up two years ago. Of course you could not bring such great institutions into operation without treading on a lot of people's toes. I have no doubt they have trodden on a lot of toes, and all honour to the trade unions for the support which they have given to the system of Labour Exchanges in spite of the perplexities and some of the embarrassments in which the system has involved them, but the success of the system is indisputable. Five thousand to six thousand persons a day are being registered in these exchanges.

We are filling more than 2,000 vacancies a day, and 500 casual jobs in addition. Last week was a record week. Seventeen thousand employers offered situations to the Labour Exchanges, and 12,800 persons were actually placed in them, exclusive of casual and shorter jobs. The 100 exchanges which have been opened actually for a year show an increase of 50 per cent. on the business transacted. Five thousand employers in the country have posted up outside their works the Board of Trade notice, "All applicants for employment to go to the nearest Labour Exchange."

Every week 1,500 to 2,000 persons are found work out of their own districts— that is to say, work which they would not otherwise have found without long and weary searching. Since the beginning of the scheme we have under the powers which the House of Commons gave to the Board of Trade advanced fares, amounting to £2,400, to 9,000 persons, and these were persons at the very last gasp in the matter of employment, to reach their destinations. Of that sum, £2,200 has already been repaid. Of course, the Labour Exchanges are still in their infancy, and in a few years, when we get greater results, we shall look back to these small beginnings in connection with what is certainly a great piece of social mechanism. In this current year I do not think it is excessive to say that we shall find employment for 80,500 persons. In Germany, after twenty years, the Labour Exchanges are scarcely finding more situations than we are doing in the present year. These results may be put forward as credentials in regard to the other half of the policy which it was my duty to announce to the House two years ago.

I must speak a word with regard to the actuarial basis of the insurance scheme. For three years this matter has been investigated. It is more than three years since the first memorandum was written at the Board of Trade on the scheme. Since the question was first taken up by the Chancellor of the Exchequer and myself, my right hon. Friend the President of the Board of Trade has come in, and he has gone over the whole field, making alterations and improvements where he found it necessary to do so. We have been three times on the threshold of introducing the scheme, and we have now got to the point where it is possible to propose it. In the meantime the facts and figures have been subjected to all the tests which industry and available information can

7.0 P.M.

[Mr. Churchill.]

supply. Of course, we admit that statistics are not exhaustive, but wherever anything in connection with the question of statistics has involved doubt we have given our decision against the Insurance Fund in every case. Let me give an instance or two. There must be one waiting week for every man who becomes unemployed before any benefit can be given. People will become unemployed several times in the course of a year. But we only count one waiting week in the year, because there will be one waiting week in regard to each period of unemployment. That is one point which we do not count in the calculation. There will be payment by employers who engage people less than a week, and perhaps several times in respect of the same man, unless they use the exchanges. We deal with that only on the basis of full weeks. We have another gain there. There is an arrangement which will give a reserve fund in the fact that everybody must pay the first twenty-six contributions before they can draw benefits. That is going to give us £1,250,000 if we begin in a good year. It is going to give us a reserve fund of that amount to face the chances of future years. That sum will yield £30,000 or £40,000 a year in interest. We shall in future years get in the contributions for the twenty-six weeks which come from new persons joining the scheme, so that the interest might easily amount to £60,000 or £70,000 a year if we begin now. We have made no calculation for that in our proposals. It is possible that the new Census may reveal figures in regard to some of the insured classes which will show that they are not quite so numerous as those on which we are acting. There again we shall get another windfall—another easement.

We have allowed nothing for the improvements in organisation and industry and the removing of the balance of fluctuation which may follow from this development. In spite of all this we have an ample margin. We have a proved margin of £200,000 a year for the solvency of the scheme. If we begin in good years there is no reasonable doubt that the fund will be solvent and equal to the emergency, but in any case if these calculations should be exceeded by the hard turn of events you can limit your risks. You can reduce the number of weeks for which benefit is payable, and in that way you can contract your obligations and secure the solvency of the fund. To reduce the unemployed benefit is different from reducing the sick

benefit. In regard to unemployment the insurance benefits are paid *pro tanto* in so far as they are payable. They do good, and they cover a considerable part. Therefore you can reduce them without destroying the effect of the benefits.

There is no proposal in the field of politics that I care more about than this great insurance scheme, and what I should like to say is that there must be no delay in carrying the unemployment insurance any more than in carrying the invalidity insurance. Strong as are the arguments for bringing forward invalidity insurance, they are no less strong—in fact, they are even stronger—for unemployment insurance. A few years ago everybody was deeply impressed with the unsatisfactory condition of affairs which left our civilisation open to challenge in this respect, namely, that a man who was willing to work and who asked that his needs might be met, could not find the means either of getting work or being provided for. That could not but make thinking men uncomfortable and anxious. Providence has ordained that human beings should have short memories, and pain and anxiety are soon forgotten. But are we always to oscillate between panic and torpor?

People talk of the improvidence of the working man. No doubt he has to bear his responsibility, but how can you expect a working man who has few pleasures and small resources, and with the constant strain that is put upon him, to scan trade cycles and to discern with the accuracy of Board of Trade officials the indications and fluctuations of world-wide markets. His failure to do so is excusable. But what can be said of the House of Commons? We have the knowledge and the experience, and it is our duty to think of the future. It is our duty to prepare and to make provision for those for whom we are responsible. What could be said for us, and what could excuse our own improvidence if the next depression found us all unprepared? There is something to be said for the working man who does not provide against unemployment. It may not fall upon him. The great majority of working men will not become unemployed in the insured trades. A working man may escape, but the State will not escape, and the House of Commons will not escape. The problem will come back to the House of Commons as sure as death and quite as cruel, and then it will be too late. It is no use attempting to insure against unemployment when it is upon you and holds you in its grip. There is no use going round then to unemployed working men and asking them to insure against unemployment. It is only in those good years that we can make provision to secure the strength of the fund which will enable us to face the lean years. All our calculations are based upon taking good years with the bad. We must begin now while unemployment is not a feature of our political life and discussion. We must begin now if the fund is to begin strong. We owe a great deal to the Chancellor of the Exchequer in connection with this great scheme. He has devised it and made it possible in the public life of this country. He has afforded us something which does give common ground for all our best efforts, and I think it will be found one of the strongest forces for the country to unite upon. There is exhilaration in the study of insurance questions because there is a sense of elaborating new and increased powers which have been devoted to the service of mankind. It is not only a question of order in the face of confusion. It is not only a question of collective strength of the nation to render effective the thrift and the exertions of the individual, but we bring in the magic of averages to the aid of the million. In the field of invalidity there is all this and more. In the field of invalidity we have not only the magic of averages, but, as we were reminded yesterday in the speech of the hon. Member for Plymouth (Mr. Astor) —a speech which excited the admiration and gratitude of all who sit on this side of the House, and the approval of every one wherever he sits—we have the genius of health. There is a third great force besides that of averages and health which is now running to waste, and which invalidity insurance brings to the surface. I mean the actuarial effects of old age pensions on those who do not get them and perhaps will never possess them. Nearly £13,000,000 a year is devoted to old age pensions to persons over seventy years of age. All others are getting no direct benefit from them, and this enormous flow of State effort is provided for every one over seventy years of age to the extent of 5s. a week. Everyone knows that he has a prospect of getting 5s. a week when he reaches that age. It is not much, unless you have not got it. Until and unless invalidity insurance is added to old age pensions the whole of the advantage of that great improvement is running to waste. But if the invalidity is added, the old age

pension will not only be enjoyed by those who now possess it, but it will cast its light backwards over all those who are approaching a pensionable age. Therefore I say we are bringing these great new forces, as valuable as if they were discoveries of new territories or of new scientific processes, to aid in overcoming the evils which we see in our social system.

The penalties for misfortune and failure are terrible to-day; they are wholly disproportionate, even when they are brought on by a man's own fault, either through the culpability of the individual or neglect of what is necessary to make him try or to make him take care. A man may have neglected to make provision for unemployment; he may have neglected to make provision for sickness; he may be below the average standard as a workman; he may have contracted illness through his own folly or his own misconduct. No doubt he is a less good citizen for that reason than others who have taken more thought and trouble. But what relation is there between these weaknesses and failings and the appalling catastrophes which occasionally follow in the wake of these failures; so narrow is the margin upon which even the industrious respectable working class family rely that when sickness or unemployment come knocking at the door the whole economy and even the status of the family are imperilled. The sickness may not be severe; the unemployment may not be prolonged. The good offices of friends and neighbours may carry the family through the crisis; but they come out with an accumulated weight of debt, and with furniture and clothing scattered at ruinous rates. Privation has weakened the efficiency of the bread-winner, and poverty has set its stamp upon his appearance. If sickness and unemployment return and knock again a second time it is all over. The home is broken up; the family is scattered on the high roads, in the casual wards, in the public houses and the prisons of the country. No one can measure the suffering to individuals which this process causes. No one can measure the futile unnecessary loss which the State incurs. We do not pretend that our Bill is going to prevent these evils. Unemployment and sickness will return to the cottage of the working man, but they will not return alone. We are going to send him by this Bill other visitors to his home, visitors who will guard his fortunes and strengthen the force of his right arm against every foe.

[8]

THE PROBLEM OF THE PUBLIC SCHOOLS

By R. H. TAWNEY

THE recent appointment by the President of the Board of Education of a Committee on Public Schools is something of a landmark in educational history. The majority of those schools, as is explained below, are already in receipt of grant-aid from the State, and comply with the obligations which that position imposes. But the popular conception of a public school has been derived from the characteristics of select specimens of the genus. As a consequence, the leading representatives of the public school system—to use the conventional, though question-begging, phrase—and the preparatory schools serving them, have been commonly regarded as forming a closed world. Their influence and prestige made it probable that interference with them would encounter tenacious opposition. The minute fraction of the rising generation which attends such schools, and the urgency of other educational requirements, caused reformers for long to doubt whether it was worth while to interfere.

The public schools exercise on English life, including English educational policy, an influence out of proportion to the number of pupils educated in them. The disposition to ignore them was never, therefore, justified. It was as short-sighted as would have been, in the fifties of last century, an apathy which left the older Universities un-reformed, on the ground that the undergraduates in both together numbered under four thousand. To-day the financial independence of the better known among the schools concerned, which made possible, if it did not excuse, that attitude of indifference, is no longer so secure as it appeared in the past. The fall in the birth-rate has hit some of them hard.[1] The improvement, both in quality and quantity, of public secondary education has exposed them to keener competition. War taxation has cut into family resources, which might, in other circumstances, have been spent on education. Some parents, perhaps many parents, who would formerly have

[1] For figures, see *Education and the Birth-Rate, A Social Dilemma*, by Grace G. Leybourne and Kenneth White, pp. 335-336, where two alternative estimates are given of the probable decline in the future population of residential public schools.

THE POLITICAL QUARTERLY

contrived, if with difficulty, to send their boys to boarding-schools, no longer feel justified in incurring the heavy costs involved ; while others, who look beyond the circumstances of the moment to the post-war situation, feel doubts whether the day when education in an expensive boarding-school was regarded as socially indispensable may not have passed for good. As a consequence, the governing bodies of some public schools are faced already, and those of some others may be faced in the near future, by a problem of declining numbers. It is natural that educational institutions, which believe that they are doing work of public value, should seek, in an unforeseen emergency, the assistance of the State. It is proper that the State, whatever the final verdict on their request, should give it serious consideration.

The particular occasion which dragged the public schools into the limelight was, therefore, a financial one. That aspect of the subject is, clearly, important, but it is only one aspect. It would be a misfortune if the discussion of the future of such schools were conducted merely or mainly on the financial plane. It is not only that grants of public money can hardly be unconditional, and that the conditions which must accompany them can be settled only after a decision as to the educational services required of their recipients. It is that, quite apart from the immediate embarrassments which have caused the question to be raised, a thorough investigation into the rôle of the public schools, of the relations which should exist between them and other parts of the educational system, and of the changes, if any, required to ensure that they make their full contribution to the educational life of the nation, is long overdue. Now that practical considerations have forced the issue to the front, an examination of the position and functions of different types of public school, in the absence of which an intelligent verdict on the desirability of assisting those not receiving State aid can hardly be given, ought not to be further postponed. The terms of reference of the Committee, which require it " to consider means whereby the association between the public schools . . . and the general educational system of the country could be developed and extended," are a recognition of that fact. Policies, however, cannot usefully be discussed, except in the light of the facts to which they are to be applied. What is a " public " school ? What was the number of such schools in existence on the eve of

THE PROBLEM OF THE PUBLIC SCHOOLS

the War? What, in respect of mere externals—school population, boarding and day; fees; grant-aid or the absence of it—were their salient characteristics?

I.—THE DIMENSIONS OF THE PROBLEM.

No legal definition of a public school appears to exist. The Public Schools Commission of 1861-64 dealt only with nine schools, but recognised that beyond them lay a mixed multitude of institutions, many of which were anxious to enjoy the same status and title, and a considerable number of which have since made good that claim. The feature emphasised as characteristic of a public school in the Report issued in 1932 by the Departmental Committee on Independent Schools is their conduct " by Governing Bodies under Trusts or other Articles of Association which limit or prevent profit." In practice, the test by which it is decided whether a particular school is or is not a " public " school is an empirical one. It depends on the answer to the question whether such a school is a member, or not, of the Head Masters' Conference. That body, which was founded in 1869, has, in addition to its other functions, supplied a criterion by which the authentic public schools can be distinguished from the mere pretenders to the title. The schools in the United Kingdom belonging to it have increased by between three- and four-fold since its establishment, from 50 in 1871 to 113 on the eve of the last war, and to 187 in 1938. The figures given below are those for 1938. They relate to public schools for boys in England only, and do not include those in Wales and Scotland. The following table[1] attempts to set out the facts, so far as it has been possible to

[1] I am indebted for the figures contained in this table, as well as for other assistance, to Mr. V. Ogilvie, of the New Education Fellowship. The principal materials used in compiling it are the list of secondary schools recognised as efficient by the Board in 1938, *The Public Schools Year-Book*, 1939; Truman and Knightley's *Schools*, 1939; and Burrows, *Schools of England*, 1939. The Board's list omits eleven schools in England represented at the Head Masters' Conference, presumably on the ground that they did not accept inspection by the Board. These schools have been included in the table. The table omits two schools of an exceptional kind, viz., Dartmouth Royal Naval College and Worcester College for the Blind. The total number of pupils over 11 in the 150 schools included in the Board's list for 1938-39 is 64,388. For the remaining eleven schools represented in the table the only published information available appears to be that given in the work of Truman and Knightley. The figures contained in it are given in round numbers, and include in some half a dozen cases boys under eleven. They total 3,900. The President of the Board stated on June 25, 1942, in answer to a question in the House, that there were 26,500 boys in the independent schools, and 64,700 in the grant-aided schools, affected by the inquiry. The Committee on Public Schools is concerned with schools which are members of the Head Masters' Conference and of the Governing Bodies' Association. Only schools which are members of the former are included in the table here given.

THE POLITICAL QUARTERLY

PUBLIC SCHOOLS IN ENGLAND, 1938

	No. of Schools Boarding & Day				No. of Pupils, Boarding and Day					No. of Schools receiving grant				Special Places		Age of Admission			
	No. of schools	Schools admitting boarders only	Schools admitting boarders and day-pupils	Schools admitting day-pupils only	Total No. of pupils	No. of boarders	%	No. of day-pupils	%	Schools not receiving grant	(1) Direct from Board	(2) Through L.E.A.'s	Schools not on grant list but approved for superannuation	Schools required to offer special places	No. of pupils whose fees are wholly or partly remitted as a result of the award of special places	Schools admitting pupils at 11	Schools having a junior school	Schools not admitting pupils at 11 nor having a junior sch'l	Uncertain
I. Schools charging fees of £150 and over	37	18	19	—	15,191	14,114	93.0	1,077	7.0	34	—	—	3	—	—	1	10	22	4
II. Schools charging fees £100–£149...	53	4	49	—	17,049	9,924	58.3	7,125	41.7	27	15[1]	1	10	15	1,165	5	30	13	5
III. Schools charging fees below £100.	70	—	37	33	35,216	2,694	7.6	32,522	92.4	4	36	29	1	65	10,970	51	17	—	2
IV. Schools charging no fees	1	1	—	—	832	832		—		1	—	—	—	—	—	1	—	—	—
Total	161	23	105	33	68,288	27,564	40.3	40,724	60.7	66	51[1]	30	14	80	12,135	58	57	35	11

[1] Including one school receiving grant on a lower scale, and not required to offer special places, though, in fact, it contained 21, out of 380, pupils whose fees had been wholly or partially remitted.

[2] The figures in this column do not include scholarships or remissions of fees other than those resulting from the grant of special places.

THE PROBLEM OF THE PUBLIC SCHOOLS

ascertain them, with regard to the 161 English public schools then in existence, in the matter of number of pupils, boarding and day; fees[1]; grant-aid; special and free places; and age[2] of admission.

It will be seen that the popular view that all or most public schools belong to one type, and that that type is represented by Eton, Harrow or Winchester, is an illusion. In reality, those schools do not form a single category, but, in certain important respects, differ somewhat widely from each other. Some receive only boarders, some only day-pupils, some both day-pupils and boarders. Some depend, to a greater or less extent, on public money; others are financed entirely from fees, or from fees *plus* endowments. Some admit pupils between eleven and twelve, others not before thirteen. Some draw a considerable proportion of their pupils from public elementary schools; others are almost completely divorced from the national system of education. The most striking fact, however, is one which would have been expected. It is that these varying characteristics are not distributed at random between different public schools, but that certain of them are normally found in combination with others, and that their presence or absence is closely related to the level of fees charged, which, in turn, is a rough index of the economic position of the families from which pupils are predominantly drawn.

The majority of schools in Group III, with boarding fees under £100, differ little, if at all, from those grant-aided secondary schools—the great majority—which do not aspire to be regarded as public schools. None of them take boarders only; over nine-tenths of their pupils are day-boys; 65 out of the 70 schools concerned are in receipt of grant, and offer special places; nine-tenths of those pupils attending public schools whose fees are wholly or partially remitted as a result of the award of special places are found in this group of schools. In all these respects the schools in Group I, which charge boarding fees of £150 and over, differ sharply from those in Group III. None of them admit

---

[1] The fees given in the table are boarding fees. The average boarding and day fees were as follows:

	Average boarding-fee of schools taking boarders		Average day-fee of schools taking day-boys
I.	£169-£170	...	£63-£64
II.	£121-£122	...	£37-£38
III.	£82-£83	...	£21-£22

[2] The figures relating to the age of admission are unreliable, and almost certainly contain more or less serious errors.

THE POLITICAL QUARTERLY

day-pupils only ; eighteen admit only boarders ; and, while nineteen admit boarders and day-pupils, the latter form less than one-tenth of the total population of the schools in the group. None of these schools receives grant,[1] or is required to offer special places. Group II is the most miscellaneous of the three. Some of the schools contained in it are hardly, if at all, distinguishable from those in Group III, and others are similar in type to those in Group I. The most significant feature of Group II is, perhaps, that, while over 40 per cent of the pupils covered by it are day-pupils, less than one-third of the schools in it receive grant or are required to admit special place pupils.

In the light of these facts, the public schools which call first for consideration can be roughly sorted out. They are those in Group I, together with something over one-half of the schools in Group II. They form, it will be observed, less than half the total number of public schools in England ; but their example has had an influence on the social outlook and educational methods of schools outside their own ranks. If the present article devotes more space to the residential schools than to the day-schools, the reason is not that the former are more important than the latter, or that the defects criticised below are found only in them. It is that they present the more difficult problem.

II.—THE LEGACY OF THE LAST CENTURY.

If the nature of that problem is to be understood, it must be seen in perspective. It may be observed in the first place, that the view sometimes heard that " the public school system " is hallowed by antiquity is a piece of mythology. Of the 161 schools included in the table given above, 59 came into existence[2] in the nineteenth century or later, and 41 of these, including some of the best-known, after 1849 ; while, of the 102 established before 1800, none, of course, were founded as public schools in the modern sense of that expression, and the majority have undergone drastic reconstructions. Particular institutions can point to links with the past of somewhat the kind as exist between the city companies of to-day and mediaeval craft-gilds. These pedigrees, dignified or picturesque, are not without their educational value ; but a long boarding-school tradition does not often

[1] Three of these schools are approved for purposes of superannuation.

[2] The dates of the foundation of schools are taken from *The Public Schools Year-Book* for 1938.

THE PROBLEM OF THE PUBLIC SCHOOLS

form part of them.[1] In reality, the assumption still prevalent among well-to-do parents in England—an assumption not countenanced[2] by the most eminent of the founders of modern public school education—that residence for four or five years at a boarding school should form, as a matter of course, a stage in the life of all boys above a certain income level, together with the existence of a group of schools which specialise in catering for that demand, are, on anything like their present scale, a thing of yesterday. Individual specimens both of the attitude and of the institution are to be encountered much earlier ; but " the public school system," in so far as these are its characteristics, has no long history behind it. It represents, in its present form, not an ancient educational tradition, but innovations which matured between 1830 and 1890.[3]

The reasons which made these two generations the golden age of the public boarding-school are not difficult to state. The moral authority and practical example of pioneers, such as Arnold and Thring, were of great importance ; but conditions peculiar to their day fixed the direction of their efforts, and it is no reflection on their originality to say that, even more than most successful reformers, they worked with the grain. Apart from the influence of individuals, the

[1] " In every case, except those of Merchant Taylors and St. Paul's, and perhaps Shrewsbury, the bulk of each school, as now existing, is an accretion upon the original foundation, and consists of boarders received by masters or other persons at their own expense and risk."—Report of Commission on Public Schools and Colleges, 1864, Vol. I, p.8, and Vol. III, pp. 502-3.

[2] A. P. Stanley, *The Life and Correspondence of Thomas Arnold* (Minerva Library ed.), pp. 72-3.

[3] The proportion of day-boys to boarders in the sixties seems to modern eyes surprisingly high. The figures below are taken partly from the Report of the Commission on Public Schools, partly from that of the Schools' Inquiry Commission, 1868, Vol. I, App. VI, pp. 150 and 322. Some of them appear to be merely estimates. The discrepancy between the total of 2,673 given below for the nine public schools and that of 2,696 given in the Report is due to uncertainty as to the Eton figures.

	Boarders	%		Day-Boys	%		Total
Nine Public Schools (end of 1861)...	1,952	73.0	...	721	26.9	...	2,673
572 Endowed Schools (1868)... ...	9,279	25.1	...	27,553	74.8	...	36,832
Proprietary Schools (1867)	15,831	30.7	...	35,674	69.2	...	51,505

The nine great public schools included in 1861 two schools, St. Paul's and Merchant Taylers, which were entirely day-schools. It will be noticed that day-boys then formed 26.9 per cent of the boys in the nine schools, as compared with 7 per cent in the thirty-seven most expensive schools in 1938, and that they accounted in 1867 for over two-thirds of the aggregate population of all schools together. Between 1840 and 1867 several boarding-schools (e.g., Marlborough, Wellington, Malvern, Rossall, Cheltenham, Clifton, Lancing, Radley) were founded, and several local grammar schools were reconstructed so as to make them available for a non-local clientèle. It is probable that, if figures for 1840 were available, they would show a substantially higher proportion of day-boys. In the present century, the proportion of day-boys attending public schools has again increased, owing to the increase in the number of day-schools belonging to the Head Masters' Conference.

THE POLITICAL QUARTERLY

decisive factors were four. They were the Industrial Revolution, with its flood of new wealth; the deficiencies, both in number and quality, of existing day-schools; the modernisation of communications; and the careers opened by the expansion of the empire, the reform of the civil service and the growth of the professions. The first greatly increased the effective demand for higher secondary education. The second and third put a premium on boarding-schools and made recourse to them practicable. The fourth ensured that the aptitudes cultivated by them would find little difficulty, when school-days were over, in securing suitable employment.

The rising middle class, if often uneducated itself, was not unaware of the advantages of education; nor was it lacking in ambition. It looked to the schools to provide, in addition to a moral and intellectual discipline, a common platform enabling its sons to associate on equal terms with those of families who, if increasingly outdistanced in income, still diffused a faint aroma of social superiority. At first, it looked in vain. The old local foundations were often in ruins. The local secondary schools of today were not yet even a dream. The condition of not a few private schools was such that the choice, parents were told by one with some title to speak, "lies between public schools and an education whose character may be strictly . . . domestic."[1] If they rejected the last course, what alternative had they but to send their sons to schools at a distance from their homes? Yet how, in the days when Arnold himself travelled to his new post at Rugby by stage-coach, and despatched his belongings by the Grand Junction Canal, could the first alternative be generally adopted?

The answer came, not from the educationalist, but from the engineer. It is not an accident that the boarding-school boom followed closely on a railway boom, that three times as many public schools were founded in the thirty years between 1841 and 1870 as in the whole century before 1841, and that enterprising grammar schools made haste to fall in with the fashion, sometimes placating their consciences for the diversion of their services from day-boys to boarders by supporting cheap day-schools for the sons of local residents. A form of education which improved communications made possible was made increasingly attractive by the requirements

[1] A. P. Stanley, *op. cit.*, p. 242.

THE PROBLEM OF THE PUBLIC SCHOOLS

of a state beginning tardily to grapple with the problems of
an empire and an urban civilisation.   The establishment in
1854 of open competition as the condition of entry to the
Indian Civil Service, the application of the same principle to
the Home Civil Service between 1855 and 1870, and the
gradual assumption by governments of functions demanding
an enlarged administrative *personnel*, combined with the
growth of law, medicine and business to create a market in
which, before the days of municipal and county secondary
schools, the products of the public schools for long met few
competitors.   Parents with means were quick to grasp the
advantages of the new dispensation.   It could be said by a
headmaster in the early seventies not only that " the ordinary
English gentleman would think that he lost caste " if he did
not send his boy to a public school, but that " there is a strong
feeling growing up among the merchant class in favour of
the public schools, and [that] hundreds go to a school now
who, thirty years ago, would not have thought of doing so."[1]
Every stage of education casts its influence back, for good or
evil, on that preceding it.   It is not surprising, therefore, that
the first preparatory school of the modern type should have
been founded, apparently, on the suggestion of Arnold.   The
increase in the number of such schools from something under
a score in the sixties to approximately four hundred[2] in 1900
supplied the public boarding-schools with a clientèle of the
social type which they desired, educated under conditions not
dissimilar from their own.   It is a commonplace that England
possesses, not one educational system, but two—a public and
a private one.   At the close of the century, the former was
still in an early stage of its history ; the latter was not far
from complete.

The " public school system " of today, therefore, in so far
as it is represented by the great boarding-schools, is not
among the more venerable of the historic treasures of the
English people.   It grew to maturity between the first and
third Reform Acts, as the child of a particular age and a
specific environment.   Like the reorganisation of local
government and the changes which followed the first Royal

[1] G. P. Parkin, *Edward Thring, Life, Diary and Letters*, II., pp. 195-196.

[2] J. Dover Wilson, *The Schools of England*, chapter on " The Preparatory School,"
by Alan Rannie, p. 65.   According to Leybourne and White, *op. cit.*, p. 190, " During
1936-37 there were in England and Wales 272 boys' preparatory schools recognised
by the Board, with 17,785 pupils, of whom 11,493 were boarders, while 6,292
attended daily.   Here, day-boys on the average paid no less than £35 7s. each year
in fees, while boarders paid as much as £148 10s."

THE POLITICAL QUARTERLY

Commission on Oxford and Cambridge, it was one phase of the great movement of middle-class reconstruction which began in 1832, reached its climax in the eighties, and then, its impetus spent, settled down to make the most of the kingdom it had won, leaving, as was inevitable, new tasks to be essayed by novel methods and in a spirit not its own. No student of English life in the latter half of the last century will question the magnitude of the improvements in the education of the propertied and professional classes which were then gathering way. No fair-minded critic, whatever his own sympathies, will depreciate the beneficial effects which those improvements produced, not only on those who directly experienced them, but on the nation as a whole. The most enlightened of reformers, however, must work with the materials to his hand; and the public boarding-schools, whether reconstituted or newly founded, took, for good and for evil, the stamp of their day. The better among them owed much, and added much, to the practical energy, the admirable moral seriousness, the respect for the hard grind of the intellect, without fancies or frills, of Victorian England. All of them, including the best, were impoverished by the feebleness of the social spirit of the same England. All of them were the victims of its precipitous class divisions, its dreary cult of gentility, its inability to conceive of education as the symbol and cement of a spiritual unity transcending differences of birth and wealth.

Two features of the period, in particular, condemned those schools to a position which they could hardly, at the time—even had they wished it—have avoided, but which later were to prove both mischievous to the nation and humiliating to them. Since no public system of education existed, in which they could take their place, they came to form, as they rose in number and influence, a separate order of their own. They developed, not as partners in a community of educational effort, welcoming the obligations which such partnership imposes and zealous to bring their contributions to the common stock, but as the apostles of an exaggerated individualism, which, at first, perhaps, was inevitable, but which survived into an age when it was no longer a necessity forced upon them by the backwardness of public education, but a cherished idiosyncracy. Isolated from what were to be the main streams of the nation's educational life, and flattered by the eminent, they were under strong inducements to become the egoists

THE PROBLEM OF THE PUBLIC SCHOOLS

of the educational world, whose pride in the uniqueness of
their excellences was stronger than their eagerness to share
them. It cannot be said that they have been notably successful
in resisting that temptation. Since, in the second place, there
was no question in their seminal period of state grants to
secondary education, the public boarding-schools were
compelled, unless blessed with endowments, to finance
themselves from fees ; and their wares, being expensive, had
to be sold in a market in which price was a secondary consideration. Here again, at first, they had no alternative ; and,
here again, till recently, they do not seem to have sought one.
Towards the end of the decade of rapid educational development which followed the Act of 1902, it was suggested by
a headmaster—now a well-known national figure—that the
public schools should accept state-aid and public supervision,
in order both to improve the quality of their education and
to reduce its cost.[1] It may be doubted whether the Government of the day would have smiled on that proposal ; but,
while the number of day-schools on the grant-list has steadily
increased, and included in 1938 some sixty-five public schools,
the public boarding-schools, as far as known to the writer,
took at the time no step in that direction. Their social
character was already fixed, and history was too strong for
them. They had grown up as the servants, not of the nation,
but of one small stratum within it. Their pupils, their staffs,
their governing bodies, were drawn from a single class. The
conversion of a luxury trade for the well-to-do into one
supplying a less select clientèle is never an easy undertaking.
Either the schools concerned did not make the effort, or it
proved beyond their power.[2]

III.—The Case for Reform.

" The public schools," observed in 1909 Dr. Norwood
and Mr. Hope, " generally produce a race of well-bodied,
well-mannered, well-meaning boys, keen at games, devoted to
their schools, ignorant of life, contemptuous of all outside

[1] Cyril Norwood and Arthur H. Hope, *The Higher Education of Boys in England*,
especially pp. 186-196 and Part III, chap. V, " The Reform of the Public Schools," by
H. Lionel Rogers.

[2] It is possible that, in more recent times, the fault has been that of the State,
rather than of the schools. According to Sir Frank Fletcher (*The Journal of Education*,
Sept., 1941), " On more than one occasion representatives of these schools [*sc.* the
leading public schools] have approached the State authorities with suggestions and
offers of co-operation, and inquiries as to the possibility of opening wider our doors
to boys of all classes—or rather of all degrees of parental wealth or poverty. The
question for us has long been not whether this is desirable, but how it can be done."

THE POLITICAL QUARTERLY

the pale of their own caste, uninterested in work, neither desiring or revering knowledge. . . . A sound economy of finance would certainly result in a considerable reduction in the cost of a public school training, to the advantage both of the often sorely-taxed parent and of the public schools themselves, since they would gain in usefulness what they lost in exclusiveness."[1] There is reason to believe that the intellectual standards of all or most public schools have improved out of recognition in the last thirty years. Good judges, for example the Master of Balliol,[2] have paid tribute to the high quality of their educational work. It is probable that, were the authors of *Higher Education in England* writing today, their strictures on the mental stagnation of public school boys would be omitted or much modified.

That point should be emphasised, especially by a critic, both on grounds of justice and because it is obviously important that reform, whatever shape it may assume, should not impair educational values, but should preserve them and extend their influence. It cannot be said with equal confidence, however, that the social idiosyncracies of the schools in question have followed the contempt for knowledge into the limbo of the past. On the prevalence of the " caste " spirit, views, doubtless, will differ, though it is significant that observers from the Dominions and the United States—not to mention Scandinavia and France—are not slow to detect its presence and to lift their eyebrows at it. " Exclusiveness," of which that spirit is the natural product, is a matter, not of opinion, but of fact. The select character of the more expensive boarding-schools, which in the eyes of their feebler-minded clients is not the least among their assets, is maintained by a scale of fees which, though qualified by scholarships and concessions to parents, automatically restricts their use to the relatively well-to-do. They are the schools for the sons of parents—before 1939 perhaps 3 per cent[3] of the population— who can afford to pay £125 to £250 and upwards a year for the education of one child. They are, in fact, public schools from which the children of the great majority of the public are rigorously excluded. In such circumstances, the

---

[1] Norwood and Hope, *op. cit.*, pp. 187 and 189.

[2] *Picture Post*, 4.1.41. " Their [*sc.* the public schools'] faults are the result of the class division, but the all-round education they give is of very high quality."

[3] "In 1935 only 4 per cent of personal incomes in the U.K. exceeded £500 per annum, while incomes above £1,000 represented . . . 1.55 per cent of the population." (Leybourne and White, *op. cit.* p. 204.)

THE PROBLEM OF THE PUBLIC SCHOOLS

charge that they are class institutions cannot seriously be contested.

Educational policy is always social policy. In the England of the later nineteenth century, when the public school system was in the making, it could plausibly be argued that the recruitment of educational institutions on the basis of wealth, if in itself unedifying, was not out of tune with the temper of the day. In their subservience to money and social position, and the tranquil, unsophisticated class-consciousness which that subservience bred, the public boarding-schools, it might be said, did not rise above the standards of their generation, but neither did they fall below them. Their virtues were genuine and their own ; their vices were of a piece with those of the society about them. Whether convincing, or not, in the past, that defence is clearly out of date. Since the public school system assumed its present shape, England has become a political democracy. The public boarding-schools continue to serve the same tiny class as in the days when Lord Balfour was at Eton and Lord Baldwin at Harrow. A national system of education has not only been created in the interval, but has revealed un-anticipated possibilities of growth, and is now on the eve of the fourth chapter in its history. It is hardly an exaggeration to say that, as far as the contact with it of the great majority of the public boarding-schools goes, it might as well not exist.[1] Institutions so immune to the stresses and demands of a changing environment may enjoy some of the advantages of an old régime, but they suffer also from its weaknesses. It is not primarily a question of the attitude of headmasters, or even of governing bodies ; for representative figures among the former have expressed themselves strongly, if with reservations, in favour of reform, and the latter, however opaque their prejudices, could not prevent it, once it had become the national policy. It is a question of the reluctance

[1] The body best qualified to express an opinion on that point is the Association of Education Committees. Its verdict (*Education*, Dec. 25, 1942, p. 585) is as follows : " It is a common characteristic of both boarding and day [public] schools that they have no present association with the general educational system, and that they profess to make, and do in fact make, educational provision for a small section of the community. Internally their organisation and the character of their community life reflect the exclusiveness which necessarily flows from these qualities. Their external relationships are similarly affected in that they have no organic, and little informal, relationship with the general educational provision of the locality in which they are found. They tend to associate, naturally enough, having regard to their circumstances, with the section of the community for which they cater and also with those who are highly placed in church and state, the professions, and the business world, to whose ranks they contribute largely and altogether disproportionately."

THE POLITICAL QUARTERLY

of a small, but influential, class to acquiesce in interference with institutions which it has come to regard as peculiarly its own ; of its fears of the keener competition for posts of profit and distinction which will result from a diminution of educational inequalities ; of a temper which values the more exclusive public schools, not only as organs of culture, but as instruments of power ; of public indifference ; of the refusal of Governments, for each and all of these reasons, to take a thorny subject up. As a consequence, the public boarding-schools have been permitted to live in isolation from the educational needs of the mass of the population and from the system which serves them. What are the results of that policy ?

(1) Its first result is obvious. The rising generation is submitted in youth to a somewhat rigid system of educational segregation, which is also a system of social segregation. Whether Disraeli's famous epigram is still applicable or not to the adult population, it certainly remains true of the young, though, thanks to the development of public education, it is less true than in the recent past. Given the existing economic order, sharp class divisions exist independently of educational organisation and policy. It is unreasonable, therefore, to speak of the public boarding-schools as creating them. But education ought to be a solvent of such divisions. It is difficult to deny that the tendency of those schools is to deepen and perpetuate them. " The very existence of the public schools, as they now are," writes Mr. Simpson, himself formerly a master at one of them, " helps to keep the different social classes ignorant of one another, and aggravates misunderstanding to an extent which public school men commonly do not realise."[1] Is it possible convincingly to challenge that criticism ?

There is something to be said for preserving some schools only loosely connected with the national educational system, on the ground that their existence is favourable to initiative, experiment, and diversity of educational type. There is nothing whatever to be said for preserving schools whose distinctive characteristic is that they are recruited almost exclusively from the children of parents with larger incomes than their neighbours. That infliction on the young of the remorseless rigours of the economic calculus is mischievous for two reasons. It is unfair to them, and it is injurious to

[1] J. H. Simpson, *The Future of the Public Schools.*

130

THE PROBLEM OF THE PUBLIC SCHOOLS

society. Children learn from each other more than the most skilful of masters can teach them. Easy, natural and un-self-conscious contacts between young people of varying traditions and different social backgrounds are not the least valuable part of their education. They are not only a stimulating influence in youth, but the best preparation for an attitude which makes the most of life in later years. An educational system which discourages them is, to that extent, not a good system, but a bad one. The one-class school is not favourable to them. Not only is an obvious injustice done when children are excluded by financial barriers from the schools in question, but the pupils admitted to them are themselves injured. They are taught, not in words or of set purpose, but by the mere facts of their environment, that they are members, in virtue of the family bank-account, of a privileged group, whose function it will be, on however humble a scale, to direct and command, and to which leadership, influence, and the other prizes of life properly belong. The capacity of youth to protect itself against the imbecilities of its elders is not the least among the graces bestowed on it by Heaven; but that does not excuse us for going out of our way gratuitously to inflict our fatuities upon it. If some of the victims continue throughout life, as unhappily they do, to see the world through class spectacles, a policy which insists on their wearing them at school must bear part of the responsibility.

Nor, of course, is it only individuals who suffer from our erection of educational snobbery into a national institution. The nation, as a whole, pays a heavy price for it. The complicated business of democratic government demands, with the world as it is, a high capacity for co-operation; and co-operation, in its turn, depends on mutual understanding. A common educational background fosters such understanding. An organisation of education which treats different sections of the population as though they belonged to different species is an impediment to it. It is precisely such a treatment which is our present practice. Its effects on public life are heightened, of course, by other factors, but they remain only too visible.

The higher ranges of the British Civil Service have many virtues. What too frequently they lack is not intelligence, or expert knowledge, or public spirit, or devotion to duty. It is personal experience of the conditions of life and habits of thought of those for whose requirements in the matter of

THE POLITICAL QUARTERLY

health, housing, education and economic well-being, they are engaged in providing. That deficiency is serious. Yet how, as long as the schools attended by a somewhat high proportion of the individuals concerned are one-class schools which no common child can enter, can they be blamed for suffering from it ? There is no reason to suppose that the *personnel* of the British diplomatic service does not possess the same virtues in abundance. If, nevertheless, some of its members surprise friendly foreign observers by their inability to mix on easy terms with any but small cliques, the reason is partly the same. It is commonly not, as their exasperated critics are apt to complain, that they are swollen with British arrogance, but that they have been immolated in youth on the altar of good form. They have breathed at school the close atmosphere of a social sect, whose conventions they have learned to regard as the right thing. Too often they continue to mistake the provincialisms of a class for the interests and manners of civilised mankind. The co-existence of a public and a private educational system is not without influence on Parliament itself. It causes the economic lines between parties to coincide in large measure with educational lines. Such a coincidence is on all grounds unfortunate. It means that education, which should be the great uniter, becomes itself a ground of division, and that not a few members, even when they themselves have no interest at stake, approach questions of importance to the mass of their fellow-countrymen in a spirit, if not of hostility, of insolent indifference, which would hardly be possible had they and their opponents rubbed shoulders at school up to sixteen or eighteen. That spirit is apt to be seen at its worst when education itself is under discussion. Members who have served on Local Education Authorities can usually be relied on, irrespective of party, to show sense and good feeling ; they have seen the children and succumbed to them. Too many of the remainder—to judge by their behaviour—find it difficult to believe that the children of common persons are human in quite the same sense as their own. They have rarely themselves been educated in schools which are directly affected by parliamentary decisions on educational policy, nor do they often send their sons to them. They can hardly be expected—apart, of course, from bright exceptions —to regard the improvement of those schools as the urgent issue which it is. On any sane view, the preparation of

THE PROBLEM OF THE PUBLIC SCHOOLS

the young for life is among the greatest of common interests. When the economic divisions of the adult world are allowed to reproduce themselves in the educational system, it is difficult for that truism to win general recognition. Thus the evil legacy perpetuates itself.

(2) The resources of character and capacity at the disposal of the nation, if larger than is often supposed, are not unlimited. The course of wisdom for it, therefore, is to make certain of turning to the best account as much of both as it commands. It is to encourage an easy movement of ability to the types of education best calculated to cultivate it, and an easy movement, again, from educational institutions to the posts which such ability is qualified to fill. *La carrière ouverte aux talents*— promotion by merit—is neither the sole object of educational policy nor, in the view of the writer, the most important one ; but it is clearly an object which should be given its due weight. The immense tasks which confront the nation during the coming generation enhance its significance.

Success in attaining that end depends on the general educational and social policy of a country, not on any particular group of schools. But all schools should co-operate, according to their opportunities, in facilitating its attainment, and none should thwart or ignore it. The existence of schools recruited primarily by an income test obstructs it in two ways. It results, in the first place, in the misdirection of ability. The children of parents of small means, whatever their natural aptitudes for the types of education which the public boarding-schools provide, are prevented by their cost from obtaining access to them. The children of the well-to-do are not infrequently sent to such schools on account of the social prestige which they confer, even when they would benefit more by an education of a different sort. Educational mal-adjustments of the kind are unjust to individuals and injurious to the nation. They prevent it from making the best use of the talents at its disposal.

The second effect of a system of selection for higher education in which, not merely the personal qualities of the young, but the financial means of their parents, play a deter-mining part, is equally serious. It is unduly to narrow the area from which recruits for positions of responsibility are drawn in later life. It is sometimes said that the peculiar function of the public boarding-schools is to " educate for leadership," and that the social life which they offer specially

THE POLITICAL QUARTERLY

fits them for that task. But, before that claim can be conceded, two considerations must be weighed. In the first place, there is no such thing as leadership in the abstract. The qualities needed by a leader depend on the social environment in which he works, on the nature of the problems that he is called upon to solve, and not least—if his métier is government—on the political psychology of those who are to be led. All three have changed profoundly, both at home and abroad, in the last half-century, nor is there any probability that that process will be arrested. Even if it be admitted that the characteristics alleged to be fostered by education at a public boarding-school were an asset in the past, what grounds are there for supposing that they are those which the world requires most to-day, or that, if they are, a secondary day-school is incapable of cultivating them? In order, in the second place, that an institution may be successful in training leaders, it is not enough that it should provide an education well suited for that purpose; it is necessary also that it should cast its net wide. The way to pick a strong team of athletes is not to exclude from it everyone with less than £10 a week, but to consider all candidates for inclusion, irrespective of their economic circumstances, and then to choose them on their merits. The way to encourage able leadership is, in principle, the same. If a school begins by ruling out as ineligible all potential leaders who cannot satisfy an exacting income test, the individuals on whom it lavishes its skill will not be those best qualified to lead, but only—a very different thing—those best qualified among the small minority who alone can comply with that initial requirement. Of course, if it is content merely to count among its old boys men who, for one reason or another, have reached positions of prominence, then money and social influence have hitherto been good horses to back. But that version of the venerable pastime of spotting the winner can hardly be intended, when the public boarding-schools are praised as the nurseries of the nation's leaders.

In reality, education for leadership, especially in a democracy, is not a simple matter. It is a question, not only of intensive cultivation, but of a wide range of selection; not only of the education of pupils actually admitted to schools, but of the principles determining the admission of some and the exclusion of others. It is likely to be a success when the right kind of education is easily accessible to those

THE PROBLEM OF THE PUBLIC SCHOOLS

best qualified to profit by it. When such education is surrounded by high financial hedges, the education itself may
still be good, but, as an aid to the production of able leadership,
it is likely to be a failure. Considered from that point of
view, the limitations of the English educational system appear
somewhat serious. No adequate statistical evidence[1] exists
showing the schools from which persons eminent in different
walks of life are drawn; nor in the nature of things, can such
evidence be up-to-date. Such scraps of information, however,
as are available suggest that Great Britain draws on the
capacity of all its citizens to a less degree than do, for example,
the United States and the Dominions, and that leadership in
politics, administration and finance is recruited—less exclusively, indeed than in the past, but still predominantly—not
from the population as a whole but from the small circle of
families—perhaps 3 per cent of the nation—who can afford
to pay for an expensive education. In the words of the
Economist,[2] " the public schools turn out, perhaps, 10,000
boys a year; from this tiny fraction we select the great
majority of those who are to be given an easy road to
the top. The selection is clearly not one of merit." Here,
again, the primary responsibility is less that of the schools
concerned than of a public which is at once indulgent to
educational privilege and parsimonious in providing for the
adequate development of secondary education. The consequences of its attitude are, however, somewhat serious. A
nation which permits the continuance of the state of things
described by the *Economist* is grappling with its problems
with one hand tied behind its back.

(3) If an educational system is to mobilise its full power,
it is not sufficient that each of the institutions composing it
should make the most of its own virtues without regard to
the remainder. It is necessary that all of them should play
their varying rôles as conscious partners in a common effort.
The pedantries of over-organisation are, of course, to be
avoided; but so also is a selfish or capricious individualism.
There should be a general recognition that, while a good
school is a community with distinctive characteristics, every
school has responsibilities, not merely to its immediate
clientèle, but to the nation as a whole; and such a relation

[1] Statistics of the schools attended by 691 persons eminent in different walks of life
will be found in the writer's *Equality*, App. I. They show that 524 (75.8 per cent)
were educated at a public school, and 330 (47.7 per cent) at one or other of fourteen
principal public schools.
[2] The *Economist*, Nov. 23, 1940.

THE POLITICAL QUARTERLY

should exist between all schools and the State as to ensure that those responsibilities are not ignored. It is not a question of mechanical systematisation, but of co-operation within a framework which finds room for wide diversities of educational type, but ensures that such diversities contribute to the common end of an educated nation.

If, judged by that standard, the public boarding-schools of to-day leave something to be desired, it is history, rather than any wilful perversity, which must be regarded as the culprit. Most of them were firmly established at a time when public education was still in its infancy. But a position of isolation, which was inevitable in the past, is unnecessary to-day, and, being needless, has become mischievous. Unfortunately, it still continues. The schools in question touch the public educational system at its apex, through their connection with the Universities ; but, being fed by expensive preparatory schools, they are rarely in touch with its lower ranges. Receiving, in most cases, no grants, they are not subject to the secondary regulations of the Board, and their contacts with it are at present confined to the voluntary acceptance of inspection by its officials. Between them and the Local Education Authorities, with their six million children and quarter of a million or so teachers, direct contacts hardly exist. The team-spirit, which leads individuals to play for their side rather than for themselves, is commonly counted among the public school virtues. It cannot be said that those schools themselves are a shining example of it. Like the Cyclops, "each governs his own children, nor do they trouble about their neighbours."

That state of things is not confined to the public boarding-schools. It is a particular case of the general problem arising from the existence of a multitude of private schools, with which no public authority has power to interfere. Its disadvantages are somewhat serious. If the nation is to make the most effective use of its educational resources, it must be in a position to bring them all under review, and to act on the conclusions which a comprehensive survey suggests. As long as one small group of important schools, and many thousand schools of inferior standing, are completely or predominantly outside the purview of the Board and the Local Education Authorities, such action is impossible. It is conceivable that the number of boarding-schools is excessive, and that some of them would be of greater service

THE PROBLEM OF THE PUBLIC SCHOOLS

if converted into day-schools. No public authority has power to reduce it, or even to prevent the foundation of additional schools of the same type. It is clearly desirable that the arrangements as to the admission of pupils to different types of secondary schools should be sufficiently similar not to impose needless obstacles on the entry of boys suited for this type or that. The fact that one group of schools is private, and another public, makes a reasonable measure of co-operation needlessly difficult of attainment. Other things being equal, diversity of social and educational experience in teaching staffs, and the easy movement of teachers between schools of different types, are an asset. Both tend to be discouraged by the same sharp cleavage. Sympathy is naturally evoked by the claim of schools for freedom to develop each its own special *ethos* and educational methods. Matters of school government and finance, however, including, where they exist, endowments and the management of boarding-houses, stand in a different category. It is not satisfactory that governing bodies should be as heavily weighted as some are at present with decorative notabilities, to the exclusion or under-representation of public education authorities ; or that fees and other costs, which are stated by a headmaster[1] to have risen greatly in the course of the last generation, should be subject to no form of public control ; or that no public authority should be responsible for seeing that the domestic economy of public boarding-schools—an aspect of school life which is not, after all, the speciality of teachers—is conducted on modern lines, and with reasonable regard to economy and efficiency. It is probable that, as far as matters of this kind are concerned, not only the public, but the schools themselves, have everything to gain from the pressure of a central authority which can pool the experience of a number of different institutions, and correct individual aberrations or laxities by reference to a range of knowledge which no single one of them can command.

IV.—Suggestions for a Policy.

The criticisms made above contain nothing novel. Nearly all of them have been from time to time advanced since, at least, the assumption by the State, in the opening decade of the present century, of the responsibility for creating an

[1] " The Future of the Public Schools," by W. F. Bushell, in *The Journal of Education*, November, 1940.

THE POLITICAL QUARTERLY

efficient system of secondary education. Nor does it appear
that the spokesmen of the public boarding-schools themselves
are unanimous in rejecting them. Leading headmasters,[1] while
emphasising that such schools have an important contribution
to make, and that a large measure of freedom is the condition
of their making it, have deplored their inaccessibility to
boys of small means ; have insisted that costs and fees can
and should be reduced ; and have urged that they " should
come to occupy a recognised place within the State system."[2]
A reasonable conclusion from recent discussions of the
question would appear to be that the existence of a group of
schools reserved for the sons of the well-to-do, and divorced
almost completely from the public educational system,
whatever its justification in the past, is commonly recognised
to be no longer defensible. If that view be accepted, to
what policy should it lead ?

The tradition of English educational policy is one of
reluctant innovation. It handles particular issues piece-meal,
when they can no longer be ignored, but has rarely been
disposed to consider them in relation to the larger problems
of which they form part. The feature of the public boarding-
schools which arouses most criticism is their social exclusiveness. It is natural, therefore, that the first proposal to be
advanced should be one for mitigating it. The suggestion
which hitherto has received most attention is that some
version of the special place system, under which, since 1907,
secondary schools aided by the State have been required to
take a certain percentage of pupils from elementary schools,
should be applied to the public boarding-schools. Several
headmasters have recently advanced the same proposal, and
the governing bodies of some schools have approached
neighbouring Local Education Authorities with an offer to
act on it. It is likely, it may be suspected, to figure prominently
among the subjects considered by the recently-appointed
Committee on Public Schools.

The free place—since 1933 the special place—system has
a distinguished history. In its present form, it is out of date,
since we can now do better ; but it has done more, nevertheless, than any other agency to build a bridge from the
elementary schools to secondary education. Nine-tenths of
the cheaper public schools, the great majority of whose

[1] Articles and letters by public school headmasters will be found in the *Journal of Education* for November and December, 1940, and January, 1941.
[2] *Journal of Education*, November, 1940, letters by C. Russell Scott and W. F. Bushell.

THE PROBLEM OF THE PUBLIC SCHOOLS

pupils are day-boys, are required to provide special places. How many boarding-schools are in present circumstances needed is a question for consideration; but, on the assumption that some such schools continue to exist, an analagous requirement in the case of those schools, which, with few exceptions, provide at present no special places, may properly be one element in any programme of reform. It is, however, only one element. To see in it a substitute for other equally essential measures would be as unreasonable as it would have been, in the early years of the present century, to regard article 20 of the then secondary school code as rendering superfluous its remaining provisions. Two points, in particular, require to be considered. The first, and most important, is the educational value of the special place system to the boys affected by it. The second relates to the liabilities which it involves for the authorities administering it.

The object of the special place system has been to make secondary education accessible to pupils in the elementary schools whose parents cannot afford the full fees. Its success has been partly due to the fact that it has combined the provision of educational opportunities with the minimum disturbance of the children's normal life. Not only do the holders of special places continue to live at home, but the schools which they enter, though often greatly superior in staffing, equipment and amenities to those which they leave, are largely, and often predominantly, attended by pupils of much the same social background as themselves. Difficulties sometimes arise; but, on the whole, the children concerned enter an environment not too different from their own, play their part in creating the social atmosphere of the school, mix on equal terms with young people some of whom they already know, and normally suffer neither from the sense of inferiority nor the tendency to exaggerated self-assertion, which are apt to be the fate of the boy whose surroundings impress on him that he is a rare exception. It would be rash to suggest that such conditions cannot exist in the case of boys transferred from elementary or grant-aided secondary schools to the more expensive boarding-schools, as the latter today are; but it can hardly be denied that they must be much more difficult of establishment. They are not likely to exist unless the proportion which such boys form of the total in-take is, not a mere trickle, but sufficiently large to enable them to exercise a decisive influence on the character of the schools;

THE POLITICAL QUARTERLY

unless it is made evident by the treatment of all places as special places that the schools are recruited on the basis of promise, not wealth; unless their living conditions are simplified and cheapened; and unless the composition of their governing bodies is radically changed.

Such reforms are, in any case, desirable; and the fact that they are necessary in order to make a special place policy a success is no argument against it. But clearly they imply a much more drastic interference with the residential public schools than is involved in the mere requirement that they shall admit a certain proportion of pupils from elementary or secondary schools. The truth is that this aspect of the subject has been gratuitously bedevilled by a fog of unconscious cant. It is sometimes implied that the public schools will be "democratised," if, while remaining predominantly academies for young gentlemen, they consent to confer on a few deserving proletarians the inestimable boon of admission to them. To that well-meant, but ill-thought-out, suggestion more than one answer will be given; it is to be feared that the least impolite will be, "Thank you for nothing." The logic of democracy involves, not the stabilisation of the educational privileges now enjoyed by wealth through their nicely-rationed extension to a few more participants, but their complete abolition. What the nation requires is, not more gentlemen, but more men with sufficient sense not to care whether they and their neighbours are gentlemen or not. If the public schools can help to produce them, the more widely their education is shared the better. If they cannot, they had better keep it to themselves, and leave the civic virtues to less fastidious institutions. The fundamental question, in short, is different from that which is usually posed. It is not how to select sons of common persons who are " capable of profiting " by attendance at a public boarding-school. It is how to modify the atmosphere, outlook, and manner of life of the more expensive boarding-schools in such a way as to make it beneficial for ordinary boys to attend them.

The administrative aspects of a special place policy require also to be considered. The problem of the age of admission is one, though not the most important, of them. Grant-aided secondary schools admit the majority of entrants between eleven and twelve; public boarding-schools between thirteen and fourteen. Various expedients have been suggested for

THE PROBLEM OF THE PUBLIC SCHOOLS

bridging the gap. Public schools could establish preparatory or junior departments, as some already have, in which case they would receive boys from schools in the public educational system at the end of the primary stage ; or they could admit boys from secondary schools between thirteen and fourteen ; or they could make the normal age of admission eleven *plus*, and reserve certain places for boys entering later from preparatory schools. It is possible, though not certain, that, given co-operation between the public boarding-schools and the Local Education Authorities—a condition not yet realised—this difficulty could be overcome. But what would be the effect on the secondary schools of the diversion or withdrawal of their ablest pupils, and of the relegation of those schools to the position of a second-best ?

The problems arising on the side of finance will not be negligible. The average boarding-fee of the cheapest group of public schools was, in 1938, £82–£83; that of the more expensive £121–£122, that of the thirty-seven aristocrats of the system £169–£170, while the fees charged by particular schools in the last group ran up to £250 or more. The average cost of a free place in a grant-aided secondary school was, on the eve of the war, in the region of £28 16s.[1] The difference is somewhat formidable. It means that the average expenditure required to educate one boy at one of the least expensive boarding-schools would educate between two and three boys at a day-school, and that between five and six boys could be educated at a day-school for one boy educated at a boarding-school in the most expensive group. That consideration is not, of course, decisive ; but the disparity of costs, even if reduced by the abolition of tuition fees, must be taken into account in planning the development of secondary education. It raises certain further issues. If the whole cost of special places at boarding-schools is to fall on the schools themselves, public authorities are not directly affected by it ; but, in that case, since few schools have large endowments, the number of special places admitted is likely to be small. If, on the other hand, the costs of special places at such schools are to be defrayed in the same way as are the costs of those at grant-aided secondary schools, by Local Education Authorities and the Board, it will be necessary for these bodies to satisfy themselves that the costs of a school place are not needlessly inflated, as some head

[1] The figure is for the year 1936–37.

THE POLITICAL QUARTERLY

masters have alleged that they are.[1] " The public schools," remarks one them, desire that their education " should be available to as large a number of boys as possible. If this is to be done, the nation will have to spend money ; but it should not be asked to spend more money than necessary."[2] That view is likely to command general assent. What precisely it involves is a matter for consideration ; but it points to, at any rate, the public control of costs at boarding-schools, and to the adequate representation of public authorities on their governing bodies. Here, again, therefore, the extension of the special place system to those schools will necessarily lead to certain further changes. It ought not, in short, to be introduced as an isolated measure, but only as part of a more general scheme of reform.

" There seems to be general agreement," wrote, two years ago, Mr. Salter Davies, " that the public schools should open their doors to a certain number of free place scholars from the elementary schools. This would be a useful beginning, but it provides no real solution. It would be a fatal mistake to rest content with first-aid treatment when a major operation is needed. . . . The public schools must become public in fact, and not merely in name."[3] The recent report of the Association of Education Committees, which rejects a special place policy as futile in the absence of " the full acceptance by the independent schools of those principles of equality of educational opportunity which the Association believe to be fundamental," says, in effect, the same. What is the nature of " the major operation " required ? What must be done if the public schools are to become " public in fact " ? The proposals made below suggest some tentative answers to those questions.

I.—Independent Schools : general provisions.

It is essential that all independent schools, whether private schools or public schools, should be brought under public supervision. They should be required, as recommended by the Association of Directors and Secretaries for Education,[4] to hold a licence from the Board of Education, to be

[1] *Journal of Education,* November, 1940, " The Public Schools and the Nation," by Hugh Elder, and " The Future of the Public Schools," by W. F. Bushell.
[2] *Ibid.* Hugh Elder, *loc. cit.*
[3] *Journal of Education,* November, 1940, leading article.
[4] *Education : a Plan for the Future,* pp. 14-15. The Report on educational reconstruction prepared for the Association of Education Committees also recommends " the licensing and effective supervision on behalf of the State of all private schools."

THE PROBLEM OF THE PUBLIC SCHOOLS

granted, in the case of local schools, after consultation with the Local Education Authority. The condition of granting such a licence would be that the schools were open to inspection, and that they complied with such requirements as the Board may lay down.

The effect of this proposal would be (1) that some 10,000[1] private schools, with perhaps 350,000 to 400,000 pupils, of which little is at present known, would be brought under the review of the Board and the Local Education Authorities. Some of them, possibly many of them, would be refused a licence, and would cease to exist. Some of them would continue, but on conditions approved by the Board and the Local Education Authorities; (2) that public schools, whether day-schools or boarding-schools, not at present in receipt of grants, would be required to be licensed, to comply with the Board's requirements, and to be inspected. Such schools numbered sixty-six in 1938. The majority of them are predominantly boarding-schools, thirty-four with fees of £150 and over, and twenty-seven with fees of £100–£149.

II.—Public Day-Schools.

The majority of public schools which are predominantly day-schools are already in receipt of grant, and must comply with the Board's Secondary Regulations. Their future depends, therefore, on the general policy of the country with regard to secondary education. Fees at secondary schools should, of course, be abolished, and all pupils should be admitted on the basis of the same test. Governing bodies should be required to include a majority of representative governors, appointed partly by Local Education Authorities, partly by the Board. When these reforms have been carried out, they will automatically apply to the day public schools receiving grant, in the same way as to other grant-aided schools. The only point which calls for special notice arises from the fact that the majority of the former are now " direct grant " schools. That position represents a concession accorded them in the past, when a public system of secondary education was in its infancy. There may be special circumstances in which it is still justified; but, now that experience has shown that Local Education Authorities can be responsible for secondary schools without impairing

[1] Report of Departmental Committee on Independent Schools (1932), p. 21.

their liberty, interfering with their teachers, inflicting party politics upon them, or otherwise injuring their *moral*, the case for that exceptional status has lost much of its validity. No additions, therefore, should be made to the list of schools receiving direct grant, and proposals from Local Education Authorities to become responsible for schools now on the list should receive favourable consideration from the Board.

III.—Public Boarding-Schools.
(1) There is nothing novel in the provision of State-aid for public day-schools. The only question which arises in their case—namely, that of the conditions on which aid is to be given—is one common to all schools on the grant-list. The public schools which cater predominantly for boarders are in a different position. A few of these also receive grant, but the great majority do not. The latter include all the more expensive schools, with fees of £150 and upwards.

The suggestion now made that the State should aid these schools is sometimes discussed in general terms, as though it involved financial assistance to all public boarding-schools desiring it and willing to comply with certain minimum requirements. Such a policy of indiscriminate assistance would be an error. In the first place, even if it is agreed that some boarding-schools ought to have a place within the national system of education, it is necessary to decide the number of such schools which, under present conditions, is required. In the second place, public boarding-schools, like other schools, vary widely in quality, and there is no reason to think that all of them are equally worth preserving. In the third place, the residential education which is the distinctive feature of the boarding-school need not necessarily aim at the same objects, or cover the same span of life, as are usual at present, and it is important to define the particular purposes to be served by the boarding-schools which it is decided to maintain. The first essential, therefore, is an investigation to determine (*a*) how many boarding-schools it is expedient to maintain in existence, (*b*) what schools are to be included in that number, (*c*) what special functions such schools are to perform. Until the results of such an inquiry are available, no offer of financial assistance to boarding-schools not already in receipt of it should be made.

(2) If it is desired to make the public schools accessible to boys of small means, the most effective and economical

THE PROBLEM OF THE PUBLIC SCHOOLS

method of doing so is obvious. It is to increase the number of day-boys. Two steps, it is suggested, ought to be taken. The first is to convert—sometimes to re-convert—into day-schools those boarding-schools which are situated in areas sufficiently populous to ensure them an adequate local clientèle. The second is to require those boarding-schools which, owing to the absence of that condition, must continue to cater predominantly for boarders to admit as large a proportion of day-boys as local circumstances allow.

The scale on which the first policy can be applied must obviously depend partly on the decision reached as to the number of residential schools required. Subject to that qualification, there is a strong presumption in favour of it. Not only, when practicable, is it the simplest method of establishing equality of access to public schools, but it is desirable for its own sake, and meets a demand which appears to be growing. Since about 1930, the tide which for long ran in favour of boarding-schools seems to have turned, and to have flowed for a time in the opposite direction. The population[1] of public boarding-schools diminished; that of public day-schools increased. That spontaneous movement may mean that the present supply of residential schools is excessive; but it is, in any case, to be warmly welcomed. Higher secondary education ought not to be concentrated in a few great centres, but to be widely diffused. Nothing would do more to heighten the intellectual vitality of English life, and to stimulate a healthy pride in local educational achievements, than the existence, not only in a few great cities, but in all considerable towns, of more day-schools resembling the best of those now in existence. There is no reason, of course, why some boarders should not be admitted to such schools; but the object of the step proposed would be to substitute day-schools, with a minority of boarders, for boarding-schools, with a minority of day-boys. The second policy—the admission to schools which are predominantly residential of a greatly increased number of day-boys—has been strongly urged by eminent head masters.[2] It is to be supported on condition—and only on condition—that the day-boys are sufficiently numerous not to be damned with a tepid toleration, but to enter fully into the life of the school, and to play an equal part with the boarders in determining its character.

[1] For facts see Leybourne and White, *op. cit.*, pp. 207-11.
[2] E.g. by Sir Frank Fletcher, in the *Journal of Education*, September, 1940.

THE POLITICAL QUARTERLY

If these reforms are to be carried through on an adequate scale and in a reasonable period, it must not be left to individual schools to initiate them, or not, as they think fit. They must become part of the educational policy of the nation. The Board should make a survey of existing residential schools, to ascertain the practicability of acting on these proposals in particular cases. It should then determine (*a*) which of these schools can with advantage be converted into day-schools, (*b*) what proportion of day-boys boarding-schools not so converted shall be required to admit. The schools in the first category would be subject to the secondary regulations of the Board. The schools in the second should be treated in the manner suggested in the following section.

(3) The policy suggested above would substantially increase the number of day-schools. There would still remain, however, a small group of schools some of which possibly could and should admit a larger number of day-boys, but which, being situated in sparsely-populated areas, would continue to be predominantly boarding-schools. It is these schools, some of them highly expensive and exclusive, which occur to the minds of most hearers when the public schools are mentioned.

The distinctive peculiarity of these schools is their residential character. It is a curious feature of the recent discussion of the public schools that the question of the special educational rôle of residence, as distinct from day attendance, has received little detailed examination. The defenders of boarding-schools appear to take it for granted that, if it is good for a boy to go to a boarding-school at all, it is necessarily good for him to remain there, as commonly to-day, for four to five years. The critics of the boarding-schools similarly seem to assume that, if they disapprove of that arrangement, they are thereby committed to denying that residence away from home can play under any conditions whatever a useful part in secondary education. Neither attitude is reasonable. Some boarding-schools of the existing type will probably continue to be required for boys in special circumstances, for example for the sons of parents living abroad; but the conditions which in the past set a premium on the boarding-school have largely disappeared. It is quite possible to believe, therefore, that boarding-schools have a valuable contribution to make, but to hold, with the Association of Education

THE PROBLEM OF THE PUBLIC SCHOOLS

Committees, that they would make it most effectively if, instead of providing four or five years' residential education for a small minority of boys, they provided it for a shorter period and for a larger number. The most useful future before some such schools may consist, for example, in supplying facilities for an advanced secondary education after sixteen for boys who have attended the secondary day-schools of a given area ; that of others in offering a secondary education closely related to the life and work of rural society ; that of a third group, in serving, as Mr. J. H. Simpson[1] has proposed, as centres to which secondary schools can send groups of boys for six to twelve months of residential education. What is needed, in short, is to cease to take for granted the routine inherited from the nineteenth century, and to consider the distinctive functions of the boarding-school in the light of the novel conditions of to-day.

Such possibilities ought to receive more consideration than has hitherto been given them. They would mean, if translated into practice, that the residential school of the future, instead of providing the whole secondary education of a small minority of well-to-do boys, would meet the needs of one stage in the education of a larger number, and ultimately, perhaps, if the new departures proved a success, of the great majority. Like most educational reforms, proposals of the kind will continue, no doubt, to be dismissed as moon-shine, until they come to be acted on, when the schools planned in accordance with them will be described as institutions peculiarly characteristic of the British genius, each blessed with a distinctive tradition of immemorial antiquity, and all offering unique opportunities for the training of character and education for leadership. In the meantime, it is necessary, in view of the suggestion that the public boarding-schools should receive financial aid from the State, to consider what other changes in their position are required. The following measures would be a step in the right direction :

(*a*) All non-local boarding-schools should be brought under public supervision, in the manner suggested in I above.

(*b*) The governing bodies of such schools should be constituted in a manner to be laid down by the Board, and should include a majority of governors consisting of

[1] See his pamphlet, *The Future of the Public Schools*.

THE POLITICAL QUARTERLY

representatives of Local Education Authorities nominated by national organisations, such as the Association of Education Committees and the County Councils Association, together with representatives of other social and educational interests appointed by the Board.

(c) The financial arrangements of such schools, including tuition fees, unless abolished, boarding-house charges, the administration of endowments (if any) and similar matters should be under the supervision of the Board. Some headmasters have expressed the view that the costs of boarding-schools are sometimes at present unnecessarily high. It should be the duty of the Board to examine living costs, and, where practicable, to reduce them. The idea to be aimed at is the maximum simplification of living conditions which is compatible with health and efficiency.

(d) Were those changes effected, the criticisms made above on a special place policy, though valid as long as that policy stands by itself, would lose part of their force. But the mere infiltration into public boarding-schools of a small minority of pupils from elementary and secondary schools would still remain of little value. Such boys should enter in substantial numbers, or not enter at all. All places should be special places. Selection for admission should be made by committees representing, in addition to the boarding-schools concerned, the Local Education Authorities and the public teaching profession.

V.—Conclusion.

Such proposals will, of course, be denounced as revealing a totalitarian contempt for educational freedom. If educational freedom requires that a small group of relatively well-to-do families shall be entitled, in virtue of their incomes, to monopolise the use of one group of educational institutions, and that the authorities controlling them shall be under no obligation to consider, in planning their arrangements, the needs of the majority who are differently circumstanced, the criticism is justified. The writer does not share that view. He regards the prevalent practice of recruiting the more expensive public schools from a single class, not only as an injustice to the young people excluded, but as injurious to the pupils educated in those schools, as well as to society. Even were he, however, of a different opinion on that point, he would still desire to see the social exclusiveness of those

THE PROBLEM OF THE PUBLIC SCHOOLS

schools completely ended, and the schools themselves made part of the public educational system.

Educational freedom, like other kinds of freedom, does not consist in the right of every individual to use such economic advantages as he may happen to possess in order to secure special privileges for himself and his children, or in the unfettered discretion of those who control educational resources to employ them, if they think fit, to gratify that natural, but anti-social, egotism. It is a reality in so far as, and only in so far as, education is organised in a manner to enable all, whatever their economic circumstances, to make the most of the powers with which they are endowed. No single group of institutions can make more than a small contribution to that end. It is none the less its duty, and should be its pride, to contribute to it what it can. To serve educational needs, without regard to the vulgar irrelevancies of class and income, is part of the teacher's honour. Schools claiming to represent the best that English secondary education has to show should be the first to offer an example of that spirit.

[9]

SOCIAL INSURANCE AND ALLIED SERVICES

PART I

INTRODUCTION AND SUMMARY

1. The Inter-departmental Committee on Social Insurance and Allied Services were appointed in June, 1941, by the Minister without Portfolio, then responsible for the consideration of reconstruction problems. The terms of reference required the Committee " to undertake, with special reference to the inter-relation of the schemes, a survey of the existing national schemes of social insurance and allied services, including workmen's compensation and to make recommendations." The first duty of the Committee was to survey, the second to recommend. For the reasons stated below in paragraph 40 the duty of recommendation was confined later to the Chairman of the Committee.

THE COMMITTEE'S SURVEY AND ITS RESULTS

2. The schemes of social insurance and allied services which the Inter-departmental Committee have been called on to survey have grown piece-meal. Apart from the Poor Law, which dates from the time of Elizabeth, the schemes surveyed are the product of the last 45 years beginning with the Workmen's Compensation Act, 1897. That Act, applying in the first instance to a limited number of occupations, was made general in 1906. Compulsory health insurance began in 1912. Unemployment insurance began for a few industries in 1912 and was made general in 1920. The first Pensions Act, giving non-contributory pensions subject to a means test at the age of 70, was passed in 1908. In 1925 came the Act which started contributory pensions for old age, for widows and for orphans. Unemployment insurance, after a troubled history, was put on a fresh basis by the Unemployment Act of 1934, which set up at the same time a new national service of Unemployment Assistance. Meantime, the local machinery for relief of destitution, after having been exhaustively examined by the Royal Commission of 1905-1909, has been changed both by the new treatment of unemployment and in many other ways, including a transfer of the responsibilities of the Boards of Guardians to Local Authorities. Separate provision for special types of disability—such as blindness—has been made from time to time. Together with this growth of social insurance and impinging on it at many points have gone developments of medical treatment, particularly in hospitals and other institutions ; developments of services devoted to the welfare of children, in school and before it ; and a vast growth of voluntary provision for death and other contingencies, made by persons of the insured classes through Industrial Life Offices, Friendly Societies and Trade Unions.

3. In all this change and development, each problem has been dealt with separately, with little or no reference to allied problems. The first task of the Committee has been to attempt for the first time a comprehensive survey of the whole field of social insurance and allied services, to show just what provision is now made and how it is made for many different forms of need. The results of this survey are set out in Appendix B describing social insurance and the allied services as they exist today in Britain. The picture presented is impressive in two ways. First, it shows that provision for most of the many varieties of need through interruption of earnings and other causes that may arise in modern industrial communities has already been made in Britain on a scale not surpassed and hardly rivalled in any other country of the world. In one respect only of the first importance, namely limitation of medical service, both in the range of treatment which is provided as of right and in respect of the classes of persons for whom it is provided, does Britain's achievement fall seriously short of what has been accomplished elsewhere ; it falls

6

short also in its provision for cash benefit for maternity and funerals and through the defects of its system for workmen's compensation. In all other fields British provision for security, in adequacy of amount and in comprehensiveness, will stand comparison with that of any other country ; few countries will stand comparison with Britain. Second, social insurance and the allied services, as they exist today, are conducted by a complex of disconnected administrative organs, proceeding on different principles, doing invaluable service but at a cost in money and trouble and anomalous treatment of identical problems for which there is no justification. In a system of social security better on the whole than can be found in almost any other country there are serious deficiencies which call for remedy.

4. Thus limitation of compulsory insurance to persons under contract of service and below a certain remuneration if engaged on non-manual work is a serious gap. Many persons working on their own account are poorer and more in need of State insurance than employees ; the remuneration limit for non-manual employees is arbitrary and takes no account of family responsibility. There is, again, no real difference between the income needs of persons who are sick and those who are unemployed, but they get different rates of benefit involving different contribution conditions and with meaningless distinctions between persons of different ages. An adult insured man with a wife and two children receives 38/- per week should he become unemployed ; if after some weeks of unemployment he becomes sick and not available for work, his insurance income falls to 18/-. On the other hand a youth of 17 obtains 9/- when he is unemployed, but should he become sick his insurance income rises to 12/- per week. There are, to take another example, three different means tests for non-contributory pensions, for supplementary pensions and for public assistance, with a fourth test—for unemployment assistance—differing from that for supplementary pensions in some particulars.

5. Many other such examples could be given ; they are the natural result of the way in which social security has grown in Britain. It is not open to question that, by closer co-ordination, the existing social services could be made at once more beneficial and more intelligible to those whom they serve and more economical in their administration.

THREE GUIDING PRINCIPLES OF RECOMMENDATIONS

6. In proceeding from this first comprehensive survey of social insurance to the next task—of making recommendations—three guiding principles may be laid down at the outset.

7. The first principle is that any proposals for the future, while they should use to the full the experience gathered in the past, should not be restricted by consideration of sectional interests established in the obtaining of that experience. Now, when the war is abolishing landmarks of every kind, is the opportunity for using experience in a clear field. A revolutionary moment in the world's history is a time for revolutions, not for patching.

8. The second principle is that organisation of social insurance should be treated as one part only of a comprehensive policy of social progress. Social insurance fully developed may provide income security ; it is an attack upon Want. But Want is one only of five giants on the road of reconstruction and in some ways the easiest to attack. The others are Disease, Ignorance, Squalor and Idleness.

9. The third principle is that social security must be achieved by co-operation between the State and the individual. The State should offer security for service and contribution. The State in organising security should

7

not stifle incentive, opportunity, responsibility ; in establishing a national minimum, it should leave room and encouragement for voluntary action by each individual to provide more than that minimum for himself and his family.

10. The Plan for Social Security set out in this Report is built upon these principles. It uses experience but is not tied by experience. It is put forward as a limited contribution to a wider social policy, though as something that could be achieved now without waiting for the whole of that policy. It is, first and foremost, a plan of insurance—of giving in return for contributions benefits up to subsistence level, as of right and without means test, so that individuals may build freely upon it.

The Way to Freedom from Want

11. The work of the Inter-departmental Committee began with a review of existing schemes of social insurance and allied services. The Plan for Social Security, with which that work ends, starts from a diagnosis of want— of the circumstances in which, in the years just preceding the present war, families and individuals in Britain might lack the means of healthy subsistence. During those years impartial scientific authorities made social surveys of the conditions of life in a number of principal towns in Britain, including London, Liverpool, Sheffield, Plymouth, Southampton, York and Bristol. They determined the proportions of the people in each town whose means were below the standard assumed to be necessary for subsistence, and they analysed the extent and causes of that deficiency. From each of these social surveys the same broad result emerges. Of all the want shown by the surveys, from three-quarters to five-sixths, according to the precise standard chosen for want, was due to interruption or loss of earning power. Practically the whole of the remaining one-quarter to one-sixth was due to failure to relate income during earning to the size of the family. These surveys were made before the introduction of supplementary pensions had reduced the amount of poverty amongst old persons. But this does not affect the main conclusion to be drawn from these surveys : abolition of want requires a double re-distribution of income, through social insurance and by family needs.

12. Abolition of want requires, first, improvement of State insurance, that is to say provision against interruption and loss of earning power. All the principal causes of interruption or loss of earnings are now the subject of schemes of social insurance. If, in spite of these schemes, so many persons unemployed or sick or old or widowed are found to be without adequate income for subsistence according to the standards adopted in the social surveys, this means that the benefits amount to less than subsistence by those standards or do not last as long as the need, and that the assistance which supplements insurance is either insufficient in amount or available only on terms which make men unwilling to have recourse to it. None of the insurance benefits provided before the war were in fact designed with reference to the standards of the social surveys. Though unemployment benefit was not altogether out of relation to those standards, sickness and disablement benefit, old age pensions and widows' pensions were far below them, while workmen's compensation was below subsistence level for anyone who had family responsibilities or whose earnings in work were less than twice the amount needed for subsistence. To prevent interruption or destruction of earning power from leading to want, it is necessary to improve the present schemes of social insurance in three directions : by extension of scope to cover persons now excluded, by extension of purposes to cover risks now excluded, and by raising the rates of benefit.

13. Abolition of want requires, second, adjustment of incomes, in periods of earning as well as in interruption of earning, to family needs, that is to say,

8

in one form or another it requires allowances for children. Without such allowances as part of benefit or added to it, to make provision for large families, no social insurance against interruption of earnings can be adequate. But, if children's allowances are given only when earnings are interrupted and are not given during earning also, two evils are unavoidable. First, a substantial measure of acute want will remain among the lower paid workers as the accompaniment of large families. Second, in all such cases, income will be greater during unemployment or other interruptions of work than during work.

14. By a double re-distribution of income through social insurance and children's allowances, want, as defined in the social surveys, could have been abolished in Britain before the present war. As is shown in para. 445, the income available to the British people was ample for such a purpose. The Plan for Social Security set out in Part V of this Report takes abolition of want after this war as its aim. It includes as its main method compulsory social insurance, with national assistance and voluntary insurance as subsidiary methods. It assumes allowances for dependent children, as part of its background. The plan assumes also establishment of comprehensive health and rehabilitation services and maintenance of employment, that is to say avoidance of mass unemployment, as necessary conditions of success in social insurance. These three measures—of children's allowances, health and rehabilitation services, and maintenance of employment—are described as assumptions A, B and C of the plan ; they fall partly within and partly without the plan itself, extending into other fields of social policy. They are discussed, therefore, not in the detailed exposition of the plan in Part V of the Report, but in Part VI, which is concerned with social security in relation to wider issues.

15. The plan is based on a diagnosis of want. It starts from facts, from the condition of the people as revealed by social surveys between the two wars. It takes account of two other facts about the British community, arising out of past movements of the birth rate and the death rate, which should dominate planning for its future ; the main effects of these movements in determining the present and future of the British people are shown by Table XI in para. 234. The first of the two facts is the age constitution of the population, making it certain that persons past the age that is now regarded as the end of working life will be a much larger proportion of the whole community than at any time in the past. The second fact is the low reproduction rate of the British community today ; unless this rate is raised very materially in the near future, a rapid and continuous decline of the population cannot be prevented. The first fact makes it necessary to seek ways of postponing the age of retirement from work rather than of hastening it. The second fact makes it imperative to give first place in social expenditure to the care of childhood and to the safeguarding of maternity.

16. The provision to be made for old age represents the largest and most rapidly growing element in any social insurance scheme. The problem of age is discussed accordingly in Part III of the Report as one of three special problems ; the measures proposed for dealing with this problem are summarised in paras. 254–257. Briefly, the proposal is to introduce for all citizens adequate pensions without means test by stages over a transition period of twenty years, while providing immediate assistance pensions for persons requiring them. In adopting a transition period for pensions as of right, while meeting immediate needs subject to consideration of means, the Plan for Social Security in Britain follows the precedent of New Zealand. The final rate of pensions in New Zealand is higher than that proposed in this Plan, but is reached only after a transition period of

9

twenty-eight years as compared with twenty years suggested here; after twenty years, the New Zealand rate is not very materially different from the basic rate proposed for Britain. The New Zealand pensions are not conditional upon retirement from work ; for Britain it is proposed that they should be retirement pensions and that persons who continue at work and postpone retirement should be able to increase their pensions above the basic rate. The New Zealand scheme is less favourable than the plan for Britain in starting at a lower level ; it is more favourable in some other respects. Broadly the two schemes for two communities of the British race are plans on the same lines to solve the same problem of passage from pensions based on need to pensions paid as of right to all citizens in virtue of contribution.

120

PART V

PLAN FOR SOCIAL SECURITY

Assumptions, Methods and Principles

300. *Scope of Social Security :* The term " social security " is used here to
denote the securing of an income to take the place of earnings when they are
interrupted by unemployment, sickness or accident, to provide for retirement
through age, to provide against loss of support by the death of another person,
and to meet exceptional expenditures, such as those connected with birth,
death and marriage. Primarily social security means security of income up to
a minimum, but the provision of an income should be associated with treatment designed to bring the interruption of earnings to an end as soon as
possible.

301. *Three Assumptions :* No satisfactory scheme of social security can
be devised except on the following assumptions :—

(A) Children's allowances for children up to the age of 15 or if in full-time
    education up to the age of 16 ;

(B) Comprehensive health and re-habilitation services for prevention and
    cure of disease and restoration of capacity for work, available to all
    members of the community ;

(C) Maintenance of employment, that is to say avoidance of mass unem-
    ployment.

The grounds for making these three assumptions, the methods of satisfying
them and their relation to the social security scheme are discussed in Part VI.
Children's allowances will be added to all the insurance benefits and pensions
described below in paras. 320-349.

302. *Three Methods of Security :* On these three assumptions, a Plan
for Social Security is outlined below, combining three distinct methods:
social insurance for basic needs ; national assistance for special cases ;
voluntary insurance for additions to the basic provision. Social insurance
means the providing of cash payments conditional upon compulsory contributions previously made by, or on behalf of, the insured persons, irrespective
of the resources of the individual at the time of the claim. Social insurance
is much the most important of the three methods and is proposed here in a
form as comprehensive as possible. But while social insurance can, and should,
be the main instrument for guaranteeing income security, it cannot be the
only one. It needs to be supplemented both by national assistance and by

121

voluntary insurance. National assistance means the giving of cash payments conditional upon proved need at the time of the claim, irrespective of previous contributions but adjusted by consideration of individual circumstances and paid from the national exchequer. Assistance is an indispensable supplement to social insurance, however the scope of the latter may be widened. In addition to both of these there is place for voluntary insurance. Social insurance and national assistance organised by the State are designed to guarantee, on condition of service, a basic income for subsistence. The actual incomes and by consequence the normal standards of expenditure of different sections of the population differ greatly. Making provision for these higher standards is primarily the function of the individual, that is to say, it is a matter for free choice and voluntary insurance. But the State should make sure that its measures leave room and encouragement for such voluntary insurance. The social insurance scheme is the greater part of the Plan for Social Security and its description occupies most of this Part of the Report. But the plan includes national assistance and voluntary insurance as well.

303. *Six Principles of Social Insurance :* The social insurance scheme set out below as the chief method of social security embodies six fundamental principles :

Flat rate of subsistence benefit

Flat rate of contribution

Unification of administrative responsibility

Adequacy of benefit

Comprehensiveness

Classification

304. *Flat Rate of Subsistence Benefit :* The first fundamental principle of the social insurance scheme is provision of a flat rate of insurance benefit, irrespective of the amount of the earnings which have been interrupted by unemployment or disability or ended by retirement ; exception is made only where prolonged disability has resulted from an industrial accident or disease. This principle follows from the recognition of the place and importance of voluntary insurance in social security and distinguishes the scheme proposed for Britain from the security schemes of Germany, the Soviet Union, the United States and most other countries with the exception of New Zealand. The flat rate is the same for all the principal forms of cessation of earning— unemployment, disability, retirement ; for maternity and for widowhood there is a temporary benefit at a higher rate.

305. *Flat Rate of Contribution :* The second fundamental principle of the scheme is that the compulsory contribution required of each insured person or his employer is at a flat rate, irrespective of his means. All insured persons, rich or poor, will pay the same contributions for the same security ; those with larger means will pay more only to the extent that as tax-payers they pay more to the National Exchequer and so to the State share of the Social Insurance Fund. This feature distinguishes the scheme proposed for Britain from the scheme recently established in New Zealand under which the contributions are graduated by income, and are in effect an income-tax assigned to a particular service. Subject moreover to one exception, the contribution will be the same irrespective of the assumed degree of risk affecting particular individuals or forms of employment. The exception is the raising of a proportion of the special cost of benefits and pensions for industrial disability in occupations of high risk by a levy on employers proportionate to risk and pay-roll (paras. 86–90 and 360).

306. *Unification of Administrative Responsibility :* The third fundamental

122

principle is unification of administrative responsibility in the interests of efficiency and economy. For each insured person there will be a single weekly contribution, in respect of all his benefits. There will be in each locality a Security Office able to deal with claims of every kind and all sides of security. The methods of paying different kinds of cash benefit will be different and will take account of the circumstances of insured persons, providing for payment at the home or elsewhere, as is necessary. All contributions will be paid into a single Social Insurance Fund and all benefits and other insurance payments will be paid from that fund.

307. *Adequacy of Benefit :* The fourth fundamental principle is adequacy of benefit in amount and in time. The flat rate of benefit proposed is intended in itself to be sufficient without further resources to provide the minimum income needed for subsistence in all normal cases. It gives room and a basis for additional voluntary provision, but does not assume that in any case. The benefits are adequate also in time, that is to say except for contingencies of a temporary nature, they will continue indefinitely without means test, so long as the need continues, though subject to any change of conditions and treatment required by prolongation of the interruption in earning and occupation.

308. *Comprehensiveness :* The fifth fundamental principle is that social insurance should be comprehensive, in respect both of the persons covered and of their needs. It should not leave either to national assistance or to voluntary insurance any risk so general or so uniform that social insurance can be justified. For national assistance involves a means test which may discourage voluntary insurance or personal saving. And voluntary insurance can never be sure of covering the ground. For any need moreover which, like direct funeral expenses, is so general and so uniform as to be a fit subject for insurance by compulsion, social insurance is much cheaper to administer than voluntary insurance.

309. *Classification :* The sixth fundamental principle is that social insurance, while unified and comprehensive, must take account of the different ways of life of different sections of the community ; of those dependent on earnings by employment under contract of service, of those earning in other ways, of those rendering vital unpaid service as housewives, of those not yet of age to earn and of those past earning. The term " classification " is used here to denote adjustment of insurance to the differing circumstances of each of these classes and to many varieties of need and circumstance within each insurance class. But the insurance classes are not economic or social classes in the ordinary sense ; the insurance scheme is one for all citizens irrespective of their means.

THE PEOPLE AND THEIR NEEDS

310. *Six Population Classes :* The Plan for Social Security starts with consideration of the people and of their needs. From the point of view of social security the people of Britain fall into six main classes described briefly as I—Employees ; II—Others gainfully occupied ; III—Housewives ; IV—Others of working age ; V—Below working age ; VI—Retired above working age. The precise definitions of each of these classes, the boundaries between them and the provision for passage from one to another are discussed in detail in paragraphs 314–319. The approximate numbers in each class and their relation to security needs, as listed in the following paragraph, are given in Table XVI. Some needs, for medical treatment and for burial, are common to all classes. In addition to this, those in Class V (Below working age) need children's allowances, and those in Class VI (Retired above working age) need pensions ; neither of

123

TABLE XVI
POPULATION BY SECURITY CLASSES
Approximate Numbers in Great Britain, July, 1939

Class	Number Million	Contribution Provisions	Security Provisions							Other Provisions
			Medical Treatment	Funeral grant	Retirement pension	Disability benefit	Unemployment benefit	Training benefit (f)	Industrial pension	
I. Employees ...	18·4	Insured by weekly contribution on Employment Book	×	×	×	×	×	—	×	Removal and lodging grant: Industrial grant.
II. Others gainfully occupied	2·5	Insured by contributions on Occupation Card	×	×	×	x(b)	—	:	—	
III. Housewives ...	9·3(a)	Insured on marriage through Housewife's Policy	×	×	×	—(c)	—(c)	×	—(c)	Marriage grant, maternity benefit (d) and grant, widows' benefit, guardian benefit, separation benefit.
IV. Others of working age	2·4	Insured by contributions on Security Card	×	×	×	—	—	×	—	
V. Below working age	9·6(g)	None	×	×	—	—	—	—	—	
VI. Retired above working age	4·3	Insured by contributions made during working age	×	×	×	—	—	—	x(e)	
	46·5									

(a) Married women gainfully occupied estimated at 1·4 million are included in the numbers shown for Class III and excluded from the numbers shown for Classes I and II.
(b) After 13 weeks of sickness.
(c) If gainfully occupied and not exempt.
(d) If gainfully occupied even though exempt.
(e) If granted before reaching the age of retirement and if higher than the retirement pension.
(f) Includes removal and lodging grant where needed.
(g) The numbers shown in Class V are on the basis of the present minimum school leaving age, viz. 14. In the Report it is assumed for the purpose of children's allowances that the minimum school leaving age is 15.

124

these classes can be called on to contribute for social insurance. The other four classes all have different needs for which they will be insured by contributions made by or in respect of them. Class I (Employees), in addition to medical treatment, funeral expenses and pension, need security against interruption of earnings by unemployment and disability, however caused. Class II, i.e., persons gainfully occupied otherwise than as employees, cannot be insured against loss of employment, but in addition to medical treatment, funeral expenses and pension they need provision for loss of earnings through disability and they need some provision for loss of livelihood. Class III (Housewives) not being gainfully occupied do not need compensation for loss of earnings through disability or otherwise, but, in addition to the common needs of treatment, funeral expenses and pension, they have a variety of special needs arising out of marriage. Class IV (Others of working age) is a heterogeneous class in which relatively few people remain for any large part of their lives : they all need provision for medical treatment, funeral expenses and retirement, and also for the risk of having to find a new means of livelihood.

311. *Eight Primary Causes of Need :* The primary needs for social security are of eight kinds, reckoning the composite needs of a married woman as one and including also the needs of childhood (Assumption A) and the need for universal comprehensive medical treatment and rehabilitation (Assumption B). These needs are set out below ; to each there is attached in the security scheme a distinct insurance benefit or benefits. Assistance may enter to deal with any kind of need, where insurance benefit for any reason is inadequate or absent.

Unemployment : that is to say, inability to obtain employment by a person dependent on it and physically fit for it, met by unemployment benefit with removal and lodging grants.

Disability : that is to say, inability of a person of working age, through illness or accident, to pursue a gainful occupation, met by disability benefit and industrial pension.

Loss of Livelihood by person not dependent on paid employment, met by training benefit.

Retirement from occupation, paid or unpaid, through age, met by retirement pension.

Marriage needs of a woman, met by Housewive's Policy including provision for :—
  (1) Marriage, met by marriage grant.
  (2) Maternity, met by maternity grant in all cases, and, in the case of a married woman in gainful occupation, also by maternity benefit for a period before and after confinement.
  (3) Interruption or cessation of husband's earnings by his unemployment, disability or retirement, met by share of benefit or pension with husband.
  (4) Widowhood, met by provision varying according to circumstances including temporary widow's benefit for readjustment, guardian benefit while caring for children and training benefit if and when there are no children in need of care.
  (5) Separation, i.e. end of husband's maintenance by legal separation, or established desertion, met by adaptation of widowhood provisions, including separation benefit, guardian benefit and training benefit.
  (6) Incapacity for household duties, met by provision of paid help in illness as part of treatment.

Funeral Expenses of self or any person for whom responsible, met by funeral grant.

125

Childhood, provided for by children's allowances if in full-time education, till sixteen.

Physical Disease or *Incapacity,* met by medical treatment, domiciliary and institutional, for self and dependants in comprehensive health service and by post-medical rehabilitation.

312. *Other Needs :* The needs listed in para. 311 are the only ones so general and so uniform as to be clearly fit subjects for compulsory insurance. There is, partly for historical reasons, a problem as to the provision to be made for fatal accidents and diseases arising out of employment, by means of an industrial grant. There are many other needs and risks which are sufficiently common to be suited for voluntary insurance, and to a varying extent are already covered by that method. They include a great variety of contingencies for which provision is made by life and endowment insurance ; there are risks of fire, theft, or accident ; there are exceptional expenditures such as those on holidays and education.

313. *Explanation of Terms :* Before defining more closely the classes into which the people must be divided for purposes of social security, it is necessary to explain three terms. " Exception " means that certain types of persons are not within a particular class, though apart from the exception they would be ; exception is general, not individual, altering the definition of a class. " Exemption " means that a person though within a particular class is exempted individually from paying the contributions of that class ; his employer, if he has one, remains liable for contributions, but these contributions are not counted in judging of the insured person's claim to benefit. " Excusal " means that contributions for which an insured person and his employer, if he has one, would otherwise be liable, are not required, but for the purpose of satisfying contribution conditions for benefit are deemed to have been paid ; excusal is normally conditional on the insured person proving that he is unemployed or incapable of work. Exemption and excusal are dealt with more fully in paras. 363–364.

314. *Employees (Class I) :* These are, in general, persons depending for their maintenance upon remuneration received under a contract of service, including apprenticeship. The exact boundaries of this class will be adjusted by certain exceptions and inclusions. There will also be provision for exemption, that is to say, for allowing persons who take work falling within Class I to escape payment of their contributions while still requiring contributions by the employer. Insured persons in this class will hold an employment book which they will present to the employer for stamping.

The principal exception suggested is for family employment, that is to say, employment of one member of a family by another forming part of the same household. This is a development of the existing exception of fathers, sons, daughters, etc., under Agricultural Unemployment Insurance, and is designed to prevent fictitious claims for benefit. Persons excluded from Class I by this exception will fall into Class II.

Persons in Class II or IV taking work temporarily under a contract of service will be allowed to claim exemption from their own contributions, and persons in Class III undertaking such work will be allowed to obtain exemption so long as they desire it. Exempt persons will present to the employer a special card to be stamped by him with the employer's contribution.

On the other hand, certain exceptions and exemptions under the present scheme will no longer apply. In particular :—

    (i) There will be no exception of employees on the ground of the regularity of their employment or that it entitles them to pension. The basis

126

of the security scheme is that all should contribute compulsorily irrespective of their personal risk. For men in the Armed Forces special arrangements for contribution will secure their rights to the benefits of the scheme when they return to civil life. For men in the merchant service there will be special arrangements for contribution adjusted to the conditions of their employment.

(ii) There will be no exception of any employees by a remuneration limit.

(iii) The right of persons above normal working age to claim exemption will cease on the introduction of the principle that pension is payable only on retirement from work and that men and women reaching the ages of 65 and 60 respectively, will have the option either of continuing to work and contribute or of retiring on pension at any time thereafter.

The possibility of either including in Class I and so insuring against unemployment certain classes of persons who are not technically under a contract of service but work in effect for employers (e.g. manual labour contractors, out-workers and private nurses) or of insuring such classes by special schemes, taking account of their special circumstances, needs further exploration. In one of these classes for instance, namely nurses, in addition to the fact that nurses work sometimes under contract of service and sometimes not, there are special needs arising out of their exposure to infection and out of the urgency of their duties, rendering necessary the possibility of intervals for rest and recuperation. The problem of giving some income security under a special scheme to share fishermen should also be explored. As stated above, apprentices generally will be included in Class I, but special arrangements may be made in regard to their rate of contribution (*see* para. 408).

315. *Others Gainfully Occupied (Class II)* : These are, in general, all persons working for gain who are not in Class I. Most of these will be persons working on their own account as employers or by themselves, including shopkeepers and hawkers, farmers, small holders and crofters, share fishermen, entertainers and renderers of professional and personal service and out-workers. They will include also persons who, though technically under contract of service, are excepted from Class I on the ground of family employment. Apart from the possibilities whose exploration is proposed above, persons gainfully occupied otherwise than under contract of service will not be insured against unemployment. Persons in Class II will pay contributions upon an occupation card. If a person in Class II gives up his independent occupation and takes insurable employment he will pass into Class I and will in due course acquire a claim to unemployment benefit in addition to the other benefits of Class II. If he takes insurable employment temporarily he will be allowed to work as an exempt person, i.e. only the employer's contribution will be paid and he will neither contribute for unemployment nor acquire a right to unemployment benefit. Conversely, a person whose main occupation is employment under a contract of service but who also works regularly or occasionally at some other gainful occupation, will be able to obtain exemption from Class II contributions. Persons in Class II will be able to apply for exemption on the ground that their income is below a certain minimum, say £75 a year (para. 363).

316. *Housewives (Class III)* : These are married women of working age living with their husbands. Any housewife who undertakes paid work as well, either under a contract of service or otherwise, will have the choice either of contributing in the ordinary way in Class I or Class II as the case may be, or of working as an exempt person, paying no contributions of her own.

127

317. *Others of Working Age (Class IV)* : These are in the main students above 16, unmarried women engaged in domestic duties not for pay, persons of private means, and persons incapacitated by blindness or other physical infirmity without being qualified for benefits under the social insurance scheme. The last of these groups will be a diminishing one. Blindness and other physical infirmities will occur in most cases after people have had a chance of contributing under the scheme and qualifying for disability benefit. At the outset there will be a number of people who became incapacitated before the scheme began. After the scheme has been established, persons in receipt of any benefit or pension in respect of contributions in other classes will be treated as still belonging to those classes and not as in Class IV. Those incapacitated or in institutions will be subject to the special arrangements appropriate in each case. All the others in Class IV will be required to hold security cards and to pay contributions thereon unless and until they pass into another class. This security card must be produced to obtain an employment book or occupation card. Persons in Class IV will be able to apply for exemption from contributions on the ground that their total income is below a certain minimum, say £75 a year (para. 363).

318. *Below Working Age (Class V)*: This class will include all persons below 16 who are in full-time education, whether compulsorily or voluntarily.

319. *Retired Above Working Age (Class VI)*: The minimum pensionable age for retirement on social insurance pension will be 65 for men and 60 for women, but persons who continue to work after these ages will pay contributions in the ordinary way and will be treated as belonging to Class I or Class II.

141

NATIONAL ASSISTANCE

369. *Assistance as part of Security :* Assistance will be available to meet all needs which are not covered by insurance. It must meet those needs adequately up to subsistence level, but it must be felt to be something less desirable than insurance benefit ; otherwise the insured persons get nothing for their contributions. Assistance therefore will be given always subject to proof of needs and examination of means ; it will be subject also to any conditions as to behaviour which may seem likely to hasten restoration of earning capacity. The cost of assistance will be met directly by the National Exchequer. But though distinct from social insurance national assistance will be combined with it in administration, as a minor but integral part of the work of the Ministry of Social Security.

370. *Transitional Scope of Assistance :* In the transitional period for pensions before contributory pensions reach subsistence level, assistance pensions will be required in a considerable number of cases and will form a large part of the total work of assistance.

371. *Limited Permanent Scope of Assistance :* The proposals in this Report (extending State insurance to new Classes, raising rates of benefit and prolonging the period of benefit) will make the permanent scope of assistance much less than that of public assistance and of the Assistance Board at present. Nevertheless there will remain a real, if limited, continuing scope for assistance covering the following main classes.

(*a*) Persons failing to fulfil contribution conditions either because they have less than the qualifying minimum (para. 366) or because they never become fit for work, or because they are not in full benefit for unemployment, disability or pensions, or because being in Class II or Class IV they claim and obtain exemption on the ground of deficient total income (para. 363).

142

(*b*) Persons failing to fulfil conditions for benefit. The most important of these are likely to be (i) men disqualified for unconditional un employment benefit through refusal of suitable employment, through leaving work without just cause, through dismissal for misconduct, and (ii) those who are disqualified for conditional unemployment benefit by failure to attend a work or training centre.

(*c*) Persons with abnormal needs in respect of diet, care and other matters.

(*d*) Persons in need through causes not suitable for insurance, e.g., some forms of desertion or separation.

372. *Unified Means Test :* The three differing tests of needs and means which are now applied by separate authorities for non-contributory pensions, supplementary pensions and public assistance, will be replaced by a test administered by a single authority on principles uniform in themselves, though taking account of the different problems which arise in relation to different classes of case. Giving of assistance involves consideration on the one hand of needs and on the other hand of the applicant's resources for meeting them. The needs of adult persons and of children should be based on estimates of what is necessary for subsistence on the principles discussed in paras. 193–232. For old persons it is reasonable to add a margin above the subsistence minimum, as is proposed in regard to contributory pensions by bringing them ultimately up to unemployment and disability benefit. Consideration of the applicant's resources raises two questions : of the ownership of the resources to be taken into account and of the treatment of resources of different kinds. As regards the ownership of the resources to be taken into account, there appears to be no reason for disturbing materially, if at all, the settlement reached under the Determination of Needs Act. As regards the treatment of resources of different kinds, this matter is now dealt with partly by Statute, partly by Regulations, and partly by administrative discretion. It is suggested that, in future, it should be wholly a matter for Regulations to be made subject to the approval of both Houses of Parliament. Regulations have the advantage over Statute both that they can be amended more easily in order to provide for changed circumstances, and that they can be more detailed than Statutes. On the other hand, they have the advantage, as compared with administrative discretion, that the making of a new Regulation calls attention of all parties concerned to any additional rights that may be granted to them. Regulations are available to all officers, members of Appeal Tribunals and the public. They set standards to which administration must conform and they ensure reasonable consistency of treatment between one place and another and between one time and another. Under the Regulations it will be possible to make suitable considered allowance for capital, for earnings, for war disability pensions, for social insurance benefits and pensions, and for other income.

373. *Cases of Special Difficulty :* At the basis of any system of social security covering all those who comply with reasonable just conditions for insurance and assistance, there must be provision for a limited class of men or women who through weakness or badness of character fail to comply. In the last resort the man who fails to comply with the conditions for obtaining benefit or assistance and leaves his family without resources must be subject to penal treatment.

374. *Some Assistance Problems :* On transfer of responsibility for assistance to a central authority it may be necessary to make some amendment of the present provisions as to (*a*) giving of assistance to persons on strike or locked-out ; (*b*) giving of assistance on loan with recovery thereafter ; (*c*) giving of assistance in kind.

143

VOLUNTARY INSURANCE

375. *Scope for Voluntary Insurance :* Compulsory social insurance provides, up to subsistence level, for primary needs and general risks. The scope of voluntary insurance is two-fold :—

(a) To go beyond subsistence level in meeting general risks, by adding to the amount of compulsory benefits ;

(b) To deal with risks and needs which, while sufficiently common for insurance, are not so common or uniform as to call for compulsory insurance.

In so far as voluntary insurance meets real needs, it is an essential part of security ; scope and encouragement for it must be provided. The State can ensure this negatively, by avoiding so far as possible any test of means for its compulsory insurance benefits, and by limiting such benefits to subsistence and primary needs. The State can ensure this positively by regulation, by financial assistance or by itself undertaking the organisation of voluntary insurance. In considering the action of the State in regard to voluntary insurance, regard must be had to the extent to which voluntary insurance has already developed in various fields and the different circumstances under which it has developed.

376. *Encouragement of Thrift :* Development of voluntary insurance and saving among persons of limited means is desirable also from another point of view. Material progress depends upon technical progress which depends upon investment and ultimately upon savings. If the distribution of the product of industry in any community is very unequal, savings come naturally either from the surplus income of the wealthy or from profits which are not distributed. If and in so far as, after the war, incomes are distributed more equally than at present or the share of wages of the total product is increased, it is important that part of the additional resources going to wage-earners and others of limited means should be saved by them instead of being spent forthwith. Increase of means brings a corresponding increase of obligations, in this as in other respects. A continuation of the War Savings movement in one form or another after the war seems likely to be an essential measure of economic policy. The same purpose can, and should be, served by development of organs for voluntary insurance to supplement State insurance.

377. *Unemployment Insurance through Trade Unions :* Voluntary insurance against unemployment is practically limited to Trade Unions, which, alone of all organisations other than the State with its Employment Exchanges, can test the genuineness of unemployment and availability of the insured person for work. Even within the Trade Unions, the sphere of voluntary insurance against unemployment is limited and it has shown no signs of growing. The number of wage-earners who by voluntary insurance now add anything substantial to what the State provides probably does not exceed one million. In the main, unemployment insurance must be compulsory, if it is to be effective. But under the existing unemployment insurance scheme scope and encouragement are afforded for voluntary insurance by arrangements under which Trade Unions giving their own benefit may act as agents for administering the State benefit and receive a grant for administrative expenses on this account.

378. *Voluntary Insurance through Special Schemes :* The Trade Union Schemes of out-of-work pay enable a limited number of skilled wage-earners to supplement their statutory unemployment benefit ; most of the insured population make no such provision and have no easy means of doing so. Both on general grounds and in view of the extension of compulsory insurance

144

to higher income ranges among non-manual workers, the possibility of extending the opportunities for supplementary insurance against unemployment should be explored. One obvious way lies in the development of special schemes for particular industries as a means not of contracting out of compulsory insurance but of adding to it. The two special schemes already established, in the Insurance industry and in Banking and Finance, cannot, under the proposals made here, continue as alternatives to the general scheme. But they might continue for the purpose of adding to statutory benefit and of administering it with their own benefit under an arrangement with the Social Insurance Fund. The principle of giving statutory sanction to special schemes for supplementary benefit is already admitted, under Section 72 of the Unemployment Insurance Act, 1935, though the powers given by that Section have not been used hitherto. In the actual special schemes for Insurance and for Banking it has been found possible to provide benefits exceeding those of the general scheme without any direct contribution from the employees or the State and a contribution from the employer of 2d. or 6d. a week. Half that sum would provide a very substantial supplementary benefit and justify the State in continuing to entrust insurance in these industries to the same agencies. If the organisation which has built up these two schemes could be directed successfully to such a new purpose, it might set a fruitful example to other industries.

379. *Friendly Benefits :* Provision for sickness is the classic ground of voluntary insurance efforts in Britain. The registered Friendly Societies, in 1939, had approved society membership of $5\frac{1}{2}$ million and expenditure on cash benefits for sickness in that year per head of this membership was practically equal to expenditure on sickness and disability per head of membership under the health insurance scheme ; that is to say, these $5\frac{1}{2}$ million members doubled by voluntary insurance the provision for sickness made for them by the State scheme. Sickness benefit given by Friendly Societies covers accidents also of all kinds ; other benefits—on death, on maternity, on old age and by way of deposit insurance—are provided on a substantial scale. The membership of the registered Friendly Societies has grown, since the introduction of national health insurance in 1911, but this growth has been steady rather than spectacular and these societies still cover not much more than a quarter of the total number for whom disability benefit is required. That proportion is too low to justify keeping compulsory disability benefit below subsistence level. It is large enough, however, to make it unnecessary for the State to take any action in regard to voluntary insurance against sickness, except to leave scope and encouragement for the Friendly Societies. One of the principal objects of the proposal to use Friendly Societies and Trade Unions giving friendly benefits as organs for the administration of State disability benefit is in order to encourage through these associations the greatest possible supplementation of State insurance by voluntary insurance in this field.

380. *Unregistered Friendly Societies :* In addition to the registered Friendly Societies mentioned in the last paragraph, there exist innumerable unregistered Societies of every degree of permanence and financial stability. Some are large and firmly established institutions with Approved Societies attached to them ; others are fleeting. Little definite information as to the scale and methods of these societies is available since they come now under no official scrutiny, but figures collected by Mr. Rowntree for York suggest that in numbers the membership of unregistered Friendly Societies is comparable to that of the registered societies. There appears to be good ground for requiring every society in whatever form which receives contributions with a view to providing payments in sickness or on death to be registered and to conform to statutory conditions.

145

381. *Superannuation Schemes :* Provision for retirement additional to or exclusive of old age pensions is now made in many occupations as a whole (civil service, local government service, teaching, railway service, public utilities) and by innumerable individual firms. No special action by the State is called for, except that of making its own development of compulsory insurance for retirement gradual, so as to give time for any necessary rearrangements of the occupational and voluntary schemes.

382. [*Life and Endowment Insurance :*] The development of insurance for funeral expenses, against death generally and for endowment through the agency of Industrial Assurance Companies and Collecting Societies is discussed in Appendix D and under Change 23 in Part II. For reasons set out there it is proposed that there should be established under the general supervision of the Minister for Social Security an Industrial Assurance Board working not for profit. This statutory corporation would have a monopoly of insurance with the use of collectors and would be authorised to undertake ordinary life assurance subject to a maximum of amount insured, say £300, in order to prevent its entry into the general field of life assurance. The Board would take over the bulk of the work of the existing Industrial Life Offices with their staffs and would bring about economies, first by eliminating competition, second by encouraging payment of premiums otherwise than through collectors, third by limiting voluntary insurance so far as possible to insurance likely to be within the permanent means of the policy-holder. This proposal is bracketed, as desirable, but not essential.

383. *Loss of Independent Earnings :* It appears impracticable to provide unemployment benefit generally, except where there is employment under contract of service. Independent earners of Class II will be able to obtain training benefit, if they need to change their occupation. For deficiency of earnings in their occupation, whether through seasonal fluctuations or through other causes, no general provision can be made, but the possibility of voluntary insurance, possibly with State aid, for particular sections of Class II needs full exploration. It might become a function of the Industrial Assurance Board.

384. *Voluntary Continuation of Compulsory Insurance :* Persons who pass out of compulsory insurance against sickness or for pensions, through change of occupation (from employment to independent earning or to no paid occupation) or through rising above the remuneration limit for non-manual workers, can now continue voluntarily in insurance. These arrangements are used extensively, there being nearly 1 million voluntary contributors for health or pensions insurance. With the extension of compulsory insurance to Classes II and IV and the removal of the remuneration limit, they will become unnecessary, though there will be problems of transition from the old system to the new system. Health service, retirement pensions and funeral grant will be available for all at all times in return for compulsory contributions. It may be argued that those who after contributing for disability benefit in Class I or Class II give up gainful occupation late in life, but before retiring age, should be allowed to continue insurance for this benefit. The answer is that cash disability benefit, as distinct from medical treatment, is compensation for earnings lost through disability ; in the case considered there are no earnings at the time when disability occurs.

[10]

Proposed Speech on Beveridge Report

John Maynard Keynes

My Lords,

I hope for the indulgence your lordships are accustomed to grant to those who address you for the first time. And, since I am closely associated with a Gov^t Dep^t, I ought, perhaps, to emphasise that anything I say to your Lordships to-day or on any other occasion is a purely personal expression of opinion. I speak because as a member of your Lordships' House who happens to be a close student of the matters under discussion

256

THE BEVERIDGE REPORT

I feel it to be a duty to express the views I have formed for what they may be worth.

I shall not attempt to cover the very wide field opened up by this Debate. I propose to confine myself to a single aspect, the question whether the country can afford what we most of us agree to be desirable. It is this financial aspect, I think, which is the chief cause of anxiety to those whom apart from this the Beveridge proposals greatly attract.

I view the Budgetary prospects after the war with great concern. It is impossible to say how constrained the position will be until we know the cost of post-war defence. And it may be a considerable time before we know that with any confidence. We must therefore be very slow to burden the Budget with any avoidable and unnecessary charges especially in the early post-war period.

On the financial side, therefore, I approach the Beveridge proposals with the question whether there is a reasonable alternative before the country which would during this period cost the Exchequer significantly less. The strange thing is that during the lengthy debate in another place no one, neither Ministers nor their critics, seems to have asked this simple question—except on the special matter of children's allowances. On that matter the Gov^t, prudently in my opinion, proposed to substitute 5s for the 8s in the plan. 5s, particularly if it is supplemented as the Lord President foreshadowed by increased services in kind, is quite enough to begin with in a new social policy which if it is a success we may carry much further when our means increase.

But assuming that the plan is amended in this way, what *other* variations does anyone propose which would save a significant amount of money? In the early period, that is to say—I will consider later on in my remarks the position twenty years hence. —I know of none.

What are the economies open to us? To slow down the development of the National Health Service? The pace of

INTERNAL POLICY

progress will be limited for reasons outside our control by the
shortage of available personnel. But neither the Gov[t] nor anyone
else proposes to make any economy here by proceeding more
slowly than we need. By offering lower rates of benefit for
unemployment and sickness? I have heard no suggestion of this
kind from Ministers or from anyone else. Indeed the Lord
President was careful to make it clear that the Gov[t] have in mind
'rates not widely different from those in the Report'. By fixing
a lower initial rate for pensions than the Beveridge figure? The
Lord President has indicated that the Gov[t] contemplate a higher
rate. These are the provisions which cost the money. There is
only one other way of saving the Budget, namely by fixing higher
contributions than those of the plan. No-one has suggested this,
though it would be easy to risk the existing readiness to peg these
increased contributions, and thus increase the charge on the
Budget, if too much of the scheme is put into the melting pot.
I am, therefore, at a loss to known how it is proposed to save
money from the Budget by *not* having the Beveridge Plan. This
is a very obvious question to ask. No-one so far has dropt even
a hint how to answer it.

Allowing for the proposed economy on children's allowances and the inevitable delays in the development of the
Health Service, it is not true that the Beveridge proposals
involve the Exchequer in any serious expense beyond what is
already inevitable.

It is, therefore, precisely because I am deeply concerned
about the Budget position in the early years after the war that
I welcome the Beveridge proposals. For these years there is no
cheaper scheme on the map. On the other hand, it would be very
easy, if we proceed piecemeal, to slip into a more expensive
scheme with higher benefits in certain directions, and with a
danger of some loss of the proposed contributions.

What I am saying is not a paradox. That Sir William
Beveridge's scheme is a relatively cheap scheme for the early
period is not an accident. He has deliberately designed it this

THE BEVERIDGE REPORT

way and that, in my judgement, is one of the great merits of the scheme which has not attracted the attention it deserves. That the Plan achieves its results at a low budgetary cost follows from one of its fundamental principles, namely that we collect to-day's pension contributions from a working population larger than corresponds to the number of today's pensioners, and we use these contributions, which are paid in return for future pensions, to defray a smaller number of current pensions. This means that the immediate financial problem is greatly eased.

But it also means that the future cost will increase progressively. The right question to ask therefore, is not whether we can afford the Beveridge Plan now, but whether the Plan brings immediate financial ease at the cost of future commitments which will prove too heavy.

This takes us into a speculative field where, admittedly, nothing can be proved certain. Speaking for myself, I can only affirm that I am not worried about the remotest future if only we can surmount our immediate post-war difficulties. On the average the cost of the Beveridge scheme will increase cumulatively by about £8 million a year as time goes on. But with merely normal technical progress such as we have experienced for many years past, the national income out of which to meet this should increase cumulatively by more like £100 million a year. Personally I expect a much greater growth of national income even than this. When the future looks black, I comfort myself with the thought that British industry can scarcely be more inefficient than it was before the war. I am confident that we could increase output both in industry and in agriculture by at least 50 per cent compared with 1938 merely by putting to work modern methods and techniques that already exist. Indeed in agriculture I fancy we have done it already. By taking on burdens we force ourselves to face the problems of organisation which it is our duty to face anyhow.

Nothing but a major reversal of fortune which would upset a great deal more than the Beveridge Plan can prevent our

INTERNAL POLICY

national income from increasing several times as fast as our obligations under the Plan.

The Gov¹ has, therefore, done well to accept the Report. I have read carefully the speeches of the Gov¹ spokesmen in another place. It is a gross travesty of what they said to represent it otherwise than as a substantial acceptance of the Plan. Nor do I see any indications of avoidable delay in putting it into force. Indeed it is obvious that we shall urgently need the Plan in operation to help us to get through the difficult period of transition from war activities. We can go into the demobilisation period without the higher contributions. We cannot go into it without the higher benefits. So how is delay going to help the Budget? I agree that there was a good deal of what the lawyers call 'without prejudice' about the Gov¹ statements. But if I am satisfied with the substance of a statement, I do not bother too much whether it has pencilled at the bottom the letters O.K. or whether the family solicitor has recommended E. and O.E. The difference between the two sets of letters is more a matter of style and temperament than substance. I hope that the noble and learned Viscount on the Woolsack will, if he can frame his lips to so convey an expression, give us a little more of the O.K. and a little less of the 'without prejudice'.

My Lords, a refusal, if it had been made, to commit later years to this modest extent would have raised the whole question of our attitude to the future. The future will be what we choose to make it. If we approach it with cringing and timidity, we shall get what we deserve. If we march on with confidence and vigour the facts will respond. It would be a monstrous thing to reserve all our courage and powers of will for War and then, crowned with victory, to approach the Peace as a bankrupt bunch of defeatists.

Moreover, to make a bogey of the economic problem is, in my judgement, grievously to misunderstand the nature of the tasks ahead of us. Looking beyond the immediate post-war period, when our economic difficulties will be genuine and must

260

THE BEVERIDGE REPORT

take precedence over all else—perhaps for the last time—the economic problems of the day [that] perplex us, will lie in solving the problems of an era of material abundance not those of an era of poverty. It is not any fear of a failure of physical productivity to provide an adequate material standard of life that fills me with foreboding. The real problems of the future are first of all the maintenance of peace, of international co-operation and amity, and beyond that the profound moral and social problems of how to organise material abundance to yield up the fruits of a good life. These are the heroic tasks of the future. But there is nothing, My Lords, in what we are discussing today which need frighten a mouse.

261

[11]

ORDERS OF THE DAY

NATIONAL ASSISTANCE BILL

Order for Second Reading read.

3.31 p.m.

The Minister of Health (Mr. Aneurin Bevan): I beg to move, " That the Bill be now read a Second time."

I am presenting to the House of Commons the last of the Measures which the Government have adopted for the expansion of the social services of this country. The House will be aware that in the last few years a number of substantial steps have been taken in transforming and enlarging the social services. Family allowances are in operation; increased old age pensions are being paid; a full scheme of National Insurance is on the statute book, and will come into operation in July next; the National Health Service is on the statute book, and will come into operation on the same date; and there is in preparation a Bill for which my right hon. Friend the Home Secretary will be responsible, for the welfare of deprived children. The National Health Service will take care of the sick. The new Child Welfare Service will, as I have said, take care of the children who are deprived of their parents and their guardians. However, there will still remain, after all these things have been done, 400,000 persons on outdoor relief, and 50,000 in institutions. There thus remain, after we have bitten into the main body of the Poor Law, these residual categories which have to be provided for. This Bill, therefore, must be seen as the coping stone on the structure of the social services of Great Britain.

The Bill itself is simple in character, and I ought not to find much difficulty in making its provisions clear to the House. I would, however, say that, simple though the Bill is, its provisions are exceedingly important, and this occasion marks the end of a whole period of the social history of Great Britain. I am sure that hon. Members in all parts of the House would wish me to take this opportunity of paying a warm and sincere tribute to the services of Beatrice and Sidney Webb. They made a most distinguished contribution towards thought on this subject, but they were not alone. There were many others, in [1603] all parties and in all fields of public activity, and now we are to see the consumation of their efforts. Indeed, the Poor Law has been humanised in its administration in the course of the last 20 to 30 years. Nevertheless, the taint remains, and, of course, many of the statutory inhibitions are still there.

The Government approach the problem from the angle that they wish to see the whole residual problem in two special categories. They wish to consider assistance by way of monetary help made a national responsibility and welfare a local responsibility. Where the individual is immediately concerned, where warmth and humanity of administration is the primary consideration, then the authority which is responsible should be as near to the recipient as possible. Therefore, it is proposed that we shall transfer to the Assistance Board, to be renamed the National Assistance Board, the responsibility for providing the financial help which will still be needed, because there must always stand behind the existing social services a national scheme to assist people in peculiar and special circumstances. There will be a number of persons who will not be eligible for insurance benefit. There will be some who will not be eligible for unemployment benefit, and there will be persons who will be the subject of sudden affliction, like fires and floods and circumstances of that kind, who will need to have help from some special organisation.

It is, therefore, proposed, as I say, that the National Assistance Board shall have the responsibility of providing help of that sort for persons in need of help. The National Assistance Board, since it has been created, has established itself as a humane system of administration, and it is, I am sure, perfectly proper that at this stage we should recruit the services of that Board as an institution to which we entrust the assistance of persons in monetary need. The scale of National Assistance will be determined by regulations, to be presented for the approval of the House of Commons by my right hon. Friend the Minister of National Insurance. There will be an opportunity for full examination when they are presented, and as hon. Members know, they will appear before the House of Commons in draft form, and every opportunity will be given for discussion when they are presented. It is [1604] not, therefore, my intention at the moment to attempt to prophesy what these scales are to be, but I do not believe they will meet with resistance when they are presented.

There are a number of persons for whom special provision will have to be made. There are, for example, the blind. Their welfare will be the responsibility of the principal local welfare authorities—the county boroughs and county councils in England and the county councils and large burghs in Scotland. For some time past we have given a special place in our social services to the welfare, care and training of the blind. Among all handicapped persons, the blind are the most handicapped. Milton expresses this in unforgettable words in "Samson Agonistes" when he says:

" Light, the prime work of God, to me's extinct,
    And all her various objects of delight Annulled. . . ."

We propose to place upon the Assistance Board the duty of providing maintenance of the blind and upon the local authorities a duty to make special schemes for their training and welfare, both domiciliary and otherwise. Of course, to some extent this has been done by some authorities on an extremely generous and humane scale under the Act of 1920, but we hope to enlarge these services in the future.

There is another category of persons for whom the Assistance Board will have a special responsibility. I refer to those who are suffering from pulmonary tuberculosis. As hon. Members will know, we have developed in this country, perhaps as much as any other country in the world, a system of mass radiography by which it is possible to detect the presence of tuberculosis even before the victim is aware of it. There was an alternative scheme adopted during the war to encourage persons in the early stages of tuberculosis to give up their jobs and to undergo treatment. Special scales were laid down in order to encourage them to do so.

We propose to continue that scheme and to extend it, but, because of the nature of its origin, because it was originally intended as a scheme to increase the labour force, it has one very grievous feature. The allowances cease when it is found that the condition is incurable.

Vol. 444

This is a cruel affliction. We propose to end it. Surely, if a person has been encouraged to give up his employment in order to undergo treatment, and if it is found that the treatment is useless, it is far better that he be kept until he dies than that he be told that because he is incurable no help can be given. Therefore, that feature will cease. The treatment of pulmonary tuberculosis, like that for other forms of sickness, will be the responsibility of the National Assistance Board, on the one side, and the regional hospital boards, on the other, it being the function of the National Assistance Board to supply the financial provision, and the hospital service to provide the treatment. This division of responsibility will run throughout the scheme and, as I hope to be able to show, it will have very important and, I hope, valuable consequences.

The National Assistance Board will provide its assistance on the basis of a determination of needs which we propose to bring up to date. If I might be allowed a personal reference, I have spent many years of my life in fighting the means test. Now we have practically ended it. In the future only the resources of the man and dependent children—that is, children under 16 years of age—will be taken into account in determining their need. Where there are other members of the household, they will be regarded as making some contribution towards the payment of rent, as at present. As a general rule, the present regulations prescribe no more than 7s. a week, and very often less.

In calculating the personal resources of applicants there will be the usual disregard of superannuation and war pensions. They will remain within definitely prescribed limits. War savings are protected, and, as regards other capital, we propose to raise the existing £25 to £50. That is to say, a person must have £75 of savings before any deduction can be made in the amount of assistance to be given, and only 6d. a week—less than 2 per cent. per annum—will be deducted where the capital is between £75 and £100. In addition to the usual disregards we are making this alteration. Of course, under the Determination of Needs Act, 1941, there are also other disregards. The owner-occupier will have disregarded his house and the effects of the household.

[Mr. Bevan.]

There is another category for which the local welfare authorities will, at first, make provision as agents of the Assistance Board. They will be the vagrants. This class of person, picturesque and very often lovers of the countryside, almost disappeared during the war. It is a fact that full employment practically extinguishes this type of person. The old method was to give help to the tramp in the form of deterrents. The Elizabethan Poor Law punished the homeless vagrant in the most savage manner. I have been looking up the Elizabethan statute. This is what it says:

" And every such person, upon his apprehension, shall, by order of a justice or constable assisted by advice of the Minister and one other of the parish, be stripped naked from the middle upwards and be openly whipped until his body be bloody."

We are a long way from that now, but we hope to take a step further still. Last year I sent a circular to the Poor Law authorities advising them that it is not the duty of the Poor Law authority now merely to pass the tramp on from one place to another, but to give him opportunities of rehabilitation towards a settled life. This system will be continued in the future on a larger scale. It will be the responsibility of the National Assistance Board to provide centres for training, education and reconditioning, and to make available to the applicants all the resources of the employment exchange. In the interregnum, until proper institutions can be created for this purpose, the National Assistance Board will use accommodation provided by local authorities.

There is another category of persons for whom we shall have to accept an even larger measure of responsibility than we have had in the past, and these are old persons. By 1970, old persons—that is, persons reaching pensionable age—will be one in five of the total population. It is a staggering figure; indeed, it can be said that, in some respects, the proper care and welfare of the aged is the peculiar problem of modern society. We have, of course, gone a long way towards it by making provision for increased old age pensions, and it is one of the more fortunate and agreeable aspects of this problem that modern medicine and better nutrition enables old people to continue working longer than they formerly did. My right hon. Friend the Minister of National In-

surance informs me that, of the 7,000 old age pensioners who become eligible for the pension every week, two-thirds continue in their employment. That is a very remarkable fact, because we all know, from our own experience, that it is very much better if we can continue to follow the rhythms of our normal life, because when those rhythms are abandoned, decay is accelerated. Further, it is a very welcome addition to the total labour force of the country.

The Nuffield Foundation Survey reports that 95 per cent. of old people live independent lives in their own homes or the homes of their children, but it does not always follow that old folk want to live in the homes of their children. Indeed, in some respects, living with their children is in many cases merely an expression of the lack of housing, and we all know how the forced juxtaposition of old and young people can produce very disagreeable domestic conditions. Where the association is voluntary and arises out of mutual love and respect, then it produces a mutual endorsement of each other's regard, but, where it is forced either by poverty or by the absence of alternative accommodation, it can be a very serious source of domestic disturbance and unhappiness. Further, it is one of the distinguishing characteristics of the psychology of old people that they cling tenaciously to privacy. They do not want to be interfered with; they want to lead their own lives. They do not want to be dependent on other people, and, as they grow older, they become jealous of their independence.

Therefore, we have decided to make a great departure in the treatment of old people. The workhouse is to go. Although many people have tried to humanise it, it was in many respects a very evil institution. We have determined that the right way to approach this problem is to give the welfare authorities, as we shall now describe them, the power to establish special homes. I have been cudgelling my brains to find a name for them, but it is very difficult.

Mr. Shurmer (Birmingham, Sparkbrook): Eventide Homes.

Mr. Bevan: No. When we talk to some old people, they think they are facing the dawn, not eventide. If we call them " Sanctuaries," it is almost as bad, and, if we call them " Retreats," it is worse, because what we are really thinking about is a type of old people who are still able to look after themselves, who can, to use a colloquialism, " do for themselves," but who are unable to do the housework, the laundry, cook meals and things of that sort. Therefore, we have to think of a type of place where these services can be rendered to the old people, and, at the same time, leave them the maximum of privacy and independence. This means that the buildings to which I now refer must not be so large as to become institutions. Bigness is the enemy of humanity. That is the reason why the Metropolis is such a bad place to live in. When hon. Members opposite nod their heads enthusiastically to this principle, let them remember that it is one of the most unfortunate features of the last 30 years that London has grown at the expense of the rest of the country.

If we have an institution too large, we might have a reproduction of the workhouse atmosphere, with the workhouse master and all the regimentation and the rules that have to be obeyed, and, therefore, it seems to us that the optimum limit for these homes must be about 25 to 30 persons. If we build them of that size, it is possible to name them and not call them by some general name at all, but to call them by some special name that belongs to each of them, in exactly the same way as a lot of residential hotels. We might call them " High Mead " or " Low Mead," or " The Limes," or whatever it may be. There is no reason at all why the public character of these places should not be very much in the background, because the whole idea is that the welfare authorities should provide them and charge an economic rent for them, so that any old persons who wish to go may go there in exactly the same way as many well-to-do people have been accustomed to go into residential hotels.

It is of the essence of the scheme, if it is to succeed, that old people who avail themselves of these institutions should be of mixed income groups, because it will at once destroy the character of these places if we have merely the most indigent persons living there. It often happens in our towns and villages that, when old people have reached this stage, they are anxious still to remain with their own neighbours and live among them. A considerable number would probably come into these places, if they were made agreeable and were not tarnished in the very slightest degree by association with the old Poor Law administration.

Mr. Lipson (Cheltenham): May I ask my right hon. Friend a question? He says that they should pay an economic rent. Does that mean that each individual must pay the rent, or that the institution, as a whole, must be economic?

Mr. Bevan: I will explain the position in more detail shortly; I was coming to that point. It is not that the institution as a whole should pay, but that the individual should pay the normal charges for accommodation there. This is the point concerning which I asked hon. Members earlier to have regard to the distinction between the functions of the National Assistance Board, on the one side, and the welfare authorities, on the other. Where an individual has not the resources to enable him to pay the normal charges for the accommodation, he goes to the National Assistance Board, and it is the Board that must put him in the position to pay the minimum charges of the hotel. In such circumstances, of course, there will be lower charges so that the home, as a whole, would not be economic; the welfare authority would itself be making a contribution, but the minimum charge would be 21s. a week. As the old age pension is 26s. a week, that would leave a margin for the individual.

Therefore, we should have in the home a number of persons, some of whom would be paying the normal charges, and the Assistance Board would be paying to the individuals and not to the authorities. The National Assistance Board puts the money into the possession of the individual old age pensioner, who then goes in a perfectly respectable and dignified way to the hotel and pays the charges that the hotel makes, with, as I have already said, a minimum of 21s. a week. This means that, so far as such a person's neighbours are concerned in the same hotel, they do not know who is putting that person in the position to pay the charges. There must be no distinction between those able to pay the full charges themselves and those who are helped to pay the minimum charges by the National Assistance Board. That is a very important consideration which must be borne in mind by everybody when they

[Mr. Bevan.]
are considering this problem. This is the main provision which we hope to make for the old people.

I have already referred to the scheme for the blind so I do not propose to refer to it any more, because the details of it will come up in Committee. There are, however, a number of other categories of persons who require assistance. For instance, there are the deaf—often neglected. Deafness is a fearful affliction, and very much more attention will have to be given to it than has been given to it in the past. When the National Health Service comes into operation, we hope to be in a position to have a large number of aural aids ready for free distribution to the deaf of this country. There are also other handicapped persons, either congenital or through accident. Such people will need to be attended to, and, in particular, to be taught occupations, either in industrial establishments or in their own homes. This will also be the responsibility of the welfare authority dovetailing into the work of the Ministry of Labour which has responsibility under the Disabled Persons (Employment) Act. Therefore, there is this clear distinction which we are drawing between the functions of the National Assistance Board and of the welfare authorities. The welfare authorities will cease to be Poor Law authorities; the public assistance committee will cease to exist. A special committee will be set up for the purpose, or the local authority might get the permission of the Ministry of Health to use one of the existing committees for this purpose.

Mr. Sydney Silverman (Nelson and Colne): Does that mean all of them?

Mr. Bevan: No, it means the welfare authorities, the county and county boroughs in England and Wales, and the counties and large burghs in Scotland. They will be the welfare authorities for this purpose. As I say, these are the main distinctions. The extent to which we can carry them out will depend on our resources, and the extent to which we can establish these new hotels for the old people will depend upon the development of our building programme. But, of course, it must be remembered that the provision of these homes is also a contribution to the housing problem itself. As we put young married people into new

homes at the one end, and thus relieve the housing problem, we can take the old people out at the other end, and, again, relieve the housing problem there. Obviously, it will not be possible for these hotels to spring up overnight; it will take some time to build and equip them. However, we have set our feet upon that road, and we intend to march upon it as quickly as possible.

These are the main provisions of the Bill—simple to state in this House of Commons, detailed to carry out in practice, but bound to have a profound effect upon the welfare and the wellbeing of large numbers of people in the country. It is, I should have thought, a very agreeable thing that, despite all our difficulties, hardships and the diminution of our resources, we are able to turn our attention to this work at the present time. The conditions in which the poor lived in the past were harsh and inhumane. Poverty was treated as though it were a crime. Those of us who have been associated with boards of guardians will know how frightfully difficult it was to administer the Poor Law in a humane fashion. Some of the rules of the old workhouses read like pieces from fiction. Here is Rule 23 which says:

" That all children from five years old to 12 shall be allowed one hour's respite from work to attend the schoolmaster for instruction in reading."

Rule 24 says:

" That encouragement be given to the industrious poor out of the profit of their labour not exceeding 2d. in the 1s. each."

Some of the Poor Law reformers of 1830 may have been humane men, but their regulations were inhuman. Sidney and Beatrice Webb, writing about the workhouse said:

" The young servant out of place, the prostitute recovering from disease, the feeble-minded woman of any age, the girl with her first baby, the unmarried mother coming in to be confined of her third or fourth bastard, the servile, the paralytic, the epileptic, the respectable, deserted wife, the widow to whom outdoor relief has been refused, are all herded indiscriminately together."

Twining, described a workhouse of the 1850's, where:

" The ' nurses ' were pauper inmates, usually infirm and more often drunk than sober, who were remunerated for their services by an amended dietary and a pint of beer, to which was added a glass of gin when their duties were peculiarly repulsive. Underneath the dining hall was the laundry, with the fumes of which it was filled four days of the week, while the lying-in ward was immediately above the female insane ward, the presence of a noisy lunatic or two in which no doubt greatly conduced to the well-being of the parturient women. The ward for fevers and foul cases contained but two beds and was separated from a tinker's shop by a lath and plaster partition.''

These are not things we are immediately leaving behind, because we have left them behind for some little while, but this is the sort of thing on which we are finally turning our backs. This is the sort of thing which has been a reproach to a civilised community. For me, personally, it is a very great honour to have the opportunity of introducing this Bill, and I am sure that to the House as a whole it is a very agreeable occasion indeed to see it read for the Second time.

Part II
Three Worlds

[12]

The three political economies of the welfare state

GØSTA ESPING-ANDERSEN *European University Institute Firenze**

Le très long débat sur la nature et les causes de l'état providence n'a pas apporté de réponses définitives à l'une ou l'autre de ces questions. Cet article a trois buts: 1/ réintégrer le débat dans la tradition intellectuelle de l'économie politique pour mieux faire ressortir les principaux problèmes théoriques; 2/ spécifier les caractéristiques principales de l'état providence, les méthodes traditionnelles de mesure de l'état providence en termes de dépenses n'étant plus satisfaisantes; 3/ 'sociologiser' l'étude de l'état providence. La plupart des études sur le sujet ont été basées sur une conception linéaire du monde: plus ou moins de puissance, d'industrialisation ou de dépenses. Cet article considère que les états providences sont d'abord des groupes de régimes-types et que leur développement doit être expliqué de manière interactive.

The protracted debate on the welfare state has failed to produce conclusive answers as to either the nature or causes of welfare state development. This article has three aims: 1/ to reintegrate the debate into the intellectual tradition of political economy. This serves to put into sharper focus the principal theoretical questions involved; 2/ to specify what are the salient characteristics of welfare states. The conventional ways of measuring welfare states in terms of their expenditures will no longer do; 3/ to 'sociologize' the study of welfare states. Most studies have assumed a world of linearity: more or less power, industrialization or spending. This article insists that we understand welfare states as clusters of regime-types, and that their development must be explained interactively.

* This is part of an ongoing project on welfare states and labor markets, funded by the Research Council of the IUE and European Community. I wish to thank Thomas Cusack, Steven Lukes, John Myles, Fritz von Nordheim Nielsen, and the participants in my IUE seminar on Political Economy, for their constructive comments and criticisms on an earlier version of this paper.

Canad. Rev. Soc. & Anth. / Rev. canad. Soc. & Anth. 26(1) 1989

11 POLITICAL ECONOMIES OF THE WELFARE STATE

THE LEGACY OF CLASSICAL POLITICAL ECONOMY

Contemporary welfare state debates have been guided by two questions. First, does social citizenship diminish the salience of class? Or, in other words, can the welfare state fundamentally transform capitalist society? Second, what are the causal forces behind welfare state development? These questions are not recent. Indeed, they were formulated by the 19th Century political economists 100 years before any welfare state can rightfully be said to have come into existence. The classical political economists – whether of liberal, conservative or Marxist persuasion – were pre-occupied with the relationship between capitalism and welfare. Their answers obviously diverged, but their analyses were unequivically directed to the relationship between market (and property), and the state (democracy). The question they asked was largely normative: what is the optimal division of responsibility between market and state?

Contemporary neo-liberalism echoes the contributions of classical liberal political economy. To Adam Smith, the market was the superior means for the abolition of class, inequality and privilege. Aside from a necessary minimum, state intervention would likely stifle the equalizing process of competitive exchange, create monopolies, protectionism and inefficiency: the state upholds class, the market can potentially undo class society (Smith, 1961: II, especially pp. 232–6).[1]

Liberal political economists were not necessarily of one mind when it came to policy advocacy. Nassau Senior and later Manchester liberals emphasized the laissez-faire element of Smith, rejecting any form of social protection outside the cash nexus. J.S. Mill and the 'reformed liberals,' in turn, were willing to let markets be regulated by a modicum of political regulation. Yet, they were all agreed that the road to equality and prosperity should be paved with a maximum of free markets and a minimum of state interference.

This enthusiastic embrace of market capitalism may now appear unjustified. But, we must take into account that the state which confronted these early political economists was tinged with legacies of absolutist privileges, mercantilist protectionisms, and pervasive curruption. They were attacking systems of governance which repressed the ideals of both freedom and enterprise. Hence, theirs was revolutionary theory, and from this vantage point, we can understand why Adam Smith sometimes reads like Karl Marx.[2]

Democracy was an Achilles heel to many liberals. Their ideals of freedom and democratic participation were grounded in a world of small property owners; not of growing property-less massses who held in their sheer numbers the possibility of seizing state power. The liberals feared the principle of universal suffrage, for it would likely politicize the distributional struggle, pervert the market and fuel inefficiencies. Many liberals discovered that democracy would contradict the market.

Both conservative and Marxist political economists understood this contradiction, but proposed of course opposite solutions. The most coherent conservative critique of laissez faire came from the German historical school; in particular from Friedrich List, Adolph Wagner and Gustav Schmoller. They refused to believe that capitalist efficiency was best assured by the pure commodity status of workers in the raw cash nexus of the market. Instead, conservative political economy believed that patriarchical neo-absolutism could provide the kind of legal, political and social framework that would assure a capitalism without class struggle.

One prominent conservative school promoted a 'Monarchical Welfare State' that would, at once, provide for social welfare, class harmony, loyalty, and productivity. It was discipline, not competition, that would guarantee efficiency. The state (or church) was the institution best equipped to harmonize conflicting interests.[3]

Conservative political economy emerged in reaction to the French Revolution and the Paris Commune. It was avowedly nationalist, anti-revolutionary, and sought to arrest the democratic impulse. It feared social levelling, and favored a society that retained both hierarchy and class. It held that class conflicts were not natural; that democratic mass participation, the dissolution of recognized rank and status boundaries were threats to social harmony.

The key to Marxian political economy, of course, was its rejection of the liberal claim that markets guarantee equality. Capitalist accummulation, as Dobb (1946) put it, disowns people of property whith the end-result being ever deeper class divisions. Here, the state's role is not neutrally benevolent, nor is it a fountain of emancipation; it exists to defend property rights and the authority of capital. To Marxism this is the foundation of class dominance.

The central question, not only for Marxism but for the entire contemporary debate on the welfare state, is whether and under what conditions the class divisions and social inequalities produced by capitalism can be undone by parliamentary democracy.

The liberals feared that democracy would produce socialism and they were consequently not especially eager to extend it. The socialists, in contrast, suspected that parliamentarism would be little more than an empty shell or, as Lenin suggested, a mere 'talking shop' (Jessop, 1982). This line of analysis, echoed in much of contemporary Marxism, leads to the conclusion that social reforms emerge in response to the exigencies of capitalist reproduction, not to the emancipatory desires of the working classes.[4]

Among socialists, a more positive analysis of parliamentarism came to prevail after the extension of full political citizenship. The theoretically most sophisticated contributions came from Austro-Marxists such as Adler and Bauer, and from German social democrats, especially Eduard Heimann. Heimann's (1929) starting point was that conservative reforms may have been motivated by desires to repress labor mobilization, but that their very presence nonetheless alters the balance of class power: the social wage lessens the worker's dependence on the market and employers. The social wage is thus also a potential power resource that defines the frontier between capitalism and socialism. It introduces an alien element into the capitalist

13 POLITICAL ECONOMIES OF THE WELFARE STATE

political economy. This intellectual position has enjoyed quite a renaissance in recent Marxism (Offe, 1985; Bowles and Gintis, 1986).

The social democratic model, as outlined above, did not necessarily abandon the orthodox assumption that fundamental equality requires economic socialization. Yet, historical experience soon demonstrated that socialization was a goal that could not be pursued realistically through parliamentarism.[5]

Social democracy's embrace of parliamentary reformism as its dominant strategy for equality and socialism was premised on two arguments. The first was that workers require social resources, health and education to participate effectively in a democratized economy. The second argument was that social policy is not only emancipatory, but it is also economically efficient (Myrdal and Myrdal, 1936). Following Marx on this point, the strategy therefore promotes the onward march of capitalist productive forces. But, the beauty of the strategy was that social policy would also assure social democratic power mobilization. By eradicating poverty, unemployment and complete wage dependency, the welfare state increases political capacities and diminishes the social divisions that are barriers to political unity among workers.

The social democratic model, then, puts forward one of the leading hypotheses of contemporary welfare state debate: the argument that parliamentary class mobilization is a means for the realization of socialist ideals of equality, justice, freedom and solidarity.

THE POLITICAL ECONOMY OF THE WELFARE STATE

Our political economy forebears defined the analytic basis of much recent scholarship. They isolated the key variables of class, state, market and democracy; and they formulated the basic propositions about citizenship and class, efficiency and equality, capitalism and socialism. Contemporary social science distinguishes itself from classical political economy on two scientifically vital fronts. First, it defines itself as a positive science and shies away from normative prescription (Robbins, 1976). Second, classical political economists had little interest in historical variability; they saw their efforts as leading towards a system of universal laws. Although contemporary political economy sometimes still clings to the belief in absolute truths, the comparative and historical method that, today, underpins almost all good political economy is one that reveals variation and permeability.

Despite these differences, most recent scholarship has as its focal point the state-economy relationship defined by 19th Century political economists. And, given its enormous growth, it is understandable that the welfare state has become a major test case for contending theories of political economy.

Below, we shall review the contributions of comparative research on the development of welfare states in advanced capitalist countries. It will be argued that most scholarship has been misdirected, mainly because it became detached from its theoretical foundations. We must therefore recast both the methodology and concepts of political economy in order to adequately

14 GOSTA ESPING-ANDERSEN

study the welfare state. This will constitute the focus of the final section of
this paper.

Two types of approaches have dominated in the explanation of welfare
states; one, a systemic (or, structuralist) theory; the other, an institutional
or actor-oriented explanation.

THE SYSTEMS/STRUCTURALIST APPROACH

System or structuralist theory seeks to capture the logic of development
holistically. It will easily focus on the functional requisites for the reproduction of society and economy; it will be inclined to emphasize cross-national
similarities rather than differences.

One variant begins with a theory of the industrial society, and argues
that industrialization makes social policy both necessary and possible. It
makes welfare states necessary because pre-industrial modes of social reproduction, such as the family, the church, noblesse oblige, and guild solidarity are destroyed by the forces attached to modernization – social mobility,
urbanization, individualism, and market dependence. The crux of the matter is that the market is no adequate substitute because it caters only to
those who are able to perform in it. Hence, the 'welfare function' is appropriated by the the nation state. The welfare state is also made possible by
the rise of modern bureaucracy as a rational, universalist and efficient form
of organization. It is a means for managing collective goods, but also a center of power in its own right, and will thus be inclined to promote its own
growth.

This kind of reasoning has informed the so-called 'logic of industrialism'
perspective, according to which the welfare state will emerge as the modern
industrial economy destroys traditional forms of social security (Flora and
Alber, 1981; Pryor, 1969). But, the thesis has difficulties explaining why
government social policy only emerged 50 or even 100 years after traditional
community was effectively destroyed? The basic response draws on Wagner's Law (1962; 1883) and on Marshall (1920), namely that a certain level
of economic development, and thus surplus, is needed in order to permit the
diversion of scarce resources from productive use (investments) to welfare
(Wilensky and Lebeaux, 1958). In this sense, the perspective follows in the
footsteps of the old liberals. Social redistribution endangers efficiency, and
only at a certain economic level will a negative-sum trade-off be avoidable
(Okun, 1975).

The new structural Marxism offers a surprisingly parallel analysis. It
breaks with its classical forebears' strongly action-centred theory. Like the
industrialism thesis, its analytical starting point is not the problems of
markets, but the logic of a mode of production. Capital accummulation
creates contradictions that social reform can alleviate (O'Connor, 1973).
This tradition of Marxism, like its 'logic of industrialism' counterpart, fails
to see much relevance in actors in the promotion of welfare states. The point
is that the state, as such, is positioned in such a way that it will serve the
collective needs of capital. The theory is thus premised on two crucial assumptions: first, that power is structural and second, that the state is 'rela-

15 POLITICAL ECONOMIES OF THE WELFARE STATE

tively' autonomous from class directives (Poulantzas, 1973; Block, 1977; for a recent critical assesment of this literature, see Therborn, 1986; and Skocpol and Amenta, 1986).

The 'logic of capitalism' perspective invites difficult questions. If, as Przeworski (1980) has argued, working class consent is assured on the basis of material hegemony, that is self-willed subordination to the system, it is difficult to see why up to 40 per cent of the national product must be allocated to the legitimation activities of a welfare state. A second problem is to derive state activities from a 'mode of production' analysis. Eastern Europe may perhaps not qualify as socialist, but neither is it capitalist. Yet, there we find 'welfare states,' too. Perhaps accummulation has functional requirements in whichever way it proceeds? (Skocpol and Amenta, 1986; Bell, 1978).

THE INSTITUTIONAL APPROACH

The classical political economists made it clear why democratic institutions should influence welfare state development. The liberals feared that full democracy might jeopardize markets and inaugurate socialism. Freedom, in their view, necessitated a defence of markets against political intrusion. In practice, this is what the laissez-faire state sought to accomplish. But it was this divorce of politics and economy which fuelled much of the institutionalist analyses. Best represented by Polanyi (1944), but also by a number of anti-democratic exponents of the historical school, the institutional approach insists that any effort to isolate the economy from social and political institutions will destroy human society. The economy must be embedded in social communities in order for it to survive. Thus, Polanyi sees social policy as one necessary precondition for the re-integration of the social economy.

An interesting recent variant of institutional alignment theory is the argument that welfare states emerge more readily in small, open economies that are particularly vulnerable to international markets. As Katzenstein (1985) and Cameron (1978) show, there is a greater inclination to regulate class distributional conflicts through government and interest concertation when both business and labor are captive to forces beyond domestic control.

The impact of democracy on welfare states has been argued ever since J.S. Mill and de Tocqueville. The argument is typically phrased without reference to any particular social agent or class. It is, in this sense, that it is institutional. In its classical formulation, the thesis was simply that majorities will favor social distribution to compensate for market weakness or market risks. If wage earners are likely to demand a social wage, so are capitalists (or farmers) apt to demand protection in the form of tariffs, monopoly or subsidies. Democracy is an institution that cannot resist majoritarian demands.

In its modern formulations, the democracy thesis has many variants. One identifies stages of nationbuilding in which full citizenship incorporation requires social rights (Marshall, 1950; Bendix, 1964; Rokkan, 1970). A second variant, developed by both pluralist and public choice theory, argues that democracy will nurture intense party competition around the median voter

16 GOSTA ESPING-ANDERSEN

that will, in turn, fuel rising public expenditures. Tufte (1978), for example, argues that major extensions of public intervention will occur around elections as a means of voter mobilization.

The democratic-institutionalist approach faces considerable empirical problems (Skocpol and Amenta, 1986). According to the thesis, a democratic polity is the basic precondition for welfare state emergence, and welfare states are more likely to develop the more democratic rights are extended. Yet, the thesis confronts not only the historical oddity that the first major welfare state initiatives occured prior to democracy, but also that they were often motivated by desires to arrest its realization. This was certainly the case in France under Napoleon II, in Germany under Bismarck, and in Austria under Taaffe. Conversely, welfare state development was most retarded where democracy arrived early, such as in the United States, Australia, and Switzerland. This apparent contradiction can be explained, but only with reference to social classes and social structure: nations with early democracy were overwhelmingly agrarian and dominated by small property owners who used their electoral powers to reduce, not raise, taxes (Dich, 1973). In contrast, ruling classes in authoritarian polities are better positioned to impose high taxes on an unwilling populace.

SOCIAL CLASS AS A POLITICAL AGENT

We have noted that the case for a class mobilization thesis flows from social democratic political economy. It differs from structuralist and institutional analyses by its emphasis on the social classes as the main agents of change, and its argument that the balance of class power determines distributional outcomes. To emphasize active class mobilization does not necessarily deny the importance of structured or hegemonic power (Korpi, 1983). But it is held that parliaments are, in principle, effective institutions for the translation of mobilized power into desired policies and reforms. Accordingly, parliamentary politics are capable of overriding hegemony, and may be made to serve interests that are antagonistic to capital. Further, the class mobilization theory assumes that welfare states do more than simply alleviate the current ills of the system; a 'social democratic' welfare state will, in its own right, establish critical power resources for wage earners and, thus, strengthen labor movements. As Heimann (1929) originally held, social rights push back the frontiers of capitalist power and prerogatives.

The question of why the welfare state itself is a power resource is vital for the theory's applicability. The answer is that wage earners in the market are inherently atomized and stratified, compelled to compete, insecure and dependent on decisions and forces beyond their control. This limits their capacity for collective solidarity and mobilization. The social rights, income security, equalization and eradication of poverty that a universalistic welfare state pursues, are necessary preconditions for the strength and unity that collective power mobilization demands (Esping-Andersen, 1985a).

The single most difficult problem for this thesis is to specify the conditions for power mobilization. Power depends on the resources that flow from the unity of electoral numbers and from collective bargaining. Power mo-

17 POLITICAL ECONOMIES OF THE WELFARE STATE

bilization, in turn, depends on levels of trade union organization, vote shares, parliamentary- and cabinet seats held by left, or labor, parties. But how long a period of sustained power mobilization is required in order to produce decisive effects? If power is measured over a brief time span (5–10 years), we risk the fallacy of a 'Blum'/'Mitterand' effect: a brief spell of left-ist power that proves ineffectual because the left is ousted again before having had a chance to act.

There are several valid objections to the class mobilization thesis. Three, in particular, are quite fundamental. One, is that in advanced capitalist na-tions, the locus of decision making and power may shift from parliaments to neo-corporatist institutions of interest intermediation (Shonfield, 1965; Schmitter and Lembruch, 1979). A second criticism is that the capacity of labor parties to influence welfare state development is circumscribed by the structure of rightist party power. Castles (1978; 1982) has argued that the degree of unity among the rightist parties is more important than is the ac-tivated power of the left. Other authors have emphasized the fact that de-nominational (usually social catholic) parties in countries such as Holland, Italy, and Germany mobilize large sections of the working classes and pursue welfare state programs not drastically at variance with their social-ist competitors (Schmidt, 1982; Wilensky, 1981). The class mobilization the-sis has, rightly, been criticized for its Swedocentrism, i.e., its inclination to define the process of power mobilization too much on the basis of the rather extraordinary Swedish experience (Shalev, 1984).

These objections address a basic fallacy in the theory's assumptions about class formation: we cannot assume that socialism is the natural basis for wage-earner mobilization. Indeed, the conditions under which workers be-come socialists are still not adequately documented. Historically, the natu-ral organizational bases of worker mobilization were pre-capitalist com-munities, especially the guilds, but also the Church, ethnicity or language. A ready-made reference to false consciousness will not do to explain why Dutch, Italian or American workers continue to mobilize around non-social-ist principles. The dominance of socialism in the Swedish working class is as much a puzzle as is the dominance of confessionalism in the Dutch.

The third and, perhaps, most fundamental objection has to do with the model's linear view of power. It is problematic to hold that a numerical in-crease in votes, unionization or seats will translate into more welfare statism. First, for socialist as for other parties, the magical '50 per cent' threshold for parliamentary majorities seems practically unsurmountable (Przeworski, 1985). Second, if socialist parties represent working classes in the traditional sense, it is clear that they will never succeed in their project. In very few cases has the traditional working class been numerically a ma-jority; and its role is rapidly becoming marginal.[6]

Probably the most promising way to resolve the combined linearity and working class minority problem lies in recent applications of Barrington Moore's path-breaking class coalition thesis to the transformation of the modern state (Weir and Skocpol, 1985; Gourevitch, 1986; Esping-Andersen, 1985a; Esping-Andersen and Friedland, 1982). Thus, the origins of the keynsian full employment commitment and the social democratic welfare state edifice have been traced to the capacity of (variably) strong working class movements to forge a political alliance with farmers organizations; additionally, it is arguable that sustained social democracy has come to depend on the formation of a new working class-white collar coalition.

The class coalitional approach has additional virtues. Two nations, such as Austria and Sweden, may score similarly on working class mobilization variables, and yet produce highly unequal policy results. This can be explained by differences in the two countries' historical coalition formation: the breakthrough of Swedish social democratic hegemony stems from its capacity to forge the famous 'red-green' alliance; the comparative disadvantage of the Austrian socialists rests in the 'ghetto' status assigned to them by virtue of the rural classes being captured by a conservative coalition (Esping-Andersen and Korpi, 1984).

In sum, we have to think in terms of social relations, not just social categories. Whereas structural-functionalist explanations identify convergent welfare state outcomes, and class mobilization paradigms see large, but linearly distributed, differences, an interactive model such as the coalitions approach directs attention to distinct welfare state regimes.

WHAT IS THE WELFARE STATE?

Every theoretical paradigm must somehow define the welfare state. How do we know when and if a welfare state responds functionally to the needs of industrialism, or to capitalist reproduction and legitimacy? And how do we identify a welfare state that corresponds to the demands that a mobilized working class might have? We cannot test contending arguments unless we have a commonly shared conception of the phenomenon to be explained.

A remarkable attribute of the entire literature is its lack of much genuine interest in the welfare state as such. Welfare state studies have been motivated by theoretical concerns with other phenomena, such as power, industrialization or capitalist contradictions; the welfare state itself has generally received scant conceptual attention. If welfare states differ, how do they differ? And when, indeed, is a state a welfare state? This turns attention straight back to the original question: what is the welfare state?

A common textbook definition is that it involves state responsibility for securing some basic modicum of welfare for its citizens. Such a definition skirts the issue of whether social policies are emancipatory or not; whether they help system legitimatation or not; whether they contradict or aid the market process; and what, indeed, is meant by 'basic'? Would it not be more appropriate to require of a welfare state that it satisfies more than our basic or minimal welfare needs?

The first generation of comparative studies started with this type of conceptualization. They assumed, without much reflection, that the level of social expenditure adequately reflects a state's commitment to welfare. The theoretical intent was not really to arrive at an understanding of the welfare state, but rather to test the validity of contending theoretical models in political economy. By scoring nations with respect to urbanization, level of

19 POLITICAL ECONOMIES OF THE WELFARE STATE

economic growth, and the share of aged in the demographic structure, it was believed that the essential features of industrial modernization were adequatly captured. Alternatively, by scoring nations on left party strength, or working class power mobilization (with complex weighted scores of trade unionism, electoral strength and cabinet power), others sought to identify the impact of working class mobilization as formulated in the social democratic model.

The findings of the first generation comparativists are extremely difficult to evaluate. No convincing case can be made for any particular theory. The shortage of nations for comparisons statistically restricts the number of variables that can be tested simultaneously. Thus, when Cutright (1965) or Wilensky (1975) finds that economic level, with its demographic and bureaucratic correlates, explains most welfare state variations in 'rich countries,' relevant measures of working class mobilization or economic openness are not included. A conclusion in favor of a 'logic of industrialism' view is therefore in doubt. And, when Hewitt (1977), Stephens (1979), Korpi (1983), Myles (1984) and Esping-Andersen (1985b) find strong evidence in favor of a working class mobilization thesis, or when Schmidt (1982; 1983) finds support for a neo-corporatist, and Cameron (1978) for an economic openness argument, it is without fully testing against the strongest alternative explanation.[7]

Most of these studies claim to explain the welfare state. Yet, their focus on spending may be irrelevant or, at best, misleading. Expenditures are epiphenomenal to the theoretical substance of welfare states. Moreover, the linear scoring approach (more or less power, democracy or spending) contradicts the sociological notion that power, democracy, or welfare are relational and structured phenomena. By scoring welfare states on spending, we assume that all spending counts equally. But, some welfare states, the Austrian for example, spend a large share on benefits to privileged civil servants. This is normally not what we would consider a commitment to social citizenship and solidarity. Others spend disproportionally on means-tested social assistance. Few contemporary analysts would agree that a reformed poor relief tradition qualifies as a welfare state commitment. Some nations spend enormous sums on fiscal welfare in the form of tax privileges to private insurance plans that mainly benefit the middle classes. But these tax expenditures do not show up on expenditure accounts. In Britain, total social expenditure has grown during the Thatcher period; yet, this is almost exclusively a function of very high unemployment. Low expenditures on some programs may signify a welfare state more seriously committed to full employment.

Therborn (1983) is right when he holds that we must begin with a conception of state structure. What are the criteria with which we should judge whether, and when, a state is a welfare state? There are three approaches to this question. Therborn's proposal is to begin with the historical transformation of state activities. Minimally, in a genuine welfare state the majority of its daily routine activities must be devoted to servicing the welfare needs of households. This criterion has far-reaching consequences. If we

20 GOSTA ESPING-ANDERSEN

simply measure routine activity in terms of spending and personnel, the result is that no state can be regarded as a real welfare state until the 1970's! And, some that we normally label as welfare states will still not qualify because the majority of their routine activities concern defence, law and order, administration and the like (Therborn, 1983). Social scientists have been too quick to accept nations' self-proclaimed welfare state status. They have also been too quick to conclude that the presence of the battery of typical social programs signify the birth of a welfare state.

The second conceptual approach derives from Richard Titmuss' (1958) classical distinction between residual and institutional welfare states. The former assumes that state responsibility begins only when the family or the market fails; its commitment is limited to marginal groups in society. The latter model addresses the entire population, is universalistic, and implants an institutionalized commitment to welfare. It will, in principle, extend welfare commitments to all areas of distribution vital for societal welfare. This approach has fertilized a variety of new developments in comparative welfare state research (Myles, 1984; Korpi, 1980; Esping-Andersen and Korpi, 1984; 1986; Esping-Andersen, 1985b; 1987). And it has forced researchers to move away from the black box of expenditures and towards the content of welfare states: targeted versus universalistic programs, the conditions of eligibility, the quality of benefits and services and, perhaps most importantly, the extent to which employment and working life are encompassed in the state's extension of citizen rights. This shift to welfare state typologies makes simple linear welfare state rankings difficult to sustain. We might in fact be comparing categorically different types of states.

The third approach is to select theoretically the criteria on which to judge types of welfare states. This can be done by measuring actual welfare states against some abstract model and then by scoring programs, or entire welfare states, accordingly (Day, 1978; Myles, 1984). The weakness of this approach is that it is ahistorical, and does not necessarily capture the ideals or designs that historical actors sought to realize in the struggles over the welfare state. If our aim is to test causal theories that involve actors, we should begin with the demands that were actually promoted by those actors that we deem critical in the history of welfare state development. It is difficult to imagine that anyone struggled for spending per se.

A RESPECIFICATION OF THE WELFARE STATE[8]

Few can disagree with T.H. Marshall's (1950) proposition that social citizenship constitutes the core idea of a welfare state. What, then, are the key principles involved in social citizenship? In our view, they must involve first and foremost the granting of social rights. This mainly entails a de-commodification of the status of individuals vis-à-vis the market. Secondly, social citizenship involves social stratification; one's status as a citizen will compete with, or even replace, one's class position. Thirdly, the welfare state must be understood in terms of the interface between the market, the family, and the state. These principles need to be fleshed out prior to any theoretical specification of the welfare state.

21 POLITICAL ECONOMIES OF THE WELFARE STATE

Rights and de-commodification

As commodities in the market, workers depend for their welfare entirely on the cash-nexus. The question of social rights is thus one of de-commodification, that is of granting alternative means of welfare to that of the market. De-commodification may refer either to the service rendered, or to the status of a person, but in both cases it signifies the degree to which distribution is detached from the market mechanism. This means that the mere presence of social assistance or insurance may not necessarily bring about significant de-commodification if they do not substantially emancipate individuals from market dependence. Means-tested poor relief will possibly offer a security blanket of last resort. But if benefits are low and attached with social stigma, the relief system will compel all but the most desperate to participate in the market. This was precisely the intent of the 19th Century poor laws. Similarly, most of the early social insurance programs were deliberately designed to maximize labor market performance (Ogus, 1979). Benefits required long contribution periods and were tailored to prior work effort. In either case, the motive was to avert work-disincentive effects.

There is no doubt that de-commodification has been a hugely contested issue in welfare state development. For labor, it has always been a priority. When workers are completely market dependent, they are difficult to mobilize for solidaristic action. Since their resources mirror market inequalities, divisions emerge between the 'ins' and the 'outs,' making labor movement formation difficult. De-commodification strengthens the worker and weakens the absolute authority of the employer. It is for exactly this reason that employers always opposed de-commodification.

De-commodified rights are differentially developed in contemporary welfare states. In social assistance dominated welfare states rights are not so much attached to work performance as to demonstrable need. Needs-tests and typically meagre benefits, however, serve to curtail the de-commodifying effect. Thus, in nations where this model is dominant (mainly in the Anglo-Saxon countries), the result is actually to strengthen the market since all but those who fail in the market will be encouraged to contract private sector welfare.

A second dominant model espouses compulsory state social insurance with fairly strong entitlements. Yet, again, this may not automatically secure substantial de-commodification, since this hinges very much on the fabric of eligibility and benefit rules. Germany was the pioneer of social insurance, but over most of the century can hardly be said to have brought about much in the way of de-commodification through its social programs. Benefits have depended almost entirely on contributions and, thus, work and employment. In fact, before the Second World War, average pensions in the German insurance system for workers were lower than prevailing poverty assistance rates (Myles, 1984). The consequence, as with the social assistance model, was that most workers would chose to remain at work rather than retire. In other words, it is not the mere presence of a social right, but the corresponding rules and preconditions that dictate the extent to which welfare programs offer genuine alternatives to market dependence.

22 GOSTA ESPING-ANDERSEN

The third dominant model of welfare, namely the Beveridge-type citizens benefit, may, at first glance, appear the most de-commodifying. It offers a basic, equal benefit to all irrespective of prior earnings, contributions or per-formance. It may indeed be a more solidaristic system, but not necessarily de-commodifying since, only rarely, have such schemes been able to offer benefits of such a standard that they provide recipients with a genuine option to that of working.

De-commodifying welfare states are, in practice, of very recent date. A minimalist definition must entail that citizens can freely, and without potential losses of job, income or general welfare, opt out of work under con-ditions when they, themselves, consider it necessary for reasons of health, family, age or even educational self-improvement; when, in short, they deem it necessary for participating adequately in the social community.

With this definition in mind, we would, for example, require of a sickness insurance that individuals be secured benefits equal to normal earnings, the right to absence with minimal proof of medical impairment, and for the du-ration that the individual deems necessary. These conditions, it is worth noting, are those usually enjoyed by academics, civil servants and higher echelon white collar employees. Similar requirements would be made of pen-sions, maternity leave, parental leave, educational leave and unemployment insurance.

Some nations have moved towards this level of de-commodification, but only recently and, in many cases, with significant exemptions. Thus, in al-most all nations benefits were upgraded to equal normal wages in the late 1960s and early 1970s. But, in some countries, for example, prompt medical certification in case of illness is still required; in others, entitlements de-pend on long waiting periods of up to two weeks; and, in still others, the du-ration of entitlements is very short (in the United States, for example, unemployment benefit duration is maximally six months, compared to 30 in Denmark). Overall, the Scandinavian welfare states tend to be the most de-commodifying; the Anglo-Saxon the least.

The Welfare State as a System of Stratification

Despite the emphasis given to it in both classical political economy and in T.H. Marshall's pioneering work, the relationship between citizenship and social class remains severely neglected, both theoretically and empirically. Generally speaking, the issue has either been assumed away (it has been taken for granted that the welfare state creates a more egalitarian society), or it has been approached narrowly in terms of income distribution or in terms of whether education promotes upward social mobility. A more basic question, it seems, is what kind of stratification system is promoted by so-cial policy. The welfare state is not just a mechanism that intervenes in, and possibly corrects, the structure of inequality; it is, in its own right, a system of stratification. It orders actively and directly social relations.

Comparatively and historically, we can easily identify alternative systems of stratification embedded in welfare states. The poor relief tradition, and its contemporary means-tested social assistance offshoot, was conspicuously

23 POLITICAL ECONOMIES OF THE WELFARE STATE

designed for purposes of stratification. By punishing and stigmatizing recipients, it promotes severe social dualisms, especially within the ranks of
the working classes. It comes as no suprise that this model of welfare has
been a chief target of labor movement attacks.

The social insurance model promoted by conservative reformers such as
Bismarck and von Taaffe was also explicitly a form of class politics. It sought,
in fact, to achieve two simultaneous stratification results. The first was to
consolidate divisions among wage earners by legislating distinct programs
for different class and status groups, each with its own conspicuously unique
set of rights and privileges designed to accentuate the individual's appropriate station in life. The second objective was to tie the loyalties of the individual directly to the monarchy, or central state authority. This was
Bismarck's motive when he promoted a direct state supplement to the pension benefit. This state-corporativist model was pursued mainly in nations
such as Germany, Austria, Italy and France and often resulted in a laby-
rinth of status-specific insurance funds (in France and Italy, for example,
there exist more than 100 status-distinct pension schemes).

Of special importance in this corporatist tradition was the establishment
of particularly privileged welfare provisions for the civil service ('Beamten').
In part, this was a means of rewarding loyalty to the state and in part, a way
of demarcating this group's uniquely exalted social status. We should,
however, be careful to note that the corporatist status-differentiated model
springs mainly from the old guild tradition. The neo-absolutist autocrats,
such as Bismarck, saw in this tradition a means to combat the rising labor
movements.

The labor movements were as hostile to the corporatist model as they
were to poor relief – in both cases for obvious reasons. Yet, the alternatives
first espoused by labor were no less problematic from the point of view of
uniting the workers as one solidaristic class. Almost invariably, the model
that labor first pursued was that of the self-organized friendly societies or
equivalent union- or party-sponsored fraternal welfare plan. This is not surprising. Workers were obviously suspicious of reforms sponsored by a hostile
state, and saw their own organizations not only as bases of class mobilization, but also as embryos of an alternative world of solidarity and justice, as
a microcosm of the socialist haven to come. Nonetheless, these microsocial-
ist societies often became problematic class ghettos that divided rather than
united workers. Membership was typically restricted to the strongest strata
of the working class and the weakest – who needed protection most – were
most likely outside. In brief, the fraternal society model contradicted the
goal of working class mobilization.

The socialist ghetto approach was an additional obstacle when socialist
parties found themselves forming governments and having to pass the social reforms they so long had demanded. For reasons of political coalition
building and broader solidarity, their welfare model had to be recast as welfare for the 'people'. Hence, the socialists came to espouse the principle of
universalism and, borrowing from the liberals, typically designed on the
lines of the democratic flat-rate, general revenue financed, Beveridge model.

24 GOSTA ESPING-ANDERSEN

As an alternative to means-tested assistance and corporatist social insurance, the universalistic system promotes status equality. All citizens are endowed with similar rights, irrespective of class or market position. In this sense, this system is meant to cultivate cross-class solidarity, a solidarity of the nation. But, the solidarity of flat-rate universalism presumes an historically peculiar class structure; one in which the vast majority of the population are the 'little people' for whom a modest, albeit egalitarian, benefit may be considered adequate. Where this no longer obtains, as occcurs with growing working class prosperity and the rise of the new middle classes, flat-rate universalism inadvertently promotes dualism because the better off turn to private insurance and to fringe-benefit bargaining to supplement modest equality with what they have decided are accustomed standards of welfare. Where this process unfolds (as in Canada or the United Kingdom), the result is that the wonderfully egalitarian spirit of universalism turns into a dualism similar to that of the social assistance state: the poor rely on the state, and the remainder on the market.

It is not only the universalist, but in fact all historical welfare state models which have faced the dilemma of class structural change. But, the response to prosperity and middle class growth has been varied and so, therefore, has been the stratificational outcome. The corporatist insurance tradition was, in a sense, best equipped to manage new and loftier welfare state expectations since the existing system could technically be upgraded quite easily to distribute more adequate benefits. Adenauer's 1957 pension reform in Germany was a pioneer in this respect. Its avowed purpose was to restore status differences that had eroded due to the old insurance system's incapacity to provide benefits tailored to expectations. This it did simply by moving from contribution- to earnings-graduated benefits without altering the framework of status-distinctiveness.

In nations with either a social assistance or a universalistic Beveridge-type system, the option was whether to allow the market or the state to furnish adequacy and satisfy middle class aspirations. Two alternative models emerged from this political choice. The one typical of Great Britain and most of the Anglo Saxon world was to preserve an essentially modest universalism in the state and allow the market to reign for the growing social strata demanding superior welfare. Due to the political power of such groups, the dualism that emerges is not merely one between state and market, but also between forms of welfare state transfers: in these nations, one of the fastest growing components of public expenditure is tax-subsidies for so-called 'private' welfare plans. And the typical political effect is eroding middle class support for what is less and less a universalistic public sector transfer system.

Yet another alternative has been to seek a synthesis of universalism and adequacy outside of the market. This road has been followed in the countries where, by mandating or legislation, the state includes the new middle classes by erecting a luxurious second-tier, universally inclusive, earnings related insurance scheme on top of the flat-rate egalitarian one. Notable examples are Sweden and Norway. By guaranteeing benefits tailored to ex-

25 POLITICAL ECONOMIES OF THE WELFARE STATE

pectations, this solution re-introduces benefit inequalities, but effectively blocks off the market. It thus succeeds in retaining universalism and, therefore, also the degree of political consensus required to preserve broad and solidaristic support for the high taxes that such a welfare state model demands.

Welfare State Regimes
Welfare states vary considerably with respect to their principles of rights and stratification. This results in qualitatively different arrangements between state, market and the family. The welfare state variations we find, are therefore not linearly distributed, but clustered by regime-types.

In one cluster, we find the 'liberal' welfare state, in which means-tested assistance, modest universal transfers, or modest social insurance plans predominate. These cater mainly to a clientele of low income, usually working class, state dependents. It is a model in which, implicitly or explicitly, the progress of social reform has been severely circumscribed by traditional, liberal work-ethic norms; one where the limits of welfare equal the marginal propensity to demand welfare instead of work. Entitlement rules are therefore strict and often associated with stigma; benefits are typically modest. In turn, the state encourages the market, either passively by guaranteeing only a minimum, or actively by subsidizing private welfare schemes.

The consequence is that this welfare state regime minimizes de-commodification-effects, effectively contains the realm of social rights, and erects a stratification order that blends a relative equality of poverty among state welfare recipients, market-differentiated welfare among the majorities, and a class-political dualism between the two. The archetypical examples of this model are the United States, Canada, and Australia. Nations that approximate the model are Denmark, Switzerland, and Great Britain.

A second regime-cluster is composed of nations such as Austria, France, Germany and Italy. Here, the historical corporatist-statist legacy was upgraded to cater to the new 'post-industrial' class structure. In these 'corporatist' welfare states, the liberal obsession with market efficiency and commodification was never pre-eminent and, as such, the granting of social rights was hardly ever a seriously contested issue. What predominated was the preservation of status differentials; rights, therefore, were attached to class and status. This corporativism was subsumed under a state edifice perfectly ready to displace the market as a provider of welfare; hence, private insurance and occupational fringe benefits play a truly marginal role in this model. On the other hand, the state's emphasis on upholding status differences means that its redistributive effects are negligible.

But, the corporativist regimes are also typically shaped by the Church, and therefore influenced by a strong commitment to the preservation of traditional family patterns. Social insurance typically excludes non-working wives, and family benefits encourage motherhood. Day care, and similar family services, are conspicuously underdeveloped, and the 'subsidiarity principle' serves to emphasize that the state will only interfere when the family's capacity to service its memnbers is exhausted. An illustrative ex-

26 GOSTA ESPING-ANDERSEN

ample is German unemployment assistance. Once a person has exhausted his/her entitlement to normal unemployment insurance, eligibility for continued assistance depends on whether one's family commands the financial capacity to aid the unfortunate; this obtains for persons of any age.

The third, and clearly smallest, regime-cluster is composed of those countries in which the principles of universalism and de-commodifying social rights were extended also to the new middle classes. We may call it the 'social democratic' regime-type since, in these nations, social democracy clearly was the dominant force behind social reform. Norway and Sweden are the clearest cases, but we should also consider Denmark and Finland. Rather than tolerate a dualism between state and market, between working class and middle class, the social democrats pursued a welfare state that would promote an equality of the highest standards, rather than an equality of minimal needs as was pursued elsewhere. This implied, first, that services and benefits be upgraded to levels commensurable to even the most discriminate tastes of the new middle classes; and, secondly, that equality be furnished by guaranteeing workers full participation in the quality of rights enjoyed by the better off.

This formula translates into a mix of highly de-commodifying and universalistic programs that, nonetheless, are tailored to differentiated expectations. Thus, manual workers come to enjoy rights identical to those of salaried white collar employees or civil servants; all strata and classes are incorporated under one universal insurance system; yet, benefits are graduated according to accustumed earnings. This model crowds out the market and, consequently, inculcates an essentially universal solidarity behind the welfare state. All benefit, all are dependent, and all will presumably feel obliged to pay.

The social democratic regime's policy of emancipation addresses both the market and the traditional family. In contrast to the corporatist-subsidiarity model, the principle is not to wait until the family's capacity to aid is exhausted, but to pre-emptively socialize the costs of familihood. The ideal is not to maximize dependence on the family, but capacities for individual independence. In this sense, the model is a peculiar fusion of liberalism and socialism. The result is a welfare state that grants transfers directly to the children, and takes direct caring responsibilities for children, the aged and the helpless. It is, accordingly, committed to a heavy social service burden, not only to service family needs, but also to permit women to chose work rather than the household.

Perhaps the most salient characteristic of the social democratic regime is its fusion of welfare and work. It is, at once, a welfare state genuinely committed to a full employment guarantee, and a welfare state entirely dependent on its attainment. On the one side, it is a model in which the right to work has equal status to the right of income protection. On the other side, the enormous costs of maintaining a solidaristic, universalistic and de-commodifying welfare system means that it must minimize social problems and maximize revenue income. This is obviously best done with most people working, and the fewest possible living off social transfers.

27 POLITICAL ECONOMIES OF THE WELFARE STATE

While it is empirically clear that welfare states cluster, we must recognize that no single case is pure. The social democratic regimes of Scandinavia blend crucial socialist and liberal elements. The Danish and Swedish unemployment insurance schemes, for example, are still essentially voluntarist. Denmark's labor movement has been chronically incapable of pursuing full employment policies due in part to trade union resistance to active manpower policies. And in both Denmark and Finland, the market has been allowed to play a decisive role in pensions.

Neither are the liberal regimes pure. The American social security system is redistributive, compulsory and far from actuarial. At least in its early formulation, the New Deal was as social democratic as was contemporary Scandinavian social democracy. In contrast, the Australian welfare state would appear exceedingly close to the bourgeois-liberal ideal-type, but much of its edifice has been the co-responsibility of Australian labor. And, finally, the European corporatist regimes have received both liberal and social democratic impulses. Social insurance schemes have been substantially de-stratified and unified in Austria, Germany, France and Italy. Their extremely corporativist character has thus been reduced.

Notwithstanding the lack of purity, if our essential criteria for defining welfare states have to do with the quality of social rights, social stratification, and the relationship between state, market and family, the World is composed of distinct regime-clusters. Comparing welfare states on scales of more or less or, indeed, better or worse, will yield highly misleading results.

THE CAUSES OF WELFARE STATE REGIMES

If welfare states cluster into three distinct regime types, we are confronted with a substantially more complex task of identifying the causes of welfare state differences. What is the explanatory power of industrialization, economic growth, capitalism, or working class political power in accounting for regime types? A first superficial answer would be: very little. The nations we study are all more or less similar with regard to all but the working class mobilization variable. And we find very powerful labor movements and parties in each of the three clusters. A theory of welfare state developments must clearly reconsider its causal assumptions if we wish to explain clusters. The hope to find one single powerful causal motor must be abandoned; the task is to identify salient interaction effects. Based on the preceding arguments, three factors in particular should be of importance: the nature of (especially working-) class mobilization; class-political coalition structures; and the historical legacy of regime institutionalization.

As we have noted, there is absolutely no compelling reason to believe that workers will automatically and naturally forge a socialist class identity; nor is it plausible that their mobilization will look especially Swedish. The actual historical formation of working class collectivities will diverge, and so also will their aims and political capacities. Fundamental differences appear both in trade unionism and party development. A key element in trade unionism is the mix of craft and industrial unions. The former is prone to particularism and corporativism; the latter is inclined to articulate broader, more universal objectives. This blend decisively affects the scope for labor party action and also the nature of political demands. Thus, the dominance of the AFL in pre-war United States was a major impediment to social policy development. Likewise, the heavily craft-oriented Danish labor movement, compared to its Norwegian and Swedish counterparts, blocked social democracy's aspirations for an active labor market policy for full employment. In the United States, craft unions believed that negotiating occupational benefits was a superior strategy, given their privileged market position. In Denmark, craft unions jealously guarded their monopoly on training and labor mobility. Conversely, centralized industrial unionism will tend to present a more unified and consolidated working class clientele to the labor party, making policy consensus easier, and power mobilization more effective. It is clear that a working class mobilization thesis must pay attention to union structure.

Equally decisive is political or denominational union fragmentation. In many nations, for example Finland, France and Italy, trade unions are divided between socialist and communist parties; white collar unions are politically unaffiliated or divide their affiliation among several parties. Denominational trade unionism has been a powerful feature in Holland, Italy and other nations. Since trade unionism is such a centrally important basis for party mobilization, such fragmentation will weaken the left and thus benefit the non-socialist parties' chances of power. In addition, fragmentation may entail that welfare state demands will be directed to many parties at once. The result may be less party conflict over social policy, but it may also mean a plurality of competing welfare state principles. For example, the subsidiarity principle of Christian workers will conflict with the socialists' concern for the emancipation of women.

The structure of trade unionism may, or may not, be reflected in labor party formation. But, under what conditions are we likely to expect certain welfare state outcomes from specific party configurations? There are many factors that conspire to make it virtually impossible to assume that any labor, or left, party will ever be capable, single-handedly, of structuring a welfare state. Denominational or other divisions aside, it will be only under extraordinary historical circumstances that a labor party alone will command a parliamentary majority long enough to impose its will. We have noted that the traditional working class has, nowhere, ever been an electoral majority. It follows that a theory of class mobilization must look beyond the major leftist party. It is an historical fact that welfare state construction has depended on political coalition building. The structure of class coalitions is much more decisive than are the power resources of any single class.

The emergence of alternative class coalitions is, in part, determined by class formation. In the earlier phases of industrialization, the rural classes usually constituted the single largest electorate. If social democrats wanted political majorities, it was here that they were forced to look for allies. Therefore, it was ironically the rural economy that was decisive for the future of socialism. Where the rural economy was dominated by small, capital inten-

29 POLITICAL ECONOMIES OF THE WELFARE STATE

sive family farmers, the potential for an alliance was greater than where it rested on large pools of cheap labor. And, where farmers were politically articulate and well-organized (as in Scandinavia), the capacity to negotiate political deals was vastly superior.

The role of the farmers in coalition formation and, hence, in welfare state development is clear. In the Nordic countries, the conditions obtained for a broad red-green alliance for a full-employment welfare state in return for farm price subsidies. This was especially true in Norway and Sweden, where farming was highly precarious and dependent on state aid. In the United States, the New Deal was premised on a similar coalition (forged by the Democratic party) but with the important difference that the labor intensive South blocked a truly universalistic social security system, and opposed further welfare state developments. In contrast, the rural economy of Continental Europe was very inhospitable to red-green coalitions. Often, as in Germany and Italy, much of agriculture was labor intensive and labor unions and left parties were seen as a threat. In addition, the conservative forces on the continent had succeeded in incorporating farmers into 'reactionary' alliances, helping to consolidate the political isolation of labor.

Political dominance was, until after World War II, largely a question of rural class politics. The construction of welfare states in this period was, therefore, dictated by which force captured the farmers. The absence of a red-green alliance does not necessarily imply that no welfare state reforms were possible. On the contrary, it implies which political force came to dominate their design. Great Britain is an exception to this general rule, because the political significance of the rural classes eroded before the turn of the century. In this way, Britain's coalition logic showed at an early date the dilemma that faced most other nations later, namely that the new white collar middle classes constitute the linchpin for political majorities. The consolidation of welfare states after World War II came to depend fundamentally on the political alliances of the new middle classes. For social democracy, the challenge was to synthesize working class- and white collar demands without sacrificing the commitment to solidarity.

Since the new middle classes have, historically, enjoyed a relatively privileged position in the market, they have also been quite succesful in meeting their welfare demands outside the state or, as civil servants, by privileged state welfare. Their employment security has traditionally been such that full employment has been a peripheral concern. Finally, any program for drastic income equalization is likely to be met with great hostility among a middle class clientele. On these grounds, it would appear that the rise of the new middle classes would abort the social democratic project and strengthen a liberal welfare state formula.

The political position of the new middle classes has, indeed, been decisive for welfare state consolidation. Their role in shaping the three welfare state regimes described earlier is clear. The Scandinavian model relied almost entirely on social democracy's capacity to incorporate them in a new kind of welfare state: one that provided benefits tailored to the tastes and expectations of the middle classes, but nonetheless retained universalism of rights.

Indeed, by expanding social services and public employment, the welfare state participated directly in manufacturing a middle class instrumentally devoted to social democracy.

In contrast, the Anglo-Saxon nations retained the residual welfare state model precisely because the new middle classes were not wooed from the market into the state. In class terms, the consequence is dualism. The welfare state caters essentially to the working class, and to the poor. Private insurance and occupational fringe benefits cater to the middle classes. Given the electoral importance of the latter, it is quite logical that further extensions of welfare state activities are resisted. Indeed, the most powerful thrust in these countries is an accent on fiscal welfare; i.e., on tax expenditures and deductions for private sector welfare plans.

The third, Continental European, welfare state regime has also been patterned by the new middle classes, but in a different way. The cause is historical. Developed by conservative political forces, these regimes institutionalized a middle class loyalty to the preservation of both occupationally segregated social insurance programs and, ultimately, to the political forces that brought them into being. Adenauer's great pension reform in 1957 was explicitly designed to resurrect middle class loyalties.

CONCLUSION

We have here presented an alternative to a simple class mobilization theory of welfare state development. It is motivated by the analytical necessity of shifting from a linear to an interactive approach with regard to both welfare states and their causes. If we wish to study welfare states, we must begin with a set of criteria that define their role in society. This role is certainly not to spend or tax; nor is it necessarily that of creating equality. We have presented a framework for comparing welfare states that takes into consideration the principles for which the historical actors willingly have struggled and mobilized. And, when we focus on the principles embedded in welfare states, we discover distinct regime clusters, not merely variations of 'more' or 'less' around a common denominator.

The salient forces that explain the crystallization of regime differences are interactive. They involve, first, the pattern of working class political formation and, second, the structuration of political coalitions with the historical shift from a rural economy to a middle class society. The question of political coalition formation is decisive.

Third, past reforms have contributed decisively to the institutionalization of class preferences and political behavior. In the corporatist regimes, hierarchical status-distinctive social insurance cemented middle-class loyalty to a peculiar type of welfare state. In the liberal regimes, the middle classes became institutionally wedded to the market. And, in Scandinavia, the fortunes of social democracy after the war were closely tied to the establishment of a middle class welfare state that benefits both its traditional working class clientele and the new white collar strata. In part, the Scandinavian social democrats were able to do so because the private welfare market was relatively undeveloped and, in part, because they were capable

31 POLITICAL ECONOMIES OF THE WELFARE STATE

of building a welfare state with features of sufficient luxury to satisfy the tastes of a more discriminating public. This also explains the extraordinarily high cost of Scandinavian welfare states.

But, a theory that seeks to explain welfare state growth should also be able to understand its retrenchment or decline. It is typically believed that welfare state backlash movements, tax revolts, and roll-backs are ignited when social expenditure burdens become too heavy. Paradoxically, the opposite is true. Anti-welfare state sentiments over the past decade have generally been weakest where welfare spending has been heaviest, and viceversa. Why?

The risks of welfare state backlash depend not on spending, but on the class character of welfare states. Middle class welfare states, be they social democratic (as in Scandinavia) or corporatist (as in Germany), forge middle class loyalties. In contrast, liberal, residualist welfare states found in the United States, Canada and, increasingly, Britain depend on the loyalties of a numerically weak, and often politically residual social stratum. In this sense, the class coalitions in which the three welfare states were founded, explain not only their past evolution but also their future prospects.

NOTES

1   Adam Smith is often cited but rarely read. A closer inspection of his writings reveals a degree of nuance and a battery of reservations that substantially qualify a delirious enthusiasm for the blessings of capitalism.

2   In the *Wealth of Nations* (Smith, 1961: II: 236), he comments on states that uphold the privilege and security of the propertied as follows: '... civil government, so far as it is instituted for the security of property, in in reality instituted for the defence of the rich against the poor, or of those who have some property against those who have none at all'.

3   This tradition is virtually unknown to Anglo-Saxon readers, since so little has been translated into English. A key text which greatly influenced public debate and later social legislation was Adolph Wagner's, Rede Ueber die Soziale Frage (1872). For an English language overview of this tradition of political economy, see Schumpeter (1954), and especially Bower (1947).

    From the Catholic tradition, the fundamental texts are the two Papal Encyclicals, Rerum Novarum (1891) and Quadrogesimo Anno (1931). The social Catholic political economy's main advocacy is a social organization where a strong family is integrated in cross-class corporations, aided by the state in terms of the subsidiarity principle. For a recent discussion, see Richter (1987).

    Like the liberals, the conservative political economists also have their contemporary echoes, although substantially fewer in number. A revival occurred with Fascism's concept of the Corporative ('Standische') state of Ottmar Spann in Germany. The subsidiarity principle still guides much of German Christian Democratic politics (see Richter, op.cit).

4   Chief proponents of this analysis are the German 'state derivation' school (Muller and Neususs, 1973); Offe (1972); O'Connor (1973); Gough (1979); and also the work of Poulantzas (1973). As Skocpol and Amenta (1986) note in their excellent overview, the approach is far from one-dimensional. Thus, Offe, O'Connor and Gough identify the function of social reforms as being also concessions to mass demands and as potentially contradictory.

32 GOSTA ESPING-ANDERSEN

Historically, socialist opposition to parliamentary reforms was principled less by theory than by reality. August Bebel, the great leader of German social democracy, rejected Bismarck's pioneering social legislation, not because he did not favor social protection, but because of the blatantly anti-socialist and divisionary motives behind Bismarck's reforms.

5   This realization came from two types of experiences. One, typified by Swedish socialism in the 1920s, was the discovery that not even the working class base showed much enthusiasm for socialization. In fact, when the Swedish socialists established a special commission to prepare plans for socialization, it concluded after 10 years of exploration that it would be practically quite impossible to undertake. A second kind of experience, typified by the Norwegian socialists and Blum's Popular Front government in 1936, was the discovery that radical proposals could easily be sabotaged by the capitalists' capacity to withhold investments and export their capital abroad.

6   This is obviously not a problem for the parliamentary class hypothesis alone; structural Marxism faces the same problem of specifying the class character of the new middle classes. If such a specification fails to demonstrate that it constitutes a new working class, both varieties of Marxist theory face severe (although not identical) problems.

7   This literature has been reviewed in great detail by a number of authors. See, for example, Wilensky et al. (1985). For excellent and more critical evaluations, see Uusitalo (1984), Shalev (1983) and Skocpol and Amenta (1986).

8   This section derives much of its material from earlier writings (see, especially Esping-Andersen, 1985a; 1985b; 1987).

REFERENCES

Bell, D.
1978 The Cultural Contradictions of Capitalism. New York: Basic Books
Bendix, R.
1964 Nation-Building and Citizenship. New York: John Wiley and Sons
Block, F.
1977 'The Ruling Class does not Rule.' Socialist Review 7 (May–June)
Bower, R.H.
1947 German Theories of the Corporate State. New York: Russel and Russel
Bowles, S., and H. Gintis
1986 Democracy and Capitalism. New York: Basic Books
Brandes, S.
1970 American Welfare Capitalism, 1880–1940. Chicago: University of Chicago
     Press
Cameron, D.
1978 'The Expansion of the Public Economy: A Comparative Analysis.' American
     Political Science Review 4
Castles, F.
1978 The Social Democratic Image of Society. London: Routledge and Kegan Paul
Castles, F. (ed.)
1982 The Impact of Parties. London: Sage
Cutright, P.
1965 'Political Structure, Economic Development, and National Social Security
     Programs.' American Journal of Sociology 70
Day, L.

33 POLITICAL ECONOMIES OF THE WELFARE STATE

1978 'Government Pensions for the Aged in 19 Industrialized Countries.' In R.
    Tomasson (ed.), Comparative Studies in Sociology. Greenwich, Conn: JAI
    Press
Dich, J.
1973 Den Herskende Klasse. Copenhagen: Borgen
Dobb, M.
1946 Studies in the Development of Capitalism. London: Routledge and Kegan
    Paul
Downs, A.
1957 An Economic Theory of Democracy. New York: Harper and Row
Esping-Andersen, G.
1985a Politics against Markets. Princeton: Princeton University Press
1985b 'Power and Distributional Regimes.' Politics and Society 14
1987 'Citizenship and Socialism: De-commodification and Solidarity in the Wel-
    fare State.' In G. Esping-Andersen, M. Rein, and L. Rainwater (eds.), Stag-
    nation and Renewal. Armonk, NY: M.E. Sharpe
Esping-Andersen, G., and R. Friedland
1982 'Class Coalitions in the Making of West European Economies.' Political
    Power and Social Theory 3
Esping-Andersen, G., and W. Korpi
1984 'Social Policy as Class Politics in Postwar Capitalism.' In J. Goldthorpe
    (ed.), Order and Conflict in Contemporary Capitalism. Oxford: Oxford
    University Press
1986 'From Poor Relief to Institutional Welfare States.' In R. Erikson et al. (eds.),
    The Scandinavian Model. Armonk, NY: M.E. Sharpe
Evans, E.
1978 Social Policy, 1830–1914. London: Routledge and Kegan Paul
Flora, P., and J.Alber
1981 'Modernization, Democratization and the Development of Welfare States in
    Europe.' In P. Flora and A. Heidenheimer (eds.), The Development of Wel-
    fare States in Europe and America. London: Transaction Books
Flora, P., and A. Heidenheimer
1981 The Development of Welfare States in Europe and America. London: Trans-
    action Books
Gough, I.
1979 The Political Economy of the Welfare State. London: Macmillan
Gourevitch, P.
1986 Politics in Hard Times. Ithaca, NY: Cornell University Press
Heimann, E.
1929 Soziale Theorie der Kapitalismus. Frankfurt: Suhrkamp (1980 reprint)
Hewitt, C.
1977 'The Effect of Political Democracy and Social Democracy on Equality in In-
    dustrial Societies.' American Sociological Review 42
Jessop, B.
1982 The Capitalist State. Oxford: Martin Robertson
Katzenstein, P.
1985 Small States in World Markets. Ithaca, NY: Cornell University Press
Korpi, W.

34 GOSTA ESPING-ANDERSEN

1980 'Social Policy and Distributional Conflict in the Capitalist Democracies.'
    West European Politics 3
1983 The Democratic Class Struggle. London: Routledge and Kegan Paul
Marshall, A.
1920 Principles of Economics (8th Edition). London: Macmillan
Marshall, T.H.
1950 Citizenship and Social Class. Cambridge: Cambridge University Press
Muller, W., and C. Neususs
1973 'The Illusion of State Socialism and the Contradiction between Wage Labor
    and Capital.' Telos 25 (Fall)
Myles, J.
1984 Old Age in the Welfare State. Boston: Little Brown
Myrdal, A., and G. Myrdal
1936 Kris i Befolkningsfraagan. Stockholm: Tiden
O'Connor, J.
1973 The Fiscal Crisis of the State. New York: St. Martin's Press
Offe, C.
1972 'Advanced Capitalism and the Welfare State.' Politics and Society 4
1984 Contradictions of the Welfare State. London: Hutchinson
1985 Disorganized Capitalism. Cambridge, Mass: MIT Press
Ogus, A.
1979 'Social Insurance, Legal Development and Legal History.' In H.F. Zacher
    (ed.), Bedingungen fur die Entstehung von Sozialversicherung. Berlin:
    Duncker and Humboldt
Okun, A.
1975 Equality and Efficiency: The Big Trade-Off. Washington, DC: Brookings In-
    stitute
Olson, M.
1982 The Rise and Decline of Nations. New Haven, Conn: Yale University Press
Polanyi, K.
1944 The Great Transformation. New York: Rhinehart
Poulantzas, N.
1973 Political Power and Social Classes. London: New Left Books
Pryor, F.
1969 Public Expenditures in Communist and Capitalist Nations. London: Allen
    and Unwin
Przeworski, A.
1980 'Material Bases of Consent: Politics and Economics in a Hegemonic System.'
    Political Power and Social Theory 1
1985 Capitalism and Social Democracy. Cambridge: Cambridge University Press
Richter, E.
1987 'Subsidiaritat und Neoconservatismus.' Politische Vierteljahresschrift 28
Rimlinger, G.
1971 Welfare and Industrialization in Europe, America and Russia. New York:
    John Wiley
Robbins, L.
1976 Political Economy: Past and Present. London: Macmillan
Rokkan, S.

35 POLITICAL ECONOMIES OF THE WELFARE STATE

1970 Citizens, Elections, Parties. Oslo: Universitetsforlaget
Schmidt, M.
1982 'The role of Parties in shaping Macro-economic Policies.' In F. Castles (ed.),
        The Impact of Parties. London: Sage
1983 'The Welfare State and the Economy in periods of Economic Crisis.'
        European Journal of Political Research 11
Schmitter, P., and G. Lembruch
1979 Trends toward Corporatist Intermediation. London: Sage
Schumpeter, J.
1944 Capitalism, Socialism and Democracy. London: Allen and Unwin
1954 History of Economic Analysis. New York: Oxford University Press
Shalev, M.
1983 'The Socialdemocratic Model and Beyond.' Comparative Social Research 6
Shonfield, A.
1965 Modern Capitalism. Oxford: Oxford University Press
Skocpol, T., and E. Amenta
1986 'States and Social Policies.' Annual Review of Sociology 12
Skocpol, T., and J. Ikenberry
1983 'The Political Formation of the American Welfare State in Historical and
        Comparative Perspective.' Comparative Social Research 6
Smith, A.
1961 The Wealth of Nations. Edited by E. Cannan. London: Methuen
Stephens, J.
1979 The Transition from Capitalism to Socialism. London: Macmillan.
Therborn, G.
1983 'When, How and Why does a Welfare State become a Welfare State?' Paper
        presented at the ECPR Workshops, Freiburg (March)
1986 'Karl Marx returning. The Welfare State and Neo-Marxist, Corporatist and
        Statist Theories.' International Political Science Review 7
Titmuss, R.
1958 Essays on the Welfare State. London: Allen and Unwin
Tufte, E.
1978 Political Control of the Economy. Princeton: Princeton University Press
Uusitalo, H.
1984 'Comparative Research on the Determinants of the Welfare State: The State
        of the Art.' European Journal of Political Research 12
Wagner, A.
1872 Rede Ueber die Soziale Frage. Berlin: Wiegandt und Grieben
1962 Finanzwissenschaft (1883), reproduced partly in R.A. Musgrave, and A.
        Peacock (eds.), Classics in the Theory of Public Finance. London: Macmillan
Weir, M., and T. Skocpol
1985 'State Structures and the Possibilities for "Keynesean" Responses to the
        Great Depression in Sweden, Britain, and the United States.' In P. Evans et
        al. (eds.), Bringing the State Back In. New York: Cambridge University
        Press
Wilensky, H.
1975 The Welfare State and Equality. Berkeley, California: University of Califor-
        nia Press

36 GOSTA ESPING-ANDERSEN

1981 'Leftism, Catholicism, and Democratic Corporatism.' In P. Flora and A.
      Heidenheimer (eds.), op.cit.
Wilensky, H., and C. Lebeaux
1958 Industrial Society and Social Welfare. New York: Russel Sage
Wilensky, H. et al.
1985 Comparative Social Policy: Theory, Methods, Findings. Berkeley: Interna-
      tional Studies. Research Series, 62

[13]

GENDER AND THE DEVELOPMENT OF WELFARE REGIMES

Jane Lewis, London School of Economics, UK

Summary

This paper builds on the idea that any further development of the concept of 'welfare regime' must incorporate the relationship between unpaid as well as paid work and welfare. Consideration of the private/domestic is crucial to a gendered understanding of welfare because historically women have typically gained entitlements by virtue of their dependent status within the family as wives and mothers. The paper suggests that the idea of the male-breadwinner family model has served historically to cut across established typologies of welfare regimes, and further that the model has been modified in different ways and to different degrees in particular countries.

It is suggested that Ireland and Britain are examples of historically 'strong' male-breadwinner states and that this helps to account for the level and, more importantly, the nature of women's (part-time) labour market participation; the lack of child care services and maternity rights; and the long-lived inequality between husbands and wives in regard to social security. Strong male-breadwinner states have tended to draw a firm dividing line between public and private responsibility. The picture is different in France, which is taken as an example of a 'modified' male-breadwinner country. The nature of French women's labour market participation has historically been stronger in that it has been predominantly full-time, and women have benefited, albeit indirectly, from a social security system that has prioritized horizontal redistribution via the wage system between families with and without children. Patriarchal control has been located within the family rather than in collective institutions, and unlike Britain and Ireland, France recognized women's claims as both wives and mothers and paid workers. Sweden is taken as an example of a 'weak' male-breadwinner country. During the late 1960s and 1970s successive Social Democratic governments consciously decided to move towards a dual-breadwinner society, pulling women into paid employment by the introduction of separate taxation and parental leaves, and by increasing child care provision.

While both the French and Swedish models would seem to offer women more than the British, the paper concludes with a cautionary note. In neither France nor Sweden did women's own demands play a significant role in determining their treatment. Paradoxically, the feminist movement has been historically stronger in Britain. This must raise issues as to what can be expected of the state and as to the possible fragility of the gains.

Résumé

NATURE ET DÉVELOPPEMENT DES RÉGIMES SOCIAUX

Cet article se fonde sur l'idée selon laquelle tout développement du concept de système de protection sociale doit intégrer le rapport entre le travail, rémméré ou non, et la protection sociale. La prise en considération du domaine privé/familial est indispensable pour comprendre la différenciation selon les sexes des formes de protection sociale: en effet, historiquement, les femmes ont acquis des droits, en raison même de leur situation de dépendance dans la famille en tant qu'épouse et mère. L'article suggère que le modèle familial dans lequel c'est l'homme qui apporte le revenu familial, a rempli, historiquement, une fonction importante qui

160   JANE LEWIS

traverse les typologies établies des systèmes de
protection sociale, et ensuite que ce modèle a
connu des modifications diverses et plus ou
moins importantes dans certains pays.

L'auteur avance que l'Irlande et la Grande-
Bretagne sont des exemples de pays fortement
marqués, historiquement, par ce modèle de
l'homme apporteur de revenu, et que ceci aide
à expliquer le niveau et, surtout, la nature de
la participation des femmes au marché du
travail (temps partiel), le manque de crèches
ou garderies, l'insuffisance de la protection de
la maternité et l'inégalité persistante entre
mari et épouse face à la sécurité sociale. Les
Etats fortement marqués par ce modèle ont eu
tendance à tracer une ligne bien nette entre
responsabilité publique et responsabilité
privés. La situation se présente autrement en
France, qui est un exemple de pays où ce
modèle centré sur l'homme s'est modifié. La
participation des femmes françaises au
marché du travail a été historiquement d'une
autre nature, en particulier du fait de la
prédominance de l'emploi à temps plein, et les
femmes ont bénéficié, quoique indirectement,
d'un système de sécurité sociale qui
privilégiait une redistribution horizontale, par
le biais due système salarial, entre les familles
avec enfants et celles sans enfants. Le contrôle
patriarcal s'est localisé au sein de la famille
plutôt que dans les institutions collectives et,
contrairement à l'Irlande et à la Grande-
Bretagne, la France a reconnu les
revendications des femmes en tant qu'épouses,
mères et travailleuses salariées à la fois. La
Suède est un exemple de pays faiblement
marqué par le modèle de l'homme apporteur
du revenu familial. Pendant la fin des années
60 et durant les années 70, les gouvernements
socio-démocrates successifs se dirigèrent
résolument vers un modèle familial à deux
apporteurs de revenu, en incitant les femmes à
un travail rémunéré par l'introduction d'une
imposition séparée et de congés parentaux et
par le développement des services de garderie.

Bien que le modèle français et le modèle
suédois semblent être plus favorables aux
femmes que le modèle britannique, l'article

s'achève par un avertissement. Ni en France,
ni en Suède, les revendications des femmes
n'ont joué un rôle significatif dans la
détermination de leur traitement. D'une façon
paradoxale, le mouvement féministe a été
historiquement plus puissant en Grande-
Bretagne. Des questions s'imposent, comme
celle concernant les attentes que l'on peut
avoir vis-à-vis de l'Etat et celle de la fragilité
éventuelle des acquis.

Gender and the development of welfare regimes[1]

Recent comparative work on modern welfare
states has emphasized the importance of the
relationship between state and economy, and
in particular between work and welfare
(especially Esping Andersen 1990). Work is
defined as paid work and welfare as policies
that permit, encourage or discourage the
decommodification of labour. While this is a
substantial advance on the older literature
which focused only on the comparative
development of policies of social
amelioration, it misses one of the central
issues in the structuring of welfare regimes:
the problem of valuing the unpaid work that
is done primarily by women in providing
welfare, mainly within the family, and in
securing those providers social entitlements.
The crucial relationship is not just between
paid work and welfare, but as Peter Taylor
Gooby (1991) recently signalled in this
journal, between paid work and unpaid work
and welfare.

The latter set of relationships is gendered,
because while it is possible to argue that the
divisions in paid work have substantially
diminished to the extent that greater numbers
of women have entered the labour market
(although not with regard to pay, status and
hours) all the evidence suggests that the
division of unpaid work remains substantially
the same (see, for example, Morris 1990).

Journal of European Social Policy 1992 2 (3)

Thus concepts such as 'decommodification' or 'dependency' have a gendered meaning that is rarely acknowledged. While Esping Andersen (1990) writes of decommodification as a necessary prerequisite for workers' political mobilization, the worker he has in mind is male and his mobilization may depend as much on unpaid female household labour as state policies. Decommodification for women is likely to result in their carrying out unpaid caring work; in other words 'welfare dependency' on the part of adult women is likely to result in the greater independence of another person, young or old. The unequal division of unpaid work thus blurs the dichotomous divisions between dependent and independent, commodified and decommodified.

As Kolberg (1991) has noted, the interface between the private in the sense of the informal provision of welfare, the market and the state has not been subjected to close analysis. Indeed, informal care was absent from Titmuss's (1963) classic threefold division of welfare into state, fiscal and occupational provision, and as Langan and Ostner (1991) comment, it is just as absent from more recent categorizations. In the work of Esping Andersen or of Leibfried (1991) women disappear from the analysis when they disappear from labour markets. Yet consideration of the private/domestic is crucial to any understanding of women's position because historically women have typically gained welfare entitlements by virtue of their dependent status within the family as wives, the justification being a division of labour perceived to follow 'naturally' on their capacity for motherhood. Women have thus tended to make contributions and draw benefits via their husbands in accordance with assumptions regarding the existence of a male-breadwinner family model (Land 1980). Furthermore, in welfare regimes where the social security system operates a dual insurance/assistance model, this in and of itself tends to be gendered, with first class (insurance) benefits going mainly to men and

second class (welfare/assistance) benefits to women (Gordon 1990). In Britain 2.5 million working women are excluded from the contributory social security system because they fall below the lower earning limit.

The development of modern welfare states in the late nineteenth and early twentieth centuries coincided with the period when the boundary between the public world of paid work and political participation and the private domain of the family was strongest in both the prescriptive literature and in reality, at least for middle class women. In its ideal form, the male-breadwinner model prescribed breadwinning for men and caring/homemaking for women. It was part of a much larger gendered division between public and private that informed the work of political philosophers after Locke, and was taken as one of the measures of a civilized society by late nineteenth century social scientists such as Herbert Spencer. Working within an evolutionary framework, Spencer argued that society was 'progressing' towards a position whereby all women would be able to stay home in their 'natural' sphere. While it may be argued that his was a shared ideal – between men and women, employees and employers and the state (Lewis 1986) – it is important to note that it was never completely achieved. The male-breadwinner model operated most fully for late-nineteenth century middle class women in a few industrialized countries. Working class women have always engaged in paid labour to some degree.

In reality, as Sokoloff (1980) and Pateman (1989) have insisted, the two spheres have been and are intimately interrelated rather than separated. Not least as a provider of welfare the family has been central to civil society, rather than separate from it. Over time, the boundary between public and private has been redrawn at the level of prescription. For example, in English the phrase 'working mother' entered the language during and after World War II, but wage earning was always deemed a secondary activity for women. Given that in modern societies independence derives primarily from wage earning (Pateman 1988), the assumption that women were located mainly in the private sphere supported by a male breadwinner also meant that women have only been partially individualized. In regard to social policies, the liberal dilemma first described by Okin (1979), whereby individuals in fact meant male heads of families, has persisted.

Modern welfare regimes have all subscribed to some degree to the idea of a male-breadwinner model. Indeed, its persistence, to varying extents, cuts across established typologies of welfare regimes. Leira (1989), for example, has shown that Esping Andersen's identification of a Scandinavian welfare regime breaks down as soon as gender is given serious consideration. The Norwegian system, which has continued to treat women primarily as wives and mothers, is closer in many respects to that of Britain than it is to Sweden. But just as the male-breadwinner model has not existed in its pure form, so the model has been modified in different ways and to different degrees in particular countries. In its pure form we would expect to find married women excluded from the labour market, firmly subordinated to their husbands for the purposes of social security entitlements and tax, and expected to undertake the work of caring (for children and other dependants) at home without public support. No country has ever matched the model completely, but some have come much closer than others. This paper looks at the way in which twentieth century welfare states have treated women as wives and mothers and as paid workers, comparing Britain (with reference also to Ireland) as historically strong male-breadwinner states with, first, France, where it is argued that the male-breadwinner model remained implicit in social policies because of the focus on children rather than on women and where women's historically stronger position in the labour market also modified the operation of the model; and second,

Sweden, where it is suggested that there has been a shift away from a strong male-breadwinner model towards something very different: a dual breadwinner model. It is suggested that the strength or weakness of the male-breadwinner model serves as an indicator of the way in which women have been treated in social security systems, of the level of social service provision particularly in regard to child care; and of the nature of married women's position in the labour market.

The paper is intended as an exploratory charting exercise, very little attempt has been made so far to gender welfare regimes.[2] While it is impossible to come to any definitive conclusion as to where women 'do best', both France and Sweden would seem to offer women more than Britain. However the paper concludes with a cautionary note. In neither France nor Sweden did women's own demands play a significant role in determining their treatment. Paradoxically, the feminist movement has historically been stronger in Britain. This must raise issues as to what can be expected of the state and as to the possible fragility of the gains.

Strong male-breadwinner states – Ireland and Britain

Ireland has been historically, and more unusually, has remained well into the late twentieth century an extremely strong male-breadwinner state. Despite the choice of export led development during the 1960s and 1970s, the labour market participation of women remained virtually the same at just under 30 per cent. Incoming electronics firms that employed 80 per cent female workers elsewhere in the world, employed 51 per cent in Ireland; in manufacturing more generally 30 per cent of the labour force was female. Pyle (1990) has argued convincingly that government policy, particularly that of the

Industrial Development Authority, played a decisive role in ensuring that men had priority in the labour market. In the civil service, a marriage bar prevented married women from working until 1977. Those married women determined to enter the labour market faced exceptionally harsh treatment under the tax system, with high marginal rates and a very low tax free allowance, and the lowest levels of child care provision in Europe. Married women's treatment under the social security system has also exhibited the kind of features that might be hypothesized for a strong male-breadwinner country until very recently, when reform was prompted in large part by EC law. Until 1984 married women received lower rates of benefit, shorter length of payment of benefit, and were not eligible for unemployment assistance. Indeed, Ireland has been the only European country to pay dependents benefits regardless of whether the wife is in paid work (Callender 1988).

Britain has also shared an historical commitment to the male breadwinner model, which, while it has been substantially modified in the late twentieth century, makes more explicable some of the differences in the position of British women, especially *vis-à-vis* the labour market.

In line with the dominant turn of the century view of gender roles in the family and their link to social stability and welfare (Lewis 1991), one Cabinet minister tried to ban the work of married women during the 1900s, and during the inter-war years a marriage bar operated in the professions. A parallel effort was put into the education of working class wives and mothers in household management and infant welfare, using the small army of female visitors attached to charities and increasingly by World War I, health visitors employed by local authorities (Lewis 1980).

This pattern of thinking about the family meant that policymakers faced a number of contradictory pulls. While women's welfare as wives and mothers was paramount, social policies were not permitted to undermine the man's responsibility to provide for dependants. Thus, national health and unemployment insurance introduced in Britain in 1911 did not cover women and children unless the woman was in full-time insurable employment (only 10 per cent were so placed). Nor was much protection offered the married woman as worker; Britain failed to implement paid maternity leave and never ratified the ILO Washington Convention provision for six weeks paid leave (Lewis and Davies 1991). Again the argument was that the father must support his family and that women's waged work was detrimental to the welfare of children and to the stability of the family. In Britain, protective labour legislation was, as Mary Poovey (1989) has commented, the obverse of control. The concern was not so much to maximize the welfare of working women as mothers, but to minimize their labour market participation, a position that was shared by male and female trade unionists and by middle class women social reformers. The position of women workers was more complicated in that while there is evidence that they supported the family wage ideal, their material circumstances dictated their need to earn.

Under the post-war Beveridgean settlement, women continued to be treated as dependants for the purposes of social security entitlements. Beveridge (PP. 1942) wrote at length of the importance of women's role as wives and mothers in ensuring the continuance of the British race (at a time of fears about population decline) and insisted on marriage as a 'partnership' rather than a patriarchal relationship (Wilson 1977; Lewis 1983). It was, however, a partnership in which the parties were to be equal but different. Hence women were defined as wives and mothers and therefore as dependent on a male wage. Married women were accordingly invited to take the 'married women's option', paying less by way of contributions and collecting less in benefits. The married women's option was not abandoned until the middle of the 1970s, with the passing of equal opportunities legislation. From the mid-

1970s, Britain offered an allowance for the unpaid work of caring for infirm dependants (the invalid care allowance) within the social security system, but, at the very same time that legislation was being passed to provide women with the means of legal redress on an individual basis against sex discrimination in pay, promotion, hiring and other mainly workplace related issues, the invalid care allowance was denied to married women on the grounds that caring was part of the 'normal' duties of such women.

The strong male-breadwinner model also predicts relatively low levels of female labour market participation and of social services such as child care. All northern European countries (except Ireland) have experienced a significant increase in women's labour market participation rates, particularly for married women. In Britain, married women's participation increased from 10 per cent in 1931 to 26 per cent in 1951, 49 per cent in 1971 and 62 per cent in 1981. On the face of it, British married women's labour participation rates have much in common with those of France. Dex and Walters' (1989) analysis of two samples of French and British women with dependent children drawn during the early 1980s found identical participation rates of 51 per cent. However, it is important that virtually the whole of the post-war expansion in married women's work in Britain is accounted for by part-time employment (44.5 per cent worked part-time in 1987, compared to 22.5 per cent in France). Sweden also has high levels of part-time work (43 per cent in 1989), but here again it is important to distinguish the meaning of 'part time'. In Britain part-time work tends to be 'precarious' (following the OECD definition), with short hours and few benefits. While, in 1979, 29.8 per cent of women in part-time manual jobs and 23 per cent in non-manual jobs worked less than sixteen hours, by 1990 these figures had become 43.7 per cent and 31.8 per cent (Lister 1992). In Sweden most women working part-time are in fact in full-time jobs

(with full benefits), but are exercising their right to work a three-quarter time day while their children are small. In Britain, the inheritance of the male-breadwinner model is reflected in the nature rather than the level of women's labour market participation.

In particular, Britain has large numbers of non-working mothers of below school age children. This is related to the low level of child care provision, which is especially striking compared to France, where some 95 per cent of 3–5 year olds are in publicly funded child care and 25 per cent of 0–2 year olds. The figures for Britain are 44 per cent and 2 per cent respectively (Phillips and Moss 1988). It is also significant that Britain tends to make less provision (thereby arguably giving less encouragement) to women workers who become mothers. Women with two years continuous service have the right to eleven weeks leave before the birth of a child and 29 weeks afterwards at 90 per cent replacement income for six of those weeks, and the right to reinstatement, but, given the precarious labour market position of British women, only 60 per cent qualify.

Strong male-breadwinner states have tended to draw a firm dividing line between public and private responsibility. If women enter the public sphere as workers, they must do so on terms very similar to men. It is assumed that the family (that is women) will provide child care and minimal provision is made for maternity leaves, pay and the right to reinstatement. During the 1980s in Britain, the public/private divide has been drawn more tightly. Thus eligibility for unemployment benefit has been linked much more firmly to recent employment and to availability for work, with attendant problems for women who interrupt paid work to care or who need to find child care. The maternity rights women won under the equal opportunities legislation of the mid-1970s have also been significantly weakened. Indeed, Britain is the only European Community member state in which maternity rights diminished during the 1980s. While no effort is now made to stop women working, the assumption is that women will be secondary wage earners and, despite the large numbers of women in paid employment, they tend to be in short part-time, low status work. Davies and Joshi's (1990) econometric analysis of gross cash earnings foregone by a woman bearing one, two or three children shows the costs in Britain (and Germany) to be similar and high at 50 per cent of income. In France and Sweden the costs are similar and low at 10 per cent or less.

Modified male-breadwinner countries –
France

The picture is different in France, where the nature of women's labour market participation has historically been stronger in that it has been predominantly full-time, and where women have benefited, albeit indirectly, from a social security system that has prioritized horizontal redistribution between families with and without children, rather than vertical redistribution between rich and poor. In 1945 twice as much flowed out in family allowances as in social insurance. The allowances enabled a French family of four to double its income, whereas in Britain it received 15 shillings from family allowances when the average male wage was 121 shillings (Pedersen 1991: 447). In 1971 the French three and four child family on median earnings received four times as much in family benefits as its British counterpart (Dawson 1979: 203).

Family policy has been dominant within the French social security system and in contrast to Britain its goals have been clear (on the conflicting goals of British policy, see Brown 1987). The primary aim of French social security has been to compensate parents for the costs of children and to this extent the system has been gender-neutral; Pedersen (1991) has described the early twentieth

century development of French family policy as following a 'parental', as opposed to a male-breadwinner model. Historically, family benefits have been financed in large measure by employers and must therefore be seen as part of the wage system. The family allowances paid by employers during the 1930s were in some regions used as a means of controlling the labour force. Allowances were forfeit if work was missed for any reason, including strikes, and were also used as a means of attaching other family members, including women, to a particular firm. In other occupations the aim was less labour force control and more straightforwardly wage control during the Depression (Pedersen 1991; Thibault 1986). While rewarding women for the unpaid work of caring for children therefore had nothing to do with the introduction of family benefits in France, the nature of the redistribution from wage earners to non-wage earners did benefit women as well as children, especially given that some benefits were increasingly paid directly to women. Unlike Britain, there was no debate about this, family allowances had never been viewed as a feminist demand as they were in Britain during the 1920s (Land 1975; Lewis 1980; Pedersen 1991) and, given French family law, which vested complete parental authority in the husband (until reform in 1970), it was assumed that the interests of husband and wife would be as one. In fact, all the research on the division of resources within the household during the last decade (e.g. Pahl 1990) has revealed the existence of substantial inequalities between family members and in so far as family allowances, the most substantial of the many family benefits (which have included pre- and post-natal allowances, family supplements, payments to single-earner families, and payments in respect of child care) have been linked firmly to wages and thus to the wage earner, it is of course impossible to be sure how far they actually benefited women and children in practice.

The case for generous family benefits was

legitimated in France by pronatalist concern. This resulted in substantial emphasis on the importance of good mothering and the pioneering French efforts to improve maternal and child welfare in the early twentieth century by, for example, the *Gouttes de Lait* were exported to Britain. Nevertheless, the percentage of women in full-time paid work increased during the late nineteenth and early twentieth centuries in France (from 30 per cent in 1866 to 37 per cent in 1911), in contrast to Britain where the percentage fell. This was in large measure attributable to the different occupational structure in France and the large number of women employed in family businesses; as late as 1968, 20 per cent of French women were employed in the rural sector (Silver 1977). While in Britain it became part of the badge of working class male respectability to keep a wife, enforced by a strong trade union movement as well as by the discourse of social reform, so in the French context this was neither so possible nor desirable. Patriarchal control was firmly located within the family rather than in collective institutions, and for a significant number of husbands it was not in their self-interest to exercise their legal right (which they held until 1965) to prevent their wives working. Thus, in France, there were no early twentieth century attempts to push women out of the labour market and paid maternity leave was introduced in 1913.

During the 1930s, pronatalist concern deepened and gave rise to increased pressure for an allowance for *la mère au foyer* (women at home raising children). Such an allowance was introduced in the 1930s, although under the 1939 *Code de la Famille* it was paid only to urban families, the reasoning being that in rural areas women could engage in both farm work and mind children (Laroque 1985). The allowance was thus conceptualized more as a compensation for earnings foregone and, as Pedersen has argued, stood in stark contrast to the British treatment of married women workers under the 1931 Anomalies Act, which effectively deprived them of the right to

unemployment insurance (see also Deacon 1976). Only during the Vichy regime were efforts made actively to prevent married women's employment and the *mère au foyer* allowance was extended and uprated.

Thus the French model recognized the reality of women's claims as both mothers and workers. In this sense it was, as Douglas Ashford (1982) has argued more generally in regard to French politics, more pragmatic than the British. As the labour force participation rate of married women increased, from 34 per cent in 1968 to 40 per cent in 1975 (Hantrais 1990), so French policy documents addressed the reality of changes in women's labour market behaviour and their implications for family policy. As Rodgers (1975) noted, this approach stands in marked contrast to the tendency of British policymakers to ignore changes in family roles and structures (see, for example, Land and Ward's (1986) comments on the Fowler Review of British social security system). In 1972 the *frais de garde* was introduced specifically for families with working mothers and a number of articles began to question the social justice of paying benefits to women staying at home when they might be better off than women in the workforce. One of the most forceful contributions came from Rolande Cuvillier in an article republished in the *Journal of Social Policy* in 1979. This line of argument played, in the manner of many Anglo-Saxon contributions of the 1980s (e.g. Murray 1984; and Mead 1986) on the rhetoric of equality in the sense of treating women the same as men, but also within the French context reflected the increasing preoccupation of the 1970s and 1980s with achieving vertical as opposed to horizontal redistribution. This was promoted by means testing and by reducing the importance of family benefits – by 50 per cent between 1955 and 1985 (Questiaux, 1985) – within the social security system. Prost (1984) has suggested that French family policy had lost its coherence by the 1980s.

French governments stated their explicit

commitment to policy-neutrality regarding women's role, but the outcomes of the shifts in both family and labour market policy during the late 1970s and 1980s have been mixed for women. In 1977 the *frais de garde* was rolled up with the allowance for single wage earners (the extended *mere au foyer* allowance) into the *complément familial*. During the course of the Senate debate on this measure, the minister, Simone Weil stated firmly: 'Le complément familial serait versait aussi bien aux mères restant a leur foyer qu'a celles qui exercent une activité professionelle. Cette neutralité nous a semblé également equitable' (Journel Officiel, Senat Debats, 22/4/76: 609). The commitment both to neutrality regarding women's choice to go out to work or not and explicitly to seeking policies that would help them (but not men) to combine 'la vie professionnelle and la vie familiale' persisted throughout the 1980s (e.g. the report of the Haut Conseil de la Population et de la Famille 1985).

However, as Pierre Laroque (1985) has pointed out, the *complément familial* continued to benefit one-earner families more than two-earner families. This was in part because the benefit (like all benefits introduced after 1970) was means tested in accordance with the new priority given vertical redistribution. Research during the 1980s (e.g. Ekert 1983) has also shown that working wives pay a disproportionate amount towards the funding of family benefits. The operation of the joint tax system also works to penalize married women's work and may account for the greater incidence of part-time work among higher paid women (Crompton, Hantrais and Walters 1990), while the interaction of the tax system with a benefit system that gives significantly more to large families may also encourage lower income women to stay at home (Hantrais forthcoming). Third children attract more family benefit via the *allocation au jeune enfant* and more tax relief; working women giving birth to a third child are entitled to longer maternity leave.

During the 1980s, while French women have done somewhat better than British women relative to men in terms of both pay and measures of vertical segregation (Hantrais 1990) and ten times as many work continuously through the childbearing and childrearing years as in Britain (Crompton, Hantrais and Walters 1990), the percentage of French women working part time has increased significantly due to conscious efforts to restructure the labour market. Between 1982 and 1986, 13,000 women lost a full-time job, while at the same time 450,000 part-time jobs were created (Jenson and Kantrow 1990: 113). Thus Jenson (1988) and Mazur (1991) have pointed out that while the 1983 Loi Roudy represented a strong measure of 'equality' legislation that notably provided for action to counter sex discrimination and segregation at the workplace level, government action also encouraged part-time work, albeit regulating it to ensure the payment of pro-rata benefits. French women giving birth to a child get between 16 and 26 weeks maternity leave at 84 per cent replacement income and 90 per cent of working mothers qualify. There is a tax allowance for child care, and public child care provision is among the best in Europe. Within the EC, France was one of only three countries in 1988 where more than 50 per cent of women with children under the age of five were in employment.

Thus pronatalist inspired social policies resulted in generous benefits to compensate for the costs of children and the way in which they have been financed also benefited women as mothers. These benefits have been diluted by more recent moves towards giving greater priority to vertical redistribution and to means testing, and also serve to penalize women workers. Nevertheless, compared to Britain or Ireland, France's modified male-breadwinner model – in which patriarchal control has been vested in husbands more than in trade unions, employers or governments, while state policy has recognized the reality of women's roles as both mothers and paid workers – has offered real gains to women.

Weak male-breadwinner countries – Sweden[3]

Sweden was not always a weak male-breadwinner state. Pre-World War II Swedish social democracy embraced the idea of difference in its thinking about the relationships between men and women, largely as a result of the great influence wielded by Ellen Key. Her ideas inspired the social democratic movement as to what was 'good and rightful' in everyday life (Key 1912, 1914). The most powerful image in Swedish social democracy has been that of building the 'people's home', which encompasses the double idea first, of society and state as a good family home, where no one is privileged, all co-operate and no one tries to gain advantage at another's expense; and second, of ensuring that productive capacity is used to the advantage of people and their families. Whether in the big 'people's home' of state and society, or the small people's home of individual household and family, women's contribution (and rewards) were allocated on the basis of wife and motherhood in line with the family wage model (Hirdman 1989).

During the 1930s and 1940s, the situation in Sweden changed to resemble the French, albeit that the policy logic was somewhat different. During this period, the Social Democrats' conceptualization of women's place in society was significantly influenced by the writings of Alva and Gunnar Myrdal, themselves members of the Party. Picking up the common theme of national suicide in the face of falling birth rates, the Myrdals insisted on 'democratic' population planning (which differentiated them from the extremes of national socialism) and the importance of society investing in the welfare of families. But alongside this maternalist politics and

policies to encourage a higher birth rate, they also insisted that state policies should aim to realize the potential of each individual. Thus while women's roles as mothers acquired 'national' significance, so it was also insisted that women had the right to develop their talents in other fields, particularly that of paid employment. The Myrdals argued that if the state wanted babies, it must also make it possible for mothers to work, albeit sequentially (Kalvemark 1980). During the late 1940s Alva Myrdal developed with Viola Klein her influential idea of 'women's two roles', whereby women should be encouraged to enter the labour market until the birth of a first child, returning when the child left school (Myrdal and Klein 1954). The state and employers were asked to support motherhood and married women's role as workers, albeit that these would be, much more than was envisaged in France, sequential and therefore separate endeavours. It was not envisaged that workers would also be the mothers of small children. In terms of Myrdal's policy inheritance in Sweden, it was important first, that she sought to reconcile women's claims both as workers on equal terms to men and as mothers within a single strategy; second, that her main justification for such a strategy was, not unlike the French, the nation's need for women's labour power and for more babies, rather than women's expressed needs; and third, that she was content to change women's lives without pressing for concomitant changes in those of men.

During the 1950s and 1960s, the labour force participation rates of women over 15 remained constant at about 30 per cent, with the low participation rates for married women in the childbearing years that were consistent with the dual roles model. But during the late 1960s and early 1970s, Swedish Social Democratic governments took conscious steps to bring all adult women into the workforce and to make 'the *two-breadwinner family* the norm' (Hirdman 1989, my emphasis). As a result, the basis for women's social entitlements was transformed

Journal of European Social Policy 1992 2 (3)

from that of dependent wife to worker. Since
the mid-1970s women have been treated as
workers and have been compensated for their
unpaid work as mothers at rates they could
command as members of the labour force.

The most important changes designed to
promote women's market work were first, the
introduction of separate taxation in 1971.
This, together with high marginal tax rates,
has meant that it has been generally
favourable for family income if a woman goes
out to work rather than the man adding extra
overtime hours (Gustafsson and Stafford
1988). In Britain, where separate taxation
was introduced in 1989, the labour market
effects are not the same because of low
progressivity in the tax system. The second
major change was the increase in the number
of places in public day care: in 1968 10 per
cent of all children under school age had
places, in 1979 27 per cent and in 1987 47
per cent. Finally, in 1974 a scheme of parental
insurance was introduced, rather than women
being given flat rate maternity benefits, they
were offered compensation for loss of market
earnings. Men were also offered the same 90
per cent replacement of earnings if they chose
to care for children. The 1974 legislation gave
a parental leave of six months to be taken
before the child reached four years together
with a ten day per year child sick leave. The
leave was extended again in 1975 and again
in 1980 to twelve months parental leave and
60 days child sick leave.

Not surprisingly the labour market
participation rate of women in Sweden
increased dramatically. Participation rates in
the 1950s and 1960s were lower than in
many other western countries, but by 1986
89.8 per cent of women aged 25–54 (only 5
per cent less than men of comparable age)
were in the labour market and 85.6 per cent
of women with children under 7 worked
compared with 28 per cent in Britain. By
1984, only 7 per cent of Swedish women
between 25 and 54 were classified as
'housewives'. Thus Sweden may be seen as
having moved away from the male-

breadwinner model towards treating women
as well as men as citizen workers, and then
grafting on women's claims as mothers
through parental leave schemes and the like.
This dual-breadwinner model which makes
social entitlements for all adults dependent on
their labour market status would seem to
offer more in terms of benefit levels (paid at
market rates) and the level of social service
provision, particularly in respect of childcare,
than strong family-breadwinner models. It is
easier to combine paid and unpaid work in
Sweden, but this is not to say that it is easier
for women to 'choose' to engage in paid
work. Women have been 'forced' into the
labour market, but they have retained their
responsibility for the unpaid work of caring;
men's behaviour has not been changed. In
terms of their labour market position,
Swedish women are better off in the sense of
finding themselves in less precarious
employment than British women, for
example. But it has been argued that the
reorganization of women's labour together
with policies such as parental leaves, which
are taken by women rather than by men, have
served to reinforce the sexual segregation of
paid labour, which is among the worst in the
western world (Jonung 1984). In this sense,
the Swedish model has less to offer than that
of strong male-breadwinner states and
considerably less to offer than France, which
provides almost as much for the working
mother (parental leave is unpaid, but child
care provision is better) and has also taken
equal opportunities legislation further than
either Sweden or the strong male-breadwinner
countries.

The various ways in which modern welfare
states have treated women as unpaid carers
and as paid workers have thus been
complicated and no one policy logic can be
said to have the undisputed advantage. The
outcomes for lone mother families provide a
useful summary illustration of this point.
Women with children and without men have
historically posed a particularly difficult
problem for governments. In Britain, policies

have tended to oscillate over time between treating these women primarily as workers (under the nineteenth century poor law) or primarily as mothers (under post-war welfare state legislation). Predicting the treatment of lone mothers in strong male-breadwinner countries is virtually impossible because their position defies the logic of the system, but governments have tended historically to categorize lone mothers firmly as either mothers or workers. In late twentieth century Britain no lone mother with a child under 16 who is claiming income support is obliged to register for work and they have the lowest labour market participation in the European Community. While 47 per cent of lone mothers were in paid work during the period 1977–9, this figure actually dropped to 39 per cent for the period 1986–8 (Millar 1989). Indeed, Britain is the only EC country where lone mothers have a lower employment rate than mothers in two parent families. In France, as Baker (1991) has pointed out, lone mothers reap the advantage of generous family benefits paid to all families with children, and while they have the highest labour force participation rate in the EC next to Denmark and Luxembourg, France is unusual in that the incomes of employed and unemployed lone mother families are very similar (Millar 1989). In Sweden, as might be expected, 87 per cent of lone mothers are in the labour force and for the most part work full-time. In material terms they are the best off, but at the price of being particularly time poor.

What can be hoped for from the state?

The position of women within different welfare regimes revolves around two related issues, the valuing of unpaid work and the sharing of it. Nowhere have these issues been addressed directly. In moving from the male-breadwinner to a dual-breadwinner model, Sweden may be judged to have gone a long way towards solving the first issue (because women get compensated at market rates for caring work), but not to have touched the second. France has also provided women with substantial, albeit indirect, rewards for mothering as a by-product of the priority it has accorded family policy, and arguably women have greater choice than in Sweden as to whether to work at home or in the labour market.

Many English speaking feminists have remained at best ambivalent as to their expectations as to what state policy can deliver. While recognizing that the outcomes of social policies have changed familial and other structures in society such that male power has been challenged, they have argued that the state has also served to perpetuate patriarchal structures (Pateman 1988; Siim 1987). On the other hand, Scandinavian feminists have insisted on the possibility of a 'woman friendly' state (Hernes 1987). Kolberg (1991: 144) has gone one step further and dismissed any idea that the Scandinavian welfare state might be patriarchal, insisting that it has increased women's 'independence, empowerment and emancipation'.

Yet it is noteworthy that in both France and Sweden women played little part in securing such advantages as accrued to them from the respective welfare regimes. In pre-war France feminists were forced to couch their claims in pronatalist terms. Pedersen (1991) suggests that paradoxically it was in large part the strength of British feminism compared to the French in putting forward a claim to family allowances as a means of both paying women as mothers (as well as providing for children) and securing equal pay for women at work (by abolishing the grounds for men's claim to a family wage) that resulted in such a weak measure. In France, family allowances were never conceptualized as a gender issue and the matter of redistribution between men and women was never articulated.

In Sweden, the Social Democratic Women's

League was an active campaigning force in the late 1960s and 1970s, but one of its most important original demands for the six hour day was not met by the body of legislation that transformed women's labour market participation because of opposition from the trade union movement. Such a measure may well have served to redistribute unpaid and paid work between men and women. On the other hand, the Swedish case may lend support to Balbo's (1987) argument that modern welfare states call forth greater female public participation. All Nordic parliaments with the exception of Iceland have reached a critical mass (30–40%) of women members and it is in part this that has led to Scandinavian women's optimism about the role of the state. (In Sweden the percentage fell from 38 to 28 as a result of the 1991 election, although the number of women ministers has remained the same at eight.) What is secured as a by-product of other concerns, for example pronatalism in France, or the desire to increase the size of the labour force as in Sweden, can be reversed. Political and institutional power is crucial not so much for securing material well-being, as for putting issues that are central to enlarging women's choices, like the division and valuing of unpaid work, onto the political agenda.

Notes

1 I am indebted to Ilona Ostner for her ideas about the concepts developed in this paper.
2 The most significant attempts to date are by Langan and Ostner (1991) and by Shaver (1990).
3 The material in this section is drawn from a larger piece of work carried out in co-operation with Gertrude Astrom.

References

Ashford, D. (1982) *British Dogmatism and French Pragmatism: Central-Local Relations in the Welfare State*, London, Allen and Unwin.
Baker, J. (1991) Family policy as an anti-poverty measure, in M. Hardey and G. Crow (eds) *Lone Parenthood*, Brighton, Harvester Wheatsheaf.
Balbo, L. (1987) Family, women and the state: notes toward a typology of family roles and public intervention, in C. S. Maier (ed.) *Changing Boundaries of the Political: Essays on the Evolving Balance Between the State and Society, Public and Private in Europe*. Cambridge, Cambridge University Press.
Brown, J. C. (1987) *The Future of Family Income Support*, London, Policy Studies Institute Studies of the Social Security System, No. 15.
Callender, R. (1988) Ireland and the implementation of Directive 79/7/EEC, in Gerry Whyte (ed.) *Sex Equality, Community Rights and Irish Social Welfare Law*, Dublin, Irish Centre for European Law.
Crompton, R., Hantrais, L. and Walters, P. (1990) Gender relations and employment, *British Journal of Sociology*, 41 (3) 329–49.
Cuvillier, R. (1979) The housewife: an unjustified financial burden on the community, *Journal of Social Policy* 8 (3): 1–26.
Davies, H. and Joshi, H. (1990) The Foregone Earnings of Europe's Mothers, Discussion Papers in Economics, 24/90, Birbeck College, University of London, London.
Dawson, P. E. (1979) Family benefits and income redistribution in France and the UK, 1891–1971, unpublished PhD thesis, York, York University.
Deacon, A. (1976) *In Search of the Scrounger. The Administration of Unemployment Insurance in Britain, 1920–1931*, Occasional papers in Social Administration, No. 60, London, London School of Economics.
Dex, S. and Walters, P. (1989) Women's occupational status in Britain, France and the USA: explaining the difference, *Industrial Relations Journal*, 20 (3): 203–12.
Ekert, O. (1983) Activite Feminine, Prestations Familiales et Redistribution, *Population* 38 (3): 503–26.
Esping Andersen, G. (1990) *The Three Worlds of Welfare Capitalism* Cambridge, Polity.
Gordon, L. (ed.) (1990) *Women, The State and Welfare*, Madison, Wisconsin, University of Wisconsin Press.
Gustafsson, S. and Stafford, F. (1988) *Daycare Subsidies and Labour Supply in Sweden*, Centre for Economic Policy Research Discussion Papers, No. 279, London.
Hantrais, L. (1990) *Managing Professional and Family Life. A Comparative Study of British and French Women*, Aldershot, Dartmouth Publishing Company.
Hantrais, L. (forthcoming) Women, work and welfare in France, in J. Lewis (ed.) *Women, Work and the Family in Europe*, Aldershot, Edward Elgar.

Haut Conseil de la Population et de la Famille (1985)
Vie Professionelle et Vie Familiale, de Nouveaux
Equilibres a Construire, La Documentation
Francaise, Paris, Ministere des Affaires Sociales et de
L'Emploi.

Hernes, H. (1987) *Welfare State and Woman Power:
Essays in State Feminism*, Oslo, Norwegian
University Press.

Hirdman, Y. (1989) The Swedish Welfare State and the
gender system: a theoretical and empirical sketch,
*The Study of Power and Democracy in Sweden
English Series* Report No. 7, Stockholm.

Jenson, J. and Kantrow, R. (1990) Labor Market and
Family Policy in France: An Intersecting Complex
for Dealing with Poverty, in G. Schaffner Goldberg
and Eleanor Kremen (eds) *The Feminization of
Poverty. Only in America?* New York, Praeger
Publications.

Jenson, J. (1988) The limits of 'and the ' discourse:
French women as marginal workers, in J. Jenson, E.
Hagen, and C. Reddy (eds) *The Feminization of the
Labour Force: Paradoxes and Promises*, New York,
Oxford University Press.

Jonung, C. (1984) Patterns of occupational segregation
in the labour market, in Gunther Schmid and Renate
Weitzel (eds) *Sex Discrimination and Equal
Opportunities*, Aldershot, Gower.

Kalvemark, A. S. (1980) *More Children of Better
Quality? Aspects in (sic) Swedish Population Policy
in the 1930s*, Stockholm, Alqvist and Wiksell.

Key, E. (1912) *The Woman Movement*, New York, G.
P. Putnam's Sons.

Key, E. (1914) *The Renaissance of Motherhood*, New
York, G. P. Putnam's Sons.

Kolberg, J. E. (1991) The gender dimension of the
welfare state, *International Journal of Sociology*,
21(2): 119–148.

Land, H. (1975) The introduction of family
allowances: an act of historic justice?, in P. Hall *et
al.* (eds) *Change, Choice and Conflict in Social
Policy*, London, Heineman.

Land, H. (1980) The family wage, *Feminist Review* 6:
55–78.

Land, H. and Ward, S. (1986) *Women Won't Benefit*,
London, National Council for Civil Liberties.

Langan, M. and Ostner, I. (1991) Gender and welfare,
in Graham Room (ed.), *Towards a European
Welfare State?*, Bristol, School of Advanced Urban
Studies.

Laroque, P. (1985) *La Politique Familiale en France
depuis 1945*, Documents Affaires Sociales, Paris,
Ministere des Affaires Sociales et de la Solidarite
Nationale.

Leibfried, S. (1991) *Towards a European Welfare
State? On the Integration Potentials of Poverty
Regimes in the EC*, TS, Bremen, Bremen University.

Leira, A. (1989) *Models of Motherhood, Welfare State
Policies and Everyday Practices: The Scandinavian

Experience*, Oslo, Institute for Social Research.

Lewis, J. (1980) *The Politics of Motherhood*, London,
Croom Helm.

Lewis, J. (1983) Dealing with dependency: state
practices and social realities, 1870–1945, in J. Lewis
(ed.) *Women's Welfare/Women's Rights*, London,
Croom Helm.

Lewis, J. (1986) The working class wife and mother
and state intervention, 1870–1918, in J. Lewis (ed.),
*Women's Experience of Home and Family, 1850–
1940*, Oxford, Blackwell.

Lewis, J. (1991) *Women and Social Action in Victorian
and Edwardian England*, Aldershot, Edward Elgar
Publishers.

Lewis, J. and Davies, C. (1991) Protective legislation in
Britain, 1870–1990: equality, difference and their
implications for women, *Policy and Politics*, 19 (1):
13–25.

Lister, R. (1992) *Women's Economic Dependency and
Social Security*, Manchester, Equal Opportunities
Commission.

Mazur, A. (1991) Agendas and egalite professionelle:
symbolic policy at work in France, in E. Meehan and
S. Sevenhuijsen (eds) *Equality, Politics and Gender*,
London, Sage.

Mead, L. (1986) *Beyond Entitlement. The Social
Obligations of Citizenship*, New York, The Free
Press.

Millar, J. (1989) *Poverty and the Lone Parent Family.
The Challenge to Social Policy*, Aldershot, Avebury.

Morris, L. (1990) *The Workings of the Household. A
US–UK Comparison*, Cambridge, Polity Press.

Murray, C. (1984) *Losing Ground. American Social
Policy, 1950–1980*, New York, Basic Books.

Myrdal, A. and Klein, V. (1954) *Women's Two Roles*,
London, Routledge and Kegan Paul.

Okin, S. M. (1979) *Women in Western Political
Thought*, Princeton, Princeton University Press.

Pahl, J. (1990) *Money and Marriage*, London,
Macmillan.

Pateman, C. (1988) The Patriarchal Welfare State, in
A. Gutman (ed.) *Democracy and the Welfare State*,
Princeton, Princeton University Press.

Pateman, C. (1989) Feminist Critiques of the Public/
Private Dichotomy, in C. Pateman (ed.) *The
Disorder of Women*, Stanford, Stanford University
Press.

Pedersen, S. (1991) Social policy and the reconstruction
of the family in Britain and France, 1900–1945,
unpublished PhD thesis, Cambridge, Mass., Harvard
University.

Phillips, A. and Moss, P. (1988) *Who Cares for
Europe's Children? The Short Report of the
European Childcare Network*, Brussels, EC.

Poovey, M. (1989) *Uneven Developments. The
Ideological Work of Gender in Mid-Victorian
England*, London, Virago.

PP. (1942) Cmd. 6404, Report of the Committee on Social Insurance and Allied Services, HMSO, London.

Prost, A. (1984) L'Evolution de la Politique Familiale en France de 1938 a 1981, *Le Mouvement Social* no. 129 Oct–Dec.: 7–28.

Pyle, J. L. (1990) *The State and Women in the Economy. Lessons from Sex Discrimination in the Republic of Ireland*, Albany, SUNY Press.

Questiaux, N. (1985) Family policy in France, in S. N. Eisenstadt and Ora Ahimeir *The Welfare State and its Aftermath*, London, Croom Helm.

Rodgers, B. N. (1975) Family Policy in France, *Journal of Social Policy* 4 (2): 113–28.

Shaver, S. (1990) *Gender, social policy regimes and the welfare state*, Social Policy Research Centre Discussion Papers, no. 26, Sydney, University of New South Wales.

Silver, C. B. (1977) France: contrasts in familial and societal roles, in J. Zollinger Giele and A. Chapman Smock (eds) *Women. Roles and Status in Eight Countries*, New York, John Wiley.

Siim, B. (1987) The Scandinavian welfare states – towards sexual equality or a new kind of male domination?, *Acta Sociologica* 30 (3/4): 255–70.

Sokoloff, N. (1980) *Between Money and Love. The Dialectics of Women's Home and Market Work*, New York, Praeger.

Taylor Gooby, P. (1991) Welfare state regimes and welfare citizenship, *Journal of European Social Policy* 1(2): 93–105.

Thibault, M.-N. (1986) Politiques Familiales, Politiques D'Emploi, *Nouvelles Questions Feministes* 14–15, Winter: 147–61.

Titmuss, R. M. (1963) The Social Division of Welfare, in R. M. Titmuss, *Essays on the Welfare State*, London, Allen and Unwin.

Wilson, E. (1977) *Women and the Welfare State*, London, Tavistock.

A
Liberal

[14]

Letter of Transmittal with the Report of the Committee on Economic Security
January 15, 1935

Dear Mr. President: In your message of June 8, 1934, to the Congress you directed attention to certain fundamental objectives in the great task of reconstruction; an indistinguishable and essential aspect of the immediate task of recovery. You stated, in language that we cannot improve upon:

> Our task of reconstruction does not require the creation of new and strange values. It is rather the finding of the way once more to known, but to some degree forgotten, ideals and values. If the means and details are in some instances new, the objectives are as permanent as human nature.
>
> Among our objectives I place the security of the men, women, and children of the Nation first.
>
> This security for the individual and for the family concerns itself primarily with three factors. People want decent homes to live in; they want to locate them where they can engage in productive work; and they want some safeguard against misfortunes which cannot be wholly eliminated in this man-made world of ours.

Subsequent to this message you created, by Executive order, this Committee on Economic Security to make recommendations to you on the third of the aspects of security which you outlined—that of safeguards "against misfortunes which cannot be wholly eliminated in this man-made world of ours."

In the brief time that has intervened, we have sought to analyze the hazards against which special measures of security are necesary, and have tried to bring to bear upon them the world experience with measures designed as safeguards against these hazards. We have analyzed all proposed safeguards of this kind which have received serious consideration in this country. On the basis of all these considerations, we have tried to formulate a program which will represent at least a substantial beginning toward the realization of the objective you presented.

We have had in our employ a small staff, which included some of the outstanding experts in this field. This staff has prepared many valuable studies giving the factual background, summarizing American and foreign experience, presenting actuarial calculations, and making detailed suggestions for legislation and administration.

We have also had the assistance of the Technical Board on Economic Security, provided for in your Executive order, and composed of 20 people in the Government service, who have special interest and knowledge in some or all aspects of the problem you directed us to study. The Technical Board, functioning as a group, through subcommittees, and as individuals, has aided the staff and the committee during the entire investigation. Many of the members have devoted much time to this work and have made very important contributions, indeed. Plus these, many other people in the Government service have unstintingly aided the committee with special problems on which their advice and assistance has been sought.

The Advisory Council on Economic Security, appointed by you and constituted of citizens outside of the Government service, representing employers, employees, and the general public, has assisted the committee in weighing the proposals developed by the staff and the Technical Board, and in arriving at a judgment as to their practicability. All members of the Council were people who have important private responsibilities, and many of them also other public duties, but they took time to come to Washington on four separate occasions for meetings extending over several days.

In addition to the Council, this committee found it advisable to create seven other advisory groups: A committee of actuarial consultants, a medical advisory board, a dental advisory committee, a hospital advisory committee, a public-health advisory committee, a child welfare committee, and an advisory committee on employment and relief. All of these committees have contributed suggestions which have been incorporated in this report. The medical advisory board, the dental advisory committee, and the hospital advisory committee are still continuing their consideration of health insurance, but joined with the public health advisory committee in endorsement of the program for extended public-health services which we recommend.

Finally, many hundreds of citizens and organization in all parts of the country have contributed ideas and suggestions. Three hundred interested citizens, representing practically every State, at their own expense, attended the National Conference on Economic Security, held in Washington on November 14, which was productive of many very good suggestions.

The responsibility for the recommendations we offer is our own. As was inevitable in view of the wide differences of opinion which prevail regard- 87 ing the best methods of providing protection against the hazards leading to destitution and dependency, we could not accept all of the advice and suggestions offered, but it was distinctly helpful to have all points of view presented and considered.

To all who assisted us or offered suggestions, we are deeply grateful.

In this report we briefly sketch the need for additional safeguards against "the major hazards and vicissitudes of life." We also present recommendations for making a beginnning in the development of safeguards against these hazards, and with this report submit drafts of bills to give effect to these recommendations. We realize that some of the measures we recommend are experimental and, like nearly all pioneering legislation, will, in course of time, have to be extended and modified.They represent, however, our best judgment as to the steps which ought to be taken immediately toward the realization of what you termed in your recent message to the Congress "the ambition of the individual to obtain for him and his a proper security, a reasonable leisure, and a decent living throughout life."

Respectfully submitted.

> *Frances Perkins,*
> Secretary of Labor (Chairman).
> *Henry Morgenthau, Jr.,*
> Secretary of the Treasury.
> *Henry A. Wallace,*
> Secretary of Agriculture.
> *Harry L. Hopkins,*
> Federal Emergency Relief
> Administrator.

Report of the Committee on Economic Security
January 15, 1935

Need For Security

The need of the people of this country for "some safeguard against misfortunes which cannot be wholly eliminated in this man-made world of ours" is tragically apparent at this time, when 18,000,000 people, including children and aged, are dependent upon emergency relief for their subsistence and approximately 10,000,000 workers have no employment other than relief work. Many millions more have lost their entire savings, and there has occurred a very great decrease in earnings. The ravages of probably the worst depression of all time have been accentuated by greater urbanization, with the consequent total dependence of a majority of our people on their
88 earnings in industry.

As progress is made toward recovery, this insecurity will be lessened, but it is not apparent that even in the "normal times" of the prosperous twenties, a large part of our population had little security. From the best estimates which are obtainable, it appears that in the years 1922 to 1929 there was an average unemployment of 8 percent among our industrial workers. In the best year of this period, the number of the unemployed averaged somewhat less than 1,500,000.

Unemployment is but one of many misfortunes which often result in destitution. In the slack year of 1933, 14,500 persons were fatally injured in American industry and 55,000 sustained some permanent injury. Nonindustrial accidents exacted a much greater toll. On the average, 2.25 percent of all industrial workers are at all times incapacitated from work by reason of illness. Each year above one-eighth of all workers suffer one or more illnesses which disable them for a week, and the percentage of the families in which some member is seriously ill is much greater. In urban families of low incomes, above one-fifth each year have expenditures for medical and related care of above $100 and many have sickness bills of above one-fourth and even one-half of their entire family income. A relatively small but not insignificant number of workers are each year prematurely invalided and 8 percent of all workers are physically handicapped. At least one-third of all our people, upon reaching old age, are dependent upon others for support. Less than 10 percent leave an estate upon death of sufficient size to be probated.

There is insecurity in every stage of life.

For the largest group, the people in middle years, who carry the burden of current production from which all must live, the hazards with which they are confronted threaten not only their own economic independence but the welfare of their dependents.

For those now old, insecurity is doubly tragic, because they are beyond the productive period. Old age comes to everyone who does not die prematurely and is a misfortune only if there is insufficient income to provide for the remaining years of life. With a rapidly increasing number and percentage of the aged, and the impairment and loss of savings, this country faces, in the next decades, an even greater old-age security problem than that with which it is already confronted.

For those at the other end of the life cycle — the children — dependence is normal, and security is best provided through their families. That security is often lacking. Not only do the children under 16 constitute above 40 percent of all people now on relief, as compared to 28 percent in the entire population, but at all times there are several millions in need of special measures of protection. Some of these need individual attention to restore, as fully as may be, lives already impaired. More of them — those who have been deprived of a father's support — need only financial aid which will make it possible for their mothers to continue to give them normal family care. 89

Most of the hazards against which safeguards must be provided are similar in that they involve loss of earnings. When earnings cease, dependency is not far off for a large percentage of our people. In 1929, at the peak of the stock-market boom, the average per capita income of all salaried employees at work was only $1,475. Eighteen million gainfully employed persons, constituting 44 percent of all those gainfully occupied, exclusive of farmers, had annual earnings of less than $1,000; 28,000,000 or nearly 70 percent, earnings of less than $1,500. Many people lived in straitened circumstances at the height of prosperity; a considerable number live in chronic want. Throughout the twenties, the number of people dependent upon private and public charity steadily increased.

With the depression, the scant margin of safety of many others has disappeared. The average earnings of all wage earners at work dropped from $1,475 in 1929 to $1,199 in 1932. Since then, there has been considerable recovery, but even for many who are fully employed there is no margin for contingencies.

The one almost all-embracing measure of security is an assured income. A program of economic security, as we vision it, must have as its primary aim the assurance of an adequate income to each human being in childhood, youth, middle age, or old age—in sickness or in health. It must provide safeguards against all of the hazards leading to destitution and dependency.

A piecemeal approach is dictated by practical considerations, but the broad objectives should never be forgotten. Whatever measures are deemed immediately expedient should be so designed that they can be embodied in the complete program which we must have ere long.

To delay until it is opportune to set up a complete program will probably mean holding up action until it is too late to act. A substantial beginning should be made now in the develoopment of the safeguards which are so manifestly needed for individual security. As stated in the message of June 8, these represent not "a change in values" but "rather a return to values lost in the course of our economic development and expension." "The road to these values is the way to progress." We will not "rest content until we have done our utmost to move forward on that road."

Summary Of Major Recommendations

In this report we discuss briefly all aspects of the problem of economic security for the individual. On many phases our studies enable us only to call attention to the importance of not neglecting these aspects of economic security and to give endorsement to measures and policies which have been or should be worked out in detail by other agencies of the Government.

Apart from these phases of a complete program for economic security with which we deal only sketchily, we present the following major recommendations:

90

Employment Assurance

Since most people must live by work, the first objective in a program of economic security must be maximum employment. As the major contribution of the Federal Government in providing a safeguard against unemployment we suggest employment assurance — the stimulation of private employment and the provision of public employment for those able-bodied workers whom industry cannot employ at a given time. Public-work programs are most necessary in periods of severe depression, but may be needed in normal times, as well, to help meet the problems of stranded communities and over-manned or declining industries. To avoid the evils of hastily planned emergency work, public employment should be planned in advance and coordinated with the construction and developmental policies of the Government and with the State and local public-works projects.

We regard work as preferable to other forms of relief where possible. While we favor unemployment compensation in cash, we believe that it should be provided for limited periods on a contractual basis and without governmental subsidies. Public funds should be devoted to providing work rather than to introduce a relief element into what should be strictly an insurance system.

Unemployment Compensation

Unemployment compensation, as we conceive it, is a front line of defense, especially valuable for those who are ordinarily steadily employed, but very beneficial also in maintaining purchasing power. While it will not directly benefit those now unemployed until they are reabsorbed in industry, it should be instituted at the earliest possible date to increase the security of all who are employed.

We believe that the States should administer unemployment compensation, assisted and guided by the Federal Government. We recommend as essential the imposition of a uniform pay-roll tax against which credits shall be allowed to industries in States that shall have passed unemployment compensation laws. Through such a unform pay-roll tax it will be possible to remove the unfair competitive advantage that employers operating in States which have failed to adopt a compensation system enjoy over employers operating in States which give such protection to their wage earners.

We believe also that it is essential that the Federal Government assume responsibility for safeguarding, investing, and liquidating all reserve funds, in order that these reserves may be utilized to promote economic stability and to avoid dangers inherent in their uncontrolled investment and liquidation. We believe, further, that the Federal act should require high administrative standards, but should leave wide latitude to the States in other respects, as we deem experience very necessary with particular provisions of unemployment compensation laws in order to conclude what types are most practicable in this country.   91

Old-Age Security

To meet the problem of security for the aged we suggest as complementary measures noncontributory old-age pensions, compulsory contributory annuities, and voluntary contributory annuities, all to be applicable on retirement at age 65 or over.

Only noncontributory old-age pensions will meet the situation of those who are now old and have no means of support. Laws for the payment of old-age pensions on a needs basis are in force in more than half of all States and should be enacted everywhere. Because most of the dependent aged are now on relief lists and derive their support principally from the Federal Government and many of the States cannot assume the financial burden of pensions unaided, we recommend that the Federal Government pay one-half the cost of old-age pensions but not more than $15 per month for any individual.

The satisfactory way of providing for the old age of those now young is a contributory system of old-age annuities. This will enable younger workers, with matching contributions from their employers, to build up a more adequate old-age protection than it is possible to achieve with noncontributory pensions based upon a means test. To launch such a system we deem it necessary that workers who are now middle-aged or older and who, therefore, cannot in the few remaining years of their industrial life accumulate a substantial reserve be, nevertheless, paid reasonably adequate annuities upon retirement. These Government contributions to augment earned annuities may either take the form of assistance under old age pension laws on a more liberal basis than in the case of persons who have made no contributions or by a Government subsidy to the contributory annuity system itself. A portion of these particular annuities will come out of Government funds, but because receipts from contributions will in the early years greatly exceed annuity payments, it will not be necessary as a financial problem to have Government contributions until after the system has been in operation for 30 years. The combined contributory rate we recommend is 1 percent of pay roll to be divided equally between employers and employees, which is to be increased by 1 percent each 5 years, until the maximum of 5 percent is reached in 10 years.

There still remains, unprotected by either of the two above plans, professional and self-employed groups, many of whom face dependency in old age. Partially to meet their problem, we suggest the establishment of a voluntary Government annuity system, designed particularly for people of small incomes.

Security for Children

A large group of the children at present maintained by relief will not be 92 aided by employment or unemployment compensation. There are the fatherless and other "young" families without a breadwinner. To meet the problems of the children in these families, no less than 45 States have enacted children's aid laws, generally called "mothers' pension laws." However, due to the present financial difficulty in which many States find themselves, far more of such children are on the relief lists than are in receipt of children's aid benefits. We are strongly of the opinion that these families should be differentiated from the permanent dependents and unemployables, and we believe that the children's aid plan is the method which will best care for their needs. We recommend Federal grants-in-aid on the basis of one-half the State and local expenditures for this purpose (one-third the entire cost).

We recommend also that the Federal Government give assistance to States in providing local services for the protection and care of homeless, neglected, and delinquent children and for child and maternal health services especially in rural areas. Special aid should be given toward meeting a part of the expenditures for transportation, hospitalization, and convalescent care of crippled and handicapped children, in order that those very necessary services may be extended for a large group of children whose only handicaps are physical.

Risks Arising Out of Ill Health

As a first measure for meeting the very serious problem of sickness in families with low income we recommend a Nation-wide preventive public-health program. It should be largely financed by State and local governments and administered by State and local health departments, the Federal Government to contribute financial and technical aid. The program contemplates (1) grants in aid to be allocated through State departments of health to local areas unable to finance public-health programs from State and local resources, (2) direct aid to States in the development of State health services and the training of personnel for State and local health work, and (3) additional personnel in the United States Public Health Service to investigate health problems of interstate or national concern.

The second major step we believe to be the application of the principles of insurance to this problem. We are not prepared at this time to make recommendations for a system of health insurance. We have enlisted the cooperation of advisory groups representing the medical and dental professions and hospital management in the development of a plan for health insurance which will be beneficial alike to the public and the professions concerned. We have asked these groups to complete their work by March 1, 1935, and expect to make a further report on this subject at that time or shortly thereafter. Elsewhere in our report we state principles on which our study of health insurance is proceeding, which indicate clearly that we contemplate no action that will not be quite as much in the interests of the members of the professions concerned as of the families with low incomes.   93

Conclusion

The program for economic security we suggest follows no single pattern. It is broader than social insurance and does not attempt merely to copy European methods. In placing primary emphasis on employment rather than unemployment compensation, we differ fundamentally from those who see social insurance as an all-sufficient program for economic security. We recommend wide application of the principles of social insurance, but not without deviation from European models. Where other measures seemed more appropriate to our background or present situation, we have not hesitated to recommend them in preference to the European practices. In doing so we have recommended the measures at this time which seemed best calculated under our American conditions to protect individuals in the years immediately ahead from hazards which plunge them into destitution and dependency. This, we believe, is in accord with the method of attaining the definite goal of the Government, social justice, which was outlined in the message of January 4, 1935. "We seek it through tested liberal traditions, through processes which retain all of the deep essentials of that republican form of government first given to a troubled world by the United States."

We realize that these measures we recommend will not give complete economic security. As outlined in the messages of June 8, 1934, and January 4, 1935, the safeguards to which this report relates represent but one of three major aspects of economic security for men, women, and children. Nor do we regard this report and our recommendations as exhaustive of the particular aspect which this committee was directed to study — "the major hazards and vicissitudes of life." A complete program of economic security "because of many lost years, will take many future years to fulfill."

The initial steps to bring this program into operation should be taken now. This program will involve considerable cost, but this is small as compared with the enormous cost of insecurity. The measures we suggest should result in the long run in material reduction in the cost to society of destitution and dependency, and we believe, will immediately be helpful in allaying those fears which open the door to unsound proposals. The program will promote social and industrial stability and will operate to enlarge and make steady a widely diffused purchasing power upon which depends the high American standard of living and the internal market for our mass production, industry, and agriculture.

[15]

INTRODUCTION

Understanding American Social Politics

MARGARET WEIR, ANN SHOLA ORLOFF,

AND THEDA SKOCPOL

Along with many other advanced-industrial democracies, the United States finds itself in the midst of debates over the future of national social policies. Since the 1970s all such democracies have endured a fiscal crisis traced by some to the growth of the welfare state. International economic recession has brought the cold grip of "stagflation" to many nations at a time when Keynesian strategies of macroeconomic management no longer seem certain to ensure steady economic growth without rising unemployment. Large population cohorts covered by mature pension systems are aging and retiring, while increasing numbers of individuals cannot depend upon traditional family ties for help during periods of difficulty. Economic pressures and social trends have thus combined to spur widespread consternation about the future of public social programs in the Western nations.

As European welfare states undergo serious reevaluations of prior policies, innovative measures continue to be debated, and the existing strong responsibilities of national states to promote social welfare are not fundamentally challenged. In the United States, however, the legitimacy of the welfare role of the federal government *is* a matter for debate, and relatively paltry public social programs are being vigorously attacked. Proponents of new social policies speak in voices barely audible on the national political stage. This is a paradoxical situation, for if any one of the advanced industrial democratic countries could afford to do more to meet domestic needs through public provision—or perhaps one should say, if any country could afford to do better and, where necessary, more—that country would be the United States.

By international standards the United States has a remarkably healthy economy, one that has consistently generated new jobs at a high rate and has recovered relatively well from the recession of the 1970s.[1] At the same

---

In preparing the final version of the Introduction, the editors benefited from comments by Fred Block, Jennifer Hochschild, and Robert Kuttner.

[1] On the remarkable generation of employment by the U.S. economy, even in the face of

4   Introduction

time, despite rising levels of social spending since 1960, the United States
has never established more than a relatively inexpensive and programmatically incomplete system of public social provision. In the mid-1970s
social spending for education, income maintenance, and health in the
United States accounted for about 16 percent of GDP, while most European nations devoted more than 20 percent of GDP to social expenditures.[2] Although the United States is above average in educational expenditures, it lacks the national health insurance and family allowances
provided by most European welfare states as well as Canada. Both public
assistance and unemployment insurance in America remain ungenerous
by international standards and uneven in their coverage across the states
and population groups at risk.[3] Only in the area of old-age, disability,
and medical insurance for retired workers who have been stably employed for most of their working lives does the United States compare
well to other industrial democracies.[4] Yet benefits in these areas are not
only channeled through the public sector but also (with encouragement
from tax breaks) through privately negotiated fringe-benefit schemes.[5]

    Why is the United States, which has one of the least generous systems
of public social provision of any of the capitalist democracies, witnessing
a period of unusually intense political attacks against its incomplete social
programs? Contrary to the accepted wisdom among conservatives and
leftists alike, the explanation does not lie in any inexorable "limit of welfare state development" or global "crisis of advanced capitalism." Although fiscal strains may be common to many countries, whether and

---

strong demographic pressures, see John Schwarz, *America's Hidden Success: A Reassessment of Twenty Years of Public Policy* (New York: Norton, 1983), p. 128.

    [2] Organization for Economic Cooperation and Development, *Public Expenditure Trends*,
Studies in Resource Allocation no. 5 (Paris: OECD, June 1978), Table 6, p. 25. For more
precise comparative figures on "income security programs" in particular, see John Myles,
Old Age in the Welfare State: The Political Economy of Public Pensions (Boston: Little,
Brown, 1984), Tables 1.2 and 1.3, pp. 17–19.

    [3] For comparisons of U.S. with Western European and Canadian social policies, see:
Myles, *Old Age in the Welfare State*; Norman Furniss and Timothy Tilton, *The Case for the
Welfare State* (Bloomington: Indiana University Press, 1977); and Robert T. Kudrle and
Theodore R. Marmor, "The Development of Welfare States in North America" in Peter
Flora and Arnold J. Heidenheimer, eds., *The Development of Welfare States in Europe and
America* (New Brunswick, N.J.: Transaction Books, 1981), pp. 81–121.

    [4] Richard F. Tomasson, "Old-Age Pensions under Social Security: Past and Future,"
American Behavioral Scientist 26 (1983): 699–723. Myles, in *Old Age in the Welfare State*,
Table 3.7, cols. 1–3, p. 69, shows that of fifteen capitalist democracies, the United States is
average or slightly above average in public pension levels for low-, average-, and high-in-
come workers.

    [5] See the paper by Beth Stevens in this volume (Chapter 3); also Alicia Munnell, *The
Economics of Private Pensions*, Studies in Social Economics (Washington D.C.: The Brookings Institution, 1982).

exactly how a "crisis" is defined, and the nature of the policy alternatives debated for the future, depend mostly upon each nation's social structure and political arrangements. Understandings of crisis and policy alternatives also depend on the ways each nation's existing policies influence political alliances and arouse debates over further policy choices. A nation's politics creates social policies; they in turn remake its politics, transforming possibilities for the future.

Contemporary American debates over "the crisis of social security" and "the need to reduce welfare dependency" do not, therefore, simply reflect economically given limits or an inexorable international crisis. To understand the shape of these debates—and also to see where American social policy might go from here—we need to explore the historical formation and remaking of social policies in the United States from the roots of the New Deal's Social Security programs through the Great Society efforts of the 1960s and on into the present. At a time when the future of U.S. public social provision is very much at issue, there is a compelling need to grasp the fundamental patterns of American social politics in historical perspective. Such is the task to which this collection of essays is devoted.

History does not speak for itself, however. It will answer only the questions we pose, and there is always more than one way to ask questions and hear answers. So we had best be explicit from the start. What features of U.S. social policy do we seek to understand? And how does our perspective on American social politics—our way of framing questions and answers—compare to important alternative perspectives that other thoughtful people have used?

The American Version of Public Social Provision

Modern welfare states, as they have come to be called, had their start between the 1880s and the 1920s in pension and social insurance programs established for industrial workers and needy citizens.[6] Later, from the 1930s through the 1950s, such programmatic beginnings were elaborated into comprehensive systems of income support and social insurance encompassing entire national populations. In the aftermath of World War II, Great Britain rationalized a whole array of social services and social insurances around an explicit vision of "the welfare state" that would universally ensure a "national minimum" of protection for all

---

[6] Peter Flora and Jens Alber, "Modernization, Democratization, and the Development of Welfare States in Western Europe," in Flora and Heidenheimer, eds., *The Development of Welfare States*, pp. 37–80. See also Furniss and Tilton, *The Case for the Welfare State*, chaps. 5 and 6.

6   Introduction

citizens against insufficient income caused by old age, disability, ill health, and unemployment. During the same period, other nations—especially the Scandinavian democracies—established "full-employment welfare states" by deliberately coordinating social policies, first with Keynesian strategies of macroeconomic management, and then with targeted interventions in labor markets.[7]

American "social policy" prior to the 1930s included state and local support for mass public education,[8] along with generous federal benefits for elderly Civil War veterans and their dependents. In contrast to the European tempo of welfare state development, neither old-age pensions nor social insurance made much headway in the United States before the Great Depression. Then, in what has been called a "big bang" of national legislation, the Social Security Act of 1935 established nation-spanning social insurance and public assistance programs, creating a basic framework for U.S. public social provision that has remained in place to the present.[9] Health insurance was omitted from the Social Security Act and later schemes for universal national health benefits also failed.[10] But three major kinds of social provision were included in the 1935 legislation: federally required, state-run unemployment insurance; federally subsidized public assistance; and national contributory old-age insurance.

Unemployment insurance was instituted in 1935 as a federal-state system. All states were induced to establish programs, but each state was left free to decide terms of eligibility and benefits for unemployed workers, as well as the amount of taxes to be collected from employers or workers or both. Unemployment benefits and taxation became quite uneven across the states, and it remained difficult to pool risks of economic downturns on a national basis or to coordinate unemployment benefits with Keynesian demand management.[11] Despite efforts in the 1930s and 1940s to

---

[7] Gösta Esping-Andersen, *Politics against Markets: The Social Democratic Road to Power* (Princeton, N.J.: Princeton University Press, 1985), chap. 7; Andrew Martin, "The Dynamics of Change in a Keynesian Political Economy: The Swedish Case and Its Implications," in Colin Crouch, ed., *State and Economy in Contemporary Capitalism* (London: Croom Helm, 1979).

[8] See Morris Janowitz, *Social Control of the Welfare State* (New York: Elsevier, 1976), p. 34; and Arnold J. Heidenheimer, "Education and Social Security Entitlements in Europe and America," in Flora and Heidenheimer, eds., *The Development of Welfare States*, pp. 269–304.

[9] The "big bang" characterization comes from Christopher Leman, "Patterns of Policy Development: Social Security in the United States and Canada," *Public Policy* 25 (1977): 261–91.

[10] Paul Starr, "Transformation in Defeat: The Changing Objectives of National Health Insurance, 1915–1980," *American Journal of Public Health* 72 (1982): 78–88.

[11] Joseph M. Becker, "Twenty-five Years of Unemployment Insurance," *Political Science Quarterly* 75 (1960): 481–99; Edward J. Harpham, "Federalism, Keynesianism, and the Transformation of the Unemployment Insurance System in the United States," in Douglas

nationalize unemployment insurance and join its operations to various measures of public economic planning, no such explicit coordination of social and economic policy was achieved in the postwar United States.

The public assistance programs subsidized under Social Security already existed in certain states by the early 1930s. Assistance for the elderly poor and for dependent children were the most important of these programs. Left free under Social Security to decide whether they would even have such programs, the states were also given discretion to decide matters of eligibility and benefits and, in practice, methods of administration. Over time, as old-age insurance expanded to cover virtually all retired employees in the United States, federal old-age assistance became less important than it had been originally. By the 1960s, the Aid to Dependent Children Program (now Aid to Families with Dependent Children—AFDC—providing benefits to caretakers as well as to the children themselves) expanded enormously with a predominately female adult clientele.[12] Labeled "welfare," AFDC has very uneven standards of eligibility, coverage, and benefits across the states, generally providing the least to the poorest people in the poorest states, and leaving many impoverished men and husband-wife families without any coverage at all.[13]

Since 1935 contributory old-age insurance, the one program originally established on a purely national basis, has usurped the favorable label "social security" that once described the whole and has become the centerpiece of U.S. public social provision. Payroll taxes are collected from workers and employers across the country. Ultimately, retired workers collect benefits roughly consistent with their employment incomes, with some redistribution to low-wage contributors to the system. After 1935, additional programs were placed under this contributory insurance rubric: programs for surviving dependents in 1939; for disabled workers in 1956; and for retirees in need of medical care in 1965. Equally important, "social security" coverage and benefits grew, as more and more employees and categories of employees were incorporated during the 1950s, and benefit levels have been repeatedly raised by Congress.[14] By the 1970s, the United States, despite the uneven and often inadequate help provided

Ashford and E. W. Kelley, eds., *Nationalizing Social Security in Europe and America* (Greenwich, Conn.: JAI Press, 1986), pp. 155–79.

[12] Winifred Bell, *Aid to Dependent Children* (New York: Columbia University Press, 1965).

[13] Furniss and Tilton, *The Case for the Welfare State*, p. 170; Harrell R. Rodgers, Jr., *The Cost of Human Neglect: America's Welfare Failure* (Armonk, N.Y.: M. E. Sharpe, 1982), pp. 56–62; David T. Ellwood and Lawrence H. Summers, "Poverty in America: Is Welfare the Answer or the Problem?" in Sheldon H. Danziger and Daniel H. Weinberg, eds., *Fighting Poverty* (Cambridge: Harvard University Press, 1986), p. 84.

[14] Martha Derthick, *Policy Making for Social Security* (Washington D.C.: The Brookings Institution, 1979).

to unemployed and dependent people, had nevertheless become reasonably generous in the benefits offered to retired people of the working and middle classes.

Properly understood, public social provision in the United States also includes many federal measures undertaken to further the well-being of broad sectors of the populace, including middle-strata employees and small property owners. Some of these measures, such as agricultural price supports to shore up the incomes of commercial farmers, were launched in the New Deal. Others—such as educational aid to military veterans and grants to localities to encourage hospital construction—were established or significantly expanded in the aftermath of World War II, when higher peacetime revenues became permanently available as a result of the extended federal income tax. Although they do not carry the explicit label of "welfare" or "social policy," these policies are often implemented by *indirect* governmental action such as "tax expenditures" (that is, incentives in the form of forgiven tax payments) rather than direct public expenditures. In other cases, federal subsidies flow to third-party providers, such as private businesses or associations or local governments, as a way to encourage the provision of goods or services to favored groups or to members of the citizenry at large. U.S. housing policies especially exemplify the use of indirect instrumentalities. Both federal mortgage insurance and the deductibility of mortgage interest payments from federal taxes have spurred widespread private home ownership; even federal programs to house the poor have relied on regulatory breaks and subsidies to private real estate developers.[15]

Welfare became an area of political controversy and policy innovation in the United States only during the 1960s, when the "War on Poverty" and the effort to create a "Great Society" were declared.[16] For the first time since 1935, major new programs of needs-tested public assistance were established in the form of in-kind aid through Food Stamps and Medicaid. In 1972, moreover, old-age and other assistance programs (originally established as federal programs under Social Security) were nationalized, ensuring more standardized benefits. Nevertheless the much larger AFDC program remained federally decentralized, and standards for

[15] On U.S. housing policies in comparative perspective, see Bruce Headey, *Housing Policy in the Developed Economy* (New York: St. Martin's Press, 1978); Arnold J. Heidenheimer, Hugh Heclo, and Carolyn Teich Adams, *Comparative Public Policy*, 2d ed. (New York: St. Martin's Press, 1983), chap. 6; and Paul Starr and Gösta Esping-Andersen, "Passive Intervention," *Working Papers Magazine* 9 (July–August 1979): 15–25.

[16] For overviews of Great Society efforts, see Sar A. Levitan and Robert Taggart, *The Promise of Greatness* (Cambridge: Harvard University Press, 1976), pts. 1 and 2; James T. Patterson, *America's Struggle against Poverty, 1900–1980* (Cambridge: Harvard University Press, 1981), pt. 3; and Eli Ginzberg and Robert M. Solow, eds., *The Great Society: Lessons for the Future* (New York: Basic Books, 1974).

other benefits such as medical care are often tied to this uneven standard bearer of the American welfare system. Welfare remains, as always, both institutionally and symbolically separate from national economic management, on the one hand, and from non-means-tested programs benefitting stably employed citizens, on the other.

In sum, a number of features of U.S. social provision require explanation. Core welfare state policies such as old-age pensions and social insurance were much slower to emerge in the United States than in Europe; some—such as national health insurance—have never been instituted at all. We need to know why America's initiation of such modern social policies was (by international standards) so belated. We also need to make sense of the two major periods of explicit social policy innovation at the national level in the twentieth century: the New Deal of the 1930s, which included the passage of the Social Security Act, and the Great Society and Nixon era reforms of the 1960s and early 1970s, which included new programs for the poor along with improvement of Social Security benefits for retirees.

The programmatic structure and modes of implementation of U.S. social provision also require explanation. The public assistance and social insurance programs established under the Social Security Act have remained disjointed and nationally uneven, and these programs operate in conjunction with a variety of indirect federal incentives and subsidies that provide scattered social benefits outside of any comprehensive vision of the goals or effects of an American welfare state. Unlike the situation in Britain following the Beveridge reforms instituted after World War II, national standards have not been established in the United States for public benefits (not even the direct ones). American "social security" has remained firmly bifurcated, both institutionally and symbolically, from welfare; and in contrast to the "full-employment welfare states" of Scandinavia, there has been little coordination of U.S. social policies with nationally rationalized public interventions in the macroeconomy or labor markets. In the United States, various social benefits remain operationally, fiscally, and symbolically separate from one another; and they are all kept quite apart from other things the national government may be doing in relation to the economy and society.

We need, in short, to understand better why the United States in the twentieth century developed *not* a Western European-style welfare state but a much more disconnected system of public social provision. Once we understand the origins and patterns of this distinctively American system, we should be better positioned to see what might come next—not what *will* come next, but what alternatives are now within the realm of political possibility.

Explaining Social Provision:
Industrialization and Liberal Values?

Among many of those seeking to understand the development of social policies in the United States, two seemingly opposite but actually complementary perspectives have long held sway. One school of thought can be dubbed the "logic of industrialism" approach because it posits that all nation-states respond to the growth of cities and industries by creating public measures to help citizens cope with attendant social and economic dislocations.[17] Once families are off the land and dependent on wages and salaries, the argument goes, they cannot easily cope with disabling accidents at work, with major episodes of illness, unemployment, or with dependent elderly relatives unable to earn their keep. As social demand for public help grows, all modern nations must create policies to address these basic issues of social security without forcing respectable citizens to accept aid under the demeaning and disenfranchising rules of traditional poor laws.

Plausible as this sounds, recent cross-national studies on the origins of modern social insurance policies have demonstrated that urbanization and industrialization (whether considered separately or in combination) cannot explain the relative timing of the passage of national social insurance legislation from the late nineteenth century to the present.[18] American social policies, in particular, are not well explained by the logic of industrialism school. Not incidentally, proponents of this perspective have tended to include data for "the U.S. case" only when doing cross-national analyses for the period after 1935. Before the 1930s the United States is an awkward outlier; this country was one of the world's industrial leaders, yet "lagged" far behind other nations (even much less urban and industrial nations) in instituting public pensions, social insurance, and other modern welfare measures.

A second school of thought—what might be called the "national values" approach—accepts many underlying principles of the logic of industrialism argument, but introduces a major modification to explain why some nations, such as Bismarck's Germany in the 1880s, initiated modern social policies at relatively early stages of urbanization and industrializa-

---

[17] For examples of this approach, see Phillips Cutright, "Political Structure, Economic Development, and National Social Security Programs," *American Journal of Sociology* 70 (1965): 537–50; Robert Jackman, *Politics and Social Equality: A Comparative Analysis* (New York: Wiley, 1975); Harold Wilensky and Charles Lebeaux, *Industrial Society and Social Welfare* (New York: Free Press, 1965); and Harold Wilensky, *The Welfare State and Equality* (Berkeley: University of California Press, 1975), chap. 2.

[18] Flora and Alber, "Welfare States in Western Europe"; David Collier and Richard Messick, "Prerequisites versus Diffusion: Testing Alternative Explanations of Social Security Adoption," *American Political Science Review* 69 (1975): 1299–1315.

tion, while others, most notably the United States, delayed behind the pace of policy innovation that would be expected from the tempo of urbanization and industrialization alone. The answer, say proponents of this approach, lies in the values and ideologies to which each nation's people adhered as urbanization and industrialization gathered force.[19] Cultural conditions could either facilitate or delay action by a nation-state to promote social security, and cultural factors also influenced the shape and goals of new policies when they emerged.

Gaston Rimlinger, one of the ablest proponents of the national values approach, argues that the early enactment of Bismarck's social insurance policies was facilitated by the weakness of liberalism and the strength of "the patriarchal social ideal" and "the Christian social ethic" in nineteenth-century Germany.[20] In the United States, however, laissez-faire liberal values were extremely strong, and a "commitment to individualism . . . and self-help" led to a "tenacious" "resistance to social protection."[21] The unusual strength and persistence of American liberal values explain why social insurance measures were not instituted before the 1930s. Rimlinger points out that "it was only when the Great Depression revealed in a shocking manner the utter defenselessness of the citizen in the American industrial state that the still potent individualistic tradition could be overcome." Besides, the American individualistic tradition was never really overcome, even in the 1930s, for the new contributory social insurance programs were deliberately rationalized as "quasi-contractual" measures in which individuals would "earn the right to benefits" through their own contributions. "This," writes Rimlinger, "was a shrewd formula, for it covered the inevitable element of compulsion with a veneer of individualism. . . . The emphasis on contractual rights was of strategic significance: in an individualistic society the individual was not to be left dependent on the benevolence of the ruling powers."[22]

Again we confront a highly plausible account. Americans *do* espouse liberal values, and virtually all public policies in this country *are* either supported or opposed with arguments invoking liberal ideals. All the same, proponents of this approach have yet to pinpoint the precise ways that cultural values influence processes of political conflict and policy de-

---

[19] This approach is advocated (especially for the United States) in Kirsten Gronbjerg, David Street, and Gerald D. Suttles, *Poverty and Social Change* (Chicago: University of Chicago Press, 1978); P. R. Kaim-Caudle, *Comparative Social Policy and Social Security* (London: Martin Robertson, 1973); Anthony King, "Ideas, Institutions, and the Policies of Governments: A Comparative Analysis, Parts I and II," *British Journal of Political Science* 3 (1973): 291–313, 409–23; and Gaston Rimlinger, *Welfare Policy and Industrialization in Europe, America, and Russia* (New York: Wiley, 1971).

[20] Rimlinger, *Welfare Policy and Industrialization*, p. 91.

[21] *Ibid.*, p. 62.

[22] *Ibid.*, pp. 214, 229.

bate—let alone how they help to determine actual policy outcomes. Arguments like Rimlinger's about national values offer a credible general gloss on "what happened," but they do not consider the subtlest value-related questions about the origins and the structure of U.S. social policies.

Laissez-faire liberal values were in many respects more hegemonic and popular in Britain than they were in the United States in the nineteenth-century. Yet in the years before World War I Britain enacted a full range of social protective measures, including workers' compensation (1906), old-age pensions (1908), and unemployment and health insurance (1911). These innovations came under the auspices of the British Liberal party, and they were intellectually and politically justified by appeals to "new liberal" values of the sort that were also spreading among educated Americans at the turn of the century.[23] Under modern urban-industrial conditions, the "new liberals" argued, governments must act to protect individual security; and governments may proceed without undermining individuals' dignity or making them dependent on the state. If British Liberals could use such ideas to justify both state-funded pensions and contributory social insurance in the second decade of the twentieth century, why could American progressives not have done the same? In both Britain and the United States, sufficient cultural transformation within liberalism had occurred to legitimate fledgling welfare states without resort to either conservative-paternalist or socialist justifications.

When American New Dealers of the 1930s at last successfully instituted nationwide social protections justified in "new liberal" terms, why did they end up with the specific policies embodied in the Social Security Act? Why was health insurance left aside, despite the availability of liberal rationales for it that were just as valid as those put forward for unemployment and old-age insurance? And why did the public assistance programs subsidized under Social Security actually cement the dependence of many individuals on the arbitrary discretion of state and local authorities, rather than furthering individual dignity and making predictable the delivery of citizen benefits as a matter of "right"? Finally, given the clear priority that Americans have always placed on getting ahead

[23] On Great Britain's "new liberalism," see Michael Freeden, *The New Liberalism: An Ideology of Social Reform* (Oxford: Clarendon Press, 1978). On parallel developments in Great Britain and the United States, see Kenneth O. Morgan, "The Future at Work: Anglo-American Progressivism, 1870–1917," in H. C. Allen and Roger Thompson, eds., *Contrast and Connection: Bicentennial Essays in Anglo-American History* (Columbus: Ohio University Press, 1976), pp. 245–71; and Charles L. Mowat, "Social Legislation in Britain and the United States in the Early Twentieth Century: A Problem in the History of Ideas," in J. C. Beckett, ed., *Historical Studies: Papers Read before the Irish Conference of Historians*, vol. 7 (New York: Barnes and Noble, 1969), pp. 81–96.

through hard work, why did the measures proposed in the 1930s and 1940s fail to achieve proposed measures to guarantee jobs for everyone willing to work? Arguably, the Social Security measures that were implemented were less in accord with longstanding American values than measures embodying a governmental commitment to full employment would have been.[24]

General deductions based on the national values approach simply cannot give us the answer to many crucial questions about the timing and programmatic structure of American social provision. At any given time some potential policy implications of liberal values are taken up, and others not; sometimes rhetorically well-crafted liberal arguments work, and sometimes not. To explain such subtle variations within American social politics, and to understand U.S. policy developments (and nondevelopments) in cross-national perspective, we must find more precise analytical tools than those offered by the national values approach. We should, however, retain the salutary emphasis on historical process and national distinctiveness that these scholars have introduced in response to the logic of industrialism argument.

Explaining Social Provision: Business Hegemony and Working Class Weakness?

Arguments stressing the impact of either industrialism or national values on the development of social policy tend to downplay political struggles and debates. Since the mid-1970s, however, many historians and social scientists have analyzed the political contributions of capitalists and industrial workers to the shaping of social policy in the Western democracies. Two sorts of class politics perspectives have been applied to American social politics; one highlights the initiatives of "welfare capitalists" and the other stresses "political class struggles" between workers and capitalists.

Proponents of the welfare capitalism approach take for granted that corporate capitalists have dominated the U.S. political process in the twentieth century, and they look for economically grounded splits between conservative and progressive capitalists as the way to explain social policy innovations.[25] Early in this century, the argument goes, certain

[24] For opinion data in support of this speculation, see Jerome S. Bruner, *Mandate from the People* (New York: Duell, Sloan, and Pearce, 1944), chaps. 8 and 9.

[25] Those who advance this argument differ in the ways they describe intracapitalist splits and relate them to policy outcomes. See, for example, Edward Berkowitz and Kim Mc-Quaid, *Creating the Welfare State* (New York: Praeger, 1980); William Domhoff, *The Higher Circles* (New York: Random House, 1970), chap. 6; Thomas Ferguson, "From Normalcy to New Deal: Industrial Structure, Party Competition, and American Public Policy in

American businesses preceded the public sector in developing principles of modern organizational management, including policies for planning and stabilizing employment and protecting the social welfare of loyal employees. Prominent "welfare capitalists" then pressed policy intellectuals and public officials to accept their ideas, so that public social insurance measures in key states and at the federal level were supposedly designed to meet the needs of progressively managed business corporations.

This perspective has served as a good lens through which to view the complementarities between public social policies—once enacted—and the labor-management practices of American corporations. For example, many American corporations accommodated nicely to Social Security's contributory old-age insurance program, meshing it with their own retirement benefits systems, especially after World War II.[26] But business groups originally opposed the passage of the Social Security Act, as well as the passage of most other federal and state-level social and regulatory measures favorable to workers, and this creates problems for the welfare capitalism thesis. Its proponents have failed to demonstrate convincingly that genuine groups or categories of U.S. capitalists—as opposed to a handful of maverick individuals not representative of any class or industrial sector—actually supported mandatory public pensions or social insurance.[27] However adaptable American capitalists have proven to be after the fact, the historical evidence is overwhelming that they have regularly fiercely opposed the initiation of public social policies. Political processes other than the initiatives of capitalists have nearly always been the cause of U.S. social policy innovations.

The "Social Democratic" or "political class struggle" perspective takes for granted that capitalists everywhere tend to oppose the emergence and expansion of the welfare state. This approach has predominated in recent cross-national research on the development of social policies in Europe and the United States.[28] To explain why American public social provision

---

the Great Depression," *International Organization* 38 (1984): 41–93; Jill S. Quadagno, "Welfare Capitalism and the Social Security Act of 1935," *American Sociological Review* 49 (1984): 632–47; Ronald Radosh, "The Myth of the New Deal," in Ronald Radosh and Murray N. Rothbard, eds., *The New Leviathan* (New York: E. P. Dutton, 1972); and James Weinstein, *The Corporate Ideal in the Liberal State, 1900–1918* (Boston: Beacon Press, 1968).

[26] William Graebner, *A History of Retirement* (New Haven, Conn.: Yale University Press, 1980), chap. 8. Also see footnote 5 to this Introduction.

[27] Many business organizations did support the state-level workers' compensation laws passed in the Progressive Era. These measures, however, did not include direct taxation or expenditures by government, and they dealt more predictably with liability issues already under the courts' jurisdiction.

[28] Those who have taken this approach include Lars Bjorn, "Labor Parties, Economic Growth, and Redistribution in Five Capitalist Democracies," *Comparative Social Research*

commenced later and has not become as generous as European public social provision, advocates of this approach underline the relative weakness of U.S. industrial unions and point to the complete absence of any labor-based political party in U.S. democracy. Given these weaknesses of working class organization, U.S. capitalists have been able to use direct and indirect pressures to prevent governments at all levels from undertaking social-welfare efforts that would reshape labor markets or interfere with the prerogatives or profits of private business. Certainly an emphasis on political class struggle between workers and capitalists helps to explain why the United States has not developed a comprehensive full-employment welfare state. As might be predicted by the political class struggle approach, American unions have frequently supported extensions of public social provision, while business groups have opposed them. Thus, policies more similar to those of Sweden probably would have been developed in the United States had American workers been as highly unionized as Swedish workers or had the modern Democratic party been a truly social-democratic party based in the organized working class.

Nevertheless, if our intention is not merely to contrast the United States to Europe but also to explain the specific patterns of modern American social policy, then the Social Democratic perspective on political class struggles is insufficient in several ways. Strict attention to conflicts of political interest between capitalists and industrial workers deflects our attention from other socioeconomic forces that have intersected with the U.S. federal state and with decentralized American political parties to shape social policies. Until recently, agricultural interests in the South and West were crucial arbiters of congressional policy making. Struggles over social welfare or labor market interventions have often involved regional, ethnic, and racial divisions. We need a mode of analysis that will help us understand why these conflicts have been equally or more influential than industrial class conflicts in the shaping of social provision in the United States.

A political class struggle approach also falls short in illuminating those

2 (1979): 93–128; Francis Castles, *The Social Democratic Image of Society* (London: Routledge and Kegan Paul, 1978); Francis Castles, "The Impact of Parties on Public Expenditures," in F. Castles, ed., *The Impact of Parties* (Beverly Hills, Calif.: Sage, 1982), pp. 21–96; Esping-Andersen, *Politics against Markets*; Walter Korpi, *The Democratic Class Struggle* (Boston: Routledge and Kegan Paul, 1983); Andrew Martin, *The Politics of Economic Policy in the United States: A Tentative View from a Comparative Perspective*, Professional Paper in Comparative Politics 01-040 (Beverly Hills, Calif.: Sage, 1973); Myles, *Old Age in the Welfare State*; and John Stephens, *The Transition from Capitalism to Socialism* (London: Macmillan, 1979). For an excellent overview of research using this approach, see Michael Shalev, "The Social Democratic Model and Beyond: Two Generations of Comparative Research on the Welfare State," *Comparative Social Research* 6 (1983): 315–51.

watersheds in American politics—especially the middle 1930s and the late 1960s and early 1970s—when broadly "democratic" forces were on the rise, and when many policies that business strongly opposed actually did pass and become a permanent part of the federal government's activities. At these junctures, why did not full-employment guarantees or more comprehensive national social policies become institutionalized as goals and programs? A political class struggle approach alone will not explain the failure of possibilities for national commitments to such measures as health insurance, or nationalized public assistance, or full-employment planning during the major reformist periods of the twentieth century. Nor can it account for the sudden political backlashes that quickly emerged in the wake of reform efforts at the end of the 1930s and the late 1960s. In short, while European social democracies have experienced the steady extension of established social policies in tandem with enhancement of labor's strength, the United States has experienced sudden bursts of reform and equally sudden backlashes, without such close correspondence to waxing and waning organizational capacities of industrial labor. The distinctive dynamics of American social politics have been rooted in shifting political coalitions that include, but necessarily go beyond, business and labor.

State Formation, Institutional Leverage, and Policy Feedbacks

Political class struggle theories have been argued with certain state and party structures in mind—namely centralized and bureaucratized states with parliamentary parties dedicated to pursuing policy programs in the name of entire classes or other broad, nation-spanning collectivities. For much of Western Europe, the existence of such features of political organization has given substance to the presumption that the industrial working class *may* translate its interests into social policies whenever "its" party holds the reins of national power over a sustained period. In contrast, the United States has never had a centralized bureaucratic state or programmatic parliamentary parties. Thus the American case highlights the importance of bringing much more explicitly into our explanations of social policy making the historical formation of each national state, as well as the effects of that state's institutional structure on the goals, capacities, and alliances of politically active groups.

Many of the puzzles about American social politics left unresolved by the alternative theoretical persuasions just surveyed can be addressed anew from what we shall call an "institutional-political process" perspective. This approach examines state formation and the state's institutional structure in both societal and historical context. Political struggles and policy outcomes are presumed to be jointly conditioned by the institutional arrangements of the state and by class and other social relationships, but never once and for all. For states and social structures are themselves transformed over time. And so are the goals and capacities of politically active groups, in part because of ongoing transformations of political and social structures, and in part because of the effects of earlier state policies on subsequent political struggles and debates.

Understanding of the patterns of American social provision can be improved from an institutional-political process perspective in several interrelated ways. First, the historical particularities of U.S. state formation, when understood in relationship to capitalist economic development, urbanization, and transformations of liberal values, explain the distinctive rhythms and limits of American social policy making more effectively than do socioeconomic or cultural processes abstracted from the institutional contexts of national politics. Second, as an alternative to overemphasis on zero-sum class struggles between capitalists and workers, pinpointing ways in which class and other social relations have intersected with the organization of the state and political parties greatly improves our ability to explain the complex political alliances that have sustained or opposed social policies in America. Finally, probing for the feedback effects of policies on subsequent politics reveals how changing policy agendas and alternative possible alliances emerge not only in response to new socioeconomic conditions but also on the basis of—or in reaction to—previous policy accomplishments.

The papers of this volume have been assembled to demonstrate the analytic value of an institutional-political process approach, and we do not want to preempt what the various authors have to say here in the introductory chapter.[29] Even so, we can briefly preview some of the insights about the development of U.S. social policies to be gained from an investigation of state formation, institutional leverage, and the political effects of preexisting policies.

"State formation" includes constitution-making, involvements in wars, electoral democratization, and bureaucratization—macropolitical processes, in short, whose forms and timing have varied significantly in capitalist-industrializing countries.[30] In sharp contrast to many European na-

---

[29] The institutional-political process perspective is not shared by all contributors to this volume, but the editors believe that the arguments of all of the papers fit within this frame of reference. Several contributors also explicitly develop analytical insights consistent with perspectives that emphasize the roles of capitalism and class relations.

[30] On variations in state formation and examples of how the U.S. case compares with others, see J. Rogers Hollingsworth, "The United States," in Raymond Grew, ed., *Crises of Political Development in Europe and the United States* (Princeton, N.J.: Princeton University Press, 1978), pp. 163–96; Samuel P. Huntington, *Political Order in Changing Societies*

tions, the United States did not have a premodern polity characterized by monarchical absolutism, a locally entrenched standing army and bureaucracy, or recurrent mobilization for land warfare against equal competitors. Instead, the American colonies forged a federalist constitutional republic in a revolution against the English monarchy, and (after some years of continued sparring with Britain) the fledgling nation found itself relatively sheltered geopolitically and facing toward a huge continent available for conquest from militarily unformidable opponents. America's greatest war—even when compared to its eventual participation in the world wars of the twentieth century—was a war about itself, the Civil War of the 1860s.[31] Both before and after that conflict, moreover, America's nineteenth-century polity was a "state of courts and parties," in which judges and lawyers made and remade private property rights, and political parties competed to mobilize the white male electorate.[32] Because such mass electoral democratization preceded state bureaucratization in the United States, public administrative arrangements were colonized by political party networks and used to nourish their organizational needs through patronage.

Not until the beginning of the twentieth century—decades after electoral democratization and well after capitalist industrialization had created private corporate giants operating on a national scale—did the U.S. federal, state, and local governments make much headway in the bureaucratization and professionalization of their administrative functions.[33] With the greatest changes coming first at municipal and state levels, bu-

---

(New Haven, Conn.: Yale University Press, 1968), chap. 2; Seymour Martin Lipset, *The First New Nation* (New York: Basic Books, 1963); Stephen Skowronek, *Building a New American State: The Expansion of National Administrative Capacities, 1877–1920* (New York: Cambridge University Press, 1982); Martin Shefter, "Party and Patronage," *Politics and Society* 7 (1977): 404–51; and Charles Tilly, ed., *The Formation of National States in Western Europe* (Princeton, N.J.: Princeton University Press, 1975).

[31] Northern and Southern battle deaths during the Civil War totaled about 600,000 (or 17,000 per million of the national population), compared with 126,000 U.S. battle deaths (1,313 per million) in World War I, and 408,300 U.S. battle deaths (3,141 per million) in World War II. Approximately 37 percent of Northern males then 15 to 44 years old, and approximately 58 percent of the Southern white males in that age-group, fought in the Civil War. This was also the only war that ever resulted in enormous destruction of property on the American mainland.

[32] The phrase "state of courts and parties" comes from Stephen Skowronek, *Building a New American State*, chap. 2; see also Morton Keller, *Affairs of State: Public Life in Nineteenth-Century America* (Cambridge: Harvard University Press, 1977), chaps. 7, 8, and 14, and Richard L. McCormick, "The Party Period and Public Policy: An Exploratory Hypothesis," *Journal of American History* 66 (1979): 279–98.

[33] Skowronek, *Building a New American State*, pts. 2 and 3; and Martin Schiesl, *The Politics of Efficiency: Municipal Administration and Reform in America, 1880–1920* (Berkeley: University of California Press, 1977).

reaucratic-professional transformations happened piecemeal through reform movements spearheaded by the new middle classes. As the various levels of government were thus partially reorganized, the fragmentation of political sovereignty built into U.S. federalism and into the divisions of decision-making authority among executives, legislatures, and courts continued throughout the twentieth century.[34] Meanwhile, American political parties have remained decentralized; and in many localities and states the major parties uneasily combine patronage-oriented and interest-group oriented modes of operation.[35] Within the federal government, Congress, with its strong roots in state and local political establishments, has remained pivotal in national domestic policy making—even during periods of strong executive initiative such as the New Deal and the world wars and the Cold War.[36]

Finally, it should also be kept in mind that the United States was, paradoxically, both the first and the last to democratize its electorate among the long-standing capitalist democracies. It was the first for white males, who were irreversibly enfranchised by the 1830s; and it was virtually the last to enfranchise *all* citizens because, except briefly during Reconstruction and its immediate aftermath, most blacks in the United States could not vote until after the post-1930s migrations from the rural South and the Civil Rights upheavals of the 1960s. During all of the twentieth century until the 1960s, the United States was a regionally bifurcated federal polity: a mass two-party democracy in the East, North, and West, coexisted with a single-party racial oligarchy in the South.[37] Only since the 1960s, as a result of major transformations that are far from completed, have American blacks been fully incorporated into the electorate, and has two-party electoral competition made headway in the deep South.

The patterns of U.S. state formation just summarized have conditioned the rhythms and patterns of social policy making from the nineteenth cen-

---

[34] Barry Karl, *The Uneasy State* (Chicago: University of Chicago Press, 1983); Skowronek, *Building a New American State*, pp. 285–92.

[35] On parties in relation to the polity, see Martin Shefter, "Party, Bureaucracy, and Political Change in the United States," in Louis Maisel and Joseph Cooper, eds., *Political Parties: Development and Decay* (Beverly Hills, Calif.: Sage, 1978), pp. 211–65; and William Nisbet Chambers and Walter Dean Burnham, eds., *The American Party Systems*, 2d ed. (New York: Oxford University Press, 1975).

[36] On the role of Congress in the U.S. state structure of the twentieth century, see Morris P. Fiorina, *Congress: Keystone of the Washington Establishment* (New Haven, Conn.: Yale University Press, 1977); Samuel P. Huntington, "Congressional Responses to the Twentieth Century," in *The Congress and America's Future*, 2d ed., The American Assembly, Columbia University (Englewood Cliffs, N.J.: Prentice-Hall, 1973), pp. 6–38; Morton Grodzins, "American Political Parties and the American System," *Western Political Quarterly* 13 (1960): 974–98; and Richard Polenberg, *War and Society: The United States, 1941–1945* (Philadelphia, Pa.: Lippincott, 1972).

[37] V. O. Key, *Southern Politics in State and Nation* (New York: Knopf, 1949).

tury to the present. America's nineteenth-century patronage democracy, with its proclivity for widely distributing benefits, fueled the late nineteenth-century expansion of de facto disability and old-age benefits for those who could credibly claim to have served the Union forces during the Civil War. Yet once American government began to bureaucratize and professionalize, the surviving structures of patronage democracy and elite perceptions that the Civil War pension system was corrupt discouraged U.S. progressive liberals from imitating the pension and social insurance innovations of their English counterparts. America's initial governmental "response to industrialism" was primarily local and state regulatory laws that often established agencies to take over functions from courts and political parties.

During the New Deal and in its aftermath, the United States launched a kind of modern welfare state, which included public assistance and social insurance measures. Nevertheless, the Social Security Act was rooted in state-level laws or legislative proposals still being actively debated in the 1930s; and congressional mediation of contradictory regional interests ensured that national standards could not be established in most programs. Most black people, still trapped during the 1930s at the socioeconomic bottom of the nondemocratic South, were excluded from or severely disadvantaged within America's original social programs. Blacks remained to be incorporated later, after social and political circumstances had sharply changed.

American mobilization for World War II—a mobilization less total and centrally coordinated by the state than the British mobilization for the same war—did not overcome congressional and local resistance against initiatives that might have pushed the United States toward a nationalized full-employment welfare state. Instead, this pivotal war enhanced federal fiscal capacities and created new possibilities for congressionally mediated subsidies and tax expenditures, but did not permanently enhance public instrumentalities for labor market intervention or the federal executive's capacities for coordinating social spending with macroeconomic management.

Geopolitics and war experiences, along with the sequencing of democratization and bureaucratization have thus powerfully set institutional parameters for social politics in the United States. Yet these fundamental patterns of state formation are only the starting point for our analysis. Political struggles and their policy outcomes have also been conditioned by the institutional leverage various social groups have gained, or failed to gain, within the U.S. state and political parties. By analyzing ways in which America's distinctive state structure has influenced possibilities for collective action and for political alliances, we can improve upon arguments that simply highlight struggles of capitalists versus industrial workers.

America's precociously (yet until the 1960s unevenly) democratized federal polity has always made it difficult for either capitalists or industrial workers to operate as a unified political force in pursuit of class projects on a national scale. Ira Katznelson and Martin Shefter have spelled out the situation for workers in a series of important publications.[38] Because in the United States manhood suffrage and competing patronage parties were in place at the very start of capitalist industrialization, American workers learned to separate their political participation as citizens living in ethnically defined localities from their workplace struggles for better wages and employment conditions. No "working class politics" joining community and workplace emerged; and American trade unions developed no stable ties to a labor-based political party during the period around the turn of the century when European social democratic movements were forged. Nationally, American workers were left without the organizational capacities to push for a social democratic program, including generous and comprehensive social policies. In localities where they did have considerable political clout, American workers tended to gain advantages on ethnic rather than class lines. Only during and after the New Deal was this situation modified, as alliances developed in many places between urban-liberal Democrats and industrial unions.[39] Yet the Democrats and the unions never went beyond flexible and ad hoc partnerships. Particular Democratic politicians put together unique constellations of supporters, sometimes including certain unions and sometimes not, while unions retained the option of supporting friendly Republicans as well as Democrats.

Although the U.S. polity has thus hardly served as a tool of broadly defined working class interests, American capitalists nevertheless, in the apt phrase of David Vogel, "distrust their state."[40] In part, this is an understandable response to a long-democratized polity prone periodically

---

[38] On the consciousness and collective action of workers, see Ira Katznelson, *City Trenches: Urban Politics and the Patterning of Class in the United States* (New York: Pantheon, 1981); Ira Katznelson, "Working-Class Formation and the State: Nineteenth-Century England in American Perspective," in Peter B. Evans, Dietrich Rueschemeyer, and Theda Skocpol, eds., *Bringing the State Back In* (New York: Cambridge University Press, 1985), pp. 257–84; and Martin Shefter, "Trade Unions and Political Machines: The Organization and Disorganization of the American Working Class in the Late Nineteenth Century," in Ira Katznelson and Aristide Zolberg, eds., *Working Class Formation: Nineteenth-Century Patterns in Europe and the United States* (Princeton, N.J.: Princeton University Press, 1986), pp. 197–276.

[39] J. David Greenstone, *Labor in American Politics* (New York: Knopf, 1969).

[40] David Vogel, "Why Businessmen Distrust Their State: The Political Consciousness of American Corporate Executives," *British Journal of Political Science* 8 (1978): 45–78.

to launch moralistic reform campaigns challenging the prerogatives of large-scale property holders. In addition, it reflects the frustrations that American capitalists recurrently experience in their dealings with this or that part of the decentralized and fragmented U.S. state structure. For not only does U.S. federal democracy impede unified working-class politics; it also gives full play to divisions within business along industrial and geographical lines.

Conflicts within the ranks of American business are readily politicized, and U.S. corporate interests have always found it difficult to provide unified support for national initiatives that might benefit the economy as a whole on terms favorable either to most sectors of business or to economically dominant sectors.[41] Within the ranks of business as well as beyond, the losers can always go to court—or back to the legislatures, or to a new bureaucratic agency—for another round of battle in the interminable struggles that never seem to settle American policy questions, especially when government intervention in the economy is at issue, as it usually is. To American capitalists the U.S. state has seemed neither coherent nor reliable. National episodes of democratic reform leading to strengthened state interventions have been resisted with the aid of any coalitional allies at hand, even though most businesses have proven able to accommodate, to reshape, and even to benefit from strengthened state interventions after the fact.

Within a state structure that so discourages unified, persistent class politics as does U.S. federal democracy, it is perhaps not surprising that social policy breakthroughs have clustered in widely separated "big bangs" of reform: during the Progressive Era from about 1906 to 1920; during the New Deal of the mid-1930s; and between the mid-1960s and the mid-1970s, during and right after the Great Society period. Each cluster of new policies was heterogeneous, a product of disparate plans previously pursued by networks of policy intellectuals (perhaps buttressed by voluntary associations or particular governmental bureaus) rather than by any political party or nationwide economic group. What is more, each cluster of policy innovations was put through by coalitions of groups in

---

[41] For examples in various policy areas, see Susan S. Fainstein and Norman I. Fainstein, "National Policy and Urban Development," *Social Problems* 26 (1978): 125–46; Ira Katznelson and Kenneth Prewitt, "Constitutionalism, Class, and the Limits of Choice in U.S. Foreign Policy," in Richard Fagen, ed., *Capitalism and the State in U.S.–Latin American Relations* (Stanford, Calif.: Stanford University Press, 1979), pp. 125–40; Steven Kelman, *Regulating America, Regulating Sweden* (Cambridge, Mass.: MIT Press, 1981); Theda Skocpol and Kenneth Finegold, "State Capacity and Economic Intervention in the Early New Deal," *Political Science Quarterly* 97 (1982): 255–78; and David Vogel, "The 'New' Social Regulation in Historical and Comparative Perspective," in Thomas K. McGraw, ed., *Regulation in Perspective* (Cambridge: Harvard Business School/Harvard University Press, 1981), pp. 155–86.

touch with sets of elected legislators, coalitions that emerged during nationally perceived crises widely understood to call for positive governmental solutions. But in each episode the coalitions favoring new social
policies were temporary, fragile, incapable of any permanent institutionalization, and very soon undone by conservative backlashes that drew on
local forces plus business and other groups resistant to enhanced state
power in the United States.

In the histories of many modern welfare states, agricultural classes have
proven to be important political allies of urban-industrial groups that
would either promote or resist enhanced state interventions.[42] In the
United States agricultural interests have been even more pivotal than elsewhere, and not only because there have always been large numbers of
family farmers in American society. The American federal state, with its
decentralized and nonprogrammatic political parties, has provided enhanced leverage to interests that could associate across many local political districts. Such widespread "federated" interests—including organizations of farmers such as the Grange and the American Farm Bureau
Federation, along with local businessmen linked to the Chamber of Commerce, and certain professional associations including the National Education Association and the American Medical Association—have been
ideal coalition partners for nationally focused forces that might want to
promote, or obstruct, or rework social policies, especially when proposals
have had to make their way through the House of Representatives.

Occasionally, such widespread federations have spurred the passage of
national social policies; the impact of the Townsend Movement is a case
in point. More often, widespread federations—especially those involving
commercial farmers and small businessmen prominent in many communities—have obstructed or gutted proposed national social policies. Thus,
for example, during the early New Deal of 1933 to 1935, federal agricultural policies had the not fully intended effect of strengthening interest-
group association among commercial farmers across the disparate crop-
areas of the South and Midwest. In turn, this meant that the American
Farm Bureau Federation could ally with business organizations, including
the Chamber of Commerce, to pressure congressional representatives
against one liberal New Deal social welfare proposal after another, from
1936 on.

Pinpointing institutional leverage through Congress also helps us to
make sense of the special role of the South in modern American social
policy making—a role that certainly rivals that of either capitalists or the
industrial working class. To be sure, the South's role cannot be under-

---

[42] Agrarian allies or opponents of welfare states are discussed in Castles, *The Social Democratic Image of Society*, and Esping-Andersen, *Politics against Markets*.

stood without underlining the class structure of southern cotton agriculture as a landlord-dominated sharecropper system from the late nineteenth century through the 1930s.[43] Nor could we ignore the explicit
racism that ensured white dominance over black majorities in all sectors
of economic and social life. Yet the South had been militarily defeated in
the Civil War, and by the 1930s this region carried little weight in the
national economy as a whole; nor were its social mores typical of the
nation's. Thus socioeconomic factors and racism alone will not explain
why Southern politicians had so much leverage during and after the New
Deal that they could take a leading role in congressional alliances opposed to the setting of national welfare standards and to any strong federal presence in economic planning.

The influence of southern agricultural interests depended on the inser-
tion of their class power as landlords and their social power as white
racial oligarchs into federal political arrangements that from the 1890s to
the 1960s allowed an undemocratized single-party South to coexist with
competitive two-party democracy in the rest of the nation. Above all,
southern leverage was registered through a congressionally centered legislative process in Washington that allowed key committee chairmen
from safe districts to arbitrate precise legislative details and outcomes.
From the New Deal onward, the national Democratic party used congressional committees to broker the divided goals of its southern and urban-
liberal northern wings.[44] This prevented the often contradictory orientations of the two wings from tearing the national party apart, but at the
price of allowing the enactment of only those social policies that did not
bring the national state into direct confrontation with the South's nondemocratic politics and racially embedded systems of repressive labor
control.

In short, taken together, the U.S. state structure as it had been formed
by the 1930s and 1940s along with the operations of the New Deal party
system, magnified the capacities of southern economic and social elites to
affect national policies—at the same time that the capacities of other interests, including those sections of organized industrial labor allied with
urban Democrats in the North, were simultaneously enhanced by the

[43] See the paper by Jill Quadagno in this volume (Chapter 6); see also Lee J. Alston and
Joseph P. Ferrie, "Labor Costs, Paternalism, and Loyalty in Southern Agriculture: A Constraint on the Growth of the Welfare State," *Journal of Economic History* 65 (1985): 95–
117, and Alston and Ferrie, "Resisting the Welfare State: Southern Opposition to the Farm
Security Administration," in Robert Higgs, ed., *The Emergence of the Modern Political
Economy*, Research in Economic History, Supplement No. 4 (Greenwich, Conn.: JAI Press,
1985), pp. 53–83.

[44] Richard Franklin Bensel, *Sectionalism and American Political Development, 1880–
1980* (Madison: University of Wisconsin Press, 1984), esp. chap. 7.

same U.S. state structure and party system. Many features of the New Deal Social Security programs—and indeed of the entire disjoint configuration of social and economic policies with which the United States emerged from the political watersheds of the New Deal and World War II—can be understood by pinpointing the social interests and the political alliances that were able to gain or retain enhanced leverage through the long-standing federal and congressional institutions of the U.S. state. As several contributors to this volume spell out for particular policy areas, the New Deal brought social policy innovators to the fore through the newly active federal executive. It also energized urban-liberal forces and created new possibilities for political alliances through the electorally strengthened and partially realigned Democratic party. Nevertheless, in the end, America's federal system and regionally uneven suffrage placed severe limits on the political alliances and policies that could prevail as the original foundations were laid for nationwide public social provision.

Especially after the New Deal (although also before that, as revealed by the effect of Civil War pensions on the social insurance debates of the Progressive Era), federal social policies themselves influenced further state formation and politics. The phrase "policy feedbacks" is used to refer to this obvious but usually insufficiently emphasized phenomenon: Once instituted, social policies in turn reshape the organization of the state itself and affect the goals and alliances of social groups involved in ongoing political struggle. Thus the Social Security Act of 1935 strongly affected subsequent possibilities for bureaucratic activism, as well as alliances and cleavages in postwar American social politics.

So many new social, economic, and military interventions by the federal government were launched in the period from the 1930s through the early 1950s that their sheer elaboration forced the growth of federal spending and employment; moreover, state and local governments expanded in response to stimuli and subsidies from the enlarged federal establishment. Because America's federal state became at all levels more bureaucratized and active, further social policy innovations were often generated from "within the state" itself. As Martha Derthick's account suggests, no better example of this phenomenon can be cited than the steady postwar extension of the one fully national program under the Social Security Act, contributory old-age insurance.[45] This program expanded to encompass virtually the entire wage and salaried population, and was also extended into related programmatic areas such as disability insurance and medicare for the elderly. According to Derthick, these developments were primarily propelled by the Social Security administrators themselves, as they adroitly deployed bureaucratic resources to man-

[45] Derthick, *Policy Making for Social Security.*

age public and expert opinion, to sooth congressional committees, and to prepare new legislative proposals for passage at opportune political conjunctures.

As they sought to expand social insurance, the Social Security administrators benefited from the increasing popularity of contributory social insurance after 1955. Within Congress and in the broader society, more and more covered groups became part of the political coalitions that protected and expanded "social security" measures. But other postwar U.S. social policies did not fare so well. In significant part this was because of the reverberations from previous policy choices, first from the internally bifurcated New Deal system and then from attempted Great Society reforms.

As has already been noted, the United States did not become a complete electoral democracy for all of its citizens until after the Civil Rights revolution of the 1960s began the process of incorporating blacks into the southern electorate, and on new terms into the national electorate and the Democratic party. The effects of these processes have been tumultuous—both on agendas for debate over social policy and on political alliances concerned with policy alternatives from the Great Society to the present.[46] Yet the incorporation of blacks into the national polity has not been happening in a social policy vacuum; it is taking place in the context of social policies inherited from the New Deal. "Social security" for the stably employed majority of citizens had become by the 1960s institutionally and symbolically separated from welfare for the barely deserving poor. And for both socioeconomic and political reasons, working-age blacks were disproportionately clients of the vulnerable welfare components of U.S. social provision.

During the social policy reforms of the 1960s and early 1970s, welfare clients temporarily benefited from the widespread recognition that the New Deal system of social policies had not adequately addressed issues of poverty or responded to the needs of blacks, who could now vote in greater numbers. As will be discussed in greater detail below, southern socioeconomic and political arrangements were finally changing in relation to the nation as a whole, and reinvigorated liberal Democrats tried to use welfare extensions and new anti-poverty programs to incorporate blacks into their—otherwise undisturbed—national and local political coalitions. But many social policy reforms of the 1960s and 1970s soon backfired to disturb rather than reinforce Democratic coalitions. National politics underwent a sea change. Since the late 1970s, conservative

[46] This is a theme emphasized by Frances Fox Piven and Richard Cloward. Although our analytic approach is different, we acknowledge their pioneering role in the study of popular impacts on social policy making.

forces hostile to expanded public social provision have found renewed strength within and beyond the Democratic party. This has left impoverished people, including many blacks, increasingly isolated in national politics, and welfare programs more than ever the unwanted orphans of social policy.

B
Corporatist

[16]

Germany: Historical Synopsis

1. The German approach to the welfare state

In terms of expenditure on social programmes, Germany certainly qualifies as a modern welfare state. As a political concept, however, the term 'welfare state' usually has negative connotations in Germany denoting excessive state intervention, and the term 'social policy' is considered preferable. In the German tradition the core of social policy is defined in a limited way by 'social insurance plus labour legislation'. This definition pervades most of the standard literature on social policy which usually excludes education and says little about health and housing. It is also reflected in the governmental division of labour which limits the competence of the Ministry of Labour and Social Affairs to the social transfer schemes and to labour law.

On the programmatic level, the term 'social market economy' is frequently used in place of 'welfare state'. In this sense, the role of the state is to supplement the market as the best mechanism for the allocation of productive resources by social benefits, compensating for market failures in the distribution of incomes. The intervention, however, should be limited and not interfere too much with the incentive structure of the free market economy. This limited definition of state activity originated in the political philosophy of neo-liberalism and the social ethics of Catholicism, but should also be understood as a reaction to the bureaucratic state control experienced in the Nazi period and the presence of Communist collectivism in East Germany. Since the late 1950s even the Social Democrats (*Sozialdemokratische Partei Deutschlands*, SPD) have been moving, albeit reluctantly, towards acceptance of the social market economy model in an attempt to widen their electoral support.

Given the lack of political support for the construction of a broadly defined welfare state, German social programmes have developed within a relatively stable institutional framework. There are four main features of German social policy.

The fragmentation of programmes

Social programmes are fragmented into a large number of uncoordinated and decentralized schemes. At the national level, income maintenance, health, housing and education are dealt with by four different Ministries: Labour and Social Affairs; Youth, Family and Health; Building, Regional Planning and Urban Development; and Education. The administration and supply of services is further decentralized in a large number of autonomous carrier organizations: for different types of benefit (e.g. various social insurance programmes); for different beneficiary groups (e.g. workers, the self-employed, etc.); and for different regions or districts (in the case of education, social assistance).

The emphasis on cash benefits

Most benefits are income maintenance cash payments, which leave consumption decisions to the beneficiary and stress the importance of the private provision of services. With the exception of education, the state provision of services is of limited importance. Outside hospitals, which may be public or private, medical goods and services are mainly provided by private suppliers (the pharmaceutical industry, private doctors and dentists, etc.). In the housing sector, state support is limited to subsidizing the supply of private housing, the provision of housing allowances for low-income families, rent regulation, and tenant protection.

The reliance on social insurance

Individuals are not normally entitled to income maintenance benefits in their capacity as citizens, but as members of social insurance programmes who have a certain contribution record. Benefits are usually earnings-related and seek to maintain the standard of living attained by the recipient during his working life. Income maintenance programmes are financed by the insured and their employers, with only a small amount of state financing.

The importance of labour legislation

All social programmes must be seen in the context of labour legislation which establishes a high degree of regulation regarding working conditions, dismissals and co-determination at the plant level. This aspect will not be dealt with further here.

2. Social protection in defence of traditional authority: the origins of the welfare state in Imperial Germany

The present structure of German welfare state institutions is not the result of a unified plan for social reorganization, but the product of long-term historical developments. The industrial revolution, which arrived relatively late in Germany, transformed society rapidly. The number of industrial workers more than doubled to 2 million in the period 1850-1867, and had risen to 6 million by 1895 [1]. This growth was accompanied by a significant increase in the organizational capacity of workers. In 1863 Ferdinand Lassalle founded the first German Labour party. In 1875 the party merged with the SPD, founded in 1869 by Bebel and Liebknecht. During the second half of the 1860s, the first trade unions were organized, and the 'social question' (*Soziale Frage* became a crucial political issue.

The Prussian state had for a long time relied on repression as the only way of reacting to the mobilization of workers. The Industrial Codes of 1845 and 1869 limited the freedom of association, and workmen's organizations were repeatedly disbanded. Nevertheless, the SPD continued to grow in parliamentary strength. Although universal male suffrage had been introduced from the outset of German unification, the government sought to combat the electoral success of the SPD with anti-socialist legislation that banned the political organization of workers and which remained in effect from 1878 until 1890 [2].

After Bismarck had opted for an interventionist economic policy with high protective tariffs for industry and agriculture, thus considerably increasing the cost of living for the working class, he realized that repression alone was not sufficient to prevent the political mobilization of the workers. With the establishment of public social insurance programmes he hoped to create a tight bond between the state and workers and to split the opposition of the SPD and the Liberals in the Reichstag who were pressing for the realization of parliamentary government.

Education never entered into Bismarck's plans for social reform. The principle of compulsory education was introduced in Prussia as early as 1717, and had become effective in all Prussian territory by 1825. The Prussian state had gained effective control of the education system by 1872 after fierce battles with the Catholic Church. The democratization of (primary) education had thus already been achieved before the political mobilization of workers began to gain momentum: nearly all workers' children attended public primary school in the last quarter of the nineteenth century, and Germany had the highest educational enrolment figures in Europe [3]. This fact may help to explain why education is not usually considered an element of German social policy.

Bismarck's social insurance bills were only passed after heated debate and several modifications. When the compulsory insurance schemes against sickness (1883), industrial accidents (1884), and invalidity or old age (1889) were finally adopted, they were the outcome of a series of compromises rather than the result of a consistent reform plan. The consideration of a broad spectrum of interests may be one of the reasons why the German social insurance schemes displayed such remarkable institutional longevity. These three programmes embodied the basic principles of present day social insurance provision: that insurance is made compulsory by law, but administered by a plurality of autonomous bodies with representatives of employers and the insured; that entitlement to benefits is based on past contributions rather than on need; that benefits and contributions are earnings-related; and that financing should, on aggregate, be tri-partite (the insured, the employer, and the state).

The successful functioning of the new social protection schemes for workers soon generated feelings of relative deprivation among other social categories. In 1901, salaried employees established an association and demanded that social insurance coverage be extended to salary earners. Pressure from the association eventually led to an important reform of the social insurance system. In 1911 the three compulsory insurance laws were consolidated in a single uniform National Insurance Code (*Reichsversicherungsordnung*). The Code included the introduction of survivors' pensions for widows and orphans [4]. In the same year, another law established a pension insurance scheme for salaried employees. Although heavily amended, the 1911 legislation is still in force today.

The provisions for salaried employees were in many respects more generous than those for workers. Employees were entitled to: an invalidity pension in cases where their earning capacity had been reduced by half (two-thirds for workers); an old age pension from the age of 65 (70 for workers); and an unconditional survivors' pension for widows of the insured (for workers, only where the widow was disabled). Employees' coverage for sickness was also preferential. The 1891 Industrial Code and the 1897 Commercial Code established full wage continuation for employees in the case of sickness lasting for a period of six weeks. Workers, instead, were only entitled to sickness insurance benefit which covered 50 percent of earnings up to a certain maximum. By institutionalizing the differentiation between workers and employees, the establishment of special social rights for salaried employees became an important element in the fragmentation of the German working class.

Apart from the revision of 1911, a second modification was the reform of sickness insurance. The Sickness Insurance Law did not regulate the relationship between insurance funds and doctors - an area which became extremely prone to conflict. In 1892 the funds won the right to determine which doctors were to be licensed with the insurance system, and to draw up individual contracts with them. The doctors, in turn, pressed for unlimited access to licenses and the collective negotiation of contracts in order to strengthen their position vis-a-vis the funds. In 1900 they formed a central association (*Hartmannbund*) in order to pursue these aims. After a series of strikes they succeeded in reaching a national agreement with the insurance funds in 1913 which introduced a system of collective bargaining. Doctors became recognized as the contracting partners of the insurance funds, the number of licences issued was regulated on the basis of the number of insured persons per district, and doctors' fees became subject to collective bargaining between the funds and doctors' associations. Although repeatedly modified, this system is still effective today.

Bismarck did not succeed in his objective of undermining the political mobilization of workers by the introduction of social reforms. The SPD voted against the social insurance bills, and by 1912 it had become the strongest faction in the *Reichstag* Nevertheless, the new social protection schemes, although not halting the growth of the SPD, effectively strengthened its revisionist wing. The administrative bodies of the social insurance schemes gave party members access to power positions and gave workers the opportunity for upward mobility to white-collar status. When an amendment to the Invalidity Insurance Law was discussed in 1899, the SPD began to vote in favour of the insurance bills. Later, at the 1902 Munich Congress, it even endorsed a public unemployment insurance scheme which was still regarded with suspicion by the unions [5]. The fact that social insurance and public education were well developed long before a Labour Party participated in government may be considered one of the reasons why the development of the German welfare state differs from that of, for example, the Scandinavian countries.

In addition to social insurance, the German *Reich* had a fairly developed public assistance scheme. In 1870, the earlier Prussian laws were transformed into a consolidated Public Assistance Law which was extended to (almost) all regions of the *Reich* after the unification. The federal structure of the Empire and the limited share of revenues accorded to the central government, however, set tight limits to the development of further initiatives in social policy. The supervision of health conditions lay within the competence of the single states. An Imperial Health Office (*Kaiserliches Gesundheitsamt*) established in 1876 only operated in an advisory capacity.

Despite very severe housing problems - especially in the rapidly growing cities - the state remained remarkably inactive in the field of housing legislation. Until World War I all initiatives to subject the housing market to a certain degree of state regulation failed. Central government activities remained limited to the granting of modest public loans to building societies, paid for the first time in 1901.

In the field of education a series of national school conferences in 1873, 1890 and 1900 sought to standardize the federally fragmented school system. The rigid differentiation between primary and secondary schooling was confirmed. Although the depression of 1873 led to a slowdown of expansion in the post-primary sectors, Germany maintained its position as one of the leaders in public education until World War I [6].

By 1913, educational expenditure (1,265 million RM) still accounted for the bulk (46 percent) of social expenditure. Outlays for social insurance and social assistance together amounted to 1,181 million RM (43 percent). Public expenditure on health (272 million RM), and housing (31 million RM) remained modest. Total social expenditure (2,749 million RM) corresponded to 37 percent of all public expenditure or scarcely 5 percent of GDP (see Graph 1).

World War I stimulated state intervention in previously neglected areas. Immediately after the onset of hostilities a federal decree introduced measures to protect tenants and control the housing market which were subsequently tightened during the war. A law of 1918 empowered the central government to subsidize the supply of housing. The state also took first steps to develop a labour market policy. In 1914 a central labour exchange was established in the Ministry of the Interior, and parts of the state's war loans were used to finance assistance payments for the unemployed. Social insurance benefits were also extended. Thus in 1916 the age limit for the receipt of old age pensions under the workers' insurance scheme was fixed at its present (regular) level of 65 years, bringing it into line with the employees' scheme.

Shortly before the end of the war in 1918, collective bargaining was recognized. In the same year a special Ministry of Labour was established. Headed by a former trade union leader, it assumed the responsibility for social policy formerly held by a department of the Ministry of the Interior. This symbolized a change in the role of social policy, from being an instrument of social order to one of social change.

3. Social policy and the democratic class struggle: the Weimar Republic

The collapse of the monarchy in November 1918 was not accompanied by a basic change in societal power structures. The change in political regime was the result of a series of compromises between old and new elites rather than of a victorious revolutionary upheaval. As plans for the nationalization of key industries were soon abandoned, social reforms to calm public unrest became necessary. Important reforms of labour relations had already been realized as part of the transition from a war to a peace economy immediately after the establishment of the Republic. Decrees of 1918 established the eight-hour working day, set up a public labour exchange, recognized collective bargaining for determining wages and working conditions, and issued rules for the formation of arbitration committees.

Labour legislation of 1923 empowered the state to declare the results of collective bargaining legally binding and to settle unresolved labour conflicts by means of obligatory arbitration. The system of local labour offices, factory inspection and arbitration committees set up under the Ministry of Labour was completed in 1926 by the introduction of special labour courts, thus creating a differentiated machinery of state intervention in labour conflict [7]. The heavy involvement of the state in labour conflicts led to an enhanced politicization of the collective bargaining process, as the conflicting parties now increasingly sought to gain control over the Ministry of Labour.

In the context of fierce domestic conflicts during the postwar economic crisis of 1919-1923, the government - led by centre-left coalitions throughout most of this period - felt constrained to implement social reforms despite a lack of resources. In the field of labour legislation, a law of 1920 consolidated the wartime provisions on workers' co-determination by making the establishment of workers' councils obligatory in all firms with more than 20 employees. In the same year another law established a nationwide corporatist Economic Council with advisory functions in economic and social matters.

Other important innovations were made in the fields of housing and education. A federal school law of 1920 abolished private primary schools preparing for entry to the *Gymnasium* and introduced a four-year comprehensive system of primary schooling for all pupils. This law led to a considerable increase in *Gymnasium* attendance [8]. In the housing sector, a law of 1920 subjected the housing market to administrative controls. Other laws to regulate rents and to strengthen tenant protection were passed in 1922 and 1923. A 1921 law introduced a special tax (subsequently extended in 1924) for the financing of the public promotion of housing construction.

The most important income maintenance reforms included the introduction of war victims' benefits (1920), which temporarily accounted for a third of the central government's budget; and the transformation of the emergency postwar unemployment relief system into a regular assistance programme, financed by employees' and employers' contributions (1923). The 1913 agreement between doctors and the insurance funds was incorporated into the National Insurance Code in 1923. The 1922 Youth Welfare Act established the basis for the present programmes for young people.

With the stabilization of the currency in late 1923, a period of economic recovery began which lasted until 1928. In the context of economic growth and a strengthened position of the unions, the social legislation of the new centre-right governments concentrated on the development of the income maintenance schemes, whilst considerably reducing the control of the housing market. A law of 1924 set up a modern public assistance scheme which replaced the old poor relief legislation of 1870, strengthening the legal position of recipients. The scope of the social insurance system was broadened through extensions to additional occupational groups and repeated increases of the income limits for compulsory coverage. The most important reform, however, was the introduction of a compulsory unemployment insurance scheme in 1927.

In late 1928 a period of economic downswing began, and the new unemployment insurance ran into financial difficulties. Its deficits had to be covered by the central government, which had itself faced deficits for several years. This generated a fierce debate in the newly formed centre-left government as to the appropriate strategy of financial consolidation. As the level of unemployment benefits sets limits to potential wage reductions, the controversy became linked to fundamental distributional conflicts. The SPD, backed by the unions, supported an increase in contribution rates, whereas the other coalition parties, supported by the employers' associations, favoured a reduction in benefits. The cabinet subsequently voted in favour of the latter, and the SPD withdrew from government. This opened the way to the replacement of parliamentary decision making by a system of presidential emergency decrees.

The new governments - first headed by Brüning - tried to balance the budget through a deflationary policy. A series of emergency decrees in 1930, 1931, and 1932 cut the public housing construction programme and drastically reduced practically all income

Graph 1

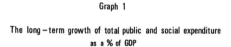

The long-term growth of total public and social expenditure
as a % of GDP

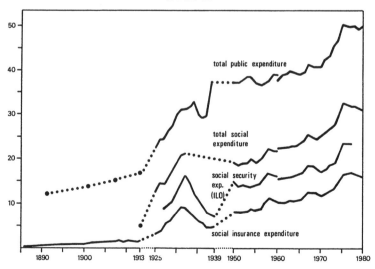

maintenance benefits. In the unemployment insurance scheme, the level of benefits was halved between 1930 and 1932, and entitlement was considerably restricted. In 1933 only 10 percent of the unemployed were in receipt of insurance benefits, and another 28 percent were in receipt of unemployment assistance payments [9].

On aggregate, social expenditure fell from 15.8 billion RM in 1930 to 12.0 billion in 1932. Social insurance expenditure (including unemployment insurance) was reduced from 10.5 to 8.5 billion RM [10]. However, as GDP shrank even faster than social expenditure, the social expenditure ratio rose, reaching an unprecedented level in 1932 (see Graph 1).

In the context of high unemployment, curtailed transfer payments and parliamentary stalemate, the National Socialist opposition increased its share of the vote in the national elections from 2.6 percent in 1928 to 37 percent in 1932. Together with the Communists it now held a majority of the seats in the *Reichstag*. Despite a setback of four percentage points at the second 1932 elections, the National Socialists came to power in 1933, and the Weimar Republic collapsed a few weeks later.

4. Social policy as an instrument of totalitarian control: the National Socialist regime

Once in power the National Socialists transformed German society rapidly. By mid-1933 all rival political parties had been dissolved. The unions were destroyed and collective bargaining was replaced by a tight bureaucratic control of the labour market. In comparison with other institutions, the body of social programmes remained remarkably intact. The fragmented structure of the social insurance system resisted all unifying and centralizing tendencies of the new regime, but its administration and functions underwent significant changes.

A law of 1934 abolished the autonomous self-administration of social insurance by employees and employers. Each social insurance fund became headed by a 'leader' chosen by the new state authorities. The high contribution rates and reduced benefit levels fixed during the depression were preserved even when economic recovery increased the funds' resources. The funds were compelled to invest a sizeable part of their surplus in government loans. In the Nazi war economy, social insurance contributions were used as an additional source of government revenues and as a means to reduce the purchasing power of the masses. The social expenditure ratio fell far below the levels of the Weimar period (see Graph 1).

The Nazi period, however, was not merely one of welfare state dismantling. The scope of social insurance was repeatedly widened. When the intensive production of heavy armaments led to a labour shortage in the late 1930s, thus strengthening the bargaining position of the working class, the regime made some improvements in social benefit levels [11]. In 1937 the option of voluntary membership of the pension insurance scheme was introduced [12]. In 1938 compulsory insurance was extended to artisans as the first major category of self-employed persons to be so covered. Pensioners were included in sickness insurance coverage in 1941. In 1942 industrial accident insurance was extended to all wage-earners regardless of occupation. Benefit levels were improved when the restrictions imposed during the economic depression were lifted, and by the extension of entitlements. Among the most important innovations were the extension of the period of sick care (unlimited duration), and the introduction of a maternity allowance for a period of six weeks before and after the birth (1942).

From the outset, the regime paid special attention to family policy. In 1933 loans to newly-wed couples were introduced with the idea of reducing female employment. A

social insurance reform which increased benefits and contributions and made some
tax reform of 1934 provided sizeable tax credits for large families. A year later an
extraordinary benefit was introduced, being payable to families with more than four
children. In 1936 this was transformed into a regular child allowance for the fifth
child and any further children. Payment of this allowance presupposed 'faithful service to the German people', and similar mechanisms for social control were incorporated into legislation on youth welfare. A law of 1938 regulating the conditions of
child employment made the minimum length of holidays dependent upon membership
of, and participation in, the *Hitlerjugend* [13].

Reorganization of the social assistance system was also used to cultivate loyalty to the
party. The autonomous public assistance organizations were dissolved, and the system
was centralized under the leadership of a National Socialist organization established
in 1933 (*Nationalsozialistische Volkswohlfahrt* NSV). Administrative guidelines specified that the function of assistance was to promote collective rather than individual
well-being and to educate recipients in National Socialist thinking.

In the health sector, a law of 1934 established health offices, still in existence today,
to supervise medical standards throughout the country. In the sectors of housing and
education, the state remained deliberately inactive. As all available resources were
channelled into the war effort, public investment on housing was significantly
reduced. Contrary to political promises, annual housing construction fell to below the
levels reached in the Weimar period [14].

Educational expenditure was reduced in real and even nominal terms [15]. In the period
1930-1939, the number of university students fell by more than half [16]. Enrolment ratios fell below the Weimar levels and also dropped to beneath the West European
average [17]. Once a 'leader' in education, Germany was now becoming a 'laggard'. The
'educational catastrophe' discovered in the mid-1960s thus originated in the Nazi
period.

Although the regime subjected the education system to strict central control and established standardized curricula, the structure of the school system remained remarkably
stable. Apart from the establishment of some new types of secondary schools, the
rigid differentiation between primary and secondary education was maintained. The
number of private schools was drastically cut, however, and religious schools were
almost completely replaced by non-denominational schools [18].

After the defeat of the Nazi regime, the financial resources of the social insurance
system were depleted, the universities were drained, and health and housing conditions were disastrous. Many able social administrators were either dead or had emi-
grated [19].

5. Security and opportunity in the social market economy: the Federal Republic

After the defeat of the Hitler regime most of the existing social programmes remained
intact. Only child allowances and some other special schemes established under Nazi
rule were discontinued. In 1946, however, the Allied Control Commission drafted a
plan for the establishment of a unified national insurance scheme based on the Beveridge model. The project immediately met with strong opposition from German
interest groups, including the trade unions. With the onset of the 'Cold War' the
Western allies lost interest in its implementation.

In the Western zones the allied authorities began to shift legislative functions to
German parliamentary bodies which were then being built up. In late 1948 the newly
established assembly (*Wirtschaftsrat*) in the Anglo-American zone passed a law on

Table 1   Major institutional changes in the German welfare state, 1949-1980

Pensions

1957   Indexation of pensions; compulsory insurance for independent farmers
1967   Abolition of income-limit for compulsory coverage
1972   Introduction of flexible age limit and other extensions of entitlements
1977   Modification of pension formula

Sickness insurance and health

1955   Regulation of relationship between doctors and insurance funds
1957   Reform of sickness insurance with partial wage-continuation for workers
1969   Full wage continuation for workers; constitutional reform strengthening the role of the federal
        government in the health sector
1970   Indexation of income-limit for compulsory coverage; introduction of preventive medical check-ups
1972   Compulsory sickness insurance for independent farmers; regulation of hospital financing with
        participation of federal government
1977   Introduction of corporatist "concerted action" to contain cost explosion in the health sector

Occupational injuries insurance

1963   Reform of occupational injuries insurance with indexation of benefits

Unemployment insurance

1956   Reform of unemployment insurance with sizeable benefit increases
1969   Major re-organization of unemployment insurance introducing instruments for an active labour
        market policy

Families and children

1954   Introduction of employer financed child allowances
1961   Youth Welfare Act
1964   Re-organization of child allowances shifting financing to federal government
1974   Introduction of universal child allowance scheme

Social assistance

1961   Major re-organization of social assistance replacing legislation of 1924
1969   Reform of social assistance extending entitlements

War consequences

1950   New benefit scheme for war victims
1952   Fund for equalization of burdens for refugees

Housing

1950   Federal subsidies for housing production; promotion of social housing
1960   De-regulation of housing market
1965   Introduction of housing allowances
1971   Legislation on tenant protection

Education

1964   Agreement among the single states to standardize the school system; compulsory education extended
        to 9 years
1969   Constitutional reform empowering federal government to legislate on education; introduction of
        education allowances
1976   First nationwide legislation on universities

structural changes to the existing schemes. The 1949 Constitution deliberately did not contain any commitment to a specific economic and social order. The result of the first national elections clearly indicated, however, that the majority of voters did not favour a socialist planning of the economy. The Communists and SPD together captured only 36.5 percent of the seats. The coalition government, formed by Christian Democrats (*Christlich Demokratische Union, Christlich Soziale Union*, CDU/CSU), FDP (*Freie Demokratische Partei*), and a conservative splinter party, opted for a liberal economic policy. Only the housing market remained subject to state controls.

The first social policy initiatives dealt mainly with a programme of subsidized housing construction, and with measures for the integration and compensation of war victims and refugees. A series of laws restored the social insurance principles of the Weimar Republic. The traditional self-administration by employers and employees was re-introduced [20]. Union and SPD plans for the establishment of a unified national insurance scheme were crushed when the first elections to the new administrative boards were overwhelmingly won by those advocating the differentiation of workers' and employees' schemes [21].

The subsequent re-establishment of a special pension insurance scheme for employees signalled the persistance of the fragmented structure of German social insurance. Two 1955 laws confirmed the traditional structure of the health system with its dominance of private suppliers, collective bargaining between doctors and insurance funds, and the limited supervisory role of the public health services. Educational matters remained the sole competence of the single states.

At the beginning of the second legislature, Chancellor Adenauer announced his intention to introduce a fundamental social reform which would restructure the highly complex welfare system. A group of experts drafted a reform plan (*Rothenfels Denkschrift*) and several academics, committees, interest groups, and parties produced a mass of elaborate proposals. In this connection a General Secretariat of Social Reform was set up within the Ministry of Labour in 1955.

In practice, few of these ambitious reform plans were implemented. This was mainly due to the deep cleavage within the CDU, between the Social Christian Workers' wing and that of the neo-liberal employers. In the cabinet this cleavage took the form of a split between the Ministry of Labour and that of Finance, with the latter advocating a highly selective social policy based on means tests. Under these circumstances, and after Adenauer had sided with the workers' wing, the idea of a complete remodelling of the welfare state gave way to the gradual extension of single programmes. Adenauer not only needed the electoral support of the growing number of pensioners, but also wished to link the extension of political rights to broader political considerations. The rebuilding of the German army needed to be balanced by improvements in social policy in order to overcome opposition from the SPD and the unions to rearmament [22].

With the sails thus set for a course of expansion, a new child allowance scheme was introduced in 1954. Subsidies to private builders were increased, with priority being given to the construction of family housing. Unemployment benefits were improved. The extension of benefits culminated in a thorough reform of pension insurance in 1957. This reform increased benefits, equalized entitlements for workers and employees, and introduced a pension scheme for farmers. Following a political strike by the unions, another law of the same year introduced partial wage continuation in the case of sickness, thus narrowing the gap between workers' and employees' entitlements.

During the third and fourth legislatures (1957-1965), reforms of social assistance (1961), child allowances (1961, 1964), and occupational injuries insurance (1963) considerably broadened the scope of individual entitlements. The deregulation of the housing market in 1960 was followed by the introduction of housing allowances for low-income families. Union demands for a further equalization of workers' and employees' sickness benefit entitlements led to an extension of workers' wage continuation in 1961. More fundamental plans to restructure sickness insurance and to introduce private cost-sharing were abandoned after a decade of contention with the unions and doctors' associations.

The mid-1960s marked the end of the expansion phase and the beginning of a period of transition. This change was linked to important political and economic changes. The rate of economic growth had declined considerably during the 1960s. The coalition government of Christian Democrats and FDP headed by Erhard, sought to develop mechanisms for increased social and economic planning. A standing committee of economic advisors (*Sachverständigenrat zur Begutachtung der gesamtwirtschaftlichen Entwicklung*) was set up to issue annual analyses of economic policy. In preparation for a reform of social policy, a committee was set up to examine the workings of social programmes. The resulting report initiated the publication of an annual governmental 'social budget', designed to link the planning of social and economic policy more closely.

In the meantime, an important political realignment brought an end to the long period of polarization between the bourgeois and social democratic camps, making all parties possible coalition partners. After a series of conflicts, the FDP moved away from the Christian Democrats. The SPD replaced its old manifesto of 1925 with a new party platform in which it reconciled itself to the social market economy and the country's integration into the Western alliance.

When a sudden recession in 1966/67 led to unresolvable conflicts between FDP and Christian Democrats over the budget, a 'grand coalition' (*Grosse Koalition*) of Christian Democrats and SPD was formed. To combat the economic crisis, the new government intended to shift public expenditure from social consumption to social investment. Various transfer payments were curbed, and for the first time, educational issues were given political priority. A wider access to higher education institutions was pursued as an investment in human capital and as a means to promote equal educational opportunities. The new coalition initiated a reform empowering the federal government to pass educational legislation and to participate in the provision of health services. A federal Ministry of Education and Science was established [23], new universities were constructed and education allowances were introduced for low-income families. Changes in income maintenance schemes met some of the long-standing demands of the SPD. As a first step towards a more active labour market policy, the competence of the unemployment insurance scheme was extended to include the promotion of vocational training. A new system of wage continuation equalized the entitlements of workers and employees, and the pension schemes of both groups were financially consolidated by an obligation to mutually balance liquidity reserves.

The drive for a new social policy gained momentum when a SPD/FDP coalition was formed in 1969 and when the renewed growth of the economy replenished federal resources. In promising to 'democratize society', the new government sought to transform social policy into a tool for active social engineering. Several commissions were set up to develop broad-based reform plans. Special attention was given to the improvement of working conditions. Social services were expanded, particularly in sickness insurance with the introduction of preventative treatment. In the educational sector, allowances were improved. Income maintenance entitlements were extended by reforms of all social insurance schemes, most notably pensions. Child allowances were increased and extended to all families with children. Housing allowances were improved and tenant protection was strengthened.

The new social policy suffered a sudden setback when the recession of the mid-1970s combined with deficits in the pension insurance scheme and a cost explosion in the health sector. Since 1975, the government has sought to bring the growth rate of social expenditure into line with that of economic growth. In this new phase of financial consolidation, most social benefits were cut (see Section V). Once again steps towards a systematic reform were initiated when the government set up a transfer inquiry commission in 1977 to examine the workings of welfare schemes and to issue recommendations for their reform. Up to the present, however, all attempts to reform the old-established fragmented system have failed. The growth of the German welfare state has therefore taken place within a fairly stable institutional order.

Notes

1. Detlev Zöllner, *Ein Jahrhundert Sozialversicherung in Deutschland.* Berlin, 1981, p.16.
2. This legislation formally prohibited the revolutionary activities of existing working class organizations, but left the party free to participate in elections.
3. See the data by Reinhart Schneider in Peter Flora, *State, Economy and Society in Western Europe 1815–1975,* Vol. I. Frankfurt, London, Chicago, 1983.
4. For a systematic summary of the most important legislative developments see Zöllner, *op. Cit.*
5. Zöllner, *op. cit.,* p. 103, and Gaston V. Rimlinger, *Welfare Policy and Industrialization in Europe, America and Russia.* New York, London, Sydney, Toronto, 1971, p. 129
6. See Hartmut Kaelble, *Soziale Mobilität und Chancengleichheit im 19. und 20. Jahrhundert Deutschland im internationalen Vergleich.* Göttingen, 1983; see also Arnold J. Heidenheimer, 'Education and social security entitlements in Europe and America', In Peter Flora and Arnold Heidenheimer (eds), *The Development of Welfare States in Europe and America.* New Brunswick and London, 1981, pp. 269–304.
7. Ludwig Preller, *Sozialpolitik in der Weimarer Republik* Düsseldorf, 1978; see also Albin Gladen, *Geschichte der Sozialpolitik in Deutschland.* Wiesbaden, 1974.
8. The proportion of 10 year olds entering the first class of the Gymnasium was 18 percent in 1928 as compared with 9 percent in 1910; see Karl Dietrich Erdmann, *Die Weimarer Republik,* Gebhardt Handbuch der deutschen Geschichte, Vol. 19. Munich, 1983, p. 226.
9. As another 38 percent received local government relief payments, one million persons or a quarter of the unemployed population, remained without any form of support from public funds. Calculated from the *Deutscher Bundestag 2. Wahlperiode,* Drucksache 1274.
10. The social expenditure data are from Suphan Andic and Jindrich Veverka, 'The growth of government expenditure in Germany since unification', *Finanzarchiv N.F.* 23, 1963/64, pp. 169–287; the social insurance data are from Detlev Zöllner, *Öffentliche Sozialleistungen und wirtschaftliche Entwicklung.* Berlin, 1963, p. 18. Both types of data are at nominal prices.
11. See Timothy W. Mason, *Sozialpolitik im Dritten Reich* Opladen, 1977. For more specialized accounts of social insurance see Gladen, *op cit.,* especially pp. 108–113, and Volker Hentschel, *Geschichte der deutschen Sozialpolitik 1880–1980.* Frankfurt, 1983, especially p. 144.
12. The option of voluntary insurance was abolished by the 1957 pension reform, but re-introduced in 1972.
13. See Heinz Lampert, 'Staatliche Sozialpolitik im Dritten Reich', In Karl Dietrich Bracher, Manfred Funke, Hans-Adolf Jacobsen (eds.), *Nationalsozialistische Diktatur 1933–1945. Eine Bilanz.* Düsseldorf, 1983, pp. 177–205.
14. See Heinz Lampert, *Sozialpolitik.* Berlin, Heidelberg, New York, 1980, p. 146.
15. Kaelble, *op. cit.,* p. 141.
16. See the data by Schneider in Flora, *op. cit.,* p. 589.

17. See Reinhart Schneider, 'Die Bildungsentwicklung in den westeuropäischen Staaten 1870–1975', *Zeitschrift für Soziologie*, 11.3.1982, pp. 207–226.
18. Karl Dietrich Erdmann, *Deutschland unter der Herrschaft des Nationalsozialismus*, Gebhardt Handbuch der deutschen Geschichte, Vol. 20. Munich, 1982, p. 168.
19. See Stephan Liebfried and Florian Tennstedt, *Berufsverbote und Sozialpolitik* 1933. Bremen, 1981.
20. Deviating from the traditional practice and following the new concept of 'social partnership' between capital and labour, workers were now also represented on the boards of occupational injuries insurance, but lost their two-thirds majority representation in sickness insurance.
21. Employees' pensions had been administered jointly with the workers' scheme since 1945.
22. On the political motives behind the social policy reforms see Hans Günter Hockerts, *Sozialpolitische Entscheidungen im Nachkriegsdeutschland*. Stuttgart, 1980.
23. A Federal Ministry of Science had already been established in 1962.

[17]

Smooth Consolidation in the West German Welfare State: Structural Change, Fiscal Policies, and Populist Politics

Claus Offe

The German welfare state, as it was originally established in the 1880s and continuously expanded and adapted without major alterations of its basic principles, is an institutional system that stands in an almost ideal correspondence with an industrial society characterized by the features of full employment, strong families, large and homogeneous corporate collective actors, and a balanced demographic structure. The German welfare state was originally uniquely designed to generate compliance, to be effective, and hence to provide stability within the parameters of this type of industrial social structure. Under present structural conditions it is far less capable of meeting these criteria. The remarkable historical robustness and continuity of the German system of social security, which has survived, since its beginnings in Bismarckian social reform, more than one century and four vastly different political regimes, must not be mistaken for a sign of continued adequacy for present conditions; on the contrary, it must be seen as a sign of institutional rigidity, with the consequence that the system fails to generate both compliance and effectiveness under the conditions to which it is now exposed. In this sense, the German welfare state can be seen as the present victim of its past success; its perfect adaptation to past conditions and ends hinders its adaptation to present conditions. These institutionally built-in rigidities

The author wishes to acknowledge insightful comments that he has received from a number of colleagues, among them in particular Karl Hinrichs, Stephan Leibfried, Frances Fox Piven, and Adrienne Windhoff-Héretier.

are the prime factor responsible for the current symptoms of inadequacy and decline – much more so than the economic turbulence that social policy-making has had to deal with since the mid-1970s or the conservative, liberal, or populist goals and values of political elites that came to power during that period.

More specifically, I shall explore three questions.

1   Which institutional features served to guarantee a high level of both compliance and effectiveness in the past?
2   To which structural social changes can we attribute the decline in the ability to generate rational support and the decline in effective goal attainment?
3   Finally, by what strategies and interpretations have political elites responded to the emergent tension between rigid institutional structures and the social environment of social policies?

The German Welfare State: Its Basic Features and Stabilizing Mechanisms

The institutional features of the German social security system[1] can be interpreted as the outcome of a strategy to maximize both the trust in the system (i.e. the condition for compliance) and the system's effectiveness, or its capacity to reach its limited goals. It generates those signals and perceptions which work as self-stabilizing cognitive feedbacks from which a high degree of "trustworthiness" of the institutions result.

What could be the potential causes of distrust, and how are the potential consequences of these causes precluded by the institutional arrangement. The greatest concern of a rational participant in an insurance system is, of course, that he might not receive (in case of the incident against which he wishes to be insured) the service or payment to which he expects to be entitled. This might possibly happen, first of all, if the insurance funds are insufficient to honor all claims. Such concerns are precluded, in the case of a social security arrangement such as the German one, by the principle of mandatory insurance, as well as by the fact that the liquidity of the fund is guaranteed through subsidies coming from the state budget, and that all members of the insurance

1   Recent accounts of the institutional structure of the German social security system and its evolution are given by J. Alber, *Der Sozialstaat in der Bundesrepublik 1950–1983* (Frankfurt: Campus, 1989), V. Hentschel, *Geschichte der deutschen Sozialpolitik 1880–1980* (Frankfurt: Suhrkamp, 1983), and M. G. Schmidt, *Sozialpolitik. Historische Entwicklung und internationaler Vergleich* (Opladen: Leske, 1988); see also G. A. Ritter, *Social Welfare in Germany and Britain* (Leamington Spa and New York: Berg, 1986), F. Tennstedt, "Sozialgeschichte der Sozialversicherung," in *Handbuch der Sozialmedizin*, vol. 3, ed. M. Blohmke (Stuttgart: Enke, 1976), pp. 385–492.

126 *Claus Offe*

enjoy an unconditional legal entitlement to cash transfers, independent of any need tests, means tests, or other restrictions.

Another rational concern might be that the funds, even though sufficient, might be diverted for purposes other than for covering the proportional entitlements of the insured – be it for (egalitarian) redistribution among the insured, or for distribution in favor of persons other than the insured and their dependents. One of the distinctive features of German social security is its "administration by para-public insurance funds,"[2] the function of which is to build trust among the insured by limiting the scope of potential political (i.e. redistributive) interference with their collective property in the common fund. Again, the system is designed to give as few reasons as possible for this kind of fear; for it guarantees the equivalence of relative status (which means that the level of benefits and the level of contributions stands in a fixed relation to the level of wages). It thus precludes concerns that either "deserving" claimants do not get what they are entitled to or that, conversely, funds are illegitimately appropriated by "undeserving" categories of people.

It also keeps the "collective private property"[3] out of the reach of governments and legislatures since the largest part of the fund is financed through contributions (not taxes, which would provide legitimate reasons for the state's interference). The use of the insurance funds and the administration of its benefits and services is organized according to the principle of "self-government," the bearers of which are a great and complex variety of semi-autonomous corporatist associations and agencies, not a centralized state administration.[4] Both these features help to insulate the system from political contingencies.

Furthermore, the whole system is centered around the core institutions of the labor contract and the family. Contributions are evenly shared by the employees and the employers in proportion to wages (except for accident insurance), and only employees who have "earned" benefits as deferred wages, together with the dependent members of their families, have access to them. The system also establishes a security premium designed for all those who, as employees, lead an ordinary and orderly work life by "earning" a full (and preferably uninterrupted) employment record. As such, the social security system contains a "hidden curriculum" which declares labor and employment to be much more than a legal and economic category, namely a form of respectable and even

2 P. Katzenstein, *Policy and Politics in West Germany* (Philadelphia, PA: Temple University Press, 1987), p. 172.
3 Cf. the discussion of the economic nature of social security funds in A. de Swaan, *In Care of the State* (Cambridge: Polity Press, 1988).
4 Cf. F. X. Kaufmann, "Die soziale Sicherheit in der Bundesrepublik Deutschland," in *Deutschland-Handbuch. Eine doppelte Bilanz 1949–1989*, ed. W. Weidenfeld and H. Zimmermann (Bonn: Bundeszentrale für politische Bildung, 1989), pp. 308–25.

dignified social existence.[5] Implicit in this curriculum is the gender division of labor in which the male breadwinner spends his economically active life in full-time employment and thus acquires the employment record necessary for full pension and other security rights, while his wife does not spend her life in (full-time) employment and hence does not earn any independent social security entitlements. The male bread-winner's wife relies on the legal rights and claims that she derives, directly or indirectly, from her institutional status within the family.

Thus the employment-centered nature of the German social security system largely implies a logic of restitution rather than one of either redistribution or investment. Restitution implies that transfers are obtained to replace market income after it is no longer earned (because of old age, disability, sickness, or unemployment), and are not an optional alternative to market income (as would be the case with basic income schemes) or designed to maintain or improve earning capacities (through human capital investment measures such as schooling, training, preventive health measures, and measures promoting social, occupational, and geographic mobility). The social security system is thus "status-maintaining" rather than "opportunity-creating,"[6] a feature which minimizes its effects upon social inequality, and hence its potential for generating status conflict.

Not only is the system insulated from political interference with social inequalities but it is also ambiguous and "overdetermined" as to the ideological principles on which it relies. Conservatives[7] accept it as an arrangement which keeps social security issues out of the arena of class conflict by giving workers a "stake in the system," and it encourages

5   Cf. U. Mückenberger, "Die Krise des Normalarbeitsverhältnisses – Hat das Arbeitsrecht noch Zukunft?," *Zeitschrift für Sozialreform*, 31 (1985), pp. 415–34, 457–75, "Zur Rolle des Normalarbeitsverhältnisses bei der sozialstaatlichen Umverteilung von Risiken," *Probleme des Klassenkampfes*, 16 (1986), pp. 31–45, and "Der Wandel des Normalarbeitsverhältnisses unter den Bedingungen einer 'Krise der Normalität'," *Gewerkschaftliche Monatshefte* (1989), pp. 211–23; A. Gorz, *Métamorphoses du travail. Quêtes du sens. Critique de la raison économique* (Paris: Editions Galilée, 1988).
6   To be sure, a new emphasis has been placed upon preventive – and in that sense "human capital forming" – measures and programs, particularly in the late 1960s and early 1970s. They aim at the preventive elimination of accidents and other health hazards, and at the retraining of labor and the upgrading of skills. The fact that these programs are also financed out of the funds of health and unemployment insurance, however, rather than general taxes, has severely limited their effectiveness, as they have to compete against strong pressures to use these funds for income maintenance and medical treatment. Cf. Katzenstein, *Policy and Politics in West Germany*, pp. 179f.
7   Cf. the discussion of the legacies of conservatism in social policy in G. Esping-Andersen, *The Three Worlds of Welfare Capitalism* (Princeton, NJ: Princeton University Press, 1990), pp. 38–41 and *passim*.

Claus Offe

employers to take some interest in the protection and maintenance of the employees' physical ability to work. Socialists may welcome it as a form of institutionalized class solidarity; and Roman Catholics or, from a different point of view, political liberals may value it for its built-in precautions against egalitarianism and state intervention. The ideologically overdetermined nature of the social security system explains the fact that basic controversies over social policies have been extremely rare in the history of the Federal Republic. The evolution of social security was mostly a bipartisan matter. Disagreements between the two major parties were limited to matters such as the timing and percentage points of increases in benefits or contributions. The policy debate has never (at least since the Federal Republic's consolidation period in the second Adenauer administration between 1953 and 1957) extended to matters of principle and basic institutional features.[8] This peculiar style of the politics of social security reflects the fact that social policy-making has consistently involved only a tiny group of legislative specialists and academic experts who mastered the vast complexity of legal, fiscal, and economic factors and who thus were able to determine the possible range and priorities of reform.

Social security benefits were originally granted as a privileged status to the "aristocracy" of industrial workers alone. The institutional features of the early system were extended, however, in the smooth and continuous inclusion of new groups (white collar workers, farmers, professionals and other self-employed groups, veterans, students, housewives), the coverage of new risks and needs (unemployment insurance, family allowances, eventually at some point in the near future also insurance covering long-term care), and the dramatic increase in benefits, in particular in old-age pensions which (since 1957) are indexed to the development of average earnings. It is as if the institutional system of social security had provided for the formation of an orderly queue which conveys to each worker-citizen what to expect, how much, and in which order.

The general picture that emerges from this brief review of the basic features of the German social security system is one of depoliticized rigidity. Social security is encapsulated in a set of principles, procedures, and institutions that seem to make it virtually immune from major changes concerning levels and sources of revenues, on the one hand, or the level of benefits and the scope of entitlements, on the other. The

---

8 The observation of this fact in German postwar politics has led Otto Kirchheimer to far-reaching generalizations about the "vanishing opposition" in democratic welfare states: O. Kirchheimer, "Germany: the vanishing opposition," in *Political Opposition in Western Democracies* ed. R. A. Dahl (New Haven, CN: Yale University Press, 1966), pp. 237–59, and "The transformation of the Western European party system," in *Political Parties and Political Development*, ed. J. LaPalobara and M. Weiner (Princeton, NJ: Princeton University Press, 1966), pp. 177–200.

system is morally undemanding in its stated objective of "security"; no one needs to believe in lofty principles of solidarity, justice, or equality to become – and remain – a rational supporter of the system. It is simply not a vehicle for the promotion of such values. Its modest goal is the guarantee of income – and of relative income status! – for employees and their dependents.[9] As a consequence, rational self-interest on the part of the "internal constituency" of the insured is sufficient as a base for consent. It can be assumed that this base of consent will remain solid even under conditions of financial strain. For, as the pension funds are seen by employees as "our" collective property, sacrifices that become necessary to restore the financial balance (such as higher contributions and/or delayed increases in benefits) will be rather readily accepted as a means to cope with temporary employment and demographic conditions and in order to prevent the premature depletion of the fund.[10]

On the other hand, the system with its property-like features is sufficiently "separated out" and insulated from pressures for intervention and reform from the "external constituency" of the democratic political process with its parties, elections, legislative process, and executive powers to preserve its "path-dependence." It is essential to understand the system's institutionally protected rigidity if we want to account for its amazing historical robustness. But when the structural environment in which the system operates is undergoing rather dramatic changes it is exactly this robustness that turns from an asset into a liability because it is not sufficiently equipped to respond or adjust.

Social Change and Social Security

In this section, I wish to pursue the following argument: the capacity of the social security system to regenerate its basis of support and its capacity to achieve inclusive social security are put in question by

9 As this system – in contrast, for instance, with the Swedish welfare state model of *folkhemmet* or "home for the people" – refrains from pursuing any inter-class redistributive or egalitarian goals, its potential for generating consent rests, so to speak, on the simple rule of "the fewer commitments made, the fewer reasons to be concerned or to complain."

10 Alber quotes survey data to this effect and commends citizens for the "understanding" and "flexible" attitudes with which they are prepared to accept cuts in social expenditures: J. Alber, "Der Wohlfahrtsstaat in der Wirtschaftskrise. Eine Bilanz der Sozialpolitik in der Bundesrepublik seit den frühen siebziger Jahren," *Politische Vierteljahresschrift*, 27 (1986), pp. 28–60, especially pp. 50–3. Ganβmann points out that the fiscal imbalance of social security may itself serve as a stabilizing mechanism, as it strengthens the preparedness of members to make sacrifices in terms of increased contributions and decreased benefits: H. Ganβmann, "Der Sozialstaat als Regulationsinstanz," in *Der gewendete Kapitalismus*, ed. B. Mahnkopf (Münster: V. Westfälisches Dampfboot, 1988), pp. 74–98, especially 84ff.

130   *Claus Offe*

ongoing changes in its social and economic environment. This environment differs sharply from what the system presupposes as "normal conditions" of work, employment, patterns of labor market participation, and security needs in an industrial society. As a consequence, the system fails to "make sense" to those whom it covers – and it also fails to cover all of whom it is meant to cover. For the first of these reasons, and as its rational sources of support begin to crumble, the social security system may become less "secure"; for the second, it may become less inclusive and "social."

Moreover, general political support for the particular arrangements of social security as they have evolved in Germany may suffer not only from the frustration of "individual utility maximizers," but also from a sense of frustration of Left political forces and movements that the "social state" ("Sozialstaat," as postulated by the Federal Republic's Basic Law in its sections 20 and 28) has failed to live up to its promise of social justice and universally inclusive security. The perception of such failure[11] is based upon the observations that a shrinking portion of the working population actually enjoys "social" security; that the way in which the system deals with its clients is alienating, incapacitating, and undermines forms of solidarity; and that it has failed to alter the system of production in progressive ways.

Moreover, the disenchantment of much of the German political Left with issues of social security and social policy may have to do with a new urgency of "post-materialist" and "anti-productivist" concerns superseding[12] the traditional emphasis of socialists on social policy and redistributive issues. On the other hand, any changes away from the core institutional features of the German welfare state (such as arguably are called for by the new conditions of labor markets, employment, and economic growth, and gender and family relations) are consistently and strongly discouraged by the industrial trade unions.

What are the structural changes, political repercussions, and support-shaping effects that attenuate and sap the rational disposition of large groups of actors to vigorously defend the social security arrangements against proposed cuts, or even to support institutional changes that would increase the scope and the political security of these institutions? In order to answer this question, we must concentrate on the changing ways in which labor markets and social policies interact and the way that this interaction is perceived and evaluated by the key actors.

Social security and the labor market interact, as is well known, in two

---

11 An often quoted statement indicating this feeling of frustration and disappointment is the claim made by Jürgen Habermas that "the development of the welfare state (*Sozialstaat*) has entered a dead end alley" and that its utopian energies are exhausted: cf. J. Habermas, "Die Krise des Wohlfahrtsstaates und die Erschöpfung utopischer Energien," *Die Neue Unübersichtlichkeit* (Frankfurt, Suhrkamp, 1985), pp. 141–63.
12 Cf. C. Offe, "Democracy against the welfare state? Structural foundations of neoconservative political opportunities," *Political Theory*, 15 (1987), pp. 501–37.

ways. First, labor markets and the position of individuals in labor markets (as to their income, employment security, and working conditions) determine the size of their contributions as well as the size, kind, and incidence of needs that are to be covered according to legal stipulations and program parameters. The labor market thus determines the size and nature of the problems which the social security system will have to absorb, as well as the financial means that the system has at its disposal. Second, social security arrangements also determine quantitative and qualitative aspects of labor market developments. The features of the system of social security and the costs and benefits it is perceived to impose upon the parties in the labor market shape the strategies of the participants and thus the overall structure of employment.[13]

This "backward linkage" between the social security system and the structure of the labor market has two effects. First, the social security system and its mode of financing increase the costs of labor and thus decrease the demand for labor by providing employers with a significant incentive to adopt labor-saving technical change ("dynamic flexibility"). Alternatively, they may find ways to escape and bypass these costs of social security by employing low-paid, poorly protected, low-skilled, "flexible," and easily fired labor in appropriately designed jobs ("static flexibility"[14]). Second, and paradoxically, the benefits of social security increase the attractiveness for (potential) employees of acquiring "full welfare state citizenship" through full-time labor market participation. At any rate, they increase the opportunity costs (among other things, in terms of social security status) of nonparticipation in formal employment. The social security system thus appears not only to be vulnerable to labor market imbalances but also to contribute to this imbalance.[15]

13 This is not, of course, to imply that the social security system is the only factor that determines the level and quality of employment.

14 The distinction of "dynamic" versus "static" flexibility as well as the general idea that social policies and their mode of financing may affect quantitative and qualitative features of employment is taken from J. Myles, "Decline or impasse? The current state of the welfare," *Studies in Political Economy*, 26 (1988), pp. 73–107.

15 An indirect indicator of the significance of these perverse steering effects that originate from the social security system itself may be seen in specific reform initiatives that have been taken by both major political parties, the Social Democrats and the Christian Democrats. In order to check the social security system's demand effect to price some labor, particularly in labor-intensive industries, out of the market, the Social Democrats favor a shift in the mode of financing social security from payroll deductions to value-added deductions which would move the financial burden of social security from the volume of employment to the volume of output. Conversely, and in order to check the undesired supply effects, the Christian Democrats have proposed and legislated since 1983, with a view to strengthening the family as an institution and to improving the long-term demographic balance, various measures to make the effect of nonparticipation in the labor market on losses in old-age pension more affordable to mothers.

132   *Claus Offe*

Apart from such endogenous paradoxes and unintended incentive effects of social security, there are a number of structural changes which render the system both less inclusive in its coverage of all labor and less able to maintain "sufficient" levels of benefits. Instead, social security seems to be in the process of becoming a "core working class fortress" discriminating against and excluding all those rapidly increasing social categories that do not conform to assumedly "normal" standards of work life and family life. Two interrelated debates on these issues have become dominant in the German social policy discourse since the mid-1970s: one of them concerns the shifting role of women, the family, and the design of the female life cycle; the other the vanishing of what has been termed the "standard employment relation"[16] (*Normalarbeitsverhältnis*). As a result, both of these debates – and the empirical findings, predictive analysis, and normative considerations that entered into them – have led to the conclusion, now widely accepted, that the structural assumptions and premises on which social security was built can no longer be taken as valid.

This applies, most importantly, to the rapid spread of "precarious" forms of employment, i.e. forms of employment which, because of their part-time character, their insecurity and lack of protection, or their low level of pay, do not involve full social security status and the entitlements derived from it. Apart from the extreme case of outright illegal ("black") employment, these forms include *de jure* self-employment (where a regular employment relation is transformed into a nominal subcontracting relation), part-time employment (in particular, employment below the threshold of nineteen hours per week beyond which compulsory social security contributions become effective), fixed-term employment, labor "rented" for short-term jobs, "telework" in "electronic cottage industries," and employment that is interrupted by stretches of voluntary unemployment. Employees working under such conditions are typically unable to build up an employment record that would provide them with sufficient claims to old-age pensions and to other transfers on which they can rely in cases of unemployment or illness. The same applies to the long-term unemployed, most of whom are transferred, after having lost their job and failed to find a new one for more than one year, from the unemployment insurance to the social assistance, or welfare, system.

The spread of these "deviant" forms of labor market participation must be explained as the synergistic effect of at least four factors. First, in response to the high and stable registered unemployment rates that

16 Cf. R. G. Heinze, J. Hilbert, and H. Voelzkow, "Qualitative Perspektiven eines Umbaus des Sozialstaates," unpublished paper, Bochum, 1989, and Hinrichs for recent summaries of these findings and related policy debates: K. Hinrichs, "Irregular employment patterns and the loose net of social security: some findings on the West German case," Center for Social Policy Research, Bremen, 1989.

reached levels unprecedented in the history of the Federal Republic
(9–10 percent in the mid-1980s), the Christian Democratic administration initiated a number of measures deregulating the supposedly overly
rigid German labor market. Second, employers in both the more and the
less competitive sectors, partly in response to the unions' work time
reduction drives in the 1980s, have adopted employment strategies
which were designed to make working time more flexible and to rely
more strongly on part-time employment. This form of employment is
significantly less well covered than full-time employment by protective
collective agreements. Similarly employers were exposed to strong incentives to escape the significant nonwage cost burdens of social security
contributions and other protective regulations by resorting either to
nominal subcontracting or to "cheap" labor employed for less than 19
hours per week. Third, high levels of unemployment forced many people
seeking jobs to accept relatively deregulated, unprotected, and insecure
forms of employment for lack of a better alternative. Fourth, cultural
changes of lifestyles, orientations towards employed work, and biographical patterns contributed to the formation of preferences for "deviant," discontinuous, and less than full-time forms of employment on
the part of many female and male workers. These shifts have provided
opportunities, and even a measure of apparent legitimacy, for employers'
inventive experimentation with forms of "flexible" manpower utilization.

Workers willing to accept such substandard forms of labor market
participation may or may not be aware of the fact that what they
sacrifice by partially or temporarily "opting out" of employment is not
just income from work, but also social security status that is tied to
continuous full-time employment. But often the line between "opting
out" and "opting in" is not easy to draw. This refers, in particular, to
married women who enter the labor market (or indicate the wish to do
so if there were an acceptable opportunity) in increasing numbers. This
phenomenon has been referred to as an "autonomous supply"[17] effect –
a phenomenon that resulted in the simultaneous increase in several years
during the 1980s of the total number of unemployed and the total of
those employed within the West German economy. The behavior underlying such seemingly paradoxical aggregate effects may be informed by
the reasoning that, since employment in general and the employment
status of the household's breadwinner in particular is perceived as precarious and endangered, it is a good idea to secure a second source of labor
market income which might be used as an intra-household safety net. In
this way, the perception of sluggish demand for labor might perversely
contribute to its increased supply. This type of motivation has probably
replaced another one that prevailed under tight labor market conditions:
the wish to "top up," through easily available part-time employment,

17 Cf. B. Lutz, "Notwendigkeit und Ansatzpunkte einer angebotsbezogenen
Vollbeschäftigungspolitik," in *Resonanzen. Arbeitsmarkt und Beruf – Forschung und
Politik*, ed. L. Reyher and J. Kühl (Nürnberg: IAB, 1988), pp. 275–89.

134   *Claus Offe*

the male breadwinner's income in order to make higher levels of consumption affordable to the household. Another way of accounting for the autonomous supply effect would be to assume that for many married women employed work plays the role of an intrinsically desirable form of activity, or of a "consumption item," which – largely regardless of the level of pay, employment security, and social security it provides – is valued for the challenge, social contact, and esteem it affords and is therefore preferred to unpaid and full-time family and household work.[18] This type of motivation is of special interest to employers, since it is assumed to be less wage elastic than that of "ordinary" labor. The continuing influx of (married) women (and mothers) into the labor market is certainly inspired also by egalitarian feminist values as well as by the rational economic consideration by married women of gaining independent access to income and social security in view of increasing rates of divorce and family breakdown. Otherwise access to social security is conditional upon the marriage relationship and the husband's income.[19]

Irregular types of employment and the loss of social security status are likely to involve the risk of (old-age) poverty if they occur outside the institutional setting of marriage and family relations. Often the family functions as a "capillary" social security system, as dependents and survivors are usually entitled to "derived" benefits of the family's breadwinner. Thus the decline of the family as an institution undermines the scope of effective social security still further. This decline, however, is one of the most consistent long-term trends to be found in German sociological and demographic time series data – whether it is measured in terms of the share of family households in all households, the number of children per married couple, the number of new marriages per 1,000 inhabitants per year, or the number of divorces per 1,000 marriages per

18 One factor that gives rise to this ordering of preferences might not be so much the intrinsic attractiveness of employed work but the lack of acceptable opportunities and the requisite social networks for "informal" work. For traditional forms of socially recognized and status-conferring activities outside formal employment (i.e. within the extended family household, associations, churches, clubs, part-time self-employment, "third sector," etc.), which used to – and might today – serve as a labor market supply buffer, have largely fallen victim within most West European societies to secular processes of modernization, urbanization, and bureaucratization; their decline causes an influx of (mostly) female labor power into the ranks of the employees and the employment seekers. For an elaboration of this line of argument, see Lutz, "Notwendigkeit and Ansatzpunkte" and *Der kurze Traum immerwährender Prosperität* (Frankfurt: Campus, 1984); see also C. Offe and R. G. Heinze, "Am Arbeitsmarkt vorbei. Überlegungen zur Neubestimmung 'haushaltlicher' Wohlfahrtsproduktion in ihrem Verhältnis zu Markt und Staat," *Leviathan*, 14 (1986), pp. 471–95.
19 Cf. D. Schäfer, "Gegenwärtige Probleme und Fragen sowie langfristige Zukunftsperspektiven der Sozialpolitik in der Bundesrepublic Deutschland," *Zeitschrift für Sozialreform*, 35 (1989), pp. 28–36.

year. These powerful trends affect both the capacity of the family to substitute for the lack of social security and, in its quality as a micro social security network, to extend the scope of social security to "inactive" or "precariously" employed dependents.

Social and labor market policies, employers' strategies, cultural changes in the conception of a desirable life course, and emerging uncertainties concerning the social role of women, men, and the family all contribute to the growth of relatively insecure and unprotected segments of the labor market and hence, conversely, to the shrinkage of that part of total labor that is covered by effective, reliable, and sufficient levels of social security. Not only in terms of pay and job security, but also in terms of social security, the distance between "good" jobs and labor market positions versus "bad" ones, or "standard" patterns of labor market participation and "irregular" ones, is increasing – a fact that is often referred to in the German labor market and social policy discourse by the suggestion of an emerging "two-thirds society" (*Zweidrittelgesellschaft*). The failure of trade unions to effectively defend the inclusive and universal nature of social security has also contributed to the rise of these disparities. This failure is due to both objective constraints and the strategic reluctance of the unions to vigorously defend, through their wage demands and collective agreements, the interests and needs of the irregularly employed who make up an increasingly important segment of the representational domain (although not of the actual membership!) of organized labor.[20]

The Politics of Adapting Social Security to the Employment Crisis

It follows from the basic institutional characteristics of an employment-centered and contributions-financed system of social security that its long-term equilibrium is particularly vulnerable to two adverse events: high and lasting levels of unemployment and demographic imbalance. Both of these disturbances hit the German welfare state in the decade 1975–84. As a consequence of the first, there will not be enough current earned income to pay for current entitlements. The second, as it becomes manifest in declining birth rates and increasing life expectancy (with its related increases in health and care needs of the aged), will exacerbate this disequilibrium – or so it came to be widely anticipated for the

20 The male-dominated German trade unions, in this respect faithful in their general policy orientation to the built-in assumptions of the German social security system, have also tended, at least until very recently, to consider only the male, skilled, full-time employed worker and family head as the model case whose interests are to be defended through union action, and virtually everyone else as a deficient deviation from this "normal" worker. Cf. Mückenberger, "Der Wandel des Normalarbeitsverhältnisses."

136   *Claus Offe*

foreseeable future – by increasing the financial burden per capita of the currently employed.[21]

The unprecedented coincidence of these two long-term problems has set the agenda for German social policy during the entire period since 1975 that interests us here. It is important to understand, however, that the simultaneous employment and demographic crises did no more than that: they called for some adequate response, but did not dictate one particular response as the only one practical and feasible. How such critical facts are responded to and coped with depends entirely upon actors, preferences, and institutions. Deterministic explanations of public policies seem to suggest that "politics did not matter," and that actual developments were in fact dictated by economic events and trends. This deceptive suggestion derives from the fact that the policy response was substantially similar whether it occurred under governments led by the Social Democrats (1975–82) or Christian Democrats (since 1982–3). In both cases, the effort was to adapt the welfare state in general, and the social security system in particular, to the emerging new conditions by preserving its institutional foundations (rather than changing or dismantling them) and by steering a careful course of austerity and financial consolidation. This means that the politics of adaptation were basically uncontroversial between the two party elites that otherwise, concerning policy areas such as foreign and defense policies, stood in sharp opposition to each other. Nevertheless, my contention is that it was not economics but politics that shaped social policies after 1975, and the false impression to the contrary derives from the fact that it happened to be bipartisan and largely uncontroversial politics. Its principles and strategies were widely shared by Christian Democrats, Social Democrats, and all major actors such as the unions, the employers' associations, the para-public social security agencies, the major representatives of the health-related industries, as well as the social policy experts. The dramatic changes taking place in the socioeconomic environment of social policy did not translate into similarly vehement political controversies. On the contrary, almost all the cuts, innovations, and adaptations that were put into effect from the "budget structure act" of 1975 to the bipartisan "old-age pension reform act" of 1989 (to become effective in 1992) were passed in a conspicuously and unusually smooth political process.

The range of policy choices that was actually considered was, from the start, much smaller than the entire "feasible set" of possible and practical responses to the crisis. In principle, the following choices were available:

21   English language summaries of the German data substantiating these twin challenges are to be found in K. H. Jüttemeier and H. G. Petersen, "West Germany," in *The World Crisis in Social Security*, ed. J. J. Rosa (Paris: Fondation Nationale d'Economie Politique, 1982), pp. 181–206, and J. Alber, "The West German welfare state in transition," in *Testing the Limits of Social Welfare*, ed. R. Morris (Hanover: Brandeis University Press, 1988), pp. 96–134.

1   cut benefits and increase burdens in negative proportion to the polit-
    ical clout of those negatively affected by such measures;
2   increase contributions to levels that are sufficient to cover existing
    entitlements and predictable future needs;
3   decrease benefits according to need, thus shifting the basis of entitle-
    ment from equivalence to need;
4   cover the deficit in social security out of general taxation, thus
    gradually shifting the financial base of social security from contribu-
    tions to taxes.

Of these options, only the first was seriously pursued. It became the
dominant response to the twin challenge. This choice cannot be explained by adverse economic and demographic conditions, and neither
can it be justified as superior economic rationality. It must be explained,
or so I wish to argue, by the realistic assessment and anticipation, on the
part of political and corporate elites, of the standards of solidarity,
popular sentiments, conceptions of group interest, and parameters of
acceptability of the political culture of social policy that has evolved
within the fragmented and "individualized"[22] West German society in
the 1980s. The policies and innovations by which the German social
security system was adapted to the new conditions that prevailed after
1975 was not uniquely "rational" in the use it made of scarce resources
or in terms of the fiscal and labor market effects it brought about. If
anything, it was "rational" in terms of the popular sentiments it catered
to and the fears it was designed to placate. The conservatism of the
adaptive moves was not a traditionalist but a strategic conservatism. Its
logic was to quell the potential for popular welfare state backlash by
pioneering a moderate version of it.

The policies of social policy adaptation and consolidation adopted by
federal governments since 1975 show a rather clear pattern of selective
protection and discriminatory exclusion which, apart from its substantive redistributive effects, has also played the role of a "hidden curriculum" by projecting images and symbolic demarcations as to which
social categories "deserve" to enjoy undiminished benefits and levels of

22   The term "individualization" has gained a currency within the German
social sciences that is itself rather symptomatic. Being the opposite of what in
British sociology has been termed "collectivism," it captures structural as well as
cultural changes that include the decomposition of encompassing moral and
associational frameworks of (class) solidarity, the erosion of biographical patterns and traditions and the certainties based upon them, and a culture of
"selfishness" that oscillates between "autonomy" and "anomie." Affinities of
this social scientific current to French debates on "postmodernism" and Anglo-
American "methodological individualism" are evident. Important sources of the
German debate include U. Beck, *Die Risikogesellschaft. Auf dem Weg in eine andere
Moderne* (Frankfurt: Suhrkamp, 1986) and W. Zapf, S. Breuer, J. Hampel,
P. Krause, H.-M. Mohr, and E. Wiegand, *Individualisierung und Sicherheit. Unter-
suchungen zur Lebensqualität in der Bundesrepublik Deutschland* (München: Beck, 1987).

security and other social categories that can justly (as well as safely, in terms of their potential for resistance and conflict) be deprived of some of their status rights. Behind the practice of adaptation, there stands an implicit theory about the kind of social justice that the renovated welfare state is meant to serve.[23]

The overall pattern is clear enough. The underlying strategy is to remove cuts and austerity measures from institutional locations where they can easily become the focal point of collective action to locations where they remain largely imperceptible to the wider public, and difficult to interpret as a collective condition and experience on the basis of which organized action might become possible. It is as if the maxim had been followed to make it more difficult to pinpoint the winners, the losers, and those responsible for the transaction. Within this pattern of adaptation to turbulences, eight components can be detected.

1   Unburdening the federal budget: in order to escape the liabilities generated by rising unemployment, more frequent early retirement, and worsening demographic balance, and to keep social security issues out of the arena of the politics of taxation and tax reform, the need to stimulate growth and employment, to lower taxes, to avoid crowding-out effects of the federal debt, and to improve the ratio of capital-forming versus consumptive components of the federal budget were cited as justifications for a strategy of "uncoupling" social security budgets from the federal budget through eliminating the federal budget's liabilities for social insurance deficits.

2   Horizontal subsidies: as the federal government is no longer, or only to a very limited extent, subsidizing the pension, health, and unemployment insurance systems, a highly complicated and opaque system was introduced according to which they are to subsidize each other.[24]

3   Cuts in preventive measures and "operative" budgets: as a balance of revenues and expenditures cannot be fully restored through horizontal redistributions, cuts in some of the programs were introduced, such as the preventive training measures of the unemployment insurance agency and some of the rehabilitative services and programs of the health insurance system. The logic of this type of consolidation measure is to

23   This two-tiered (instrumental and symbolic/expressive) nature of political communications can be illustrated in one of the favorite slogans of the conservative and market liberal political Right in the early 1980s, namely "*Leistung muß sich wieder lohnen!*" ("effort is to become worthwhile again!"). At its instrumental surface, this slogan serves to advocate the demand for lowering taxes and tax progression; it designates a desirable future. But on a deeper level it expresses something about the deplorable present which must be brought back to order "again": effort does not pay today, because those making "efforts" are not properly rewarded and people are rewarded without making an appropriate effort (e.g. to find a job).

24   Cf. K. J. Bieback, "Leistungsabbau und Strukturwandel im Sozialrecht," *Kritische Justiz*, 17 (1984), pp. 257–78, especially p. 262.

disperse risks in time, as current needs which are neglected will often cause greater costs in the future.

4   Cuts in entitlements to cash payments, including delayed increases to compensate for inflation, and increases in contributions: these measures make individual employees and social security recipients pay in terms of their current income for some of the costs of adaptation.

5   Shifting the burden to local governments: as the number of long-term unemployed (who are no longer entitled to unemployment insurance benefits[25]) increases and as the real income from the lowest range of old-age pensions falls below the poverty line, the local state is made to carry the burden of increasing expenditures for social assistance (*Sozialhilfe*), which in turn prevents it from spending its budget on (presumably employment-generating) investment programs.[26]

6   Selective termination or reduction of programs funded by the federal government: these have mostly affected high school and university students and the long-term unemployed, thus shifting the burden to either families or individuals.

7   Local and state experiments with secondary and unprotected labor markets: these programs have mostly been targeted at unemployed youth and other "marginal" workers, as well as recipients of local social assistance, thus creating a new status of "deregulated" labor.

8   Cuts in local expenditures on social services and the reintroduction or increase of user-fees.[27]

The overall logic of these fiscal and legislative measures can be compared with that of a giant domino effect which starts in the labor market and goes on to affect the federal budget, the social security systems, local governments, marginal segments of the labor force, families (in particular women within families), clients of services, and individuals. This immensely complex process of adaptation, retrenchment, and carefully designed consolidation explains why social policy expenditures have indeed remained roughly constant in absolute terms – though certainly not in proportion to the dramatically increased levels of need that were caused by unemployment and demographic factors. What still remains to be explained, however, is the fact that these cuts and substantial

25   As early as 1982, 1.3 million registered unemployed no longer received any benefits from the unemployment insurance; as a consequence, a majority of them became dependent upon federal and local support.
26   A growing number of local governments have adopted an ingenious strategy in this game of "vertical dispersion" that is being played between the unemployment insurance and local governments: they fight back by nominally employing unemployed persons for a limited period of time in order to make them eligible for unemployment benefits, and then laying them off and thus making the Federal Employment Agency liable for their income – until the point where the next round of "recycling" the fiscal burden of unemployment may start.
27   Cf. H. Zacher, "Der gebeutelte Sozialstaat in der wirtschaftlichen Krise," *Sozialer Fortschritt*, 33 (1984), pp. 1–12, especially p. 3.

140   *Claus Offe*

relative losses in no way provoked a significant level of opposition or social and political conflict.

In order to come to terms with this question, we turn from the policies of consolidation to the politics of social policy and the conspicuous absence of polarized conflict about reform and retrenchment. The adaptation has taken place in a slow and gradual rather than sudden and abrupt manner, beginning with restrictive regulations of the unemployment insurance in 1975 and fiscal consolidation laws adopted in 1977 and 1978, and the cuts were dispersed across social categories and institutions. This pace stands in sharp contrast with, for instance, the British sea change in public policy after 1979.[28] Moreover, most of the changes were adopted by a *de facto* bipartisan coalition. In making these cuts, both the Christian Democrats[29] and the Social Democrats were rationally inclined to grant relative protection to active labor market participants[30] and thus the constituency of trade unions. Under these tactics of careful,[31] gradual, and largely consensual[32] management of

28   Cf. H. Michalsky, "Sozialstaat als Programm und Praxis. Die Sozialpolitik der SPD als Regierungspartei (1966–1982), Habilitationsschrift," unpublished, Heidelberg, 1985, chs VI and VII; also Alber, "The West German welfare state in transition," who observes that "the mid-1970s stand out as a watershed in social policy development" (p. 104) – not the coming-to-power of the conservative–liberal coalitions government in 1982–3.
29   The party itself contains a significant Christian socialist (mostly Roman Catholic) minority which is very careful to present itself as based in the working class and representing its interests; this is particularly the case as the Christian Democratic Minister of Labor and Social Affairs, Norbert Blüm, is also the Christian Democrats' designated challenger for the prime minister's office in Northrhine-Westphalia, the largest West German federal state which is now firmly controlled by Social Democrats – again, a significant difference if compared with Britain where "wet" and "one nation" Conservatives have been virtually eliminated from government posts and party leadership.
30   Cf. Alber, "The West German welfare state in transition," p. 111: "Labor force participants passed through the austerity period in, relatively, the most favorable terms."
31   Both Social Democratic and Christian Democratic governments have been remarkably sensitive to the evidence that cuts did occasionally turn out to be detrimental to their respective electoral prospects, in which cases reversals or compensatory measures were quickly adopted. A case in point is a measure that severely cut the amount of cash payments made available to the inmates of old-age homes. After this cut drew wide publicity, payments were quickly restored to the original levels. Cf. A. Windhoff-Héritier, "Sozialpolitik der mageren Jahre," in *Sparpolitik. Ökonomische Zwänge und politische Spielräume*, ed. H. Mäding (Opladen: Westdeutscher Verlag, 1983), pp. 77–99, especially p. 86.
32   This consensual nature of consolidation policies was not only based upon inter-party agreements and forms of collaboration, most importantly in the drafting of the old-age pension reform passed by the Bundestag in 1989. The consensus was also engineered through a specific corporatist arrangement for the health sector, the "health sector concerted action," in which all major organized

potential conflict, a polarized politicization of social policy issues could not emerge. Cuts were made acceptable to the electorate by virtue of their coming in small doses and at the expense of highly diverse social categories, rather than in the form of vehement and sudden assaults upon specific groups. The government that programmatically insisted upon cuts and introduced them was reelected[33] both in 1976 and in 1987.

But the absence of open and polarized political conflict was not only due to the tactics of its containment. The potential for conflict and the rational disposition of large parts of the population to defend the welfare state and to advocate its further growth was much more limited than many critics of the consolidation policies tend to assume. The success of conflict containment must then be partly explained by the fact that there was not much conflict potential to be contained in the first place. According to this hypothesis, the conspicuously smooth course of events reflects the fact that collectivist priorities and encompassing solidarities had widely vanished in the electorate. Positive individual incentives to defend the welfare state, its maintenance and further expansion, were weakened as fewer and fewer groups could expect to be in a position to make an unequivocal redistributive net gain. At the same time the negative collective incentive lost much of its persuasiveness as the West German society was exposed to the experience that large-scale and lasting unemployment and rapidly increasing numbers of people dependent on social assistance did not constitute, as had been widely feared, a threat to social peace.

In sum, the smoothness of the adaptation process must be accounted for not only in terms of the skillful management of possible conflict through political elites, but also in terms of changing perceptions and priorities on the part of large segments of the electorate which correspondingly have "good reasons" to comply with and even advocate austerity policies, rather than to engage in social and political protest over it. The declining allegiance to collectivist ideas about generous and further increasing levels of welfare state spending must in turn be seen in the context of the ongoing labor market restructuring described before.

"The contemporary welfare state has become a strategic environment

---

interests relevant to that sector were involved. Cf. H. Wiesenthal, *Die Konzertierte Aktion im Gesundheitswesen* (Frankfurt: Campus, 1981), and D. Webber, "Krankheit, Geld und Politik: Zur Geschichte der Gesundheitsreform in Deutschland," *Leviathan*, 16 (1988), pp. 156–203.

33 Alber, "The West German welfare state in transition," p. 115, quotes survey data according to which the "percentage of stern welfare state defenders had drastically declined by thirty percentage points between 1975 and 1983." Confronted with the alternative of either having to pay for higher taxes and contributions in order to maintain levels of transfers or having to cut both, increasing numbers of people were rationally disposed towards giving priority to the latter alternative.

142   *Claus Offe*

in which people operate as calculating entrepreneurs."[34] The ongoing
policy discourse on the need for austerity and consolidation measures
has certainly sensitized people to their own position and the pay-offs
connected with it within the social security game; it has thus undermined attitudes of both "trust in others" and "trust in the future" that
together make up a conventionalist and collectivist orientation to social
security issues. As people begin to calculate and to compare, some
portion of rational support is likely to decline. This applies both to the
individual and collective levels, and within both the upper middle class
and the lower working class.

Increasing portions of the upper middle class can, with good economic
reasons, adopt the perspective that they do not really need and depend
upon much of the social security provisions that they are entitled to as
members of the system. They are therefore inclined to object to the fiscal
burdens the welfare state imposes upon their income.

At the same time, an increasing portion of the working class, particularly of workers in the lower income brackets, loses its rational reason for
supporting the income-graduated social security system because the level
of benefits that they will eventually derive from it is not substantially
higher than the level of social assistance benefits to which they would be
entitled even without having made any contributions. To them the social
insurance differential is individually[35] unattractive.

Nor does the opposition to, or at any rate lack of strong support for,
the social security system to which these two very diverse social categories are rationally disposed necessarily remain a matter of opinion and
resentment. It can translate itself in collective as well as individual
action. On the collective level, "tax resistance" and "welfare state backlash" are political syndromes on which rightist populist parties and
movements have thrived not just in highly developed welfare states such
as Denmark and Norway but also in Britain. Apart from the now rather
obsolete approach of Victorian moralizing,[36] such political forces can
either, in their more benign version, invoke meritocratic and market-
liberal principles of property rights, or they can openly rely on racist,
xenophobic, and sexist sentiments. The common logic of these
approaches is to question the legitimacy of entitlements to transfers and
services, be it those of working mothers, foreign workers, "welfare
scroungers," farmers, civil servants, the unemployed, or some other
supposedly "undeserving" social category.

34 de Swaan, *In Care of the State*, p. 229.
35 Although, obviously, a "fallacy of composition" is involved in this argument; it is true on the individual level, but becomes meaningless if all the lower
working class would rely on social assistance, thus dramatically lowering the per
capita funds available through it.
36 L. Mead, *Beyond Entitlement: The Social Obligations of Citizenship* (New York:
Macmillan, 1986); M. Spieker, *Legitimationsprobleme des Sozialstaats* (Bern: Haupt,
1986).

In the German case, the neo-conservative populist approach has constituted a noticeable ingredient of the political discourse of the 1970s and 1980s without assuming anything like the hegemonic role it enjoys in Britain.[37] This approach was accompanied by active efforts, on the part of governing political elites, to promulgate issues and themes which served to distract attention from the older collectivist agendas and thereby disorganize and discredit large-scale collectivities and bonds of solidarity within civil society through a cross-cutting and cross-coding "politics of interpretation".[38] These semantic and symbolic forms of politics are designed to dramatize nonclass issues of either an all-inclusive ("moral order," "national identity," terrorism, "technological competitiveness," ecological issues) or a particularizing variety (focusing on particular institutions – such as the family – or isolated issues such as drugs or AIDS, or specific groups such as asylum-seeking foreigners or *Aussiedler*).

The legal and administrative treatment of the unemployed – and the change of rules that was adopted in Germany in the period we consider here – is a more specific case in point. First, the rules of the unemployment insurance are set up in such a way that a sort of zero-sum game of the employed against the unemployed emerges under conditions of a more than moderate level of unemployment and long-term unemployment, particularly if the perceived probability of one's self becoming unemployed is highly differentiated according to branch of industry, age, region, and other criteria.[39] That is, workers who are employed and who expect to remain so will take an interest in lowering or at least not having increased the amount that is deducted from their wages as their contribution to mandatory unemployment insurance, while unemployed workers will have the reverse interest. More generally, some of the unemployed perceive – or are led to believe by successful rightest populist

37   The basic insight that this political approach seeks to promulgate is nicely captured in a statement by Margaret Thatcher that is noteworthy for its explicitness, its absurdity, and its cleverness: "There is no such thing as society. There are individual men and women, and there are families."

38   As an illustration of what I call "politics of interpretation" I would cite a chief analyst of the Federation of German Employers' Associations who maintained that about half the present number of the unemployed are not in fact unemployed but unemployable, due to their suffering from irreversible physical, mental, or skill deficiencies. This redefinition of unemployment suggests a dissociation between "us" (i.e. normal people, employed or unemployed) and "them," who suffer from special handicaps that cannot conceivably be overcome by collectivist strategies. The implication is clear: if this code is accepted as valid, demands for policies aiming at full employment become meaningless. For a contrasting use of the "politics of interpretation" in this area, one might look at the Swedish practice of coding all persons who are presently undergoing retraining or are employed on nominal or "protected" jobs as "wage earners."

39   That is, if the "veil of ignorance" becomes thin; cf. for an application of this Rawlsian metaphor to social policies J. Elster, "The possibility of rational politics," *Archives Européennes de Sociologie*, 28 (1987), pp. 67–103.

campaigns – their interests to be opposed to those of the employed, as wage increases successfully fought for by the latter will push the price of labor up and diminish the prospects of the unemployed finding jobs. These intra-class conflicts and the concomitant distributional conflicts among workers are exacerbated by policies which virtually abolished state subsidies to unemployment insurance. Furthermore, the cuts have taken the highly and intentionally divisive form of differentiating the claims of unemployed persons according to their age, family status, employment record, and duration of unemployment, thus individualizing the condition of unemployment and not only pitting the employed against the unemployed but also fragmenting the interests of the latter. A similar logic of division and fragmentation seems to apply in recent reforms and developments in the health system and with regard to the income of old-age pensioners where we also find an almost endless variation of individual cases, conditions, and the rules that apply to them, thus making the definition of a collectively shared interest and its organizational representation much more difficult than it otherwise would be.

As a result of these strategies and developments, one can anticipate the emergence and consolidation of a class-divided society in which each class is defined by its relation not to the means of production but to the state-organized resources of welfare, and therefore by the differing degree to which it is vulnerable to being deprived of its share.[40] Let me propose the following five-class model. The upper class within this system is made up of the public sector employees, foremost the civil servants (*Beamte*); the latter enjoy a rather unique combination of privileges, such as old-age pensions without prior deduction of contributions, job security, and extensive coverage of their health expenditures through public funds. The second and largest class consists of "normal" employees – "normal" in the (both descriptive and slightly moralizing) sense that they have full-time and relatively stable jobs, live in equally stable families, enjoy the advantages of a strong representation through unions, and are covered by the mandatory social security systems. A third class is made up of all those who have been in employment but are presently no longer so because of old age, invalidity, or unemployment; they are less numerous and much less well organized than the second class and hence more vulnerable to cuts, but are still able to defend themselves against the worst attacks. In the fourth category, we find the disparate and heterogeneous group of those who depend on means-tested social assistance transfers and/or (as clients and patients) state-organized services. Finally, there is the lower class of the welfare state made up of people who (as refugees, foreign workers, illegal aliens, or

40   The notion of society being divided into several "welfare classes" was first used by R. M. Lepsius, "Soziale Ungleichheit und Klassenstrukturen in der Bundesrepublik Deutschland," in *Klassen in der europäischen Sozialgeschichte*, ed. H. U. Wehler (Göttingen: Ruprecht, 1979), pp. 166–209.

asylum seekers) do not unequivocally enjoy the basic privileges that are tied to national citizenship. Needless to say, such a class system is vastly regressive in its distributional impact, as it privileges the middle classes enjoying stable employment in the public and private sectors at the expense of virtually everyone else.[41]

In economic terms, this decline of class politics can be explained by the fact that by the mid-1970s the model of the Keynesian welfare state was rendered a highly unpromising one by the changed realities of the international economy. Major advances seemed no longer feasible and probably counterproductive, as they would involve budget increases and rates of inflation that no major social and political group would be willing to advocate. From a sociological point of view, the largely homogeneous *Arbeitnehmergesellschaft* (society of employees) had given way, in the eyes of political elites, and probably to some extent in reality, to a fragmented social structure generating a multiplicity of issues, cleavages, and identities which could no longer be responded to by politics in terms of social class, economic growth, and political redistribution. As early as 1976, the Christian Democrats came up with a widely appealing populist political formula. The axis of conflict was no longer labor versus capital but the organized against the unorganized – and, most emphatically, women, children, and families versus male-dominated and employment-centered corporate actors.[42] Much less appealing was the Social Democratic response which emphasized economic decline, rising unemployment, new poverty, and the "two-thirds society", with one-third of the population allegedly marginalized and excluded from prosperity. This formula, accurate though it certainly was and still is to some extent, makes little sense from the point of view of politics. It appeals to benevolence rather than to the interests of the majority of the electorate which still lives under conditions of prosperity and will not easily be mobilized by social policy demands favoring small disadvantaged groups.

The failure of the Left to regain the social policy initiative is a further element of our answer to the question how the massive socioeconomic shocks experienced by the West Germans in the course of the late 1970s and 1980s could be absorbed as smoothly as was actually the case. The victorious Kohl campaigns in both 1983 and 1987 failed to pay more than occasional lip service to a problem that as late as 1982, the last year of the Schmidt government, was generally assigned the position of the

41 Zacher, "Der gebeutelte Sozialstaat in der wirtschaftlichen Krise," p. 5.
42 In fact, it is probably no exaggeration to observe that during the 1980s a new ideological formation and policy orientation has evolved within the Christian Democratic Party that can be described as "conservative state feminism." As a consequence, social policies focusing on the social security status of women were virtually the only area within social policies where not cuts, but substantial improvements – such as the granting of pension claims for mothers, graduated by the number of children – prevailed. Cf. Schmidt, *Sozialpolitik*, pp. 89–90.

146   *Claus Offe*

single most important social and economic problem that the Germans had to face, namely unemployment, which had risen to 2.5 million registered (and about another 1.5 million unregistered) people without jobs who wanted jobs. This abrupt transformation of a dominant issue into a virtual nonissue must be attributed, according to my analysis, to the three interrelated factors that I have discussed in this chapter, namely:

1 the perceived job security and social security of those within employment, as they had as much to lose as they had little to fear and could afford to acquiesce in the economic and social condition of their less fortunate fellow citizens;
2 the growing heterogeneity of interests, values, and identifications within the social structure which became manifest in the rise of issues and demands having to do with regional interests, age categories, gender categories, health, and agriculture, among numerous others; this centrifugal and "disorderly" pattern of political issues dominating domestic politics over the last decade was not suitable for integration into a coherent and potentially hegemonic program of social reform (such as might have been expected from the political Left);
3 the fact that this multiplicity of cleavages, issues, and identities could only be – and was in fact quite effectively – over-arched, as it were, by the political Right's populist and partly nationalist advances and its general emphasis on "moral" rather than social and economic reform and leadership, with a particular emphasis on austerity as the fiscal equivalent to populism.

C
Social Democratic

[18]

OFFICIAL PROGRAMS AND LEGISLATIVE ACTS

THE new and imperative problem of population and family was presented to the Swedish people in the fall of 1934 in the framework of ideas set forth in preceding chapters. It was immediately grasped and discussed as a problem with the dimensions and content of a new social policy. From the beginning the discussion took cognizance of the magnitude of the changes involved, of the many different aspects of life that had to be harmonized, and of the need for conscious planning to supersede the automatic adjustments relied upon in the past. There was enough factual knowledge about demographic trends, especially about the prospects of impending decline in population, to give reality to the question whether something needed to be done. Less complete data, but still enough to make the challenge to social action concrete, had been compiled to show the effect which childbearing, even at a level below that required for stabilizing population, had on the plane of living of those families which had the children. It became public knowledge that the poverty of many Swedish families was due primarily to the fact that there were children in those families. Consequently, poverty was selective, and it particularly affected children.

The people realized vaguely that any remedial program must be revolutionary in scope. While emotional reactions to the situation and practical suggestions for reform may have been divergent, there was national agreement that population problems must be placed at the top of society's agenda. When the Swedish Riksdag opened in January, 1935, all the political parties were ready to declare their concern.[1] The Conservatives signed a party motion, significantly the first of the year's session in both parliamentary chambers. It opens with a solemn reminder:

No sooner have the relief cares of mass unemployment become lighter as a result of business recovery, and consequently the political tension about employment remedies relaxed, than a crisis of infinitely greater scope demands an answer from the Swedish people: namely, the population question.

[1] See records of the Riksdag for 1935.

158   NATION AND FAMILY

The motion goes on to describe the factual situation and then gives an interpretation of the national crisis.

Against the background of the above facts the population question appears as the most important question of our day. It is not like others, just one question among many; it is the very frame for a multitude of social problems of great urgency. With it is connected the whole problem of national economy; it affects all problems of production and distribution; upon it depends the possibility of utilizing our country's natural resources, of maintaining our culture and our national integrity. The population question is literally a question of the life of the Swedish people.

More tragic than anything is the fact that in this whole field of population policy the most profound contradictions appear between what we, on the one hand, have been willing to do, and what, on the other hand, we seem to find we can just as obviously omit doing. For the children who are permitted to come into this world, our community will provide educational institutions which are generally recognized as being of high quality. The aged, the infirm, and the dependent we care for in such a manner as to arouse the recognition of foreign observers. None is allowed to suffer from want or privation with the knowledge or consent of communal or state authorities. Medical science tries its utmost to keep alive a flickering life flame. All this seems natural and is accepted in a society with an old Christian tradition like our own. But we go further in our concern for the future: modern society not only assumes responsibility for the people's own welfare and happiness, but it also furnishes prudent advice and diligent care as to how the material resources shall best be preserved. We consult as to the best means of preventing soil wastage or utilization of other resources of nature. We try to save for posterity the living capital in our forests, so valuable for the maintenance of our people, through forestry laws which forbid excessive cutting and provide for reforestation. It is only for its own renewal that this same Swedish people fails to provide. In so far as this failure is caused by selfish motives of individuals, it shows a way of life which is in no way unique in history, but wherever it has appeared earlier, it foreboded retrogression for the people themselves and the culture which they made flourish. Here, if ever, it can truly be said that the lessons of history are frightening.

The Conservative party therefore declares its willingness to support reforms, which naturally enough bear the special coloring of its attitudes.

Furthermore, these serious questions must always be judged from the life philosophy of Christian ethics in which Swedish legal principles and social institutions are fundamentally grounded. The chances of influencing the development of the population problem through direct socio-political measures on the part of the community are undoubtedly very limited. The knowledge of this, however, should not deter us from conscientiously following any suggestions along this line. . . . The national and social ideals of the Conservative party make it our duty to cooperate with such a policy without, at the same time, surrendering our principle that the greatest social resource consists in the responsibility individuals themselves are assuming.

An inventory of possible reforms is then given which almost coincides with the ones presented by opposing ideological groups at the opening of the whole population discussion. Greater stress is, however, laid on reforms in taxation, on developing single-family homes as the solution of the housing problem, on new colonization and greater security for the farming population, and on domestic training for girls. Economic reforms, on the other hand, are less explicitly encouraged, advocacy being in inverse relationship to expense. Still, considerable advances are envisaged; for instance, in relation to maternity bonuses and delivery care. Birth control is spoken of evasively. A definite change in opinion is indicated in the treatment of married women's right to work.

It is just as apparent that this problem is not solved by more or less restrictive regulations concerning married women's right to gainful employment. It seems rather more appropriate to believe that the chief aim will be better advanced through giving self-supporting women greater security in their employment relations.

This proclamation was immediately followed by a similar one from leaders of the liberal middle party (*Folkpartiet*). The most remarkable feature of this proclamation was that the practical consequence of all this anxiety, namely, having to make an economic redistribution in favor of children, was explicitly realized.

In the discussion of the population question a series of measures has been recommended which might contribute to increasing the birth rate by decreasing the economic burden connected with the birth of children, their education and support. Such proposals are founded on the *principle of equalizing the economic costs of childbearing*. If the extra expense in the family budget entailed by childbearing can be decreased, one of the most important factors leading to family limitation would be eliminated. A systematic survey of all practical possibilities in such a direction should be undertaken. It is, in fact, a main feature of a positive population policy that the costs of childbearing, and thus also the costs for the maintenance of the population stock, should not fall entirely upon the parents but should be shared by all alike.

To effect an increase in fertility or not literally means life or death for our people. It is only necessary to imagine for a moment what continuous depopulation would mean in order to understand that we should not hesitate in the adoption of radical social reforms if there is reason to suppose that they would considerably increase fertility and contribute toward the improvement of mental and physical growth conditions for our children, so that they might become good citizens. There is considerable unanimity in this respect in all political quarters. For our part, we have wanted to declare our point of view and our willingness to cooperate for the achievement of positive results.

Substantially the same position was taken by the National party of the extreme right (*De Nationalla*), insignificant in itself, since it then had only

160   NATION AND FAMILY

three members in the Riksdag and now has none, but interesting because it reveals the most drastic shift. There is a declaration in favor of legal security for married women in the labor market by the same party, even by the same man, who had during the previous session of the Riksdag presented a motion in exactly the opposite direction.

In so far as a married woman is employed she considers herself in many instances prohibited from bearing children. Many times she risks losing her position because in most cases she is not irreplaceable. It has also occasionally happened that an employer has summarily dismissed an employed married woman when she became pregnant in order to avoid the inconveniences resulting from interruption of her services.

It is in our opinion both proper and possible to give recourse to legal action against these abuses. There is already a law which forbids the discharge of an employee in certain cases, namely, for military service . . . and, as far as we know, no inconveniences have been suffered from this law. A law providing for prohibition of discharging married prospective mothers would not, according to our lights, meet any obstacles in principle. . . . It is the public duty to protect and shield maternity in every possible way. It would thus be an important step for the state to provide that the married woman, who wants to assume the obligations of motherhood, should not thereby risk the destruction, perhaps complete, of her whole economic existence.

Simultaneously with these party motions came the first expression of attitude on the part of any official body. The Committee on Social Housing (on which were some of the experts who had been most influential in arousing social concern about the family and population situation) dwelt at some length on "the serious demographic status of our country" in its report published in January, 1935. [*18*] "It must be stressed," the report points out, "that for any population policy just the next few decades furnish the respite. We are then still going to enjoy the numbers of persons in the productive, both in an economical and in a biological sense, middle ages born during times of greater fertility. If social measures are instituted during that critical period, they might, if successful, serve to maintain the very conditions, both demographic and economic, for the continuance of such a social population policy in the future." Economic reforms to help the families with children were brought to the forefront and complete redirection of public housing schemes toward families with children was advocated.

In the Riksdag the population question received much attention. The Standing Committee unanimously supported the demand for research and planning. The Riksdag itself voted in favor of this and declared that "the Riksdag wants forcefully to stress the necessity of a positive population policy by the state." The immediate result was a request that the Cabinet appoint

OFFICIAL PROGRAMS AND LEGISLATIVE ACTS   161

such a study and planning commission, and on May 17, 1935, the Population Commission was appointed.

MANDATE FOR THE POPULATION COMMISSION

As the Social Democratic Labor party was in power and as the revival of the population discussion had emanated from Social Democratic groups, there had been no necessity to demonstrate its opinion by any party motion in the Riksdag. This opinion was vigorously summed up, however, in the mandate to the Commission prepared by the Minister of Social Affairs:

No people with unimpaired energy and the will to live can observe such a tendency toward its own decline as is now obvious in this country and at the same time fail to undertake strong measures to combat the situation. First of all, measures will have to be instituted to encourage marriage, particularly in the younger age groups, and the bearing of children. Through wise diffusion of information, a feeling of responsibility for our people's future and welfare may be awakened in all social classes. But no matter how important this may be, the need of a large amount of socio-political intervention in order to create economic security and to improve the material welfare of our people must be frankly faced. It will be necessary to weigh different alternatives for attaining a state in which children will not be a pressing economic burden on the parents to the same extent as at present. These measures must, therefore, provide for decreasing the individual family expenses for rearing, educating, and supporting the children. The more favorable environmental conditions thereby achieved will contribute to the healthy growth of children and young people and lead to a better utilization of our human material.

After thus briefly outlining the main purposes which stand out for the investigation as demanded by the Riksdag, which investigation should be begun without further delay, I want to dwell upon some of the basic practical questions which must be considered for the achievement of our purposes.

Especially important from an ideological point of view is a comprehensive and truly vigorous educational campaign to clarify aims as well as means regarding the population question. It should be considered axiomatic that the sociological, eugenic, and ethical arguments for and against encouragement of childbearing under different circumstances be duly presented. As our social conscience protests, however, that economically weak homes should not be burdened by too many children, and that the physically or mentally unfit should not be encouraged to reproduce, such matters must not be neglected in the projected program of public instruction.

The list of social family reforms is of particular interest, as it outlined the reform proposals that were to be expected from the Commission.

Among the socio-political measures which have been proposed during the recent lively debate, and which are of more immediate practicality for the maintenance of the population, quantitatively and qualitatively, it has been suggested that taxes on married persons and on large families should be alleviated. . . .

Consideration must also be given to widening the possibilities for the care and education of children during the part of the day when the mother is gainfully employed outside the home. . . . The raising of a family is now further being discouraged when, as so often happens, an employer refuses to continue the employment of a woman upon marriage or when she becomes pregnant. . . . Ways and means of furnishing public loans or subsidies for homemaking and thus for founding a family at an earlier age should also be considered. The question of furthering the same purpose through planned and organized savings and the possibility of giving increased public aid to invalid persons or to single mothers who are the chief support of minor children are obviously steps in the same direction.

In order to ameliorate the position of mothers we have first to continue along the same road the state has already entered upon through maternal welfare measures. This will mean demands for a more effective expansion of that scheme for support and at the same time increased and improved social resources for maternal as well as for infant care.

As far as the obligatory school ages are concerned, there is reason to inquire to what extent and by what means individual educational expenses can further be decreased. In this connection, the questions of furnishing free school supplies and free school meals should be given particular attention. It also seems to me important in this same connection to develop measures for providing children and young people with efficient and rational medical care, utilizing such schemes as have proved successful both in some foreign countries and in certain endeavors in our own country.

In order to secure employment for the young people, present experience teaches that occupational training is most important. . . . The public has probably not sufficiently realized this circumstance. If the necessary means for training had existed earlier, unemployment in the younger age groups could probably have been decreased more rapidly during the present upturn of economic conditions. Under such circumstances it becomes an important duty to provide opportunity for all young people in town and country to acquire definite training in order to ensure their own economic support in the future.

It is evident that a positive population policy along the lines indicated presupposes that huge public measures be undertaken in order to guarantee the general living standard of the people at a desired level, even when children increase the size of the family. As far as housing is concerned, the point of view of simultaneously guaranteeing consumption and creating employment by encouraging specific production of family houses has gained consideration from the state for some time and especially during the recent crisis. But neither should, in my opinion, the problems of food and clothing for children be neglected, highly important as they are in the family budget.

No matter how praiseworthy specific measures may be in the different fields, no practical results can be expected without comprehensive planning embracing all forms of assistance from the community to the family. Seen from this angle, the problem becomes so wide as to include the whole task of creating economic security for the adults and proper growth opportunities for the young among our people as a whole.

OFFICIAL PROGRAMS AND LEGISLATIVE ACTS 163

The Population Commission, given this mandate to investigate the problem and construct a program, was composed of nine members, the chairman being a highly placed administrator, a politician of Conservative affiliations, and a former professor of statistics. The others were a professor of economics, who was also a member of the Riksdag; a professor of statistics; a professor of hereditary biology; a woman doctor; three members of the Riksdag representing the Conservatives, Liberals, and Social Democrats, the first being a farmer, the second a newspaper editor, and the third a factory worker; and finally the leader of the Social Democratic women's organization. For each special problem a committee of experts and representatives of various organizations and interests was set up with a member of the Population Committee serving as chairman.

In Sweden the usual procedure of such committees is to prepare reforms and propose them to the government in the form of printed publications. Then the proposals are sent out to administrations and local governments and to civic agencies and interested organizations in order to get their signed opinions. In case a change in civil or criminal law is involved, a vote on the legal aspects of the proposal has to be taken by the Supreme Legislative Council, an advisory body of high-ranking lawyers. If and when the Cabinet finally wants to submit the proposal, changed or unchanged, to the Riksdag, it has to take these opinions into consideration and publicly accept or refute them. As soon as they are delivered, these opinions become official documents and are eagerly seized upon by the press, which then widely publicizes the technical arguments on both sides of the questions. The Swedish press not only treats social questions as news but also by sustained discussion, by interviewing people, and by organizing feature articles on the various subjects it serves as an educational vehicle of tremendous importance. A large reading public is alert to these discussions. The whole training of the people in adult education and their participation in civic organizations prepare them to regard questions of social and economic policy as something more than politics. Reforms are thus not only prepared through a laborious and careful administrative process but also analyzed in detail through the critical study by the press and the people. All interested organized bodies express their views. They may in a sense be called pressure groups but their pressure is regulated and exerted in the open. It is fundamentally pressure on public opinion and its ultimate appeal is to reason.

THE COMMISSION AT WORK

The first step of the new Commission was to propose an extra census, to be taken at the end of the year 1935, between the regular censuses of 1930 and 1940. The Cabinet without delay sent this proposal as its own to the Riksdag where the proposition was carried without any opposition.

164   NATION AND FAMILY

The first report of the Commission was issued in the fall of 1935,[2] proposing a change in the status of married women in civil service positions so
that the bearing of children would be facilitated by allowing women leave of
absence with more generous pay. [1] Taking the point of view that the state
should act as a model employer and thus be a leader in humanizing labor
conditions, the Commission made the proposals with the hope that they
would influence public attitudes and thus prepare for the time when more
thoroughgoing reforms for harmonizing women's work with motherhood
could be proposed.

In 1935 also a most important step was taken toward reducing the housing
costs of families. It was initiated not by the Population Commission but by
the Committee on Social Housing. [18] Proposals for public housing schemes
for families with three or more children and state grants for rent reduction
according to size of family were published at the time the Riksdag convened.
As may be deduced from what has been related above about party consensus,
the Riksdag was ready to act favorably. The new housing bill (1935) was
the first result of the new orientation with regard to population policy.

Early in 1936, the Population Commission presented additional install-
ments of its plan, proposing free delivery care for all women, [2] state organization of maternity and infant clinics, a maternity bonus to all women
at the birth of children, and special maternity aid to destitute women as
an emergency measure. [5] In the same year the Commission proposed state
marriage loans combined with a system of planned voluntary saving. [4]
It further elaborated a scheme for the reorganization of state and local income taxation, aiming at considerable tax exemptions for families with children. [3]

In the waves of rising and falling public sympathy which were likely to
surround such a complex question as that of population, the latter scheme
caused a temporary setback. Touching practically everybody in his everyday
life, as direct taxation affects extremely low-income levels in Sweden, it
aroused the antagonism of the bachelors and the childless people who would
have to meet an increase in taxation while others were enjoying a decrease.
And it should be pointed out that the bachelors and the childless are in the
majority. So egotistically direct is the formation of opinion in regard to
taxation that from the publicly asserted opinions one could practically determine the family status of the speaker. An unfortunate similarity to the punishment taxes levied on bachelors in dictator countries accounted for the
most severe attacks by columnists, actors, and others. Even if such public
ridicule helped to kill one or two of the specific proposals, it should not be

---

[2] A brief chronological survey of the reports is given here, as the treatment under separate
headings of these and related proposals in the following chapters may not indicate the close
integration of the various phases of the Commission's work.

OFFICIAL PROGRAMS AND LEGISLATIVE ACTS 165

inferred that it was altogether unwholesome. The treatment of population problems even in these forms of publicity, year after year, served the purpose of keeping popular interest alert to the fact that here was Public Problem No. 1.

Another such reaction occurred in connection with the extra census, which shows how varied public opinion is when the complex-ridden questions of sex and family are involved. The extra census of 1935–1936 was requested in order to secure definite answers to some specific questions rarely included in the regular census: size of family, women's work, etc. The chief novelty, however, was the proposal to send enumerators to collect the census returns, filled by every fifth household, and to amplify these written answers by oral statements. The Swedish census, inaugurated in 1749, has consisted only of a balance sheet prepared from material already in the official registers as a result of the continuous, compulsory registration that has been in force since 1686. The most violent criticism was aroused by this change in administrative detail, which provided for visits to the homes by enumerators. Accusations of "invasion of privacy," "violation of domicile," and similar affronts filled the newspapers, and it was intimated that this was Nazism, communism, or something even worse. Exactly the same results are feared in countries where the enumerators are part of the customary census system, while the inauguration of a registration is thought to imply "regimentation" and "intrusion upon civic liberty." This incident is an example of the problems associated with a thoroughgoing democracy, such as Sweden. When something happens in their social sphere, all have to take their stand and articulate their attitudes. The educative process of purging public opinion of rash sentiments by referring all issues to discussion and reason requires considerable time. New experiments are therefore likely to require more educational preparation and to result in more gradual realization than in other political systems. Such things may contribute to an understanding of why the Scandinavian countries, although so uncompromisingly on their way to quite a radical social system, proceed with such conservative caution as to methods and tempo.

In 1936–1937 the Population Commission broached a new phase of its gigantic problem, proposing a thorough revision of antiquated legislation on sexual problems. This implied considerable liberalization of laws on contraception, [7] abortion, [9] sex education, [8] and sterilization. [6] In order to lay the groundwork for family reforms by public honesty on sexual matters, occasion was taken for a comprehensive discussion of principles. The Report on the Sexual Question is to be considered as the main ideological discussion of the Commission. It stresses the necessity of universal access to birth control techniques and to sex education. Curiously enough, the atmosphere was again completely calm and sympathetic.

166   NATION AND FAMILY

Soon after the publication of these new reports, the proposals contained in the previous ones were carried by the Cabinet to the Riksdag. A delay of a year is practically always to be expected as a result of the procedure described above. The proposals were all favorably accepted. Some related schemes for children's pensions and state-advanced support were also carried on the tide of public opinion. So decidedly was the social program of population policy accepted and so free from opposition were the major reforms enacted that this session has been called the "Riksdag of Mothers and Children."

In 1938 most of the previous year's proposals for sex legislation bore fruit in actual reforms enacted by the Riksdag. At the same time a new series of reports from the Commission was published. At the very beginning of the year came proposals for a social policy with regard to nutrition [10] and to clothing for children. [11] Especially in the field of nutrition a far-reaching economic program was envisaged. It involved heavy expenses, as food is such a large item in the family budget. Although the new reforms to a considerable extent implied only the transfer of already instituted subsidies to agriculture, replacing export premiums by state purchases of surplus products, they had the power again to arouse public discussion. The apparent adding of tens of millions to the expenditures for a whole series of reforms already enacted, or at least authoritatively sanctioned in the name of population policy for later enactment, caused the public once more to react unfavorably. In the adverse publicity campaign which followed, the school meal was particularly singled out for ridicule. But again the agitation died down. Moreover, the school luncheon is now partly realized in the new social ventures on which the country prides itself.

The latter part of 1938 saw the publication of various residual proposals. Two of these sought to build on reforms already provided for: legal protection for women against being dismissed when marrying or giving birth to children, legitimate or not, [12] and subsidies for nursery education. [15] They were received without great stir. There further appeared a set of more fundamental research findings about depopulation of rural areas, [13] some specific demographic studies in differential fertility, [16] and a report on the ethical implications of the population problem. [14] Then, at the end of 1938, the final report appeared, [17] embodying the working compromise at which the members of the Commission had arrived.

The unanimity of the highly varied group of Population Commission members had been considerable. In itself it testifies that here was a problem view as a national concern above politics and party quarrels, with a considerable consensus as to how it should be tackled. Differences of opinion arose only in some of the later instances, namely, in regard to the projects on nutrition, clothing, married women, and nursery education. The Con-

OFFICIAL PROGRAMS AND LEGISLATIVE ACTS 167

servative party representative published his different views on these topics, and in the case of the proposals with regard to married women he was supported by the representatives of the Liberal party and of the Employers' Association. The strength of the process of clarification within the voting mass through widespread public discussion and appeals to rationalism may be concluded from the fact that the people voiced no opposition to the certainly quite radical revisions of attitudes and laws concerning sexual problems. With regard to the later financially expensive proposals, however, unification of opinion was more difficult to obtain. That the radical intentions of the Population Commission in general obtained a victory over the conservatives was certainly an important turn of affairs. The explanation is not only that the people as a whole had moved in that direction but also that the radical members always carried the strategic positions simply because in the whole population discussion it was the radical side that formulated goals and programs. The conservative ideology was on the defensive and thus, when forced to reason things through at the conference table, either conceded the point or stalled in a dilemma.

The reactions of the general public to the work of the Population Commission are also interesting. Apparently there was fear on the part of the public of the large-scale changes proposed but also respect for the scope and coherence of the program and a realization that the reports constitute a storehouse from which blueprints for future reforms can be drawn.

Basic Principles Endorsed by the Commission

The general attitudes underlying the work of the Population Commission may be summarized at some length as they illuminate the factual and detailed description to follow. With respect to the interrelation of social and individual aspects of the population problem, the Commission took the following position:

The population question has been taken up for official investigation as a problem of social prominence. By so doing it is principally recognized that the changes within the sexual life of individuals, which have caused a problem to arise for society, do not concern the individuals alone in the sense that society remains indifferent as to what happens in this field. Still these conditions are of fundamental importance in the life happiness of individuals.

It is the opinion of the Population Commission that the latter consideration must be given primary weight in democratic cultures of the Western world. But at the same time it is also the opinion of the Commission that in this field social and individual interests are not antagonistic but converging. The Commission is not of the opinion that individual interests in and of themselves can be expected infallibly to lead to individually and socially satisfactory progress but believe that human attitudes and the social order could and should be so altered as to lead

168   NATION AND FAMILY

to individual and social harmony. The measures that should be undertaken to assure such harmony must obviously, as far as individuals are concerned, work through better instruction and education and as far as the community is concerned, through certain radically extensive changes of that society itself, particularly in its economic relations. [8]

Fixing the goal for society's interest in a population policy is, however, strictly limited by social facts themselves. Thus the possibility of an increasing population had to be discarded from the beginning.

A population increasing in the long run — even if this were considered desirable by anyone — has been assumed to be so far outside the realm of practical possibility that this alternative is not considered worthy of further discussion. [17]

The quantitative goal for the new population policy thus was formulated as follows:

The goal for Swedish population development should, according to the opinion of the Population Commission, be such a fertility as would keep population in the long run at least constant with as low mortality as possible. [17]

There are numerous reasons for choosing this goal: popular attitudes of a vague emotional character implying direct valuations, international considerations, economic advantages, and psychological implications. The Commission took account of these as follows:

Popular attitudes concerning population decline
The Commission wants to remark that this conclusion as to the quantitative goal arrived at through intellectual reflection — through a social evaluation built upon as rational a knowledge of causes and effects as possible — corresponds exactly to the immediate feeling that a citizen normally experiences when he becomes cognizant of the existing tendency in Swedish population development. This immediate attitude is founded upon the citizen's natural feeling that he is a member of a people which, unlike himself, lives through generations.

International implications
The detailed effects as to international relations are hardly possible to anticipate. . . . If Sweden is looked upon as part of a greater international body, it is evident that if the country cannot solve its own population problem, it will have decreasing possibilities of acting as an influence for peace and social culture, a role that for many reasons seems to be given us and our neighbors. . . . Looking to ourselves, it becomes just as evident that a country with a declining population will not in the long run be able to erect bars against other national groups seeking a new home or resist the pressure from more crowded countries. To a certain extent it is not desirable that such bars be erected. Immigration to our country should by and large not be considered as harmful but oftentimes rather as advantageous. Even without considering our own interests we must for the present recognize our duties to alleviate the political distress and the homelessness of

large groups. But with mass immigration imminent, there would follow certain problems which must not be concealed. The smaller our own part in the new generations becomes, the less will our culture be the dominant one.

Economic implications

Certain economic effects, dynamic in character, are apt to follow the shrinkage in population. A more regressive population development must in the somewhat longer run increase the risks of losses of investments. Also in other ways capital investments would become depressed. The result in general is to be foreseen as a slowing up of economic progress.

Basic for the still greater economic effects to appear after the present transition period, when persons in the middle-aged groups are excessive in number, will be the predominance of aged persons needing support, which characterizes a shrinking population while the predominance of young or young middle-aged persons has been typical of our society in its expansive phase.

Psychological implications

The age composition of a people, however, has also other, although much more evasive, effects. The psychological differences between the generations must show their effect not only on economic but also on political behavior and on the general atmosphere in our culture.

When passing judgment on this question it would be wrong to underevaluate the importance of the calm deliberation, the discriminating caution, and the greater practical experience which accompany aging. But already the age composition prevalent in a stationary population would give full assurance of a sufficient predominance of the age groups which possess these valuable traits in highest degree. The age composition in a declining population would on the contrary constitute a real danger that in the life of the nation there would be lacking those traits, which before all belong to youth: courage, will to sacrifice, initiative, creative imagination. [*17*]

With respect to the undesirable effects of a shrinking population as compared with a constant population there is the final point that the family itself tends to become built up in small units. All the psychologically and sociologically ascertainable relations seem to indicate that if what is commonly called family values are to persist as values, they must be related to a fairly complete family. The Population Commission asserts that three or four children in a family would lead to more harmony and happiness than is now found either in the very small or in the very large family, the assumption being that social and economic stress should not, as now, have to be regarded. Thus individual interests seem to be fairly well reconcilable with social interests in the goals for a population policy.

Constancy of population thus would best be realized in a much wider distribution of middle-sized families, the two extremes becoming less frequent. Determined more exactly in terms of individual family size this aim requires the following:

170   NATION AND FAMILY

The number of childless and child-poor marriages with 1 or 2 children must be decreased from one-half of all marriages to about one-third. The majority of the remaining marriages must have not 3 but 4 children. Despite this, 5 children must be born in a small number of marriages, if the proportion of married in the adult population cannot be increased.

Through special investigations by the Population Commission it has thus been demonstrated that not only the so-called 2-child system but also a 3-child norm is irreconcilable with the aim of keeping population constant. This means in practical terms that the nonsterile family must aim at producing more than 3 children. [8]

When family size is spoken of in such rationalistic terms, it becomes evident that the Population Commission was sanctioning birth control at the same time that it was deploring its excess. The latter part of the double postulate needed no further development and was not dealt with at any great length save for the statistical calculation of distribution of children per family under different assumptions of fertility. The former position was the more difficult one to get into verbalized public opinion and so became one of the fundamental contributions of the Commission. As instances are rare in which official bodies take a clear stand in defense of revised sex attitudes, some verbatim quotations may be given:

Taking the long view, the solution of the population problem must be sought in the birth of normally large numbers of children by couples in all social classes. If it is desired to apply any scheme of public education to more positive family attitudes and at the same time to afford space to important social improvements for children . . . it is necessary that *the starting point be the principle of voluntary parenthood, conscious of responsibility for one's own and others' welfare.*

The first necessity was to bring into the open the whole complex of social questions which have long been taboo because of their connection with individual sex problems.

The Commission notes that it is particularly important that sexual problems be discussed more sincerely and from a more practical standpoint in civic discussions than has been the case up to now. It is especially true that the question as to the extent and valuation of consciously practiced birth control has not usually been discussed with the frankness and seriousness that it warrants.

The Commission feels that in the future this problem should not be avoided through evasive and generalized terms. The lack of honesty which has characterized the publicly sustained and especially the official attitude is not the least danger to the morality of our people. The Commission has seen, to be sure, particularly on the part of youth a beginning of a tendency toward greater frankness and seriousness in the discussion of this question as in the discussion of sex problems in general. But this trend toward a better state of public opinion has not yet fully percolated through the population in general. [8]

OFFICIAL PROGRAMS AND LEGISLATIVE ACTS 171

The public sanction of birth control in positive terms was one of the most urgent tasks for the Population Commission.

The level of fertility existing at present in Sweden testifies that birth control is being practiced in the vast majority of cases inside marriage and in extra-marital relations of a common-law marriage type. It is self-evident that birth control is also used in most other sex relations, such as promiscuous extramarital intercourse. In the majority of cases the method is one of prevention of conception, that being the connotation in which the term birth control is used here thus excluding abortion as a means for limitation of births.

On rationalization in sex attitudes the Commission took the following position:

The direct reason for the fall in the birth rate has been shown to be principally the more and more extensive and intensified birth control consciously practiced within the greater part of the population. The population crisis is, therefore, caused by a change on the part of the individuals themselves in their attitude toward procreation. This change is usually expressed in the following way: Sex life used to be without deliberation as to procreation, whereas at present sex life has entered the area of intellectually governed life in that intercourse is accompanied by deliberation and a decision as to whether procreation is intended or not. As far as bearing of children is concerned, sex life has become rationalized.

When this judgment is passed it ought to be emphasized, in order to avoid misunderstanding, that sex life already had been rationalized to a great extent by having individuals arrange it within a monogamic, durable, and personal union. When sexual relations in the order of marriage have been sanctioned by society, there is not only an acceptance but also an approval of and demand for some such rationalization of sex life. From a general cultural standpoint, the sexual urge may carry great possibilities of happiness for individuals, but only if it is to a certain extent exercised according to mores within the society and according to moral norms upheld by the people. Sexual impulses, totally unrestrained by volitional forces, will, on the contrary, become judged by society as hostile to life and happiness. One of the hardest problems of human life is to strike the right balance between instinct and culture. The spread of consciously practiced birth control during the last two generations as here discussed thus implies a growing rationalization of sex life only in so far as the relationship between sex intercourse and reproduction is concerned.

Notice, however, should be taken of the fact that this conception of the historical development has only relative validity. There are reasons for supposing that birth control was consciously practiced in other periods before the recent fall in the birth rate. The change is a quantitative one. Birth control as such is not new, but it is being used by more and more individuals and more and more intensively.

From the point of view of the principle involved the following consideration is important: In the olden days sex intercourse may have been just as rationally considered as far as reproduction was concerned as it is today, but in this rational

172   NATION AND FAMILY

process the reasons against childbearing may not have been so strong or may not have been considered so strong as to exercise an influence on fertility. During the last century, with rapidly proceeding industrialization and the migration from agricultural occupations to industrial occupations, together with urbanization generally, on the one hand, and with the general increase in the standard of living and culture and raised demands in child welfare, on the other hand, children have become less valuable in the productive process or in the household. At the same time, the costs of bringing up and educating children falling upon the individual family have been considerably increased. The basis for what was rational thus was a different one.

As far as the judging of such a rationalization of the sex life in its relation to reproduction is concerned, many viewpoints may be considered, but, according to the opinion of the Commission any one-sided view runs the danger of being superficial.

On the one hand, we have to realize that the reduced fertility up to a certain point has had consequences which must be regarded as beneficial. Large families, especially in the poorer classes, had to endure need and privation. The parents often had to neglect the care and the education of the children. Food and proper housing were often lacking. Physical and mental health of mothers and children suffered. Thus a check in infant mortality came chiefly through intentionally decreasing the number of children born. Through the conscious practice of birth control it has further become possible to space the birth of children in such a way as to promote the health and growth of the children themselves, the strength of the mother, and the welfare of the whole family. If this conscious birth control is practiced in the proper way and to the proper extent, it may be considered as veritable cultural progress for many reasons, some of which are suggested.

On the other hand, grave anxiety is found in many quarters as to whether a people which has generally placed reproduction under the reign of calculating reason can survive through the ages. In so far as we feel that a people's continued survival is of value, we must fear that birth control would be harmful and should thus be condemned as dangerous to life in its innermost sense. In our work for creating a better society in the future through wisdom, work, and sacrifice, we all count upon the survival of our nation. Otherwise our efforts, except the narrowest egotistical ones, would be wasted.

The risk is that immediate needs be considered so pressing as not to permit enough births to reproduce the living generation in the next generation. It cannot be denied that the trend now present points in exactly this direction. But the question which should be further posed is whether this consequence of the rationalization of reproduction is really necessary or whether it is not due to socially and individually faulty adjustment, which in turn may be partly due to a passing reaction . . . against earlier conditions. The extreme limitation of the birth rate which now threatens the people's very existence is, however, in the long run certainly a ground for less and not more happiness within the families, that is, if there need not be sufficient reasons for such a limitation. [8]

The Commission then discussed the need for coupling educational and economic measures in reforming society for the benefit of children.

OFFICIAL PROGRAMS AND LEGISLATIVE ACTS   173

This means that the tendency itself could be reversed if certain economic and social reforms could be instituted partly to decrease the existing reasons for extreme limitation in individual families and partly to enlighten people as to their own real interests and to give them a healthier and more positive attitude toward the family. All of our population policies strive, in the last analysis, toward measures along these two lines.

These two types of remedial means will be followed in their many ramifications. The Population Commission realized the importance of relating them not only as parallel influences working in the same direction but also as mutually insuring each other. Only economic reforms could make it defensible to encourage the morale of the middle-sized family through education, and only education could prepare the political soil for obtaining social reforms.

An important observation is the following: In the lower population strata, where young people have experienced at close quarters the effects of very large families, and where they have thought, rightly or wrongly, that attempts have been made through the anticontraceptive law and other measures with corresponding aims to keep the lower social classes in ignorance of reliable preventive methods no longer prevalent in the higher social classes, great mistrust has been entertained toward all social population policy. Only when the whole of this field has been swept clean; when the rightfulness of birth control has been openly recognized in different political, ideological, and religious quarters; when in connection therewith the reliability of the applied technique itself has been recognized as a public health concern; when all efforts to hinder sound education on this subject have been liquidated; and when the trade in contraceptives has been brought into the open will a true groundwork have been created among the young people in all social classes for a new, sincerely endorsed, positive attitude toward a population policy, which is of so vital importance for both family and people. [8]

When all of its work was concluded, the Population Commission prepared a Final Report. In order to show the spirit in which the work was carried forward the concluding passages of that report may be quoted, again utilizing the solemnly phrased generalities rather than the practical policies of which the remaining chapters will show abundant evidence.

There is probably no one who does not want the Swedish people themselves to solve their own economic and cultural problems of the future. To adopt a population policy founded upon continued and increasing immigration would be the same as giving up the fundamental assumption of our positive population policy, namely the maintenance of the Swedish people and the Swedish culture.

Not of least importance in our day is the assertion that the Swedish people have a valuable inheritance of culture to guard. We are fortunate enough to have within boundaries delimited by nature a people of favorable endowment for successful cooperation, thanks to homogeneity of language, religion, and cultural traditions. There is today in Sweden a national folk communion which cuts through the social classes and which, in spite of all remaining deficiencies, is a good foundation for the development of the future. Everybody has the feeling that it is worth while to work for our people's future. If we are allowed to work in peace in our own Swedish way, we may even accomplish something of significance for the world at large in times to come. But a sufficiently large population is one of the most important presuppositions for such an undisturbed development. Without this, sooner or later, we may have such a large immigration that unity will be endangered and the Swedish tradition broken. Anyone who knows young people will recognize that this reasoning meets with understanding. It would certainly be a great mistake to propagandize for such viewpoints in a society which could not assure parents and children work and a self-respecting subsistence. But, in so far as these are assured, it would also be just as great a mistake not to capitalize upon the viewpoints specified.

During the course of its work, the Population Commission has gained a deep understanding of the economic worries of the masses of the Swedish people and an insight into many social evils still existing in Sweden. The Commission also understands that many people seriously hesitate to bring children into the world in these disturbed and threatening times. Facing not only economic and social insecurity but also the alarming war scares constantly before them, they have a pessimistic attitude toward life in general. But in spite of this no people and no nation, today as in times past, can survive and be of service to humanity if they do not have faith in the future and in the ultimate victory of the forces for good. Neither a people nor an individual should rely upon the fatalistic belief that whatever happens is inevitable and predestined. As far as the population question is concerned, it is just as true that it is in our power to work changes as it is true that no one should fool himself that the trend will turn in a favorable direction unless such special measures are adopted. Nothing can be more foolish than such a belief and nothing more dangerous than such a comfortable optimism. It is important for our people to be conscious of the still more severe population crisis which is pending. Even if the time is not ripe as yet for the radical social reforms which soon will become required by such a crisis, social enlightenment on the population question should be pushed so that public opinion may be further informed and in order that when the decrease in population is fully under way, there may not be an atmosphere of panic with less deliberate or even desperate measures undertaken.

The Population Commission does not believe in its own competency to answer the question as to whether within our people the will to life is sufficiently strong on which to build a general educational program in order to create a really positive attitude toward the family, both on the part of the individual and in society as a basis for a policy of family welfare. This fateful question can only be answered finally in the development of society itself and of the nation during generations to come. It has, however, fallen as a duty on our generation to attempt to lead the development of Swedish population in such a direction that the answer will be in the affirmative and that the future of our people will be assured. [*17*]

References

Population Commission

1. Unpublished report on Married Women in Civil Service, 1935.
2. Report on Maternity Care. *Betänkande angående förlossningsvården och barnmorskeväsendet samt förebyggande mödra-och barnavård.* S.O.U. 1936:12.
3. Report on Family Taxation. *Betänkande angående familjebeskattningen.* S.O.U. 1936:13.
4. Report on Planned Saving and Homemaking Loans. *Betänkande angående dels planmässigt sparande och dels statliga bosättningslån.* S.O.U. 1936:14.
5. Report on Maternity Bonus and Maternity Aid. *Betänkande angående moderskapspenning och mödrahjälp.* S.O.U. 1936:15.
6. Report on Sterilization. *Betäkande angående sterilisering.* S.O.U. 1936:46.
7. Report on Repeal of the Anticontraceptive Law. *Yttrande angående revision av 18 kap. 13 § Strafflagen m.m.* S.O.U. 1936:51
8. Report on the Sexual Question. *Betänkande i sexualfrågan.* S.O.U. 1936:59.
9. Report on Abortion. *Yttrande i abortfrågan.* S.O.U. 1937:6.
10. Report on Nutrition. *Betänkande i näringsfrågen.* S.O.U. 1938:6.
11. Report on Clothing, etc. *Betänkande angående barnbeklädnadsbidrag m.m.* S.O.U. 1938:7.
12. Report on Married Women. *Betänkande angående förvärvsarbetande kvinnors rättsliga ställning vid äktenskap och barnsbörd.* S.O.U. 1938:13.
13. Report on Rural Depopulation. *Betänkande angående "landsbygdens avfolkning."* S.O.U. 1938:15.
14. Report on the Ethical Aspect of the Population Question. *Yttrande med etiska synpunkter på befolkningsfrågan.* S.O.U. 1938:19.
15. Report on Day Nurseries, etc. *Betänkande angående barnkrubbor och sommarkolonier m.m.* S.O.U. 1938:20.
16. Report on Demographic Investigations. *Betänkande med vissa demografiska utredningar.* S.O.U. 1938:24.
17. Final Report. *Slutbetänkande.* S.O.U. 1938:57.

Committee on Social Housing

18. *Betänkande med förslag rörande lån årliga bidrag av statsmedel för främjande av bostadsförsörjning för mindre bemedlade barnrika familjer.* S.O.U. 1935:2.

[19]

The development of the Swedish welfare state in a comparative perspective

The welfare state in Sweden emerged at a relatively late stage but developed rapidly after the Second World War. Its distinguishing characteristics are social programmes covering citizens at high and middle income levels as well as low income earners, an integration between social policy and labour market participation, and a heavy emphasis on maintaining full employment. The development of the Swedish welfare state has been intimately related to political currents in the country.

Ideas and guiding principles

It is probably fair to say that the Swedish welfare state has developed through a series of political compromises and piecemeal solutions to practical problems rather than as the result of ideological blueprints within the Social Democratic Party, which came to stay in government for some half a century. Nevertheless, over the years a number of guiding principles were developed and these have come to put their mark on the institutional structures of the Swedish welfare state.

The Minister of Social Affairs who did much of the groundwork for the Swedish welfare state or *folkhem* (People's Home) was Gustav Möller, who was in office for much of the period from 1924 until 1951. The abolition of poverty was a central goal during this period of development, and was emphasized by Möller in his pronouncement (made in the 1930s) that, given Sweden's powers of production, there could be no justifiable reason for any Swedish citizen to suffer need. The only possible explanations for poverty continuing to exist in Sweden were, according to Möller, the lack of the will to combat it or poor organisation.

Another of the main guiding principles in the development of social policy in Sweden was that the stigmatising means test, associated with the Poor Law that dated back to 1763, should be abolished. It was a central conviction that benefits should be given as a universal right, not as a charity. The political goal was thus the gradual marginalisation of means testing; social insurance was seen as one of the important ways of achieving this goal.

The Social Democrats' most pressing social policy aim was thus the creation of a system of social insurance which gave a real sense of security to the citizens of the country. The system they strove to achieve would ensure security against hardship in the case of accident, illness, unemployment, and in old age.

The Swedish system of social insurance came to be developed according to the principle of *people's insurance*. In other words, it took the form of overarching programmes which did not separate occupational groups and which covered all citizens, rather than only low income earners. In line with the Social Democrats' aim to do away with means testing and to distance policies from principles associated with the old Poor Law, flat-rate benefits were seen, in the early stages, as reasonable and desirable. During the postwar period, however, salaried employees in particular came to demand benefits which were related to previous levels of income. The political response to these demands was to develop income-related benefits within the framework of existing universal programmes, something which deterred the better-off from creating separate systems of their own. The principle of universality and equality in social insurance, with standards high enough to satisfy high income earners, was applied in the social services, including the health services.

Another important guideline for the development of Swedish social policy has been the stress on full employment and economic growth and efficiency. Providing a job for everybody able to work was seen not only as the best way of preventing poverty and reducing social inequalities but also as a way of improving overall standards of living and efficiency in the country. The fact that income-related benefit levels made social protection dependent on work participation tended to contribute to work incentives, which naturally benefitted the Swedish economy as a whole.

The reduction of inequality has long been one of the explicit goals of social, fiscal and economic policies in Sweden. This goal was seen as easier to achieve in an environment where all those able to work were actually working, where resources were growing, and where all citizens shared similar rights within the welfare state programmes and had the same access to publicly provided education, health and social services of high standard.

The values which have been of importance for the development of the Swedish welfare state were later to be summarised in the lofty formulations of the Social Services Act of 1982 *(Socialtjänstlag)*, where the goals are defined as follows: "Public social services are to be established on the basis of democracy and solidarity, with view to promoting economic and social security, equality of living conditions, and active participation in community life. ... Social services are to be based on respect for the self-determination and privacy of the individual."

Prewar developments

In the 1920s, Sweden was still largely a rural and relatively poor country. In 1929, its gross domestic product (GDP) per head of population ranked about tenth among western nations, after those of the United States, Switzerland, Belgium, Australia, Canada, the United Kingdom, the Netherlands, France and Denmark. At that time, social insurance programmes protecting citizens in old age and in the case of sickness, work accidents and unemployment had already been legislated in Germany, Austria, Belgium, the Netherlands, the United Kingdom, Ireland and Belgium. In

Sweden, although there was a tradition of social welfare services which goes back to mediaeval times, social insurance programmes covered only state subsidies to voluntary sickness insurance schemes with relatively low coverage in the population and low income replacement levels (1891), a basic public pensions system (1913), and compulsory work accident insurance (1916).

In the early stages, the development of social insurance in Sweden came to diverge from the German and continental European pattern. The latter is characterised both by income-related benefits and separate programmes for different occupational categories, initially only industrial workers. Sweden came instead to follow the British pattern, with low flat-rate benefits but a wide coverage in the population. The basic pension system, legislated in 1913 and covering practically the whole population, was the first major step in this direction.

During the economic difficulties of the 1920s, the social policy debate in Sweden focused on measures to combat unemployment. Central issues here were (i) whether the unemployed should be put into work projects at below market wages and whether the unemployed could be requested to accept work in workplaces with ongoing strikes, or (ii) whether work projects for the unemployed should be organised on normal market wages and terms. Two Social Democratic minority governments which favoured the second alternative were forced to resign over these issues (1923 and 1926).

In 1932, in the trough of the Great Depression, the Social Democrats and the small Communist Party for the first time won a narrow majority in the direct elections to the second chamber of the *Riksdag* (Parliament). A Social Democratic government was formed as a result. This government then reached an understanding with the Agrarian (later Centre) Party in the so-called "Cow Deal". According to this agreement, support for agriculture was traded in return for support for policies of social reform. The combatting of unemployment became the centrepiece of the policies of the new government. This full employment policy came to form the basis for a close future cooperation between the government and LO, the Swedish Trade Union Confederation for blue-collar workers (the largest such confederation in the country).

During the period up to the Second World War, moves towards the gradual extension of other forms of social protection were added to the fight against unemployment. An unemployment insurance scheme which was state-supported and union-based was introduced in 1934 and pensions were later improved somewhat (1937). The development of a Swedish family policy involving measures to help families with children also dates from this period. In line with attempts to reduce social inequalities, this policy aimed to promote financial equality both between families with children and those without. It was also hoped that such measures would help to increase Sweden's low birth rate.

5

A variety of new provisions, such as home-furnishing loans, subsidies for housing construction, housewives' vacations and school health programmes, were developed during this period. Benefits and medical services for mothers and young children were introduced, public medical and dental services were extended, abortion legislation was passed, and an annual two-week paid vacation period was legislated in 1938. Thus, these prewar years gave rise to a wide number of provisions which aimed to counter poverty and social inequalities. It was, however, only in the years after the Second World War that the development of the Swedish welfare state came to gather speed.

Postwar policies. Full employment and economic efficiency

In 1945, the wartime four-party coalition government was replaced by a Social Democratic one. The expansion of the Swedish welfare state during the postwar years was based on the view that full employment was the very foundation of the welfare state and essential as a preventive social policy. The social protection of citizens was to be achieved through a combination of labour market policies, social insurance, social services and an efficient economy able to compete on international export markets.

In the postwar years, however, low levels of unemployment were generally linked with high inflation rates. The Swedish solution to the problem of combining full employment with stable prices was developed by Gösta

Rehn and Rudolf Meidner of the LO staff. The so-called Rehn-Meidner model was based on the assumption that full employment cannot be created through the maintenance of high general demand in the economy, since this will foment inflation. Since the level of demand generally varies between different sectors of the economy, government policy should instead be directed towards maintaining a moderate overall demand. A relatively restrictive economic policy should be combined with a selective labour market policy, designed to handle the pockets of unemployment that would arise. This type of "active labour market policy" would involve not only work projects for the unemployed but also the stimulation of geographical and occupational mobility and the retraining of the labour force. The aim of this "work strategy" against unemployment was thus to put the unemployed not on the dole but rather back into work on market wages.

LO developed the so-called "solidaristic wages policy", according to which wages were to be determined by the nature of the job rather than by the profitability of the company, and wage differentials were to be reduced. In the mid-1950s, economy-wide wage bargaining was introduced. This combination of a solidaristic wages policy and economy-wide wage bargaining put strong pressure on the least profitable areas of the economy, while the more efficient sectors of industry could retain relatively high profits to be used for investment. The active labour market policy thus helped to

6

increase efficiency and maintain full employment in Sweden.

Social reforms

On the basis of the work of parliamentary commissions, social insurance systems were reformed and extended in the postwar years. In the changed political climate, social policy reforms generally had wide political support. These reforms included free school meals, introduced in 1946, and universal child allowances (1947). In 1948, the low, flat-rate pension levels were raised and income testing was abolished. The reform of the sickness insurance system led to much debate, both within and between the political parties, about the principle of flat-rate benefits. The outcome was a universal, compulsory health insurance system with income-related benefits which protected against loss of income. This came into force in 1955. The state-supported yet union-based unemployment insurance system was, however, retained.

Basic pensions became index-linked in 1951. The proposal to reform the pension system and to introduce an income-related superannuation generated a major political struggle in the 1950s, which led to the break up of the Social Democratic-Agrarian coalition government (1951—57), a national referendum and an extra parliamentary election (1958), before the proposal was finally passed in 1959 with a one-vote parliamentary majority.

In 1962, the legislation and administration of

basic pensions *(folkpension)*, national supplementary pensions *(ATP)*, health insurance and the parental insurance system were coordinated under the terms of the National Insurance Act *(Lag om allmän försäkring)*.

As a result of the alterations to the sickness and pensions programmes legislated during the second half of the 1950s, Swedish social insurance came to combine the British principle of universal coverage with the Continental principle of income-related benefits. The general raising of benefit levels during the postwar years came to relegate means-tested social assistance to a marginal position in terms of relative expenditure. In the Swedish welfare state, the right to most benefits is thus shared by all citizens, not only the poor. As a consequence, in spite of the very high levels of taxation, Swedish welfare state policies have tended to get relatively strong political support, something which was to become evident during the political debates on cutbacks which took place during the 1980s.

The financing of Swedish social insurance programmes has changed over the years. In the early 1950s the major part of the financing came from the insured themselves, while pensions, on the other hand, were largely financed from central government revenue. Contributions by insured employees were abolished in 1974 and the main sources of financing have since then been employers' payroll taxes and central government revenue.

A housing policy has been one of the central elements of Swedish social policy since relatively early on, when it was regarded as one of the means of abolishing poverty and promoting social equality. In the 1940s, government loans for housing construction at guaranteed rates of interest had been introduced, as were rent controls and rent allowances for pensioners and for large families. By the 1960s, however, increasing urbanisation had generated an acute housing shortage. To counteract this, in the ten-year period following the mid-1960s, no fewer than one million new apartments were constructed by local public housing authorities as part of the so-called Million Programme.

The 1960s saw the beginning of a rapid expansion of public sector social services, to a considerable extent financed through the introduction of indirect taxation (sales tax) and increases in proportional local taxes. This expansion was especially marked in the areas of education and health care. A comprehensive school system was legislated in 1962 and a major expansion of the county councils' medical and health care services and of the municipal social services was carried out during this decade.

The expansion of social insurance pro-grammes continued in the 1970s. Thus, in 1973 unemployment benefits were introduced for those not covered for unemployment insurance through membership of a trade union. In 1974, sickness benefits were made taxable, with a 90% net replacement rate,

while the health insurance system came also to include dental care. As part of the government's policy to encourage equality of opportunity between the sexes, a parental insurance available to both fathers and mothers for a six-month period after the birth of a child was introduced in 1974 and the building of day care centres and pre-schools expanded rapidly. During the postwar period annual paid vacations for employees were gradually lengthened and have been five weeks since 1978.

Further major legislation was passed in the 1980s. 1982 saw the new Social Services Act come into force followed, in 1983, by a new Health and Medical Care Act *(Hälso- och sjukvårdslag)*, an enabling act which emphasises the overall goal of good health and medical care on equal terms for the entire population.

The 1980s also witnessed the extension of the parental insurance system, with parents in 1990 entitled to a total of 450 days' parental leave between them. In 1989, the net replacement rates in unemployment insurance were raised to 90% and waiting days were abolished. (For more detailed information, see publications listed under **Further reading**, page 13.)

Employment policy

During the postwar period the role of the Labour Market Board *(Arbetsmarknads-styrelsen, AMS)*, created in 1948 and the institution in charge of Sweden's characteristic active labour market policy,

8

Table 1. Total expenditures on labour market policies as percent of GDP, expenditures on active labour market measures, and unemployment in 18 OECD countries, 1987

		Total expenditures on labour market policies as % of GDP	Of which "active" measures (%)	Unemployment as % of labour force
1	Ireland	5.1	28	17.5
2	Denmark	5.0	23	7.8
3	Belgium	4.4	25	11.0
4	Netherlands	4.0	28	9.6
5	France	3.1	24	10.5
6	Sweden	2.7	70	1.9
7	United Kingdom	2.6	35	10.2
8	Finland	2.4	32	5.0
9	Germany	2.3	42	6.2
10	Canada	2.2	25	8.8
11	New Zealand	1.7	38	4.1
12	Australia	1.5	21	8.0
13	Austria	1.5	28	3.8
14	Italy	1.3	36	11.2
15	USA	0.8	29	6.1
16	Norway	0.8	54	2.1
17	Japan	0.6	29	2.8
18	Switzerland	0.4	43	0.7

was strengthened. Compared with other countries, Sweden spends a much larger proportion of its labour market policy expenditure on "active" programmes (job creation, training, etc) than on "passive" measures (unemployment benefits or early retirement). OECD data indicate that in 1987 Sweden spent about the same proportion of its GDP on labour market policies as France and the United Kingdom. However, in contrast to the latter countries, Swedish expenditures were directed largely to active measures and helped to generate a much lower level of open unemployment than in France or the United Kingdom. Ireland, Denmark, Belgium and the Netherlands spent proportionally far more on labour market policies than Sweden, but a much smaller proportion on active measures and had considerably higher levels of unemployment (see Table 1).

The Swedish welfare state and its commitment to full employment has generated an especially high rate of labour force participation among women. In the late 1980s, close to 80 per cent of all women aged 15—64 years were working, the highest proportion among the OECD countries. Since the 1960s, women have increasingly found employment in the public sector, which in the 1980s employed about one third of the total labour force. Because of female participation in the labour market, and because unemployment is low, working time per capita, that is per person in the population, is actually higher in Sweden than in many other OECD countries, in spite of the long paid vacation and the many provisions made by the social insurance programmes for employees to stay off work for a variety of reasons.

Income inequality and growth

In the 1930s and 1940s, the differences in disposable household incomes in Sweden tended to decrease, largely as a result of diminishing levels of unemployment and a shrinking agricultural population. During the 1950s and up to the mid-1960s, this development tapered off. However, from the mid-1960s to the early 1980s the reduction in income inequalities accelerated again.

While income transfers in the Swedish welfare state have not generally been selective in the sense of being directed only to the poor, they have nevertheless been of such a large volume that the distribution of gross income (including, for instance, child allowance), has become considerably less unequal than that of factor income. Up to the end of the 1980s, the taxation system, primarily the progressive state tax, contributed to making disposable incomes less unequal than gross income.

The measures adopted in Sweden to achieve a relatively low degree of economic inequality may also be of relevance for the amount of inequality existing in other areas of society. Thus, for example, health differences between socio-economic classes appear to be somewhat smaller in Sweden than in Britain.

International perspective

Around 1980, the degree of inequality in disposable household income (after transfers and taxes, equivalenced for household size), differed considerably between the twelve western countries for which good comparative data are available. Inequalities in disposable income were especially large in Israel and the USA, and were also considerable in France, the Netherlands, Canada, Australia and Switzerland. The United Kingdom and the Federal Republic of Germany had higher levels of income inequality than the Nordic countries, among which Sweden at this time had the lowest levels (see Table 2).

OECD figures indicate that since 1960 economic growth (changes in the gross domestic product per capita) in Sweden has come close to the average of the 18 countries listed in Table 1. Changes in the Swedish standard of living in terms of average purchasing power have also followed those of other wealthy countries.

In comparison with other western countries, the Swedish welfare state has been characterised during the postwar period by the fact that it gives **all** citizens basic protection and some measure of income security in difficult circumstances. On the other hand, during the first decades of the postwar period, Swedish social insurance

10

Table 2. Inequality in distribution of
disposable household income (equivalenced) in twelve countries around 1980
(Gini index x 100)*

	Gini
Israel	33.3
USA	32.4
France	30.9
Netherlands	30.6
Canada	29.8
Australia	29.7
Switzerland	29.6
United Kingdom	27.6
Germany	26.2
Norway	23.8
Finland	22.5
Sweden	20.2

* The Gini index is a measure of income inequality.

programmes were not particularly generous
in terms of the amount of money received by
the individual.

In 1960, for example, the basic pension
system covering all residents paid pensions
which corresponded to about one third of the
net wage of an industrial worker. At that
time, pension levels for industrial workers
were higher in Austria, Belgium, Denmark,
Finland, France, Germany, Italy, the
Netherlands, New Zealand, and the United
States. It was only with the maturation of its
supplementary pension scheme in the 1980s
that Sweden came to have the highest
pension levels for workers. In the field of
sickness insurance, income replacement was
somewhat higher in Germany, Austria and
Norway than in Sweden in the 1980s. As for
unemployment insurance, it was not until the
late 1980s that Sweden came to have higher
replacement levels than those of many other

western countries. Thus, it is primarily when
we consider the wide range of Swedish
social programmes and the longstanding
commitment to full employment that the
distinctiveness of the Swedish welfare state
becomes apparent.

Increasing controversy

During the 1960s and 1970s, the expansion
of the welfare state and the public sector as
well as the maintenance of full employment
were policies largely accepted and supported
by all the major political parties in Sweden.
The non-socialist coalition governments
which were in power 1976—1982 accordingly maintained welfare programmes and
made major economic commitments to
safeguard full employment in the difficult
economic situation following the international recession in the wake of the oil
crises of 1973 and 1979. As a result of the
deteriorating economic situation and external
balances, the non-socialist governments in
the early 1980s saw themselves forced to
propose some cutbacks in social insurance
programmes, a factor which contributed to
their defeat in the 1982 elections.

Over recent years, against internationally
very high rates of unemployment and
increasing tensions on the Swedish labour
market, the welfare state has become a
controversial issue, in Sweden as elsewhere.
The welfare state, the public sector and the
high levels of taxation have been subjected to
sustained attacks by different political
parties, groups within the business world and
academics.

11

It has thus been argued over the past few years that the welfare state distorts the functioning of markets and personal incentives, thereby generating low work intensity, a black economy, the search for tax loopholes, etc. These distortions have been held to decrease the rate of economic growth. A major tax reform, legislated in 1990, comes into force in January 1991. This reduces rates of marginal taxation, abolishes state income tax for most employed people and increases the number of goods and services upon which value-added tax is payable.

On a political level it has also been argued in recent years that welfare state policies have negative consequences for the role of the family, for freedom of choice and for the independence of the individual in relation to the State. There has been much discussion of the potential need for alternative solutions to those traditionally adopted in Sweden. Thus, in the early 1990s, the present and future shape of the Swedish welfare state is generating intense debate.

References

Elmér, Åke: *Svensk socialpolitik*. Liber, Stockholm 1989

Heckscher, Gunnar: *The Welfare State and Beyond. Success and Problems in Scandinavia.* University of Minnesota Press, Minneapolis 1984

Korpi, Walter: *The Working Class in Welfare Capitalism. Work, Unions and Politics in Sweden.* Routledge, London 1978

Korpi, Walter: *The Democratic Class Struggle*. Routledge, London 1983

Lindbeck, Assar: "Consequences of the advanced welfare state". *World Economy* Vol. 11 (March) 1988, pp. 19—37

Lindbeck, Assar: "Individual freedom and welfare state policy". *European Economic Review* Vol. 32 (March), pp. 295—318

Olson, Sven: "Sweden" in Flora, P: *Growth to Limits. The Western European Welfare States since World War II*. pp. 1—16. De Gruyter, Berlin & New York 1986

Vågerö, Denny and Lundberg, Olle: "Health inequalities in Britain and Sweden". *The Lancet* (July 1) London 1989

OECD *Employment Outlook* (September) 1988

OECD *Economic Outlook* (No. 46, December) 1989

OECD *National Accounts 1960—1988* (Vol. 1) 1990

Part III
Other Worlds

[20]

Catherine Jones

Hong Kong, Singapore, South Korea and Taiwan: Oikonomic Welfare States[1]

THE 'LITTLE TIGERS'' REPUTATION AMONGST WESTERNERS (and for that matter with the Japanese) is rich in negatives. Exploitative, unprincipled, uncontrolled; minimalist on welfare, maximalist on profit: the unacceptable face of capitalism indeed, to those feeling themselves on the receiving end of the Tigers' determination to compete and get rich quick. Nevertheless the image is misleading. These are no chance miracles of laissez-faire capitalism unbound. On the contrary, the rise 'from nowhere' to world trading notoriety has to an extent been contrived in every case.

Moreover it has been contrived in a particular fashion: via the 'household management'[2] of each national 'household economy' (*oikos* in classical Greek), with the aid (amongst other things) of 'Western-style' social services. Hence the expression 'Oikonomic welfare states'. This paper looks first at some of the explanatory characteristics (see Table 1), before commenting (see Table 2) on the Tigers as welfare states.

MOTIVATION, OPPORTUNITY

They grew because they were pushed. This is scarcely a sufficient explanation of the speed of take-off and rates of economic growth

---

[1] Ideas presented in this paper stem from researches originally conducted into social policy development in Hong Kong (ESRC personal research grant 1984–85). C. Jones, *Promoting Prosperity: The Hong Kong Way of Social Policy*, Hong Kong, Chinese University Press, 1990.

[2] Literally, Aristotle's 'household management' style of government, e.g., E. Barker (trans. and ed.), *The Politics of Aristotle*, Oxford, Clarendon Press, 1946, p. 12: 'Rule over wife and children, and over the household generally, is a...kind of rule, which we have called by the name of household management. Here the rule is either exercised in the interest of the ruled or for the attainment of some advantage common to both ruler and ruled.'

TABLE 1: 'Pacific Challenge'

	HONG KONG	SINGAPORE	SOUTH KOREA	TAIWAN	JAPAN
Population (millions)	5.7	2.6	42.6	19.8	122.6
GNP (US$m. 1986)	37,360	19,160	98,370	72,621	1,559,720
GNP per capita	6,720	7,410	2,370	3,750	12,850
Percentage unemployed	1.7 (87)	4.2 (86)	3.8 (86)	2.2 (86)	2.8 (87)
Percentage labour force in agriculture					
1960	7.8	7.5	66.4	56.0	32.9
1970	4.3	3.4	51.0	35.0	19.0
1986	1.8	0.9 (87)	22.7	15.3	8.0 (87)
Percentage labour force in industry					
1960	51.6	23.0	9.3	11.0	29.5
1970	54.8	30.3	20.1	16.0	34.5
Percentage labour force in manufacturing					
1986	35.8	26.7	23.7	35.0 (87)	23.4
GDP annual average growth					
1965 – 80	8.5	10.4	9.5	10.0	6.3
1970 – 77	8.0	8.6	9.9	7.7	5.0
1980 – 86	6.0	5.3	8.2	7.2	3.7
Percentage population					
0 – 14	23.1 (86)	23.4 (87)	29.9 (85)	29.3 (86)	20.0 (88)
60 +	11.5	8.2	6.8	8.3	16.0
Government expenditure as percentage GNP (86 – 7)	18.29	33.6*	25.11	30.33	27.48
Percentage Government expenditure					
Defence/L&O	13.1	18.0	32.8	35.3	6.5
Education	18.3	11.4	20.6	20.5	8.6
Social security	5.8**	1.4	5.4	18.2**	18.3
Health care	9.7	3.0	2.6	2.2	17.0 (80)
Housing	11.9	8.1			

*The remainder of this column has been computed from material contained in *Singapore 1988*.
**Includes 'social welfare'

SOURCES
Encyclopaedia Britannica, *Britannica Book of the Year*, 1990. Tai, Hung-chao (ed.), *Confucianism and Economic Development: An Oriental Alternative?*, Washington, Washington Inst. Press, 1989.

TABLE 2: 'Gang' Social Service Provision as of 1989

SERVICE	HONG KONG	SINGAPORE	SOUTH KOREA	TAIWAN
SOCIAL SECURITY	Statutory public assistance. Spec. Allowances (indexed) for elderly/disabled.	Discret. pub. assistance. Central Provident Fund (compuls. nat. savings; employer 10%/ employee 25%); — Medisave (hosp. bills), — housing deposits etc, — lump sum for annuity.	Discret. pub. assistance. National Pension (1988): compuls. for ind. empl./wkers total (shared) contrib = 3%; pension after 20 yrs.	Discret. pub. assistance. Labour Insurance compuls. for nrly all wkers; employer (4/5) employee (1/5): total 7%; lump sum on retirement.
HEALTH	Government & Govt subs. clinic & hosp. services. No stat. health ins. Extensive/expensive private medicine.	Govt low fee health servs. Medisave (above) re insured + dependants in go⁺t & private hosps.	Medical ins. schemes for civil servts, teachers, wkers, farmers . . . (c.66% of pop. 1988). Govt subs. health servs. (some).	Ltd compuls. wker health ins. Sep. schemes for civil servts, + teachers. 78% of econ. active (38% of pop.). Special provision for children/students. Ltd free/subs. servs. for needy. Govt + vol. (e.g. missnary) hosps; most hosps. = private.
HOUSING	47% pop. in 'govt hsing' (incl. home ownership). High rise.	86% + pop. in 'govt hsing' (maj. = home ownership). High rise.	1982 — govt hse-blding drives (pro urban home ownership). Increasing high rise (urban).	1976 — 10 yr Hsing Plan — but:- poor qual./image/sites, costly/big downpayments. Pro home ownership. High rise (unpopular).
EDUCATION	Govt/govt aided schls: 1033; private (us. small): 1580; grad. expans. of free/subs. places owing to demand; v. competitive. Curriculum/lang. complics.	Govt/govt aided schls: 386; private: 4. Streaming/v. competitive. Govt controlled curricula. Lang. complications. (Education = largest Min.)	Govt & private schools. 12 yrs compuls educ. (7 free). Govt controlled curricula. V. competitive; hence lottery (e.g. to high schl)!	100% government schools. 9 yrs free education (+ free textbooks for poor).
SOCIAL WELFARE	Social Welfare Department; extens. subventions system; extens. network vol. orgs.; Council of Social Service, Community Chest etc.	Min. of Community Devt (former Soc. Welfare Dept); extens. network vol. orgs.; Council of Social Service; Community Chest (+ employee payroll deduction scheme).	Min. of Health & Soc. Affairs; extens. reliance vol. agencies + 'traditional Confucianism'. Increasing govt investment.	Department of Social Affairs & county welfare services. Subventions to vol. agencies. Increasing govt investment.

thereafter, but it is certainly *part* of the explanation. Ironically enough, all four countries had been occupied by the Japanese, their latterday examplar.[3] Hong Kong was 'first off' after 'liberation': once massive immigration from the mainland — compounded by the Korean War blockade on trade with China — had ruined its prospects as an *entrepôt* by the early 1950s. Whereas for Taiwan (coming to terms with the need for long-term viability), South Korea (in the wake of war and military takeover) and Singapore (thrust into high-risk independence from the Federation of Malaysia), it was rather in the 1960s that industrialization was 'forced' to the forefront.

There were (and remain) further pressure points in common. Notwithstanding huge variations in land area and population size, all were bereft of natural resources other than people and were short even of land for easy development.[4] Moreover, the population resource, so-called, was suspect to the extent it was presumed to be either 'rootless'[5] or 'alienated'[6] — this for a collection of peoples and places for whom the notion of vulnerability (physical, social, geo-political, military, in varying combination) was to remain a primary fact of life.

But naturally there was also a positive side to the coin. There was no shortage of cheap, eager manpower, as has already been remarked. In the case of Hong Kong, in particular, there was the bonus of the 'Shanghai translation': of entrepreneurs possessed of some capital, some plant and frequently a nucleus of skilled labour to what had hitherto been that great city's poor relation(s). In the case of both Hong Kong and Taiwan there was some industrial base on which to build. In the case of both Hong Kong and Singapore there was a powerful trading tradition upon which to build. In the case of all four there was ready access to maritime trading routes. And in the case of all four, most decisively, there was massive incentive on every side to seek out the fastest path to profitability.

[3] No mere 'wartime occupation' in the cases of Taiwan (from 1895) and Korea (from 1910).

[4] NB. Inhospitable terrain in the case of Taiwan and South Korea; sheer lack of space in the case of Singapore; lack of space *and* inhospitable terrain in the case of Hong Kong.

[5] The migrant Chinese of Hong Kong and Singapore; refugees in South Korea.

[6] The indigenous inhabitants of Taiwan and of New Territories' Hong Kong.

POPULAR CULTURE

They were (and remain) populations Chinese (Taiwan), overwhelmingly Chinese (Hong Kong), predominantly Chinese (Singapore) and Chinese acculturated (Korea). None of them, of course, is or was to be accounted a Chinese society of high tradition.[7] Nonetheless shared 'Chineseness', in this context, has meant a common core of attitudes and beliefs of particular significance for the conduct of society; so pervasive and persistent has been the force of Chinese tradition.

At the heart of this tradition is Confucianism: or rather a set of precepts and axioms popularly associated with the teachings of the great philosopher and, as such, still commanding overwhelming respect.[8] Foremost amongst these is the notion of the family as the key unit of society, indeed its model unit. The ideal family has a place for everyone — and has everyone in his or her place. Filial piety ensures due deference 'upwards'; family honour ensures due care and protection 'downwards'. The ideal family epitomises harmony, solidarity, pride, loyalty as between members of the group. And the ideal family goes on for ever.

Of course, in recent times real families have rarely approximated to any such ideal; least of all in conditions of migration, modernization and competition. With ancestors left behind,[9] urban accommodation tight-packed and even wives going out to work, the old ways have seemingly been stretched to breaking point. Yet this has not meant that traditional values associated with family life have been robbed of all significance. On the contrary, it is in the image of the ideal family — and hence the well-run household — that the good society is seen as resting not on individuals but on interlocking *groups*, not on equal rights but on ascending orders of duty and obligation, not on 'constructive conflict' — perish the thought — but on the maintenance of stability and harmony at all costs. Once again, reality may be at a conspicuous remove from the ideal; yet the ideal has been enough to ensure some show of popular deference to elders and betters.

Members of government and administration rank higher or lower in such a hierarchy according to the weight (or otherwise) of influence they are presumed to possess. Chinese popular culture

---

[7] The commercial rationale per se was antithetical to 'high' Chinese tradition.

[8] Confucius (K'ung-Fu Tzu or K'ung Tzu) 551–479 BC.

[9] Literally, in family graves.

has had no place for abstract concepts of government per se; none at all for notions of government as being the property of 'the people'. The tradition was one of subjects, not citizens; of coming to terms with officials (as and when necessary), not of exercising 'rights'. It was only when 'normal bargaining' was perceived to have broken down or to have given rise to an unacceptable (and rejectable) outcome that people 'in general' were liable to protest (i.e. riot) against government 'in general': though when this happened the mayhem could be awesome indeed.

It was not until the coming of age of educated young people entertaining Western notions (however etiolated in practice) of 'citizen rights' and 'government for the people', that any real change of attitude was to be expected. Yet even here the evidence remains uncertain. Had it not been for mounting concern over 1997, for instance, the articulate, vociferous young 'social professionals' of Hong Kong would probably have been no more interested in championing grassroots democracy than was anyone else in the colony. Hitherto their ambition had seemed rather to secure entry for themselves to the Hong Kong Establishment, in order (not least) to represent the interests, as they understood them to be, of the ricebowl classes. Assumptions of due authority and deference die hard.

GOVERNANCE

Constitutionally this is a motley collection: one British Crown Colony (Hong Kong), one former British Crown Colony now a 'parliamentary, prime ministerial democracy' (Singapore), one ex-military dictatorship now a 'presidential democracy' (South Korea) — and the 'democratic' Republic of China (ROC) which is Taiwan. Nevertheless there are characteristics of governance in common. Whatever the extent or otherwise of notional democratization, Western-style politics does not come easily — or fit easily when/if ever it arrives. Arguing on public issues in public, taking sides on the basis of rival points of view, engaging — heaven forbid — in open pressure group activity: such are still more likely to be viewed as proofs of government failure than political maturity.

Successful government, in this context, is government with least appearance of politics. The proper place for politics is behind the scenes, out of sight, absorbed into the administration.[10] There is in consequence not much place — or respect — for 'professional politicians'. People who matter will as far as possible have been recruited, co-opted or assiduously cultivated, as appropriate, by representatives of the ruling establishment. Meanwhile ordinary people are there to be watched, instructed, protected, encouraged, rewarded, reproved as the corporate ('household') interest dictates. It is not a recipe for minimum rule.

Indeed, only in 'capitalist paradise', low-profile colonialist Hong Kong has there been so much as a pretence of minimum rule. And even here the analogy characteristically drawn has been between running Hong Kong (whoever is supposed to be in real charge at the top)[11] and managing a corporation. This is not corporatism — there being no serious independent voice for labour — but 'corporationism' or rather (given the tradition of family firms in Hong Kong) household management writ large: top-down direction calling for bottom-up compliance, in the interests of society as a whole. It is an image which more than holds good for the other three countries.

SOCIAL POLICY

The Three Principles said to underly the Constitution of ROC Taiwan are Nationalism, Democracy and Social Welfare.[12] The constitution of 'Fifth Republic' South Korea requires the state to promote 'social security and welfare' over and above guaranteeing human rights 'to the greatest possible extent'.[13] Singapore and Hong Kong are not possessed of such constitutional niceties, yet have nonetheless accumulated social policies at a conspicuous rate.

Initially there was never anywhere any question of 'social investment' as recompense for popular effort or desert.[14] Nor

[10] Witness A. Y. C. King, 'Administrative Absorption of Politics in Hong Kong: Emphasis on the Grass-Roots Level', *Asian Survey*, Vol. 15, No. 5, May 1975, pp. 422–39.

[11] In the words of the old cliché: 'Power in Hong Kong resides in the Jockey Club, Jardine Matheson, the Hong Kong and Shanghai Bank and the Governor — in that order.'

[12] *Republic of China: A Reference Book*, Taipei, Government Information Office, 1983.

[13] *Korea Annual 1987*, pp. 114–115.

[14] Cf. the 'war then welfare' line of accounting for the British welfare state.

was it a case of responding to popular demand — for there was none to speak of. The priority was rather to build a sense of community where none — or none sufficient — was deemed to exist. 'Community' stood for order, discipline, loyalty, stability, collective self help: all the traditional virtues so conspicuously lacking in the pathological non-societies of postwar, post-revolution East and South-East Asia. Without order, there could be no sustained economic growth; without economic growth there could be no future. It was in just such terms that ordinary people were to be instructed in the facts of life.

In particular, community building was about restoring the family to its role as bulwark of society and rendering the neighbourhood (e.g the apartment block) the functional equivalent of a traditional village: scarcely trivial undertakings either of them, yet appropriate targets for 'good government' as already discussed. Witness (even) the Hong Kong authorities' eventual high-profile, multi-faceted investment in 'Family Life Education', not to mention Mutual Aid Committees to promote 'good neighbourliness' in their own housing estates. There was not much 'from the grassroot' about either development,[15] any more than there was about 'Parent Education' or the formation of Residents' Committees in Singapore.[16] Then again, President Park's *Saemaul Undong* (New Community Movement) seems to have pulled few punches in its determination to instil the spirit of 'self-help, diligence and mutual cooperation' into the common folk of South Korea,[17] just as 'planned change' was also being pressed on the designated 'new communities' of Taiwan.[18]

[15] Understandably, the colonial authorities of 'anachronistic' Hong Kong, were the latest to get around to explicit community building. It took the 'Cultural Revolution' riots of 1967 – 68 to convince Government-and-Establishment that (even) Hong Kong required to be rendered a proper Chinese society. The first prescribed tasks of Mutual Aid Committees (from 1973) were to help 'Fight Violent Crime' and keep down litter in each their own housing block. By definition they were not intended to serve as vehicles for 'spontaneous' let alone confrontational community action. See C. Jones, op. cit.

[16] e.g. S. Vasoo, 'Residents' Organisations in the New Towns of Hong Kong and Singapore: A Study of Social Factors Influencing Neighbourhood Leaders' Participation in Community Development', PhD thesis, University of Hong Kong, 1986.

[17] Chung Hee Park, *Korea Reborn: A Model for Development*, Englewood Cliffs, N.J., Prentice Hall, 1979.

[18] e.g. W. Chao, 'Planned Change in Community Development: Its Application in Taiwan' in P. C. Lee (ed.), *Dimensions of Social Welfare Transition: Sino-British Perspectives*, Taipei, Chu Liu Book Company, 1988.

Clearly, ordinary people were too important to be left alone or taken for granted.

Yet there was another side to the picture. Ordinary people thus exposed to 'active government' could develop notions of their own importance hitherto unforeseen by either side; at the same time as government 'in the service of the economy' could increasingly be coming to mean government as *a provider of services* useful to the economy. Once exposed to such services 'courtesy of government' — and to the extent they themselves perceived them to be useful — ordinary people were liable to demand more of the same: if not as a right then certainly as a perk to go for in the perennial struggle to get ahead. Just so has a popular learning exercise been taking place, beyond the bounds of any formal public education programme.

So practical community building could be as much about striking bargains as imposing grand designs. It was Sir Murray MacLehose (former reforming Governor of Hong Kong) who remarked, not before time in 1976, that 'people will not care for a society which does not care for them'.[19] And it was Hong Kong's by then 'social services' that he had in mind as the basis for a *quid pro quo*: putative pillars, as he saw them, for a new form of consensual society; not because these services had been designed and introduced with any such end in view, but because they happened (in the meantime) to have proved their popularity on the ground.

True, with the situation in Hong Kong so fraught of late, it is not surprising to find 'social services' prominent amongst items of concern: not least in the wake of hints from the New China News Agency that people should not expect to be so lucky in this respect after 1997. Without the same quality of threat hanging over it (and without the burden of 'colonial embarassment' to boot), it would be unrealistic to expect similar frankness from government spokesmen in Singapore. But this scarcely signifies that the popularity (or otherwise) of key services has come to be taken any the less seriously there. On the contrary, popular service satisfaction is recognised as critical to the maintenance of Singapore's variety of 'socialism that works'.[20]

Naturally, the longer and better established the provision of popular useful services, the further advanced any such learning

[19] Address at the Opening Session of the Legislative Council, 6 October 1976.

[20] C. V. Devan Nair (ed.), *Socialism That Works... The Singapore Way*, Singapore, Federal Publications, 1976.

process is likely to be. In the cases of Taiwan and South Korea —
wherein compulsory contributory social insurance seems to have
continued more as a community-building imposition than a truly
'popular' device (see below) — positive expectations of
government have been slower to develop.[21] Though this seems
set to change as social services in-kind proliferate, not least in
consequence of the quest for First World status and
respectability.[22]

Nowhere has there been a popular call for 'social justice' in
principle — let alone for (forced) redistribution in practice,
whether across or between generations. Nor has there been much
enthusiasm for the idea of selective social services targeted
explicitly and exclusively at 'the poor' (though services loosely
designed to help 'the less well off' have had a different ring to
them). Again (to repeat), there seems to be a distinct lack of
enthusiasm for long-term 'earned welfare' in the sense of
wage/contribution- conditional old age insurance. The preference
has been rather for services and benefits which everyone can see
the immediate use of — and which many families, if not most,
will endeavour to gain particular advantage from. Services for
minorities — particularly 'non-economic' minorities — tend
naturally to lose out in the face of such competition.

SOCIAL SERVICES

The most popular service, from the point of view of governments
and peoples alike, has been education. After defence (not even
that, in the case of Hong Kong) it is the largest single item of
government expenditure. Then again, it ranks as the single most
important item go-ahead families are wont to invest in, with or
without government help. So persuading parents to send their
children to school has never been much of a problem; the problem
has been rather one of reconciling parental expectations and
demands with schooling capacity and perceived national
requirements.

Respect for learning is traditional; but no less traditional has
been the perception of education as being instrumental to family

---

[21] N. W. S. Chow, 'Social Security Provision in Singapore, Hong Kong, Taiwan and
South Korea: A Comparative Analysis', *Journal of International and Comparative Social
Welfare*, Vol. II, Nos 1–2, 1986, pp. 1–10.

[22] Both of these are regimes more anxious than average to win friends in the West.

success.[23] The parental ideal is for an academic education of the sort (and extent) to command prestige and open doors to a promising career for their offspring and hence (as it were) for the family at large. Traditionally (again), prestige is only to be acquired via competiton; so today's parents tend to value forms of education and educational institution according to the number and difficulty of examinations required to qualify for entry. On the other hand, today's governments tend to be less concerned with exams for their own sake but more concerned about manpower requirements.

The scope for mismatch is obvious. There is (or at any rate has been) not so much competition for and (hence) prestige attached to forms of vocational, non-academic education. Whereas in the case of mainstream academic education, the difficulties and embarrassments are of an opposite order: too many people self-defeatingly in pursuit of targets which, by definition, are bound to elude most of them.[24]

In the case of Hong Kong it has meant the proliferation of government-aided 'Anglo-Chinese grammar schools', at the expense of other forms of secondary education[25] — and the proliferation of seemingly semi-literate, semi-confident 'worst of all worlds' teachers and pupils as a result.[26] In the case of Singapore, by contrast, it has prompted government (1980) to impose a system of streaming on all schools, whereby degrees of ability are first identified by examination at the end of Primary Three and educational schedules distributed accordingly.[27] In the case of South Korea, most intriguingly, it has led to the imposition of lotteries in place of exams to settle entry to middle school, high school and now at last college[28] — so destructive and expensive had the 'examinations hell' become, not least for parents faced with out-of-school tutoring fees.

Naturally, the extent to which governments have been able to moderate or manipulate parental preferences in practice has been

[23] NB. The Chinese tradition of entry to the Mandarinate by competitive examination — well worth an ambitious family's investment.

[24] cf. F. Hirsch, *Social Limits to Growth*, Cambridge, Mass., Harvard University Press, 1976.

[25] Not least at the expense of Chinese-style secondary education.

[26] 'Possibly the best memorizers in the world.'

[27] *Singapore 1988*.

[28] Between candidates already possessed of basic entry qualifications, *Korea Annual 1987*.

a function, in part, of the extent to which each government is seen as being in charge of its own schools system as opposed merely to being its principal financier. The government of Hong Kong — studiously careful not even to seem to be dictating curriculum content within and between schools which are by and large government-aided rather than government-run — occupies the least directive position on this spectrum; in greatest contrast, probably, to the nationalist government of Taiwan. But none can afford to appear neglectful of parental preferences altogether. They are, after all, in the business of encouraging ambition and enterprise (within bounds) not passive dependency.

Meanwhile, by contrast, two other sorts of service are of anything but traditional appeal. Rather the popularity of housing and (Western-style) health care facilities has been of governments' own making. The initial concern was with public health and safety measures as a precondition for economic growth. Too much dirt and disease was bad for trade; urban squatters constituted a fire and health hazard (quite apart from taking up valuable development land); orphans (not to mention 'orphaned parents') cost money to support. Naturally these were not the only sorts of sentiment to find official expression, but they were the sorts presumed to carry most weight as grounds for government intervention. Just so did the government and establishment of postwar Hong Kong become convinced of the need for a (renewed) public health/health education campaign backed up by cheap health services available on demand — and eventually, even, of the need for a mass public housing programme.

It was to prove an embarrassing success story all round. So popular does cheap Western medicine become there are soon charges of government favouritism from the defenders of traditional *Chinese* medicine,[29] as the colony's Medical and Health Department struggles to keep pace (never to catch up) with mounting demand for its services. Hence, as queues and waiting lists lengthen, health care becomes a principal focus for popular dissatisfaction with government — only to be rivalled by mounting discontent over public housing also.

Mass resettlement estates had never ever been intended as an exercise in consumerism in Hong Kong. The object had rather been to clear squatters from valuable sites and decant them in to

---

[29] i.e., there are demands for government subsidies to be made equally available for Chinese as for Western medicine.

blocks of units ('apartments' would be much too grand an expression) cheap enough for them to be able to afford and hence for them to be likely to stay in. It also came to be seen as a good way of concentrating labour supplies where convenient for industrial development. What was *not* apparently envisaged was that such housing estates themselves would come to require positive management if they were not to sink into total social chaos; nor was it foreseen that the better the standard of amenity eventually provided, the more likely were such estates to emerge as a desirable (i.e. useful) 'service' in their own right.

Still, not looking too far ahead has long been a hallmark of defensive government in colonialist Hong Kong. The evolution of health and housing services in Singapore has been more contrived and, as most would have it, much more successful. Here too there has been extensive investment in cut-price primary health care services 'to bring health care within the reach of all'.[30] Unlike in Hong Kong, however, there is self-financing Medisave to take care of most people's hospital bills, thus relieving one major call on the government purse at the same time as (presumably) boosting the utilization of private in addition to government hospital facilities.

The investment in public housing has, meanwhile, been that much more spectacular. Proportionately speaking there is more of it. Absolutely speaking, Singapore's Housing and Development Board has been able to offer a greater variety of product, to apparent greater popularity effect, than anything the Hong Kong Housing Authority has been able to match. Notably, this has included the promotion of home ownership on a mass scale: a strategy designed deliberately to 'root' the so-called transients of Singapore. (The efforts of Hong Kong's Housing Authority to do the same in respect of its own tenants have been inevitably less successful.[31])

Without such dramatic population pressures experienced anything like so soon, the governments of South Korea and Taiwan have taken longer to go in for mass housing provision. Creeping urbanization — as compared with the threat of imminent social collapse — seems to have been the problem characteristically perceived. Thus Taiwan's first Ten-Year

---

[30] *Singapore 1988*, p. 198.

[31] Most of those responding to the Hong Kong Housing Authority's home purchase schemes have been families disqualified from applying for public rental accommodation (by reason of income at time of application) or else simply tired of waiting for it.

Housing Plan dates only from 1976 and Korea's (five-year) Socio-Economic Development Plan only includes a mass housing component from 1982. First achievements, furthermore, were disappointing. The Korean construction industry proved (not surprisingly) incapable of delivering quite the requisite number of units within the requisite time set[32] — whilst Taiwan's first public house-building efforts seem to have resulted, most embarrassingly, in quantities of accommodation nobody actually wanted to purchase.[33] Nevertheless it was a beginning in each case, not an end.

Meanwhile government and government-subsidized health services continue thinner on the ground in South Korea and Taiwan by comparison with Hong Kong and Singapore. Yet in this case there is a clear difference — rather than mere 'deficiency' — of policy to be observed. The former have characteristically gone in for compulsory, employer/worker social insurance in general — and medical insurance in particular — to an extent quite removed from the norms of Singapore and especially Hong Kong. The less 'rootless' the mass of the population — perhaps the more American-influenced the content of government — the stronger the apparent prospects for thrusting this particular form of compulsory self-help (as against expensive services in kind) on key sections of a labour force and their employers.[34]

Though even in Korea and Taiwan the emphasis has always been on *minimum* and above all short-term social insurance benefits. Pensions provision in Taiwan, for instance, still consists of a lump sum on retirement — no less than it does courtesy of the Central Provident (forced savings) Fund of Singapore.[35] It

[32] Though it did manage 81.5% of target, 1,166,000 instead of an intended 1,431,000 for 1982 – 86. (*Korea Annual 1987.*)

[33] Note the prime object in each case was to produce homes *for purchase.* But building standards (in the Taiwan case) had evidently been appalling. Sites were inconvenient if not downright disreputable (what *fung-shui*-respecting Chinese would wish to live next to cemetery, for instance?) and the price (plus level of downpayment) was too high. See for instance Hsiao-Hung Nancy Chan 'Public Housing Development Plan Experience in the Republic of China' in P. Ching-Yung Lee (ed.), *Dimensions of Social Welfare Transition: Sino-British Perspectives*, Taipei, Chung-Lin Book Company, 1988.

[34] e.g. N. W. S. Chow, op. cit., and cf. Bismarck's exercise in social insurance.

[35] By definition *not* social insurance, since the sum thus saved represents the amount — no more no less — deposited by the individual worker and his employer on his behalf. Though nowadays, 'beneficiaries' can be compelled to keep enough in the Fund at least to purchase an annuity on their retirement (*Singapore 1988*, p. 126).

remains to be seen how far South Korea's latest-launched plan (1988) for a part-earnings-related pensions scheme serves, in practice, to break this particular mould.[36] Meanwhile, the most generous of short-term responses to the needs of the elderly remains the 'no strings' Special Allowances system of Hong Kong.[37]

Chinese tradition has had little to say about the needs (let alone rights) of the disadvantaged per se. The emphasis has rather been on the duties of families and villagers [sic] to take care of their own. As a strategy for social welfare, it was inseparable from notions of good family and good community behaviour in general — and as such ill-equipped to travel well on its own. In the changed, charged circumstances of Tigerlands in take-off, there was no natural fount of public sympathy — let alone sense of public responsibility — for 'anonymous unfortunates' littering the streets. If anything, indeed, competition between strangers heightened a sense of fatalism: losers were people not 'destined' to succeed — and so were best to be avoided.[38] Hence the signficance in this context of one particular Western innovation: specialized, professionalized, 'free standing' social welfare.

True, there was precious little 'free-standing' about the original missionary presence.[39] Nevertheless caring institutions could outlast excesses of proselytizing zeal[40] — and stand as examples for others to emulate or improve on. In the case of Hong Kong, 'second stage' expansion took place exceptionally and most spectacularly in the years of China's Communist Revolution, as (Western) international charities scrambled to offer each their own care and relief services to refugees in flight from the Red Menace.[41] Eventually (again) people moved on, many of them, but agencies remained. Hence the names of prominent voluntary organizations, in present-day Hong Kong as elsewhere, can still strike Western audiences as familiar.

---

[36] *Int. Soc. Sec. Review 1988*, Vol. 2, pp. 202–3; *1989* Vol. 3, p. 265.

[37] Non-means-tested, indexed-linked payments for the severely disabled and the elderly aged 70+.

[38] e.g. L. Ching, *One of the Lucky Ones* being the 'true story of a blind Chinese girl's triumph over prejudice', Hong Kong, Gulliver Books, 1980.

[39] NB The principal attraction of Hong Kong et al. for nineteenth-century missionaries seems to have been as a launching pad for forays into China.

[40] Note that the Chinese were reckoned 'impervious to religion' in any case.

[41] C. Jones, op. cit.

But then names can be deceptive. Economic growth has been forcing and facilitating Western social welfare's patriation for a long time. The more impressive the economic performance (and the more 'unscrupulous' the trading reputation) the less deserving of international aid (or an expatriate presence) were the Tigers liable to appear (no matter how many refugees there might yet be to cope with — as Hong Kong was to find to its cost).[42] So: to the extent that Western-style welfare services had in the meantime 'proved their credentials', here was another deficiency for governments — and thence community-building — to endeavour to make good.

Witness the efforts to inculcate 'charity-mindedness' amongst the peoples of Hong Kong and Singapore, via massive annual Community Chest campaigns and a 'voluntary' payroll deduction scheme, respectively:[43] campaigns designed not to impose 'Western' values so much as to revive and modernize traditional Chinese sentiments of social obligation — not to mention familial self-respect. Yet giving to the anonymous 'other' was never likely (or intended) to be the same as volunteering, personally, to help unknown individual strangers in need. Hence what some have declared to be the 'misleading' successes of high profile fundraising: the sums raised are not proof necessarily of a shift of attitudes towards the disadvantaged per se, so much as of a renewed awareness that charitable giving constitutes a component of correct, respectable behaviour for families and societies alike.

But then again, the social workers typically responsible for such remarks have scarcely themselves been of Western ideal-type. Theirs is a new profession: still finding its level and very much in search, therefore, of 'status supports'. Witness the eagerness to impress 'upwards' that they are no 'free lunch merchants' at the same time as impressing 'downwards' that they can be relied upon to know and do best for ordinary (not just disadvantaged) people. There is not much scope or call here for the likes of non-directive casework or mere 'enabling' community action. The requirement is rather for social workers confident enough to tell people what to do, with conviction. As seems already to have been

---

[42] e.g. in the wake of China's Cultural Revolution: long before the advent of boat people from Vietnam.

[43] NB. in the wake of this scheme in 1984 — 85 the people of Hong Kong raised as much for Oxfam's Ethiopian Famine Appeal as did the entire population of the United States. They had emerged as givers indeed.

appreciated — witness the expansion of professional social work education in Hong Kong, Singapore and latterly Taiwan. And witness the evidence, such as it is, of growing popular respect for the profession per se: not least as evinced by the return of no less than 20 out of 22 community social work candidates standing for District Board election in Hong Kong 1985. A modest triumph, at least.[44]

THE OIKONOMIC WELFARE STATE

The 'household economy', as here portrayed, is no more open-ended in its promises than egalitarian in its philosophy. Economic success stands as the prime objective, indeed rationale, for everyone's sake. Success — in these most modern of Chinese societies — is deemed to rest on the exercise of informed authority by some over others, complemented by the said others' recognition and performance of their duty.

So these are not 'leveller regimes'; they are not participatory democracies; there is no sentimental tradition of indiscriminate, unconditional citizen rights — let alone of indiscriminate, unconditional social obligation; there is no mystique attached to concepts of welfare state or social service per se: quite the reverse. It is the pursuit of prosperity which here calls for discipline and duty no less than family ambition. In which cause social services (like any other sort of service) are there to be useful, no more no less.

It is an 'ideal' which will strike some Western audiences as unappealing and others as plain inconvenient: the 'no frills' welfare state. Or alternatively, as yet, welfare capitalism that works.

---

[44] Given the distinctly modest status and 'powers' of the District Boards.

[21]

CHIARA SARACENO

The Ambivalent Familism of the Italian Welfare State

Welfare states have developed as ways of assuming public responsibilities for the conditions of reproduction. Therefore, they interact with families and contribute to shaping the particular form of the gender division of labor both inside and outside of families. In this capacity, they frame a significant part of the material, juridical, and cultural conditions in which negotiations concerning gender and family roles and relations occur.

The shape of the Italian welfare state has been deeply influenced by assumptions about the family and its gender and intergenerational responsibilities: the family is both an economic unit in which there are dependents (e.g., children, wives, parents, and disabled adults) and "family heads" who redistribute income, and a caregiving unit in which there are also dependents and those (i.e., women, wives, and adult daughters) who "redistribute" care. Within the family, as defined by welfare state provisions, married women are expected to be the main care providers for family members and kin and therefore, at least in part, economically dependent on their husbands. At the same time, most of the caring needs of individuals—children, infirm older and disabled persons, but also healthy adult men—are defined as best served by the caring of wives, mothers, and/or daughters.

The welfare state follows this definition to such an extent that even those social services which exist in this area are often defined

Social Politics   Spring 1994

interchangeably as "services for the family," "services for women," and "services for children" (or the disabled, etc.). As a matter of fact, and somewhat paradoxically, women may be defined (if not denounced) as dependent on the state when they ask for, or use, services for their children. Older people's dependency is labeled as such more clearly when they use public money and services than when they are cared for within household and kin boundaries. Dependency within and on one's own family and kin for money or care is expected and positive, although not all forms of individual dependency are formally acknowledged in the same way: men's dependence on women's caring for them and their children is perceived more as a vested right (which might become a shortcoming when they are not married), while husbands' responsibility toward their "dependents" is acknowledged in many labor policies which privilege "family heads" with regard to decisions on hiring and layoffs. On the other hand, children's and older people's dependence on women's caring provides few rights for women, apart from maternity leaves for working women. Rather, that dependence makes women appear as irresponsible or unduly dependent on the state— or even as rendering their family "dependent on the state" (e.g., Donati 1981)—when they try to redistribute "their" care-giving work.

The family, with its gendered and generational division of responsibility and labor, as well as its asymmetrical structure of interdependencies, is therefore the explicit partner of the Italian welfare state (Balbo 1977; Balbo 1984). In contrast to other welfare state regimes that also stress the importance of the family (Langan and Ostner 1991), the Italian state's emphasis on the family has not always resulted in policies that either strengthen the (male) family head or materially support the "traditional family" (e.g., paying higher child allowances either to the mother or father). Rather, reference to family responsibilities and solidarity serves to ration access to benefits and restrict individual rights. Thus, at-home professional care for invalid older people is provided only on the basis of a test of both economic means and the unavailability of a care-giving woman within the kinship network. All tests of means are household- and sometimes kin-based (e.g., a separated woman with no economic means might be referred by social assistance to her distant brother, who by law should offer her economic support).[1] At the same time, many income support measures targeted at the less privileged groups and regional areas can be interpreted as a means of acknowledging that many families cannot really have an economic "head," and therefore, must be "dependent" on the state.

The way the state defines family responsibilities and interdepen-

62 ◆ Saraceno

dencies determines to a great degree when and how use of public resources is defined as dependence on the state. The longstanding debate about the specific status of personal social services (i.e., caring services) is a case in point: insofar as these services are defined as surrogates for an inadequate family (i.e., a care-giving mother or daughter), rather than as services granting individual social rights irrespective of family membership, they are likely to be perceived as creating dependency. Analogously, the lack of universal unemployment benefits, while fragmenting the unemployed into many categories, exposes the weakest among them (all those looking for their first job) to both the risk of receiving nothing and of being labeled as inadequate and thus dependent on public assistance.

From this point of view, we see a kind of pendulum in the recent history of the Italian welfare state: during the seventies a number of caring needs were at least partially defined as individual social rights (health care, day care and education for preschool children, and basic education); in the nineties the increasing recourse to family-based means testing has tended to weaken individual rights in favor of family rights and (compulsory) family solidarity, at the same time relabeling as "dependencies" what had been previously defined as individual social rights. Exemplary of this shift is the reform of the National Health Service approved in 1992 (discussed later in this article).

General Features of the Italian Welfare State

According to the Italian Constitution, Italy is a republic based on labor. Older or disabled workers have a right to live according to their previous standard of living, while nonworkers must be granted "the minimum necessary for survival." Full citizenship, therefore, is reached through participation in paid work, although it is not at all certain that having a job is a citizenship right.

In the Constitution, the disparity in rights for workers and nonworkers is expressed not only in different pension rights of older persons even at the minimum level (the social assistance pension is much lower than the minimum work pension), but also in the fragmented, discretionary protection granted to nonworkers. At the same time, the Constitution protects the family as a "natural society" and a "natural right"—so much so that successive legislation has established the principle that children have a right to an adequate family, through adoption if they have none or foster care if they have a temporarily inadequate one.

The Constitution stipulates that men and women, husbands and wives, are equal in the family, "granted that the unity of the fami-

The Familism of the Italian Welfare State ◆ 63

ly is not hampered." A principle of hierarchy between the sexes is therefore inscribed in Italy's fundamental law, pointing to a possible conflict between individual rights (of women) and family and community rights, to be resolved in favor of the latter. The unity of the family—the caring it must provide in the "republic based on work"—is based on women's willingness to reduce their individual rights in favor of their husbands' rights. This, in turn, reduces women's opportunities to secure social rights based on paid work. Women should be dependent on their husbands' incomes because their husbands and children are dependent on their care-giving.

While this analysis of the Constitution is brief and incomplete, it is important to identify the constitutional framework of social rights in Italy. As in most countries, social rights are generally linked to working status: to both the fact of working for pay and specific job location in the occupational structure and in the social security system. Not having a paid job constitutes a barrier to access to other rights: public or subsidized housing, emergency lodging when evicted, low cost loans, and so on (Saraceno 1992a). Subordinately, access to social rights is granted through a family relationship (as a wife or child) to someone having such working status.

The Italian welfare state developed during the seventies and early eighties, approaching average European levels of protection.[2] During this period of development, the social services (kindergartens, day care, after school activities, at-home care for older persons) experienced maximum expansion, and important legislation concerning gender roles and the family was approved (e.g., divorce, abortion, extension of coverage for working mothers, and parental leaves available also to working fathers).

Social analysts define the Italian welfare state as a "clientelistic" variant of the "particularistic-meritocratic" social state typical of continental Europe (Paci 1984; Paci 1989; Ferrera 1985; Ascoli 1986; Esping-Andersen 1990): the state is heavily shaped by the control and negotiation of political parties and trade unions, which in the past used social expenditures as a means to gain consensus. Social analysts attribute the lack of autonomy of civil society with regard to the state in Italy as "clientelistic dependency" (Farneti 1978; Tarrow 1979; Paci 1989), and the Italian case as one of "party government" (Rusconi and Scamuzzi 1981).[3]

This does not mean that there are not universalistic measures: compulsory education and, to a large extent, high school education (which in Italy is not compulsory) are free in Italy. Public (state or local government organized) or local government subsidized kindergartens for children three to five years old[4] cover about 90 percent of the youngsters in this age bracket. Even university education is inexpensive, and some analysts interpret this as perverse re-distribution, insofar as the costs of university education are supported by all tax payers, but particularly by the large majority whose children do not attend the university.

Aside from education, however, universalism in Italy developed belatedly and weakly. M. Ferrera points out that although discussion of pension reform is recurrent in Italian history, particularly in republican history, the Italian pension system is still one of the most stratified and internally diversified (1993). Even the quite radical reform finally approved in the fall of 1992 has not unified the different systems, and there still is not a universal basic old age pension. Instead, there is a so-called social pension which is about half of the minimum work pension; it is means-tested on the basis of family income and is paid to those (mostly women) who did not "earn" a work pension.

Canceling the many diversified systems that had developed over more than a century, the single universalistic reform of the seventies introduced the National Health System in 1978. This system made health care a citizenship right that was granted to all Italian citizens as well as to all foreigners legally residing in the country.[5]

A variety of public or publicly financed social services also developed in that period, with the aims of both supporting families (women) in meeting the caring needs of their dependents and of granting individuals some degree of care and resources (intellectual stimuli, leisure and sports activities, etc.) not exclusively linked to individual and family resources. To be sure, controversy around the social rights feature of these services continued; while many conservatives denounced the "state intrusion in private life," many leftists overplayed the social rights dimensions of services which in reality were often undeveloped and scarce or used some explicit or implicit criteria for screening prospective users.

Personal social services and social assistance in Italy are a responsibility of municipal governments, which finance them out of funds received from the central government. Municipalities may or may not offer particular services; these decisions are based on their analysis not only of "need," but of local lobbies and political priorities. Exclusive local responsibility for offering services, therefore, has an important consequence for citizens: there are substantial differences both in the quality and quantity of services available in a given locale. This is particularly true in the case of social services such as day care for children under three, at-home care for older or disabled persons, school cafeterias, and family clinics—that is, services that most directly assist (women's) family work. For example, although the fertility rate is higher in the South than in the

Center-North and the proportion of preschool children in the population is higher, until the early eighties there were no day care centers in Sicily, and kindergartens, although their number had risen substantially since the early seventies, are still fewer and offer on average a reduced schedule. In addition, school cafeterias, at-home care for older persons, services for the disabled, and services for drug addicts are considerably less available in the South than in the Center-North. This, in turn, makes individuals more dependent on their family and kin for meeting their needs.

Local residence in Italy makes a great difference not only in terms of job opportunities, but also in terms of the acknowledgment and accessibility of social rights. Territorial differentiation in Italy makes it difficult to delineate any "average" description of processes and situations. Many social analysts maintain that the interplay of local political and social traditions, economic development, and formal and informal systems of social protection give rise to distinctive social formations, which cannot be analyzed along a continuum, but must be understood in their specificity and interplay. This does not mean that these disparities and inequalities remain the same over time or that the general regional divisions used in routine presentation of data (North, Center, and South, or North-West, North-East, Center, South, and Isles) are internally homogeneous. Reforms introduced in late 1992, aimed at decreasing the heavy public debt, have reduced the scope of the universalism of the health system and increased geographical differentiation in the provision and cost of social services.

As a consequence of its clientelistic-particularistic characteristics, the Italian system of social protection has four specific features. First, different measures of income support have been continually privileged over not only the provision of services but also over a full employment policy since the postwar years (with the notable exception of the seventies when most of the social service system was developed [Paci 1984; Ascoli 1986; Artoni and Ranci Ortigosa 1989]). This in turn has led to the second feature, a steady reliance on the family and its gender division of labor and intergenerational solidarity for the provision of caring work and services as well as for the integration of inadequate income support measures. The family is the explicit partner of social policies in Italy, although this partnership has been emphasized differently over the years. A third feature is the wide differentiation not only between provisions for workers and nonworkers, but among various categories of workers and "people in need." There are differences in rights and coverage between state employees and private sector employees, and, within the latter, between those employed in large industries and

Regional divisions in Italy: North-West (1, 2, 3, 7); North-East (4, 5, 6, 7, 8); Central (9, 10, 11, 12); South (13, 14, 15, 16, 17, 18); and Isles (19, 20).

those who work for small firms. Differences occur not only in the coverage for unemployment, but also, at least up to fall 1992, in regulations concerning pensions (Castellino 1976; Commissione per l'Analisi dell'Impatto Sociale 1990). Since women and men are likely to be located in different sectors of the labor market, they generally receive different kinds of benefits even though explicit formal gender discrimination in the labor market has been banned since 1961. Women are more likely to be concentrated either in the less protected sectors, such as small industries and workshops, shops, and small offices, or in the best protected state and public administration sector. Fourth, social assistance measures are widely differentiated: there are as many poverty lines, vital minima, and so on, as there are means-tested measures and providing groups.

Welfare state measures differ significantly across the country, particularly along the line between the Center-North and South, and also among provinces. Within an overall constant privileging of income support, as opposed to social service provisions, not only is there a great variance in the kind of income support distributed, but also in the availability, quality, and cost of public social services (e.g., education, health, and care for children, the disabled, and older persons). Since local governments do not have financial autonomy, insofar as they cannot raise taxes, these differences are due, on the one hand, to a differential territorial distribution of directly state-provided resources (e.g., schools and hospitals) and pressure by local governments to obtain, monitor, and even use them; on the other hand, such differences are due to local governments' use of the money distributed to them by the central state.

Ambivalences and Contradictions in the State's Gender Structure

The categorical and clientelistic features of the Italian welfare system, together with its heavy reliance on family unity and solidarity, have specific and sometimes ambivalent or contradictory consequences for gender divisions and inequalities.

Italian women receive social benefits (e.g., health care and services for their children) as mothers and wives, rather than as citizens or workers. In this the democratic republic, with the exception of the extension of political rights to women, was not really discontinuous with Fascism. The fascist regime, in fact, while pushing women out of the labor market and denying them control of their bodies through punishment of contraception and abortion, created the first widespread system of social and health services (ONMI) catering to mothers and their children; ONMI even sup-

68 ◆ Saraceno

ported unwed mothers in their efforts to persuade their children's fathers to accept their responsibilities (Saraceno 1991). At the same time, women's family relationships were the basis for legally restricting their access to the social rights attached to the full status of (paid, male) worker (a feature carried into the sixties with the legislation of the post-fascist republic): until the mid-fifties women were legally barred from the best social security-protected and paid jobs as well as from the higher employment ranks and could be fired if they married or bore children.

Yet the very family-centered social definition of women, together with the high value attributed in Italy to the family not only as a social and moral institution, but also as the main redistributive and caring social agency, resulted in social legislation which for a long time privileged the model of a family with a male breadwinner and a full-time housewife. Health insurance was progressively extended to cover all family dependents, but only if the insured worker was the husband-father. Survivors' pensions were extended to many categories of workers, but only for survivors of husband-fathers. Male workers were entitled to a family allowance for their "dependents." Tax rebates might (and still may) be obtained for dependent wives and children. As a consequence, wives and mothers were discouraged from working—at least in the official, social security-covered labor market—particularly if they could not obtain a wage high enough to compensate for the loss of benefits for the family.

If women worked, their contributions toward health insurance and old age pensions carried less weight than those of men, since women's benefits could not be extended to family dependents. Thus, the Christian Democratic governments of the fifties did not change from the fascist approach; they only widened the social groups (and families), which were covered, and included rural workers and farmers. The most discriminatory provisions among these (the different worth of men's and women's contributions) were removed only in the mid-seventies, either because they were declared unconstitutional (in the case of survivors' pensions paid only to surviving wives[6]) or because of the institution of the National Health Service.

Since the 1950s, the focus on the family and its well-being resulted in a close and constant examination of the conditions of working mothers by the Socialist, Communist, and Christian Democratic Parties, and the Catholic Church. While Catholics disapproved of mothers working for pay and were in favor of a men's family wage, they were concerned about the problems faced by women who "had to work" due to economic hardships. They were, therefore, in favor of long, paid maternity leaves, but they opposed the provision of pub-

The Familism of the Italian Welfare State ◆ 69

lic child care services campaigned for by the Left, trade unions, and lay religious groups. Catholics resented what they perceived as an "intrusion" of the state into family responsibilities and into an area—services for children and families—that traditionally had been controlled by the church and religious associations.

These somewhat contrasting views and interests inspired a number of legislative and social policy measures aimed at helping working mothers cope with their dual responsibilities: (1) one of the best European laws on maternity leaves, (2) a system of public kindergartens that now covers almost 80 percent of 3–5 year olds, and (3) a system of public day care centers for children under age three, which, although greatly underdeveloped, in some areas covers 30 percent of all children in that age bracket. The law granting extended paid, part compulsory, part optional maternity leaves to working mothers was supported by the Catholic Party in 1971. The Left and women's associations requested that child care services (day care and kindergartens) be provided and financed by the state. Both measures were eventually approved, partly due to the pressure of a then highly visible women's movement. At present all working mothers are entitled to two months of paid leave before and three months after delivery, followed by an additional leave period with reduced pay (this period may now be taken by the father or mother). At the same time children of working mothers receive priority placement in day care and kindergartens.

The great majority of three-to-five-year-old children in Italy attends kindergarten (mostly state organized), regardless of their mothers' working status. In the urban areas of the Center-North, the provision of day care for children under three is one of the acknowledged responsibilities of the local government, although with less emphasis than kindergartens: day care in the Center-North costs more and there are fewer centers, compared to kindergartens. The difference in availability and cost to families depends on a definition of the need: kindergartens have become increasingly defined as a school service, connected to children's education; therefore, the mother's working status is only an additional entitlement to the service. Day care services for children under three, on the contrary, notwithstanding changes in legislation, are defined as personal social services, which (1) are not compulsory local responsibilities, (2) must be partly paid for by users, although on a sliding scale based on family income, and (3) are rationed on the basis of "need." Day care services also are still primarily for children of working mothers or of families defined as suffering from some kind of stress (e.g., divorced parents, unwed mothers, or parents receiving social assistance). A mother's full-time care-giving remains the ideal for this

70 ◆ Saraceno

age bracket.[7] A paradoxical consequence of this is that nonworking mothers do not receive any social support in raising their children (under age three), since these mothers are defined as totally adequate and self-sufficient.

The focus on women's family responsibilities, combined with a categorical/clientelistic approach to social security, motivated the granting of controversial privileges to specific categories of working mothers: if they are state employees, they receive credit toward seniority for each child they bear. They also receive full pay (not just the legislated 70 percent) during maternity leaves and may take longer leave periods. Finally, until the fall 1992 reform, working mothers constituted the main group that took advantage of the opportunity for state employees to retire after sixteen (instead of the minimum twenty) years of work and begin receiving a pension, without waiting to reach the general retirement age (these women are called "baby pensioners"). To be sure, these pensions are relatively low, because they are based on a reduced contributive period. These women, therefore, are liable to become poor in old age if for some reason they lose access to an additional (husband-derived) income. Yet this reduced pension is higher than the minimum pension in the private sector and grants an income well before old age. Most women who chose this solution in the past did so within a family strategy: their pension supplemented their husband's income, and their availability for family work (caring for husbands, children, and kin) was de facto financially supported by the state.

While the legislation for working mothers benefited mostly middle-class women, another measure was targeted at rural mothers and derived from an analogous mixture of (1) a definition of women as family members and secondary income providers, and (2) a categorical/clientelistic approach. Aimed at supporting the family income of rural workers in the most economically undeveloped areas, particularly in the South, this legislation grants unemployment benefits, paid maternity leaves, and pension rights to rural employees who work a minimum number of days per year. Women in rural areas of the South (where men have difficulty earning a living wage) use this legislation not so much in order to have a wage for some months or to have the ridiculous unemployment indemnity, but to have paid leaves during pregnancy and after birth, and to assure themselves a minimum work pension. While there are employers who offer jobs as a "favor" toward this benefit, therefore maintaining very low wages, there are also women (and men) who pay to be registered as workers and then pay the contributions themselves without doing one day of work. While this phenomenon may

The Familism of the Italian Welfare State ♦ 71

be analyzed as part of the clientelistic system encouraged by governmental policies, it has a special gender feature: social policy in this case does not so much encourage the male breadwinner principle as discourage women from finding an autonomous economic base as workers. Women define themselves as workers only as part of a family strategy aimed at gathering as many "income bits" as possible (see also Balbo 1977). But their main, and often only, work remains unpaid family work with little support from social services or husbands.

These policies on working mothers and rural workers, therefore, provide family income support and continue the traditional gender division of labor within the family by acknowledging some kind of paid working status for wife-mothers even when they do not (or no longer) work. While requiring citizens to have a high degree of ingenuity and knowledge of the administration of social security and social policies, the policies risk branding women who use them as "cheating" the system, and as being overly dependent on public funds. The recent, legitimate, widespread outcry against the women "baby pensioners" among state employees, as well as against "fake workers" receiving undeserved benefits, hides not only political parties' and trade unions' responsibilities in creating this situation, but also their failure to develop generalized, more universalistic income support measures and minimum pension benefits. These legitimate denunciations also failed to address the costs for women due to the lack of acknowledgment of women's family work.

Other measures, such as the means-tested family allowances[8] and tax deductions for dependent spouses, as well as the recently introduced family income threshold which determines access to free health care,[9] discourage working women from insisting on receiving social security benefits, if their pay is not high enough to offset the loss of other conjugal status-linked benefits as well as the increased taxation on two-income households.

Women are entitled to workers' rights even if they have at best only a partial work history; or women may hide their paid work activity (therefore relinquishing their workers' rights). In both of these cases, married women are defined and encouraged to perceive themselves first and foremost as family members, insofar as the adequacy of their income, as well as its visibility and benefits, depends on the immediate family convenience, regardless of individual long-term risks. Depending on the circumstances, however, women may or may not be encouraged to appear as workers, regardless of ideology and cultural values. Family *interdependence,* more than women's *dependence* is encouraged in Italy: given the gender division

72 ◆ Saraceno

of labor in the family and gender stratification and segregation in
the labor market, the emphasis on interdependence may result more
in women's economic dependency than in men's independence.

Another less gender specific social security measure was amply
used until the 1992 pension reform: workers who paid contributions for at least fifteen years were entitled to receive the minimum
work pension when they reached the pension age, without regard
to the value of the contributions. The difference between the amount
earned through contributions and the minimum pension was supplemented by public funds. The only requirement was that the individual's personal income was no higher than twice the minimum
pension. On the average, these minimum pensions are 70 percent
supplemented by public funds—only about 30 percent of the pension is "earned" through contributions. Many self-employed artisans and shopkeepers may take advantage of the minimum pension
because their contributions are very low compared to other workers. Many women who were formerly wage workers receive a supplemented minimum pension because they worked up to the minimum contributive years, or sometimes left work and paid voluntary
contributions until they reached the minimum requirements: they
left paid work in order to devote themselves to family work, but
counted on small pensions in old age to supplement their husbands'
incomes.

The fall 1992 reform, which grants the supplement only on the
basis of a means test applied to the couple's income (analogous to
what happened to the social assistance pension), has not only rendered this strategy impossible for younger generations, it has also
disrupted the expectations of those now reaching the pension age
and who see their pension "cut" often by more than half, since they
will receive only what they contributed. They are now confronted
with the results of a strategy they were encouraged by social policies to undertake some years ago, and while others accuse them of
wanting more than they earned, they perceive themselves as cheated in their legitimate rights. This is an interesting, if painful, case
of social policies shaping and then disrupting life trajectories.

Women, particularly older women, are more likely to be exposed
to this risk, since criteria are now applied to them which were not
in the past. Further, the costs of women's dual burden and marginalization in the labor force are ignored. Younger women are strongly
encouraged to become economically independent if they want to
assure their economic well-being as individuals, even into old age.
At the same time the conditions under which young women make
their choices continue to encourage (if not force) them to consider
family interdependencies within a framework shaped by a persis-

tent gender division of labor. Long-term individual and family economic strategies and short-term family strategies may be increasingly at odds.

Women's rights to incomes, social security, and support have been best protected when they worked for a wage, rather than when they were full-time care-givers. In fact, the highly extolled figure of the full-time homemaker does not receive any substantial support through social policy: her children, particularly those under three, have little or no entitlement to places in a public child care service, after-school activities, and so on; and her older parents have less entitlement to at-home care (which is a means-tested measure anyway). If she divorces, the value of her unpaid family work is only partially acknowledged.

The family law approved in 1975 stipulates that the economic regime of marriage is "community property" (although exceptions are possible on demand), regardless of the income of either spouse.[10] The law also explicitly points to the contribution of family work to this property. But the only wealth taken into consideration is "visible" property and savings, not the "command over resources" gained through career and work experience and seniority. This "command" remains her husband's property, although through family work a woman has offered him the opportunity to invest in his career (Oliver 1983; Pahl and Pahl 1971; Barbagli 1990; De Singly 1987). Moreover, there is an increasing tendency by tribunals (courts), in the name of gender equality, to withhold alimony from wives if they are able-bodied, even if they have forfeited career opportunities in order to care for families or are too old to enter the labor market (Barbagli 1990).

There is only one type of woman who is "privileged" in comparison to men or women in similar economic conditions: the solo (widowed, separated, unwed) mother, with dependent children, whose income is below the poverty level (Saraceno 1992a). In this case motherhood entitles women to some form of specific (not work-linked) rights or "legitimate" social dependency. Widows are entitled to social pensions if their husbands died before achieving the minimum pension. Separated or unwed mothers are entitled to some kind of income support at the local level, to a higher degree and for a longer time than adults with no dependent children or male-headed families. But this "privileging" of motherhood occurs within a framework that defines solo mothers who receive support as failed, or interrupted, wives. There is, in addition, a hierarchy within this group: widowed mothers receive more secure entitlements than separated, divorced, or unwed mothers.

Women as wives and mothers are expected to act as a resource

74 ◆ Saraceno

of the welfare state (and of course also of the labor market, through their reproductive work): school schedules, the scarce availability of school cafeterias, the scarce availability of at-home help for older and disabled persons, and the structure of care in hospitals and old age homes require homemakers to fill the gaps and connect the services (see also Balbo 1984). There are, however, important regional differences. It is significant that in regions (such as the Center-North, where there is a high labor force participation rate by women) with increased numbers of working mothers, and where the women's movement in the seventies and eighties succeeded in lobbying for women's interests at the local government level, the number of social services for children and older persons is high. It is low (and mostly in the form of institutionalization rather than at-home and community care services) where women's employment rate is low, although both their employment and unemployment rates are rising (Saraceno 1992b).

In other words, within a persistent cultural and social policy framework, which points to the family as the locus and women as the main providers of care, changes in women's choices and actions somewhat shifted the balance toward the state and social services in the most developed areas of the country (while leaving substantially untouched men's responsibilities and actions). Moreover, the spread of social services in these areas helped to develop, and was accompanied by, a culture of individual rights, particularly of social rights defined as individual rather than family rights (see also Bimbi 1992): child care services have been partly redefined as catering to children's rights and needs; "family clinics" cater first to individuals' (mostly women's) demands for control of their health, body, and reproductive rights. These are also the areas of the country where the birthrate is one of the lowest in the world, and in some regions (Emilia Romagna, Piemonte, Liguria) the divorce rate approaches that of the Nordic countries. All of this points to renegotiations and redefinitions of the marriage contract, including the gender division of labor and power (Barbagli 1990).

Current Trends and their Impact on Between-gender and Within-gender Inequalities

In recent years, a public debt apparently out of control, budget reforms required by the Maastricht deadline, and heavy criticism increasingly leveled at the delivery of public services have prompted a "hidden" reform of the Italian welfare state. This reform became more explicit with the measures approved in fall 1992: (1) a

The Familism of the Italian Welfare State ◆ 75

further shift of responsibilities from state to local governments in the areas of social assistance and services, (2) a re-privatization/re-familization of responsibilities for the cost of some services or goods (starting from needs, services, and goods in health care), and (3) an increasing institutionalization of "social partnership" between state or local governments and nonprofit or volunteer associations. At the same time, work-related social security benefits have been "purified" of "improper" meanings and aims (cutting all improperly defined work pensions), without instituting alternative non-work-related income support measures. As a consequence, an increasing number of welfare state provisions has moved from the area of either social security or citizenship rights to that of means-tested social assistance and has been labeled as public dependency.

Changes in the National Health Service are particularly important for understanding not only how family interdependence is used and constructed (by Italian policymakers to cut costs and ration individual rights), but also the deviousness and ambiguity of the state's redistributive mechanisms. Accelerating a process initiated in the eighties, the universalistic features of the National Health Service have been greatly restricted. Health services remain free for all citizens only in the cases of hospital care and prescriptions for specified chronic or life threatening illnesses. In all other cases, citizens are exempted from paying only if they are poor older persons, (i.e., receiving only a social or minimum pension), permanently disabled with an invalidity pension, or "certified poor," receiving income support from local authorities.[11] People who are not exempted from charges are divided into two categories on the basis of household income and family size. Those below the threshold pay, for example, a percentage on prescriptions, laboratory exams, and specialists' visits. Those above the threshold pay the full cost of those services, up to a certain amount.[12]

These measures might be interpreted as a further redistribution from those with higher incomes, who have already paid higher contributions and taxes, to those with lower incomes. Difficulties in accepting this interpretation derive from the ambiguous mixture through which the system is financed. Insofar as wage workers' contributions are the major part of the financing system, they expect to be entitled to services without further costs. Moreover, since taxes are derived more from wages than from any other income in Italy, workers above the income threshold feel cheated by a system that not only protects the poor, but rewards tax evaders.[13] Further, although family size is considered in the income threshold (an improvement with regard to the first formulation of the norm), the formula is too simplistic: the age of family members is not considered, particularly the age of children, a crucial element in determining needs and expenses for health care.

The risk is that, given the higher costs, households just above the income threshold will delay seeking specialist care as long as possible, and the benefits of preventative health care will be lost, with consequences for individuals and the community. This may influence as well the use of services that relate to the individual's freedom and privacy: if young girls, on the basis of their parents' income, will be asked to pay for a gynecologist's exam at the family clinic (which earlier had been free) and for birth control pills or other contraceptives and laboratory exams, it is predictable that many of them will renounce all such services and advice.[14]

Finally, given the abrupt rise in costs, a family just above the income threshold may decide it is more convenient for the wage earner with the lower income (usually the wife) to drop out of the official labor force. The consequences are clear not only for tax evasion, but for the social security and labor history of that earner. The new, long-term social security requirements and the short-term family-based requirements are in conflict here, particularly for "secondary" wage earners—married women. More generally, health care has returned to the status of a family-linked right, after about fifteen years as an individual right.

These trends are not univocal in meaning and consequences, however, although they all point to a retrenchment of direct state responsibilities in providing rights. Shifting the responsibilities of supporting the cost of services, such as health care and personal social services, back to families widens social inequalities and may have contradictory effects on the gender division of labor: it may encourage women who can command only low wages to abandon their jobs (or to enter the "black" labor market[15]) in order to keep the family income low enough to be exempted from the various kinds of charges and/or to exchange too costly social services with "free" family work. It may also encourage other families to remain or become dual-income families in order to bear the costs of those same services.

There is a further, and possibly increasing, differentiation of rights and provisions granted at the local level depending, on the one hand, on politically defined priorities (child care or services for older persons; at-home care or institutionalization) and clienteles, and, on the other hand, the availability of "social partners" (volunteer and nonprofit agencies). For example, it is already clear that while there are geographical areas where a synergy exists between public and

nonprofit and volunteer services, in other areas many needs are left
to family resources or unsupported small volunteer associations (Saraceno 1992b). This situation affects citizens regardless of gender,
but it also has a gender specificity insofar as the lack of a system
of public and/or nonprofit services has consequences for family incomes and women's care-giving work. Moreover, the limitations on
social expenses due to budget constraints will probably be hardest
on the weakest "clienteles": poor older persons (mostly women),
solo mothers, and so on.

The institutionalization of social partnership—cooperation between local government and nonprofit and volunteer associations—
certainly grants neither a reduction of public expenses nor a control on clientelism. Yet it constitutes a public admission that the
family is no longer the only adequate alternative to state-provided
services. Women's family work is no longer the only resource to be
called on when social provisions are scarce or inadequate. The increasing labor force participation rate among younger women (Gesano 1990; Pristinger 1992), together with the aging of the population (with an accompanying increase in demands for care), are
probably as relevant for this change as the more ideological shift
which values civil society and private (profit and nonprofit) initiatives against the "statist" model of the welfare state.

The various regional laws encouraging the maintenance of disabled persons within their homes, through income support for the
caring costs (whoever provides the caring work), have ambivalent
meanings and point in different directions.[16] On the one hand, the
laws acknowledge not only the individual's right to be cared for
without being institutionalized, but also the economic value of the
caring performed. On the other hand, while the standards of care
are not always granted, the short- and long-term impact on the caregivers (mostly women), as well as on their families, has not been
sufficiently considered, particularly since it will be the poorest group
who will use such income support, offering in exchange a woman's caring work, instead of using the income provided to partly
pay for a non-family care-giver.

From these observations, we see a high differentiation in both
families' and womens' options and conditions depending on their
locality, in terms of the local context and culture of social policy
and citizenship rights, and on the resources they have with regard
to the labor market—that is, depending on their location within the
two dimensions which now more than ever frame citizenship in Italy: local (regional) residence and participation in the labor market. Both are equally important in defining the degree of women's

78 ◆ Saraceno

autonomy from family responsibilities and ties, insofar as they determine the degree to which a portion of the reproductive work will
be cared for by social services instead of being defined as women's
unpaid work.

In turn, such specific circumstances might also encourage with-
in-family, between-sexes renegotiations of the gender structure of
family responsibilities and power, and the structuring and acknowledgment of dependencies and interdependencies, although there is
not a linear relationship between these phenomena. In any case,
women living in less favorable circumstances are likely to experience an even greater reduction of their individual social rights and
remain entangled in a double-edged family solidarity that makes
them dependent on their husbands' incomes.

NOTES

1. Provisions concerning youth unemployment allow that 18–29 (and
in some cases up to 35) year-old youths be hired under temporary—training—contracts at a minimum wage, under the assumption that they do not
have family responsibilities. No matter that the average age at marriage
for men in Italy is 27 and for women is 23: the "young" are by definition
still children living in their parents' household and partly still dependent
on them.

2. During the 1950s, social insurance coverage in Italy was the lowest
in western Europe due to the reduced pension and unemployment coverage (Ferrera 1985; Ferrera 1993; Flora and Alber 1981; Ascoli 1986).

3. Ferrera wrote: "Nowhere else (not even in countries characterized
by a high institutional fragmentation of provisions and policies) can one
detect such an intense diffusion of particularistic patterns of providing
benefits. . . . The party-clientelistic manipulation of social security provisions is an almost unique phenomenon of our country" (1985, 271–72).
Explanations of this usually refer to the presence of a strong class conflict
and of strongly conflicting ideological identities and memberships (e.g.,
Catholic and Communist) and to the impossibility of really changing government coalitions during the Cold War. Party government and clientelism
were ways of dealing with and controlling conflict, and consequences of
the lack of change among those in power.

4. In Italy there are two kinds of publicly-subsidized preschool services: crèches, or day care (*asili nido*), are for children three months to three
years old; kindergartens (*scuola materna,* or *scuola per l'infanzia*) are for
children three to five years old. Crèches are open about eight hours a day,
five days a week, eleven months a year; kindergartens are open six to eight
hours a day, five days a week, ten months a year. The creches are more
expensive for parents (who pay a fee based on family income), less widespread, and a municipal responsibility; kindergartens are almost free for
parents (who pay only a nominal fee plus the price of the school meal),
more widespread, and mostly a state responsibility. Both offer care and

The Familism of the Italian Welfare State ◆ 79

education, although historically creches have been defined more as a caring and social assistance service, while kindergartens have been defined more in educational terms.

5. In principle, this system should have been financed through general taxation. This part of the reform, however, was never implemented and the system maintained a dual financing system: through workers' and employers' contributions, as in the old systems, and through taxation for the self-employed. Given the inefficiency of the Italian fiscal system, the burden of financing the National Health Service for all citizens remained heavier for wage workers and for citizens living not only in the richer regions of the country, but in the regions where the quota of (official) wage work was higher. This phenomenon, combined with bureaucratic inefficiency and political clientelism, eventually led to the present financial crisis of the National Health Service: each year the state has to cover each region's budget deficit in health care and, at the same time, regions are not always able to hire the needed personnel or finance needed purchases of medical equipment and restructuring of hospitals. These problems lie behind the reform of the system inaugurated in fall 1992.

6. A surviving husband may now receive a survivor's pension. Survivors' pensions are paid even to people (men and women) who have a pension or income already. Surviving children no longer receive it when they reach the legal age of eighteen.

7. In recent years women's and parents' groups, as well as day care workers' groups, have been campaigning for the acknowledgment of day care as an educational rather than only as a caring service. These groups insist that it is a working mother's and a child's right, because of the changes in family composition and the increasing awareness of the importance of early intellectual stimulation and education.

8. In Italy there is no universal child benefit, as there is in England or France. Fascism introduced family allowances for wage workers: family allowances were paid to wage workers who were family heads, usually husbands, for their dependents (mothers received allowances if they were wage workers without husbands). This system continued until the mid-eighties, when the amount was raised and means testing introduced. Now these allowances are paid to families of wage workers and pensioners below family income thresholds. These thresholds are indexed and differ according to family size and are higher if it is a one-parent family or if there is a disabled family member. In Italy, "family income" exists only for means-testing purposes, not for taxation. Income taxes, in fact, are based on individually earned income, and citizens are taxed separately on their income. Economically dependent spouses, children, and parents entitle the taxpayer to a tax deduction.

9. Italian citizens have been divided into three categories based on family income: (1) the "poor" (particularly older persons and the disabled poor), who receive health services and prescription drugs free of charge, (2) the "low income," who must pay a percentage for each prescription and lab exam, and (3) the "rich," who must pay the full cost of prescriptions and lab exams. The income threshold is defined in relation to family size.

80 ◆ Saraceno

10. It is interesting, at any rate, that among younger couples an increasing number chose not to have community property. This is true for over 50 percent of new marriages in the larger towns of the Center-North. It increases among women who are more educated and is directly linked with their having paid jobs (Barbagli 1993). Apparently more women are choosing not to consider the family as an economic unit, even if this might weaken their economic rights if and when their marriage breaks up.

11. In order to avoid abuse (and instead of controlling general practitioners), these "exempted" persons are given stamps which are withdrawn one by one with each prescription. When they exhaust their stamps, they may receive some other assistance based on the general practitioner's advice.

12. In order to use the general practitioner they must also pay an annual charge of L.85.000 for each household member. This last charge is compulsory, whether one uses the National Health Service general practitioner or not.

13. The question is complicated further by the fact that the income considered refers to 1992 but, due to the economic crisis, many (both blue- and white-collar) families' incomes have been reduced because of cuts in overtime pay and regular working hours, or, worse still, job loss. More generally, many families are not at all secure that their income will be assured even through one year—they may lose their jobs.

14. Further changes are envisaged in the Financial Law to be approved at the end of 1994. These changes take account more of age than of household size and income. Children under age twelve and people over age sixty-five should receive services free of charge. It is not possible to be more precise about this because the law is at present being debated and there are new proposals almost daily.

15. The black (or informal) labor market is, of course, not covered by social security. Both wages and employers' profits evade taxation. These may include jobs as servants, housecleaners, or childminders, or work in small workshops and offices. Many women, as well as young people, work in this market. Many men with social-security covered jobs also hold a job in this informal market.

16. The amount paid may vary, although it usually ranges between the social and minimum pensions. At the national level, laws stipulate that disabled individuals who are not self-sufficient may be entitled to an "accompanying person" indemnity and that an individual who forfeited working in order to care for a disabled person will receive a social pension when old. Employed people may take temporary unpaid leaves, with seniority guaranteed, in order to care for a disabled person.

REFERENCES

Artoni, R., and E. Ranci Ortigosa. 1989. *La Spesa Pubblica per L'assistenza in Italia.* Milano: F. Angeli.

Ascoli, U. 1986. "The Growth in the Social Welfare System in the Post-War Period." Pp. 108–41 in *Time to Care in Tomorrow's Welfare Systems,* ed. L. Balbo and H. Nowotny. Wien: Eurosocial.

Balbo, L. 1977. "Un caso di Capitalismo Assistenziale: La Società Italiana."
    Inchiesta 7:1–5.

———. 1982. "'Patchwork': Una Prospettiva sulla Società di Capitalismo
    Maturo." Pp. 32–53 in *Ricomposizioni,* ed. L. Balbo and M. Bianchi.
    Milano: F. Angeli.

———. 1984. "Famiglia e Stato nella Società Contemporanea." *Stato e
    Mercato* 10:3–32.

Barbagli, Marzio. 1990. *Provando e Riprovando: Matrimonio e divorzio
    in Italia e Negli Altri Paesi Occidentali.* Bologna: il Mulino.

———. 1993. "Comunione o Separazione dei Beni? I rapporti Patrimoni-
    ali fra Coniugi in Italia: 1975–91." *Polis* 7, no. 1: 143–62.

Bimbi, F. 1992. "Tre Generazioni di Donne: Le Trasformazioni dei Modelli
    di Identità Femminile in Italia." Pp. 65–98 in *Educazione,* ed. Ulivieri.

Castellino, O. 1976. *Il Labirinto delle Pensioni.* Bologna: il Mulino.

Commissione per l'analisi dell'Impatto Sociale. 1990. *Pensioni, Lavoro,
    Equità: Effetti della Formula di Calcolo della Pensione.* Roma: Poligrafi-
    co dello Stato.

De Singly, Françoise. 1987. *Fortune et Infortune de la Femme Mariée.* Paris:
    Presses Universitaires de France.

Donati, P. P. 1981. *Famiglia e Politiche Sociali.* Milano: F. Angeli.

Esping-Andersen, Gosta. 1990. *The Three Worlds of Welfare Capitalism.*
    Oxford: Polity Press.

Farneti, P. 1978. *La Democrazia Italiana tra Crisi e Innovazione.* Torino:
    Edizioni Fondazione Agnelli.

Ferrera, M. 1985. *Il Welfare State in Italia.* Bologna: il Mulino.

———. 1993. *Modelli di Solidarietà.* Bologna: il Mulino.

Flora, P., and J. Alber. 1981. "Modernization, Democratization, and the
    Development of Welfare States in Western Europe." Pp. 37–80 in *The
    Development of Welfare States in Europe and America,* ed. P. Flora and
    A. J. Heidenheimer. New Brunswick and London: Transaction Books.

Gesano, G. 1990. Dieci anni di Evoluzione del Mercato del Lavoro Ital-
    iano: 1978–87: Un'Analisi per Generazioni nel Nord-Centro e nel Mez-
    zogiorno. Working paper, Consiglio Nazionale delle Ricerche/Istituto di
    Ricercho Sulla Popolazione.

Langan, M., and I. Ostner. 1991. "Gender and Welfare: Towards a Com-
    parative Framework." Pp. 127–50 in *Towards a European Welfare
    State?* ed. G. Room. Bristol: SAUS Publications.

Oliver, J. 1983. "The Caring Wife." In *The Public and the Private,* ed.
    Eva Garmanikov. London: Heinemann.

Paci, M. 1984. "Il Sistema de Welfare Italiano tra Tradizione Clientelare
    e Prospettiva di Riforma." In *Welfare State all'Italiana,* ed. U. Ascoli.
    Bari: Laterza.

———. 1989. *Pubblico e Privato nei Moderni Sistemi di Welfare.* Napoli:
    Liguori.

Pahl, J. 1989. *Money and Marriage.* Macmillan: London.

Pahl, J. M., and R. E. Pahl. 1971. *Managers and their Wives: A Study of
    Career and Family Relationships in the Middle Class.* London: Allen
    Lane.

82 ◆ Saraceno

Pristinger, F. 1992. "Il Lavoro delle Donne: Passato e Presente." Pp. 143–76 in *Educazione*, ed. Ulivieri.

Rusconi, G. E., and S. Scamuzzi, eds. 1981. "Italy: An Eccentric Society," special issue. *Current Sociology* 29, no. 1 (Spring).

Saraceno, C. 1991. "Redefining Maternity and Paternity: Gender, Pronatalism and Social Policies in Fascist Italy." Pp. 196–221 in *Maternity and Gender Policies: Women and the Rise of the European Welfare States, 1880s-1950s*, ed. G. Bock and P. Thane. London and New York: Routledge.

———. 1992a. "EC Observatory on Policies to Combat Social Exclusion." Consolidated National Report. Lille.

———. 1992b. "EC Observatory on Policies to Combat Social Exclusion." Part II: Social Services. National Report: Italy. Turin.

Tarrow, S. 1979. *Tra Centro e Periferia: Il Ruolo degli Amministratori Locali in Italia e in Francia.* Bologna: il Mulino.

Ulivieri, S., ed. 1992. *Educazione e Ruolo Femminile.* Firenze: La Nuova Italia.

[22]

New Gold Plan

Revised Ten-Year Strategy to Promote Health Care and Welfare for the Elderly
(New Gold Plan)

December 18, 1994

An Agreement of the Ministers of Finance, Health and Welfare and Home Affairs

(Basic Direction for the Revision)

- The development of health care and welfare services for the elderly has been steadily promoted under the "Ten-year Strategy to Promote Health Care and Welfare for the Elderly" (an agreement of the Ministers of Finance, Health and Welfare and Home Affairs in December 1989). However, in the Local Health and Welfare Plans for the Elderly prepared by nationwide local public bodies in the previous year, the necessity of developing health and welfare services for the elderly which substantially exceeded the objectives of the Gold Plan was identified. Since the drawing up of the Gold Plan, various measures concerning health and welfare services for the elderly have been improved upon. It was then decided to make an extensive review of the Gold Plan to further improve measures concerning personal care for the elderly.

- In reviewing the Gold Plan, taking into consideration regional needs, it is vital to upgrade the goals related to the urgent development of infrastructures for care services for the elderly as well as establishing a new basic framework for future measures. To achieve this, specific measures will be taken paying special consideration to securing revenue sources up to 1999.

- The total project expenditure between FY 1995 and 1999 will be over nine trillion yen including projects already begun in the on-going Gold Plan.

> **Upgrading the Goals Related to the Urgent Development
> of Infrastructures for care services for the Elderly, etc.
> (Current development goals up to te end of FY 1999)**

(1) In-home Services

	At present	After the revision
· Home helpers	100,000 helpers	170,000 helpers
(Home helper stations)	—	10,000 stations
· Short Stay	50,000 beds	60,000 beds
· Day services/Day care	10,000 centers	17,000 centers
· In-home care support centers	10,000 centers	10,000 centers
· Home-visit nursing care stations for the elderly	—	5,000 stations

(2) Facility Services

	At present	After the revision
· Special nursing homes for the elderly	240,000 beds	290,000 beds
· Health service facilities for the elderly	280,000 beds	280,000 beds
· Living welfare centers for the elderly	400 centers	400 centers
· Care houses	100,000 beds	100,000 beds

(3) Staff Development

	At present	After the revision
· Matron & care staff	—	200,000 persons
· Nursing staff, etc.	—	100,000 persons
· OTs & PTs	—	15,000 persons

> **Basic Framework for the Development of the Care Service Infrastructure for the Elderly**

⟨Basic Principles⟩

> To establish a system through which all elderly people can maintain their dignity and live their lives independently even if they are mentally and/or physically handicapped and to provide everyone who needs care — the most serious concern for the elderly — with the services necessary for their independence.
>
> i   User-oriented support for independence
>
>   To support the independence of the elderly by providing high quality user-oriented services respecting the intention and choice of each elderly person.
>
> ii   Universality
>
>   To provide necessary services universally for every elderly person who needs support.
>
> iii   Supply of comprehensive services
>
>   To provide effective and comprehensive services to meet the diverse needs of the elderly which extend over health care, medical treatment and welfare centering on in-home services.
>
> iv   Regionalization
>
>   To establish service provision systems centering on municipal offices so that necessary services can be provided carefully within the community where residents feel most at-home.

〈Goals of the Measures〉

I   **Development of the Comprehensive Care Service Infrastructure for the Elderly**

Ⅰ. Upgrading Regional Care Services for the Elderly

(1) In-home Services

1) Making 24-hour continuous (mobile) home help services widely available.

2) Encouraging the effective use of short stay and care services offered at health care facilities for the elderly as well as making these services widely available.

3) Promoting the establishment of small scale day service centers, etc. by easing the requirements for the establishment of day service centers.

4) Reinforcing general counseling and care management functions of in-home care support centers by integrating in-home services and establishing service networks as well as providing easy access to health and welfare service information provision support systems.

5) Promoting home-based medical treatment by upgrading professional standards for personal physicians. For example, the broad application of comprehensive medical fees for the bedridden elderly at home

6) Increasing the number of service providers by easing restrictions on in-home welfare service providers.

7) Conducting service quality evaluation of in-home and facility services from the users' viewpoint and encouraging the drawing up of care plans for individual elderly persons to provide them with appropriate care.

(2) Facility Services

1) Promoting the development of medical care wards for the elderly which have the environment and staff with the health care skills suitable for physical and mental conditions of elderly persons.

2) Upgrading the nursing care environment at facilities and hospitals focusing on the continuity of living. For example, the expansion of basic room areas of special nursing homes for the elderly (promoting private rooms) and the improvement of dining halls and conversation rooms at medical care wards for the elderly.

3) Promoting the modernization of facilities and independence support functions through the active introduction of technical aids including personal care equipment.

4) Taking supportive measures to develop small scale special nursing homes for the elderly in urban areas.

5) Promoting the comprehensive improvement of day-care centers, welfare centers for the elderly, municipal health care centers and other local public facilities and the utilization of unused classrooms.

6) Utilizing land and buildings, which have become available as a result of the reorganization of national hospitals and national sanatoriums, for the development of health service facilities for the elderly.

2. Implementation of Comprehensive Measures to Support the Independence of the Elderly Needing Care

(1) Implementing the Renovated Campaign to Reduce the Number of Bedridden Elderly People to Zero

1) In order to prevent the elderly from becoming bedridden and to actively support their independence, regional rehabilitation systems will be reinforced. To do this, regional rehabilitation programs centering on local health care centers will be promoted.

2) Upgrading health care programs to prevent cerebral apoplexy, bone fractures, etc.

3) Development of municipal health care centers to act bases for local health care services for the elderly will be promoted.

4) Recruiting local public health nurses to provide instructions on preventive measures and in-home care for the bedridden and elderly dementia patients on a local basis.

(2) Implementing Healthy Independence Support Programs

Implementing healthy independence support programs to assist the elderly in actively living out their old age.

(3) Making Meal Services and Emergency Communication Systems Widely Available

Making meal services for frail elderly persons at home and emergency communication systems for elderly persons living alone at home widely available.

3. Implementation of Comprehensive Measures for elderly dementia patients

(1) Improvement of Educational Activities and Counseling and Information Services

1) Disseminating accurate information on senile dementia.

2) Reinforcing the cooperation of regional counseling bodies such as in-home care support centers, medical care centers for elderly dementia patients and municipal health care centers.

3) Promoting the development of medical care centers for elderly dementia patients.

(2) Senile Dementia Prevention and Early Detection and Treatment

Senile dementia prevention and early detection and treatment systems will be established by upgrading senile dementia training programs for personal physicians, public health nurses, care staff, etc.

(3) Improvement of Treatment and Care for elderly dementia patients

   1) Promoting the acceptance of elderly dementia patients through existing health care and welfare service facilities.

   2) Developing day services and day care facilities specializing in senile dementia.

   3) Improving health care facilities specializing in senile dementia.

   4) Improving medical care wards for senile dementia.

   5) Upgrading home-based care services such as small scale communities (group homes) and day services.

(4) Establishing Cures for Senile Dementia and Promoting Research and Development

   1) Research into the actual condition of senile dementia will be promoted. In addition, as part of the research on aging and health, various research and study programs will be promoted to identify the true nature of senile dementia and devise cures.

   2) Development of care processes and treatment methods for elderly dementia patients will be promoted.

(5) Protecting the Rights of elderly dementia patients

   Systems to protect the rights of elderly dementia patients, including legislation, will be considered.

4. Promotion of Measures which Support Productive Aging and the Social Involvement of the Elderly

Efforts will be made to effectively implement the "Project to Promote the Health of the Elderly and to Provide the Elderly with a Fulfilling Life." The social involvement of the elderly will be promoted by supporting old people's culb activities.

> II   Implementation of Comprehensive Support Measures for the Development of the Care Service Infrastructure

Ⅰ. Measures to Develop and Secure Staff to Care for the Elderly

(1) Improving Training Facilities

In-home nursing care training facilities will be improved at training facilities for OTs and PTs, certified care workers and nurses.

(2) Improving the Skills of Care Staff and the Establishment of Training Systems

Training programs for home helpers, newly employed facility workers and home-visit nurses will be upgraded and training centers to support in-home medical treatment will be developed.

(3) Improvement of Working Environment to Help Recruit Quality Staff

In order to recruit quality staff on a stable basis, the working environment for health and welfare related staff will be improved by introducing labor saving measures, reducing working hours and upgrading welfare programs.

2. Promoting the Development and Use of Technical Aids

(1) Promoting Research and Development into Technical Aids

In order to help the elderly and handicapped become independent and reduce the burden on care providers, the development of technical aids will be promoted.

To achieve this, proceeds resulting from the operation of the Longevity Social Welfare Funds will be provided to support research and development activities. Various programs including research into health care equipment at the National Rehabilitation Center for the Disabled will be promoted on a national level.

(2) Promoting the Broad Use of Technical Aids

1) In order to cultivate the broad use of technical aids, 59 practical health care training and dissemination centers will be established throughout the nation and counseling, information services and hands-on programs concerning technical aids will be promoted.

2) To support the independence of those who need care at home, an extensive review will be made of equipment provision programs, etc. and a system will be established through which all those elderly people needing support will be able to choose appropriate technical aids depending on their individual needs.

3) The active introduction of technical aids to institutions and hospitals will proceed along with the modernization of these facilities by streamlining care providing procedures, etc. and improving the measures which support patient independence by upgrading rehabilitation programs.

3. Wide Ranging Improvements to the Provision of Easy-to-Use Service Systems

Specific measures will be taken to provide residents with a wide variety of care related information. To do this, the development of in-home care support centers will be promoted and their information providing functions will be enhanced.

In addition, the development of more practical systems to provide information about the use of in-home health care services and the condition of service users will be promoted.

4. Diversification and Flexibility in the Provision of Services Including the Utilization of Private Services

(1) Diversification and flexibility in the provision of services through the active utilization of private institutions in addition to public services will be promoted to allow the elderly to choose independently those services which meet their diverse and increasing needs for care services and to promote effective and quality care service supply through sound competition.

To achieve this,

1) deregulation of core organizations which provide care services will be deregulated and a contract arrangement awarded to exemplary private service providers will be established.

2) To secure quality private services, service evaluation systems including the broad establishment of the Silver Mark system will be in place.

5. Promotion of In-depth Research on Aging and Health

In-depth research into old age science and health ranging from basic areas to the development of preventive measures and cures for old age diseases, nursing and health care, the development of support equipment, and social sciences will be promoted.

6. Promotion of Housing and Community Development Measures

(1) Housing Developments for the Elderly and Handicapped

1) Developing care houses and government managed apartments.

2) Taking supportive measures for the development of small scale care houses in urban areas, etc.

3) In order to upgrade private residential buildings focusing on the elderly and handicapped, governmental loans will be provided to facilitate the construction and renovation of residential buildings as well as to private businesses which supply domiciles including condominiums for the elderly and handicapped.

4) Drawing up residential manuals and design guidelines focusing on the elderly as well as upgrading the professional standards of renovation advisors, etc.

(2) Development of Domiciles Equipped with Life Supporting Functions for the Elderly

1) Developing care houses with home helper stations and day service centers.

2) The development of domiciles equipped with life supporting functions combining domiciles and in-home welfare services will be promoted. For example, the development of silver housing and senior residences and the integration of public apartments and day service centers.

(3) Promotion of Community Developments Carefully Designed for the Convenience of the Elderly or Handicapped

1) Further promotion of "Community Developments with Special Consideration Being Paid to the Elderly and Handicapped"

2) The development of comprehensive private health and welfare facilities will be promoted.

3) Promoting community developments to provide the elderly and handicapped with comfortable living environments by eliminating barriers in public spaces such as public buildings and roads.

7. Promotion of Volunteer Activities, Welfare Education and Public Involvement

(1) Promotion of Volunteer Activities and Welfare Education

Volunteer activities will be promoted by upgrading volunteer center programs as well as establishing volunteer activity bases such as local welfare centers. Student volunteer activities will also be encouraged.

(2) Promotion of Public Involvement

Public involvement will be encouraged by enhancing the general public's access to practical information and techniques on health care.

⟨Implementation of the Measures⟩

To achieve these objectives, the national, prefectural and municipal governments will implement appropriate programs depending on their roles and capacity as well as supporting measures to care for the elderly which will be carried out independently by local public bodies taking advantage of regional characteristics.

⟨Involvement with Future Tax Reforms, etc.⟩

● With respect to measures to care for the elderly, certain financial measures was decided upon as part of the latest tax reform. However, in order to ensure stable development of the care service infrastructure for the elderly, the means to secure the funds required in the context of securing the necessary social security budget in connection with revisions to the national and local consumption tax rates is now under consideration.

● In addition, to furnish care services which the general public can use effectively and smoothly, it has been decided to develop comprehensive measures to care for the elderly including the establishment of a new public care system.

Previous Gold Plan

Japan now leads the world in terms of longevity with an average life expectancy of 80 years. In the 21st century, one out of four citizens will be 65 years old or older. It is vital to make the silver society in the 21st century a society where everyone is healthy, has something to live for and is able to live their whole lives with peace of mind.

To achieve this, taking into account the reason for the introduction of the consumption tax, it has been decided to develop the public service infrastructure in the field of health care and welfare for the elderly as well as promoting in-home and facility service development programs with 10-year goals to be achieved by the end of this century.

1 . Urgent Development of Measures for In-home Services on a Municipal Level
    ——Ten-Year Project to Promote In-home Services for the elderly
  (1) Home helpers   100,000 helpers
  (2) Short stay   50,000 beds
  (3) Day service centers   10,000 centers
  (4) In-home care support centers   10,000 centers
  (5) Short stay centers, day service centers and in-home care support centers will be established in all municipalities.
  (6) In-home service providers (incorporated foundations such as public corporations) will be established in all municipalities.
  (7) Promoting the "Project to Develop Welfare Communities for Comfortable Living" (including municipalities with a population of less than 50,000.)

2 . Campaign "to Reduce the Number of Bedridden Elderly People to Zero"
  (1) Systems will be developed to provide practical training to anyone who wishes to receive functional training.
  (2) A cerebral apoplexy information system will be developed covering the entire population.
  (3) Recruiting staff
       In addition to increasing the number of home helpers, staff including nurses and public health nurses will be systematically assigned to in-home care support centers.
       · In-home care instructors (nurses, public health nurses, etc.)   20,000persons
       · In-home care consultants and assistants (community volunteers) 80,000persons
  (4) Health education, etc. will be improved to prevent cerebral apoplexy, bone fractures, etc.

3 . Establishment of the "Longevity Social Welfare Fund" to Upgrade In-home Welfare Services, etc.
  (1) In order to promote in-home welfare services, a 70-billion yen fund will be established.
  (2) The fund will be mainly used for the following projects:
       (a) To support in-home welfare and medical services

(b) To promote measures to provide the elderly with something to live for and to enhance the health of the elderly.

4. Urgent Development of Facilities————10-Year Project to Promote the Establishment of Facilities

(1)	Special nursing homes for the elderly	240,000 beds
(2)	Facilities for health care services for the elderly	280,000 beds
(3)	Care houses	100,000 beds
(4)	Living welfare centers for the elderly in depopulated areas	400 centers

5. Promotion of Measures for Productive Aging

(1) "Organizations to Promote a Prosperous Old-Age Society" will be established in all prefectures.

(2) A "Model Project to Promote the Health of the Elderly and to Provide the Elderly with a Fulfilling Life" will be established.

6. 10-Year Project to Promote Research on Aging and Health

(1) The National Research Center for the Science of Old Age will be established to improve the research base, and at the same time a foundation will be established to suport research on aging and health

(2) Conducting in-depth research on aging and health ranging from basic areas to the development of preventive measures and cures, nursing and health care and social sciences.

(3) In addition, measures will be taken to ensure that the children who will have to support the silver society in the future are born and raised in a healthy environment. In particular, health care measures and medical services for mothers and children to ensure lifelong health will be further promoted from a medium to long term perspective.

7. Development of Comprehensive Welfare Facilities for the Elderly

(1) Development of comprehensive private health care and welfare facilities for the elderly will be promoted. ("Furusato (My Home Town) 21: a program to develop communities where the residents can live long and healthy lives.)

(2) Development of comprehensive facilities centering on public service providers which provide the elderly with domiciles, nursing care and opportunities for health improvement and productive activities will be considered together with the utilization of land which has become available as a result of the reorganization of national hospitals and national sanatoriums

In addition to the above, support will be given to health care and welfare services for the aged which local public bodies develop and implement independently taking advantage of regional characteristics.

[23]

Needs-Based Strategies of Social Protection in Australia and New Zealand

Francis G. Castles

For much of the past century – although to different degrees in different periods and to different degrees in the two countries – Australia and New Zealand have been the clearest examples of a particular approach to social protection. That approach rests on guaranteeing minimum levels of social protection to those who meet certain conditions. One such condition is need, with the emergence, in these countries, of the world's most comprehensive systems of means tested income support benefits. Means testing is not, of course, unique to the Antipodes, but what has been unique is a further set of guarantees providing minimum income levels for those in employment also supposedly related to a social policy definition of need. Together these guarantees have underpinned a model of the welfare state quite unlike those of Western Europe and North America.

Earlier this century, the emergent Antipodean nations were frequently regarded as laboratories for path-breaking social experiments. In 1913, an American scholar felt it appropriate to point to 'the ideals which have animated the Australian people and the Australian lawmakers in placing on the statute book the body of social legislation which has drawn the eyes of all the World to Australia, and which marks the most notable experiment yet made in social democracy' (Hammond, 1913: 285). In 1949, the ILO would note that the New Zealand Social Security Act of 1938 has 'more than any other law, determined the practical meaning of social security, and so has deeply influenced the course of legislation in other countries' (ILO, 1949: iii). More recently, however, the combination of low aggregate social expenditure and widespread means testing manifested by these nations gave them the reputation of being amongst the worst laggards of social development during the Golden Age of the welfare state. Now, with the Golden Age but a memory, an account of the features making the Antipodean welfare state model distinctive may be instructive in widening the repertoire of policy options for those seeking to achieve the basics of social protection in an era in which 'choices of restraints and innovation' (Heidenheimer et al., 1990: 17) are unquestionably the order of the day.

The wage earners' welfare state

Social protection by other means

During the third of a century or so following the Second World War, the Antipodean nations were amongst those for which a very strong case can be mounted that the exigencies threatening disruption to the 'working class life course' (Myles, 1990: 274) had been largely tamed. In 1950, Australia's and New Zealand's GDP per capita levels were respectively fifth and sixth highest in the world (Summers and Heston, 1991) and in both countries there was an extensive and state regulated system of minimum wages leading to greater wage compression than in most other comparable nations (Lydall, 1968: 153; Easton, 1983). Nor were the wage packets of most workers much reduced by taxation, with a very strong preference for progressive income taxation on the well-off rather than on indirect taxes or social security contributions that impacted on ordinary wage earners.

Most important of all, in both countries, a combination of Keynesian demand management and measures protective of local industries had led to extremely low levels of unemployment. In New Zealand 'in March 1956 only 5 unemployment benefits were being paid, and thus there was some substance to the claims of politicians that they knew the unemployed by name' (Shirley, 1990). According to the economists, Australia 'enjoyed brimful employment' in the 1950s (Karmel and Brunt, 1962) and an increase to over 2 per cent in 1961 very nearly toppled the long-running Liberal government and forced it into instant reflationary measures. Australia maintained full employment until the mid 1970s and New Zealand until the early 1980s. Given these conditions, plus the strong ties of family dependency implicit in high fertility rates, low divorce rates (UN, 1970) and rates of female labour market participation well below OECD norms until the late 1960s (OECD, 1992: Table 2.8), it is arguable that wage earners and those dependent on them experienced a relatively high level of social protection throughout this period.

On the surface, at least, it would not appear that the same could be said of those outside the labour force and dependent on social security. In Australia, all social security benefits other than child allowances were incomes tested and, in New Zealand, the only exceptions to incomes testing were, again, child allowances plus a universal, but income taxed, super-annuation benefit payable at age 65. In both countries, all benefits were flat-rate and all were financed directly from the General Exchequer. After 1960, Australia and New Zealand were the only OECD countries without any form of contributory social insurance, a fact which does much to explain the lack of pressure for greater universalism: contributions not only fund benefits, they also create a view that all should benefit!

Replacement rates in Australia varied from genuine subsistence level (unemployment and sickness benefits) to no more than the basis for a frugal existence (the age pension) (see Henderson et al., 1970). In New Zealand, overall expenditure levels were high at the beginning of the period

(ILO, 1972), allowing very generous provision in certain areas. However, over a long period of right-wing political dominance, benefit levels were eaten away by inflation. In 1972, Labour governments were elected in both countries with a mandate to increase welfare spending, but that followed a decade in which the Antipodean nations had been the only ones in the OECD experiencing a decline in income maintenance expenditure as a percentage of GDP (OECD, 1976). It is these features which have made contemporary European observers and domestic critics alike point to the weaknesses of the Antipodean welfare states.

Nonetheless, for the period discussed here, the evidence does not suggest that inadequacies in the benefit systems translated into working class life courses that were more subject to fluctuation than in other advanced nations. The most obvious reason why this should have been so was, of course, the fact that unemployment was minuscule and almost entirely frictional. But there were other factors intrinsic to the design of Antipodean social policy which also served as important offsets to the supposed weaknesses of the welfare state system. Incomes tests on unemployment, sickness and invalidity benefits are of rather less practical significance than is sometimes supposed by the social policy community (cf. Esping-Andersen, 1990: 78), given that the conditions which define entitlement automatically prevent disqualification on income grounds. Over time, moreover, there was a gradual shift in emphasis, with means tests designed less to target the very poor and more to exclude the middle class. Universal superannuation in New Zealand and progressive age pension incomes test liberalization in Australia made for an increasingly residual definition of the excluded rather than the included group, with the prevailing notion being one of a welfare state in retirement for 'the battlers' (the preferred Australian term) or 'the ordinary bloke' (a New Zealand formulation).

Apart from these factors, mitigating the supposedly deleterious effects of widespread means testing, were others modifying the impact of relatively low, flat-rate benefits. Most important was the institution of supplementation for dependants on the basis of need, so that a relatively small flat-rate unemployment or sickness benefit might be doubled or trebled where a beneficiary supported a spouse and dependent children. It should be remembered, too, that flat-rate benefits are singularly more favourable to maintaining the living standards of those at or below average wage levels than to preserving the life styles of those in higher income echelons. All other things being equal, the means tested, flat-rate, welfare state is far more redistributive than the universal, income-related one (see Åberg, 1989).

As important as these intrinsic factors were institutional arrangements, rarely considered aspects of the welfare state as such, which mitigated the impact of low and/or declining transfers in these countries. It is these distinctive institutional features of the Antipodean welfare states that explain why sickness and, in particular, old age were not, for the great majority, significant threats to income maintenance across the life cycle.

Although spending on social insurance sickness benefits in this period was extremely low by OECD standards (Varley, 1986) and remains so (Kangas, 1991), the reason was that the same system of wage regulation which enjoined minimum wage levels also guaranteed workers stipulated numbers of sickness leave days paid for by the employer at full wage rates. In Australia, this obligation dated back to the interwar period, and meant that, in practical terms, Australia was a pioneer in respect of this form of social provision (Castles, 1992).

Looked at from a comparative perspective, two factors mitigated the impact of old age on poverty in the Antipodes. The first arose from a far more youthful age profile than in most parts of Europe. The second, which served to offset the low replacement rate of pensions, was a highly institutionalized and culturally ingrained system of private home ownership, with figures for owner-occupation being around 70 per cent in both countries during much of the post-war era (on New Zealand, see Thorns, 1984; on Australia, see Kemeny, 1980). For older couple households, ownership free of mortgage obligations is nearly universal, with recent figures for both countries of around 85–90 per cent (on New Zealand, see Thorns, 1993, 98; on Australia, see Gruen and Grattan, 1993: 184). Since home ownership leads to an appreciable diminution of the need for cash income (see St John, 1993: 124), this must be regarded as a very important offset to the low replacement rates of income support payments in these countries.

This system resting on wage compression and low-level, needs-based, income support did not, of course, mean that poverty and destitution in these countries was wholly absent. There is, however, no reason to suppose that gaps in Australasian safety-net provision at this time were any greater than in other advanced nations. They were, however, differently located. The author of Australia's major poverty study of the late 1960s, Ronald Henderson, argued that the crucial difference between Australia and most other OECD countries lay in the lower percentage of the poor to be found in the workforce. In the OECD, overall, half the poor were working, a figure which contrasted with around a quarter in Australia, and suggested that 'the high level and comprehensive coverage of minimum wage legislation in Australia . . . meant that Australia had a much smaller group of "working poor"' (Henderson, 1978: 169). Given that, in New Zealand, the prevailing architecture of the welfare state was also based on 'enforcing minimum wage regulations and subsidising those outside the wage system with selective benefits' (Davidson, 1989: 250), it seems reasonable to suppose that the New Zealand system was similarly biased.

The use of wage regulation as the primary instrument of social protection and the distinctive pattern of social policy outcomes resulting from it have been the basis for labelling the Antipodean nations as 'wage earners' welfare states' (Castles, 1985: 102–9), a description and, in many cases, a designation which has achieved some currency in both countries (on Australia, see e.g. Brown, 1989: 51 and Bryson, 1992: 89–99; on New

Zealand, see the analysis of Davidson, 1989 and the comments of Walsh, 1993b: 190 and Rudd, 1993: 240). The typical life cycle profile produced by the wage earners' welfare state in this period is clearly distinguishable from those emanating from other welfare state types – most notably in its unusually equalizing thrust within both the working population (reduced wage dispersion) and the group dependent on benefits (flat-rate provision) combined with a somewhat greater discrepancy between the two life cycle stages as a result of the system's lesser generosity to all beneficiaries other than those on below average wages or with above average needs.

Origins and logic

In very simple terms, what made for a distinctive set of strategies of social protection in the Antipodes was a different historical context. Perhaps to a greater degree even than in Europe and Scandinavia, social advances were a function of growing affluence and working class politics. However, what was different about the Antipodes was that these countries were rich from the latter part of the nineteenth century onwards (for Australia, see Maddison, 1991; for New Zealand, see Rankin, 1992: 46–9) and that, in these newly democratized settler societies, the labour movement was politically strong far earlier than in Europe (the world's first Labour government was a minority government in the State of Queensland in 1899). This meant that the push for social amelioration occurred in a quite different intellectual climate to that of Europe of the 1930s and 1940s – a climate in which the issue of addressing the problem of want was seen in terms of what was commonly called 'the problem of wages' rather than of state expenditure for welfare.

Turn-of-the-century Antipodean social reformers with strong labour movement support set out to tackle 'the problem of wages' directly, with their most important innovation being courts of arbitration with the power to set wage rates. The outcome was to make wage awards subject to forces other than those of the market, and, in particular, to allow some room for wage-fixing on the basis of social policy criteria. Contemporary New Zealand commentators talked of a 'theory of fair wages . . . sufficient to give the worker a decent living according to the colonial standard' (Le Rossignol and Stewart, 1910: 239) and the Australian Court of Arbitration suggested that a 'fair and reasonable wage' was one which met 'the normal needs of the average employee regarded as a human being living in a civilised community' (Higgins, 1922). Since the 'average employee' of the time was a male, and since his 'normal needs' included his domestic responsibilities, a 'fair wage' was very rapidly defined as a wage sufficient to support a wife and two or three children. In this sense, the notion of the 'family wage' has been at the heart of Antipodean social and wages policy since the first quarter of the century.

But by itself, the institution of compulsory arbitration could not be regarded as a sufficient basis for resolving the issue of social protection in a capitalist economy. Getting an adequate wage was one part of the problem; the other, as amply demonstrated by recent economic conditions, was getting a job. What made compulsory arbitration the basis for a distinctive strategy of social amelioration was that it was fashioned into a more or less explicit political deal, which has been dignified by some authors as a 'historic compromise' paralleling those of Scandinavia in the 1930s (on Australia, see Castles, 1988: 110–32; on New Zealand, see Davidson, 1989: 177–87). The substance of this deal was that fair wages were to be complemented by policy measures, in principle, regarded as ensuring the capacity of employers to provide sufficient high-wage jobs. These policy measures, which in combination have been described as constituting a strategy of 'domestic defence' (Castles, 1988), involved high levels of tariff protection to restrict foreign competition and to foster the basis of a domestic manufacturing industry, and controls on migration designed simultaneously to exclude low-wage ('Asiatic') labour and to allow population growth within parameters set by the need to maintain a reasonably tight labour market.

The logic by which a strategy of domestic defence was transformed into the wage earners' welfare state is transparent enough. To the degree that wage regulation delivered all male employees an adequate family wage, and in so far as the assumption was that all women and children were dependent on male wage earners, it followed that only when men were unemployed or had been insufficiently provident to provide for their old age could there be a need for additional intervention by the state. But with wages as the frontline weapon against poverty and, supposedly, sufficient high-wage jobs generated by the protection of tariff walls and controls on migration, social policy could be doubly residual: to be given only to the poor and only where it was apparent that the wages mechanism was inadequate. In other words, the unusually needs-based character of income support measures in the Antipodean nations was a function of the fact that the needs of most families were supposed to be guaranteed by a wage-setting process which gave heed to social policy objectives.

These considerations explain why schemes of social expenditure in these countries have tended to be selective and laggard and why the tax state has been both small and redistributive in emphasis. Targeting benefits only to those in need followed from seeing them as a secondary safety-net only for those who somehow fell through the mesh of the primary wage control mechanism. With the exception of the means tested age pension, other benefits tended to be introduced rather later than in many European countries, because the initial assumption was that private savings from supposedly adequate wages would be sufficient to meet short-term emergencies such as frictional unemployment or to insure privately for foreseeable medical costs. Certainly from the latter part of the nineteenth century until the Second World War, these were countries in which small scale savings societies, often organized as friendly societies, with a clientele largely of ordinary working men, flourished mightily.

Only when the assumption of wage adequacy proved demonstrably inaccurate over a long period of time were new benefits introduced and, even then, the initial tendency was to seek remedies through the wage awards system, as was the case in respect of sickness leave. The logic by which an emphasis on fair wages led to means testing and the small tax state was replicated on the revenue side. An aversion to heavy tax burdens on average working families, and, hence, a strong preference for reliance on progressive income taxes, followed naturally from the conception that wages from employment were the legally established minimum required for a civilized existence. Overall, the closely intertwined set of preferences for redistributive instruments on both the expenditure and the revenue sides of the tax-transfer system gave the wage earners' welfare state in its heyday a distinctively egalitarian or 'radical' cast (see Castles and Mitchell, 1993).

Judicially determined wage levels set on the basis of social policy considerations also account for other important features of the Antipodean wage earners' welfare state. The extremely low levels of female (particularly married) labour force participation in both countries were a direct consequence of the family wage concept, which led the arbitration courts to set female base wage rates at around half those of men on the ground that women generally were not responsible for the support of dependants (on Australia, see Bryson, 1992: 167–70; on New Zealand, see Brosnan and Wilson, 1989: 21–34). Given this legally institutionalized construction of female dependency, feminist commentators have properly seen the Antipodean model of the early post-war decades as a 'male wage earners' welfare state' (Bryson, 1992; Du Plessis, 1993). Finally, the high wage rates stemming from the relative affluence of these nations, together with the relatively low dispersion of wages produced by the arbitration system, created circumstances highly propitious to high levels of private home ownership, with mortgage repayments serving, in effect, as a functional alternative to European earnings-related welfare as a means of horizontal life cycle income distribution. Certainly, by the 1950s and 1960s, governments in Australia and New Zealand were treating home ownership as a welfare good to be provided for all classes of the population through subsidized or interest-regulated loans, with the most dramatic instance of the equation between ownership and welfare being the New Zealand Labour initiative in 1958 of permitting the 'anticipation' of some part of future child benefits as a lump sum payment towards private house purchase (Thomson, 1991: 39–40).

The story told here of an evolving economic policy strategy of domestic defence contributing to the maturation of a wage earners' welfare state is, of course, an ideal typical representation of developments occurring over many decades and with many important differences in the two Antipodean nations. In this context, the difference that most demands attention is that which led to New Zealand developing a system of social security in the 1940s and 1950s which, in all respects bar its selectivity, was as extensive as any in the world. This difference is attributable most particularly to the fact that, as in Scandinavia, the party which assumed the reigns of government after the Depression of the 1930s was Labour. Over a period of 14 years of continuous majority rule, Labour sought to marry the institutional design of a comprehensive and generous social security state, including the world's first national health service, with the wage guarantees for the broad mass of wage earners provided by the arbitration system. Arguably, the resulting welfare state was highly ambiguous – 'neither fish nor fowl' – but it was sufficient to convince contemporary observers that New Zealand was amongst the world's leaders in social security development.

In the first half of the post-war period, the wage earners' welfare state in New Zealand re-emerged by stealth as more or less continuous government by the right-wing National Party undermined the generosity of social security provision. Nevertheless, the First Labour Government left an important legacy of legitimation for a welfare state along European lines, which resurfaced with legislation by the Third Labour Government, 1972–5, to introduce a funded, earnings-related, superannuation scheme. But the ambiguities built into New Zealand's welfare state were to continue. Basing its appeal on what has been described as 'a blatant electoral bribe', the National Party returned to office with a 'national superannuation' scheme which was reasonably generous in replacement rate terms, but extraordinarily so in reducing the age of entitlement to 60 and in offering the benefit as a demogrant. The ambiguities – and obvious future fiscal difficulties – lay in tying the old to the new by making superannuation flat-rate and funding it from the Exchequer on exactly the same basis as the other benefits of the wage earners' welfare state.

By contrast, whilst never as generous, the Australian development was far more consistent. Although the Australian Labor government of the 1940s had brought into existence the standard range of social security schemes – child, unemployment, sickness and widows' benefits – all, bar the child benefit, were in the traditional selective, ungenerous and flat-rate mould of the 1908 pension and represented an extension of the residual safety-net of the wage earners' welfare state, not its supersession. The wartime Labor government had unsuccessfully attempted to create a national health system along New Zealand lines, but otherwise believed that the crucial tasks of post-war economic reconstruction were full employment and economic growth which would make welfare 'palliatives . . . less and less necessary' (Chifley, 1944: 1). Its long-term Liberal successor never challenged the existing social policy model and believed that it had proved successful in wiping out absolute poverty in Australia (Wentworth, 1969: 3). When Labor next came to office in 1972–5, it finally succeeded in introducing a national health system, increased the generosity of benefits and even took a cautious step towards universalism in respect of pensions for those over 70. However although, as in New Zealand, ideas of earnings-related pensions were in the air, they were ultimately rejected because of 'the clash of principle between this earnings-related scheme and the traditional Australian practice of flat-rate benefits according to need'

96   *Advanced Welfare States*

(Henderson, 1978: 175). Finally, the Fraser Liberal government which took office in 1975 saw monetarism as the correct response to the developing economic crisis and had absolutely no intention of moving beyond the traditional confines of Australia's low-taxation welfare state.

Changing the shape of social protection

A new social laboratory

If it is appropriate to regard the Antipodes at the turn of the last century as a social laboratory in which state experiments were carried out for the greater edification of other nations, the same may be no less true of the last two decades of this century. In the 1980s and early 1990s, Australia and New Zealand were amongst a group of largely Anglo-American nations which did more than simply seek incremental and piecemeal ways of coping with the economic and social policy consequences of major new disruptions in their external economic environment (Castles, 1993: 3–34). Instead, departing from a premise that the end result of many decades of state intervention had left a substantial legacy of economic inefficiency, these countries committed themselves to making a substantial overhaul of their entire panoply of economic and social policy institutions and, in particular, sought to reshape institutions in such a way that they would become more responsive to market disciplines. This more comprehensive policy response to the economic disruptions of the 1970s is generally seen as emanating from the ideas of the 'new right', although in Australia – and perhaps a significant indicator of differences in that nation's approach – a rather less overtly political label of 'economic rationalism' (see Pusey, 1991; King and Lloyd, 1993) has found some favour, at least in regard to the home-grown product.

Nor can it be said that the policy response of the Antipodean nations was merely a minor echo of the new right mainstream of Thatcherism in the United Kingdom and Reaganomics in the United States. What makes the dramatic economic and social reforms of the past decade in Australia and New Zealand so fascinating is that they were initiated by governments traditionally associated with the interventionist state and with measures of social protection. In Australia, the architect of reform was a Labor government that was first elected in 1983, and which has subsequently proceeded to win the next four elections. In New Zealand, economic reform directions were established by the Fourth Labour Government which ruled from 1984 to 1990, and were markedly accelerated, particularly in the labour market and social policy areas, by its National Party successor.

The kinds of economic policy and welfare outcomes associated with the new right triumphant – a greater emphasis on price stability than un-employment, labour market deregulation, reduced taxation, cuts in public expenditure and stringent targeting of benefits, and greater inequality in the distribution of income – are simultaneously the outcomes often associated with a post-industrial future in which the supposed fate of the welfare state is 'poor, nasty, brutish and short'. In a sense, then, it would appear that the Antipodean nations over the course of the past decade provide a perfect laboratory for testing the limits of those theories which suggest that the economic reforms set in motion by contemporary societal developments are inimical to the maintenance of social protection at the levels established in the early post-war decades. Two countries on the periphery of the world economic system embarked on extensive policy reforms explicitly designed to make their economies respond more efficiently to market signals under the auspices of governments without any previous predilection for pro-market interventions or for rightist outcomes. Had the experience of the two countries been a common move towards outcomes uniformly destructive of social progress, it might have been argued that this was proof sufficient that, even in countries with a tradition of social protection and under governments supposedly committed to socially protective goals, the very fact of seeking to conform to the demands of international competitiveness was an inevitable recipe for the destruction of the welfare state.

In fact, as the remainder of this chapter demonstrates, whilst welfare state outcomes in Australia and New Zealand manifested certain common trends over the period, they were, in substantial ways, very different. A vital component of that difference was the fact that, despite quite similar economic objectives, the governments in the two countries sought to achieve their ends by quite distinctive policy means. At a minimum, this seems to imply that the future trajectory of welfare state development is far more open than some commentators appear to believe. Just as important, the tenor of the account offered here, as of the previous section, which noted the pivotal role of labour movement politics in articulating the agenda of social protection in the Antipodes, suggests that, however much the general trajectory of welfare state development is shaped by broad societal and economic developments, an account which leaves out political choice and agency will always be, to some degree, flawed.

Processes of economic and social change

The areas in which common trends have been most apparent are those in which economic and social factors have impinged most directly on the life cycle prospects of workers and potential workers. They are the areas in which the forces unleashed by the breakdown of the post-war economic settlement and post-industrial transformation have been least mediated by policy, whether because policy has been ineffective, because policy-makers have consciously retreated from former interventionist strategies or because the transformation has been at a level too fundamental to admit of policy solutions. Table 4.1 summarizes a variety of these outcomes in Australia and New Zealand and contrasts them with those of other groupings of advanced nations featuring in this volume.

What Table 4.1 shows is the extent to which the world had changed since

Table 4.1 *Economic and social indicators of economic slowdown and post-industrial change*

	Australia	New Zealand	North America	Continental Europe[1]	Scandinavia
Economic slowdown					
Per capita growth 1979–90[2] (%)	1.6	0.8	1.7	1.8	2.2
Unemployment 1992[3] (%)	10.7	10.3	9.4	10.2	8.8
Labour force composition					
Service sector 1980–90[2] (%)	65.9	59.3	68.9	60.4	63.0
Male labour force 1992[3] (%)	85.8	82.2	84.2	77.2	83.4
Female labour force 1992[3] (%)	62.5	63.2	68.5	54.7	74.9
Part-time employment 1992[3] (%)	24.5	21.6	17.2	16.1	20.4
Social structure					
Divorce rate 1990 (or nearest)[4] (per 1000)	2.5	2.6	3.9	1.5	2.5
Tertiary education 1991[5] (%)	38.6	44.8	79.7	36.2	41.4
Female tertiary education 1991[5] (%)	42.0	48.0	87.8	34.8	44.9

[1] Average for Belgium, France, Germany, Italy and the Netherlands.
Sources:
[2] From OECD, 1992.
[3] From OECD, 1993.
[4] From UN, 1992.
[5] From UNESCO, 1993.

the end of the Golden Age. A decade or more of low economic growth and cyclical recessions had by the early 1990s everywhere produced levels of unemployment uncontemplated in the 1950s and 1960s. The character of the labour force had also changed. Everywhere services had become dominant, everywhere male participation rates had declined significantly and everywhere women were entering the labour force in unprecedented numbers. In respect of social structure the transformation was no less pronounced, with increased rates of family break-up, a more educated population and, within that population, far greater opportunities for women.

However, despite these common trends, there were, as emphasized by Gøsta Esping-Andersen in his contributions to this volume, quite major differences between different national groupings, especially with respect to labour force development. Of the groupings, continental Europe experienced a lesser move towards service employment, a higher attrition of the male workforce and a lower rate of entry by female workers. By contrast, Australia and New Zealand's male workforce is comparable with that of the North American and Scandinavian nations. However, in respect of female participation rates, the Antipodes lags behind these latter groupings, although clearly on a trajectory towards their higher levels, with part-time employment as the vehicle of that transformation. In respect of social structure, it is again clear that continental Europe is different, with the Antipodean nations rather similar to Scandinavia in respect of marriage break-up, and falling somewhere between Scandinavia and continental Europe in respect of educational expansion.

Turning to the specifics of the Antipodean development, it is apparent that, from the mid 1970s onwards, the economic and labour market outcomes, which through the 1950s and 1960s had been the main testimony to the success of the wage earners' welfare state in delivering a decent and even-tenored standard of life, had begun to deteriorate or to be transformed. Relative GDP per capita levels in both countries remained in the top half of the OECD distribution until the mid 1970s, but declined appreciably thereafter as a consequence of slow productivity growth and a serious downturn in the terms of trade. In 1985, Australia had a GDP per capita level 98 per cent of the OECD average and New Zealand 90 per cent; in 1992, the Australian figure was 91 per cent and the New Zealand level was 76 per cent (Easton, 1993: 11). By the latter date, New Zealand, with an economic growth rate shown in Table 4.1 to be substantially lower than even the modest norm for the period, had a GDP per capita which, amongst the OECD nations, only exceeded those of Ireland, Greece, Portugal, Spain and Turkey (OECD, 1994).

The decline in the Antipodean nations' relative economic standing was, of course, one of the most significant factors promoting a sense of the need for policy change that might lead to enhanced international competitiveness. In particular, it promoted moves to financial deregulation and the phasing out of the barriers of external protection which had been such a central component of the traditional 'domestic defence' strategy. Deregulation across all spheres of policy was a particularly compelling platform for policy reform in nations which had historically seen economic regulation as the sovereign remedy for all problems, and, most particularly, for problems perceived as emanating from the international economy. Hardly surprisingly, this new deregulatory ethos, signalled by the defeat of conservative governments which had confronted the economic crisis of the late 1970s by a further battening down of the regulatory hatches, made for substantial pressures on the no less traditional wage earners' welfare state strategy of wage compression in a full employment economy.

Research suggests that, as late as the mid 1980s, the dispersion of male earnings in Australia was still relatively low compared with a range of other OECD nations, being roughly comparable with that of Sweden, but that it increased markedly thereafter (Bradbury, 1993). An emerging trend towards greater wage inequality in Australia over the past decade or so is compatible with evidence concerning the progressive disappearance of the middle of the income distribution· as part-time employment at low wages has been substituted for full-time jobs at standard wage rates (Gregory, 1993). Similar wage distribution trends were also clearly apparent in New Zealand during the period of the Fourth Labour Government and have continued under the National government (Brosnan and Rea, 1992). Whilst some critics have argued that these trends constitute a particular cause for condemnation of domestic economic policy in these nations, in actual fact the wage distribution tendencies described are common to many OECD countries, and criticism, if that is appropriate, should be directed more to the removal of the barriers that had hitherto insulated these countries from world market trends. However the consensus of economists in both countries, and not merely those with new right and economic rationalist views, is that such barriers could not have lasted much longer in any case and that, whatever their past rationale, they had, by the early 1980s, become wholly counter-productive.

Transformation rather than deterioration is the appropriate description for other aspects of the change occurring in these decades. Greater service employment was partly a function of enhanced productivity levels in other economic sectors, and was accompanied by a great expansion in educational opportunity and economic independence for women. However these nations rated in comparative terms, the structural shifts which occurred were of mammoth proportions. In Australia, services grew from 50.1 per cent of civilian employment in 1960 to 69.0 per cent in 1990 and, in New Zealand, from 46.8 to 64.8 per cent (see OECD, 1992). Female labour force participation as a percentage of the female population from 15 to 64 grew from a level well below the OECD average to one somewhat above it – in Australia, from 34.1 per cent in 1960 to 62.5 per cent in 1992 and, in New Zealand, from 31.3 to 63.2 per cent over the same period (OECD, 1993). In Australia, part-time employment as a percentage of total employment increased from 11.9 to 24.4 per cent between 1973 and 1992, and in New Zealand the comparable figures were 11.2 and 21.6 per cent (OECD, 1993). Finally, turning to the educational correlates of employment change, between 1980 and 1991 tertiary enrolment ratios in Australia increased from 25.4 to 38.6 per cent (for females, from 23.4 to 42 per cent), and in New Zealand from 28.6 to 44.8 per cent (for females, from 23.7 to 48 per cent) (see UNESCO, 1993).

One area in which transformation was somewhat less pronounced than in many OECD nations was in respect of the reduction in the male labour force stemming from the decline in industrial manufacturing and the more general labour market deterioration since the early 1970s. In Australia between 1960 and 1992, the reduction was only 11.4 percentage points; in New Zealand, it was 11.6 points. Together with the figures for the expansion in the female labour force, this demonstrates that Australia and New Zealand did not utilize labour supply reduction strategies of the kind common in Western Europe during this period (see Esping-Andersen, 1990; von Rhein-Kress, 1993). However, unlike the Scandinavian countries, the expansion of aggregate labour supply in these countries was not a function of an expansion of public employment. Rather the employment story of these countries into the mid 1980s, at least, is quite analogous to that of the other Anglo-American countries during the same period, with the main factor facilitating female labour force entry being a taxation system providing substantial incentives to part-time work and the precise level of overall employment depending on a particular government's willingness to utilize measures of fiscal stimulus.

It is not the case that the changes in workforce composition which have taken place in Australia and New Zealand in this period have been inherently inimical to the life cycle security of most wage earner families, although they have certainly altered the typical profile of the interface between family and work. Indeed, the fact that it is now the norm for most families during early and later stages of the life cycle to have more than one member in some form of paid employment may have been an important factor in maintaining the very high level of Antipodean home ownership despite two decades of economic slowdown and periodic unemployment (Castles, 1994). On the other hand, part-time working for men and employment for married women have made the wage earners' welfare state notions of the 'family wage' and female dependence increasingly antediluvian.

That is all the more so as a result of changes in social mores and legal norms. Divorce law reform in both countries since the 1970s has markedly facilitated family break-up, and crude divorce rates per 1000 of the population are amongst the highest in the world (see UN, 1992; and see Table 4.1). As a consequence, the percentage of sole-parent families has also increased greatly: in New Zealand, from 5 per cent of households in 1971 to 9 per cent in 1991 (Statistics New Zealand, 1993), and in Australia, from 6 per cent of family households in 1976 to 9 per cent in 1991 (Australian Bureau of Statistics, 1994). While changing workforce composition *per se* may not undermine the security of the standard wage earner life course, family break-up clearly does, and, in common with the experience of most other advanced nations, single-parent households in these countries are likely to be those with the greatest risk of poverty.

Employment and social changes relating to women, unquestionably, have been the single most important manifestation of post-industrial transformation in Australia and New Zealand in the past two decades. One interesting response, and hardly one that would have been expected on the basis of the more apocalyptic prognoses of the consequences of postindustrial change, has been the development of a strong women's policy machinery within the bureaucracies of both nations, and a series of policy changes under the two Labour governments (but not National) which have created greater gender equality within the welfare system (on Australia, see Sawer, 1990 and Shaver, 1993; on New Zealand, see Curtin, 1992) and have modified and extended (i.e. by childcare subsidies) the welfare state to facilitate still greater female labour force participation. On this score, it would appear that the most recent periods of Labour rule in these countries have seen initiatives pushing Australia and New Zealand in policy directions more Scandinavian than continental European (low female labour force participation) or North American (no state involvement).

However, the Antipodean nations still have a very long way to go. A wage earners' welfare state premised on female dependency is hardly the best nurturing environment for an income support system which caters adequately for women seeking to combine labour force participation and caring duties within the family. There remain many impediments. For single mothers, these include the lack of generosity of benefits (although cf. Table 4.2 below and associated comment) and means tests imposing high effective marginal tax rates which deter women from re-entering the work-force to an appreciably greater degree than in Scandinavia or, indeed, other Anglo-American nations. For all working women, there is the difficulty of the very limited range of benefits facilitating workforce re-entry and job retention. These are clearly important targets for welfare reform in these countries.

Interestingly, although the wage earners' concept has been an impediment to some of the substance of women's welfare needs, what shift there has been towards greater gender equality has owed not a little to the traditional mechanisms of the wage earners' welfare state. The arbitration system, which had once stood as institutional guarantor of the family wage, became in the late 1960s and early 1970s a mechanism actively promoting equal pay for women through award decisions. As a consequence, in recent decades, Australia and New Zealand have maintained relatively low gender wage inequalities by international standards, only now under threat as a result of the recent decentralization, and, in New Zealand, destruction of traditional wage-fixing institutions (on New Zealand, see Hammond and Harbridge, 1993). Most recently, the Australian trade union movement has been pressing for both maternity and parental support payments to become a new type of occupational benefit established under the wage award system, bearing first fruit in a lump sum, means tested (but along standard Australian lines, only excluding the top 15 per cent of income earners) maternity benefit announced in the May 1995 budget. In general, the use of the state as a 'user-friendly' mechanism to achieve women's welfare goals is one which has strong resonances with the regulatory and interventionist modes of Antipodean government that gave birth to the wage earners' model.

Obviously, the change which has broken most dramatically with the even-tenored working class life cycles of the immediate post-war decades has been the growth of unemployment. As of 1993, the jobless figure was around 11 per cent in both countries, although declining to below 9 per cent by mid 1995 (all unemployment figures bar the most recent are from OECD, 1993). In Australia, Labor in 1983 inherited around 10 per cent unemployment from its monetarist predecessor and in the early 1990s again experienced levels of this magnitude, not least as a consequence of a high real interest rate policy at the end of the 1980s. In the interim, however, there was a substantial decline in unemployment to a low of around 6 per cent in 1989. In New Zealand, unemployment was to some extent contained by Keynesian and state-led investment policies until the mid 1980s, standing at less than 6 per cent in 1983 and under 4 per cent in 1986. Thereafter, unemployment in New Zealand was to increase annually to 1993, not so much in tune with cyclical trends in the world economy, but rather as a consequence of the policy initiatives of the Fourth Labour Government and its successor, and, in particular, its successive use of monetarist and real interest rate remedies against inflation from the mid 1980s onwards.

The wage earners' welfare state in jeopardy

To say the very least, the broadly common outcomes of economic policy development in these countries over the past decade mean that there are major areas in which the wage earners' welfare state either no longer delivers or in which it delivers outcomes markedly less favourable than was previously the case. The Antipodean economies and labour markets no longer guarantee living standards comparable with the best in the world, no longer guarantee full employment and no longer guarantee a high level of wage equality, although they do still appear to provide an extraordinarily high level and, indeed, standard of home ownership. Moreover, the guarantees that are no longer there were precisely those on which rested the claim for the efficacy of the Antipodean welfare strategy *vis-à-vis* European welfare state models. Nevertheless, from the mid 1980s onwards, there also were major differences in labour market policies and labour market outcomes between the two countries, and differences also in the tax policies which transformed the economic rewards of labour market participation into family incomes. These differences very clearly demonstrate the greater commitment of the Australian Labor government than its New Zealand Labour and National counterparts to insulating its natural constituency of support amongst average and below average income earners from the full impact of its programme of economic deregulation.

One very important area of difference has been in employment policy. In New Zealand, thorough going economic restructuring initiatives were taken to remove external barriers to trade, to corporatize state enterprises as a precursor to privatizing them, to reduce assistance to industry and agriculture, to remove price controls and, above all, to reduce inflation. However, there were no serious efforts to address the likely employment effects of these policies, and, indeed, they took place at the same time as the active labour market schemes already in existence were being phased out (Shirley et al., 1990: 84–6). On the contrary, what Roger Douglas, the Labour Finance Minister, and the Treasury, seen by many commentators (Jesson, 1989; Easton, 1994b) as the intellectual powerhouse of the monetarist and Hayekian doctrines shaping policy from 1984 onwards, wanted was for their measures to bite with immediate effect so as to realize structural adjustment gains as rapidly as possible. The result was to decimate employment in whole areas of the economy and regions of the country.

In Australia, by contrast, a deregulatory thrust which was of major dimensions by OECD standards, but nevertheless far less gung-ho than in New Zealand, was managed by tripartite industry plans and negotiated micro-economic reform in the context of government and trade union negotiated policy settings encouraging stable business expectations and high levels of investment (Chapman et al., 1991). Labor's primary policy instrument in this was a consciously established set of corporatist or quasi-corporatist arrangements and understandings known as the Accord, which, for more than a decade, have made the government and trade unions partners in the process of economic transformation (see Matthews, 1991: 191–218; Gruen and Grattan, 1993: 111–34). A telling contrast, pertinent to both the style and content of labour market policy on both sides of the Tasman in the latter half of the 1980s, was that whereas in New Zealand, policy was driven by a Chicago School enthused Treasury, in Australia policy was presided over by a Prime Minister (Bob Hawke) who had been President of the Australian Confederation of Trade Unions (ACTU) for many years. In employment terms, at least, the difference made by this contrast of policy approaches was extremely dramatic. Between 1982 and 1990, Australia recorded employment growth of 2.6 per cent per annum, much the best performance in the OECD, whilst New Zealand, with an average of 0 per cent per annum, was the second worst performer after Ireland (OECD, 1993: 5).

The other crucial area of difference related to issues concerning wages, conditions of employment, and taxation of income from employment. In Australia, the Accord mechanism was initially used, in conjunction with the traditional arbitration machinery, to manage the decline in real wages adjudged necessary to enhance competitiveness, whilst simultaneously providing continuing minimum wage guarantees for workers in low-wage industries. Whilst wage inequality has clearly increased in Australia, there has been, at least, some attempt to preserve wage fairness. Changes on the industrial relations front have also seen a progressive shift towards more decentralized, enterprise-based, wage-setting (Plowman, 1990: 155–6), but the Accord mechanism has prevented any serious undermining of those features of the centralized industrial relations system protecting minimum wage levels and working conditions and preventing wage break-outs. The demands of competitiveness also impinged in the area of taxation, where economic rationalist reformers argued that progressivity reduced the incentives stemming from what they saw as necessary wage inequalities. However, again as a consequence of the Accord relationship between Labor and the trade unions, the government backed away from plans to impose a general consumption tax in return for a reduction in marginal rates of taxation. Although reducing the top marginal rate from 60 to 49 per cent, the traditional wage earners' welfare state aversion to consumption taxes triumphed. Instead, Labor instituted both a capital gains tax and a progressive fringe-benefits tax on business expenses, measures very much against the regressive trend of 1980s OECD tax reform (cf. Heidenheimer et al., 1990: 209–14).

The crucial difference between the two countries in respect of managed wage restraint was the absence in New Zealand of a working relationship between unions and the Labour government in any way comparable to the Australian Accord (Sandlant, 1989). The absence of such a relationship also showed up clearly in the tax arena, with a complete lack of popular, much less trade union, consultation prior to the imposition of a general consumption tax and a far less progressive income tax regime than any contemplated in Australia, with a top marginal rate of 33 per cent (Heidenheimer et al., 1990: 211). On the other hand, and with the exception of radical reforms in respect of state sector employment, industrial relations was an area in which the Fourth Labour Government, perhaps for once mindful of traditional allegiances, manifested rather less deregulatory zeal than was its wont (Walsh, 1991). However, the National Government after 1990 was far less circumspect, seeing labour market deregulation as the major missing building-brick in the edifice of economic restructuring. The Employment Contracts Act, passed in 1991, did away with almost 100 years of labour market protection, abolishing the last remnants of the arbitration system and severely curtailing the right to strike, as well as removing much of the basis of trade union freedom to organize. According to one commentator, the consequences are already apparent in 'a substantial, perhaps irreversible, fall in trade union membership and collective bargaining coverage, the continued erosion of employment conditions and employment security, a growing sense of employer strength and (in some quarters) militancy' (Walsh, 1993a: 74).

106   *Advanced Welfare States*

Rolling back or refurbishing the welfare state

If the keystone of the institutional arch of the wage earners' welfare state used to be the institutions of wage control which regulated and pacified the conflict of labour and capital, then the Employment Contracts Act marks the end of the wage earners' welfare state in New Zealand. The contrast here with Australia is one not just of outcomes, but of the integrity of institutions and of their potential for social protection. As we have already noted, the Australian labour market has offered a markedly lower degree of protection over the past decade, but it does still contain institutions designed to resolve the conflicts of labour and capital by adjudicating the outcomes of the wage bargaining process; it does maintain important protections against the exploitation of weaker groups of workers in the labour market; and there are still tax mechanisms which seek to moderate the growing inequality of wages. Moreover, in the adverse external circumstances of the past decade, and with the general realization that it is impossible any longer to pursue the traditional strategy of domestic defence, the established wage-fixing apparatus has been made more flexible without undermining its inherited legitimacy and has been simultaneously augmented by the development of quasi-corporatist links between Labor and the trade unions. In Australia, arguably, the verdict on what has happened in the labour market in the Labor decade is that, whilst the traditional institutional props of the wage earners' welfare state have ceased to operate as effectively as in the past, there has been a genuine attempt to refurbish their role as, at least, a secondary line of defence of life cycle security for the broad mass of wage and salary earners.

In the traditional wage earners' model, wage control was the primary instrument of welfare and social security was residual. Now, the roles have been reversed, partly as a consequence of the failure of the traditional labour market strategy, but also because, as in many other countries, changes in mores, family structures and patterns of female labour force participation have transformed traditional ties of family dependence. Under these circumstances, it might have been reasonable to assume that New Zealand, with a stronger policy tradition of universalism and expenditure generosity, would have responded more positively than Australia. In fact, the reverse has been the case and, as of the mid 1990s, it seems clear that social protection through social security rests on firmer foundations in Australia than in New Zealand and, indeed, arguably, on firmer foundations than in any other English-speaking nation.

This has not happened as a consequence of any sudden shift towards universalism or massive growth of generosity on Australia's part. On the contrary, in respect of social security income maintenance expenditure, the Labor decade has been one in which selectivism has been intensified, with an assets test imposed on age pensions, and the one non-income-tested benefit, the child allowance, becoming tested against both income and assets. There have been a whole host of more minor adjustments designed to target need more precisely and to encourage the transition from benefits to labour market participation, the latter emphasis being the theme of Labor's major Social Security Review of the latter part of the 1980s. Crucially, however, the budgetary impetus for such change has come from a wish not so much to cut back public expenditure as to control its growth. In consequence, means tests have been drawn not at the line separating the poor from the rest, but rather at the line which obviates 'middle class welfare'. In the new stringently targeted Australian world of means tests, the one-child family earning less than $60,000 (approximately US$42,000) still receives child benefit, and 72 per cent of the aged qualify for the age benefits (Gruen and Grattan, 1993: 192).

Moreover, real benefits, whilst they have not increased substantially, did move up gradually over the course of the 1980s (Saunders, 1991: 302) and, taking account of both social wage and indirect tax changes, the living standards of the bottom three income deciles improved by 5 per cent or more over the period from 1984 to 1988–9 (Saunders, 1994: 183). There is also some evidence that this trend of the high employment growth years has been maintained in respect of unemployment and family benefits throughout the recessionary period of the early 1990s (Harding, 1994: 16). Indeed, family poverty, and particularly that of one-parent families, has been a specific target of Labor policy, with the introduction of an additional child payment for low-income families and the very substantial enhancement of the rent allowance as a means of targeting family poverty arising from the lack of private home ownership. If recent simulation estimates are to be believed, these measures appear to have been rather successful, leading to a marked decline in both poverty rates and poverty gaps for families with children between 1989–90 and early 1994 (Harding, 1994: 15–17).

In New Zealand, initial social policy measures by the Fourth Labour Government had some similarities to the tighter targeting measures in Australia, with a whole series of cost containing modifications of the existing system. Given the flagrant generosity of certain aspects of national superannuation – its status as a flat-rate demogrant from age 60 – it became an early candidate of the new government's zeal for budget stringency. The imposition of a tax surcharge on the benefit effectively amounted to an incomes test on the benefit. As an additional means of containing superannuation costs, the government further announced the gradual phased-out eligibility of the 60–65 age group. In the area of family support, the real value of universal child benefits was allowed to decline, despite evidence of increasing family poverty, but, as in Australia, a new targeted benefit was introduced for families with low incomes. By 1987, major divisions emerged within Labour, with those who had earlier spearheaded economic reform arguing for a major rationalization and cut-back of social expenditure. This view was contested, not least by a major Royal Commission on Social Policy, which reaffirmed a commitment to a New Zealand society in which there is 'a sense of community responsibility and collective values that provide an environment of security' (Royal Commission, 1988: 11). Labour, nevertheless, went into the 1990 election with proposals for a single base-rate for all benefits other than superannuation that would have meant substantial reductions for many classes of beneficiaries (O'Brien and Wilkes, 1993: 79).

These proposals lapsed when the Nationals won in 1990, but, as in the labour market arena, the new National Government took up the running where Labour left off. The National Government's new policy programme, 'Welfare that works', included a scheme for a global system of abatement of all forms of social assistance, including health and hospital care. So far, this has proved too complex to implement, and the piecemeal introduction of parts of the package has compounded existing poverty traps resulting from means testing. In its initial form, the programme also included a proposal to make superannuation a direct, means tested, benefit targeted exclusively at the poor, but this generated enormous opposition and National had to be satisfied with an increase in the surcharge, a three-year freeze on benefit levels and an acceleration of the timetable for making benefits payable from age 65. Despite these reverses, moves towards 'an ever more tightly targeted welfare state' continued apace (St John and Heynes, 1993: 3), with the total abolition of the universal child benefit and a means tested regime of health care that much diminished the concept of a universal, national health system (Kelsey, 1993: 85–8), being only amongst the more conspicuous examples. Moreover, in its early months in office, National reduced real benefit levels for virtually all classes of beneficiaries, leading to an estimated increase in poverty of no less than 40 per cent over the two-year period 1989–90 to 1991–2 (Easton, 1993: 1–23).

Although it is not possible to measure benefit replacement rates in the Antipodean nations as percentages of prior earnings as in the European and Scandinavian earnings-related systems, a rough and ready comparative yardstick may be provided by relating benefits to GDP per capita in much the same manner as Esping-Andersen does in his analysis of the social minima in Western Europe (Chapter 3). This is done in Table 4.2, which examines the replacement rates of various benefits for claimants with and without spouses and specified dependants. The contrast between the countries at the end of the period we have been examining shows the extent to which Australia has now caught up with New Zealand in the area of income support. In respect of both unemployment and sickness benefits, Australia is now somewhat the more generous of the two nations and, for unemployment beneficiaries between 21 and 24 years of age, it is appreciably so. In respect of single parents, New Zealand remains marginally more generous than Australia, and only in respect of age superannuation does New Zealand maintain a large margin of advantage.

There is, in fact, an almost point for point reversal in the welfare policy transformation that has taken place in New Zealand and Australia since the advent of Labour governments in both countries in the first half of the 1980s. In respect of income maintenance expenditure, New Zealand started

Table 4.2 *Benefit rates as a percentage of per capita GDP, 1993*

Benefit	Australia	New Zealand
Unemployment		
Under 18	14.4	20.4
Youth	26.4 (18–20 years)	25.6 (18–24 years)
Full	34.7 (21 years +)	30.8 (25 years +)
Couple	57.9	51.3
Couple + 2 children	76.3	69.3
Sickness		
Full	34.7	32.1
Couple	57.9	58.3
Couple + 2 children	76.3	73.1
Single parent		
+ 1 child	47.1	53.8
+ 2 children	56.4	62.9
Aged		
Single	34.7	43.9
Couple	57.9	67.6

Sources: calculated from official data from the Australian Department of Social
Security and the New Zealand Department of Social Welfare. Since New
Zealand benefits are taxed, the figures in the table are calculated net of tax.
Figures for families with children include all applicable child benefits

out both more generous in respect of all forms of income maintenance
expenditure and less selective. However, by the mid 1990s the changes we
have described had led to a situation in which some benefit levels were
higher in Australia and only age benefits remained markedly more generous
in New Zealand. Moreover, Australian incomes tests, again with the
exception of age pensions, cut in at rather higher levels than in New
Zealand. In the early 1980s, New Zealand also possessed a national health
system which, dating back to the late 1930s, had some claim to be the
oldest in the world, whilst the Australian Liberals had just abolished
Labor's Medibank scheme introduced for the first time in 1974. But in
1984, Australia's new Labor government restored the universal, national
health scheme under the name of Medicare and less than a decade later
New Zealand made user charges a major component of its once universal
health care system. Finally, even New Zealand's long-standing record as
the more generous provider of age pensions may well disappear over the
course of the coming decades. Initially introduced in the traditional wage
earners' welfare state context of a general wage award, the Australian
arbitration system delivered an earnings-related, employer-funded, scheme
in 1986. This has now been codified in legislation and expanded, so that
nearly all Australian wage earners will eventually benefit from a scheme
which, by early next century, will be funded by 9 per cent employer, 3 per
cent employee and 3 per cent general revenue contributions. Although
contributions are compulsory, they go into privately administered funds

and are not generally counted as part of public expenditure. According to official estimates, a retiree on average wages in the year 2031 might expect superannuation benefits amounting to 60 per cent of pre-retirement income (Clare and Tulpulé, 1994).

The enormous difference between the termination points of these processes of welfare state transformation is poignantly underlined by a juxtaposition of the titles of recent books published in the two countries. In 1992, a group of well-known New Zealand social scientists contributed to an edited volume called *The Decent Society?* (Boston and Dalziel, 1992), the question mark prefiguring a critical onslaught on the entire policy record of the National Party Government which had used 'the decent society' as its 1990 election slogan. In complete contrast, an Australian book, co-authored by a social policy specialist and an economist, and based on extensive survey research using analytical techniques similar to those of the Scandinavian level-of-living studies of the 1970s, could use the title *Living Decently* (Travers and Richardson, 1993) to epitomize its conclusions as to the character of the life courses of average Australians in the late 1980s.

This history of a decade of welfare reversal in the Antipodes is of more than parochial interest. The willingness and capacity of the Australian Labor government to introduce reforms to the system of social amelioration as significant as universal health care and earnings-related superannuation offer an extraordinary contrast to the 'there is no alternative' brand of public expenditure cut-backs in New Zealand and the United Kingdom in the same period. Interestingly, too, the superannuation reform was initiated as an adjunct to the wages system and may, properly, be considered an extension of the wage earners' welfare state. Indeed, the usual myopia of domestic and foreign commentators concerning features of the Antipodean welfare model applies to this scheme, which, presumably because it counts as neither public expenditure nor taxation, is frequently unmentioned in debate on social security development in the Labor decade – an omission roughly equivalent, in real terms, to describing the Swedish system of social protection without mentioning the ATP system of age superannuation. The contrast between the social policy initiatives of the Australian and New Zealand governments in these years is a still more clear-cut instance of the difference in policy stances already noted in the area of labour market reform. What both differences demonstrate is that there are, in fact, alternatives: that policy may be harnessed to refurbishing the welfare state, as in Australia (see Castles, 1994), or to destroying any kind of welfare state, as in New Zealand. In this account, policy clearly matters.

Some lessons

That policy matters is one important lesson that may be drawn from this analysis of the development of social policy in the Antipodean nations before, during and after the Golden Age. There are others. Another emerges as a kind of a postscript to the emergence of differences between the two nations' responses to economic disruption and postindustrial change in the past two decades. This is a lesson that human institutions – and, perhaps, particularly institutions of social protection (see Polanyi, 1944) – are often more resilient than we give them credit for. That lesson is clearly underlined by recent developments in New Zealand which offer some prospect of preserving what is left of the welfare state and, perhaps, even reversing some of the losses. After almost a decade in which the New Zealand Treasury's views have been pushed through Parliament by majority governments with both Labour and National partisan labels, in 1993 the electorate used the referendum mechanism to ditch the first-past-the-post electoral system blamed for producing majority governments unresponsive to popular opinion (Mulgan, 1994). Arguably, governments elected under the new system will be more wary of policies designed to 'crash through or crash'. It should give aid and comfort to those who favour the cause of social development when, however belatedly, attacks on established standards and institutions of social protection inspire popular reaction and counter-attack.

A further lesson is that while policy matters, it is not the only thing that matters. The world of the Golden Age cannot be recovered by policies which wish it so. Policy options are broadly shaped by the economic forces and social and cultural structures which shape a generation's dilemmas and opportunities. Sadly, this generation's dilemmas involve many of the same kinds of economic constraints and trade-offs that characterized the choices of the pre-Golden-Age generation. More hopefully, in areas such as greater female emancipation and greater educational opportunity, at least some of the options offered by a postindustrial society seem to allow for an extension of the limits of social protection beyond those allowed by the institutional structures of the Golden Age. That the sexist assumptions of the wage earners' welfare state have been subject to a slow process of dissolution over the past two decades is a gain not a loss for social development in Australia and New Zealand.

A final lesson provides a challenge to those who are too ready to assert that there is one best way of pursuing the cause of social development. The countries examined in this chapter have frequently been criticized for low levels of social protection implicit in low income support replacement rates. In the Golden Age, the best retort was to point to the wage earners' welfare state's capacity to deliver 'social protection by other means' (Castles, 1989) – through guaranteed wage levels and high levels of home ownership. Even today, however, with wage guarantees under threat or destroyed, there remain some defences of a system resting on needs-based guarantees, as, of course, there are also for systems resting on social insurance (the entrenchment of entitlements) or universalism (equality of treatment).

Table 4.2 above shows that the Antipodean systems of income support do genuinely adjust for need stemming from dependency. The figures in that table cannot be compared with the social minima reported by Esping-Andersen (see Table 3.1), because the latter are not adjusted for additional payments for dependants. However, very recent research (Bolderson and Mabbett, 1995), which compares replacement levels (as a percentage of the average production worker's wage) for single beneficiaries and for couples with two children in respect of age, invalidity and unemployment benefits in Sweden, the Netherlands, France, Germany, Britain, the USA and Australia, does allow some tentative conclusions to be drawn. As one might expect, for single beneficiaries, flat-rate benefits lead to replacement levels in Australia generally lower than in most other countries. However, for couples with two children the results are quite different and Australia is in the top half of the distribution for every type of benefit. For second-string unemployment benefits (i.e. when social insurance is exhausted and social minima apply), Australia is second only to the Netherlands. New Zealand does not figure in this analysis, but extrapolation from Table 4.2 suggests that quite similar conclusions must apply in this case also. What this means is that in the area where a needs-based system should deliver – i.e. where need is greatest – it does, at least, deliver outcomes at least as satisfactory as those of most other types of welfare state. That is a feature of such systems which may be of very considerable appeal to nations seeking to establish viable systems of social protection for the first time or to streamline existing systems under the pressure of fiscal exigency.

References

Åberg, R. (1989) 'Distributive mechanisms of the welfare state – a formal analysis and an empirical application', *European Sociological Review*, 5(2): 167–82.

Australian Bureau of Statistics (1994) *Australian Social Trends 1994*. Canberra: AGPS.

Bolderson, H. and Mabbett, D. (1995) 'Mongrels or thoroughbreds: a cross-national look at social security systems', *European Journal of Political Research*, 28: 119–39.

Boston, J. and Dalziel, R. (eds) (1992) *The Decent Society? Essays in Response to National's Economic and Social Policies*. Auckland: Oxford University Press.

Bradbury, B. (1993) 'Male wage inequality before and after tax: a six country comparison'. University of NSW, Social Policy Research Centre Discussion Paper, no. 42.

Brosnan, P. and Rea, D. (1992) 'Rogernomics and the labour market', *New Zealand Sociology*, 7(2): 188–221.

Brosnan, P. and Wilson, M. (1989) 'The historical structuring of the New Zealand labour market', Victoria University of Wellington, Industrial Relations Centre, Working Paper no. 4.

Brown, R.G. (1989) ' Social security and welfare', in K. Hancock (ed.), *Australian Society*. Cambridge: Cambridge University Press.

Bryson, L. (1992) *Welfare and the State*. London: Macmillan.

Castles, F.G. (1985) *The Working Class and Welfare: Reflections on the Political Development of the Welfare State in Australia and New Zealand, 1890–1980*. Sydney: Allen and Unwin.

Castles, F.G. (1988) *Australian Public Policy and Economic Vulnerability*. Sydney: Allen and Unwin.

Castles, F.G. (1989) 'Social protection by other means: Australia's strategy of coping with external vulnerability', in F.G. Castles (ed.), *The Comparative History of Public Policy*. Cambridge: Polity Press.

Castles, F.G. (1992) 'On sickness days and social policy', *Australian & New Zealand Journal of Sociology*, 28(1): 29–44.

Castles, F.G. (1993) 'Changing course in economic policy: the English-speaking nations in the 1980s', in F.G. Castles (ed.), *Families of Nations*. Aldershot: Dartmouth.

Castles, F.G. (1994) 'The wage earners' welfare state revisited: refurbishing the established model of Australian social protection, 1983–1993', *Australian Journal of Social Issues*, 29(2).

Castles, F.G. and Mitchell, D. (1993) 'Worlds of welfare and families of nations', in F.G. Castles (ed.), *Families of Nations*. Aldershot: Dartmouth.

Chapman, B.J., Dowrick, S.J. and Junankar, P.N. (1991) 'Perspectives on Australian unemployment: the impact of wage-setting institutions', in F.H. Gruen (ed.), *Australian Economic Policy: Conference Proceedings*. ANU: Centre for Economic Policy Research. pp. 21–57.

Chifley, J.B. (1944) *Social Security and Reconstruction*. Canberra: Government Printer.

Clare, R. and Tulpulé, A. (1994) 'Australia's ageing society', EPAC, Background Paper no. 37.

Curtin, J.C. (1992) 'The ministry of women's affairs: where feminism and public policy meet'. MA dissertation, University of Waikato.

Davidson, A. (1989) *Two Models of Welfare: the Origins and Development of the Welfare State in Sweden and New Zealand, 1888–1988*. Uppsala: Acta Universitatis Upsaliensis.

Du Plessis, R. (1993) 'Women, politics and the state', in B. Roper and C. Rudd (eds.), *State and Economy in New Zealand*. Auckland: Oxford University Press.

Easton, B. (1983) *Income Distribution in New Zealand*. Wellington: NZ Institute of Economic Research.

Easton, B. (1993) 'Poverty and families: priority or piety?' Unpublished paper, Economic and Social Trust on New Zealand, Wellington.

Easton, B. (1994a) 'Economic rationalism in New Zealand', 'Australia, New Zealand and economic rationalism: parallel or dividing tracks'. Institute of Ethics and Public Policy, Monash University, Occasional Paper no. 7, pp. 15–30.

Easton, B. (1994b) 'The ideas behind the New Zealand reforms', *Oxford Review of Economic Policy*.

Esping-Andersen, G. (1990) *The Three Worlds of Welfare Capitalism*. Cambridge: Polity Press.

Gregory, R.G. (1993) 'Aspects of Australian and US living standards: the disappointing decades 1970–1990', *The Economic Record*, 69(204): 61–76.

Gruen, F. and Grattan, M. (1993) *Managing Government*. Melbourne: Longman Cheshire.

Hammond, M.B. (1913) 'Judicial interpretation of the minimum wage in Australia', *Annals of the American Academy of Political and Social Science*.

Hammond, S. and Harbridge, R. (1993) 'The impact of the Employment Contracts Act on women at work', *New Zealand Journal of International Relations*, 18: 15–30.

Harding, A. (1994) 'Family income and social security policy'. Unpublished paper, University of Canberra, National Centre for Social and Economic Modelling.

Heidenheimer, A.J., Heclo, H. and Adams, C.T. (1990) *Comparative Public Policy*, 3rd edn. New York: St Martin's Press.

Henderson, R. (1978) 'Social welfare expenditure', in R.B. Scotton and H. Ferber (eds), *Public Expenditures and Social Policy in Australia*, vol. I. Melbourne: Longman Cheshire.

Henderson, R.F., Harcourt, A. and Harper, R.J.A. (1970) *People in Poverty: a Melbourne Survey*. Melbourne: Cheshire.

Higgins, H.B. (1922) *A New Province for Law and Order*. London: Constable.

ILO (1949) *Systems of Social Security: New Zealand*. Geneva: International Labour Office.

ILO (1972) *The Cost of Social Security*. Geneva: International Labour Office.

Jesson, B. (1989) *Fragments of Labour*. Auckland: Penguin.

Kangas, O. (1991) *The Politics of Social Rights*. Stockholm: Swedish Institute for Social Research.

Karmel, P.H. and Brunt, M. (1962) *The Structure of the Australian Economy*. Melbourne: Cheshire.

Kelsey, J. (1993) *Rolling Back the State.* Wellington: Bridget Williams Books.

Kemeny, J. (1980) 'The political economy of housing', in E.L. Wheelright and K. Buckley (eds), *Essays in the Political Economy of Australian Capitalism*, vol. 4. Sydney: Australian and New Zealand Book Company.

King, S. and Lloyd, P. (1993) *Economic Rationalism: Dead End or Way Forward?* Sydney: Allen and Unwin.

Le Rossignol, J.E. and Stewart, W.D. (1910) *State Socialism in New Zealand.* London: Harrap.

Lydall, H. (1968) *The Structure of Earnings.* London: Oxford University Press.

Maddison, A. (1991) *Dynamic Forces in Capitalist Development.* Oxford: Oxford University Press.

Matthews, T. (1991) 'Interest group politics: corporatism without business?', in F.G. Castles (ed.), *Australia Compared.* Sydney: Allen and Unwin.

Mulgan, R. (1994) *Politics in New Zealand.* Auckland: Auckland University Press.

Myles, J. (1990) 'States, labor markets and life cycles', in R. Friedland and A.F. Robertson (eds), *Beyond the Marketplace.* New York: Aldine de Gruyter.

O'Brien, M. and Wilkes, C. (1993) *The Tragedy of the Market: a Social Experiment in New Zealand.* Palmerston North: Dunmore Press.

OECD (1976) *Public Expenditure on Income Maintenance Programmes.* Paris: OECD.

OECD (1992) *Historical Statistics 1960–1992.* Paris: OECD.

OECD (1993) *Employment Outlook*, July. Paris: OECD.

OECD (1994) *OECD Observer*, June/July. Paris: OECD.

Plowman, D. (1990) 'The stone the builders rejected', in M. Easson and J. Shaw (eds), *Transforming Industrial Relations.* Sydney: Pluto Press. pp. 145–59.

Polanyi, K. (1944) *The Great Transformation.* New York: Rinehart.

Pusey, M. (1991) *Economic Rationalism in Canberra.* Melbourne: Cambridge University Press.

Rankin, K. (1992) 'New Zealand's gross national product: 1859–1939', *Review of Income and Wealth*, 38(1).

Royal Commission on Social Security (1988) *Towards a Fair and Just Society.* Wellington: Government Printer.

Rudd, C. (1993) 'The welfare state: origins, development and crisis', in B. Roper and C. Rudd (eds), *State and Economy in New Zealand.* Auckland: Oxford University Press.

St John, S. (1993) 'Income support for an ageing society', in P.G. Koopman-Boyden (ed.), *New Zealand's Ageing Society.* Wellington: Daphne Brasell Associates Press.

St John, S. and Heynes, A. (1993) 'The welfare mess'. Unpublished paper, University of Auckland, Department of Economics.

Sandlant, R.A. (1989) 'The political economy of wage restraint: the Australian accord and trade union strategy in New Zealand'. M Arts thesis, Auckland, Department of Political Studies.

Saunders, P. (1991) 'Selectivity and targeting in income support: the Australian experience', *Journal of Social Policy*, 20(3): 299–326.

Saunders, P. (1994) *Welfare and Equality: National and International Perspectives on the Australian Welfare State.* Melbourne: Cambridge University Press.

Sawer, M. (1990) *Sisters in Suits: Women and Public Policy in Australia.* Sydney: Allen and Unwin.

Shaver, S. (1993) 'Women and the Australian social security system: from difference towards equality'. University of NSW, SPRC Discussion Paper, no. 41.

Shirley, I. (1990) 'New Zealand: the advance of the right', in I. Taylor (ed.), *The Social Effects of Free Market Policies.* London: Harvester/Wheatsheaf.

Shirley, I., Easton, B., Briar, C. and Chatterjee, S. (1990) *Unemployment in New Zealand.* Palmerston North: Dunmore Press.

Statistics New Zealand (1993) *All About Women in New Zealand.* Wellington.

Summers, R. and Heston, A. (1991) 'The Penn World Table (Mark 5): an expanded set of international comparisons, 1950–88', *Quarterly Journal of Economics*, 106(2): 327–68.

Thomson, D. (1991) *Selfish Generations.* Wellington: Bridget Williams Books.

Thorns, D. (1984) 'Owner occupation, the state and class relations', in C. Wilkes and I. Shirley (eds), *In the Public Interest: Health, Work and Housing in New Zealand*. Auckland: Benton Ross.

Thorns, D. (1993) 'Tenure and wealth accumulation: implications for housing policy', in P.G. Koopman-Boyden (ed.), *New Zealand's Ageing Society*. Wellington: Daphne Brasell Associates Press.

Travers, P. and Richardson, S. (1993) *Living Decently*. Melbourne: Oxford University Press.

UN (various dates) *UN Demographic Yearbook*. New York: United Nations.

UNESCO (1993) *UNESCO Yearbook*.

Varley, R. (1986) *The Government Household Transfer Data Base 1960–1984*. Paris: OECD.

von Rhein-Kress, G. (1993) 'Coping with economic crisis: labour supply as a policy instrument', in F.G. Castles (ed.), *Families of Nations*. Aldershot: Dartmouth.

Walsh, P. (1991) 'The State Sector Act 1988', in J. Boston, J. Martin, J. Pallot and P. Walsh (eds), *Reshaping the State: New Zealand's Bureaucratic Revolution*. Auckland: Oxford University Press.

Walsh, P. (1993a) 'The Employment Contracts Act', in J. Boston and P. Dalziel (eds), *The Decent Society? Essays in Response to National's Economic and Social Policies*. Auckland: Oxford University Press.

Walsh, P. (1993b) 'The state and industrial relations in New Zealand', in B. Roper and C. Rudd (eds), *State and Economy in New Zealand*. Auckland: Oxford University Press.

Wentworth, W.C. (1969) 'Social services and poverty', in G.C. Masterman (ed.), *Poverty in Australia*. Sydney: Australian Institute of Political Science.

[24]

AFTER THE FAMILY WAGE
Gender Equity and the Welfare State

NANCY FRASER
Northwestern University

T HE CURRENT CRISIS OF THE WELFARE STATE has many roots—
global economic trends, massive movements of refugees and immigrants,
popular hostility to taxes, the weakening of trade unions and labor parties,
the rise of national and "racial"-ethnic antagonisms, the decline of solidaristic
ideologies, and the collapse of state socialism. One absolutely crucial factor,
however, is the crumbling of the old gender order. Existing welfare states are
premised on assumptions about gender that are increasingly out of phase with
many people's lives and self-understandings. They therefore do not provide
adequate social protections, especially for women and children.

The gender order that is now disappearing descends from the industrial
era of capitalism and reflects the social world of its origin. It was centered
on the ideal of the family wage. In this world, people were supposed to be
organized into heterosexual, male-headed nuclear families, which lived
principally from the man's labor market earnings. The male head of the
household would be paid a family wage, sufficient to support children and a
wife and mother, who performed domestic labor without pay. Of course,
countless lives never fit this pattern. Still, it provided the normative picture
of a proper family.

The family-wage ideal was inscribed in the structure of most industrial-era
welfare states.[1] That structure had three tiers, with social-insurance programs
occupying the first rank. Designed to protect people from the vagaries of the

*AUTHOR'S NOTE: Research for this article was supported by the Center for Urban Affairs and
Policy Research, Northwestern University. For helpful comments, I am indebted to Rebecca
Blank, Joshua Cohen, Fay Cook, Barbara Hobson, Axel Honneth, Jenny Mansbridge, Linda
Nicholson, Ann Shola Orloff, John Roemer, Ian Schapiro, Tracy Strong, Peter Taylor-Gooby,
Judy Wittner, Eli Zaretsky, and the members of the Feminist Public Policy Work Group of the
Center for Urban Affairs and Policy Research, Northwestern University.*

POLITICAL THEORY, Vol. 22 No. 4, November 1994 591-618
© 1994 Sage Publications, Inc.

592   POLITICAL THEORY / November 1994

labor market (and to protect the economy from shortages of demand), these programs replaced the breadwinner's wage in case of sickness, disability, unemployment, or old age. Many countries also featured a second tier of programs, providing direct support for full-time female homemaking and mothering. A third tier served the "residuum." Largely a holdover from traditional poor relief, these programs provided paltry, stigmatized, means-tested aid to needy people who had no claim to honorable support because they did not fit the family-wage scenario.[2]

Today, however, the family-wage assumption is no longer tenable—either empirically or normatively. We are currently experiencing the death throes of the old, industrial gender order with the transition to new, postindustrial phase of capitalism. The crisis of the welfare state is bound up with these epochal changes. It is rooted in part in the collapse of the world of the family wage, and of its central assumptions about labor markets and families.

In the labor markets of postindustrial capitalism, few jobs pay wages sufficient to support a family single-handedly; many, in fact, are temporary or part-time and do not carry standard benefits.[3] Women's employment is increasingly common, moreover—although far less well-paid than men's.[4] Postindustrial families, meanwhile, are less conventional and more diverse.[5] Heterosexuals are marrying less and later, and divorcing more and sooner. And gays and lesbians are pioneering new kinds of domestic arrangements.[6] Gender norms and family forms are highly contested, finally. Thanks in part to the feminist and gay and lesbian liberation movements, many people no longer prefer the male breadwinner/female homemaker model. As a result of these trends, growing numbers of women, both divorced and never married, are struggling to support themselves and their families without access to a male breadwinner's wage.[7]

In short, a new world of economic production and social reproduction is emerging—a world of less stable employment and more diverse families. Although no one can be certain about its ultimate shape, this much seems clear: the emerging world, no less than the world of the family wage, will require a welfare state that effectively insures people against uncertainties. If anything, the need for such protection is increased. It is clear, too, that the old forms of welfare state, built on assumptions of male-headed families and relatively stable jobs, are no longer suited to providing this protection. We need something new, a postindustrial welfare state suited to radically new conditions of employment and reproduction.

What then should a postindustrial welfare state look like? Conservatives have lately had a lot to say about "restructuring the welfare state," but their vision is counterhistorical and contradictory; they seek to reinstate the male breadwinner/female homemaker family for the middle class, while demanding that poor single mothers work. Neoliberal proposals have recently emerged in the United States, but they too are inadequate in the current context. Punitive, androcentric, and obsessed with employment despite the absence of good jobs, they are unable to provide security in a postindustrial world.[8]

Both of these approaches ignore one crucial thing: a postindustrial welfare state, like its industrial predecessor, must support a gender order. But the only kind of gender order that can be acceptable today is one premised on gender equity.

Feminists, therefore, are in a good position to generate an emancipatory vision for the coming period. They, more than anyone, appreciate the importance of gender relations to the current crisis of the industrial welfare state and the centrality of gender equity to any satisfactory resolution. Feminists also appreciate the importance of care work for human well-being and the effects of its social organization on women's standing. They are attuned, finally, to potential conflicts of interest within families and to the inadequacy of androcentric definitions of work.

To date, however, feminists have tended to shy away from systematic reconstructive thinking about the welfare state. Nor have we yet developed a satisfactory account of gender equity that can inform an emancipatory vision. We need now to undertake such thinking. We should ask: What new, postindustrial gender order should replace the family wage? And what sort of welfare state can best support such a new gender order? What account of gender equity best captures our highest aspirations? And what vision of social welfare comes closest to embodying it?

Two different kinds of answers are presently conceivable, I think, both of which qualify as feminist. The first I call the universal breadwinner model. It is the vision implicit in the current political practice of most U.S. feminists and liberals. It aims to foster gender equity by promoting women's employment; the centerpiece of this model is state provision of employment-enabling services such as day care. The second possible answer I call the caregiver parity model. It is the vision implicit in the current political practice of most Western European feminists and social democrats. It aims to promote gender equity chiefly by supporting informal care work; the centerpiece of this model is state provision of caregiver allowances.

Which of these two approaches should command our loyalties in the coming period? Which expresses the most attractive vision of a postindustrial gender order? Which best embodies the ideal of gender equity?

In this article, I outline a framework for thinking systematically about these questions. I analyze highly idealized versions of universal breadwinner and caregiver parity in the manner of a thought experiment. I postulate, contrary to fact, a world in which both of these models are feasible in that their economic and political preconditions are in place. Assuming very favorable conditions then, I assess the respective strengths and weaknesses of each.

The result is not a standard policy analysis. For neither universal bread-winner nor caregiver parity will in fact be realized in the near future, and my discussion is not directed primarily at policy-making elites. My intent, rather, is theoretical and political in a broader sense. I aim, first, to clarify some dilemmas surrounding "equality" and "difference" by reconsidering what is meant by gender equity. In so doing, I also aim to spur increased reflection on feminist strategies and goals by spelling out some assumptions that are implicit in current practice and subjecting them to critical scrutiny.

These aims converge in the overall logic of my argument. Starting from some widely held moral intuitions, I arrive by the end of the thought experiment at a surprising and controversial conclusion: with respect to social welfare, at least, the deconstruction of gender difference is a necessary condition for gender equity.

My discussion proceeds in four parts. In the first section, I propose an analysis of gender equity that generates a set of evaluative standards. Then, in the second and third sections, I apply those standards to universal bread-winner and caregiver parity, respectively. I conclude, in the fourth section, that neither of those approaches, even in an idealized form, can deliver full gender equity. To have a shot at that, I contend, we must develop a new vision of a postindustrial welfare state, which effectively deconstructs gender difference as we know it.

I. GENDER EQUITY: A COMPLEX CONCEPTION

To evaluate alternative visions of a postindustrial welfare state, we need some normative criteria. Gender equity, I have said, is one indispensable standard. But of what precisely does it consist?

Feminists have so far associated gender equity with either equality or difference, where equality means treating women exactly like men, and where difference means treating women differently insofar as they differ from men. Theorists have debated the relative merits of these two approaches as if they represented two antithetical poles of an absolute dichotomy.[9] These arguments have generally ended in stalemate. Proponents of difference have successfully shown that equality strategies typically presuppose "the male as norm," thereby disadvantaging women and imposing a distorted standard on everyone. Egalitarians have argued just as cogently, however, that difference approaches typically rely on essentialist notions of femininity, thereby reinforcing existing stereotypes and confining women within existing gender divisions. Neither equality nor difference, then, is a workable conception of gender equity.

Feminists have responded to this stalemate in several different ways. Some have tried to resolve the dilemma by reconceiving one or another of its horns; they have reinterpreted difference or equality in what they consider a more defensible form. Others have concluded "a plague on both your houses" and sought some third, wholly other, normative principle. Still others have tried to embrace the dilemma as an enabling paradox, a resource to be treasured, not an impasse to be gotten around. Many feminists, finally, have retreated altogether from normative theorizing—into cultural positivism, piecemeal reformism, or postmodern antinomianism.

None of these responses is satisfactory. Normative theorizing remains an indispensable intellectual enterprise for feminism, indeed for all emancipatory social movements. We need a vision or picture of where we are trying to go, and a set of standards for evaluating various proposals as to how we might get there. The equality/difference theoretical impasse is real, moreover; it cannot be simply sidestepped or embraced. Nor is there any "wholly other" third term that can magically catapult us beyond it. What then should feminist theorists do?

I propose that we reconceptualize gender equity as a complex, not a simple, idea. This means breaking with the assumption that gender equity can be identified with any single value or norm, whether it be equality, difference, or something else. Instead we should treat it as a complex notion comprising a plurality of distinct normative principles. The plurality will include some notions associated with the equality side of the debate, as well as some associated with the difference side. It will also encompass still other normative ideas that neither side has accorded due weight.

Assume, for example, that gender equity requires not only equal respect for women and men, but also some more substantive kind of equality, such as equality of resources or equality of capabilities. Assume, in addition, that it requires not only parity of participation in socially valued activities, but also the decentering of androcentric measures of social value. In that case, each of four distinct norms must be respected for gender equity to be achieved. Failure to satisfy any one of them means failure to realize the full meaning of gender equity.

This kind of approach promises several advantages. Treating gender equity as a complex idea lets us spot possible tensions among its component norms. We can see, for example, that some efforts to equalize resources between women and men can work at cross-purposes with some efforts to achieve parity of participation in socially valued activities, and we can look for ways to minimize such conflicts. No longer restricted to the two meganorms of equality and difference, moreover, we have more conceptual resources at our disposal. We can develop more fine-grained appraisals of alternative political strategies and goals.

In what follows, I assume that gender equity is complex in this way, and I propose an account of it that is designed for the specific purpose of evaluating alternative pictures of a postindustrial welfare state. This account might not be perfectly suited to handling issues other than welfare. For such issues, it might be best to devise a somewhat different package of component norms. Nevertheless, I believe that the general idea of treating gender equity as a complex conception is widely applicable. The analysis here may serve as a paradigm case demonstrating the usefulness of this approach.

For this particular thought experiment, in any case, I unpack the idea of gender equity as a compound of five distinct normative principles. Let me enumerate them one by one.

Antipoverty Principle

The first and most obvious objective of social-welfare provision is to prevent poverty. Preventing poverty is crucial to achieving gender equity now, after the family wage, given the high rates of poverty in solo-mother families and the vastly increased likelihood that U.S. women and children will live in such families.[10] If it accomplishes nothing else, a welfare state should at least relieve suffering by meeting otherwise unmet basic needs. Arrangements, such as those in the United States, that leave women, children, and men in poverty, are unacceptable according to this criterion. Any postindustrial welfare state that prevented such poverty would constitute a major advance. So far, however, this does not say enough. The antipoverty principle might be satisfied in a variety of different ways, not all of which are acceptable. Some ways, such as the provision of targeted, isolating and stigmatized poor relief for solo-mother families, fail to respect several of the following normative principles, which are also essential to gender equity in social welfare.

Antiexploitation Principle

Antipoverty measures are important not only in themselves, but also as a means to another basic objective: preventing exploitation of vulnerable people.[11] This principle, too, is central to achieving gender equity after the family wage. Needy women with no other way to feed themselves and their children, for example, are liable to exploitation—by abusive husbands, by sweatshop foremen, and by pimps. In guaranteeing relief of poverty then, welfare provision should also aim to mitigate exploitable dependency.[12] The availability of an alternative source of income enhances the bargaining position of subordinates in unequal relationships. The nonemployed wife who knows she can support herself and her children outside of her marriage has more leverage within it; her "voice" is enhanced as her possibilities of "exit" increase.[13] The same holds for the low-paid nursing home attendant in relation to her boss.[14] For welfare measures to have this effect, however, support must be provided as a matter of right. When receipt of aid is highly stigmatized or discretionary, the antiexploitation principle is not satisfied.[15] At best, the claimant would trade exploitable dependence on a husband or a boss for exploitable dependence on a caseworker's whim.[16] The goal should be to prevent at least three kinds of exploitable dependencies: exploitable dependence on an individual family member, such as a husband or an adult child; exploitable dependence on employers and supervisors; and exploitable dependence on the personal whims of state officials. Rather than shuttle people back and forth among these exploitable dependencies, an adequate approach must prevent all three simultaneously.[17] This principle rules out arrangements that channel a homemaker's benefits through her husband. It is likewise incompatible with arrangements that provide essential goods, such as health insurance, only in forms linked conditionally to scarce employment. Any postindustrial welfare state that satisfied the antiexploitation principle would represent a major improvement over current U.S. arrangements. But even it might not be satisfactory. Some ways of satisfying this principle would fail to respect several of the following normative principles, which are also essential to gender equity in social welfare.

Equality Principles

A postindustrial welfare state could prevent women's poverty and exploitation and yet still tolerate severe gender inequality. Such a welfare state is not satisfactory. A further dimension of gender equity in social provision is redistribution, reducing inequality between women and men. Equality, as we saw, has been criticized by some feminists. They have argued that it entails treating women exactly like men according to male-defined standards, and that this necessarily disadvantages women. That argument expresses a legitimate worry, which I will address under another rubric below. But it does not undermine the ideal of equality per se. The worry pertains only to certain inadequate ways of conceiving equality, which I do not presuppose here. At least three distinct conceptions of equality escape the objection. These three are essential to gender equity in social welfare.

Income equality. One form of equality that is crucial to gender equity concerns the distribution of real per capita income. This kind of equality is highly pressing now, after the family wage, when U.S. women's earnings are less than 70% of men's, when much of women's labor is not compensated at all, and when many women suffer from "hidden poverty" due to unequal distribution within families.[18] As I interpret it, the principle of income equality does not require absolute leveling, but it does rule out arrangements that reduce women's incomes after divorce by nearly half, whereas men's incomes nearly double.[19] It likewise rules out unequal pay for equal work and the wholesale undervaluation of women's labor and skills. The income equality principle requires a substantial reduction in the vast discrepancy between men's and women's incomes. In so doing, it tends, as well, to help equalize the life-chances of children, because a majority of U.S. children are currently likely to live at some point in solo-mother families.[20]

Leisure-time equality. A second kind of equality that is crucial to gender equity concerns the distribution of leisure time. This sort of equality is highly pressing now, after the family wage, when many women, but only a few men, do both paid work and unpaid primary care work, and when women suffer disproportionately from "time poverty."[21] One recent British study found that 52% of women surveyed, compared to 21% of men, said they "felt tired most of the time."[22] The leisure-time equality principle rules out welfare arrangements that would equalize incomes while requiring a double shift of work from women, but only a single shift from men. It likewise rules out arrangements that would require women, but not men, to do either the "work of claiming" or the time-consuming "patchwork" of piecing together income from several sources and of coordinating services from different agencies and associations.[23]

Equality of respect. A third kind of equality that is crucial to gender equity pertains to status and respect. This kind of equality is especially pressing now, after the family wage, when postindustrial culture routinely represents women as sexual objects for the pleasure of male subjects. The principle of equal respect rules out social arrangements that objectify and denigrate women—even if those arrangements prevent poverty and exploitation, and even if, in addition, they equalize income and leisure time. It is incompatible with welfare programs that trivialize women's activities and ignore women's contributions—hence with welfare reforms in the United States that assume AFDC claimants do not "work." Equality of respect requires recognition of women's personhood and recognition of women's work.

A postindustrial welfare state should promote all three of these conceptions of equality. Such a state would constitute an enormous advance over present arrangements, but even it might not go far enough. Some ways of satisfying the equality principles would fail to respect the following principle, which is also essential to gender equity in social welfare.

Antimarginalization Principle

A welfare state could satisfy all the preceding principles and still function to marginalize women. By limiting support to generous mothers' pensions, for example, it could render women independent, well provided for, well rested, and respected, but enclaved in a separate domestic sphere, removed from the life of the larger society. Such a welfare state would be unacceptable. Social policy should promote women's full participation on a par with men in all areas of social life—in employment, in politics, in the associational life of civil society. The antimarginalization principle requires provision of the necessary conditions for women's participation, including day care, elder care, and provision for breast-feeding in public. It also requires the dismantling of masculinist work cultures and woman-hostile political environments. Any postindustrial welfare state that provided these things would represent a great improvement over current arrangements. Yet even it might leave something to be desired. Some ways of satisfying the antimarginalization principle would fail to respect the last principle, which is also essential to gender equity in social welfare.

Antiandrocentrism Principle

A welfare state that satisfied many of the foregoing principles could still entrench some obnoxious gender norms. It could assume the androcentric view that men's current life patterns represent the human norm and that women ought to assimilate to them. (This is the real issue behind the previously noted worry about equality.) Such a welfare state is unacceptable. Social policy should not require women to become like men, nor to fit into institutions designed for men, to enjoy comparable levels of well-being. Policy should aim instead to restructure androcentric institutions so as to welcome human beings who can give birth and who often care for relatives and friends, treating them not as exceptions, but as ideal-typical participants. The antiandrocentrism principle requires decentering masculinist norms—in part by revaluing practices and traits that are currently undervalued because they are associated with women. It entails changing men as well as changing women.

Here then is an account of gender equity in social welfare. On this account, gender equity is a complex idea comprising five distinct normative principles, one of which—equality—is internally complex and encompasses three distinct subprinciples. Each of the principles is essential to gender equity. Thus no postindustrial welfare state can realize gender equity unless it satisfies them all.

How then do the principles interrelate? Some of the five tend usually to support one another; others could well work at cross-purposes. Everything, in fact, depends on context. Some institutional arrangements permit simultaneous satisfaction of several principles with a minimum of mutual interference; other arrangements, in contrast, set up zero-sum situations, in which attempts to satisfy one principle interfere with attempts to satisfy another. Promoting gender equity after the family wage, therefore, means attending to multiple aims that are potentially in conflict. The goal should be to find approaches that avoid trade-offs and maximize prospects for satisfying all—or at least most—of the five principles.

In the next sections, I use this approach to assess two alternative models of a postindustrial welfare state. First, however, I want to flag three sets of relevant issues. One concerns the social organization of care work. Precisely how this work is organized is crucial to human well-being in general and to the social standing of women in particular. In the era of the family wage, care work was treated as the private responsibility of individual women. Today, however, it can no longer be treated in that way. Some other way of organizing it is required, but a number of different scenarios are conceivable. In evaluating postindustrial welfare state models then, we must ask: how is responsibility for care work allocated between such institutions as the family, the market, civil society, and the state? And how is responsibility for this work assigned within such institutions: by gender? by class? by "race"-ethnicity? by age?

A second set of issues concerns differences among women. Gender is the principal focus of this article, to be sure, but it cannot be treated en bloc. The lives of women and men are cross-cut by several other salient social divisions, including class, race-ethnicity, sexuality, and age. Models of postindustrial welfare states, then, will not affect all women—nor all men—in the same way; they will generate different outcomes for differently situated people. For example, some policies will affect women who have children differently from those who do not; some, likewise, will affect women who have access to a second income differently from those who do not; and some, finally, will affect women employed full-time differently from those employed part-time, and differently yet again from those who are not employed. For each model then, we must ask: which groups of women would be advantaged and which groups disadvantaged?

A third set of issues concerns desiderata for postindustrial welfare states other than gender equity. Gender equity, after all, is not the only goal of social welfare. Also important are nonequity goals, such as efficiency, community, and individual liberty. In addition, there remain other equity goals, such as racial-ethnic equity, generational equity, class equity, and equity among nations. All of these issues are necessarily backgrounded here. Some of them, however, such as racial-ethnic equity, could be handled via parallel thought experiments: one might define racial-ethnic equity as a complex idea, analogous to the way gender equity is treated here, and then use it, too, to assess competing visions of a postindustrial welfare state.[24]

With these considerations in mind, let us now examine two strikingly different feminist visions of a postindustrial welfare state, and let us ask: which comes closest to achieving gender equity in the sense I have elaborated here?

II. UNIVERSAL BREADWINNER MODEL

In one vision of postindustrial society, the age of the family wage would give way to the age of the universal breadwinner. This is the vision implicit in the current political practice of most U.S. feminists and liberals. (It was also assumed in the former state-socialist countries!) It aims to achieve gender equity principally by promoting women's employment. The point is to enable women to support themselves and their families through their own wage earning. The breadwinner role is to be universalized, in sum, so that women too can be citizen-workers.

Universal breadwinner is a very ambitious postindustrial scenario, requiring major new programs and policies. One crucial element is a set of employment-enabling services, such as day care and elder care, aimed at freeing women from unpaid responsibilities so that they can take full-time employment on terms comparable to men.[25] Another essential element is a set of workplace reforms aimed at removing equal-opportunity obstacles, such as sex discrimination and sexual harassment. Reforming the workplace requires reforming the culture however—eliminating sexist stereotypes and breaking the cultural association of breadwinning with masculinity. Also required are policies to help change socialization, so as first, to reorient women's aspirations toward employment and away from domesticity, and second, to reorient men's expectations toward acceptance of women's new role. None of this would work, however, without one additional ingredient: macroeconomic policies to create full-time, high paying, permanent jobs for women.[26] These would have to be true breadwinner jobs in the primary labor force, carrying full, first-class social-insurance entitlements. Social insurance, finally, is central to universal breadwinner. The aim here is to bring women up to parity with men in an institution that has traditionally disadvantaged them.

How would this model organize care work? The bulk of such work would be shifted from the family to the market and the state, where it would be performed by employees for pay.[27] Who then are these employees likely to be? In the United States today, paid institutional care work is poorly remunerated, largely feminized, and largely racialized,[28] but such arrangements are precluded in this model. If the model is to succeed in enabling all women to be breadwinners, it must upgrade the status and pay attached to care work employment, making it too into primary labor force work. Universal breadwinner, then, is necessarily committed to a policy of "comparable worth"; it must redress the widespread undervaluation of skills and jobs currently coded as feminine and/or "non-White," and it must remunerate such jobs with breadwinner-level pay.

Universal breadwinner would link many benefits to employment and distribute them through social insurance. In some cases, such as pensions, benefit levels would vary with earnings. In this respect, the model resembles the industrial era welfare state.[29] The difference is that many more women would be covered on the basis of their own employment records, and many more women's employment records would look considerably more like men's.

Not all adults can be employed, however. Some will be unable to work for medical reasons, including some not previously employed. Others will be unable to get jobs. Some, finally, will have care work responsibilities that they are unable or unwilling to shift elsewhere. Most of these last will be women. To provide for these people, universal breadwinner must include a residual tier of social welfare that provides need-based, means-tested wage replacements.[30]

Universal breadwinner is far removed from present realities. It requires massive creation of primary labor force jobs—jobs sufficient to support a family single-handedly. That, of course, is wildly askew of current postindustrial trends, which generate jobs not for breadwinners, but for "disposable workers."[31] Let us assume for the sake of the thought experiment, however, that its conditions of possibility could be met, and let us consider whether the resulting postindustrial welfare state could claim title to gender equity.

Antipoverty

We can acknowledge straight off that universal breadwinner would do a good job of preventing poverty. A policy that created secure breadwinner-quality jobs for all employable women and men—while providing the services that would enable women to take such jobs—would keep most families out of poverty, and generous levels of residual support would keep the rest out of poverty through transfers. Failing that, however, several groups are especially vulnerable to poverty in this model: those who cannot work, those who cannot get secure, permanent, full-time, good-paying jobs— disproportionately women and/or people of color; and those with heavy, hard-to-shift, unpaid care work responsibilities—disproportionately women.

Antiexploitation

The model should also succeed in preventing exploitable dependency for most women. Women with secure breadwinner jobs are able to exit unsatis-factory relations with men, and those who do not have such jobs but know they can get them will also be less vulnerable to exploitation. Failing that, the residual system of income support provides back-up protection against exploitable dependency—assuming that it is generous, nondiscretionary, and honorable. Failing that, however, the groups mentioned above remain espe-cially vulnerable to exploitation—by abusive men, by unfair or predatory employers, by capricious state officials.

Equality

Income equality. Universal breadwinner is only fair, however, at achieving income equality. Granted, secure breadwinner jobs for women—plus the services that would enable women to take them—would narrow the gender wage gap.[32] Reduced inequality in earnings, moreover, translates into reduced inequality in social-insurance benefits, and the availability of exit options from marriage should encourage a more equitable distribution of resources within it. But the model is not otherwise egalitarian. It contains a basic social fault line dividing breadwinners from others, to the considerable disadvan-tage of the others—most of whom would be women. Apart from comparable worth, moreover, it does not reduce pay inequality among breadwinner jobs. To be sure, the model reduces the weight of gender in assigning individuals to unequally compensated breadwinner jobs, but it thereby increases the weight of other variables, presumably class, education, race-ethnicity, and age. Women—and men—who are disadvantaged in relation to those variables will earn less than those who are not.

Leisure-time equality. The model is poor, moreover, with respect to equality of leisure time, although it improves on current arrangements. It assumes that all of women's current domestic and care work responsibilities can be shifted to the market and/or the state. But that assumption is patently unrealistic. Some things, such as childbearing, attending to family emergencies, and much parenting work, cannot be shifted—short of universal surrogacy and other presumably undesirable arrangements. Other things, such as cooking and (some) housekeeping, could be shifted—provided we were prepared to accept collective living arrangements or high levels of commodification. Even those tasks that are shifted, finally, do not disappear without a trace, but give rise to burdensome new tasks of coordination. Women's chances for equal leisure, then, depend on whether men can be induced to do their fair share of this work. On this, the model does not inspire confidence. Not only does it offer no disincentives to free riding, but in valorizing paid work, it implicitly denigrates unpaid work, thereby fueling the motivation to shirk.[33] Women without partners would, in any case, be on their own. And those in lower-income households would be less able to purchase replacement services. Employed women would have a second shift on this model then, albeit a less burdensome one than some have now; and there would be many more women employed full-time. Universal breadwinner, in sum, is not likely to deliver equal leisure. Anyone who does not free ride in this possible postindustrial world is likely to be harried and tired.

Equality of respect. The model is only fair, moreover, at delivering equality of respect. Because it holds men and women to the single standard of the citizen-worker, its only chance of eliminating the gender respect gap is to admit women to that status on the same terms as men. This, however, is unlikely to occur. A more likely outcome is that women would retain more connection to reproduction and domesticity than men, thus appearing as breadwinners manqué. In addition, the model is likely to generate another kind of respect gap. By putting a high premium on breadwinner status, it invites disrespect for others. Participants in the means-tested residual system will be liable to stigmatization, and most of these will be women. Any employment-centered model, even a feminist one, has a hard time construct-ing an honorable status for those it defines as nonworkers.

Antimarginalization

This model is also only fair at combating women's marginalization. Granted, it promotes women's participation in employment, but its definition of participation is narrow. Expecting full-time employment of all who are able, the model may actually impede participation in politics and civil society. Certainly it does nothing to promote women's participation in those arenas. It fights women's marginalization, then, in a one-sided, "workerist" way.

Antiandrocentrism

Finally, the model performs poorly in overcoming androcentrism. It valorizes men's traditional sphere—employment—and simply tries to help women fit in. Traditionally, female care work, in contrast, is treated instru-mentally; it is what must be sloughed off to become a breadwinner. It is not itself accorded social value. The ideal typical citizen here is the breadwinner, now nominally gender neutral. But the content of the status is implicitly masculine; it is the male half of the old breadwinner/homemaker couple, now universalized and required of everyone. The female half of the couple has simply disappeared. None of her distinctive virtues and capacities has been preserved for women, let alone universalized to men. The model is androcentric.

We can summarize the merits of universal breadwinner in Figure 1. Not surprisingly, universal breadwinner delivers the best outcomes to women whose lives most closely resemble the male half of the old family-wage ideal couple. It is especially good to childless women and to women without other major domestic responsibilities that cannot easily be shifted to social ser-vices. But for those women, as well as for others, it falls short of full gender equity.

III. CAREGIVER PARITY MODEL

In a second vision of postindustrial society, the era of the family wage would give way to the era of caregiver parity. This is the picture implicit in the political practice of most Western European feminists and social demo-crats. It aims to promote gender equity principally by supporting informal

	Universal Breadwinner
Antipoverty	Good
Antiexploitation	Good
Income equality	Fair
Leisure-time equality	Poor
Equality of respect	Fair
Antimarginalization	Fair
Antiandrocentrism	Poor

Figure 1.

care work. The point is to enable women with significant domestic responsibilities to support themselves and their families, either through care work
alone or through care work plus part-time employment. (Women without
significant domestic responsibilities would presumably support themselves
through employment.) The aim is not to make women's lives the same as
men's, but rather to "make difference costless."[34] Thus childbearing,
childrearing, and informal domestic labor are to be elevated to parity with
formal paid labor. The caregiver role is to be put on a par with the breadwinner
role—so that women and men can enjoy equivalent levels of dignity and
well-being.

Caregiver parity is also extremely ambitious. On this model, many (although not all) women will follow the current U.S. female practice of
alternating spells of full-time employment, spells of full-time care work, and
spells that combine part-time care work with part-time employment. The aim
is to make such a life pattern costless. To this end, several major new
programs are necessary. One is a program of caregiver allowances to compensate childbearing, childraising, housework, and other forms of socially
necessary domestic labor; the allowances must be sufficiently generous at the
full-time rate to support a family—hence equivalent to a breadwinner wage.[35]
Also required is a program of workplace reforms. These must facilitate the
possibility of combining supported care work with part-time employment
and of transitioning between different life states. The key here is flexibility.
One obvious necessity is a generous program of mandated pregnancy and
family leave so that caregivers can exit and enter employment without losing
security or seniority. Another is a program of retraining and job search for
those not returning to old jobs. Also essential is mandated flextime so that
caregivers can shift their hours to accommodate their care work responsibilities, including shifts between full- and part-time employment. Finally, in the
wake of all this flexibility, there must be programs to ensure continuity of all

the basic social-welfare benefits, including health, unemployment, disability, and retirement insurance.

This model organizes care work very differently from universal breadwinner. Whereas that approach shifted care work to the market and the state, this one keeps the bulk of such work in the household and supports it with public funds.[36] Caregiver parity's social-insurance system also differs sharply. To assure continuous coverage for people alternating between care work and employment, benefits attached to both must be integrated in a single desert-based system. In this system, part-time jobs and supported care work must be covered on the same basis as full-time jobs. Thus a woman finishing a spell of supported care work would be eligible for unemployment insurance benefits on the same basis as a recently laid off employee in the event she could not find a suitable job, and a supported care worker who became disabled would receive disability payments on the same basis as a disabled employee. Years of supported care work would count on a par with years of employment toward eligibility for retirement pensions. Benefit levels would be fixed in ways that treat care work and employment equivalently.

Caregiver parity also requires another, residual tier of social welfare. Some adults will be unable to do either care work or waged work, including some without prior work records of either type. Most of these people will probably be men. To provide for them, the model must offer means-tested wage and allowance replacements.[37] Caregiver parity's residual tier should be smaller than universal breadwinner's, however; nearly all adults should be covered in the integrated breadwinner-caregiver system of social insurance.

Caregiver parity, too, is far removed from current U.S. arrangements. It requires large outlays of public funds to pay caregiver allowances, hence major structural tax reform and a sea change in political culture. Let us assume for the sake of the thought experiment, however, that its conditions of possibility could be met. And let us consider whether the resulting postindustrial welfare state could claim title to gender equity.

Antipoverty

Caregiver parity would do a good job of preventing poverty—including for those women and children who are currently most vulnerable. Sufficiently generous allowances would keep solo-mother families out of poverty during spells of full-time care work, and a combination of allowances and wages would do the same during spells of part-time supported care work and part-time employment. (Wages from full-time employment must also be sufficient to support a family with dignity.) Because each of these options

608   POLITICAL THEORY / November 1994

would carry the basic social-insurance package, moreover, women with feminine work patterns would have considerable security. Adults with neither care work nor employment records would be most vulnerable to poverty in this model; most of these would be men. Children, in contrast, would be well protected.

Antiexploitation

Caregiver parity should also succeed in preventing exploitation for most women, including those who are most vulnerable today. By providing income directly to nonemployed wives, it reduces their economic dependence on husbands. It also provides economic security to single women with children, reducing their liability to exploitation by employers. Insofar as caregiver allowances are desert based and nondiscretionary, finally, recipients are not subject to caseworkers' whims. Once again, it is adults with neither care work nor employment records who are most vulnerable to exploitation in this model, and the majority of them would be men.

Income equality. Caregiver parity performs quite poorly, however, with respect to income equality. Although the system of allowances plus wages provides the equivalent of a basic minimum breadwinner wage, it also institutes a "mommy track" in employment—a market in flexible, noncontinuous full- and/or part-time jobs. Most of these jobs will pay considerably less even at the full-time rate than comparable breadwinner-track jobs. Two-partner families will have an economic incentive to keep one partner on the breadwinner track rather than to share spells of care work between them; given current labor markets, making the breadwinner the man will be most advantageous for heterosexual couples. Given current culture and socialization, moreover, men are generally unlikely to choose the mommy track in the same proportions as women. So the two employment tracks will carry traditional gender associations. Those associations are likely in turn to produce discrimination against women in the breadwinner track. Caregiver parity may make difference cost less then, but it will not make difference costless.

Leisure-time equality. Caregiver parity does somewhat better, however, with respect to equality of leisure time. It makes it possible for all women to avoid the double shift if they choose, by opting for full- or part-time supported care work at various stages in their lives. (Currently, this choice is available only to a small percentage of privileged U.S. women.) We just saw, however, that this choice is not truly costless. Some women with families will not want to forego the benefits of breadwinner-track employment and will try to combine it with care work. Those not partnered with someone on the caregiver track will be significantly disadvantaged with respect to leisure time, and probably in their employment as well. Men, in contrast, will largely be insulated from this dilemma. On leisure time, then, the model is only fair.

Equality of respect. Caregiver parity is also only fair at promoting equality of respect. Unlike universal breadwinner, it offers two different routes to that end. Theoretically, citizen-workers and citizen-caregivers are statuses of equivalent dignity. But are they really on a par with one another? Caregiving is certainly treated more respectfully in this model than in current U.S. society, but it remains associated with femininity. Breadwinning likewise remains associated with masculinity. Given those traditional gender associations, plus the economic differential between the two lifestyles, caregiving is unlikely to attain true parity with breadwinning. In general, it is hard to imagine how "separate but equal" gender roles could provide genuine equality of respect today.

Antimarginalization

Caregiver parity performs poorly, moreover, in preventing women's marginalization. By supporting women's informal care work, it reinforces the view of such work as women's work and consolidates the gender division of domestic labor. By consolidating dual labor markets for breadwinners and caregivers, moreover, the model marginalizes women within the employment sector. By reinforcing the association of caregiving with femininity, finally, it may also impede women's participation in other spheres of life, such as politics and civil society.

Antiandrocentrism

Yet caregiver parity is better than universal breadwinner at combating androcentrism. It treats caregiving as intrinsically valuable, not as a mere obstacle to employment, thus challenging the view that only men's traditional activities are fully human. It also accommodates feminine life patterns, thereby rejecting the demand that women assimilate to masculine patterns. But the model still leaves something to be desired. Caregiver parity stops short of affirming the universal value of activities and life patterns associated with women. It does not value caregiving enough to demand that men do it too; it does not ask men to change. Thus caregiver parity represents only one-half of a full-scale challenge to androcentrism. Here, too, its performance is only fair.

Caregiver parity's strengths and weaknesses are summarized in Figure 2. In general, caregiver parity performs best for women with significant care work responsibilities. But for those women, as well as for others, it fails to deliver full gender equity.

IV. CONCLUSION: GENDER EQUITY IN A POSTINDUSTRIAL WELFARE STATE REQUIRES DECONSTRUCTING GENDER

Both universal breadwinner and caregiver parity are highly utopian visions of a postindustrial welfare state. Either one of them would represent a major improvement over current U.S. arrangements. Yet neither is likely to be realized soon. Both models assume background preconditions that are strikingly absent today. Both presuppose major political-economic restructuring, including significant public control over corporations, the capacity to direct investment to create high-quality permanent jobs, and the ability to tax profits and wealth at rates sufficient to fund expanded high-quality social programs. Both models also assume broad popular support for a postindustrial welfare state that is committed to gender equity.

If both models are utopian in this sense, neither is utopian enough. Neither universal breadwinner nor caregiver parity can actually make good on its promise of gender equity—even under very favorable conditions. Although both are good at preventing women's poverty and exploitation, both are only fair at redressing inequality of respect: Universal breadwinner holds women to the same standard as men while constructing arrangements that prevent them from meeting it fully; caregiver parity, in contrast, sets up a double standard to accommodate gender difference while institutionalizing policies that fail to assure equivalent respect for feminine activities and life patterns. When we turn to the remaining components of gender equity, moreover, the two models' strengths and weaknesses diverge. Whereas universal breadwinner is better at preventing women's marginalization and at reducing income inequality between men and women, caregiver parity is better at redressing inequality of leisure time and at combating androcentrism. Neither model, however, promotes women's full participation on a par with men in politics and civil society. And neither values female-associated practices enough to ask men to do them, too; neither asks men to change. (The relative merits of universal breadwinner and caregiver parity are summarized in Figure 3.)

	Caregiver Parity
Antipoverty	Good
Antiexploitation	Good
Income equality	Poor
Leisure-time equality	Fair
Equality of respect	Fair
Antimarginalization	Poor
Antiandrocentrism	Fair

Figure 2.

Neither model, in sum, provides everything that feminists want. Even in a highly idealized form, neither delivers full gender equity.

If these were the only possibilities, we would face a very difficult set of trade-offs. Suppose, however, we reject this Hobson's choice and try to develop a third alternative. The trick is to envision a postindustrial welfare state that combines the best of universal breadwinner with the best of caregiver parity, while jettisoning the worst features of each. What third alternative is possible?

So far, we have examined—and found wanting—two initially plausible approaches: one aiming to make women more like men are now, and the other leaving men and women pretty much unchanged, while aiming to make women's difference costless. A third possibility is to induce men to become more like most women are now—that is, people who do primary care work.

Consider the effects of this one change on the models we have just examined. If men were to do their fair share of care work, universal breadwinner would come much closer to equalizing leisure time and eliminating androcentrism, whereas caregiver parity would do a much better job of equalizing income and reducing women's marginalization. Both models, in addition, would tend to promote equality of respect. If men were to become more like women are now, in sum, both models would begin to approach gender equity.

The key to achieving gender equity in a postindustrial welfare state, then, is to make women's current life patterns the norm. Women today often combine breadwinning and caregiving, albeit with great difficulty and strain. A postindustrial welfare state must ensure that men do the same, while redesigning institutions so as to eliminate the difficulty and strain. Such a welfare state would promote gender equity by dismantling the gendered opposition between breadwinning and caregiving. It would integrate activities that are currently separated from one another, eliminate their gender coding, and encourage men to perform them too.

	Universal Breadwinner	Caregiver Parity
Antipoverty	Good	Good
Antiexploitation	Good	Good
Income equality	Fair	Poor
Leisure-time equality	Poor	Fair
Equality of respect	Fair	Fair
Antimarginalization	Fair	Poor
Antiandrocentrism	Poor	Fair

Figure 3.

This, however, is tantamount to a wholesale restructuring of the institution of gender. The construction of breadwinning and caregiving as separate roles, coded masculine and feminine respectively, is a principal undergirding of the current gender order. To dismantle those roles and their cultural coding is in effect to overturn that order. It means subverting the existing gender division of labor and reducing the salience of gender as a structural principle of social organization.[38] At the limit, it suggests deconstructing gender.[39]

President Clinton has proclaimed that his goal is to end welfare as we know it. The present thought experiment has led us to a different goal: to end gender as we know it. Only by embracing the aim of deconstructing gender can we mitigate potential conflicts among our five component principles of gender equity, thereby minimizing the necessity of trade-offs. Rejecting that aim, in contrast, makes such conflicts, and hence trade-offs, more likely. Achieving gender equity in a postindustrial welfare state, then, requires deconstructing gender.

A thought experiment, I noted at the outset, is not a policy analysis. But it can nevertheless have political implications. By clarifying that gender equity requires deconstructing gender, the reasoning here suggests a strategy of radical reform. This means building movements whose demands for equity cannot be satisfied within the present gender order. It means organizing for reforms that "advance toward a radical transformation of society."[40]

Crucial to such a strategy is a third—deconstructive—vision of a postindustrial welfare state. What then might such a welfare state look like? Unlike caregiver parity, its employment sector would not be divided into two different tracks; all jobs would assume workers who are caregivers, too; all would have a shorter work week than full-time jobs have now; and all would have employment-enabling services. Unlike universal breadwinner, however, employees would not be assumed to shift all care work to social services. Some informal care work would be publicly supported and integrated on a par with paid work in a single social-insurance system. Some would be

· performed in households by relatives and friends, but such households would not necessarily be heterosexual nuclear families. Other supported care work would be located outside of households altogether—in civil society. In state-funded but locally organized institutions, childless adults, older people, and others without kin-based responsibilities would join parents and others in democratic, self-managed care work activities. This approach would not only deconstruct the opposition between breadwinning and caregiving; it would also deconstruct the associated opposition between bureaucratized public institutional settings and intimate private domestic settings. Treating civil society as a site for care work offers a wide range of new possibilities for promoting equal participation in social life, now no longer restricted to formal employment.

Much more work needs to be done to develop this third—deconstructive—vision of a postindustrial welfare state. A key is to develop policies that discourage free riding. Contra conservatives, the real free riders in the current system are not poor solo mothers who shirk employment. Instead, they are men of all classes who shirk care work and domestic labor, and especially corporations who free ride on the labor of working people, both underpaid and unpaid.

A good statement of the deconstructive vision comes from the Swedish Ministry of Labor: "To make it possible for both men and women to combine parenthood and gainful employment, a new view of the male role and a radical change in the organization of working life are required."[41] The trick is to imagine a social world in which citizens' lives integrate wage earning, caregiving, community activism, political participation, and involvement in the associational life of civil society—while also leaving time for some fun. This world is not likely to come into being in the immediate future. But it is the only imaginable postindustrial world that promises true gender equity, and unless we are guided by this vision now, we will never get any closer to achieving it.

NOTES

1. See Abramowitz (1988), Fraser (1987), Gordon (1988), and Land (1978). An exception is France, which from early on had high numbers of female workers (Jenson 1990).

2. This account of the tripartite structure of the welfare state represents a modification of my earlier (1987) view. Heretofore, I followed Nelson (1984, 1990) in positing a two-tier structure of ideal-typically "masculine" social insurance programs and ideal-typically "feminine" family support programs. Although that view was a relatively accurate picture of the U.S. social-welfare system, I now consider it analytically misleading. The United States is unusual in that the second and third tiers are conflated. The main program of means-tested poor relief—Aid to Families

with Dependent Children (AFDC)—is also the main program that supports women's child raising. Analytically, these are best understood as two distinct tiers of social welfare. When social insurance is added, we get a three-tier welfare state.

3. See Harvey (1989), Lash and Urry (1987), and Reich (1991).

4. Smith (1984).

5. Stacey (1987).

6. Weston (1991).

7. Ellwood (1988).

8. Fraser (1993).

9. Bartlett and Kennedy (1991).

10. Ellwood (1988).

11. Goodin (1988).

12. Not all dependencies are exploitable. Goodin (1988, 175-6) specifies the following four conditions that must be met if a dependency is to be exploitable: (1) the relationship must be asymmetrical; (2) the subordinate party must need the resource that the superordinate supplies; (3) the subordinate must depend on some particular superordinate for the supply of needed resources; and (4) the superordinate must enjoy discretionary control over the resources that the subordinate needs from him or her.

13. See Hirschman (1970), Okin (1989), and Hobson (1990).

14. Piven and Cloward (1971), Esping-Andersen (1990).

15. Goodin (1988).

16. Sparer (1970).

17. See Orloff (1993). The antiexploitation objective should not be confused with current U.S. attacks on welfare dependency, which are highly ideological. These attacks define dependency exclusively as receipt of public assistance. They ignore the ways in which such receipt can promote claimants' independence by preventing exploitable dependence on husbands and employers (Fraser and Gordon 1994).

18. Lister (1990), Sen (1990).

19. Weitzman (1985).

20. Ellwood (1988, 45).

21. Hochschild (1989), Schor (1991).

22. Bradshaw and Holmes (1989, as cited by Lister, 1990).

23. Balbo (1987).

24. A fourth set of issues is also extremely important, but I do not have space to consider it here. It concerns the bases of entitlement to provision. Every welfare state assigns its benefits according to a specific mix of distributive principles, which defines its basic moral quality. That mix, in each case, needs to be scrutinized. Usually it contains varying proportions of three basic principles of entitlement: need, desert, and citizenship. Need-based provision is the most redistributive, but it risks isolating and stigmatizing the needy; it has been the basis of traditional poor relief and of modern public assistance, the least honorable forms of provision. The most honorable, in contrast, is entitlement based on desert, but it tends to be antiegalitarian and exclusionary. Here one receives benefits according to one's contributions, usually tax payments, work, and service—where tax payments means wage deductions paid into a special fund, work means primary labor force employment, and service means the military, all interpretations of those terms that disadvantage women. Desert has been the primary basis of earnings-linked social insurance in the industrial welfare state. (Actually, there is a heavy ideological component in the usual view that public assistance is need-based, whereas social insurance is desert-based. Benefit levels in social insurance do not strictly reflect contributions. Moreover, all government programs are financed by contributions, in the form of taxation. Public assistance programs are

financed from general revenues, both federal and state. Welfare recipients, like others, contribute to these funds, for example, through payment of sales taxes [Fraser and Gordon 1992].) The third principle, citizenship, allocates provision on the basis of membership in society. It is honorable, egalitarian, and universalist, but also expensive and hence hard to sustain at high levels of quality and generosity; some theorists worry, too, that it encourages free riding. (The free-rider worry, incidentally, is typically defined androcentrically as a worry about shirking paid employment. Little attention is paid, in contrast, to a far more widespread problem, namely, men's free riding on women's unpaid domestic labor. A welcome exception is a recent unpublished paper by Peter Taylor-Gooby [1993].) Citizenship-based entitlements are typically found in social-democratic countries, where they may include single-payer universal health insurance systems, universal family or child allowances, and universal flat-rate old-age pensions; they are virtually unknown in the United States—except for public education. In examining models of postindustrial welfare states then, one must look closely at the construction of entitlement. It makes considerable difference to women's and children's well-being, for example, whether day care places are distributed as citizenship entitlements or as desert-based entitlements (i.e., whether or not they are conditional on prior employment). It likewise matters, to take another example, whether care work is supported on the basis of need, in the form of a means-tested benefit for the poor, or whether it is supported on the basis of desert, as return for work or service, now interpreted nonandrocentrically, or whether, finally, it is supported on the basis of citizenship under a universal basic income scheme.

25. On what basis would these benefits be distributed? In theory, employment-enabling services could be distributed according to need, desert, or citizenship, but citizenship accords best with the spirit of the model. Means-tested day care targeted for the poor cannot help but signify a failure to achieve genuine breadwinner status, and desert-based day care sets up a catch-22: one must already be employed in order to get what is needed for employment. Citizenship-based entitlement is best then, but it must make services available to all. This rules out Swedish-type arrangements, which fail to guarantee sufficient day care places and are plagued by long queues (Hobson 1993).

26. That, incidentally, would be to break decisively with U.S. policy, which typically assumes that job creation is for men; Bill Clinton's much-touted industrial and infrastructural investment policies are no exception in this regard (Fraser 1993).

27. This could be done in several different ways. Government could itself provide day care, and so on, in the form of public goods, or it could fund marketized provision through a system of vouchers. Alternatively, employers could be mandated to provide employment-enabling services for their employees, either through vouchers or in-house arrangements. The state option means higher taxes, of course, but it may be preferable nevertheless. Mandating employer responsibility creates a disincentive to hire workers with dependents, to the likely disadvantage of women.

28. Glenn (1992).

29. It too conditions entitlement on desert and defines contribution in traditional androcentric terms as employment and wage deductions.

30. Exactly what else must be provided inside the residual system will depend on the balance of entitlements outside of it. If health insurance is provided universally as a citizen benefit, for example, then there need be no means-tested health system for the nonemployed. If, however, mainstream health insurance is linked to employment, then a residual health care system will be necessary. The same holds for unemployment, retirement, and disability insurance. In general, the more that is provided on the basis of citizenship, instead of on the basis of desert, the less has to be provided on the basis of need. One could even say that desert-based entitlements create the necessity of need-based provision; thus social insurance creates the need for means-tested public assistance.

616   POLITICAL THEORY / November 1994

31. Kilborn (1993).

32. Exactly how much depends on the government's success in eliminating discrimination and in implementing comparable worth.

33. Universal breadwinner apparently relies on persuasion to induce men to do their fair share of unpaid work. The chances of that working would be improved if the model succeeded in promoting cultural change and in enhancing women's voice within marriage. But it is doubtful that this would suffice.

34. Littleton (1991).

35. On what principle(s) would these benefits be distributed? Caregiver allowances could in theory be distributed on the basis of need, as a means-tested benefit for the poor—as they have always been in the United States. But that would contravene the spirit of caregiver parity. One cannot consistently claim that the caregiver life is equivalent in dignity to the breadwinner life, while supporting it only as a last-resort stopgap against poverty. (This contradiction has always bedeviled mothers' pensions—and later Aid to Dependent Children—in the United States. Although these programs were intended by some advocates to exalt motherhood, they sent a contradictory message by virtue of being means tested and morals tested.) Means-tested allowances, moreover, would impede easy transitions between employment and care work. Because the aim is to make caregiving as deserving as breadwinning, caregiver allowances must be based on desert. Treated as compensation for socially necessary service or work, they alter the standard androcentric meanings of those terms.

36. Susan Okin (1989) has proposed an alternative way to fund care work. In her scheme the funds would come from what are now considered to be the earnings of the caregiver's partner. A man with a nonemployed wife, for example, would receive a paycheck for one-half of his salary; his employer would cut a second check in the same amount payable directly to the wife. Intriguing as this idea is, one may wonder whether it is really the best way to promote wives' independence from husbands, because it ties her income so directly to his. In addition, Okin's proposal does not provide any care work support for women without employed partners. Caregiver parity, in contrast, provides public support for all who perform informal care work. Who then are its beneficiaries likely to be? With the exception of pregnancy leave, all of the model's benefits are open to everyone; so men as well as women can opt for a "feminine" life. Women, however, are considerably more likely to do so. Although the model aims to make such a life costless, it includes no positive incentives for men to change. Some men, of course, may simply prefer such a life and will choose it when offered the chance; most will not, however, given current socialization and culture. We will see, moreover, that caregiver parity contains some hidden disincentives to male caregiving.

37. In this respect, it resembles the universal breadwinner model: whatever additional essential goods are normally offered on the basis of desert must be offered here too on the basis of need.

38. Okin (1989).

39. J. Williams (1991).

40. Gorz (1967, 6).

41. As quoted in Lister (1990, 463).

REFERENCES

Abramowitz, Mimi. 1988. *Regulating the Lives of Women: Social Welfare Policy from Colonial Times to the Present.* Boston: South End.

Balbo, Laura. 1987. "Crazy Quilt." In *Women and the State*, edited by Ann Showstack Sassoon. London: Hutchinson.

Bartlett, Katharine T., and Rosanne Kennedy, eds. 1991. *Feminist Legal Theory: Readings in Law and Gender*. Boulder, CO: Westview.

Ellwood, David T. 1988. *Poor Support: Poverty in the American Family*. New York: Basic Books.

Esping-Andersen, Gosta. 1990. *The Three Worlds of Welfare Capitalism*. Princeton, NJ: Princeton University Press.

Fraser, Nancy. 1987. "Women, Welfare, and the Politics of Need Interpretation." *Hypatia: A Journal of Feminist Philosophy* 2, no. 1: 103-21. (Reprinted in Fraser, *Unruly Practices: Power, Discourse, and Gender in Contemporary Social Theory*. Minneapolis: University of Minnesota Press, 1989.)

————. 1993. "Clintonism, Welfare, and the Antisocial Wage: The Emergence of a Neoliberal Political Imaginary." *Rethinking Marxism* 6, no. 1: 9-23.

Fraser, Nancy, and Linda Gordon. 1992. "Contract versus Charity: Why Is There No Social Citizenship in the United States?" *Socialist Review* 22, no. 3: 45-68.

————. 1994. "A Genealogy of 'Dependency': Tracing a Keyword of the U.S. Welfare State." *Signs: Journal of Women in Culture and Society* 19, no. 2: 309-36.

Glenn, Evelyn Nakano. 1992. "From Servitude to Service Work: Historical Continuities in the Racial Division of Paid Reproductive Labor." *Signs: Journal of Women in Culture and Society* 18, no. 1: 1-43.

Goodin, Robert. 1988. *Reasons for Welfare: The Political Theory of the Welfare State*. Princeton, NJ: Princeton University Press.

Gordon, Linda. 1988. "What Does Welfare Regulate?" *Social Research* 55, no. 4: 609-30.

Gorz, Andre. 1967. *Strategy for Labor: A Radical Proposal*. Translated by Martin A. Nicolaus and Victoria Ortiz. Boston: Beacon.

Harvey, David. 1989. *The Condition of Postmodernity: An Inquiry into the Origins of Cultural Change*. Oxford: Basil Blackwell.

Hirschman, Albert O. 1970. *Exit, Voice, and Loyalty: Responses to Decline in Firms, Organizations, and States*. Cambridge, MA: Harvard University Press.

Hobson, Barbara. 1990. "No Exit, No Voice: Women's Economic Dependency and the Welfare State." *Acta Sociologica* 33, no. 3: 235-50.

————. 1993. "Economic Dependency and Women's Social Citizenship: Some Thoughts on Esping-Andersen's Welfare State Regimes." Unpublished typescript.

Hochschild, Arlie. 1989. *The Second Shift: Working Parents and the Revolution at Home*. New York: Viking.

Jenson, Jane. 1990. "Representations of Gender: Policies to 'Protect' Women Workers and Infants in France and the United States before 1914." In *Women, the State, and Welfare*, edited by Linda Gordon, 152-77. Madison: University of Wisconsin Press.

Kilborn, Peter. 1993. March 15. "New Jobs Lack the Old Security in Time of 'Disposable Workers.' " *The New York Times*, pp. A1, A6.

Land, Hilary. 1978. "Who Cares for the Family?" *Journal of Social Policy* 7, no. 3: 257-84.

Lash, Scott, and John Urry. 1987. *The End of Organized Capitalism*. Cambridge: Polity.

Lister, Ruth. 1990. "Women, Economic Dependency, and Citizenship." *Journal of Social Policy* 19, no. 4: 445-67.

Littleton, Christine A. 1991. "Reconstructing Sexual Equality." In *Feminist Legal Theory: Readings in Law and Gender*, edited by Katharine T. Bartlett and Rosanne Kennedy, 35-56. Boulder, CO: Westview.

618 POLITICAL THEORY / November 1994

Nelson, Barbara. 1984. "Women's Poverty and Women's Citizenship: Some Political Conse-
quences of Economic Marginality." *Signs: Journal of Women in Culture and Society* 10, no.
2: 209-31.
———. 1990. "The Origins of the Two-Channel Welfare State: Workmen's Compensation and
Mothers' Aid." In *Women, the State, and Welfare*, edited by Linda Gordon, 123-51. Madison:
University of Wisconsin Press.
Okin, Susan Moller. 1989. *Justice, Gender, and the Family*. New York: Basic Books.
Orloff, Ann Shola. 1993. "Gender and the Social Rights of Citizenship: The Comparative
Analysis of Gender Relations and Welfare States." *American Sociological Review* 58, no. 3:
303-28.
Piven, Frances Fox, and Richard A. Cloward. 1971. *Regulating the Poor*. New York: Random
House.
Reich, Robert. 1991. *The Work of Nations: Preparing Ourselves for 21st Century Capitalism*.
New York: Alfred A. Knopf.
Schor, Juliet. 1991. *The Overworked American: The Unexpected Decline of Leisure*. New York:
Basic Books.
Sen, Amartya. 1990. "More Than 100 Million Women Are Missing." *The New York Review of
Books* 37, no. 20: 61-6.
Smith, Joan. 1984. "The Paradox of Women's Poverty: Wage-Earning Women and Economic
Transformation." *Signs: Journal of Women in Culture and Society* 9, no. 2: 291-310.
Sparer, Edward V. 1970. "The Right to Welfare." In *The Rights of Americans: What They
Are—What They Should Be*, edited by Norman Dorsen, 65-93. New York: Pantheon.
Stacey, Judith. 1987. "Sexism By a Subtler Name? Postindustrial Conditions and Postfeminist
Consciousness in the Silicon Valley." *Socialist Review* 96: 7-28.
Taylor-Gooby, Peter. 1993. "Scrounging, Moral Hazard, and Unwaged Work: Citizenship and
Human Need." Unpublished typescript.
Weitzman, Lenore. 1985. *The Divorce Revolution: The Unexpected Social Consequences for
Women and Children in America*. New York: Free Press.
Weston, Kath. 1991. *Families We Choose: Lesbians, Gays, Kinship*. New York: Columbia
University Press.
Williams, Joan. 1991. "Deconstructing Gender." In *Feminist Legal Theory: Readings in Law
and Gender*, edited by Katharine T. Bartlett and Rosanne Kennedy, 95-123. Boulder, CO:
Westview.

*Nancy Fraser is Professor of Philosophy and Faculty Fellow of the Center for Urban
Affairs and Policy Research at Northwestern University, where she is also an affiliate of
the Women's Studies Program. She is the author of* Unruly Practices: Power, Discourse
and Gender in Contemporary Social Theory *(University of Minnesota Press and Polity
Press, 1989), the co-author of* Feminist Contentions: A Philosophical Exchange
(Routledge, 1994), and the co-editor of Revaluing French Feminism: Critical Essays on
Difference, Agency, and Culture *(Indiana University Press, 1992).*

[25]

RICHARD T. ELY LECTURE

The Postsocialist Transition and the State: Reflections in the Light of Hungarian Fiscal Problems

By JÁNOS KORNAI*

I deal here with only one of the innumerable problems that arise during the transformation of the postsocialist countries: the role of the state in the economy. My treatment is based on the experiences of Hungary, but I believe the problems I discuss are quite general and will arise sooner or later in all postsocialist countries, though they may vary in intensity and form. Although my illustrations are from Hungary, the lecture is not intended to offer an overall survey of the Hungarian economy. One feature, perhaps, is worth noting: while several countries in the region face grave economic problems and may even be threatened by chaos, the transition in Hungary is taking place under orderly conditions, and there are signs of promising economic development.

I. The Suggestions in Western Writings

Of course the first trip that academic economists like ourselves make in search of guidance is to the library, where the body of writing on the division of labor between the state and the market is certainly abundant, even embarrassingly so.

Many economists in the postsocialist region, disillusioned with central planning, are prone to make an uncritical, mythical cult of the market. One effective cure for this disorder is to read Western writings on the shortcomings of the market mechanism. They convincingly prove the existence of several fundamental problems to which the market alone has no reassuring solution: for example, preserving the macroequilibrium of the economy, ensuring a fair distribution of income, accounting for the effect of externalities, supplying an adequate quantity of public goods, and limiting the power of monopolies. The writers suggest that, where market failure occurs, the state should actively intervene.[1]

There is another strand of Western literature, however, that persuasively shows how political action, politicians, and bureaucrats, perhaps even more significantly than the market, can fail to coordinate the economy. This doubt, voiced long ago by the Austrian school and then reformulated in the arguments of public-choice theory, has induced

*Harvard University and the Institute of Economics, Hungarian Academy of Sciences, Budaörsi ut 45, 1112 Budapest, Hungary. Great assistance was given to me by E. Erdélyi, M. Kovács, M. Móra, L. Muraközy, M. Z. Petschnig, A. Seleny, I. Gy. Tóth, and A. Vacroux in gathering the information that serves as the background for the analysis, and I take this opportunity of thanking them for their support. I am grateful to B. McLean and J. Parti for translating the text, which was originally written in Hungarian. I received valuable comments on the first draft of the study from Francis M. Bator, Tamás Bauer, Zsuzsa Dániel, Martin S. Feldstein, George Kopits, Álmos Kovács, Michael Marrese, and László Urbán. Of course, the author alone bears the responsibility for any errors that remain. The research was supported by the Hungarian National Science Foundation (OTKA).

[1] Earlier summaries of the theories of market failure can be found in the works of Francis M. Bator (1958) and William J. Baumol (1965). For a present-day survey, see Joseph E. Stiglitz et al. (1989). As research progresses, light is shed on the shortcomings of an unfettered market in more and more areas. Consideration, for instance, of imperfect competition and economies of scale leads to several alterations in the earlier concept vindicating free trade and suggests that, under certain conditions, the state may be justified in playing a more active role. An overall account of the wide-ranging research that followed the pioneering work by Paul R. Krugman, Elhanan Helpman, and others can be found in Helpman (1990).

economists to reconsider the problem (see James Buchanan and Gordon Tullock, 1962; William A. Niskanen, 1971). Are those who intervene in the economy in the state's name intent only on serving the public interest? The question strikes a strong chord in anyone who has lived under the socialist system. Similarly relevant is the analysis critical of the welfare state for imposing a high level of redistribution that dulls the incentive for investment, innovation, and enterprise (see e.g., Assar Lindbeck, 1988).[2]

However, when an Eastern European economist comes out of the library, he stops in confusion. He is still unfamiliar with capitalism from within; he would like to rely on the professional literature, but at least at first glance it seems to be giving him strongly conflicting directions. What should he be fighting for after all: a more or a less active state?

This confusion can be contained to some extent by studying the literature more thoroughly. The normative proposals to be drawn from the theoretical literature are always *conditional*. The conditions under which the arguments apply are either stated explicitly or implied. Any Western expert giving advice to a postsocialist economy or any economist in a postsocialist country using Western literature when reaching his position has a duty to clarify these assumptions very carefully before citing "authoritative" Western economic writings. Let me mention just two typical assumptions.

1. The cited literature refers to a mature market and a stable, deeply rooted, and well-established democratic state that operates in the advanced capitalist countries of our time. The trouble is that the market and state in Hungary and the other postsocialist countries differ from this situation in several respects: the private sector is still immature, and the democratic institutions are weak and not yet fully developed.

2. The literature assigns roles to the state and to the market assuming a capitalist system with permanent or slowly changing institutions and operating under robust rules of behavior. In contrast, the postsocialist system is in the midst of a revolutionary transformation: institutions vanish at breathtaking speed, others are just appearing, the legal system is changing at a very rapid rate by historical standards, and the behavior of every player in the economy keeps changing accordingly. So, a special kind of dynamic analysis is needed.

II. The Political and Governmental Spheres in Postsocialist Hungary

Let me try to outline briefly, in almost telegraphic style, the characteristics of the political and governmental sphere in Hungary today.[3] I do not give a similar description of the present state of the market here, because this will emerge in the later part of the lecture.

Although a measure of political liberalization had begun earlier, the turning point in Hungary came in 1989–1990. The communist party's monopoly over government ended, other parties became free to organize, and free elections were held for the first time in 43 years. A government with a parliamentary majority was formed. The main roadblock to the development of a market economy, the political domination of a communist party that had liquidated or sought to liquidate capitalism, was removed

[2]An account of left- and right-wing criticisms of the welfare state is given by Claus Offe (1984).

[3]Rather than using an overall, comprehensive definition of "the state," I will try to break the political sphere down into its components. Different approaches to this can be distinguished in political science, among them functionalist models, the public-choice theory of economics referred to earlier, analyses that examine the conflicts between groups and classes, and the various institutionalist approaches. In my view, these are, for the most part, complementary, rather than mutually exclusive explanations, and I have tried to draw on the ideas of all the trends in this lecture. Summaries can be found in the works of Joel D. Aberbach et al. (1981) and Peter A. Hall (1986).

by this radical change in the structure of power.

The legislature, executive administration, and judiciary were only formally separate under the socialist system. In fact, the officials filling all the posts in each branch were selected by the communist party, which directed their activities. The separation of the branches of state power only became institutionalized after the political turning point.

Parliament is now mastering its new role. The myriad of rules required for a constitutional state evolved in the developed democracies over a long historical period, while in Hungary the most essential laws are being drafted at a forced pace. The sluggishness and constant delay with which the government drafts legislation and the rate at which Parliament can cope with its legislative load form one of the most distressing bottlenecks in the advance toward a modern market economy. Most members of Parliament are political novices; they do not have enough time or a sufficiently large staff of experts and advisers to conduct a thorough study of the bills, let alone to devise legislative proposals of their own. Therefore, Parliament cannot really be said to be supervising the work of the administration closely. The courts too are inexperienced in imposing law and order on a market economy.

Before the political turning point came, the anticommunist forces were united in the face of a common enemy. This cooperation between them has been replaced by bitter political clashes between the governing and opposition parties, and even within the governing coalition. There is nothing surprising about it, as the same phenomenon occurs under all parliamentary systems. However, the absence of a broad political consensus almost precludes the possibility of resolving the grave problems on the agenda, such as curbing inflation, bringing about budgetary stability, and restructuring production, because they all involve unpopular measures that require serious sacrifices. I hardly need to explain here, to my American economist colleagues in 1992, that when the political rivalry for power becomes acute, politicians aim to maximize their electoral chances, not a "social welfare function."

According to the normative theory of a classical democracy, there should be a clear demarcation line between the politicians directly responsible to the electorate and the bureaucracy that loyally serves each successive constitutional government, regardless of political program. Political appointments and "civil service" positions should be clearly distinguished by law or respected convention. In the postsocialist political system, this distinction is not yet made unambiguously. The governing parties of today have thoroughly learned the oft-quoted slogan of Vladimir Ilyich Lenin: the question of power is the fundamental question. Political loyalty is a far more important criterion than competence when a great many posts are to be filled.

The bureaucracy has greater expertise in Hungary than in other postsocialist countries because the partial reforms commenced in 1968 induced it to adapt to the requirements of a market economy. Yet it has nothing like the knowledge or experience required to perform the administrative tasks of a modern capitalist economy. The change of system, moreover, puts the bureaucrats' livelihoods at risk: who knows who will be dismissed when? Servility spreads. Many of the more-talented specialists leave the state service for more lucrative and secure jobs in the private sector. State discipline is lax due to inexperience and uncertainty, and there is great friction in the process of enforcing the laws and state regulations.[4]

We are dealing neither with the philosopher-statesmen of Plato, who rise above all selfish criteria, nor with the expert, law-abiding, punctilious bureaucracy of Max Weber. Nor are we dealing with the political decision-makers described in studies of

---

[4]Theda Skocpol (1985) pointed out that the "capacity" of the state, defined as its actual ability to perform specific tasks, is an important determining factor of state activity. The scarcity of this capacity, which I mentioned in connection with drafting and enacting of legislation, also hinders law enforcement.

welfare economics, who exclusively serve the public interest. Therefore, any economist arguing that market forces should be curtailed must soberly consider that *this* is the kind of state to which he now wishes to assign a function, and this is the kind of state it will remain for some time to come.

The only components of the political sphere discussed so far have been the organizations of the state and the political parties. Two other important phenomena that can affect the operation of both the state and the market must be mentioned.

First, it is inestimably important that the press, often called the fourth arm of government in the mechanism of checks and balances, is now free in Hungary.[5] Anyone trying to abuse the state's power or to mismanage the state's money runs a risk of being exposed in the press.

Second, what political scientists call the "civil society," the public's capacity to organize itself, is steadily awakening. Organizations embodying certain strata, groups, and occupations are forming in succession and are making their voices heard. Such special-interest groups are often referred to disparagingly in the United States and can certainly play a detrimental part as well, but the citizens of a country where all kinds of voluntary and spontaneous association were persecuted are better placed to value the advantage of people's freedom to associate and apply political pressure. It must be added that, in the economic sphere, the expression of civil society remains obscure. The rearguard actions of the unions surviving from the old order, combined with the weakness of the new unions, leave employees without a mature and effective system of representation. The employers' organizations are immature as well. In other words, the kind of European extraparliamentary representative associations capable of overriding narrow professional interests and negotiating with each other with a sense of

responsibility for the nation have yet to develop or gain strength. There is a danger, therefore, of populist organizations winning over large numbers of people and impeding the process of political and economic consolidation. This is one of the vulnerable points in the new democracy, for such populist movements can prevent the conclusion of a "social contract" among broad layers of society willing to show moderation in order to help overcome the economic difficulties.[6]

My general position on the division of labor between the state and the market is supported strongly by the current situation in Hungary's political and governmental sphere. (In fact, I could call it my prejudice, since my opinion is clearly based on a value judgment.) I am ready to ask for government intervention so long as it is clear in the case concerned that the market left to itself will decide badly and there is a very strong likelihood that state intervention will improve matters. I must be convinced that the authority concerned is in expert, impartial, and honest hands, and that in this particular case it is really possible to ensure a public scrutiny which will force the state to act wisely. However, if I am in doubt about which to leave the decision to, an ill-operating market or an ill-operating state, and I can only make a random choice, my instincts tell me to choose the market. One factor here is certainly that I am an Eastern European, for my compatriots and I have been disappointed very often by the state, and our confidence is not easily restored. This preference will be the underlying philosophy of the rest of the lecture.

III. Four Fiscal Problems

Socialism before the reforms was marked by totalitarian power, in other words, by a

---

[5] The increasing freedom of the press ties in with the fact that a sizable proportion of the press has passed into private ownership.

[6] In 1990, one small group in Hungary, the taxi drivers, who were well organized through their radio links, managed to cripple the capital with a blockade to protest a rise in gasoline prices. Many employees were sympathetic to the taxi drivers, with whom members of the government negotiated before television cameras.

TABLE 1—SUMMARY OF GENERAL GOVERNMENT
OPERATIONS: INTERNATIONAL COMPARISON
(as a Percentage of GDP)

Country	Year	Revenue	Expenditure
Austria	1989	46.9	49.7
Canada	1989	40.3	43.9
Denmark	1989	59.6	59.4
France	1989	46.2	47.8
Greece	1988	32.7	46.3
Netherlands	1989	51.1	56.6
Portugal	1988	40.7	45.0
Spain	1987	35.0	38.6
Sweden	1988	59.1	56.9
United States	1988	34.3	36.5
West Germany	1989	45.7	45.9
Hungary	**(1989)**	**61.3**	**63.7**

Notes: The data refer to consolidated general government revenues and expenditures (i.e., they include revenues and expenditures of central and local governments and extrabudgetary funds).
Source: Compiled by L. G. Kopits and L. Muraközy, based on International Monetary Fund (1990).

TABLE 2—SUMMARY OF HUNGARIAN GENERAL
GOVERNMENT OPERATIONS
(as a Percentage of GDP)

Year	Revenue	Expenditure	Deficit (−) or surplus (+)
1981	61.0	63.9	− 3.2
1982	59.1	61.2	− 2.1
1983	60.9	62.0	− 1.1
1984	60.8	59.4	+ 1.4
1985	60.0	61.2	− 1.1
1986	63.2	66.0	− 2.9
1987	60.3	64.1	− 3.9
1988	63.7	63.6	+ 0.0
1989	61.3	63.7	− 2.5
1990	61.5	61.5	+ 0.0
1991	62.2	66.4	− 4.2
1992	60.1	62.3	− 2.2

Notes: The data refer to consolidated general government revenues and expenditures (i.e., they include revenues and expenditures of central and local governments and extrabudgetary funds). The methodology used to compile the IMF data and that used by Hungarian sources are slightly different. Data for 1991 and 1992 are official government forecasts.
Source: Compiled by L. Muraközy. Figures for the period 1981–1989 are based on International Monetary Fund (1990); those for 1990 are based on Központi Statisztikai Hivatal [Central Statistical Office] (1991); and for 1991 and 1992 are based on projections by Magyar Köztársaság Kormánya [Government of the the Hungarian Republic] (1991).

hyperactive state which sought to control all activity in society. Although the process of partial reform that began in 1968 produced some reduction in the role of the state in many respects, the new democratic system has still inherited "big government."[7]

The weight and scale of the state can be measured in several ways, one of the most important measures being the ratio of the government budget to GDP. Table 1 shows that the government in Hungary withdraws and redistributes almost two-thirds of GDP, whereas the typical proportion in Western Europe is 40–45 percent, and it is even lower, in fact, in countries with a level of development similar to Hungary's. Table 2 does not register any clearly perceptible tendency toward a decline in this ratio, which is stubbornly stuck at a size close to two-thirds.

As the subtitle of this lecture suggests, I am primarily concerned here with fiscal questions. What policy would be required in

order to reduce the proportion of production withdrawn and spent by the state? Given political, social, and economic conditions, what is the probability of a policy producing "smaller government?" For reasons of space, I do not even intend to cover the whole sphere of fiscal problems.[8] I will

[7]The role of the state under the socialist system is dealt with in my (1992a) book.

Let me mention specifically two subjects that are omitted from this lecture even though they tie in closely with a discussion of the role of the state. One is the restoration of macro equilibrium and macro management of the economy in general; the other is the role of the state in the privatization of firms hitherto under state ownership. Discussion of them has been avoided not because I consider them unimportant, but because there is already a wealth of literature analyzing them both. I have also attempted to discuss them myself, for instance in my 1990 and 1992b works. I prefer in this lecture to bring up a few questions that have received less attention so far.

discuss the following four topics: administrative expenditures, assistance to loss-making firms and unemployment benefits, taxation of the private sector, and welfare expenditures. Although all four topics are connected with the budget, I would like to go beyond the scope of public finance in the narrow sense and examine each problem in its political, social, and general economic context; and to that extent the subject of my lecture falls under the category of *political economy*.

A. *Administrative Expenditures*

Demands for cuts in administrative spending are heard in every budget debate in every parliament in the world. They are particularly apposite in Hungary, where spending on general public services and public order and safety in 1990 was equivalent to 8.8 percent of GDP, which is inadmissibly high. For comparison's sake, the same item accounted for 5.5 percent of GDP in 1988 in West Germany, 5.1 percent in Chile, and 4.4 percent in Denmark.[9] The government of the new democracy promises to cut such expenditures year after year, and the opposition, rightly, calls for a far more vigorous reduction in the overall size of the budget.

Two opposing trends can be observed. On the one hand, earlier administrative expenditures have ceased or decreased, while on the other, new administrative expenses have appeared. Let me give four examples.

1. The vast bureaucracy of the communist party, which almost duplicated the state apparatus in size, has been disbanded. At the same time, a new professional political apparatus, made up of the employees of all the parties and the staff assisting all the members of national and local assemblies, has been formed.
2. Many institutions of the centralized planned economy are being eliminated; for example, the planning and price of-

fices have shut down, and several ministries that previously controlled production amalgamated, with a smaller combined staff. The new system, however, requires some new agencies: offices for privatization, bank regulation, insurance regulation, monitoring the observance of anti-monopoly legislation, an agency dealing with small business, an auditor-general's office to supervise the financial affairs of the state bureaucracy, and so on.
3. The secret police, a pillar of the old system, has been disbanded, but there is a demand for more police to combat an appalling increase in common crime. Among the reasons for the crime wave are the dissolution of the nationwide network of informers, the easing of the obligation to register changes of residence with the police, and the opening of the borders, which makes drug trafficking easier. In other words, the increase in crime is partly explained by the harmful side-effects of a healthy process, namely the abolition of the police state.
4. Under the old system, many disputes were settled arbitrarily by the party secretary or some administrative organization, but in a constitutional state this becomes mainly the task of the courts. As the private sector and the prestige of the law increase, so does the number of court cases.[10] The backlog of undecided cases will continue to grow unless the present staff of the courts is enlarged.

To sum up point A, an effort must be made to cut back administrative expenses, but high hopes cannot be placed on this effort contributing to a substantial reduction of the budget:GDP ratio in the near future.

---

[9]Calculated by L. Muraközy based on data from the International Monetary Fund (1990).

[10]The Budapest courts received 9,000 new civil cases in 1988 and 16,400 in 1990. The numbers of requests for payment injunctions received by the courts in the same two years were 31,000 and 64,000, respectively (statement by the president of the Metropolitan Judiciary in the daily paper *Népszabadság*, 23 November 1991).

TABLE 3—SUBSIDIES AND TRANSFERS TO FIRMS:
INTERNATIONAL COMPARISON
(as Percentage of GDP)

Year	Bulgaria	Czechoslovakia	Hungary
Total current expenditures:			
1985	48	51	53
1989	52	55	57
Subsidies and transfers to firms:			
1985	13	15	21
1989	15	19	16

Notes: Subsidies and transfers to firms include product-specific price subsidies, explicit interest-rate subsidies, and debt servicing on behalf of firms and institutions. Subsidies and transfers constitute one component of total current expenditures (i.e., the data in the first lines of the table).
Source: George Kopits (1991 pp. 22–3).

B. *Assistance to Loss-Making Firms and Unemployment Benefits*

It is apparent from Table 3 that the subsidies and transfers to firms in Hungary have been showing a tendency to fall for a long time (unlike those in Czechoslovakia and Bulgaria, also shown in the table, where they tended to grow before the political changes). However, a further, more vigorous dismantling of assistance brings up some sensitive problems that require detailed analysis.

The socialist system produced a curious phenomenon which I termed in my earlier writings the syndrome of the *soft budget constraint*.[11] In this situation the firm's spending is not strictly constrained by its financial position or, ultimately, in a dynamic context, by its revenues. Even if it should land in serious financial difficulties, make steady losses, and become insolvent, it can count on help from the state. Such a firm will be given tax concessions or allowed to postpone payment of its taxes, it will receive a subsidy, or it will gain access to soft loans. It is quite safe in building into its expectations a state bail-out to ensure its

survival. This softness of the budget constraint has a number of baneful consequences, among them that it leads to toleration of inefficiency, postponement of adjustment to demand, and mistaken investment decisions.

It is a widely accepted view that this harmful phenomenon is incompatible with a market economy, so that in the postsocialist transition period the budget constraint on state-owned firms must be hardened at last. The question is: to what extent will this requirement receive only lip service and to what extent will it be acted upon? No clear answer can be given because at present there are conflicting tendencies at work, and it is unclear which of them will prevail.

The situation of firms varies, and so does their behavior.[12] Some have moved toward privatization, converting themselves into joint-stock companies or planning to do so in the near future, and have negotiated with prospective Hungarian or foreign private owners. However, I wish to focus attention here on the ones that have not yet taken any practical steps towards privatization. Some of these have adapted quite successfully to the new situation, but others are facing serious problems, and in the latter cases the typical attitude is to try and muddle through. That means on the physical or real side of production that they utilize stocks hoarded under the shortage economy without replacing them, neglect maintenance and renewal, and perhaps sell off a plant or an office building. There is continual disinvestment; in other words, the firm eats itself up by consuming its own assets. Parallel events occur on the monetary side, where the steady losses increase the firm's indebtedness. It no longer makes punctual or full payments of its taxes and social-security contributions, or of the interest and repayments on its debts to the commercial banks.[13] Most commonly of all, the firm

---

[11] For an explanation of the concept see Kornai (1986).

[12] On the position of loss-making state-owned firms, see the article by Mária Móra (1991) and the more detailed study (Móra, 1990) on which it is based.

[13] The sum of the first two debts (unpaid taxes and social-security contributions) in mid-1991 was greater than the entire budget deficit planned for 1992.

8					AEA PAPERS AND PROCEEDINGS					MAY 1992

stops paying the bills of the firms that supply its inputs. There is no voluntary credit contract in any of these cases; the debtor is forcing the creditor to lend by refusing to pay. This brings me to the other side of the problem: how the creditor reacts to this kind of behavior by the firm.[14]

Softness of the budget constraint actually means that the involuntary creditor tolerates the debtor's default. In postsocialist Hungary, the present situation is ambivalent, as mentioned earlier, because the accustomed tolerance continues to be shown in some of the cases, but the opposite also occurs. Already there are, albeit infrequently, instances of the tax or social-security authorities or the banks taking measures to wind up a debtor firm. More commonly, the suppliers initiate liquidation proceedings against firms that are unable to pay their bills (see Kamilla Lányi, 1991 p. 64).

Although firms had also been liquidated earlier, that constituted *administrative selection*, because the death sentence or the reprieve came from the bureaucracy. Now one can see the first signs of *natural selection*. The latter, once it really develops to the full, will take place as a decentralized market process. Instead of matters of life and death being decided by an arm of the state, proceedings against defaulting debtors will be taken by creditors acting in their own best financial interest.

In fact, there has been liquidation legislation on the statute books in Hungary for some time, and the legal framework for the exit of insolvent firms was available in other respects as well. These were not taken advantage of before, but it now seems as if there is a movement to do so. A surge of liquidations in the state sector is forecast for this year, and if it takes place, it will be accurate to say that the budget constraint has hardened.

How this change should be appraised is the subject of much debate. For my part, I consider it painful but healthy. Let me recall Joseph A. Schumpeter's well-known concept of *creative destruction*.[15] Renewal and reorganization of production, technical progress, and innovation are normally accompanied by destruction of the old product lines, organizations, and institutions. This cleansing is essential for development. For a number of reasons, the socialist system was incapable of it. The old industrial dinosaurs, the distended, sluggish, clumsy giants, survived, and the softness of the budget constraint served as the financial mechanism for warding off creative destruction; but the destruction has now begun, in the form of various corrective measures. Five closely connected processes can be cited:

1. Anti-inflationary monetary policy inevitably entails a contraction of production. In some cases this means the total closure of firms, and in others it means curtailment of production. The Schumpeterian interpretation of the business cycle seems to be justified in this context; a macro recession accelerates natural selection and the destruction that clears the decks for creation. There was no way that the planned economy, with its drive for continual expansion and forced growth, could perform this selection.

2. There is a restructuring in the sectoral composition of production. The share of manufacturing in total output is falling, and the share of services is rising. This involves a halt or cut in the activity of certain manufacturing firms.

3. Closely related to the previous process is the restructuring of exports. The collapse of the Comecon market has brought dire problems for firms that specialized in

---

[14] Hardening the budget constraint is partly a *fiscal* matter, since it is closely related to state subsidies and to taxation. However, the problem is far more complicated in nature than that, and so I must go beyond the subject-matter of this lecture outlined earlier, for instance by touching briefly on aspects of *monetary* policy as well.

[15] Schumpeter (1912) wrote about the benefits of destroying loss-makers in his first classical work. The expression "creative destruction" was introduced in his 1942 book (see Schumpeter, 1976 pp. 81–8). The Schumpetarian aspect of the transition process is emphasized in the work of Peter Murrell (1990).

supplying it and prove to be incapable of satisfying the demands of new markets.

4. Restructuring takes place in the size distribution of firms. There was an excessive concentration of production under the socialist system in Hungary, as there was in the other socialist countries. Firms were oversized, even in branches where there were no economies of scale to justify it. Moreover, small undertakings were almost completely eliminated under prereform classical socialism, and too little scope was left for medium-sized firms. Part of the corrective process consists of closing a good many firms that are oversized to the point of being inviable and cannot be broken down into smaller units.

5. The majority of the bureaucratically controlled state-owned firms under the socialist system operated at a low level of efficiency. Unemployment on the job was widespread. Efficiency has to improve as a result of the corrective process. Even if the volume of production were to stay the same, it could be made with a far smaller workforce.

All five corrective processes have serious side effects: jobs are eliminated on a massive scale. However, some of these processes (numbers 2–4) create as well as destroy: they provide new jobs, mainly in the private sector, and primarily in the small and medium-sized segments. This will be discussed again later. All that needs to be said in advance is that the creation of new jobs is failing to keep pace with the loss of old ones. Therefore, unemployment rises. This is a shattering experience under any system, but it is doubly painful under postsocialism, for people in Hungary's part of the world have been used not only to full employment but to absolute job security and even a chronic shortage of labor for a long time. Table 4 presents a short time-series. May 1991 was the particular moment in history when the number of unemployed persons exceeded the number of vacancies for the first time and the labor market switched over from a state of excess demand to one of excess supply. The rate of unemployment reached 7.3 percent in

TABLE 4—VACANCIES AND UNEMPLOYMENT IN HUNGARY

Month	Number of registered vacancies	Number of registered unemployed persons
1/1990	37,711	23,426
2/1990	38,335	30,055
3/1990	34,048	33,682
4/1990	35,191	33,353
5/1990	37,938	38,155
6/1990	37,859	43,506
7/1990	36,222	50,292
8/1990	33,732	51,670
9/1990	26,969	56,115
10/1990	22,763	60,997
11/1990	17,150	69,982
12/1990	16,815	79,521
1/1991	12,949	100,526
2/1991	14,721	128,386
3/1991	13,583	144,840
4/1991	16,478	167,407
5/1991	14,919	165,022
6/1991	14,860	185,554
7/1991	15,186	216,568
8/1991	14,124	251,084
9/1991	15,351	292,756
10/1991	15,389	317,692
11/1991	13,021	351,285

Source: Data for the period January 1990 through August 1991 are in Országos Munkaügyi Központ [National Labor Center] (1991a p. 20); for September 1991, data are from Országos Munkaügyi Központ (1991b p. 4); for October and November 1991, data are from Országos Munkaügyi Központ (1991c p. 4).

November 1991, which is quite high even for countries accustomed to unemployment. Unfortunately, there will be a further rise in unemployment this year, according to the forecasts.[16]

What should the government do under the circumstances? Before trying to answer that question, let me say just a few words on what it should *not* try to do. It should not, in my opinion, yield to the pressure to relax its monetary policy at the macro level and use casually dispersed loans and export subsidies, rashly raised nominal incomes, and

---

[16]On the present state of the Hungarian labor market and unemployment, see the studies by János Köllő (1990, 1991).

budget-financed grand investments to whip up aggregate demand, particularly not in the state sector. The Hungarian inflation rate, which has been curbed with great difficulty and still lingers around 35 percent, would suddenly take off, with frightening consequences.

Another warning is needed, concerning the micro level. Now, amid the first signs that the budget constraint on firms is hardening, the government should not relapse into softening it again. I am convinced that it is better to accept the serious problem of unemployment openly (giving effective assistance, of course, to those losing their jobs) than to continue the policy of trying to cover up the superfluity of many inefficient workplaces by artificially sustaining terminally ill firms and perpetuating unemployment on the job. The danger of a relapse into the earlier soft-budget-constraint syndrome persists even under the present political conditions. The image of a politician intervening to bail out a firm in financial trouble is not unknown in the United States; nor is the prospect of interest groups lobbying for a protectionist policy to favor some sector or another. Another danger is that some of the banks may be ready to grant soft loans irresponsibly, calculating that their survival will be ensured no matter what, even in the last resort, at the taxpayer's expense. This attitude, recently observed in the Savings-and-Loan sector and parts of the banking system in the United States, is prevalent and deeply embedded in the postsocialist economy and its financial sphere.

It is desirable for many reasons that the ownership of the overwhelming majority of formerly state-owned firms should pass into private hands; but let no one think that the problem just outlined, the task of "creative destruction," can be comfortably solved by privatization. No buyer, domestic or foreign, willingly purchases a hopelessly insolvent firm with a view to carrying on its operations. At most there will be a buyer for the physical assets and human capital that belong to the firm. In some other instances, it will not be clear from the outset whether the privatized firm has any chance of financial recovery. If it does not succeed, the new

owners (be they individual shareholders, mutual funds or other institutional owners) will no doubt shut it down as soon as it becomes apparent that the firm cannot operate at a profit. This is no less bitter a pill for those concerned, and it may be even more brutal than if the liquidation had preceded the privatization. Another possibility is that, after the privatization, the employers and employees of the private firm together may set about salvaging it by lobbying the connections they have built up under the new regime. This possibility brings us back to the starting point, the softness of the budget constraint.

I will now turn to the advisable measures. *A one-time, temporary* subsidy or loan could be granted to firms that the government wishes to give a last chance, just in case they can adapt to actual market conditions after all. However, it must be strictly stipulated that the subsidy is to be phased out and that the loan will not be repeated if the adaptation does not succeed. I feel somewhat uncertain about raising this possibility at all, because there remains the danger that all the phenomena that emerged in connection with the soft budget constraint may arise here as well.

The state must establish an adequate system of unemployment insurance. This should provide temporary assistance to cushion the shock, but it should not be allowed to weaken the incentive for the jobless to seek work and be prepared to adjust to the demand for labor. One favorable feature of the economic transformation in Hungary is that the organization of unemployment insurance was begun much earlier than in other postsocialist countries. The present system, however, leaves much to be desired; the amount, duration, and conditions of the benefit are all questionable.

The insurance must be accompanied by the organization of employment exchanges and retraining. This is undoubtedly a task for the state. It is laudable that it has begun in Hungary, although performance thus far leaves much room for improvement.

Finally, there is the most important task: job creation, primarily in the private sector.

This leads to the problem discussed in the next section.

To sum up point B, the policy of hardening the budget constraint sets a *fiscal trap*. On the one hand, the state budget reduces expenditures by withdrawing subsidies for state-owned firms that are incapable of surviving. The tougher fiscal discipline applied to state-owned firms should bring about an increase in tax revenues, assuming that firms will be capable of paying taxes at all. On the other hand, the hardening of the budget constraint may cause economic activity to contract more sharply, thereby reducing the tax base and, therefore, budgetary revenue. Meanwhile, spending on unemployment benefits represents a growing burden on the budget.[17] There is no way of predicting the net result of these conflicting trends accurately: will they improve or aggravate the overall fiscal situation? I consider a deterioration to be the more likely outcome in the next few years, but I think nonetheless that the grave short-term drawbacks must be accepted in order to gain the longer-term, lasting advantages: the development to be expected from the "creative destruction."

C. *The Taxation of the Private Sector*

Perhaps the most important tendency in the process of the transition is the very fast growth of the private sector. Mention was made in the last section of the destructive side of Schumpeter's "creative destruction." The mushrooming of new private enterprise forms perhaps the most conspicuous manifestation of the other side, creation. The private sector is the most likely source of mass job creation, the introduction of innovations, better supply to the consumer, and the winning of new export markets.

Unfortunately, given the system of statistical records in Hungary (and in the other postsocialist countries), for the time being it is not possible to measure the expansion of the private sector.[18] Expert estimates vary, but most of them fall inside the range of 25–35 percent for the private sector's contribution to GDP.[19]

Part of the private sector operates within the framework laid down by law. The tax authorities had records of 111,700 economic organizations in August 1991 (see Pénzügyminisztérium, 1991 p. 848). For comparison's sake, one should recall that a decade earlier there were some 3,000 large state-owned firms and a few thousand other large, quasi-state agricultural cooperatives in operation. The number of registered private undertakings has certainly grown very rapidly.

Private businesses have appeared in particularly large numbers in the service sector and in domestic and foreign trade. The latter observation is supported by Table 5. It is worth noting the appearance between 1989 and 1991 of more than 4,500 exporters that were not exporting at all in 1989. The change is still more conspicuous if a comparison is made with earlier periods. In the prereform, classical socialist economy, the entire foreign trade turnover was monopolized by about two dozen giant, state-owned foreign trading firms.

Alongside the legal private undertakings there is a very extensive semilegal segment. This informal economy existed even under prereform classical socialism and grew very

---

[17]Unemployment benefits in Hungary are paid out of an extrabudgetary insurance fund formed out of contributions from employers and employees. This separate handling is expedient, but it does not alter the fact that this is *ultimately* a fiscal problem in two senses. Contributions to the fund are compulsory, not voluntary, and a kind of tax. If the fund should fall into deficit, the state budget guarantees to make it up out of other tax revenue.

[18]Researchers are trying to gain a picture of the true extent of the private sector through confidential interviews, but they run up against great difficulties. Nóra Esti (1991 p. 23) writes in her report on a survey of private entrepreneurs that when questions were asked about income in the interviews, "it occurred on several occasions that an entrepreneur who had been patient so far declared the interview to be over at that point." In the main it was precisely those doing well who refused to respond.

[19]The production of the private sector is compared here with the true GDP, in which both officially recorded production and the unrecorded contribution of informal private undertakings are included.

TABLE 5—HUNGARIAN FIRMS ENGAGING IN HARD-CURRENCY EXPORTS

	Number of firms		Volume of trade (million $)	
Size classes	1989	1990	1989	1990
> $10 million	136	158	4,422	5,268
$0.5–10 million	668	1,115	1,700	2,554
< $0.5 million	1899	5,108	172	347
Total	2,703	6,381	6,294	8,169

Source: Lányi and György Oblath (1991 p. 76), based on figures drawn from the data bank of KOPINT-DATORG.

fast during the reform process. Defining real crime as black and undertakings that meticulously observe all the laws and regulations as white, the sphere I would like to mention here can be depicted as various shades of gray. Since the political turning point, there has been a considerable expansion of the "gray segment," to which a variety of kinds of activity belong. These include "moonlighting," the activity of people who have one foot still in the state sector, but who have stepped into the private sector with the other. There are others whose entire working time is spent in the private sector, but they evade the legal regulations. Many officially registered private undertakings operate partly in the white and partly in the gray segment.[20]

However varied the forms of gray activity may be, they have one feature in common: they involve *invisible earnings* that the tax authorities are unable to get their hands on.

---

[20]A further indicator of the growth of the informal and formal private sector is the rapid increase in the hard-currency bank deposits of individuals. The source of such deposits is not asked of the depositors, but it is widely believed that a large part originates in private business activities, like exports or services to tourists in Hungary.

In the first nine months of 1991, the net increment of individuals' hard-currency deposits (called "net unrequited transfers" in official statistics) contributed 40 percent of the total positive balance of the current account. (National Bank of Hungary, 1991 p. 24).

That brings me to the fiscal side of the problem.

It was comparatively simple under the classical socialist system for the financial authorities to "get hold" of a large state-owned firm. The business accounts were easily checked, and the monobank simply deducted the sum due to the budget from the firm's account. These days, as I have mentioned, it is not easy to collect money even from state-owned firms. As far as the private sector is concerned, the "dark gray" part of it entirely evades its tax obligations and the "light gray" part evades at least some of them. This is not confined to personal income tax and corporate profits tax, for it extends to total or partial evasion of value-added tax, social-security contributions and all other kinds of payroll tax. It seems that as Hungary moves towards a market economy, citizens and authorities have adopted an "Italian style" attitude to taxation, rather than a Dutch or Swedish one, in which people dutifully pay their taxes.

This evaporation of tax returns is one of the gravest obstacles to budgetary equilibrium. This situation, moreover, turns into the most serious infringement of the principle that taxation should be fair. The main factor in progressivity is not the formula used to decide the rates of taxation on visible earnings. The highest degree of regressivity results from the fact that the direct burdens of taxation are placed on visible earnings, while invisible earnings escape being taxed at all.

One task under these conditions is clearly to improve the efficiency of tax collection, which involves a great many things: more in situ inspections, more frequent and thorough audits and accounting requirements, and legal action when rules are broken (see Milka Casanegra de Jantscher et al., 1991). This task creates one of the great political and economic dilemmas. On the one hand, both fiscal and fairness criteria demand forceful tax collection, but on the other, it must be recognized pragmatically that a large proportion of the new businesspeople are emerging into the twilight world of a curious "early capitalism." Nothing will be gained here by brutal crackdowns or harassment of private entrepreneurs. That would only push some people deeper into illegality and discourage others from private enterprise altogether.

The measures against those breaking the law must be strict but within the bounds of legality and the norms of a civilized constitutional state, and as a complement there must be a range of changes to make it *advantageous* to abide by the law. A growing proportion of the private sector must be guided to legality by combinations of stick and carrot, as in the following examples of appropriate incentives.[21]

A businessman thinking of stepping out of semi-legality into the light of day might consider his choice as a kind of "deal." The service he receives is the rule of law, and the price he pays is tax. One major factor in the growth of the private sector is the impressive speed at which the legal system has developed. A range of new laws have been passed, including company, bankruptcy, banking, and accounting acts. A succession of others are being drafted, but it would be desirable to speed up the process. Let us hope that this legislative process will be accompanied by reinforcement of the courts and acceleration of their work. Private entrepreneurs will be attracted toward legality if that is the only way they can gain legal protection for their property. They will also be able to count on the just treatment of their complaints at court if they come into conflict with the bureaucracy.

Legalization of business transactions helps in enforcing private contracts. This benefits both the entrepreneur and the other party to the contract, which provides grounds for hoping that the state can find allies among the public. Here, however, all parties to a contract encounter a dilemma. Let me give two illustrations.

The rate of value-added tax is very high at present. If no receipt is provided by the seller or requested by the buyer, both sides can gain at the state's expense. However, a buyer who wants to complain later, for instance, because the quality is poor, has no legal redress. The more active the legal protection of buyers becomes in the future, the more common it will become for buyers to demand a receipt, even if that means paying a higher price, covering the value-added tax.

For the second example, consider that nowhere else in the world do the employer and the employee together have to pay a higher sum for social security, pension contributions, and unemployment insurance than they do in Hungary. It amounts to 55 percent of gross wages at present, and there are plans to raise it further to cover the increasing expenditures on unemployment benefits.[22] If employers fail to register employees or if wages are underreported, then employers and employees can divide the saving in wage-related mandatory contributions between them. In many cases, employees do not lose much by it, since they can still qualify for many social benefits.[23] However, if a higher proportion of social benefits depended on the employer's and employee's own contributions, employees could become the treasury's allies in legalizing employment.

All these issues tie in with the question of the citizens' relations with the law and the state. The suspicion, indifference, and even antagonistic feelings toward the state which are very prevalent among citizens are a legacy from the old order. A sizable part of

[21] The economic development in Italy and Spain is enlightening in this respect. The legalization process there continued for some years and has probably not ended yet (see Charles Sabel, 1982; Lauren A. Benton, 1990). The problems of legalizing the Hungarian informal private sector are analyzed by Ildikó Ékes (1992) and Anna Seleny (1992).

[22] In comparison, the social-security contributions as a proportion of wages are in the range of 30–40 percent in Austria, Portugal, Spain, and Sweden, and 20–30 percent in Greece (U.S. Department of Health, 1990 pp. 12, 98, 208, 238, and 246).

[23] There are a great many opportunities for this. People may be on sick leave, paid maternity leave, or registered as unemployed, and they can receive benefits on that basis. Or, they may spend some of their working time in the state sector, which qualifies them for social-security benefits, while doing work illegally, without registering, in the private sector as well, thus saving part of the wage-related taxes.

the population does not consider tax evasion to be immoral.[24] For a long time it was a form of civil courage to defy the state, and that attitude cannot be altered by ceremonial pronouncements alone. Experience has to prove that the state will be a good steward of the taxpayers' money; it must win the public's trust by its actions.[25]

The private sector will be drawn towards legality if it can expect far greater *economic* advantages than it does at present. Here let me mention just one example: access to the legal credit and capital market. The large commercial banks, for instance, treat small private firms quite ungenerously because they are used to links with the large state-owned firms, with which they are closely bound up, and because they consider it riskier to lend to the private sector. If the behavior of the financial sector changes, and banks show more readiness to extend credit to legal private businesses, including small and medium-sized undertakings and new ventures, private businesspeople will have one more reason to become legal.[26]

To sum up point C, the transition sets yet another *fiscal trap*. The larger the private sector's share of production, the harder it becomes to collect taxes. To put it another way, the more successful the transformation of property relations, the greater is the risk of budgetary troubles. All incentives that help to increase the relative weight of the law-abiding, tax-paying segment within the private sector as a whole must be used. This

may bring with it an increase in tax revenues. Regrettably, I cannot rule out the possibility of the process being protracted and, thus, plagued with severe fiscal problems caused by loss of budget revenue in the meantime.

D. *Welfare Expenditures*

One of the largest items in the consolidated budget, which also includes for statistical purposes various funds handled separately, is "welfare expenditures," under which the following can be grouped: (i) benefits in cash such as old-age pensions, disability pensions, maternity and child-care allowances, sick pay, family allowances, student scholarships, social assistance, and unemployment compensation; (ii) benefits in kind, such as medical care, medicines, public education, training, nursery schools and after-school centers, nursing homes, and labor-market services provided free or at concessionary prices; and (iii) price subsidies on consumer goods and services, including the prices (and rents) of housing.[27] Most of the observations in this lecture refer to welfare spending as a whole; there is no room to deal here with special problems posed by education, culture, and housing.

Tables 6 and 7 use international comparisons to show that welfare expenditures are very high in Hungary. Considering only the aggregate figures as a proportion of GDP, such spending in Hungary exceeds the level in the group of countries close to it in terms of economic development (Greece, Spain, and the lower-income OECD countries as a whole). Although the ratio is lower than in the developed "welfare states" (Sweden or Denmark), it approaches those in such developed European countries as West Ger-

---

[24]A public-opinion poll of the Hungarian Gallup Institute found that 44 percent of respondents agreed with the following statement: "People prosper in whatever way they can, and so they should not be blamed if they hide some of their earnings from the tax authorities" (Robert Manchin and Lajos Géza Nagy, 1991a pp. 8-9).
[25]Hungary still has a long way to go in this. People were asked in one survey whether various institutions really served the public interest. Only 42 percent of respondents said this was so of the government, while the churches, the press, the Constitutional Court and the parliamentary opposition received far higher confidence ratings (Manchin and Nagy, 1991b pp. 10-11).
[26]Erzsébet Gém (1991) provides a thorough description and analysis of the credit-supply situation of private firms.

[27]Several thorough studies of these issues have been made in Hungary. I recommend in particular the works by Zsuzsa Ferge (1991, 1992) and the report by the company Fraternité Rt. (1991). The descriptions and analyses prepared under the auspices of international agencies are extremely instructive, particularly the studies of the World Bank (Kessides et al., 1991) and the International Monetary Fund (Kopits et al., 1990). My lecture draws many ideas from these studies.

TABLE 6—SOCIAL EXPENDITURES: INTERNATIONAL COMPARISON (Government Expenditure as a Percentage of GDP)

Country	Total social expenditures		Health		Pensions	
	1980	1986	1980	1986	1980	1986
GR	12.6	19.5	3.6	3.7	5.8	10.6
IT	23.7	26.4	5.6	5.2	12.0	12.2
NO	24.2	24.8	6.5	6.6	7.9	8.8
SP	15.6	17.0	4.3	4.3	7.3	7.6
SW	33.2	32.0	8.8	8.3	10.9	11.4
US	18.0	18.2	3.9	4.5	6.9	7.2
WG	26.6	25.2	6.3	6.3	12.1	11.4
HU	**21.8**	**24.4**	**3.3**	**4.1**	**7.8**	**9.1**

Notes: In line with OECD definitions, the Hungarian data on total social expenditures do not include consumer and housing subsidies. Countries: GR = Greece, IT = Italy, NO = Norway, SP = Spain, SW = Sweden, US = United States, WG = West Germany, and HU = Hungary.
Source: Christine Kessides et al. (1991 p. 7). Statistics for OECD countries are based on OECD data bank sources; Hungarian data are extracted from Central Statistical Office *Statistical Yearbooks* (Központi Statisztikai Hivatal, various years), information provided by the Social Security Administration, government officials, and estimates by World Bank staff.

TABLE 7—NET SOCIAL INSURANCE TAX AND TRANSFERS: INTERNATIONAL COMPARISON (as a Percentage of GDP)

Statistic	OECD lower-income states,[a] 1986	OECD welfare states,[b] 1986	Hungary, 1989
Total social insurance contributions (employees + employers)	8.3	12.0	15.2
Total social expenditures	21.0	31.0	25.4[c]

Source: Kessides et al. (1991 p. 13). Statistics for OECD countries are based on OECD data bank sources; Hungarian data are extracted from Central Statistical Office *Statistical Yearbooks* (Központi Statisztikai Hivatal, various issues), information provided by the Social Security Administration, government officials, and estimates by World Bank staff.
[a]Average of Greece, Ireland, Portugal, Spain, and Turkey.
[b]Average of Belgium, Denmark, Finland, France, Netherlands, Norway, and Sweden.
[c]In accordance with OECD definitions; see note to Table 6.

TABLE 8—MAJOR SOCIAL-SECURITY PROGRAMMES IN HUNGARY

Year	Expenditure on Benefits	
	Billions of forints	As percentage of GDP
1985	167.0	16.2
1986	181.5	16.7
1987	200.3	16.3
1988	255.2	18.1
1989	317.1	18.6
1990	414.7	19.9

Note: The OECD data are compiled in accordance with a definition of social-security programs that is narrower than the definition underlying the World Bank statistics presented in Tables 6 and 7. Nevertheless, both Table 6 and 8 reveal a similar trend of increasing social expenditures.
Source: Organization for Economic Co-operation and Development (1991 p. 67).

many or Italy, which are not normally placed in the "welfare-state" category.

Table 8 presents a Hungarian time-series demonstrating that governmental expenditures on social-security programs are increasing continually. Meanwhile, one hears many complaints from the Hungarian public, and a substantial part of them are quite warranted. For example, though the numbers of doctors and hospital beds per capita are very high, there are serious problems with medical care, such as tragically low life expectancy and high infant mortality. While the system of old-age pensions goes a very long way in some respects, pensions are only partially indexed, so in times of rapid inflation the retired face devastating difficulties. Moreover, inequality is increasing: the postsocialist transition allows some of the population to grow rich, but others are impoverished or actually sink into penury, and the regulations and institutions in existence up to now are insufficient to halt the process of decline. This paradoxical situation presents perhaps one of the gravest dilemmas of all the problems discussed in this lecture.

The Hungarian welfare state was born "prematurely." There is generally a close positive correlation between a country's level of economic development and the scale of its welfare services. Development is not the only factor, but it is undoubtedly among the decisive ones. Hungary was "ahead of itself" in this respect. To a certain extent, the classical, prereform socialist system rushed ahead when it made a constitutional commitment that it would satisfy a number of basic needs free or for minimal recompense. It introduced free medical services and education and introduced a pension scheme covering almost the entire population, it subsidized the prices of foodstuffs, set rents for state housing at an almost nominal level, and so on. Later on it proved incapable of keeping its promises. Chronic excess demand appeared for the free or unrealistically cheaply priced services, and the quality of them was often very poor.

Added to the unkept promises of the classical system were the new concessions introduced during the process of reform that began in 1968. It was one of the characteristics of the Hungarian reform, sometimes referred to as "goulash communism," that it tried to turn its back on the previous policy of forced industrialization and devote greater attention to the needs of the general public. A measure of liberalization was accompanied by a growth in the political influence of the forces known as the "living-standard advocates." However, the gulf between promises and their fulfillment remained and in fact widened due to the slowdown and then the stagnation in economic growth. Some new concessions were granted, while others were withdrawn.

Finally came the political turning point, and the population—understandably from a psychological point of view—expects the new system to fulfill the promises made, but not kept, by the old. People are irritated by the state interfering in their private lives and harassing individuals, but many of them still want a caring, paternalist state as well.

So what can be done? Everyone agrees that the institutions of welfare policy and social security must be reformed. There could also be a substantial improvement in utilization of resources and allocative efficiency.[28] The incentives for the providers of

services could be substantially improved, and the administrative costs could be reduced. Detailed proposals have been prepared, and they extend to these details and beyond. It may be that they could all achieve some cost reductions. However, it would be wrong to convey the impression that the problem can be solved by improving administrative efficiency.

Some radical proposals have also been put forward for rapidly and greatly reducing the state's role in this sphere, at least to the scale found, for instance, in the present-day United States. It is argued that a fast rate of decentralization and privatization should take place in both medical care and the pension system, apart from a narrow band financed by the state.

I do not feel it is my task in this lecture to comment on the American situation. There is a debate going on, for example, about whether there should be a national health service or whether the health care of the majority of the population should continue to be based mainly on private insurance. All I would like to underline here, in the spirit of the first sections of the lecture, is this: it is extremely important to remember where one is moving from and to. It is one thing to decide whether a state should give its citizens a right they have not enjoyed before and another to decide to withdraw from them a right they have gained and become accustomed to. A curious *institutional ratchet-effect* can be seen here. The cogwheel of historical development turns one way, but it cannot turn back in the opposite direction. If Britain had not had a national health service already, the government of Margaret Thatcher would certainly not have proposed introducing one; but as it existed before Mrs. Thatcher's time, her government did not suggest closing it down.

The citizens of postsocialist society are suffering many uncertainties they did not know before. I have already mentioned the

---

[28] For example, there are too few nursing homes for the aged in Hungary, and the majority of them are ill-equipped. On the other hand, the hospitals are used to a great extent to care for old people who in fact do not need hospital care. This is far less beneficial for the old people concerned, and at the same time it is much more costly.

depressing experience of unemployment. Many people's sense of security would be shaken if in addition the medical care, pension system, and other welfare services ensured by the state were to collapse around them.

There is great resistance to the idea of a swift drastic cut in the welfare services provided by the state, along with decentralization and privatization of welfare assignments. In fact, the economic problems of the transition even add new expenditures to the list. Mention has already been made of unemployment benefits. In addition it must be said that the great transformation of society is accompanied by a redistribution of incomes, and there are many sections in society whose material living conditions are rapidly deteriorating. They expect the social-security net at least to save them from crashing to the ground. Unfortunately, the net has big holes, and to weave a denser one would generate additional demands on the state budget at a time when drastic cuts in budget spending are desperately needed.

No easy escape from this dilemma exists, and it will take patience and tact to get closer to a more acceptable situation. The most important guide should be the principle of *voluntariness and free choice*.[29] Let me give a few illustrations of how these principles can be applied in this field.

The evolution of a decentralized network of for-profit and nonprofit insurance companies and pension funds which employers and employees can join voluntarily must be affirmatively promoted, not just permitted. It would be worth introducing a law that specifies that these new institutions should receive valuable, truly income-generating portfolios of securities during the privatization of the state-owned firms, as a free contribution to their initial capitalization.

More leeway must be given to private medical practice and private providers of other social services ranging from child care, through nursing of the sick, to care for the aged. They should receive a market rate of remuneration for their activities.[30]

In other words, it would be worthwhile to ensure that the private sector grows rapidly in this sphere as well, under appropriate governmental supervision. I agree with the view that the desirable *final state* after the transformation would be a combination of three basic forms: a minimal level of certain services must be guaranteed as a civil right; other services must be provided in accordance with contributions paid by the beneficiaries and their employers; and finally, some services can be available to individuals through private insurance or through a direct act of purchase on the market. Let individuals be given as much scope as possible to choose between schemes providing welfare benefits. However, in view of the initial conditions, this final state can only be approached gradually. Those who have no means of making a real choice cannot be presented with a fait accompli.[31]

Something perhaps more important still than providing a choice between various mechanisms for social services is to give citizens the chance to express their will through the *political process*. A far greater role in monitoring the institutions providing social services should be given to various voluntary associations for safeguarding interests. Apart from that, the legislature must have the final word on welfare expenditure and in matters of social insurance and the levies connected with it. The political parties cannot avoid this complex of problems.

---

[29]In an earlier work of mine (Kornai, 1988), I tried to shed light on how the reforms taking place in the socialist countries have a bearing on the growth of *individual freedom* through the expansion of economic choice.

[30]It is another matter to decide who should pay this remuneration. In some cases, it could be the clients availing themselves of the services or their insurers; in others it could be the state or the social welfare fund; and in still others remuneration could be provided by a combination of the two.

[31]A young man today, for instance, can make a choice between alternative pension schemes, but someone near retiring age cannot be forced to transfer to a private pension fund. The state made a "contract" with him or her under the pension laws in force when they were working, and it cannot be broken arbitrarily and unilaterally.

A far clearer connection must be made between what citizens receive from the state and quasi-state organizations and how much tax they pay for them. Not the least of the economists' obligations in this respect is to protest against cheap prevarication and to expose politicians who promise a cut in taxes alongside an unchanged welfare program. The proportion of the state's welfare spending should decrease to the extent that well-informed voters *consent to* and desire it, in order to lessen the burden of taxation. Conversely, the welfare expenditures can only be maintained in the proportion that the citizens are prepared to finance with their taxes.

To sum up point D, there is yet another fiscal trap ahead, and this may be the most painful one to writhe in. A drastic cut in state welfare spending will bring insecurity and a grave deterioration in the quality of life of many people. However, to maintain current levels of welfare spending, and still more to increase them, would be accompanied by levels of taxation that would discourage investors and therefore hold back economic growth. It is a self-evident truism to say that more production is needed to cover the welfare services provided: a bigger pie is easier to divide.

It is difficult to make a forecast about expected welfare expenditures in the years to come. I believe the likeliest outcome will be that welfare services will be partially decentralized and marketized, but with agonizing slowness.

IV. General Conclusions

I have examined four problems through an analysis of experiences in Hungary. Nowadays there are countries (such as the republic-states being formed in the former territory of the Soviet Union) battling with problems even more staggering and elemental in force than these, such as deciding what to do to ensure that the population has food, that money has real purchasing power, and that the dive in production is halted. There is hope, however, that sooner or later all postsocialist countries will progress beyond the baneful state of chaos

and crisis, and then they will all find the questions I have discussed in my lecture on their agendas.[32]

Bitter conclusions can be drawn from this discourse. Even where the elemental tasks of macro stabilization have been more or less accomplished, grave problems are constantly reproduced. Even where there has been some success in approaching budgetary stability, serious pressure on public finances persists. On the one hand, an increase in various kinds of spending is still being urged by a variety of political and social forces, and on the other, the difficulties of collecting taxes are increasing. The danger of budgetary deficit is here to stay. Covering the deficit with loans from the central bank can constitute a perilous contribution to the inflationary pressure. Any success in monetary macro stabilization can easily slip through our fingers. Covering the deficit by issuing state bonds can crowd out productive investments, which will impede growth.

Any kind of quick-fix solution can only be proposed by economic dilettantes or political tricksters. I have repeatedly mentioned potential traps in order to underline that there is no easy way out of any of the problems discussed in the lecture. What present themselves are painful trade-offs and choices between bad and worse.

Strong and persistent efforts must be made to repress the former hyperactivity of the state and concurrently to reduce state spending, while combatting the bureaucratic, centralizing tendencies that constantly revive. The change is likely to occur slowly; it will be a good while before today's big government has been reduced to government on a desirable scale, far smaller than the present one.

Although I cannot make optimistic short-term forecasts, the outlook in the

---

[32]Among the factors compelling a reduction in state spending and taxation is Hungary's desire, shared with several other Eastern European countries, to join the Economic Community. One requirement for membership is that these rates should not exceed the far lower European norms.

longer term is more favorable. The political change has released the spirits of autonomy, freedom, and entrepreneurship, and these are the primary driving forces of economic progress. It seems justified to expect the low point to be followed by a rise in production, one effect of which will be to make it easier to solve the fiscal problems discussed in this lecture. This will broaden the tax base, which is a precondition for a reduction in the tax rates. The latter stimulates investment, which in turn creates new jobs. A decrease of unemployment ultimately reduces the social-security burdens of the state.

A wise and efficient government can accelerate this development, and governmental errors and omissions can impede it, but the final outcome of the transition is not in the government's hands. Under the new postsocialist system, the state can at most influence the economy. It cannot run the economy, which is propelled by the interests of those participating in it. This is one of the main advantages a market economy has over centrally managed socialism.

REFERENCES

Aberbach, Joel D., Putnam, Robert D. and Rockman, Bert A., *Bureaucrats and Politicians in Western Democracies*, Cambridge, MA: Harvard University Press, 1981.

Bator, Francis M., "The Anatomy of Market Failure," *Quarterly Journal of Economics*, August 1958, 72, 351–79.

Baumol, William J., *Welfare Economics and the Theory of the State*, Cambridge, MA: Harvard University Press, 1965.

Benton, Lauren A., *Invisible Factories: The Informal Economy and Industrial Development in Spain*, Albany: State University of New York Press, 1990.

Buchanan, James and Tullock, Gordon, *The Calculus of Consent: Logical Foundations of Constitutional Democracy*, Ann Arbor: University of Michigan Press, 1962.

Ékes, Ildikó, "A második gazdaság az átmenet időszakában és a piac fejlődése" ["The Second Economy in the Period of Transition and the Development of the Market"], unpublished manuscript, Központi Statisztikai Hivatal [Central Statistical Office], Budapest, 1991.

Esti, Nóra, *A magyarországi kisvállalkozások helyzetének és lehetőségeinek alakulása 1991-ben* [*The Trend in the Situation and Outlook for Small Business in Hungary in 1991*], Budapest: Gazdaságkutató Intézet, 1991.

Ferge, Zsuzsa, "The Social Safety Net in Hungary: A Brief Survey," in *Social Safety Nets in East/Central Europe*, mimeo, Kennedy School of Government, Harvard University, 1991.

_____, "Marginalization, Poverty, and Social Institutions," *Labor and Society*, 1992 (forthcoming).

Gém, Erzsébet, *Hitelt—de honnan? A vállalkozásfinanszirozás rendszere Magyarországon* [*Credit—But Where From? The System of Financing Entrepreneurship in Hungary*], Budapest: Kopint-Datorg, 1991.

Hall, Peter A., *Governing the Economy: The Politics of State Intervention in Britain and France*, New York: Oxford University Press, 1986.

Helpman, Elhanan, *Monopolistic Competition in Trade Theory*, Princeton: Princeton University Press, 1990.

Jantscher, Milka Casanegra de, Silvani, Carlos and Vehorn, Charles L., *Modernizing Tax Administration in Eastern Europe*, Washington, DC: International Monetary Fund, 1991.

Kessides, Christine, Davey, Kenneth, Holzman, Robert, Micklewright, John, Smith, Andrew, and Hinayon, Carlos, *Hungary: Reform of the Social Policy and Distribution System*, Washington, DC: World Bank, 1991.

Kopits, George, *Fiscal Reform in European Economies in Transition*, Washington DC: International Monetary Fund, 1991.

_____, Holzman, R., Schieber, G. and Sidgwick, E., *Social Security Reform in Hungary*, Washington, DC: International Monetary Fund, 1990.

Köllő, János, "Munkaerőpiac: mitől legyünk pesszimisták" ["Labor Market: Why One Should Be a Pessimist"], in R. Andorka, T. Kolosi, and G. Vukovich, eds., *Társadalmi riport 1990* [*Social Report 1990*], Budapest: TÁRKI, 1990, pp.

259–71.

———, "A foglalkoztatáspolitika igazi dilemmája" ["The Real Dilemma of Employment Policy"], *Figyelő*, 22 August 1991, *35*, 3.

Kornai, János, "The Soft Budget Constraint," *Kyklos*, 1986, *39*, 3–30.

———, "Individual Freedom and Reform of the Socialist Economy," *European Economic Review*, March 1988, *32*, 233–67.

———, *The Road to a Free Economy*, New York: Norton, 1990.

———, (1992a) *The Socialist System: The Political Economy of Communism*, Princeton: Princeton University Press, 1992.

———, (1992b) "The Principles of Privatization in Eastern Europe," *De Economist*, 1992 (forthcoming).

Lányi, Kamilla, ed., *A gyors változások területei a magyar gazdaságban* [*The Areas of Rapid Changes in the Hungarian Economy*], Budapest: Kopint-Datorg, 1991.

——— **and Oblath, G.,** eds., *A világgazdaság és a magyar gazdaság helyzete és kilátásai 1991 végén* [*The Conditions and Prospects for the World Economy and the Hungarian Economy at the end of 1991*], Budapest: Kopint-Datorg, 1991.

Lindbeck, Assar, "Consequences of the Advanced Welfare State," *World Economy*, March 1988, *11*, 19–37.

Manchin, Robert and Nagy, Lajos Géza, (1991a) *Ismeretek és vélemények az adóról* [*Information and Opinions on Taxes*], Budapest: Hungarian Gallup Institute, 1991.

——— **and** ———, (1991b) *Vélemények gazdaságról, életszinvonalról, politikai intézményekről* [*Opinions on the Economy, Living Standard, and Political Institutions*], Budapest: Hungarian Gallup Institute, 1991.

Móra, Mária, *Az állami vállalatok (ál)privatizációja* [*The Pseudo-Privatization of State-Owned Firms*], mimeo, Budapest: Gazdaságkutató Intézet, 1990.

———, "The (Pseudo-) Privatization of State-Owned Enterprises (Changes in Organizational and Proprietary Forms), 1987–1990)," *Acta Oeconomica*, 1991, *43* (1-2), 37–58.

Murrell, Peter, "An Evolutionary Perspective on Reform of the Eastern European Economies," unpublished manuscript, University of Maryland, College Park, 1990.

Niskanen, William A., *Bureaucracy and Representative Government*, Chicago: Aldine, 1971.

Offe, Claus, *Contradictions of the Welfare State*, Cambridge, MA: MIT Press, 1984.

Sabel, Charles, *Work and Politics*, Cambridge: Cambridge University Press, 1982.

Schumpeter, Joseph A., *The Theory of Economic Development: An Inquiry into Profits, Capital, Credit, Interest and the Business Cycle*, Leipzig: Duncker & Humblot, 1912 (in German); English translation, Cambridge, MA: Harvard University Press, 1934.

———, *Capitalism, Socialism and Democracy*, New York: Harper, 1942; reprinted, New York: Harper and Row, 1976.

Seleny, Anna, *The Political Economy of Property Rights and the Transformation of Hungarian Politics: 1949–1989*, unpublished manuscript, MIT, 1991.

Skocpol, Theda, "Bringing the State Back In: Strategies of Analysis in Current Research," in P. B. Evans, D. Rueschemeyer, and T. Skocpol, eds., *Bringing the State Back In*, Cambridge: Cambridge University Press, 1985, pp. 3–37.

Stiglitz, Joseph E., et al., *The Economic Role of the State*, Oxford: Blackwell, 1989.

Fraternité Rt., *Jelentés a társadalombiztosítás reformjáról* [*Report on the Reform of Social Insurance*], Budapest: Fraternité Rt., 1991.

International Monetary Fund, *Government Finance Statistical Yearbook*, Washington, DC: International Monetary Fund, 1990.

Központi Statisztikai Hivatal [Central Statistical Office], *Magyar statisztikai évkönyv 1990* [*Hungarian Statistical Yearbook 1990*], Budapest: Központi Statisztikai Hivatal, 1991.

Magyar Köztársaság Kormánya [Government of the Hungarian Republic], Állami költségvetés *1992* [*State Budget 1992*], Budapest: Magyar Köztársaság Kormánya, 1991.

National Bank of Hungary, *Quarterly Review*, No. 4, Budapest, National Bank of Hungary, 1991.

Organization for Economic Cooperation and Development, *OECD Economic Surveys: Hungary 1991*, Paris: Organization for Economic Cooperation and Development, 1991.

Országos Munkaügyi Központ [National Labor Center], (1991a) "Munkaerőpiaci helyzetkép. Havi jelentés. Augusztus" ["Monthly Report on the State of the Labor Market: August"], *Munkaerőpiaci Információk*, 1991, *9*, 20.

_____, (1991b) *Munkaerőpiaci helyzetkép. Havi jelentés. 1991. október* [*Monthly Report on the State of the Labor Market: October 1991*], Budapest: Országos Munkaügyi Központ, 1991.

_____, (1991c) *Munkaerőpiaci helyzetkép. Havi jelentés. 1991 november* [*Monthly Report on the State of the Labor Market: November 1991*], Budapest: Országos Munkaügyi Központ, 1991.

Pénzügyminisztérium [Ministry of Finance], "Az 1991. I-VII-VIII. havi és várható éves gazdasági folyamatokról" ["On Actual and Expected Economic Development in the January–July–August Period and for the Whole Year"], *Pénzügyi Szemle*, November 1991, *35*, 847–52.

U.S. Department of Health, *Human Services Research Report*, No. 60, Washington, DC: U.S. Department of Health, 1990.

[26]

Public Action for Social Security: Foundations and Strategy*

Jean Drèze
Amartya Sen

1. INTRODUCTION

'As you all know,' said Hecate, the mistress of the witches in *Macbeth*, 'security is the mortals' chiefest enemy.' His exaggerated sense of security certainly did not help Macbeth, but the 'chiefest enemy' that the majority of humanity face is the almost total *absence* of security in their fragile and precarious existence. The lives of billions of people are not merely nasty, brutish, and short, they are also full of uncertain horrors. An epidemic can wipe out a community, a famine can decimate a nation, unemployment can plunge masses into extreme deprivation, and insecurity in general plagues a large part of mankind with savage persistence.

It is this general fragility, on top of chronic and predictable deprivations, that makes the need for social security so strong and palpable. That recognition is part of the background of this chapter, but not the whole of it. The case for public action in this field requires us to go beyond the negative diagnosis of what isn't there, to the positive identification of what can, in fact, be achieved through a programme of social security. The motivation here is to investigate what the problems are, why some special actions are needed, what forms such actions should take, and in general how we should think about devising public action for social security.

It is useful to distinguish at the outset between two different aspects of social security—what we may call respectively 'protection' and 'promotion'. The former is concerned with preventing a decline in living standards in general and in the basic conditions of living in particular. The problem of protection is paramount in the context of famine prevention, and also in dealing with other kinds of sudden economic crises and sharp recessions.

This contrasts with the objective of enhancing the normal living conditions and dealing with regular and often persistent deprivation. This promotional aspect of social security is, in a sense, more ambitious, in wanting to eradicate

* Several sections of this chapter draw substantially on our recent book *Hunger and Public Action* (Drèze and Sen 1989). We are most grateful to John Hills and Nicholas Stern for helpful comments on an earlier draft, and to Asad Ahmad, Peter Lanjouw and Shantanu Mitra for research assistance.

4   JEAN DRÈZE AND AMARTYA SEN

problems that have survived thousands of years. The strategic issues involved
in promotional social security may differ very considerably, as we shall see,
from those in protective social security.

It may be useful to make three clarificatory remarks to prevent misunderstanding of the distinction and in particular of the terms chosen. First, while
both 'promotion' and 'protection' have superficially a somewhat paternalistic
ring, the terms refer in fact to the objects of the exercise, rather than to the
agency that may bring about those objects. As we shall argue, public action for
social security is neither just a matter of State activity, nor an issue of charity,
nor even one of kindly redistribution. The activism of the public, the unity and
the solidarity of the concerned population, and the participation of all those
who are involved are important features of public action for social security.
There is no assignment of any paternalistic role to the State—or to any other
body—in clarifying the plurality of the objectives involved.

Second, the contrast between protection and promotion arises in different
contexts in our analysis. For example, we may be concerned with the distinction
in the context of the generation of incomes, and we may then distinguish
between the promotion of incomes (changing persistently low incomes) and
the protection of incomes (preventing sharp declines). The distinction may
apply, similarly, in the context of entitlements, living standards, and so on.
There will then be a need to differentiate between entitlement promotion and
entitlement protection, between the promotion of living standards and the
protection of those standards, and so forth. The protection–promotion distinction has to be integrated with other discriminations that will be used in this
chapter.

Third, while the objectives of protection and promotion are distinct, the
pursuits of these objectives are not, of course, independent of each other. Nor
is the importance of one independent of the achievement of the other. For
example, success with the promotional objectives may make protection easier
(for example, individual insurance may be less difficult when one's normal
level of prosperity is higher). It can also make protection less intensely crucial
(for example, a decline from a higher standard of living may cause hardship but
not the kind of starvation and extreme deprivation that a fall from a lower—
more precarious—level would entail). There are other interdependences
between the two aspects of social security and their respective pursuits. It is
perhaps as important to note the interdependences as it is to clarify the
distinction.

The plan of this chapter is something like this. In Section 2, we discuss the
nature of well-being and deprivation and try to characterize the focus variables
underlying the analysis of social security. This section deals with the normative
foundations of the problem, and asks the question: what is the object of the
exercise? In Section 3, we examine whether the desired results can be achieved
through normal economic and social processes, without needing to devise

systems of social security as such. Why do we specifically need social security? The next section discusses a central problem of protective social security, namely, the prevention of famines through public action. What can be done to make communities safe from famines? In Section 5, the attention is shifted to the prevention of chronic deprivation. How can promotional social-security programmes combat regular and persistent hunger and hardship?

In Section 6, the nature of public action for social security is examined, and the role of the public in public action is analysed. We also discuss the problem of integration of State activities with those of the public in general and of non-governmental institutions in particular. Some concluding remarks are made in Section 7.

2. WELL-BEING, DEPRIVATION, AND SECURITY

The basic idea of social security is to use social means to prevent deprivation, and vulnerability to deprivation. What counts as deprivation is, of course, a matter of valuation, and the values involved can be characterized in different ways.

2.1. *Utility versus Objective Deprivation*

The utilitarian notion of value, which is invoked explicitly or by implication in much of welfare economics, ultimately sees value only in individual utility, itself defined in terms of some mental condition, such as pleasure, happiness, desire-fulfilment. This subjectivist perspective has been extensively used, but it can be very misleading, since it may fail to reflect a person's real deprivation. A thoroughly deprived person, leading a very tough life, might not appear to be badly off in terms of the mental metric of utility, if the hardship is accepted with non-grumbling resignation. In situations of long-standing deprivation, the victims do not go on sighing all the time, and very often make great efforts to take pleasure in small mercies and to cut down personal desires to modest— 'realistic'—proportions. A person's deprivation, then, may not at all show up in the metrics of pleasure, desire-fulfilment, and so on, even though he or she may not have the ability to be adequately nourished, comfortably clothed, minimally educated, and so on.[1]

This issue, aside from its foundational relevance, may have some immediate bearing on practical public policy. Smugness about continued deprivation and vulnerability is often made to look justified on grounds of lack of strong public demand and forcefully expressed desire for removing these impediments. For example, the persistence of massive illiteracy in India, especially among

---

[1] On this subject, see Sen (1985*b*).

women (the proportion of the literate among all Indian women above 5 years of age is still only around 28 per cent according to the last census), is often 'rationalized' in terms of the absence of a clamouring demand (especially among rural women) for elementary education. At a more removed—but still fairly immediate—level, similar arguments are used about the quiet tolerance of endemic undernutrition in many parts of the world, including India. These demand-centred arguments tend to hide the enormity of actual social deprivations.

2.2. *Commodities, Incomes, and Quality of Life*

An alternative approach is to focus on a person's 'real income', or command over essential commodities. This concrete perspective need not be subjectivist in the way utilitarian valuation is, since it is not exclusively dependent on the mental metrics of utility. Indeed, this type of 'non-psychological' accounting has been enormously influential in the recent literature on economic development, largely through the use of the 'basic needs' approach, which concentrates on the requirement to provide some specified minimal amounts of necessary goods (such as food, clothing, shelter) to all.[2]

The approach has, however, the disadvantage that commodities—and therefore income and wealth—are *means* to well-being, rather than *constituent elements* of it. In fact, the conversion of commodities into personal achievements may vary greatly between one person and another, and also between communities. For example, the calorie requirement for being well-nourished varies greatly with metabolic rates, body size, sex, pregnancy, age, parasitic ailments, climatic conditions, and so on, and an interpersonal comparison of deprivation or of poverty cannot be adequately performed just in terms of comparing commodity commands.[3]

Focusing only on incomes for analysing poverty and deprivation—as is frequently done—is problematic on two counts. The value of income lies in its use for commanding commodities, and therefore the variability in the relation between commodities and the quality of life applies also to that between incomes and the quality of life. But on top of that there are additional problems in the conversion of incomes into commodities. There are variations in the power of income to establish command over goods and services, because of market limitations in such forms as imperfect competition, presence of externalities, and the unavailability of certain goods in particular markets (for example, the

---

[2] See Streeten *et al.* (1981).

[3] The variability of the relation between commodities possessed and personal states is discussed in Sen (1980, 1985*b*). The 'basic needs' literature, which has played an enormously important and creative part in development economics, has also increasingly focused its evaluative attention on living conditions (being nourished, being disease-free, etc.) rather than on needs defined in terms of command over essential commodities as such (food, health services, etc.). See Streeten (1984) and Stewart (1985, 1988).

absence of educational services on offer in the rural markets of many developing economies). Therefore the problem of conversion of commodities into living standards is compounded by the problem of conversion of incomes into commodities.[4]

2.3. *Living Standards and Capabilities*

If neither the subjectivist utilitarian view, nor the means-oriented (commodity or income) view, is adequate, we need some other focus variable for analysing quality of life in general, and deprivation and poverty in particular. One approach, which has been explored recently, focuses on the capability to perform certain basic functionings.[5] The foundations of the approach go back, in a particular form, to Aristotle. Aristotle examined the problem of 'political distribution' in terms of his analysis of 'the good of human beings', and this he linked with his investigation of 'the function of man' and his exploration of 'life in the sense of activity'.[6] The Aristotelian theory is, of course, a very specific one, and involves elements (such as objectivity of valuation, a particular reading of human nature, and so on) that may or may not be compelling to all of us. But the argument for seeing the quality of life in terms of valued activities (and the ability to choose these activities) has much broader relevance and application.[7]

If life is seen as a set of 'doings and beings' that are valuable, the exercise of assessing the quality of life takes the form of evaluating these functionings and the capability to function. This valuational exercise need not be performed by simply counting pleasures or desires (as in the utility-based accounting), or by focusing on commodities or incomes instead of doings and beings (as in the commodity-based accounting). The task is that of evaluation of the importance of the various functionings in human life, going beyond what Marx called

---

[4] See Sen *et al.* (1987), with the 1985 Tanner Lectures at Cambridge by Amartya Sen (1987*b*), and comments by Muellbauer (1987), Kanbur (1987), Hart (1987), Williams (1987), and Hawthorn (1987). See also Schokkaert and van Ootegem (1989).

[5] See Sen (1982, 1985*a*, *b*).

[6] Aristotle (1980: bk 1, pp. 12–14). Note that Aristotle's term 'eudaimonia', which is often misleadingly translated simply as 'happiness', stands for fulfilment of life in a way that goes well beyond the utilitarian perspective. Though pleasure may well result from fulfilment, that is a consequence rather than the cause of valuing that fulfilment. For an examination of the Aristotelian approach and its relation to recent works on functionings and capabilites, see Nussbaum (1988).

[7] Among the classical political economists, both Adam Smith and Karl Marx explicitly discussed the importance of functionings and the capability to function as determinants of well-being; see Smith (1776: particularly 351–2) and Marx (1844). Marx's approach to the question was closely related to the Aristotelian analysis (and indeed was apparently directly influenced by it, on which see de Sainte Croix 1981, and Nussbaum 1988). One part of the Marxian reformulation of the foundations of political economy is clearly related to the importance of seeing the success of human life in terms of fulfilling the needed human activities. Marx (1844) put it thus: 'It will be seen how in place of the *wealth* and *poverty* of political economy come the *rich human being* and *rich human need*. The rich human being is simultaneously the human being *in need of* a totality of human life-activities—the man in whom his own realization exists as an inner necessity, as *need*.'

8   JEAN DRÈZE AND AMARTYA SEN

'commodity fetishism'.[8] The functionings themselves have to be examined, and the capability of the person to achieve them has to be appropriately valued. The evaluation is a reflective activity, and not a matter of identifying valuation with some mental metric or other, such as pleasure or desire.[9]

2.4. *Poverty and Deprivation*

The approach of focusing on capabilities and functionings can be used in a variety of evaluative problems.[10] In the case of studying poverty, it is the failure to have the capability to achieve minimal levels of certain basic functionings that would occupy the centre of the stage. The capabilities to be adequately nourished, to be comfortably clothed, to avoid escapable morbidity and preventable mortality, and so on, become the appropriate focus variables. This general approach yields a policy perspective that takes us well beyond an income-centred or a commodity-centred analysis, and also forces us to abandon smugness based on socially conditioned, unreflected acceptance of traditional inequities, deprivations, and vulnerabilities. The practical import of this reflective foundation, built on evaluating human functionings and capabilities, becomes clear as strategic problems in devising social-security programmes are seriously considered.[11]

Seeing poverty as capability failure may, at first sight, appear to be quite a departure from the traditional idea of poverty, which is typically associated with a shortage of income. The poor are taken to be those whose incomes fall below a certain specified level, namely, the so-called 'poverty line', and there is an extensive literature on (1) how the poverty line may be fixed, and (2) how the conditions of the different people below the poverty line may be put together to provide an aggregate measure of poverty.[12] However, the motivation under-

[8] Marx (1887: chap. 1, sec. 4, pp. 41–55). See also Marx (1844).

[9] It is sometimes presumed that to depart from a person's own pleasures or desires as the measuring rod is to introduce paternalism into the evaluative exercise. This view overlooks the important fact that having pleasure and desiring are not themselves valuational activities, even though the latter (desire) can often result from valuing something, and the former (pleasure) can often result from getting what one values. A person's utility must not be confused with his or her own valuations, and thus tying the evaluative exercise to the person's own utility is quite different from judging a person's success in terms of the person's own valuation. On these and related issues, see Sen (1985a).

[10] See Sen (1980, 1982, 1985a,b, 1987b); Culyer (1985); A. Williams (1985); Helm (1986); Kakwani (1986); Brannen and Wilson (1987); Hart (1987); Hawthorn (1987); Hossain (1987); Kanbur (1987); Muellbauer (1987); Osmani (1987); B. Williams (1987); Griffin and Knight (1988). See also the related literature on social indicators and general development goals, e.g., Adelman and Morris (1973); Sen (1973); Adelman (1975); Griffin and Khan (1978); Morris (1979); Streeten (1981, 1984); Stewart (1985); Dasgupta (1986); Lall and Stewart (1986).

[11] See, for instance, Drèze and Sen (1989) on the implications of the capability approach for public action aimed at removing nutritional and related deprivations.

[12] Some of the conceptual problems in the identification and aggregation of poverty, with suggested solutions, are discussed in Sen (1976a, 1981a); Atkinson (1983); Foster (1984). Foster in particular provides an extensive critical review of the literature.

ACTION FOR SOCIAL SECURITY   9

lying the concern with deprivation of income is indeed the likely impact of
income shortage on the lives that people can lead. The income view of poverty
is derivative, related to the effects of income on people's basic capabilities to
lead minimally acceptable lives. The ultimate concern of poverty analysis has
to be with the deprivation of living conditions, for example, lack of nourishment (rather than of the income to buy nutrients), exposure to preventable
diseases (rather than inability to buy medicine), and so on.

The concentration on income in the poverty literature, while ultimately
justifiable only derivatively, happens to be quite helpful, up to a point, for the
analysis of policy issues, since the shortage of real income (appropriately
defined) is one of the most visible and crucial factors restricting the basic
capabilities of many people. It is because of the recognition of this important
fact that the very idea of poverty has got associated with a shortfall of income
rather than with a failure to have the ability to achieve certain basic functionings
(such as being adequately nourished, minimally sheltered, and so on). That
causal connection is an important one to keep constantly in view, and in
particular contexts—such as famine prevention—the creation of income may
indeed be the crucial policy instrument to use.

But it is precisely because income shortage and poverty *seem* so inseparably
tied that we ought to be careful about those cases in which the ties are qualified
by other factors which may also have significant policy relevance. First of all,
the deprivation of particular members of a family may have a close but
somewhat variable relation with total family income, since the intrahousehold
distribution may itself vary. No analysis seriously concerned with poverty can
leave the matter of, say, child poverty merely to the size of the family income
available to support the children, ignoring altogether how that family income
is, in fact, used to support the lives that the members of the family—children
and adults—can lead. Similarly, no serious poverty analysis can fail to take
note of the important needs of women, related to social as well as biological
factors, including of course pregnancy. There are also other parameters of age
and ability, of health and disease, and so on that must be considered in
determining the relationship between income and the capability to lead
adequate lives.

While in devising policy strategies note must obviously be taken of the
crucial and far-reaching role of income in providing the means of minimally
acceptable living conditions, the subtler aspects of policy choice may well be
lost unless we also see the importance of income as being ultimately derivative
and contingent. Once an adequately comprehensive view of poverty and
deprivation has been taken, it is possible to make good use of the diagnosis of
income shortage and of the instrumental importance of income creation
without losing sight of the ends in the anxiety about the means.

10   JEAN DRÈZE AND AMARTYA SEN

3. WHY SOCIAL SECURITY?

The basic problems that call for social-security programmes are of two different general types. There is, first of all, the problem of widespread, persistent deprivation, and there is also the issue of fragility of individual security.

3.1. *Persistent Deprivation*

Much of humanity has come to terms with systematic denials of decent living conditions, and experiences failures of elementary capabilities. The overall picture is one of extreme deprivation across the world. The 'under-5 mortality rate', which is 13 per thousand in the USA, 11 in the UK, 9 in Switzerland and Japan, and 7 in Finland and Sweden, is more than 50 in eighty countries in the world, more than 100 in sixty countries, and more than 200 in twenty-three countries (among those for which data have been processed by UNICEF 1988). These are average figures, including the rich and the poor, the urban and the rural, and mortality rates for the rural poor would far exceed even these astonishingly high figures.

    While life expectancy at birth is more than 75 years in many of the countries of Europe and North America, the corresponding figure is below 60 years for most poor countries, below 50 years for a great many of them, and even below 40 years for some.[13] Similarly, the incidence of avoidable mortality is incomparably higher in many of the poorer developing countries than in the richer nations of the world. The failure of actual basic capabilities, compared with what is potentially possible, is remarkably widespread and intense.

3.2. *Vulnerability and Fragile Living Conditions*

In addition to the problem of persistent deprivation, there is also the issue of vulnerability. The average experience of the poorer populations understates the precarious nature of their existence, since a certain proportion of them undergo severe—and often sudden—dispossession, and the threat of such a thing happening is ever-present in the lives of many more. The decline may result from changes in personal circumstances (such as illness or death of earning members of the family), or from fluctuations in the social surroundings (such as a crop failure, a general recession, or a civil war).

    There are two different, but interrelated, problems raised by this feature of human existence. There is, first, the problem of how to counter the effects of the decline in the lives of those who experience it. And there is, second, the

---

[13] UNICEF (1988).

problem of how to increase the security in the lives of all, so that people do not live in constant fear of a calamity visiting them. The phenomenon of sudden decline affects the interests not only of those who succumb to it, but also those of others who are made to live diminished lives as a result of the ever-present threat (even though they may, in the event, not succumb to it).

3.3. Opulence, Public Support, and Capability Expansion

How can we deal with these problems of (1) persistent deprivation, and (2) fragility of individual security, involving irregular declines and persistent vulnerability? What, in particular, is the role of social security in encountering these challenges?

The latter question can be put in a different—and somewhat negative—way also. Why can't these problems be dealt with through standard channels of economic growth and social progress? It could be argued that the rich economies avoid most of these problems simply because of the average level of their opulence. That surely is the way to go? Or, at least, the need for taking the social-security route has to be established by showing the inadequacy of the more non-interventionist, traditional path.

In fact, the basic premises of this 'negative' view are themselves far from sound. Improvements in living standards in the rich economies have often been the direct result of social intervention rather than of simple economic growth. The expansion of such basic capabilities as the ability to live long and to avoid preventable mortality has typically gone hand in hand with the development of public support in the domains of health, employment, education, and even food in some important cases. The thesis that the rich countries have achieved high levels of basic capabilities simply because they are rich is, to say the least, an oversimplification.

The point can be illustrated by looking at the time pattern of expansion of longevity in Britain and in Japan. Table 1.1 presents the increase in life

Table 1.1. Increase in life expectancy in England and Wales per decade (years)

Decades	Male	Female
1901–11	4.1	4.0
1911–21	6.6	6.5
1921–31	2.3	2.4
1931–40	1.2	1.5
1940–51	6.5	7.0
1951–60	2.4	3.2

Source: Based on data presented in Preston *et al.* (1972: 240–71). See also Winter (1986) and Sen (1987*a*).

12   JEAN DRÈZE AND AMARTYA SEN

expectancy at birth in England and Wales in each of the first six decades of this century (starting with a life-expectancy figure that was no higher than that of most developing countries today). Note that while the increase in life expectancy has been between one to four years in each decade, there were two decades in which the increase was remarkably greater (around seven years approximately). These were the decades of the two world wars, with dramatic increases in many forms of public support including public employment, food rationing, and health care provisions.[14] The decade of the 1940s, which recorded the highest increase in British life expectancy during the century, was a decade of enormous expansion of public employment, extensive and equitable food rationing, and the birth of the National Health Service (introduced just after the war).

The Japanese figures come in less regular intervals, but a similar picture emerges of accelerating increase in life expectancy during the decade of the Second World War and post-war reconstruction (see Table 1.2). This was, again, a period of rapid expansion of public support.[15] These are suggestive

Table 1.2. Increase in life expectancy in Japan (months)

Period	Male		Female	
	Total	Per year	Total	Per year
1908–40	55.2	1.73	87.6	2.74
1940–51	136.8	12.44	144.0	13.09
1951–64	100.8	7.75	123.6	9.51

Source: Based on data provided in Preston *et al.* (1972: 420–39).

---

[14] See Winter (1986) for an illuminating analysis of the effects of the First World War on public distribution and public involvement, and their impact on living conditions in Britain. The experience of the Second World War is discussed in great detail by Titmuss (1950: chap. 25), who examined the evidence indicating a strong relationship between the surprisingly good health conditions of the British population during the war (including a rapid improvement of the health status of children) and the extensive reach of public support measures in that period. As Titmuss put it, 'by the end of the Second World War the Government had, through the agency of newly established or existing services, assumed and developed a measure of direct concern for the health and well-being of the population which, by contrast with the role of Government in the nineteen-thirties, was little short of remarkable' (p. 506). According to Titmuss, the most influential part of social policy during the war related to employment provision and food rationing. This conclusion is strongly corroborated by Hammond's detailed study of the 'revolution in the attitude of the British State towards the feeding of its citizens' which took place after 1941 (Hammond 1951). On these issues, see also Marrack (1947); McKeown and Lowe (1966: 131–4); McNeill (1976: 286–7); Szreter (1988).

[15] In Japan, it seems that the years of most rapid expansion of longevity were those immediately following the Second World War. Indeed, according to census estimates, the expectation of life for males leaped from 50 in 1947 to 60 in 1950–2, and that for females from 54 to 63 (unpublished figures from the Ministry of Health and Welfare). We are grateful to Akiko Hashimoto for helpful

ACTION FOR SOCIAL SECURITY   13

facts, even though any detailed analysis of cause–effect relations would have to take into account other associated factors (such as the significantly increased tempo of medical innovation during the wars). No matter how exactly the credit for expansion of longevity during the war and post-war years is divided, it is extremely unlikely that the role of public support and social intervention could be shown to be inconsequential. There is more to the expansion of life expectancy than the simple story of economic growth and increased average opulence.

3.4. *Distribution, Provisioning, and the Quality of Life*

The association between the average prosperity of a nation (given by such indicators as GNP per head) and the basic capabilities enjoyed by its population is substantially weakened by a number of distinct factors: (1) inequalities in the distribution of incomes; (2) variations over time of incomes of any person; and (3) the dissonance between personal incomes and individual capabilities.

The first issue has been much discussed in the development literature. There can be remarkable disparities in the sharing of the fruits of economic growth. Even the presumption that there must be substantial 'trickle down' effects has been contradicted by the actual experience of a number of countries.[16] Enhancing the average income level is, thus, an undependable route to the promotion of living standards. Average income is also a capricious variable for protecting entitlements of the population, since different occupation groups can go to the wall and perish even when average income rises, and indeed several major famines have occurred in overall boom situations. The need for social security thus remains strong even when a country is successful in its attempt to generate economic growth.

The second problem concerns variations of income over time even for a given person. A person's earnings may change not merely with age (with little income when one is very old or very young), but also with business fluctuations, international slumps, crop failures, agricultural seasonality, and so on. The time pattern of earnings may not at all match the time pattern of needs. Indeed, sometimes the needs are maximal precisely when incomes tend to be minimal (for example, when a person is seriously ill). This intertemporal mismatch would not matter greatly if capital markets were 'perfect', allowing adjustment of expenditure to needs even without altering the pattern of earnings. The

discussions on the empirical evidence relating to this observation. On the demographic transition in Japan, and its relation to public support, see Taeuber (1958); Shigematsu and Yanagawa (1985); and Morio and Takahashi (1986).

[16] The problem of unequal sharing of economic expansion was extensively discussed by Griffin and Khan (1977, 1978). There have been in recent years several empirical studies on the sharing issue, and while sharing has been, evidently, more equal in some cases than others, altogether 'trickle down' is clearly an unreliable means of reducing poverty.

14   JEAN DRÈZE AND AMARTYA SEN

problem of unexpected fluctuations could similarly be encountered if insurance
markets were versatile and efficient. But capital markets and insurance
markets are frequently non-existent or feeble (especially in developing countries). Social security has a special role in these circumstances.[17]

The roots of the third problem have already been discussed in earlier
sections of this paper. The conversion of commodity holdings into personal
capabilities depends on a number of contingent circumstances (for example,
the relation between nourishment and food intake can vary greatly with age,
sex, pregnancy, climate, and many other factors). Furthermore, often the vital
commodities needed for the protection or promotion of living conditions (such
as public-health provisions) cannot easily be individually owned, and the
public sector may well be able to deliver them more efficiently than the market.
Thus, the relation between individual income and individual capabilities is
weakened not merely by the influence of variables other than commodities (as
was discussed earlier), but also by the importance of delivery mechanisms (this
issue will be further examined in Section 5).

The last point indicates that the unreliability of GNP as a guide to living
conditions must not be seen merely as a problem of distributional inequality of
the aggregate GNP. The problem of the delivery mechanism and the related
questions of converting incomes into capabilities require us to go well beyond
the usual concern with income distribution as a supplement to the GNP and
other aggregate measures.[18]

These factors put together indicate why economic growth alone cannot be
relied upon to deal either with the promotion or with the protection of living
standards. The strategy of public action for social security has to take adequate
note of the problems that limit what aggregate expansion can do in enhancing
living conditions. In the next section we turn to an acute problem of protection
of entitlements and living standards, namely, the conquest of famines, and in
Section 5 we move on to the more diverse problem of promotion of living
standards to combat the persistent deprivation that has been the lot of much of
humanity for much of history. Which way should the strategy of public action
for social security take us in facing these momentous challenges?

---

[17] On this general question, see Chap. 2 below.

[18] To illustrate the point, the Indian State of Kerala has one of the lower GNP per head among
the different Indian States, but has remarkable achievements in generating a high quality of life
(e.g., a life expectancy in the upper 60s—far above that of any other Indian State). If the crude
aggregate measures of GNP per head are corrected by taking note of distributional inequalities,
Kerala's relative position does not go up very much, and it still remains one of the poorest Indian
states in terms of distribution-adjusted real incomes (on this see Sen 1976b, and Bhattacharya et al.
1988). It is in the public delivery of health, food, and education that we have to seek an answer to
Kerala's achievements in living standards. On Kerala's experience of public support, see the
literature cited in Sec. 5.3 below.

4. FAMINE PREVENTION

Starvation is clearly among the most acute forms of deprivation, and famine prevention must, therefore, be—explicitly or implicitly—one of the most elementary functions of social-security systems. At the same time, the social-security perspective itself can, as we shall see, throw fresh light on famine prevention issues. While exploring these interconnections, much of our attention will focus on sub-Saharan Africa. This is natural enough, since famine vulnerability afflicts this part of the world more than any other.

4.1. *Famines and Public Action*

In the short term, preventing famines is essentially an *entitlement protection* exercise. In the long term, much more is involved, including entitlement promotion, aimed at a durable elimination of vulnerability—through greater general prosperity, economic diversification, and so on. But even within a long-term perspective, the task of setting up reliable entitlement protection systems remains a central one. Indeed, in most cases it would be very naïve to expect that efforts at eliminating vulnerability could be so successful as to allow a country to dispense with distinct and specialized entitlement protection mechanisms.[19] While entitlement protection does not subsume all aspects of famine prevention, it is undoubtedly the most vital part of the problem.

Any particular exercise of entitlement protection is intrinsically a short-term one. But it should not be confused with the popular notion of 'famine relief' which conjures up the picture of a battle already half lost and focuses the attention on emergency operations narrowly aimed at containing large-scale mortality. The task of devising planned, coherent, effective, and durable entitlement protection mechanisms is a much broader one. Entitlement crises have many repercussions on the rural economy and on the well-being of affected populations, and a comprehensive strategy for dealing with the scourge of famine must seek to ensure not only that human beings have secure lives but also that they have secure livelihoods.

---

[19] The entitlements that need to be protected in a famine situation naturally relate, to a large extent, to food itself. Indeed, the initiation of famine mortality typically follows enfeeblement caused by hunger as well as other destitution-related phenomena such as population displacements. However, given the prominent role often played by water contamination and epidemic diseases in the propagation of famine mortality, measures also have to be taken to guarantee adequate access to basic health care and safe water supply. Many empirical studies have shown that simple measures for the protection of entitlements to staple food and basic public services can lead to a dramatic reduction of excess mortality in famine situations. For some examples (historical as well as contemporary) see Valaoras (1946); Ramalingaswani *et al.* (1971); Berg (1973); Krishnamachari *et al.* (1974); Binns (1976); Smout (1978); Will (1980); Kiljunen (1984); Otten (1986); Drèze (1988); and de Waal (1989) among others.

16   JEAN DREZE AND AMARTYA SEN

This is not just a question of immediate well-being, but also one of development prospects. Consider, for instance, the so-called 'food crisis in Africa'.[20] The current débâcle of agricultural production in much of sub-Saharan Africa has, not without reason, been held partly responsible for this region's continued vulnerability to famine. But it is also legitimate to wonder how farmers who are condemned every so often to use up their productive capital in a desperate struggle for survival can possibly be expected to save, innovate, and prosper. Improved entitlement protection systems in Africa would not only save lives, but also contribute to preserving and rejuvenating the economy of this continent. The alleged dilemma between 'relief' and 'development' is a much exaggerated one, and much greater attention has to be paid to the *positive* links between famine prevention and development prospects.

Seeing famine prevention as an entitlement protection problem draws our attention to the plurality of available strategies for dealing with it. Just as entitlements can be threatened in a number of different ways (which may or may not involve a decline in the overall availability of food), there are also typically a number of feasible routes for restoring them. Importing food and handing it over to the destitute is one of the most obvious options. The overwhelming preoccupation of the journalistic and institutional literature on famine prevention in Africa has been with the logistics of food aid, reflecting the resilient popularity of this approach.[21] But there is a good case for taking a broader view of the possible forms of intervention, and indeed the historical experience of famine prevention in different parts of the world actually reveals an impressive variety of approaches to the protection of food entitlements.

At a general level, a reliable system of famine prevention can be seen to consist essentially of two distinct elements. The first is a mechanism to ensure that an early decision to act is taken by the responsible authorities in the event of a crisis. This part of the system has, inevitably, an important political dimension. The second indispensable element of a famine prevention system is of a more administrative nature, and involves an intelligent and well-planned intervention procedure, ensuring that the political decision to act translates into effective action for the protection of entitlements. In the remainder of this section we shall investigate both aspects of the problem of famine prevention.

[20] For analyses of the main issues involved, see Berry (1984); IDS Bulletin (1985); Rose (1985); Eicher (1986, 1988); FAO (1986); Whitehead (1986); Mahieu and Nour (1987); Mellor *et al.* (1987); Rukuni and Eicher (1987); Platteau (1988); Drèze (1989).

[21] International agencies, it must be said, bear some responsibility for the perpetuation of archaic intervention strategies. For instance, the persistent reluctance of the international donor community to undertake multi-year food aid commitments, or to allow the 'monetization' of food aid, have been an important factor of rigidity in famine prevention policies.

4.2. *Early Warning and Early Response*

Effective entitlement protection calls, *inter alia*, for early and decided action in the event of a crisis. The advantages of early intervention are of course well recognized, even from the narrow point of view of saving human lives. Extraordinary difficulties are encountered with containing mortality once large-scale population displacements have been allowed to begin. The penalties of reluctant or apathetic response to a crisis are dramatically visible in the disastrous human toll of unrelieved famines, such as the Bengal famine of 1943 and the Chinese famines of 1959–61.[22]

The blame for delayed action is often put on inadequately detailed *information* about the existence, or the exact character, of a crisis. There has, in fact, recently been a surge of interest and involvement in so-called 'early warning systems'.[23] However, it would be hard to see a central part played by formal early warning techniques in the recent experiences of successful famine prevention, whether in India, Botswana, Zimbabwe, or Cape Verde.[24]

Indeed, most often the warnings of imminent dangers have tended to come from general reports of floods or droughts or economic dislocations, and from newspaper coverage of early hardship and visible hunger. In countries with relatively pluralistic political systems (such as India and Botswana), open channels of protest have also helped to direct forcefully the attention of the authorities to the need for preventive action without delay. Varieties of administrative, journalistic, and political communications have served the 'early warning' role in the absence of elaborate systems of famine prediction or of formal procedures of early warning.

Of course, informal ways of anticipating famine threats can sometimes mislead. But so can formal systems of early warning, which are often based on some rather simple model (explicitly invoked or implicitly presumed), paying attention to a few variables and ignoring many others. There is undoubtedly scope for improving famine-warning systems based on economic analysis.[25] But there is little chance that a formal model can be developed that would be practically usable (with all the necessary data inputs being obtainable at the required speed) and that would take adequate note of all the variables that may well be relevant in the wide variety of cases that can possibly

---

[22] On the inadequate nature of government response in these events, and the political factors involved, see Sen (1981a, 1983); Peng (1987); Brennan (1988).

[23] One study finds the current situation of duplication and heterogeneity of independent efforts to be quite 'surrealistic' (CILSS 1986: 67). That study, which is not meant to be exhaustive, identifies no fewer than 39 different early-warning systems in the Sahel alone, of which 14 are engaged in primary data collection and 25 'recycle' information collected by 'more or less competing agencies' (p. 69).

[24] On this see Drèze and Sen (1989: chap. 8).

[25] On different lines of possible improvement, see e.g. Cutler (1985b); Desai (1986); Borton and York (1987); Autier (1988); Walker (1988); Autier *et al.* (1989); Swift (forthcoming).

18   JEAN DRÈZE AND AMARTYA SEN

arise. The supplementation of formal economic models by more informal systems of communication and analysis is, to a great extent, inescapable.

It would, moreover, be a mistake to see the problem of early warning only in terms of the gathering and analysis of information. The informational exercise has to be seen in the broader context of the need to trigger early and resolute action on the part of the concerned authorities. Indeed, most cases of unmet famine threats reflect not so much a lack of knowledge that could have been remedied with more reliable systems of prediction, but negligence or smugness or callousness on the part of the non-responding authorities.[26] In this context it is important to note that such informal systems of warning as newspaper reports and public protests carry not only information that the authorities *can* use, but also elements of pressure that may make it politically compelling to respond to these danger signals and do something about them urgently. It is no accident that the countries that have been most successful in famine prevention in the recent past have typically had relatively pluralistic politics with open channels of communication and criticism.

Official tolerance of political pluralism and public pressure in many African countries is, at the moment, quite limited. The opposition is often muzzled. Newspapers are rarely independent or free. The armed forces frequently suppress popular protest. Further, to claim that there are clear signs of change in the direction of participatory politics and open journalism in Africa as a whole would be undoubtedly premature. However, there is now perhaps a greater awareness of the problem and of the need for change. The long-term value of creative dissatisfaction should not be underestimated.[27]

4.3. *Cash Support and Employment Provision*

As was discussed earlier, an effective system of famine prevention requires not only a mechanism to ensure early response in the event of a crisis, but also a sound procedure of entitlement protection. One factor which has frequently accounted for belated and somewhat unsuccessful famine prevention efforts is the dependence of entitlement protection measures on the timely arrival of food aid, and generally on the complicated logistics associated with the direct delivery of food to potential famine victims. The greater use of 'cash support' to protect the entitlements of vulnerable groups is an important option to consider in remedying this problem.

Cash support is not a new idea. It has, in fact, a rich history covering many

---

[26] This applies, *inter alia*, to the famines in Bengal in 1943 and in China in 1959–61, mentioned earlier. In the case of the African famines of 1983–5, too, it has been observed that 'early warnings were given in almost all instances' (World Food Programme 1986: 4).

[27] On the role of the press and adversarial politics in the context of African famines, and the emerging signs of change in some countries, see Yao and Kone (1986); Mitter (1988); Reddy (1988); Drèze (1989).

parts of the world.[28] But the suggestion that it has a contribution to make to famine prevention strategies in Africa today is often met with resilient suspicion. This suspicion cannot reasonably arise from the belief that the conversion of cash into food might prove impossible in a famine situation. Indeed, a plethora of recent sudies have shown that the acquisition of cash (for subsequent conversion into food through the market) is now one of the most important survival strategies of vulnerable populations in famine-prone countries.[29] But there is a deeper problem. If it is clear enough that cash can almost always help an *individual* to acquire food and avoid starvation, it is less obvious that cash support can improve *collective* security. After all, one person's ability to command food through cash support may adversely affect other people's entitlements—for example, by exerting an upward pressure on prices. The merits of cash support do, therefore, require careful scrutiny.

Assessing the likely impact of entitlement protection measures backed by cash rather than by food involves a careful consideration of market responses.[30] Indeed, an immediate effect of cash-based entitlement protection is to exert an upward pressure on food prices (since the effective demand for food increases), and this in turn can have complicated repercussions on the allocation of food in the economy. Needless to say, this increase of prices has altogether different implications from the sort of inflationary pressure that might result from, say, speculative hoarding or a boom in the urban economy. In this instance, the increase of prices has its origin in the greater purchasing power of the needy and is part of the process of improving (rather than undermining) their command over food. In order to assess the precise impact of a cash-based entitlement protection strategy on the allocation of food in the economy, one must examine carefully the effects it is likely to have, via the price mechanism, on (1) the net *aggregate* amount of food consumed in the region under consideration, and (2) the *distribution* of consumption between different sections of the population.

Price increases are likely to lead to an improvement in the availability of food in the affected region through changes in production, trade, and storage. The potential for reducing the forces of famine by inducing interregional food movements towards severely affected regions through the channel of private trade is particularly important to consider.

[28] Cash relief has a long history both in India (Loveday 1914; Drèze 1988) and in China (Mallory 1926; Will 1980; Li 1987), and has also been an important feature of famine prevention in a number of African countries more recently, including Botswana (Hay *et al.* 1986), Cape Verde (van Binsbergen 1986), Tanzania (Mwaluko 1962), and Ethiopia (Kumar 1985; Padmini 1985).

[29] See Drèze and Sen (1989: chap. 5), and the literature cited there.

[30] Our concern here is with the wisdom of cash-based entitlement protection measures that are carried out *without* a corresponding amount of food being released on the market by the relief system. This 'cash injection' issue has to be distinguished from what one might call the 'cash medium' issue, which is concerned with comparing the merits of giving food directly with those of giving cash *with* a corresponding amount of food being released on the market. See Drèze and Sen (1989: chap. 6), for further discussion of this distinction, and of the cash medium issue itself.

In the common international perception, connected largely with the nature of media reports, African famines are often seen in terms of acute and more or less uniform 'shortages' of food everywhere in the affected country or countries. This is, however, largely a myth, and in fact the scope for interregional food movements to alleviate the intensity of distress is often considerable. Large variations in food output between different regions are common in Africa, and frequently a marketable surplus does remain in or near the famine-affected territory. There is also considerable evidence that private trade in Africa is alive to economic opportunities when it is allowed to operate without bureaucratic restrictions. Of course, sharp contrasts exist between different countries in these respects, and it may well be that in some places a major reliance on the operation of private food trade to respond to the demands generated by cash support would be problematic. There are, however, no serious grounds for general pessimism in this respect.[31]

Despite the possibly important effects of cash support on the total supply of food in the affected region, it is very likely that the increase in food availability will fall short of the increase in the consumption of those receiving cash support. Indeed, the same price rise which has an expanding effect on supply will also have a contracting effect on the demand for food of those who do not receive cash support but now face higher prices. To that extent, a *redistribution* of consumption towards the protected groups will take place.

The prospect of dealing with the threat of famine partly by inducing a redistribution process operating within affected areas strikes terror in the heart of many observers. They see this as a failure to respond to the 'real problem' of 'shortage', and as an attempt 'to transfer food from one victim to another'. It must be remembered, however, that large inequalities are a pervasive feature of most famine-prone societies. There is, moreover, considerable evidence that the consumption patterns of even relatively privileged households are quite responsive to price changes in situations of economic adversity.[32] The scope for redistribution from these groups to the most vulnerable may therefore be far from negligible. When direct delivery of food through the public relief system is hampered or slowed down by administrative and logistic difficulties, redistribution through selective cash support may be a crucial option.

The success of the redistributive strategy, however, depends to a great extent on the ability of the relief system to provide preferential support to the entire vulnerable population. If substantial numbers of vulnerable people are excluded from entitlement protection measures but have to take the consequences of price increases, the overall vulnerability of the population could conceivably be exacerbated rather than diminished by the relief system.[33] An

---

[31] For further discussion of this issue, and of the evidence, see Drèze and Sen (1989: chap. 6).

[32] The evidence is discussed in Drèze and Sen (1989: chap. 5).

[33] It should, however, be mentioned that some of the excluded groups could gain from *derived benefits* obtained from the income support provided to other groups. For instance, a reduction of

ACTION FOR SOCIAL SECURITY   21

important question therefore concerns the need to cover all the major vulnerable groups, while continuing to exclude the more privileged in order to preserve the redistributive bias on which the success of the strategy of cash support depends.

In this respect, much can be said in favour of a strategy of open-ended employment provision. The element of 'self-selection' involved in this strategy makes it possible to carry out comparatively large transfers to vulnerable households, while at the same time imparting a strong redistributive bias to the entitlement protection process.

In fact, often the only effective and politically acceptable method of providing large-scale cash support is precisely that of employment provision with cash wages. The case for this strategy receives added strength from a number of other advantageous features of employment-based entitlement protection. These include: (1) being compatible with intervention at an early stage of a subsistence crisis (when affected people are looking hard for alternative sources of income but do not yet suffer from severe nutritional deprivation); (2) obviating the necessity of movements of entire families to feeding camps; (3) at the same time, obviating the necessity of taking food to every village (as in a system of decentralized distribution), to the extent that the work-seeking adult population is mobile; (4) inducing positive market responses in the form of an upward pressure on local wages; (5) providing women (who are, very often, a majority of the work-force on public-works programmes) with an independent source of income and thereby increasing their bargaining power within the household.[34]

Cash support and employment provision have strong and mutually reinforcing advantages, which have been well illustrated in a number of recent experiences of famine prevention, both in Africa and in South Asia.[35] These advantages deserve greater recognition, even though it is also important not to fall into the trap of assuming the existence of a universally attractive model of public intervention in famine situations.

distress livestock sales on the part of those who receive support could substantially benefit vulnerable livestock owners outside the relief system by arresting an impending collapse of livestock prices. The increased purchasing power of those who do receive support can also have helpful 'multiplier effects', e.g., through their purchases of labour services from other vulnerable groups.

. [34] For further discussion of these and other advantages of employment provision as a strategy of entitlement protection, see Drèze and Sen (1989: chaps. 6, 7).

[35] See Drèze (1988, 1989); and Drèze and Sen (1989: chap. 8), for case-studies of famine prevention in India, Botswana, and Cape Verde. Of course, the provision of employment has to be supplemented by measures of unconditional relief for those who are not able to work and cannot rely on the support of able-bodied dependants. Such measures have been part of the entitlement protection systems of each of these three countries. Also, highlighting the contribution that cash support and employment provision can make to the protection of entitlements should not be seen as dismissing the role of food supply management. The latter can be important too, but it need not be *tied* to income generation measures, as in systems of direct feeding or 'food-for-work'.

22   JEAN DRÈZE AND AMARTYA SEN

5. CONFRONTING DEPRIVATION

We noted earlier (in Section 3) the possible dissonance between the average opulence of a country and the basic capabilities of its population. Despite this possible dissonance, there are good grounds for expecting a positive *general* association between the two. This is partly because the increased private incomes associated with greater general affluence do indeed offer the opportunity to obtain command over a number of commodities which are crucially important to basic capabilities, such as nutritious food, sound shelter, and adequate fuel. But, in addition, greater opulence provides resources for extending public support in areas such as health, education, employment, food distribution, and social insurance. While some of the best things in life may not be purchasable in the market, and while the command over them may depend to a great extent on public provisions made by the State, it is also true that what the State can provide may, in turn, be much facilitated by greater general opulence.

5.1. *Alternative Strategies: Growth-Mediated Security and Support-Led Security*

Given the distinct, though interconnected, roles played by overall opulence and public support in enhancing capabilities, it is possible in principle to distinguish two contrasting approaches to the removal of precarious living conditions. One approach is to promote economic growth and take the best possible advantage of the potentialities released by greater general affluence, including not only an expansion of private incomes but also an improved basis for public support. This may be called the strategy of 'growth-mediated security'. Another alternative is to resort *directly* to wide-ranging public support in domains such as employment provision, income redistribution, health care, education, and social assistance in order to remove destitution without waiting for a transformation in the level of general affluence. Here success may have to be based on a discriminating use of national resources, the efficiency of public services, and a redistributive bias in their delivery. This may be called the strategy of 'support-led security'.

The possibility of success through either approach is credible enough in principle. But there have been, in fact, serious detractors questioning the viability of each of these avenues of action. The merits of the respective strategies have to be assessed against the actual experiences of different countries in the world. Intercountry comparisons of performance may, of course, be quite misleading, but they do provide a preliminary and suggestive bias for noting certain elementary relationships and possibilities.

We shall examine briefly the comparative performance of different countries in terms of one particular indicator, namely the observed percentage reduction in combined infant and child mortality (hereafter 'under-5 mortality') between 1960 and 1985.[36] The ten best performers among the developing countries according to this criterion are the following: Hong Kong, United Arab Emirates, Chile, Kuwait, Costa Rica, Cuba, China, Singapore, Jamaica, and South Korea.[37] The actual figures are presented in Table 1.3.

Table 1.3. Proportionate reduction in under-5 mortality rates: the top ten countries (1960–1985)

Country	% reduction in U5MR (1960–85)	% growth rate of GNP/capita (1965–85)	GNP per head in US$ (1985)	Level of U5MR (1985)
Hong Kong	83	6.1	6 230	11
Chile	82	−0.2	1 430	26
United Arab Emirates	82	n.a.	19 270	43
Costa Rica	81	1.4	1 300	23
Kuwait	80	−0.3	14 480	25
Cuba	78	n.a.	n.a.	19
Singapore	76	7.6	7 420	12
China	75	4.8	310	50
Jamaica	72	−0.7	940	25
South Korea	71	6.6	2 150	35

Note: Excluded from the comparison are the countries of Eastern and Western Europe, Japan, New Zealand, Australia, USA, USSR, and Canada.

Sources: UNICEF (1987: Table 1); World Bank (1987: Table 1).

On the basis of the information contained in Table 1.3, and of what is known about the experiences of the countries involved, it is possible to divide these ten countries into two distinct groups. Growth-mediated security has clearly been an important part of the experiences of Hong Kong, Singapore, South Korea, Kuwait, and the United Arab Emirates. These countries have experienced outstandingly high rates of economic growth between 1960 and 1985, and their remarkable success in reducing under-5 mortality has been much helped by their rising opulence.[38] Thus, a half of the ten highest performers in terms of

[36] The information on under-5 mortality rate (U5MR) for 130 countries, on which this exercise. is based, appears in table 1 of UNICEF (1987). The nature of the U5MR index is explained in UNICEF (1987: 126). This index must not, of course, be interpreted as an overall indicator of the quality of life, but it clearly relates to a very important aspect of it.

[37] North Korea was excluded from the initial list because we learned from the statistical agencies involved that the figures for North Korea were not independently obtained but simply *assumed* to be the same as those for South Korea.

[38] The first three of these countries have been among the five fastest-growing countries during the period under consideration (World Bank 1987: table 1). The last two (Kuwait and the United

percentage reduction of under-5 mortality seem to have resorted to a strategy of growth-mediated security, of one sort or another.

On the other hand, the other five countries (namely, Chile, Costa Rica, Cuba, China, and Jamaica) have had quite different experiences. Their growth rates have been comparatively low. Moreover, as we shall see shortly, these countries stand out sharply in having achieved far lower mortality rates than most other countries at a comparable income level. The basis of their success does not seem to rest primarily in rapid income growth, and suggests the possibility of support-led security.[39]

There is, in fact, considerable evidence that direct public support has indeed been the driving force behind the success of each of these five countries.[40] We shall return to this question in Section 5.3.

5.2. Economic Growth and Public Support: Interconnections and Contrasts

The distinction made in the preceding section between growth-mediated security and support-led security reflects an important strategic aspect of public action, but it can also be easily misunderstood. A few remarks may help in clarifying the precise nature of the contrast.

First, the distinction involved is definitely not a question of activism versus disengagement on the part of the State. The governments of the countries which have pursued a strategy of growth-mediated security have, in fact, often been extremely active both in bringing about economic growth and in disseminating its fruits. The constructive role of the State in these countries has in varying extents included: (1) promoting economic growth through skilful planning; (2) facilitating wide participation of the population in the process of economic expansion, particularly through the promotion of skills and education and the maintenance of full employment; and (3) utilizing a substantial part of the resources generated by rapid growth for extensive public provisioning of basic necessities. This applies even to countries such as South Korea or Singapore, which are often presented as examples of the fecundity of '*laissez-faire*', but whose experiences are in fact rich illustrations of the diverse roles that State activism can play within a strategy of growth-mediated security.[41]

Arab Emirates) have not experienced high growth rates of GNP over that period in terms of conventional measures, but this is mainly because the phenomenal increase in their incomes that has in fact taken place as a result of changes in relative prices (in this case involving oil) is not well captured in the growth rate of the real *quantity index* of GNP per capita (see World Bank 1984*b*).

[39] The Chinese growth rate appearing in Table 1.3 is quite impressive, and might be seen as suggesting that the basis of China's success may well lie as much in economic growth as in direct public support. It can be shown, however, that (1) China's growth rate during the period of interest has been much exaggerated, and (2) economic growth has *followed* rather than preceded the wide-ranging measures of public support which must be seen as the main source of China's success. On this question, see Drèze and Sen (1989: chap. 11).

[40] See the case-studies in Drèze and Sen (1989: chaps. 11, 12), and the literature cited there.

[41] See the case-studies in Drèze and Sen (1989: chap. 10).

Second, the contrast we have pursued is also not a simple one of market versus State provisioning. The masses can gain a share in general opulence not only through the increase of private incomes, but also through wide-ranging public provisioning. A striking example is provided by Kuwait, where rapid growth has created the material basis for what is clearly one of the most munificent 'Welfare States' in the world.[42] The general notion that one of the important fruits of economic growth can be to facilitate public support is also visible from other successful experiences of growth-mediated security. These experiences contrast sharply with those of countries such as Brazil where there has been little effort to combine rapid growth with social provisioning, and where, as a result, living conditions remain shockingly poor for a large part of the population.[43]

Third, the distinction made in the last section has little to do with the dilemma that has sometimes been construed between the pursuit of 'growth' and the fulfilment of 'basic needs'. A strategy of 'growth-mediated' security is not at all the same thing as the pursuit of economic growth *tout court*, or what might be called 'unaimed opulence'. The former need not conflict with the satisfaction of basic needs—indeed it is an approach to their satisfaction. Conversely, support-led security does not imply surrendering the goal of economic growth. In fact, sometimes improvements in the quality of human life (for example, through better health and education) also enhance the productivity of the labour-force. And economic growth can be crucial to the sustainability of a strategy based on generous public support.' The interconnections and contrasts between the two strategies are more extensive and more complex than would be captured in a simple dichotomy between growth and basic needs.

The real source of the contrast lies in the fact that the countries that have made substantial use of the strategy of support-led security have not *waited* to grow rich before resorting to large-scale public support to guarantee certain basic capabilities. The contrast is a real one, but it should not obscure the complementarities that exist between economic growth and public support— and in particular, the prominent role played by public support in the strategies of growth-mediated as well as support-led security.

Despite these complementarities, dilemmas can arise in seeking a balance between the two strategies. Both growth-oriented measures and support-oriented measures make substantial claims on public resources as well as on public administrative capabilities. There are choices to be made in public policy-making, and nothing is gained in obscuring the conflicts involved.

---

[42] On the extensive nature of public provisioning in Kuwait, see Ismael (1982), who describes this country as 'a total service society with almost every human need from the cradle to the grave serviced by institutional arrangement' (p. 105). It should be mentioned, however, that the welfare state in Kuwait discriminates sharply between Kuwaiti citizens and non-Kuwaiti residents.

[43] On this experience of 'unaimed opulence' in Brazil, see Sachs (1986).

26   JEAN DRÈZE AND AMARTYA SEN

5.3. *The Strategy of Support-Led Security*

In Section 5.1 we noted how a number of countries (including China, Costa Rica, Jamaica, Chile, and Cuba) have achieved outstanding success in reducing under-5 mortality rates.in spite of unremarkable rates of growth of GNP per head. We have also suggested that these experiences can be seen as illustrative of a strategy of 'support-led security', which consists of embarking on ambitious programmes of public support at an early stage of development.

The causal links between public efforts and social achievements in these as well as other countries have received a good deal of attention in the recent development literature.[44] The investigations have taken different forms. One group of studies has been concerned with examining similarities in the nature of public support efforts in *different countries* (each with good records in mortality reduction and other achievements), and the commonalities involved in their respective efforts have been assessed, especially in contrast with the experience of other countries.[45] A second group of studies has been concerned with *interregional* comparisons within single countries, comparing the achievements of regions which have greater or lesser involvement in public support.[46] A third set of studies has presented *intertemporal* comparisons within single countries of public efforts and social achievements.[47] A fourth set of studies has examined the direct impact of public support measures, such as health and nutrition programmes, at the *micro* level.[48] The causal links between public support provisions and social achievements have been clearly brought out in different ways in these diverse empirical investigations.

Public support can take various forms, such as public health services, educational facilities, food subsidies, employment programmes, land redistribution, income supplementation, and social assistance, and the respective country experiences have involved various combinations of these measures. While there are significant contrasts in the relative importance of these different forms of public support in the different country experiences, the

---

[44] In addition to the 5 countries mentioned above, two further experiences of successful support-led security deserve special mention here: those of Sri Lanka, and of the State of Kerala in India. In the case of Sri Lanka, the main expansion took place *prior* to 1960, and this country is thus not included in the list of top performers for 1960–85 in Sec. 5.1. Kerala, on the other hand, did not appear in this list because it is not a country but only a State in a federal country (India). On these two experiences of support-led security, see Isenman (1980); Halstead *et al.* (1985); Basu (1986); Caldwell (1986); Anand and Kanbur (1987); Kumar (1987); Sen (1987*a*); Drèze and Sen (1989), among others. See also Chap. 7 below.

[45] See e.g. Sen (1981*b*); Flegg (1982); Halstead *et al.* (1985); Stewart (1985); Caldwell (1986).

[46] See e.g. Castaneda (1984, 1985), Jain (1985), Nag (1985), Prescott and Jamison (1985), Morrison and Waxler (1986), Kumar (1987), Mata and Rosero (1987).

[47] See e.g. Castaneda (1984, 1985) on Chile, Anand and Kanbur (1987) on Sri Lanka, and Mata and Rosero (1987) on Costa Rica.

[48] See e.g. Gwatkin *et al.* (1980); Harbert and Scandizzo (1982); Garcia and Pinstrup-Andersen (1987); Berg (1987); Mata and Rosero (1987).

ACTION FOR SOCIAL SECURITY   27

basic commonality of instruments is quite striking (especially in view of the great diversity of the political and economic regimes).[49] Underlying all this is something of a shared approach, involving a public commitment to provide direct support to raise the quality of life, especially of the deprived sections of the respective populations.

The empirical investigations cited earlier also throw some useful light on the resource requirements (and affordability) of the kind of public support measures that have been found crucial to the strategy of support-led security. Scepticism regarding the feasibility of large-scale public provisioning in a poor country often arises precisely from the belief that these measures are inordinately 'expensive'. Several experiences of support-led security (particularly those that have succeeded in spite of a low GNP per capita, as in China, Sri Lanka, and Kerala) suggest that this diagnosis is, at least to some extent, misleading.

Indeed, the costs of social-security programmes in these countries have been in general astonishingly small. This applies, in particular, to public provisioning of health care and education. It has been estimated, for instance, that in China the percentage of GDP allocated to public expenditures on health has been only around 2 per cent. Moreover, only about 5 per cent of total health expenditure has tended to go to preventive health care, which has been one of the major influences behind the fast retreat of infectious and parasitic diseases.[50] There are similarly striking figures for other experiences of support-led success.[51]

The relatively inexpensive nature of public provisions in the domains of health and education in developing countries is partly a reflection of the low level of wages. Aside from this, several considerations would tend to reduce the real burden of public support in these countries. First, financial costs are not always a good reflection of social costs, and in particular a good case can often be made for regarding the social costs of labour in labour-surplus economies as being lower than the market wage.[52] Second, the opportunities for raising revenue are not independent of the existence of a social-security system. For instance, the scope for resorting to exacting indirect taxation may be much

---

[49] See the case studies presented in Drèze and Sen (1989: chaps. 11, 12).

[50] Bumgarner (1989). On this general question, see also World Bank (1984a) and Jamison (1985).

[51] The percentage of GDP allocated to public expenditures on health in Sri Lanka in 1981 was barely 1% (Perera 1985: table 8). The corresponding figure for Cuba was around 2.7% (Muniz *et al.* 1984: tables 6.1 and 6.6). In Kerala, per capita government expenditure on health is not much greater than in the rest of India (Nag 1985: table 16). For further evidence and discussion of the scope of low-cost public provisions in the domain of health, with special reference to China, Costa Rica, Kerala and Sri Lanka, see various contributions in Halstead *et al.* (1985), and also Caldwell (1986).

[52] On the distinction between financial costs and social costs, see Drèze and Stern (1987), and the literature reviewed there.

28   JEAN DRÈZE AND AMARTYA SEN

larger when vulnerable groups are protected from possibly severe deprivation. Third, there is an element of investment in public provisioning (for example, through the relation between health, nutrition, education, and productivity). This reduces the diversion from investment opportunities that is apparently involved in a programme of public support.

Resource constraints should not be overlooked, but it would be a mistake to regard these constraints as the most important obstacle to be overcome in attempts to provide social security through direct public support in developing countries. The distinction of China, Kerala, Sri Lanka, or other countries with a distinguished record of support-led security does not lie in the size of financial allocations to particular public provisions. Their real success seems to be based on creating the political, social, and economic conditions under which ambitious programmes of public support are undertaken with determination and effectiveness, and can be oriented towards the deprived sections of the population.

It is not enormously surprising that efforts to provide extensive public support are rewarded by sustained results, and that public sowing facilitates social reaping.[53] Perhaps what is more remarkable is the fact that the connections studied here are so frequently overlooked in drawing up blueprints for economic development. The temptation to see the improvement of the quality of life simply as a consequence of the increase in GNP per head is evidently quite strong, and the influence of that point of view has been quite pervasive in policy-making and policy-advising in recent years. It is in the specific context of that simple growth-centred view that the empirical connections between public support measures and the quality of life deserve particular emphasis.

6. THE NATURE OF PUBLIC ACTION

Before closing this chapter we must address some general issues regarding the strategy of public action for social security. These issues are implicit in many of the discussions that we have already presented, but there is a case for addressing them separately and explicitly.

Public action must not be confused with State action only. Public action includes not merely what is done *for* the public by the State, but also what is done *by* the public for itself. We have to recognize *inter alia* the role of non-governmental organizations in providing social security (particularly in times

---

[53] Hunger and deprivation are, to a large extent, social conditions that cannot be seen only in isolated individual terms. There are strong interdependences and so-called 'externalities' involved in health (e.g. through the spread of diseases), education (e.g. through influencing each other), and nutrition (e.g. through food habits being dependent on social customs). The importance of social intervention in ensuring adequate entitlements to 'public goods', and in dealing with externalities generally, has been well recognized for a long time in economics (see Samuelson 1955; and Arrow 1963).

of distress), and the part that social, political, and humanitarian institutions can play in protecting and promoting living conditions.

Among the actions that can be undertaken by the public, the political role of pressuring the government to act is a particularly important one. As was discussed earlier, there is considerable evidence, for instance, that early action in preventing famines has often been precipitated by newspaper reports of early cases of starvation and by pressure from political and social organizations demanding action.[54] Public involvement and activism may have the role both of drawing the attention of the government to problems that may otherwise be neglected and of forcing the hands of the government by making it politically impossible—at least unwise—for it to ignore impending threats.

While this informational and adversarial role of action by the public operates through the government, there are other non-governmental, public activities that directly contribute to the support of entitlements and living conditions of the vulnerable population. The problem of integration of governmental and non-governmental activities is an important one in a programme of public action for social security.[55]

There is also an important problem of integrating State actions in supporting living conditions with what emerges from the market mechanism. While it is true that the need for State action partly arises from the failure of the market to provide adequate protection and promotion of living conditions, it does not follow that State action for social security must dispense altogether with reliance on the market. In so far as the market mechanism contributes to economic expansion, provides effective means of matching supplies to demands, and yields widespread entitlement generation (particularly through employment creation), it can be a very significant ally in providing social security through public action.

A purist strategy—relying only on the market or only on State action—can be awfully short of logistic means. The need to consider the plurality of levers and a heterogeneous set of mechanisms is hard to escape in the pursuit of social security. In the context of discussing famine prevention, we had the occasion to discuss both the possible failure of the market mechanism to provide adequate guarantee of entitlements and the possibly helpful role of markets in meeting demands generated by public relief programmes (Section 4). Similarly, in discussing the elimination of systematic and persistent deprivations and the promotion of living standards in general, we had the opportunity to discuss the part that economic growth—even when promoted by market-related processes —can play provided that the fruits of growth are sensibly used for the purpose of social security (Section 5).

[54] See Sec. 4.2. See also Sen (1983); Ram (1986); Drèze (1988); Drèze and Sen (1989); Reddy (1988).
[55] For further discussion of this issue, with special reference to sub-Saharan Africa, see Chap. 9 below.

30   JEAN DRÈZE AND AMARTYA SEN

   In this context we have to guard against two rather disparate and contrary dangers. One is to ignore the part that the market mechanism can play in generating growth and efficiency (despite its various limitations as an allocative device), with the State trying to do it all itself through administrative devices. The other is to be over-impressed by what the market mechanism can do and to place our reliance entirely on it, neglecting those things that the government can effectively undertake (including various policies for the promotion of health and education).

   The Chinese success during the pre-reform period (that is, prior to 1979) in enhancing the quality of life, despite its low GNP per head, illustrates the important role that the State can play in the direct promotion of social security. But it also shows how easily inefficiencies can be bred and how the engine of economic growth can be rigidly constrained by an over-reliance on administration and a severe neglect of the market. The remarkably fast economic expansion (particularly in agriculture) since the reforms, including the reinstatement of many markets and market-type institutions, brings out the part that the market can creatively play. And yet, there is evidence that there has been some set-back in the sharp decline of mortality rates and related features of the quality of life since the reforms of 1979, and that this may be connected with some withdrawal from public provisioning (especially communal health delivery in the rural areas).[56] In emphasizing the problem of integration, our aim is to warn against both types of problems (namely, over-reliance on as well as neglect of markets).[57]

7. PUBLIC ACTION FOR SOCIAL SECURITY

This chapter has been concerned with foundational as well as strategic issues involved in public action for social security. We began by distinguishing between two different but interrelated challenges, namely, the *protection* of living standards from serious declines (for example, by preventing famines), and the *promotion* of these standards to permanently higher levels (for example, by eliminating endemic hunger, chronic hardship, and rampant morbidity). Social security is concerned with both these challenges (Section 1).

---

[56] See Sen (1987a, 1988); Hussain and Stern (1988); and Drèze and Sen (1989: chap. 11). Some of the reported increases in mortality rates have other explanations (e.g., changes in reporting bias, changing age composition of the population) but some part of the increased mortality rates does seem to be both (1) real, and (2) related to declining arrangements of public provisioning.

[57] The Chinese experience is, in fact, a storehouse of important lessons for social-security planning. In drawing attention to the problems faced, we must not, of course, ignore the basic fact that public action in China has achieved remarkable results in improving various aspects of the Chinese quality of life to levels that are totally unusual in countries with comparably low per-capita income. On this see particularly Riskin (1987), and also Chap. 6 below.

Second, a foundational issue concerning the whole idea of social security is the choice of 'evaluative space', that is, the variables in terms of which the success or failure of social security is to be judged. We have argued in favour of using a suitably adapted version of an old evaluative tradition (associated with the works of Aristotle, Smith, and Marx, among others) which focuses on the capability that people have—based on their individual as well as social characteristics—to achieve valuable functionings (doings and beings). This provides a useful way of interpreting the standard of living and the positive freedom to achieve valued living conditions. This focus contrasts with purely subjective criteria such as utility-based accounting (used in mainstream welfare economics), and also with various criteria that focus only on *means* that are useful in living a good life (such as real incomes, entitlements, Rawlsian 'primary goods', Dworkinian 'resources') rather than on the nature of that life and the freedom to lead a less deprived life. The means are, of course, helpful in achieving ends, and thus the strategy of social security must pay attention to them, but ultimately the successes and failures of social security would have to be judged in terms of what it does to the lives that people are able to lead (Section 2).

Third, another foundational issue concerns the question as to why we need a separate and explicit policy for social security, rather than expecting that it will be taken care of by general economic growth and overall expansion. The popular belief that it is through economic growth as such that the rich countries of today have overcome their own inheritance of massive deprivation can be shown to be a gross oversimplification, and conscious public efforts to enhance living conditions have played a substantial part in that achievement. Even among the poorer countries today, some have achieved a great deal more than others through deliberately planning social security and expanding public support. Any reliance on GNP per head either as a means of protection, or as a vehicle of promotion, can be extremely treacherous, partly because of distributional inequalities but also because of the limitations of private markets in generating good living conditions (Section 3).

Fourth, as far as the protective aspect of social security is concerned, we analysed the phenomenon of famines and experiences in controlling and eradicating them. The prevention of famines has to be sought in entitlement protection rather than only in the marshalling and distribution of food. Public action has to be geared to the variety of economic and social influences that determine the ability of people (particularly vulnerable groups) to command and use food. The study of actual experiences of famine prevention in different countries brings out particularly the importance of both (1) an administrative system that is systematically aimed at recreating lost entitlements (when these are disrupted by droughts, floods, wars, economic slumps, or whatever), and (2) a political system that can act as the prime mover in getting the administrative system to work as and when it is required.

32   JEAN DRÈZE AND AMARTYA SEN

Various specific lessons were also discussed, including (1) the advantages of cash support as a method of quickly recreating lost entitlements (without waiting for prior food movements through bureaucratic channels); (2) the crucial role of employment creation in a comprehensive anti-famine strategy; (3) the power of informal communication channels and political activism in precipitating early action, in comparison with formal 'early warning' techniques; and (4) the need to see famine prevention as a matter not just of containing excess mortality, but also of minimizing hardship, avoiding loss of capital and productive resources through distress disposal, and preventing a lasting disruption of economic and social systems (Section 4).

Fifth, we then shifted our attention from the urgent imperatives of entitlement protection to the more general problem of the promotion of living standards. In this context, we discussed the effectiveness of different kinds of policies, and distinguished in particular between two general approaches, which we respectively called 'growth-mediated security' and 'support-led security'. A comparison of the contrasting performances of different countries brings out the plurality of routes through which living standards have been promoted, in some cases involving the achievement of elevated GNP per head (as in Hong Kong, Singapore, South Korea, the United Arab Emirates, Kuwait) and in others without remarkable increase in GNP per head (as in China, Costa Rica, Cuba, Chile, Jamaica, Sri Lanka). The experience of the latter group of countries brings out the possibility of not waiting for GNP expansion before achieving substantial breakthroughs in guaranteeing minimal living standards to all. This strategy of 'support-led security' involves public action in a particularly crucial and indispensable way.

On the other hand, the experience of the former group suggests that growth too can be an engine of promotion of social security, if the fruits of growth are skilfully used for social objectives. It is, in fact, the misuse of the opportunities provided by enhanced opulence that has been the cause of the most severe disappointments with the route of economic growth (for example, in Brazil). Here too there is a positive role for public action in ensuring productive use of the fruits of growth in enhancing living conditions and in achieving social security (Section 5).

Finally, we discussed some general issues regarding the nature of public action for social security (Section 6). It is particularly necessary to distinguish between actions undertaken *for* the public and *by* the public. The former are, of course, important in achieving social security, but can be both incomplete (requiring integration with efforts of the public in general and non-governmental institutions in particular), and in need of a political push (requiring an informed and active role of public pressure groups). In both these respects, public action for social security has to be seen in a much wider perspective than that of State action only.

References

Adelman, I. (1975), 'Development Economics: A Reassessment of Goals', *American Economic Review*, Papers and Proceedings, 66.

—— and Morris, C. (1973), *Economic Growth and Social Equity in Developing Countries*. Stanford: Stanford University Press.

Anand, S., and Kanbur, R. (1987), 'Public Policy and Basic Needs Provision: Intervention and Achievement in Sri Lanka', mimeo, to be published in Drèze and Sen (1990).

Aristotle (1980), *The Nicomachean Ethics* (trans. W. D. Ross). Oxford: Clarendon Press.

Arrow, K. (1963), 'Uncertainty and the Welfare Economics of Health Care', *American Economic Review*, 53.

Atkinson, A. B. (1970), 'On the Measurement of Inequality', *Journal of Economic Theory*, 2; repr. in Atkinson (1983).

—— (1983), *Social Justice and Public Policy*. Brighton: Wheatsheaf, and Cambridge, Mass.: MIT Press.

—— and Bourguignon, F. (1982), 'The Comparison of Multi-Dimensional Distributions of Economic Status', *Review of Economic Studies*, 49; repr. in Atkinson (1983).

Autier, P. (1988), 'Nutrition Assessment Through the Use of a Nutritional Scoring System', *Disasters*, 12.

—— d'Altilia, J. P., Delamalle, J. P., and Vercruysse, V. (1989), 'The Food and Nutrition Surveillance System of Chad and Mali: The "SAP" After Two Years', mimeo, European Association for Health and Development, Brussels.

Basu, K. (1986), 'Combatting Chronic Poverty and Hunger in South Asia: Some Policy Options', paper presented at a Conference on Food Strategies held at WIDER, Helsinki, 21–5 July 1986; to be published in Drèze and Sen (1990).

Berg, A. (1973), *The Nutrition Factor*. Washington, DC: Brookings Institution.

—— (1987), *Malnutrition: What Can be Done?* Baltimore: Johns Hopkins University Press.

Berry, S. S. (1984), 'The Food Crisis and Agrarian Change in Africa: A Review Essay', *African Studies Review*, 27/2.

Bhattacharya, N., Chatterjee, G. S., and Pal, P. (1988), 'Variations in Level of Living across Regions and Social Groups in India', in Srinivasan and Bardhan (1988).

Binns, C. W. (1976), 'Famine and the Diet of the Enga', *Papua New Guinea Medical Journal*, 19.

Borton, J., and Clay, E. (1986), 'The African Food Crisis of 1986', *Disasters*, 10.

—— and York, S. (1987), 'Experiences of the Collection and Use of Micro-level Data in Disaster Preparedness and Managing Emergency Operations', *Disasters*, 11.

Brannen, J., and Wilson, G. (eds.) (1987), *Give and Take in Families*. London: Allen & Unwin.

Brennan, L. (1988), 'Government Famine Relief in Bengal, 1943', *The Journal of Asian Studies*, 47.

Bumgarner, R. (1989), 'China: Long-Term Issues in Options for the Health Sector', mimeo, The World Bank, Washington, DC.

34   JEAN DRÈZE AND AMARTYA SEN

Caldwell, J. C. (1986), 'Routes to Low Mortality in Poor Countries', *Population and Development Review*, 12.

Castaneda, T. (1984), 'Contexto Socioeconomico y Causas del Descenso de la Mortalidad Infantil en Chile', Documento de Trabajo No. 28, Centro de Estudios Publicos, Santiago.

——(1985), 'Determinantes del Descenso de la Mortalidad Infantil en Chile 1975–1983', *Cuadernos de Economia*, 22.

CILSS (Comité Permanent Interétats de Lutte Contre la Sécheresse dans le Sahel), (1986), *La Prévision des situations alimentaires critiques dans les pays du Sahel: Systèmes et moyens d'alerte précoce*. Paris: OECD.

Cornia, G., Jolly, R., and Stewart, F. (eds.) (1987), *Adjustment with a Human Face*. Oxford: Clarendon Press.

Culyer, A. J. (1985), 'The Scope and Limits of Health Economics', *Okonomie des Gesundheitswesens*, 1985.

Cutler, P. (1985a), 'Detecting Food Emergencies: Lessons from the 1979 Bangladesh Crisis', *Food Policy*, 10.

——(1985b), 'The Use of Economic and Social Information in Famine Prediction and Response', report prepared for the Overseas Development Administration. London: Overseas Development Administration.

Dalby, D., Harrison Church, R. J., and Bezzaz, F. (eds.) (1977), *Drought in Africa 2*. London: International African Institute.

Dasgupta, P. (1986), 'Positive Freedom, Markets and the Welfare State', *Oxford Review of Economic Policy*, 2.

Desai, M. (1986), 'Modelling an Early Warning System for Famines', paper presented at a Conference on Food Strategies held at WIDER, Helsinki, 21–5 July 1986; to be published in Drèze and Sen (1990).

de Sainte Croix, G. E. M. (1981), *The Class Struggle in the Ancient Greek World*. London: Duckworth.

de Waal, A. (1989), *Famine That Kills: Darfur 1984–1985*. Oxford: Oxford University Press.

Drèze, J. P. (1988), 'Famine Prevention in India', Discussion Paper No. 3, Development Economics Research Programme, London School of Economics; to be published in Drèze and Sen (1990).

—— (1989), 'Famine Prevention in Africa', Discussion Paper No. 17, Development Economics Research Programme, London School of Economics; to be published in Drèze and Sen (1990).

—— and Sen, A. K. (1989), *Hunger and Public Action*. Oxford: Clarendon Press.

——(eds.) (1990), *The Political Economy of Hunger*, 3 vols. Oxford: Oxford University Press.

—— and Stern, N. (1987), 'The Theory of Cost-Benefit Analysis', in A. Auerbach and M. Feldstein (eds.), *Handbook of Public Economics*. Amsterdam: North-Holland.

Eicher, C. K. (1986), 'Transforming African Agriculture', The Hunger Project Papers, No. 4, The Hunger Project, San Francisco.

——(1988), 'Food Security Battles in Sub-Saharan Africa', paper presented at the VIIth World Congress for Rural Sociology, Bologna, 25 June–2 July 1988.

FAO (Food and Agriculture Organization), *African Agriculture: The Next 25 Years*. Rome: FAO.

Flegg, A. T. (1982), 'Inequality of Income, Illiteracy and Medical Care as Determinants of Infant Mortality in Underdeveloped Countries', *Population Studies*, 36.

Foster, J. (1984), 'On Economic Poverty: A Survey of Aggregate Measures', *Advances in Econometrics*, 3.

—— (1986), 'Inequality Measurement'. In H. P. Young (ed.), *Fair Allocation*, vol. 33 of Proceedings of Symposia in Applied Mathematics. American Mathematical Society.

Garcia, M., and Pinstrup-Andersen, P. (1987), 'The Pilot Food Price Subsidy Scheme in the Philippines: Its Impact on Income, Food Consumption, and Nutritional Status', Research Report No. 61, International Food Policy Research Institute, Washington, DC.

Glantz, M. (ed.) (1987), *Drought and Hunger in Africa: Denying Famine a Future*. Cambridge: Cambridge University Press.

Grant, J. (1978), *Disparity Reduction Rates in Social Indicators*. Washington, DC: Overseas Development Council.

Griffin, K., and Khan, A. R. (eds.) (1977), *Poverty and Landlessness in Rural Asia*. Geneva: International Labour Organization.

—— (1978), 'Poverty in the World: Ugly Facts and Fancy Models', *World Development*, 6.

—— and Knight, J. (1988), 'Human Development in the 1980s and Beyond', report for the United Nations Committee for Development Planning.

Gwatkin, D. R., Wilcox, J. R., and Wray, J. D. (1980), *Can Health and Nutrition Interventions Make a Difference?* Washington, DC: Overseas Development Council.

Halstead, S. B., Walsh, J. A., and Warren, K. S. (eds.) (1985), *Good Health at Low Cost*. New York: Rockefeller Foundation.

Hammond, R. J. (1951), *History of the Second World War: Food*. London: HMSO.

Harbert, L., and Scandizzo, P. (1982), 'Food Distribution and Nutrition Intervention: The Case of Chile', World Bank Staff Working Paper No. 512, The World Bank, Washington DC.

Hart, K. (1987), 'Commoditisation and the Standard of Living', in Sen *et al.* (1987).

Hawthorn, G. (1987), 'Introduction', in Sen *et al.* (1987).

Hay, R., Burke, S., and Dako, D. Y. (1986), 'A Socio-Economic Assessment of Drought Relief in Botswana', report prepared by UNICEF/UNDP/WHO for the Inter-Ministerial Drought Committee, Government of Botswana, Gaborone.

Helm, D. (1986), 'The Assessment: The Economic Borders of the State', *Oxford Review of Economic Policy*, 2.

Hossain, I. (1987), 'Poverty as Capability Failure', mimeo, University of Stockholm.

Hussain, A., and Stern, N. (1988), 'On the Recent Increase in Death Rates in China', mimeo, London School of Economics.

IDS (Institute of Development Studies) Bulletin (1985), *Sub-Saharan Africa: Getting the Facts Straight*, special issue, 16/3.

Isenman, P. (1980), 'Basic Needs: The Case of Sri Lanka', *World Development*, 8.

Ismael, J. S. (1982), *Kuwait: Social Change in Historical Perspective*. Syracuse, NY: Syracuse University Press.

Jain, A. K. (1985), 'Determinants of Regional Variation in Infant Mortality in Rural India', *Population Studies*, 39.

Jamison, D. (1985), 'China's Health Care System: Policies, Organization, Inputs and Finance', in Halstead *et al.* (1985).

36　　　　　JEAN DRÈZE AND AMARTYA SEN

Kakwani, N. (1986), 'On Measuring Undernutrition', Working Paper No. 8, WIDER, Helsinki.

—— (1987), *Analysing Redistributive Policies*. Cambridge: Cambridge University Press.

Kanbur, R. (1987), 'The Standard of Living: Uncertainty, Inequality and Opportunity', in Sen *et al.* (1987).

Kiljunen, K. (ed.) (1984), *Kampuchea: Decade of the Genocide*. London: Zed.

Krishnamachari, K. A. V. R., Rao, N. P., and Rao, K. V. (1974), 'Food and Nutritional Situation in the Drought Affected Areas of Maharashtra: A Survey and Recommendations', *Indian Journal of Nutrition and Dietetics*, 11.

Kumar, B. G. (1985), 'The Ethiopian Famine and Relief Measures: An Analysis and Evaluation', mimeo, UNICEF, New York.

—— (1987), 'Poverty and Public Policy: Government Intervention and Levels of Living in Kerala', D.Phil. thesis, University of Oxford.

Lall, S., and Stewart, F. (eds.) (1986), *Theory and Reality in Development: Essays in Honour of Paul Streeten*. London: Macmillan.

Li, L. M. (1987), 'Famine and Famine Relief: Viewing Africa in the 1980s from China in the 1920s', in Glantz (1987).

Loveday, A. (1914), *The History and Economics of Indian Famines*. London: A. G. Bell and Sons; repr. New Delhi: Usha Publications, 1985.

McKeown, T., and Lowe, C. R. (1966), *An Introduction to Social Medicine*. Oxford: Blackwell.

McNeill, W. H. (1976), *Plagues and People*. Garden City, NY: Anchor Press.

Mahieu, F. R., and Nour, M. M. (1987), 'The Entitlement Approach to Famines and the Sahelian Case: A Survey of the Available Literature', mimeo, WIDER, Helsinki.

Mallory, W. H. (1926), *China: Land of Famine*. New York: American Geographical Society.

Marrack, J. R. (1947), 'Investigations of Human Nutrition in the United Kingdom During the War', *Proceedings of the Nutrition Society*, 5.

Marx, K. (1844), *Economic and Philosophic Manuscripts of 1844*. English trans. Moscow: Progress Publishers, 1977.

—— (1887), *Capital*, i, trans. S. Moore and E. Aveling. London: Sonnenschein; repub. London: Allen & Unwin, 1946.

Mata, L., and Rosero, L. (1987), 'Health and Social Development in Costa Rica: Intersectoral Action', document prepared by the Instituto de Investigaciones de Salud (INISA), University of Costa Rica.

Mellor, J. W., Delgado, C. L., and Blackie, C. L. (eds.) (1987), *Accelerating Food Production in Sub-Saharan Africa*. Baltimore: Johns Hopkins University Press.

Mitter, S. (1988), 'Managing the Drought Crisis: The Zimbabwe Experience, 1982–1983', undergraduate essay, Harvard University.

Morio, S., and Takahashi, S. (1986), 'Socio-Economic Correlates of Mortality in Japan', in Ng Shui Meng (ed.), *Socio-Economic Correlates of Mortality in Japan and ASEAN*, National Institute for Research Advancement, Japan, and Institute of Southeast Asian Studies, Singapore.

Morris, M. D. (1979), *Measuring the Conditions of the World's Poor: The Physical Quality of Life Index*. Oxford: Pergamon.

Morrison, B., and Waxler, N. (1986), 'Three Patterns of Basic Needs Distribution within Sri Lanka: 1971–1973', *World Development*, 14.

Muellbauer, J. (1987), 'Professor Sen on the Standard of Living', in Sen *et al.* (1987).

Muniz, J. G., Fabián, J. C., and Mauriquez, J. C. (1984), 'The Recent Worldwide Economic Crisis and the Welfare of Children: The Case of Cuba', *World Development*, 12.

Mwaluko, E. P. (1962), 'Famine Relief in the Central Province of Tanganyika, 1961', *Tropical Agriculture*, 39.

Nag, M. (1985), 'The Impact of Social and Economic Development on Mortality: Comparative Study of Kerala and West Bengal', in Halstead *et al.* (1985).

Nussbaum, M. (1988), 'Nature, Function and Capability: Aristotle on Political Distribution', *Oxford Studies in Ancient Philosophy*, supplementary volume.

Osmani, S. R. (1982), *Economic Inequality and Group Welfare*. Oxford: Clarendon Press.

—— (1987), 'Nutrition and the Economics of Food: Implications of Some Recent Controversies', Working Paper No. 15, WIDER; to be published in Drèze and Sen (1990).

Otten, M. W. (1986), 'Nutritional and Mortality Aspects of the 1985 Famine in North Central Ethiopia', mimeo, Centre for Disease Control, Atlanta, Ga.

Padmini, R. (1985), 'The Local Purchase of Food Commodities: "Cash for Food" Project', mimeo, UNICEF, Addis Ababa.

Peng, X. (1987), 'Demographic Consequences of the Great Leap Forward in China's Provinces', *Population and Development Review*, 4.

Perera, P. D. A. (1985), 'Health Care Systems of Sri Lanka', in Halstead *et al.* (1985).

Platteau, J. P. (1988), 'The Food Crisis in Africa: A Comparative Structural Analysis', Working Paper No. 44, World Institute for Development Economics Research, Helsinki; to be published in Drèze and Sen (1990).

Prescott, N., and Jamison, D. (1985), 'The Distribution and Impact of Health Resource Availability in China', *International Journal of Health Planning and Management*, 1.

Preston, S., Keyfitz, N., and Schoen, R. (1972), *Causes of Death: Life Tables for National Populations*. New York: Seminar Press.

Pyatt, G. (1987), 'Measuring Welfare, Poverty and Inequality', *Economic Journal*, 97.

Ram, N. (1986), 'An Independent Press and Anti-Hunger Strategies', paper presented at a conference on Food Strategies held at the World Institute for Development Economics Research, July 1986; to be published in Drèze and Sen (1990).

Ramalingaswami, V., Deo, M. G., Guleria, J. S., Malhotra, K. K., Sood, S. K., Om, P. and Sinha, R. V. N. (1971), 'Studies of the Bihar Famine of 1966–1967', in G. Blix *et al.* (eds.), *Famine: Nutrition and Relief Operations in Times of Disaster*. Uppsala, Sweden: Swedish Nutrition Foundation.

Ravallion, M. (1987), *Markets and Famines*. Oxford: Clarendon Press.

Reddy, S. (1988), 'An Independent Press Working Against Famine: The Nigerian Experience', *Journal of Modern African Studies*, 26.

Riskin, C. (1987), *China's Political Economy: The Quest for Development since 1949*. Oxford: Clarendon Press.

Rose, T. (ed.) (1985), *Crisis and Recovery in Sub-Saharan Africa*. Paris: OECD.

Rukini, M., and Eicher, C. K. (eds.) (1987), *Food Security for Southern Africa*. Harare: UZ/MSU Food Security Project, Department of Agricultural Economics and Extension, University of Zimbabwe.

Sachs, I. (1986), 'Growth and Poverty: Lessons from Brazil', paper presented at a Conference on Food Strategies held at WIDER, Helsinki, 21–5 July 1986; to be published in Drèze and Sen (1990).

Saenz, L. (1985), 'Health Changes During a Decade: The Costa Rican Case', in Halstead *et al.* (1985).

Samuelson, P. A. (1955), 'Diagrammatic Exposition of a Theory of Public Expenditure', *Review of Economics and Statistics*, 37.

Schokkaert, E., and van Ootegem, L. (1989), 'Sen's Concept of the Living Standard Applied to the Belgian Unemployed', Public Economics Research Paper No. 1, Centre for Economics Studies, Leuven.

Sen, A. K. (1973), 'On the Development of Basic Income Indicators to Supplement GNP Measures', *Economic Bulletin for Asia and the Far East*, 24.

——(1976a), 'Poverty: An Ordinal Approach to Measurement', *Econometrica*, 44; reprinted in Sen (1982).

——(1976b), 'Real National Income', *Review of Economic Studies*, 43; reprinted in Sen (1982).

——(1980), 'Equality of What?', in S. M. McMurrin (ed.), *Tanner Lectures on Human Values*, i, Cambridge: Cambridge University Press; reprinted in Sen (1982).

——(1981a), *Poverty and Famines*. Oxford: Clarendon Press.

——(1981b), 'Public Action and the Quality of Life in Developing Countries', *Oxford Bulletin of Economics and Statistics*, 43.

——(1982), *Choice, Welfare and Measurement*. Oxford: Blackwell; and Cambridge, Mass: MIT Press.

——(1983), 'Development: Which Way Now?', *Economic Journal*, 93.

——(1984), *Resources, Values and Development*. Oxford: Basil Blackwell.

——(1985a), 'Well-being, Agency and Freedom: The Dewey Lectures 1984', *Journal of Philosophy*, 82.

——(1985b), *Commodities and Capabilities*. Amsterdam: North Holland.

——(1986), 'India and Africa: What do we Have to Learn from Each Other?', C. N. Vakil Memorial Lecture delivered at the Eighth World Congress of the International Economic Association, New Delhi, Dec. 1986.

——(1987a), *Hunger and Entitlements*. Helsinki: WIDER.

——(1987b), 'The Standard of Living', in Sen *et al.* (1987).

——(1988), 'Food and Freedom', Sir John Crawford Memorial Lecture, The World Bank; to be published in *World Development*.

—— *et al.* (1987), *The Standard of Living* (ed. G. Hawthorn). Cambridge: Cambridge University Press.

Shigematsu, I., and Yanagawa, H. (1985), 'The Case of Japan', in J. Vallin and A. Lopez (eds.), *Health Policy, Social Policy and Mortality Prospects*. Liège: International Union for the Scientific Study of Population.

Smith, A. (1776), *An Enquiry into the Nature and Causes of the Wealth of Nations*. Repub. Oxford: Clarendon Press, 1976.

Smout, T. C. (1978), 'Famine and Famine-Relief in Scotland', in L. M. Cullen and T. C. Smout (eds.), *Comparative Aspects of Scottish and Irish Economic History 1600–1900*. Edinburgh: Donald.

Srinivasan, T. N., and Bardhan, P. K. (eds.) (1988), *Rural Poverty in South Asia*. New York: Columbia University Press.

Stewart, F. (1985), *Planning to Meet Basic Needs*. London: Macmillan.

—— (1988), 'Basic Needs Strategies, Human Rights and the Right to Development', Luca d'Agliano–Queen Elizabeth House Development Studies Working Paper No. 2, Queen Elizabeth House, Oxford.

Streeten, P. (1981), *Development Perspectives*. London: Macmillan.

—— (1984), 'Basic Needs: Some Unsettled Questions', *World Development*, 12.

—— *et al.* (1981), *First Things First: Meeting Basic Needs in Developing Countries*. Oxford: Oxford University Press.

Swift, J. (forthcoming), 'Planning Against Drought and Famine in Turkana: A District Contingency Plan', to be published in T. E. Downing *et al.* (eds.), *Coping with Drought in Kenya: National and Local Strategies*. Boulder, Colo.: Lynne Rienner.

Szreter, S. (1988), 'The Importance of Social Intervention in Britain's Mortality Decline *c*.1850–1914: A Re-Interpretation', *Social History of Medicine*, 1.

Taeuber, I. B. (1958), *The Population of Japan*. Princeton: Princeton University Press.

Titmuss, R. M. (1950), *History of the Second World War: Problems of Social Policy*. London: HMSO.

UNICEF (United Nations Children's Fund) (1987), *The State of the World's Children*. New York: UNICEF.

—— (1988), *The State of the World's Children*. New York: UNICEF.

Valaoras, V. G. (1946), 'Some Effects of Famine on the Population of Greece', *Milbank Memorial Fund Quarterly Bulletin*, 24.

van Binsbergen, A. (1986), 'Cape Verde: Food Aid Resource Planning in Support of National Food Strategy', paper presented at a Conference on Food Aid for Development, Abijan, Sept. 1986.

Walker, P. (1988), 'Famine and Rapid Onset Disaster Warning Systems: A Report by the International Institute for Environment and Development for The Red Cross', mimeo, International Institute for Environment and Development, London.

Whitehead, A. (1986), 'Rural Women and Food Production in Sub-Saharan Africa', paper presented at a Conference on Food Strategies held at WIDER, Helsinki, 21–5 July 1986; to be published in Drèze and Sen (1990).

Will, P. E. (1980), *Bureaucratie et famine en Chine au 18ᵉ siècle*. Paris: Mouton.

Williams, A. (1985), 'Economics of Coronary Bypass Grafting', *British Medical Journal*, 3 Aug.

—— (1987), 'What Is Health and Who Creates It?', mimeo, University of York.

Williams, B. (1987), 'The Standard of Living: Interests and Capabilities', in Sen *et al.* (1987).

Wilson, G. (1987a), *Money in the Family: Financial Organisation and Womens' Responsibility*. Aldershot: Avebury Publishers.

—— (1987b), 'Patterns of Responsibility and Irresponsibility in Marriage', in Brannen and Wilson (1987).

Winter, J. M. (1986), *The Great War and the British People*. London: Macmillan.

Wyon, J. B., and Gordon, J. E. (1971), *The Khanna Study*. Cambridge, Mass.: Harvard University Press.

World Bank (1984a), *China: The Health Sector*. Washington, DC: World Bank.

—— (1984b), *World Development Report*. Washington, DC: The World Bank.

—— (1987), *World Development Report*. Washington, DC: The World Bank.

World Food Programme (1986), 'Lessons Learned from the African Food Crisis', mimeo, World Food Programme, Rome.

Yao, F. K., and Kone, H. (1986), 'The African Drought Reported by Six West African Newspapers', Discussion Paper No. 14, African Studies Center, Boston University.

Name Index

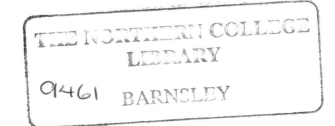